AFRICAN ETHNOGRAPHIC STUDIES OF THE 20TH CENTURY

Volume 71

THE BANTU OF NORTH KAVIRONDO

THE BANTU OF NORTH KAVIRONDO
Volume I

GÜNTER WAGNER

First published in 1949 by Oxford University Press for the International African Institute.

This edition first published in 2018
by Routledge
2 Park Square, Milton Park, Abingdon, Oxon OX14 4RN

and by Routledge
711 Third Avenue, New York, NY 10017

Routledge is an imprint of the Taylor & Francis Group, an informa business

© 1949 International African Institute

All rights reserved. No part of this book may be reprinted or reproduced or utilised in any form or by any electronic, mechanical, or other means, now known or hereafter invented, including photocopying and recording, or in any information storage or retrieval system, without permission in writing from the publishers.

Trademark notice: Product or corporate names may be trademarks or registered trademarks, and are used only for identification and explanation without intent to infringe.

British Library Cataloguing in Publication Data
A catalogue record for this book is available from the British Library

ISBN: 978-0-8153-8713-8 (Set)
ISBN: 978-0-429-48813-9 (Set) (ebk)
ISBN: 978-1-138-59924-6 (Volume 71) (hbk)
ISBN: 978-0-429-48581-7 (Volume 71) (ebk)

Publisher's Note
The publisher has gone to great lengths to ensure the quality of this reprint but points out that some imperfections in the original copies may be apparent.

Disclaimer
The publisher has made every effort to trace copyright holders and would welcome correspondence from those they have been unable to trace.

A Vugusu mother

THE BANTU
OF
NORTH KAVIRONDO

VOLUME I

BY

GÜNTER WAGNER

Published for the
INTERNATIONAL AFRICAN INSTITUTE
by the
OXFORD UNIVERSITY PRESS
LONDON NEW YORK TORONTO
1949

Oxford University Press, Amen House, London E.C. 4.

GLASGOW NEW YORK TORONTO MELBOURNE WELLINGTON
BOMBAY CALCUTTA MADRAS CAPE TOWN

Geoffrey Cumberlege, Publisher to the University

PRINTED IN GREAT BRITAIN

PREFACE

THE present book is the first volume of a monograph on a number of Bantu tribes living in the North Kavirondo District of the Nyanza Province of Kenya. It contains part of the results of two periods of fieldwork which the author has carried through under a research appointment by the International African Institute awarded to him on the recommendation of Professor Westermann. The investigations extended from 1934 until 1938, about two and a half years having been devoted to the actual work in the field. I wish to acknowledge my indebtedness to the Institute and its directors, and especially to Dr. J. H. Oldham, for having financed the two expeditions to Kenya as well as granting the funds that enabled me to write up my material.

I also make grateful acknowledgement to the Rockefeller Foundation for having extended my original fellowship in the U.S.A. for a second year to be spent on preliminary training for this special task at the London School of Economics under the inspiring tutorship of the late Professor Malinowski. It is to him that I owe the greatest possible tribute. I was privileged to work for many months in close personal contact with this brilliant scientific personality, who also started me off in the field.

My approach to the magico-religious side of native life, to which a substantial part of the present volume is devoted, has been greatly stimulated by Professor Evans-Pritchard's admirable book on Zande witchcraft (*Witchcraft, Oracles, and Magic among the Azande*, Oxford, 1937) which, by a fortunate coincidence, I was asked to review shortly before embarking upon my second expedition to Kenya.

While writing my book I benefited greatly from discussing the various problems with my fellow workers in London (chiefly Professor Raymond Firth, Dr. Meyer Fortes, Dr. Lucy P. Mair, and Dr. Kalervo Oberg) and later, when in Germany, with Professor Westermann and Professor Thurnwald.

In Kenya itself I enjoyed unlimited support for my work both from the Central Government at Nairobi and from the Provincial and District Administrations as well as the various Government Departments. Mr. (now Sir Armigel) de Vince Wade, then Colonial Secretary and later Acting Governor of Kenya, apart from kind hospitality, granted me valuable facilities and made those all-important initial arrangements for me which proved most helpful in establishing close contacts with the local authorities. I would thank also a great many Government officials for taking an interest in my work that went far beyond their routine duties. The study of modern contact conditions and of their repercussions on present-day native life, which forms the central theme of the second volume, could hardly have been accomplished without the assistance and co-operation of the Administration and the various departmental services, especially the Agricultural and the Education Departments.

I am further greatly indebted to many missionaries, both Protestant and Catholic, for the understanding and helpful attitude which they have shown on every possible occasion. In particular, I wish to express my gratitude to the Church Missionary Society, the Church of God Mission, the Friends' African Mission, and the Roman Catholic Mill Hill Mission, as well as to Mr. James W. C. Dougall, then liaison officer between the Kenya Government and the Kenya Missionary Board.

Besides, my wife and I wish to take this opportunity to express our grateful appreciation of the generous hospitality which we received in all quarters, both official and private.

Last, but not least, I would thank my African friends and informants, both old and young, pagan and Christian. Without their untiring and unselfish co-operation I should not have got very far. Especially four of them, Christopher Mtiva and William Serenge of South Maragoli, James Tsindakha of Bunyore and Javan Nandoli of North Kitosh, have taken such a genuine and keen interest in helping me 'to get at the facts' that their names must be connected with this book.

Hamburg
April 1946.

Since the above foreword was written I have to extend my thanks to Professor A. R. Radcliffe-Brown and Professor Daryll Forde, the present Director of the Institute, to both of whom I am deeply indebted for having recommended and arranged for the publication of the manuscript *in extenso*. My particular thanks, finally, are due to Mrs. Beatrice Wyatt, the Secretary of the Institute, for her careful revision of the proofs.

July 1947.

NOTE ON NATIVE TERMS

TO facilitate the use of the material contained in the present book for comparative studies as well as to document certain passages, I have included a number of native terms and quotations in the vernacular, putting them in brackets after their (approximate) equivalents in English. I have endeavoured to render the phonetic transcription as simple as possible. The vowel sounds *e* and *o* always being open in all Bantu Kavirondo dialects, no special symbols have been used to denote their open quality. Futhermore, no distinction has been made between bilabial and labio-dental *v*, a point which, however, will be discussed in connexion with the publication of my linguistic material. *l* and *r* frequently being interchangeable, I cannot vouch for having been entirely consistent in differentiating between these two sounds. ʃ (cap Σ) denotes a voiceless palato-alveolar fricative, *x* a voiceless velar fricative. All other consonants are pronounced as in English. Stress is usually on the penultimate; in all other cases it has been marked by an accent on the stressed syllable (for instance, *tsimbú*).

For readers not familiar with the Bantu system of class prefixes I refer to the chart on p. 26. I may add that the prefix *ovu-* (*vu-*) always denotes the idea of abstraction. Thus: *omuvila*, the sorcerer (plural: *avavila*), but *ovuvila*, sorcery. The different rendering of native terms in different contexts is explained by dialectic differences: for instance, the term for 'witch' is *omulogi* in Lurogoli (the dialect spoken by the Logoli tribe living in Maragoli) and *omulosi* in Luvugusu (the dialect spoken by the Vugusu living in Kitosh); the term for 'cow' is *eŋombe* (plural: *edziŋombe*) in Lurogoli and *éxafu* (plural: *tjíxafu*) in Luvugusu, &c.

CONTENTS

LITERATURE ON THE BANTU KAVIRONDO . . . xix

Part I. INTRODUCTORY

A. THE COUNTRY 3
The Nyanza Province and the three Kavirondo Districts—Distribution of Bantu and Nilotes—Geographical situation and boundaries of North Kavirondo—Soil—Climate—Rivers—Kisumu and the Nyando Valley—From the Nyando Valley to the North Kavirondo plain—Traffic on the road—Scenery in the southern part of the District—Symptoms of European influence—Native dukas—A native market—The Kakamega goldfields—The township of Kakamega—Natural features in the eastern part of the District—Native agriculture in Kitosh—The Vugusu's wealth in cattle—Remains of former village fortifications—The caves of Mt. Elgon—Malakisi—Scenery in the central portion of the District—Mumias—Density of the population in Bunyore.

B. THE PEOPLE 15
Non-Bantu living in North Kavirondo—Neighbouring tribes—Population figures of the Bantu Kavirondo tribes—Population movement—The sex ratio—The Bantu Kavirondo politically, linguistically, and culturally not a unit—The name Kavirondo—The tribal groups and chieftaincies (locations) of the North Kavirondo District—Tribal traditions (origins and migrations)—The chief dialects—Political relations between the tribes—Cultural differences between the sub-tribes—Physical appearance of the Bantu Kavirondo—Features of mind and character.

C. SURVEY OF THE HISTORY OF EUROPEAN PENETRATION AND PRESENT 'CONTACT SITUATION' IN KAVIRONDO . . 30
First Europeans to visit North Kavirondo—Opening up the first District Station at Mumias—Pacification of the various tribes and cessation of intertribal warfare—Introduction of taxation—The Uganda Railway and the opening up of Kavirondo—'Time-table' showing the development of the District—Beginnings of missionary work in North Kavirondo—The present contact situation: (1) The Administration of the District and the activities of the Government Departments, (2) Missions, (3) Gold-mining, (4) Natives in the employment of Europeans, (5) The native production of cash crops.

Part II. ELEMENTS OF KINSHIP STRUCTURE

A. THE FAMILY 40
Types of family structure—Terminological data—Establishing the family status—The family as a residential and economic unit—The father as the head of the family—Matrimonial and family status of husband and wife—Relationship pattern between parents and children—Relations between siblings—Structure of the polygynous family.

B. CLAN AND LINEAGE 53
Definition of the clan—Clan and tribe—Sub-groups of the clan—Sub-clan and lineage—Terminological data—Clans are territorial units—Departures from the territorial principle—Clan-lists and clan traditions of various sub-tribes (Logoli, Tiriki, Idaxo, Tsotso, Vugusu, Wanga)—Origin of new clans and its causes: (1) Quarrels and disputes, (2) Peaceful segregation, (3) Natural growth of sub-groups and the gradual establishment of their independence—Classificatory use of kinship terms along clan lines—Significance of the classificatory extensions of kinship relations—Clan-taboos—Qualities attributed to clans.

CONTENTS

CLAN-HEAD AND CLAN-ELDERS 76
Conditions of political leadership: Authority of age (principle of seniority)—Qualities of character—Reputation as a warrior—Religious qualifications—Economic wealth—The ideal type of a clan-head—Terminological data—Rights and duties of a clan-head—Installation of the clan-head.

C. MANIFESTATIONS OF KINSHIP 83
Bilateral orientation of effective kinship relations—Stress laid on paternal kin—Manifestations of kinship: Kinship terms, kinship behaviour (avoidances—joking relations), fulfilment of ceremonial duties, gift obligations, rights of residence and land tenure, claims to inheritance and succession, readiness to grant help, status in the marriage law of the tribe.

D. LIST OF KINSHIP TERMS 86
Among the Logoli: (i) Consanguineous kin, (ii) Affinal kin—Among the Vugusu: (i) Consanguineous kin, (ii) Affinal kin.

PART III. THE MAGICO-RELIGIOUS

A. INTRODUCTORY 90
Reasons for dealing with magic and religious phenomena under a joint heading—Plan of presentation of the magico-religious beliefs and practices—Mystical and common-sense notions—Double causation.

B. AGENTS AND FORCES BELIEVED TO EXERCISE A MYSTICAL INFLUENCE OVER HUMAN WELFARE 95
Different categories of human agents: Ordinary people—Persons or animals as passive vehicles of a dangerous mystical power (temporary ritual impurity)—Specialists.

(1) ORDINARY PEOPLE POSSESSING AND HANDLING PUBLIC ACTIVE MAGIC . 96
(a) *Promotive Magic* 96
Public magic defined—The relation between promotive, preventive, and protective magic—Rare occurrence of promotive magic—Agricultural magic—Talismans—Love magic.

(b) *Curses and Blessings* 101
The major types of curses: (1) Against definite persons; (2) Against unknown offenders—Occasions for the uttering of curses—The victims of curses—Examples of curses—Blessings.

(2) PERSONS AND ANIMALS IN A STATE OF RITUAL IMPURITY . . . 106
The notion of ritual impurity—The states of *luswa* and *kiragi*—Typical situations producing these states—The dangers arising from ritual impurity—The disposition for falling *luswa* inherited—Other kinds of ritual impurity: *Vuxútjakáli* of widows, *ovukáli* of warriors, *vusixu*, *vuxwana* of twins.

(3) SPECIALISTS:
(a) *Avalogi (avalosi)* 111
Ovulogi (ovulosi) always anti-social and secret—Types of *avalosi* distinguished among the Vugusu and techniques used by them: *ovinásitjula* and *omuvini, omurori, omusíndixilisi, ómuxupi owe vílasila* and *omuxondoli, omufúndilili*—Conditions of practising *ovulosi*—The powers of the *omulosi* inherited—The breaking forth of the inherited disposition—Instruction in *ovulosi*—Succession—Motives for practising *ovulosi*—Attitude towards *ovulosi* and behaviour adopted towards persons suspected of *ovulosi*—Types of *avalogi* distinguished among the Logoli—Transfer of *ovulogi*—Attitude towards *avalogi* among the Logoli—*ovulogi* among the Marama.

(b) *Avavila* 132
Difference between *ovulogi* and *ovuvila*—*Ovuvila* socially condoned—Aims of *ovuvila*—Harmful magic wielded by *avavila*—The technique employed by the *avavila*—Cases of *ovuvila*—Curative magic employed by *avavila*—Motives for practising *ovuvila*—Transfer of *ovuvila*—Ambivalent nature of *ovuvila*—*Ovuvila* among the Marama and Wanga.

(c) *The Rain-magician* 144
(i) The importance attached to rain-magic: Social status of the rain-magician—Distribution of rain-magicians in Kavirondo—(ii) The technique of rain-control: Bunyole, Marama, Butsotso, Kitosh—Elements of rain-magic—(iii) The origin of rain-magic according to the local tradition—(iv) Succession to the office of rain-magician—(v) Tribute paid to the rain-magician.

(4) THE SPIRITS OF THE DEAD 159
Essential qualities of living beings: Body, heart, shadow—Physical death and the process of transformation which it implies—Transitional phase through which spirits pass and their initial restlessness—Permanent abode of spirits—Visitations by spirits and effects produced by them—Range and limitations of their powers—Motives for the antagonistic attitude of the spirits towards the living—Positive attitude of the 'Tame Spirits' towards the living.

(5) THE SUPREME BEING 167
The Supreme Being among the Logoli—The concept of the High God among the Vugusu—Wele as creator—Prayers to Wele—Origin myths—Wele as sustainer and promoter—Wele's personification—Relation between Wele and the Sun (*liuwa*)—Sun-myths—Wele's relations to the antagonistic powers—The White God and the black god (*Wele Omuwanga* and *wele gumali*)—The ancestral spirits as helpers and servants of the white and the black gods—The White God no judge over good and evil—The White God not omnipotent.

C. MEASURES OF PROTECTION AND PREVENTION

(1) INTRODUCTORY 178
The need for protection and prevention—Protective and preventive measures a well-organized system of activities—Relation between beliefs and practices—Different types of protective and preventive magic.

(2) ORDINARY PRECAUTIONS AGAINST DISEASE AND MISFORTUNE . . 179
Insight into empirical causes and effects—Mystical notions do not clash with empirical knowledge—Relation between protective magic and ordinary measures of precaution.

(3) PROTECTIVE MEASURES BASED ON THE EMPLOYMENT OF CHARMS AND MEDICINES 181
Amulets and medicines—General and specific protective virtues of amulets—Protective magic performed on definite occasions—Garden magic to afford protection from hail and from the evil eye—Protective magic performed for the benefit of cattle—Conspicuous absence of protective magic in hunting and warfare.

(4) AVOIDANCES AND OTHER RITUAL PROHIBITIONS . . . 189
(a) *Avoidances between Persons* 190
Following a quarrel or a curse—Avoidance of persons in a state of ritual impurity—Avoidances between in-laws—Ritual prohibitions observed between kinsmen.

(b) *Other Avoidances and Ritual Prohibitions* 198
Prohibition against killing certain animals—Food avoidances (Food prohibitions on a clan basis—Food prohibitions on a sexual basis—Avoidance of milk by unmarried girls and young wives—Observance of temporary food taboos by pregnant women—Personal food avoidances—Abstention from food on certain occasions)—Miscellaneous avoidances and prohibitions.

(5) GOOD AND BAD OMENS 207
Omens in the proper sense of the word—Significance of dreams and dream prophecy—Forecasting the future from the inspection of entrails.

D. THE TAKING OF COUNTER-MEASURES AND THE APPEAL TO HIGHER AUTHORITIES 219

(1) DIVINATION 219
Consulting the diviner the chief prerequisite for the taking of counter-measures—Situations in which the diviner is consulted—A visit to the diviner—Questioning the client—Technique of oracular consultation among the Logoli—The procedure of divination—Techniques of consulting the oracles among the Vugusu—Accounts of two consultations—The psychology of divination—Confidence in the diviner—The diviner's fees—Succession to the office of a diviner.

(2) RITES OF PURIFICATION AND RECONCILIATION 245
The aim of these rites the restoration of one's 'ritual status'—Lustration from the state of *luswa*—Lustration from contamination by death and human blood—Lustration after the violation of taboos (*emigilu*)—Lustration after having committed a crime—Lustration after having come into contact with harmful magic—Lifting of curses—Reconciliation to terminate a state of mutual avoidance.

(3) COMBATING AND NEUTRALIZING HARMFUL MAGIC . . . 257
Introductory remarks—Detection and destruction of harmful magic (*okuliula*)—Removing *vilasila* or *evikoko* by means of the cupping horn—Burning of *vifúndilila*-particles—Destruction of *ovovila*—Reversing the direction in which the evil magic will strike—Combating evil magic by antidotes (counter-magic)—Reparation by the perpetrator of the harmful magic—Ordeals and punishment of sorcerers and witches.

(4) THE CULT OF THE ANCESTORS AND OF THE SUPREME BEING
(a) *Family Sacrifices* 277
Twofold significance of the ancestor cult—The nature of the funeral and mourning rites—Different types of family sacrifices—Occasions for offering a sacrifice—Sacrificial objects—Native terms for sacrificial rites—Sacrificial shrines among the Logoli and the Vugusu—Consecration of the sacrificial shrine—The sacrificial priest—The procedure at a sacrificial offering—The ancestral name.

(b) *Warding off and destroying persistently troublesome Spirits* . . 288
Excavating and burning the bones of persistently troublesome spirits—Trapping *visieno* spirits among the Vugusu—Warding off visitations by evil spirits.

(c) *Tribal Sacrifices* 290
Sacrifices on a tribal scale performed only among the Logoli—Objectives of tribal sacrifices—The sacrificial priests—Announcing the tribal sacrifice and preparatory observances—Kindling the sacrificial fire (*ovwali*)—Offering an animal sacrifice in the sacrificial cave.

PART IV. THE RITES OF PASSAGE

A. BIRTH

(1) INTRODUCTORY 295
THE SOCIAL SIGNIFICANCE OF CHILDBIRTH

(2) CONCEPTION AND PREGNANCY 295
Factors alleged to influence conception—Measures taken to aid conception (counter-magic—extramarital intercourse of the wife)—Symptoms of pregnancy—Determining the time of delivery—Notions on the respective share of both parents in the process of reproduction—Explanation of miscarriages—Rules to be observed during pregnancy—Behaviour of husband—*okugasidza* rite for a pregnant woman.

CONTENTS

(3) DELIVERY 300
Place of delivery—Midwifery—Disposal of the navel cord and the afterbirth—Rites performed in cases of difficult delivery—Neglect of a child whose mother has died in childbirth.

(4) THE RITUAL SITUATION AT CHILDBIRTH 302
Ritual impurity of mother and child—Taboos on sexual intercourse—The newborn child still lacks a social status—The birth of a child affects the social status of the parents.

(5) CONFINEMENT AND RITUAL SECLUSION 303
Seclusion of the ritually contaminated mother—Her behaviour during the period of segregation—Ceremonial cleansing of the mother and the child—Ceremonies performed in connexion with the first suckling (or feeding) of the infant—Ample supply of food for the young mother—Testing the legitimacy of the child—Making the *mulivu*-skirt for the ritually contaminated mother—Continence of the young mother.

(6) THE TERMINATION OF CONFINEMENT AND THE PRESENTATION OF THE INFANT TO ITS KINDRED 307
Visit paid by the child's maternal kin—Presentation of the child to its kin—Placing the child under the eaves in front of the hut and dropping water on it—Ceremonial anointing with ghee—Abuse levelled by the husband's mother at her guests and refusal of the latter to eat the food offered to them—First joint meal of the husband's and the wife's relatives—Gifts presented by the wife's mother—Kindling a fire in the young mother's hut—Taking the *ovwivu*-leaves to the wife's mother and terminating the period of ritual impurity—Resumption of marital relations between husband and wife—First touching of the child by its father—Sexual regulations.

(7) THE LISWÁKILA RITE 311
Offering the first ancestral sacrifice in the child's name—Choice of the sacrificial animal—Cutting up the *oluvinu* plant—Persons officiating at the sacrifice (*omusálisi, ombili, ombiki*)—Consecration and killing of the sacrificial goat—Inspection of entrails—Ceremony of piercing the stomach—Smearing the mother and the child with the stomach-content of the goat—Spitting with *ovwanga*—The sacrificial meal—Kindling a sacrificial fire with the branches of the *oluvinu* plant.

(8) NAMING 313
Different kinds of names: childhood name, puberty name, ancestral name—Special significance of the ancestral name—Time of its bestowal—Choice of the ancestral name—Bestowal of two ancestral names—Relations between the ancestral spirit and the child named after it—Subsequent bestowal of the ancestral name and 'confirmation' of the ancestral name—Use of the ancestral name.

(9) CUTTING TEETH AND WEANING 322
Lustration rite in case of abnormal cutting of teeth—Time of weaning—Weaning the child and new pregnancy of its mother—Manner of weaning a child.

(10) ATTITUDE TOWARDS TWINS AND CEREMONIES CONNECTED WITH THEIR BIRTH 323
Opposite attitudes adopted towards twins among the Logoli and the Vugusu—No particular native theory to account for the birth of twins—Ritual danger (*vuxwana*) emanating from twins and their ceremonial seclusion inside the hut—Birth ceremonies performed in honour of twins: ceremonial 'opening of the twins'; presents brought by kinsmen; holding a dance in celebration of the birth of twins—Protective measures taken against the *vuxwana*—Ancestral sacrifice to benefit the twins—Fertility magic performed by the father of the twins—Gradual ebbing away of the *vuxwana*.

CONTENTS

(11) CEREMONIES PERFORMED FOR WEAK AND SICKLY INFANTS . . 330
Consulting the diviner—Depositing the child in the bush and having it nursed by a neighbour—A cobra as the cause of a child's weakness—Rite performed to placate the spirit of the cobra—Ceremonies of piercing the ear and coaxing the life-flame for a sickly child.

B. CIRCUMCISION AND INITIATION RITES

(1) INTRODUCTORY 334
General significance of initiation rites—The problem of their meaning (symbolism and function)—Differential distribution of circumcision among the Bantu tribes of North Kavirondo—Question of their age.

(2) CONDITIONS OF CIRCUMCISION AND PREPARATORY OBSERVANCES . . 337
Deciding to hold circumcision rites—Consulting the omens preparatory to holding the rites—Age of the circumcision candidates—Resistance offered by fathers to their sons' desire to be circumcised—Circumcision no condition of marriage—The main phases of the initiation rites—Time of holding the circumcision rites—Behaviour of the candidates: Among the Vugusu—Among the Tiriki—Among the Idaxo—Among the Logoli.

(3) THE DAY OF THE OPERATION 346
The office of the circumcision doctor (*omukevi*)—Arrival of the *omukevi*—His attire and his behaviour—Place of circumcision—Behaviour of the candidates before the operation—The operation (tribal variants)—Attitude of the candidates during the operation—Treatment of the wound—Behaviour of the girls towards the initiates (Vugusu)—Dances performed by the novices' sisters and mothers after the operation—Fees paid to the circumcision doctor.

(4) THE LIFE OF THE INITIATES IN THE HUT OF SECLUSION . . . 353
Office of the male tutors (*avadili*) and of the female sponsors or guardians (*avadili avakana*)—Social composition of the novices living in the same hut—The initiation hut (*etumbi*)—Ceremonial way of entering the hut—Food observances by the novices—Ritual cleansing of the novices by the circumcision doctor—Further treatment of the circumcision wound—Hushing up the death of a novice—Manufacturing the circumcision masks and cloaks—Grass skirts of the novices—Behaviour of the novices when outside the initiation hut—Their attitude towards cowards—Instruction given to the novices by their tutors—Hunting and war practices by the initiates—Pilfering raids—Ritual enactment of the initiates' death and rebirth among the Tiriki—Lustration rites performed for them.

(5) THE FEAST OF COMING OUT 363
Time of the feast of dismissal from the hut of seclusion—Preparatory actions of the novices: Among the Vugusu (ceremonial kindling of a fire in the open; washing off the clay; putting on the new skins; giving of commandments by the novices' father)—Among the Logoli (plaiting and hiding of the *dzisume*-rings; ceremonial spearing of the hut of seclusion with the *dzindanga*-staffs; burning down the hut of seclusion; dance of the novices; ancestral sacrifice and sacrificial meal)—Among the Idaxo (*vuxulu* dance; burning of the objects used by the novices during their seclusion; hiding the *tsimbú*-sticks; devastating the banana-grove; putting on the new skins; public demonstration of their marksmanship by the novices)—Variations among the Tiriki and Isuxa—Round of visits paid by the novices—Establishing the *virongo*-friendship among the Logoli.

(6) CIRCUMCISION AGE-GRADES 373
System of the circumcision age-grades—Names of the age-grades among the Logoli—Significance of the names—Age-grades among the Tiriki—Age-grade cycle and sub-grades among the Vugusu—Attitude of the age-mates towards one another—Legal, economic, &c., relations between age-mates.

C. MARRIAGE

(1) ATTITUDE TOWARDS MARRIAGE 379
    Valuation of matrimony and parenthood by the social community—An early marriage advantageous for the husband—Women seek to defer their marriage—Considerations determining the attitude of parents towards their children's marriages.

(2) THE CHOICE OF THE MARRIAGE PARTNER 382
    Rules limiting the number of people eligible as marriage partners—The laws of clan exogamy—The notions of *vuleve* and *vusoni*—Observance of the rule of exogamy—Procedure adopted in the case of a violation of these rules—Alleged consequences entailed by violations of the marriage prohibitions—Social significance of clan exogamy—No intermarriage between cousins—Marriage prohibition between clans that have concluded a ceremonial friendship—Marriage prohibitions resulting from a blood feud—Marriage prohibitions resulting from the conclusion of the *virongo*-friendship—Disapproval of the simultaneous sororate as well as of marriage between two sisters and two brothers—Notions on which the marriage prohibitions and restrictions are founded—Suspicion of sorcery or witchcraft as a bar to marriage—Economic wealth as a factor influencing the choice of the marriage partner—Other factors: tendency towards tribal endogamy; relative age of the marriage partners; personal qualities of the marriage partners; attitude towards virginity.

(3) COURTSHIP AND BETROTHAL 396
    Different forms of concluding a marriage—Distinction between playful love-making and serious courtship—Formal behaviour of the betrothed towards one another—Engaging the services of a go-between when courting a girl—Influence of a father upon his son's courtships—Marital age of girls—Sending an emissary to the girl's father—Settling the amount of the bridewealth and drinking the beer of *enganana*—Inspection of the marriage-cattle—Driving the cattle to the homestead of the girl's father—Logoli text on courtship and betrothal—Length of betrothal—Work and services rendered by the betrothed to their future parents-in-law—Pattern of behaviour between the betrothed couple—Dissolution of a betrothal—Forced betrothals.

(4) THE WEDDING-FEAST AND THE CONSUMMATION OF MARRIAGE . . 409
    The wedding a series of festive occasions—Variability of the marriage customs—Feast at the homestead of the bride's father—Ceremonial preparations—The nature of the festivities—The bride's first visit to the bridegroom's homestead—Selecting the bridesmaids—Adorning the bride and performing a rite of fertility-magic for her—Departure of the bride from her parental homestead—The bridal party—Fetching of the bride by the bridegroom's sisters and sham resistance offered by the bridal party—Haughty attitude displayed by the relatives of the bride towards those of the bridegroom—Hospitality offered to the bridal party—Sexual licence—Ceremonial segregation of the bride and 'opening the bride' by the bridesmaids—The bride's return to her parental home—Ceremonial rules observed upon her return to the parental homestead—Counter-visit paid by the relatives of the bridegroom and hospitality offered to the bridegroom's party—Rules of marital conduct given to the bride by her maternal uncle—Symbolic exchange of foodstuffs between the bride and her sister-in-law—Second visit paid by the bride to the bridegroom's homestead—Test of virginity—The wedding night—Paying the 'goat of defloration' to the bride's paternal aunt—Handing the *evilisio* gifts to the bride.

(5) THE ECONOMIC ASPECT OF THE CONCLUSION OF MARRIAGE . . 430
    The exchange of gifts and hospitality an important aspect of the marriage procedure—Expenses incurred and gifts made by the bridegroom's kin—Expenses incurred and gifts made by the bride's kin—Strict reciprocity of the gifts—Their threefold significance.

CONTENTS

(6) OTHER TYPES OF MARRIAGE 433
The full marriage procedure observed in less than 30 per cent. of all marriages concluded—(a) Marriage by elopement: motives for eloping with a girl; legitimizing such a marriage; tension between the bridegroom and the girl's kin; individual cases—(b) Marriage by abduction—(c) Various other forms of marriage: marriage of a girl with an illegitimate child; remarriage of a divorced woman; remarriage of a widow.

(7) DISSOLUTION OF MARRIAGE 440
Stability of the matrimonial bond—Motives for the dissolution of a marriage—Return of the marriage-cattle—Deductions proportionate to the number of children borne by the wife and to the services rendered by her.

D. DEATH AND MOURNING

(1) INTRODUCTORY 447
Physical death a transition to a new phase of existence—Analogy with the other crises of life—Cultural significance of the ceremonial observances—The situation at death differing according to the former status of the deceased in the community.

(2) THE APPROACH OF DEATH 449
Removing the dying person from his hut—Last sacrificial rite performed by the dying person—Sacrificial meal as ordeal for the originator of the disease—Behaviour of kinsmen at the moment of death.

(3) WAILING AND CEREMONIES PERFORMED IN HONOUR OF THE DECEASED . 451
Outbreak of wailing at the moment of death—Spreading the death-message—The death watch of the widows—Ceremonial round of wailing made by the widows—The cattle-drive—The sham fight—Behaviour of the mourners—Social composition of the mourners—Dirges.

(4) BURIAL 469
Mode of burial and tribal variations—Time of interment—Burial site and digging of the grave—Shape of the grave and mode of burial—Ceremonial observed when placing the corpse in the grave—The vigil at the grave—The burial of clan-heads deviating from the norm.

(5) THE CEREMONIAL CONDUCT OF THE WIDOWS DURING THE FUNERAL RITES 480
Putting on the mourning attire—Ceremonial consumption of the first meal after the husband's death—Collecting bananas—Hiding a rafter of the death-hut in the bush—Tribal variations.

(6) THE HAIR-SHAVING CEREMONY 485
Ritual significance of the hair-shaving ceremony—Settling the debts and claims of the deceased—Discussing the cause of his death—The office of the *omuseni* (comforter)—Inheritance of the widows—Protocols on the course of procedure followed at several hair-shaving ceremonies.

(7) THE RITUAL STATUS OF THE WIDOW AND OF THE WIDOWER . . 496
Ritual impurity of the widow—Rules of avoidance—Behaviour of the widow during the period of mourning—Removing of the *ekisuli* (*sisuli*) staff from the roof of the deceased's hut—Termination of the period of mourning—Special status of widows throughout their lives—Conduct of widowers—Death customs observed in the case of women and unmarried persons.

(8) THE FIRST SACRIFICE FOR THE DECEASED AND THE CARE OF THE GRAVE . 501
The first sacrifice for a deceased establishes his status in the spirit world—Time for offering the sacrifice and ritual observances connected with it—Ceremony of cleaning the grave—Ceremony performed at one's father's grave when attaining to the full status of a family head.

INDEX 505

ILLUSTRATIONS

A Vugusu mother . . . . . *Frontispiece*

PLATE
1. A. Nandi Range and Nyando Valley
   B. Descent from Equator Hill, South Maragoli . *facing page* 10
2. A. Maragoli homestead
   B. A teacher's house: Butsotso . . . ,, 11
3. A. Donera, an elder of South Maragoli
   B. A woman in her traditional attire: South Kitosh ,, 40
4. A. A Kitosh homestead
   B. Maxeti, a Kitosh elder wearing a cowrie-shell cap ,, 41
5. A garden magician: South Maragoli . . ,, 152
6. Inspection of entrails: South Kitosh . . ,, 153
7. Diviner consulting the pebble oracle: Butsotso . ,, 186
8. Diviner consulting the rubbing-board oracle: South Kitosh . . . . . . ,, 187
9. A. A widow wailing for her husband in front of a sacrificial hut: North Kitosh .
   B. Offering meat on a spear-point to ancestral spirits: South Kitosh ,, 230
10. Skinning a sacrificial calf: South Kitosh . . ,, 231
11. Idaxo novices dancing in their grass masks . . ,, 296
12. Dance of the novices: Idaxo. . . . ,, 297
13. A. Taking gifts from bride's to bridegroom's place: North Kitosh
    B. Dancing at a wedding in the *lidegeriza* fashion: South Maragoli ,, 352
14. A. A maternal uncle giving rules of matrimonial conduct to the bride: North Kitosh
    B. Beer-drinking in the shade of a banana grove: South Maragoli ,, 353
15. A. A widow decked out in her husband's clothes: North Kitosh
    B. Driving cattle to a funeral feast: South Maragoli ,, 382
16. A. Accordion player accompanying *ovukana* dance: South Maragoli
    B. Decorating a grave: North Kitosh ,, 383

LITERATURE ON THE BANTU KAVIRONDO

1. BRYK, F. *Neger-Eros*, Berlin, 1928.
2. —— Einige 'Parallelen' zum Alten Testament aus Kavirondo (Kenya Colony, East Africa). *Völkerkunde*, Vienna, 1928, p. 104.
3. BUNCHE, R. J. The Land Equation. *Journal of Negro History*, vol. xxiv. 1, pp. 33-43.
4. BURNS, F. Trial by Ordeal among the Bantu-Kavirondo. *Anthropos*, vol. v, p. 808.
5. (*Carter Report*), *Report of Kenya Land Commission*, London, 1934.
6. DUNDAS, K. The Wanga and Other Tribes of the Elgon District. *Journal of the Royal Anthropological Institute*, London, 1913.
7. HOBLEY, C. W. Kavirondo. *The Geographical Journal*, London, 1898, vol. vii.
8. —— *Eastern Uganda, an Ethnological Survey*. Anthropological Institute, Occasional Papers, No. 1, London, 1902.
9. —— Anthropological Studies in Kavirondo and Nandi. *Journal of the Royal Anthropological Institute*, London, 1903, pp. 325-59.
10. —— *From Chartered Company to Crown Colony*, London, 1929.
11. HUNTINGFORD, G. W. B. Tribal Names in the Nyanza and Kerio Provinces. *Man*, London, 1930, pp. 124-5.
12. —— Further Notes on Some Names for God. *Man*, London, 1930, p. 102.
13. JOHNSTON, SIR HARRY. *The Uganda Protectorate*, London, 1902.
14. Kenya Colony and Protectorate: *Native Affairs Department Annual Reports* (N.A.D.A.R.).
15. KITSON, SIR ALBERT E. *Interim Report on the Kakamega Goldfields*, Nairobi, 1932.
16. LINDBLOM, G. *I vildmark och negerbyar*, Stockholm, 1921.
17. —— Forskningar bland niloter och bantu i Kavirondo, särskild med hänsyn till äldre kulturelement. *K. Svenska Vetenskapsakademiens Årsbok*, 1927.
18. —— *Notes ethnographiques sur le Kavirondo septentrional et la Colonie du Kenya*, Universidad Nacional de Tucuman, Tucuman 1932.
19. MARQUARD, F. Bericht über die Kavirondo. *Zeitschrift für Ethnologie*, Berlin, 1909, pp. 753-7.
20. MILLIKIN, A. S. Burial Customs of the Wa-Kavirondo. *Man*, London, 1906, pp. 54-5.
21. NORTHCOTE, G. A. S. The Nilotic Kavirondo. *Journal of the Royal Anthropological Institute*, London, 1907, pp. 58-66.
22. PETERS, CARL. *Die Deutsche Emin-Pascha-Expedition*, Leipzig, 1891.
23. RAVENSTEIN, E. G. Vocabularies from Kavirondo, British East Africa. Collected by Mr. C. W. Hobley. *Journal of the Royal Anthropological Institute*, London, 1899, pp. 338-42.
24. *Report of the Committee on Native Land Tenure in the North Kavirondo Reserve*, Oct. 1930. Nairobi, 1931.
25. STAM, N. The Religious Conceptions of the Kavirondo. *Anthropos*, vol. v, pp. 359-62.
26. —— Bantu Kavirondo of Mumias District. *Anthropos* (1919-20), vols. xiv-xv, pp. 968-80.
27. —— The Bahanga. *Publ. of the Catholic Anthropological Conference, Washington, U.S.A.*, vol. i, no. 4, pp. 143-79. 1 plate, 2 illustrations.

xx   LITERATURE ON THE BANTU KAVIRONDO

28. THOMSON, JOSEPH. *Through Masai Land*, London, 1884.
29. WAGNER, G. The Background of Sex and Sex-Teaching among the Maragoli. *Christianity and the Sex-Education of the African*, London, 1937, pp. 43-65.
30. —— Native Institutions and Local Government. *Oxford University Summer School on Colonial Administration, Second Session*, 1938, pp. 80-3.
31. —— The Changing Family among the Bantu Kavirondo. Supplement to *Africa*, vol. xii, no. 1, London, 1939.
32. —— Reifeweihen bei den Bantustämmen Kavirondos und ihre heutige Bedeutung. *Archiv für Anthropologie, Neue Folge*, vol. 25, no. 1. Brunswick, 1939, pp. 1-35.
33. —— The Political Organization of the Bantu of Kavirondo. *African Political Systems*, edited by M. Fortes and E. E. Evans-Pritchard, London, 1940, pp. 197-236.
34. —— Das Luxo-Spiel der Bantu-Kavirondo. *Mitteilungen der Deutschen Gesellschaft für Völkerkunde*, no. 10, 1940, pp. 76-80.
35. —— Die Religion der Bantu-Kavirondo. *Zeitschrift für Ethnologie*, 71. Jahrgang, pp. 201-18.
36. —— Die moderne Entwicklung der Landwirtschaft bei den Bantu-Kavirondo. *Zeitschrift der Gesellschaft für Erdkunde zu Berlin*, 1940, no. 7-8, pp. 264-87.
37. —— Das quantitative Verfahren in der völkerkundlichen Feldforschung. *Beiträge zur Kolonialforschung*, vol. i, Berlin, 1942, pp. 111-28.
38. WESTERMANN, D. Afrikaner erzählen ihr Leben. *Essener Verlagsanstalt*, Essen, 1938, pp. 228-53.
39. Phillips, Arthur. *Report on Native Tribunals*, Government Printer, Nairobi, 1946.
40. Humphrey, Norman. *The Liguru and the Land*: Sociological Aspects of Some Agricultural Problems in North Kavirondo, Nairobi, 1947.

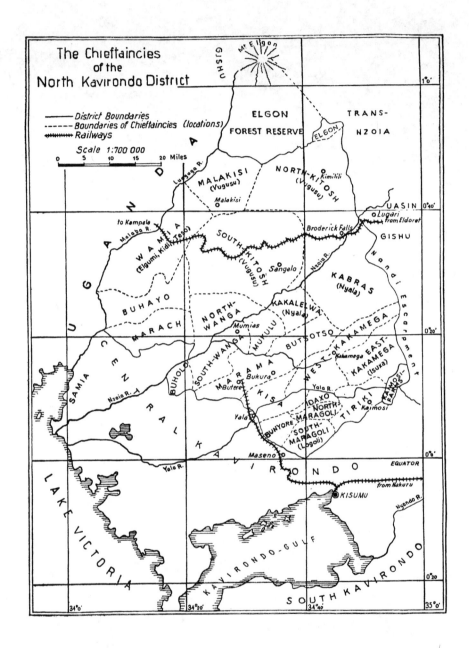

PART I
INTRODUCTORY
A. THE COUNTRY
I

KAVIRONDO is situated to the north-east of Lake Victoria on either side of the Equator. The Kavirondo Gulf and its natural extension towards the east, the Nyando Valley, divide Kavirondo into three geographically distinct areas: (1) the Nyando Valley and the low-lying coastal regions to the north of the gulf (Central Kavirondo); (2) the elevated, undulating plain extending between the Nyando Valley and the slopes of Mount Elgon (North Kavirondo); and (3) the elevated country to the south of the gulf and of the Nyando Valley which gradually passes over into the western Masai steppe (South Kavirondo). Politically, Kavirondo forms part of Kenya Colony and Protectorate (British East Africa).[1] The three administrative districts of North, Central, and South Kavirondo essentially correspond to the geographical divisions. Together with the Districts of Kisumu-Londiani and Kericho they form the Nyanza Province, the westernmost of the six provinces of the colony.[2]

The native population of the three Kavirondo Districts amounted, in 1937, to 1,072,382.[3] It consists of approximately equal parts of Nilotes (Jaluo, Gaya, Nyifwa) and of Bantu, to which must be added a few minor groups speaking Nilo-Hamitic languages (see below, p. 16). The Nilotic tribes, which as regards language and culture are closely related to the Acholi and Alur in Uganda, inhabit Central Kavirondo as well as the low-lying coastal strip of South Kavirondo (Gaya). The Bantu-speaking tribes, on the other hand, are found chiefly in North Kavirondo and in the high-lying regions of South Kavirondo (in the Kisii Highlands). The Bantu tribes of Kavirondo, accordingly, do not show a continuous distribution, but the area inhabited by them is broken by the Nyando Valley with its Nilotic population. The tribes investigated by the author of the present book comprise only the Bantu of North Kavirondo, while he paid only a flying visit to the southern group, the Kisii (or more properly Gusii) and related tribes.

---

[1] Since 1 April 1902. Before that date Kavirondo formed part of what was then the Eastern Province of Uganda. See Thomas and Scott, *Uganda*, London, 1935, p. 41.

[2] The three Kavirondo Districts, excluding the water area, comprise:

Central Kavirondo	1,762 sq. miles
North Kavirondo	2,684 ,,
South Kavirondo	2,956 ,,
	7,402 sq. miles

[3] *Blue Book*, 1937.

INTRODUCTORY

The North Kavirondo District extends from 0° 56' northern latitude, the northernmost point of the chieftaincy Elgon on the slopes of Mount Elgon, to 0° 0', the southern boundary of the chieftaincy of South Maragoli, and from 34° 5' eastern latitude near Busia on the Uganda border to 34° 59' on the Nandi escarpment. The maximum extension of the district from north to south is 64·6 miles and the maximum distance from east to west 64·0 miles, its total area comprising 2,684 square miles.[1] In the east and the north the boundaries of the district are clearly marked by the Nandi escarpment and the slopes of Mount Elgon. In the west the boundary line follows for many miles the course of the Malaba River, which also marks the Kenya and Uganda border. From the confluence of the Sanga and the Sio Rivers onwards, the south-western and southern boundaries of the district are determined chiefly by the ethnical dividing line between Bantu and Nilotes.

The altitude of the district varies between roughly 3,600 feet in the western part near Busia and 7,500 feet on the slopes of Mount Elgon, by far the greatest part of North Kavirondo lying between 4,500 and 5,000 feet. It forms a well watered undulating plain gradually sloping away towards the west and slightly also towards the north until it rises again to the foot-hills of Mount Elgon. In the southern and south-eastern part of the district the topographical forms created by the numerous rivers and rivulets show a pleasing variety of features. Ridges and valleys, often of but miniature dimensions, constantly alternate, so that the natives must dig their fields largely on steeply sloping ground, a fact which, in view of the absence of terrace-cultivation, aggravates the danger of soil erosion. In the remaining parts of the district the river valleys are wide with flat bottoms and gentle slopes. Here and there isolated elevations, among which Sangalo Hill, crowned by two huge vertical granite slabs, forms a particularly striking landmark, rise up to a thousand feet above the surrounding plain.

The prevailing type of soil is the extremely fertile 'red earth'. Its depth, however, varies considerably in accordance with the topographical features. In the chieftaincies of Bunyole and Maragoli, and also in Tiriki, the original granite at many points comes to the surface and the homogeneous, deeply red weathered soil is strewn with granite boulders and rocks of all sizes.

The climate of North Kavirondo is agreeable, with the exception of the height of the dry season (from the middle of December until the middle of February) when the dry easterly wind, blowing from the Nandi escarpment, can be rather trying. Owing to the comparatively high altitude the temperatures are not excessive, despite the immediate vicinity of the Equator. While during the noonday hours the heat of the sun is considerable it is never oppressive, as it is down in the Nyando Valley, since there is nearly always a light breeze. The evenings and nights are rather cool, and during the rainy season a nightly fire is often quite welcome.

The annual rainfall—as far as the available records show—varies between

[1] *Blue Book*, 1937.

61·7 inches and 76·3 inches in the different parts of the district. It is heaviest in the east (Lugari) and south-east of the district (Kakamega and Kaimosi), less heavy in the central part (Bukura, Sangalo), and stronger again on the slopes of Mount Elgon and in the western part of the district, for which, however, there exist no records. As will be seen from the diagram below, there are two rainy seasons, a major one in the months

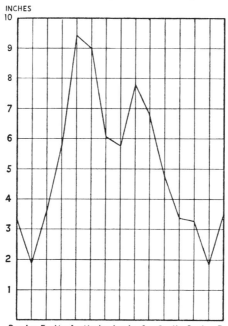

April–May, and a minor one in August–September, the driest month being January, but even that month seldom passes entirely without rain. On the other hand, even during the height of the rainy season it does not by any means rain every day everywhere. Observations extending over six years show for the months of April and May an average of 16 and 15·5 rainless days in the immediate vicinity of the locality at which precipitation was registered. The actual rains are exceedingly heavy. In 1937 the daily rainfall in Maragoli on 13 days was between 1 and 2 inches, while on 7 days it reached more than 2 inches, with a maximum rainfall of 2·75 inches in the course of a single downpour. During the rainy and especially the cooler months precipitation often takes the form of hail-storms, and in those months even fogs occasionally occur. The typical daily cycle of the weather is about as follows: The day begins with blue skies and brilliant sunshine; towards noon heavy clouds gather together in the east over the Nandi escarpment, and in the early afternoon, following a strong windstorm, there is a short but heavy downpour, usually accompanied by a violent thunder-storm.[1] Soon the sky clears up again, and the evening hours are again calm and pleasant.

Rainfall in North Kavirondo
(by inches)

Months	Kaka-mega	Kaimosi	Lugari	Maragoli	Bukura	Sangalo	Monthly average
January	2·4	3·0	1·1	2·1	1·4	1·7	1·9
February	4·5	3·9	2·6	4·4	2·8	3·6	3·6
March	5·7	6·3	5·6	6·6	5·7	5·3	5·8
April	8·8	10·0	9·8	10·1	8·3	9·2	9·4
May	11·4	9·8	8·0	8·8	8·3	7·6	9·0
June	7·6	6·8	6·0	5·9	5·0	5·2	6·1
July	7·3	5·8	8·1	3·5	5·1	5·0	5·8
August	9·7	7·6	9·2	5·8	8·1	6·2	7·8
September	7·4	7·1	10·3	5·0	6·2	4·9	6·8
October	5·0	5·5	3·7	4·2	4·9	5·3	4·8
November	3·6	4·2	0·9	4·5	3·6	3·5	3·4
December	2·9	2·9	1·0	5·0	3·6	4·2	3·3
TOTAL	76·3	72·9	66·3	65·9	63·0	61·7	67·7

Years to which the observations refer:

Kakamega	. 1921–35		Maragoli	. 1932–7
Kaimosi	. 1914–35		Bukura	. 1924–35
Lugari	. 1930–2 and 1935		Sangalo	. 1933–7

The numerous rivers and streams in Kavirondo carry water throughout the year. Coming from the slopes of Mount Elgon, the Uasin-Gishu Plateau and the Nandi Plateau, they flow mainly in a south-westerly direction and drain into Lake Victoria. The longest and most important of them is the Nzoia River, which flows almost exactly through the centre of the district; next follows the Yala River in the south, and then the Sio and Malaba Rivers in the north-west. All rivers abound with palatable fish, the major rivers like the Nzoia and the Yala also containing crocodiles.

II

The European visitor who approaches Kavirondo by the Uganda Railway, coming from Mombasa or Nairobi, catches the first glimpses of the wide Nyando Valley and of the grey expanse of the distant Kavirondo Gulf as the train in numerous curves and turnings descends the slopes of the Mau Plateau (10,000 feet). As it reaches the bottom of the valley the almost European character of the climate and the scenery changes into a typical

---

[1] Cf. C. W. Hobley, 1929, p. 90: 'One of the principal drawbacks to the life in Kavirondo is the prevalence of tropical storms of the most violent character. . . . Hail often falls, and on one occasion some of the hailstones were two and three-quarter inches in diameter, lenticular in shape, and about one and a half thick, and the ground was covered with ice for a couple of hours afterwards. The native huts are often struck by lightning and the people killed.'

THE COUNTRY 7

African savannah of tropical character, with numerous umbrella-shaped acacias, euphorbias, aloes, and wild figs, growing some in clusters, some singly, as well as an occasional grotesque-looking sausage tree. Picturesquely dotted over the landscape are the Jaluo kraals, fenced by thorn-bush or euphorbia hedges. Herds of cattle are grazing on the sparse pasture, broken now and again by barren patches. The scanty banana-groves, maize-, and sorghum-fields visible from the train window do not yet let the visitor anticipate that the greater part of Kavirondo is one of the most fertile and economically farthest advanced regions of the whole colony. Repeatedly the train crosses wide sandy river-beds. Their appearance indicates that the trickles of water which they ordinarily contain swell after a heavy rain to gushing streams which for hours—and during the rainy season for days or for weeks—render the dips impassable for motor-cars.

Kisumu, the terminus of the Uganda Railway on the Kavirondo Gulf— 600 miles from the coast—is the provincial headquarters of the Nyanza Province and the administrative centre of the Districts of Central Kavirondo and Kisumu–Londiani. Economically, its position as a port of transhipment for the goods traffic between the coast and Uganda was threatened after the completion of the direct railway line to Uganda (Nakuru–Jinja–Kampala) in the year 1931. However, the development of the transcontinental air-service on the Cairo–Capetown route, on which Kisumu forms one of the chief intermittent landing-stations, the discovery of gold in the North Kavirondo District (Kakamega) in the year 1931, and the steady economic progress of the native reserves in the three Kavirondo Districts have given its development new vigorous impulses. To-day Kisumu is one of the busiest centres in the colony with a population of over a hundred Europeans and several thousand Indians.

Kisumu and the Native Reserve, the scene of the present study, are two different worlds. However, the very contrast which they offer is in itself significant and instructive to the social anthropologist bent on the study of culture contact and social change.

But also within the reserve the scene is varied enough, revealing already at first sight many of the problems the study of which forms the principal concern of the present book. To give a general impression of this scene it will therefore be well to describe what one sees when travelling through the district in a motor-car.

III

Starting out for Kakamega, the administrative headquarters of the district and the centre of gold-mining, situated some thirty miles to the north-east of Kisumu, we drive along a modern all-weather road.[1] After having crossed the bottom of the Nyando Valley, the road, climbing the slope of a short side-valley covered with low thorn-bush vegetation, reaches the top of the first terrace of the Kavirondo plain. Soon the ever-grey

[1] In 1937 the average daily load amounted to 600 tons.

sheet of water of the gulf, the spreading township of Kisumu, and the Nyando Valley, from the brownish-yellow tints of which the green of an Indian sugar-plantation stands out as a bright spot, are lying far below us. Looking back, they melt into a homogeneous whole with the mountain ranges of South Kavirondo as a picturesque background.

The road, however, requires our full attention. On narrow paths which frequently cross the winding highway we meet hundreds of Africans. They are mostly women and children carrying their produce—maize, sorghum, bananas, vegetables—to the Kisumu market or balancing on their heads the heavy boxes or suitcases which their husbands want to take along on their way to a labour contract in the 'European Highlands' or on the coast. They have become so accustomed to motor traffic that they hardly step aside to let the car pass. But the numerous herds of goats and sheep grazing on either side of the road command even more attention than the natives. They have the awkward habit of darting across the road right in front of the car, while the herd-boy either runs away or looks on passively from a safe distance.

As we reach the top of the first terrace the scenery becomes far more friendly than it was down in the valley. Native cultivation becomes more frequent. Euphorbia and acacia disappear and their places are taken by various kinds of leafy trees. A nursery of black wattle and a side-road lined by an avenue of trees point to the presence of a mission station, the extensive buildings of which soon become visible in a pleasant setting a few hundred yards away from the main road. While down in the valley the native settlements to the right and the left of the road consisted of the typical kraals of the Nilotic Jaluo, their places are now taken by individual homesteads and huts. They are dotted at random over the whole country-side and furnish a visible indication that we have left the territory occupied by the Nilotes and are now in the Bantu-inhabited part of Kavirondo.

After a few miles' drive through exceedingly fertile and densely populated country the scenery changes abruptly. Having climbed a ridge, from the highest point of which we obtain a last glimpse of the Kavirondo Gulf and the gracefully curved outlines of Mount Homa rising behind it, a valley with stony slopes spreads out before us. It is almost completely bare of vegetation, and its reddish waste stands in striking contrast to the fertile garden land which we have just passed through. Less than twenty years ago, it is said, the valley and the slopes of the ridges on either side were as fertile as the surrounding lands. As a result of careless methods of cultivation the fertile top-soil has been washed off until the once fertile land eventually turned into a desert. To-day the Government authorities are endeavouring by means of a laborious scheme of soil reclamation to restore the vegetation and so to reclaim the so-called 'red ridge' at least for use as pasture land.

Steadily climbing and following the numerous bends and turnings of a valley literally strewn with rocks and boulders of all sizes, the road reaches

—about 15 miles from Kisumu—the last of the terraces and thereby the top level of the North Kavirondo plain. Before our eyes the pleasant scenery of a fertile garden land unfolds itself. Laid out in an irregular fashion, the gardens (*shambas*) of the Africans shine in a large variety of different hues, giving a kaleidoscopic impression. Maize-, sorghum-, and eleusine-fields, interspersed with ground-nut, simsim, and beans, alternate with one another. Dotted over the landscape are patches of a darker, saturated green, the banana-groves that surround almost every hut or homestead in a semicircle. Only occasionally the native cultivations are broken by a stretch of pasture land or by a swampy valley-bottom lined by trees and bushes. A rather un-African note in this setting is presented by the numerous eucalyptus trees which everywhere grow profusely, as individual specimens, in rows or small clusters, or even in unbroken patches as in a tree nursery. Thanks to their rapid growth increasing quantities of them are planted by the natives so that they threaten to supersede the indigenous trees. The impressive background of this garden scenery and the dominating feature of the whole of North Kavirondo is formed by the squat, pyramid-shaped outline of Mount Elgon (14,000 feet), extending nearly along the entire northern horizon. To the east we discern another imposing landmark, the Nandi escarpment. Running from north to south, it is likewise visible from all points of the North Kavirondo plain which it separates from the Nandi plateau as distinctly as a cliff coast marks off the land from the sea.

Over gentle hills and through flat-bottomed valleys the winding road for the next fifteen miles leads through a garden land of idyllic beauty. With about 590, and in some areas far more, inhabitants per square mile, it belongs to the most densely populated regions not only of Africa but of the whole world. The majority of native huts, with their low, circular mud walls and their peaked straw roofs, still look exactly as Joseph Thomson, the first European who visited the district in the year 1883, has described them. Nevertheless, we meet with numerous symptoms indicating that the country has undergone great changes since that time. The road frequently passes native bush and village schools. The rectangular shape of the school building, the flower garden surrounding it, the neatly laid-out lawns, and the football ground with its goal-posts, all form a striking contrast to the ordinary native homestead. Every now and then our attention is caught by a red brick house with a straw or corrugated-iron roof, the home of an African teacher, trader, or chief. Here and there we see a pasture or a field marked off by a fence, or an attempt in that direction; an obvious sign that its native owner is adopting European notions of property. At the cross-roads native dukas or stores catch the eye. They are mostly primitive huts in which enterprising Africans who have learned from their Indian tutors are selling 'King Stork' cigarettes, soap, matches, sugar, salt, tea, kerosene in bottles, safety-pins, glass beads, thread, and similar commodities of European manufacture that have come to form part of the present-day native standard of living. Some of them also sell maize porridge or boiled rice to native labourers travelling through the country to or from their place of work in European employment. These native dukas serve at the same time as the favoured meeting-places for the 'do-nothings' of the neighbourhood. For hours they sit about, smoking and gossiping, and hoping to pick up the latest news of the world from the next native-driven bus or lorry that passes by. In the open veranda, the so-called baraza, a young African sits behind a Singer sewing-machine. From cheap khaki or calico he sews clothes for the women or shirts and trousers for the men, for the completion of which his customers can wait on the premises.

On we drive, crossing numerous clear streams and deeply gorged rivers often fringed by luxuriant tropical forest, passing primitive but adequate water-mills which the Africans have constructed under the guidance and supervision of a missionary and which they now run on a co-operative basis. Strings of women walking along the road and carrying on their heads baskets with grain or fruit or large earthenware pots, of which three or four are often skilfully tied together, indicate a nearby market. Soon we pass a large pasture, situated at the boundary between two chieftaincies, where on market-days thousands of people gather to barter their produce or to sell it for money. Here numbers of native tailors sit behind their sewing-machines. Meat, fish, grain, salt, sugar, glass beads and other ornaments, pots of all sizes and shapes, clay pipes, grindstones, and many other things are offered for sale to native customers.

A few miles before reaching Kakamega we meet with the first visible signs of the gold-mining industry which has developed here in the course of the last few years.[1] While in most parts of the three Kavirondo Districts only alluvial gold is mined, here in the neighbourhood of Kakamega a number of companies are engaged in reef-mining. In the year 1934, 6,360 Africans were directly employed in the gold-mining industry of the North Kavirondo District.[2] But the economic life of a far greater number has been affected by the market which the mining companies and the individual European claim-holders offered for foodstuffs, timber for building and mining purposes, mats, &c. On the other hand, a total of 65,000 acres of native lands has been required for mining purposes—a fact which, especially during the first few years after the discovery of the gold-fields, caused considerable anxiety among the native population.

Kakamega, until the discovery of the gold-fields a quiet district station with a few Indian dukas and a native market, is to-day bustling with life. As the administrative centre of the North Kavirondo District, Kakamega is the seat of the District Office (Boma), of a Government Hospital for natives, a Government African School, the District Court of Appeal, and a Seed-farm of the Agricultural Department.

[1] In the year 1934 the number of European gold-miners varied between 360 and 420 persons (*N.A.D.A.R.*, 1934, p. 13).   [2] *N.A.D.A.R.*, 1934, p. 166.

PLATE 1

A. *Nandi Range and Nyando Valley*

B. *Descent from Equator Hill, South Maragoli*

PLATE 2

A. *A Maragoli homestead*

B. *A teacher's house: Butsotso*

THE COUNTRY

Immediately to the north of Kakamega the scenery changes again. The country becomes more open and level, the density of the population decreases, and the garden landscape prevailing in the southern part of the district gradually changes into grassland and bush steppe. Along the watercourses and on the slopes and tops of the isolated hills we encounter also here in the north a dense and varied growth of trees. Groups of boulders, consisting mostly of quickly weathering porphyritic granites, form an even more striking feature of the landscape than farther to the south. In places they are so numerous that the road can avoid them only by means of frequent curves and turnings. Fifteen miles to the north-east of Kakamega, having nearly reached the base of the Nandi escarpment, the road leads for a short stretch through a magnificent forest[1] of which larger unbroken areas are still to be found in the south-eastern part of the district (Kaimosi Forest) and on the adjoining Nandi plateau. They probably form the remainder of a large forest area which, prior to the settlement of Kavirondo by its present Bantu inhabitants, extended over the greater part of the district but which largely fell victim to native hoe-cultivation.[2]

Continuing in a northerly direction, the road leads through the chieftaincy of Kabras, passing the former village of the same name. It has gained a certain historical significance, for here the Scotsman Joseph Thomson, in the year 1883, on his expedition through Masai Land to Lake Victoria, entered Kavirondo as the first European to visit that part of the world. With 54 heads per square mile, the native population here reaches its lowest level in the whole district. The neighbourhood of the Nilo-Hamitic Nandi and the lasting influence of the nomadic Kwafi–Masai who formerly inhabited the Uasin-Gishu Plateau to the north-east of Kavirondo are still clearly reflected in the attire of the Nyala, the inhabitants of Kabras. Many of them carry Masai spears and their women wear the full leather garments of the Nandi; in their physical appearance also and in their facial features they show a distinct Nilo-Hamitic admixture.

On a high bridge we soon cross the Nzoia River (cf. above, p. 6). Carrying plenty of water all the year round, it teems with palatable fish and supplies the tribes living along its course with an important part of their diet. A mile farther on we cross the railway line to Uganda (Nakuru–Kampala) constructed in the late twenties. It has essentially contributed towards advancing the agricultural development of the northern part of the district which previously had hardly been touched by European influence.

[1] Sir Harry Johnston, 1902, vol. i, p. 44, writes about this forest: '... those forests which follow the western slope of the Nandi Plateau are certainly among the densest and richest of the Protectorate' (i.e. of Uganda).

[2] Cf. Sir Harry Johnston, 1902, vol. ii, p. 738: 'The whole of Kavirondo was once covered with dense forest of a rather West African character, but trees are now scarcely ever seen, except in the river valleys. The people would hew down all the trees they could fell, and burn the branches and trunks, mixing the ashes with the soil as manure.... After the land had borne two or three good crops it was abandoned and a fresh piece opened up.'

INTRODUCTORY

Within only five years after the completion of the railway line the native maize export from this area increased from a few hundred bags per year to 36,577. In contrast to the small irregular fields characteristic of the densely peopled southern and central parts of the district, we see here in the north large, plough-cultivated maize- and sorghum-fields up to 30 or even 40 acres, almost giving the impression of a European farming district. Enterprising Africans have exploited the traditional rights of every tribesman to cultivate as much unused land as he cares to. With the assistance of native wage labour and European methods of cultivation they have taken up the production of cash crops on a large scale. They have thereby started a development which is bound to entail far-reaching changes in the social and economic structure of native life. Native agricultural enterprise in the northern part of the district has also been greatly stimulated by the European farming areas in the adjoining districts[1] which recruit most of their agricultural labour from these parts.

We now leave the road leading to the European settlements of Kitale and Eldoret and turn off in a westerly direction. Driving along the foot-hills of Mount Elgon—no longer impressive from near by—we are following a great African highway. It is the chief motor-road between Nairobi, the capital of Kenya, and Kampala, the capital of Uganda. Nevertheless, this section of it is only a poor road which after heavy rainfalls often becomes impassable.

For the next 30 or 40 miles we are traversing the territory inhabited by the Vugusu or Kitosh, as they are called by the Masai. Although no mean agriculturists, the chief concern and pride of their men is cattle-keeping, and they have, in fact, been influenced in many ways by the cattle customs of their nomadic neighbours. In the year 1937 201,134 head of cattle and 50,144 sheep and goats were counted[2] in the three Bantu chieftaincies to the north of the Nzoia River. Having a total population of 51,139,[3] this makes 4 head of cattle to every person, an unusually large number for a Bantu tribe with a well-developed hoe-culture.[4] Despite their wealth in cattle, the Vugusu do not lead a nomadic life but are sedentary like the other tribes of the district. Until British rule was established they lived in walled villages which have been described by Thomson, Hobley, and Sir Harry Johnston. The circular mud-walls were about 10 feet high and 1 or 2 feet thick, and they had several entrances which could be tightly closed with heavy logs. Round the wall ran a moat-like ditch 3 or 4 feet deep. These village fortifications are said to have offered an effective protection against the frequent raids by the Uasin-Gishu Masai from

[1] The Trans-Nzoia and Uasin-Gishu Districts of the Rift Valley Province.
[2] Personal information supplied by the Veterinary Officer, Sangalo Veterinary Station.　　　　　　　　　　　　　　　　　　　　[3] Census of 1932.
[4] By way of comparison it may be mentioned that the Kenya Masai who, according to the official estimates of the year 1930, own more cattle than any other pastoral tribe in Kenya, possessed 720,000 head of cattle with a tribal population of 48,381 (*Report of the Kenya Land Commission*, September 1933, Cmd. 4556, p. 190).

the east and by the Teso from the west. Their remains, from which may be gauged the size of the villages, the thickness of the walls, and the depth of the ditches, may still be seen at various places in the Vugusu country; but of the huts themselves no traces are left. Nowadays the Vugusu, like the tribes in the southern part of the district, live in individual huts or homesteads scattered all over the country.

An excursion of a few miles to the wooded lower slopes of Mount Elgon takes us to the large and roomy caves, discovered by Joseph Thomson, which extend along a good part of the mountain always at the same level. Until the beginning of the present century many of them were inhabited by the El Kony, a small tribe speaking a language closely akin to that of the Nandi. Leading a timid and retiring life in the shelter of these caves, they defended themselves as best they could against the numerically superior Bantu tribes who, with their herds of cattle and their cultivations, encroached more and more upon their domain. When intertribal wars were stopped, the El Kony began to venture from their mountain retreat and to settle again in the plain. To-day they form the northernmost chieftaincy of the district and live—outwardly at least—in peaceful neighbourhood with the Vugusu.

After a drive of about 25 miles in a westerly direction through a tree- and bush-steppe, well watered by numerous streams flowing in the valleys between the ridges jutting out from the Elgon massif, we reach Malakisi, a typical Indian trading-centre. In addition to a few dozen corrugated-iron dukas, it contains a ginnery, the busy centre of this small settlement. It is the first sign that we have entered the cotton-growing area which extends from here in a westerly and south-westerly direction until it links up with the great cotton country, Uganda. A special feature of Malakisi is a dairy, the only European-operated economic enterprise in the whole reserve, apart from the gold-mining industry in the Kakamega area and the economic activities of the missions. This one dairy suffices to turn the entire surplus of cream, supplied by the 200,000 head of Vugusu cattle, into dairy products for the town populations of Kenya and Uganda.

From Malakisi we turn to the south again, making the return journey to Kisumu via Mumias and the western part of the district. Except for a mission station or two, an occasional bush school, and a few native dispensaries, the part of the reserve through which we are now passing does not yet show any marked change as compared with the old days. The homesteads and cattle enclosures do not yet betray any European influence. Many people still wear their traditional garb, a cow- or goatskin tied together over the shoulder, or a single blanket which they don in the same fashion. Soon after we have crossed the railway line for a second time, we pass Sangalo, the Government Veterinary Station and School. Africans of all tribes, after having finished their general school education, are trained here in European methods of cattle-keeping and breeding. It also serves as an experimental station in the fight against cattle diseases.

INTRODUCTORY

Gradually the bush-steppe through which we have been driving gives way to an open, undulating grassy plain, characteristic of the whole central and western part of the district, especially of the area along the central reaches of the Nzoia River.[1] Despite its scarcity of trees, this grassy plain is far from being monotonous: its ample and varied vegetation is in blossom nearly all the year round, so that the rolling plains always present a colourful and cheerful sight. Especially in the months of March and April, at the beginning of the big rains, the steppe is a vast expanse blazing with colour hardly surpassed even by neighbouring Uganda with its luxuriant vegetation.

A peculiar feature which we see in many parts of Kavirondo, but which here in the open plain is particularly striking, are the frequent quail traps of the natives. In the vicinity of many homesteads we see a tall pole (30 to 35 feet long) standing upright in the ground. Attached to it is a long row of cage-like, conically shaped baskets, each of which contains a male quail as a decoy. Radiating in all directions from the base of these poles are narrow paths in the course of which numerous noose-traps are laid for the quails.

On a modern steel suspension-bridge we cross—about 25 miles to the south of Malakisi—the Nzoia River for the second time. Its clear water flows swiftly over numerous rocks and boulders. Half a mile farther on we pass through Mumias, the residence of the Wanga chief Mumia and the former administrative centre of the North Kavirondo District.[2] The clan of the Wanga chiefs is the only one among the various tribes of Bantu Kavirondo which already in pre-European days commanded an authority extending—at least at times—beyond the tribal limits. In acknowledgement of this fact, the present Chief Mumia, who was in office when the British Administration was opened up in the year 1894, was appointed to the rank of a Paramount Chief over all tribes of the North Kavirondo District. His residence—a number of particularly large and neatly built huts grouped in a semicircle round a spacious yard—is located at some distance from the Indian dukas which make up the township proper.

At Butere, about 10 miles to the south of Mumias, we reach the terminus of another railway line, built some years ago as a branch-line from Kisumu to open up the maize-growing area in the south-western part of the district.

[1] Sir Harry Johnston was obviously referring to the central portion of North Kavirondo when he wrote: 'The whole of the Kavirondo country is most grateful to the eye. It consists of rolling downs (though there is a little marsh in the valley of the Nzoia) covered with the greenest of grass, and made additionally beautiful by the blending with the green of fleecy white, shining mauve or pale pink, effects which are caused by the grass being in flower or fluffy seed.... Where the land is not actually under cultivation in Kavirondo, the prairies are gorgeous with wild flowers at almost all times of the year. Prominent amongst these are the sunflowers (Coreopsis), which cause certain hill-sides to blaze with yellow.' (*The Uganda Protectorate*, vol. i, pp. 44 and 50–1.)

[2] In the year 1920 the District Office was moved to Kakamega, which has a more healthy climate.

The scenery encountered during the last stage of our trip resembles again the garden land through which we passed between Kisumu and Kakamega. As we approach the south-western corner of the district the density of the population steadily increases. In the chieftaincy of Bunyore it reaches the remarkable figure of 1,137 persons to the square mile. In these parts the native homesteads stand close together; every inch of arable soil is exploited to the utmost, and pasture land is so scarce that not only sheep but also cattle are tethered while grazing or even stable-fed. But even the extraordinary fertility of the soil and the two full crops which it yields every year cannot sustain such a dense population. Clear symptoms of overpopulation begin to show: not only do adults take up labour-contracts in European employment, but to an increasing extent children also, who work chiefly as tea-pickers in the Kericho tea plantations. But whereas some of the people have to look for work outside the reserve to buy foodstuffs out of the money which they earn, others grow maize for export even here in Bunyore.

At Maseno, a central mission station of the Church Missionary Society located right on the Equator, the road leaves the North Kavirondo District and enters the territory of the Nilotic Jaluo. In a steady decline it descends into the plain adjoining the Kavirondo Gulf and soon reaches our starting-point, Kisumu.

Although we have covered scarcely 170 miles, we have gained a great variety of impressions. Within the compass of less than 3,000 square miles we have encountered many different types of scenery, ranging from highly developed garden land to sparsely settled bush-steppe and tropical rain-forest. We have passed through regions settled by tribes who by intensive methods of cultivation feed more than a thousand persons per square mile, and through others inhabited by tribes whose wealth in cattle is not far behind that of the major pastoral tribes of Africa. We have obtained glimpses of the most varying shades and degrees of the process of culture change. From the Kakamega mining district, where in the course of a few years the living conditions of the natives have come to resemble those prevailing in South Africa, to the comparatively untouched chieftaincies in the north-western part of the district, where the great majority of the native population still largely maintains its traditional mode of life. North Kavirondo thus presents itself as a field of study which promises to be fruitful not only for a widening of our knowledge of Bantu life but also for an understanding of the problems with which the African native of our days is confronted.

B. THE PEOPLE

THE area occupied by the Bantu Kavirondo on the whole corresponds to the political boundaries of the North Kavirondo District. An exception is formed by the north-western part of the district which is inhabited by the Nilo-Hamitic Mia (called Kidi[1] by the Swahili and Elgumi by the Masai), a sub-group of the Teso. According to the 1937 census they number 26,066, and they occupy an area of 208 square miles. Other minor non-Bantu groups living within the district are the El Kony (numbering 3,475 souls) on the slopes of Mount Elgon, and the Lago and Ngoma (Ngomanek) who have been politically absorbed within the tribe of the Vugusu, all three of whom speak a Nandi dialect; furthermore, there are remnants of the Uasin-Gishu Masai living among the Kabras (about 1,200), 11,000 Luo, most of whom have intermarried with Bantu in the south-western part of the district or are working in the Kakamega gold-mines, and finally several hundred Swahili, Ganda, and Nubians who are chiefly to be found at Mumias where, in the early days, they formed part of the British garrison (cf. p. 31). The only major Bantu Kavirondo tribe living outside the district in Central Kavirondo are the Samia, who extend as far as Uganda. They and the Gishu, who adjoin the Vugusu in the extreme north-western corner of the district, are the only Bantu tribes who form a territorial link between the Bantu Kavirondo and the neighbouring Bantu groups of Uganda, the Soga, Gwe, and Nyuli.

All other neighbours of the Bantu Kavirondo are non-Bantu tribes: to the south and south-west the Nilotic Jaluo, to the south-east and east the Nilotic Nandi and Nyangori (a sub-group of the Nandi), and in the north-east (formerly) the Uasin-Gishu Masai.[2] Prior to the establishment of British rule the Bantu Kavirondo lived in a state of more or less permanent warfare with all these neighbouring groups. In their relations with the Masai and the Nandi they were chiefly on the defensive; their contests with the Jaluo seem to have been characterized by an approximate equality of military prowess, while they were obviously clearly superior to the Teso and El Kony whose villages they claim to have frequently raided.

In 1937 the Bantu Kavirondo (with the exception of the Samia) numbered 312,000 souls. As far as can be judged from the available data,[3] the population is moving on the upward grade. The following comparative figures, which, however, comprise only about two-thirds of the chieftaincies of the district, indicate an increase of 9·65 per cent. in 14 years, which is the equivalent of an annual increase of 0·69 per cent.

[1] Probably the same word as the term 'kedi' used in Uganda to designate the Nilotes.

[2] After 1860 the greater part of the Uasin-Gishu Masai (Kwafi) was decimated by wars with the main Masai bands, so that at the time when Joseph Thomson travelled through Masai Land the greater part of the Uasin-Gishu Plateau was already uninhabited (cf. J. Thomson, *Through Masai Land*, 2nd edition, p. 243). In connexion with the transfer of the Masai which the British Administration carried through in the years from 1904 to 1906 the Uasin-Gishu Plateau was cleared of the remaining Masai bands roaming there and it has since been developed as a European farming district. In 1937 (*Blue Book*), 1,997 Europeans were living in the Uasin-Gishu District of the Rift Valley Province.

[3] They are based on hut-counts (undertaken for purposes of taxation) which comprise only the adult part of the population.

THE PEOPLE

	Census of 1918[1]	Census of 1932
Buholo	6,783	8,687
Bukhayo	12,826	16,816
Butsotso	5,215	8,457
Kabras	9,252	10,829
Kakalelwa	5,358	4,859
Kakamega	30,264	31,406
Kitosh	47,632	51,139
Marach	12,213	14,864
Marama	22,287	18,957
Mukulu	4,993	6,154
Wanga	24,072	26,187
Total	180,895	198,355

Comparative figures for the entire native population of the district are: 340,917 for 1932 and 354,505 for 1937, which means an annual increase of 0·8 per cent. It is, however, impossible to ascertain to what extent this increase is due to the immigration of natives from other districts since the discovery of the Kakamega gold-fields, rather than to a biological increase of the population. The Native Affairs Department Annual Report for 1932 states that the population of the North Kavirondo District shows an annual increase of 1·2 per cent., a figure which, however, in view of the available data appears to be rather on the high side. In the absence of any vital statistics—when I left the district in 1938 births and deaths were not yet registered, but it was proposed to establish marriage registers in the more progressive chieftaincies—it is as yet impossible to do more than guess at the trend of the biological population movement.

As has already been mentioned, the population is rather unevenly distributed over the district. While the average density is 140·84 per square mile, it rises to several hundred in the southern and south-eastern chieftaincies (with a maximum of 1,137), whereas in the north and the north-east it drops to less than 80 per square mile (with a minimum of 54·15).

The sex ratio is characterized by a considerable surplus of male births which—as far as the scanty observations at hand reveal—does not appear to be neutralized by the higher mortality of male infants. Hobley, on the basis of figures compiled by him, gives the following comparative figures showing the ratio of male and female births for the Bantu Kavirondo, Jaluo, and Nandi:[2]

	Male births, per cent.	Female births, per cent.
Bantu Kavirondo	57·5	42·5
Jaluo	42	58
Nandi	48·75	51·25

[1] According to data supplied by N. Stam, 1919, p. 969.
[2] C. W. Hobley, 1903, p. 354.

INTRODUCTORY

Figures obtained by myself from the maternity wards of the American Friends Mission Hospital at Kaimosi (chieftaincy Tiriki) and of the Church of God Mission at Kima (chieftaincy Bunyore) show the following ratio:

(1) *Kaimosi*

Year	Male births	Female births
1929	51	31
1930	77	57
1931	50	52
1932	68	57
1933	136	101
1934	60	72
Total	442	370

Year	Male births	Female births	Stillborn Male	Stillborn Female
1935	76	68	28	23
1936	93	83	28	18
1937	97	84	21	21
1938 (Jan.–Apr.)	23	19	5	6
	289	254	82	68
Less	82	68		
Live births	207	186		
Live births, per cent.	52·6	47·4		

(2) *Kima*[1]

Year	Male births	Female births	Sex not registered
1936	45	34	5
1937	54	35	1
Total	99	69	6

Inquiries concerning the sex ratio which I have undertaken at a number of schools by questioning the pupils as to their living and deceased siblings likewise show a surprising predominance of the male sex, and this not only among the Bantu but, in contrast with Mr. Hobley's observations, also among the Jaluo.

[1] The figures contain 8 stillbirths for the year 1936 and 9 for 1937, the sex not being stated. By way of comparison it may be mentioned that in the Mengo Hospital at Kampala, Uganda, out of a total of 1,097 births 570 were male and 527 female.

I. *Bantu*

School	Living children		Deceased children	
	Male	Female	Male	Female
Kima Mission (Bunyore) . . .	165	118	114	97
Friends Mission (Kaimosi) . . .	136	91	78	74
Catholic Mission (Yala) . . .	219	202	..	..

II. *Nilotes (Jaluo)*

Kima Mission (Bunyore) . . .	58	68	27	24
Catholic Mission (Yala) . . .	182	122	..	..

This strong preponderance of the male sex over the female may, to some extent, be due to the fact that the pupils of the schools where I have made my inquiries are recruited from families boasting on the whole a higher percentage of male children than would be the tribal average. Such a tendency might have its explanation in the fact that fathers with more daughters than sons would have less reason to send their sons to a boarding-school than fathers with more sons than daughters. Such a tendency, however, even if it existed, would not entirely explain the preponderance of the male sex.

A careful inventory which I made of all the inhabitants of a Christian village in North Kitosh confirms the results obtained from the inquiries made in native schools. The inventory shows that the 36 Christian families living in the village had a total of 47 living sons and of 31 living daughters, the average age of the male children being 4·03 years and that of the female children 6·7 years.[1] The number of the deceased male children amounted to 15 as against 23 female children. The sex ratio of the total number of children in the Christian village which had been 62 : 54 at birth had—owing to the higher mortality rate of the female children—changed in favour of the male children, instead of the female ones as one would have expected.

From the ethnical, linguistic, and political points of view the Bantu Kavirondo do not form a homogeneous group, even though they are clearly distinct from the surrounding tribes. The term 'Kavirondo', the origin and etymology of which are still obscure, never appears to have been used by the natives themselves. Nor does there seem to exist any word in the various Bantu Kavirondo dialects from which the term 'Kavirondo' could possibly have been derived. According to Sir Harry Johnston's inquiries the term 'Kavirondo' was employed and spread by Swahili and Arab traders.

'The word Kavirondo', writes Sir Harry, 'probably appeared first on the maps drawn by Mr. E. G. Ravenstein at the end of the seventies from information given him by Mombasa missionaries, such as the late Mr. Wakefield.

---

[1] The year of birth could be ascertained for all children with a high degree of accuracy.

INTRODUCTORY

It is certain that the Swahili and Arab caravans who first reached the north-east coast of Lake Victoria Nyanza came back with the impression that the people in that direction were styled "Kavirondo" and communicated these views to Mr. Wakefield.[1]

Owing to its constant use by Europeans, the term 'Kavirondo' has nowadays been to some extent adopted by the natives, but they use it with reference to the district rather than to themselves. When talking to other natives—even outside the district—they always style themselves by the name of their respective sub-tribe, such as Wanga, Vugusu, Logoli, Nyole, &c. Among politically minded natives who for a number of years have been pleading for a political unification of all Bantu Kavirondo tribes under a paramount chief according to the Buganda pattern, the word *avaluhia*, meaning 'those of the same tribe', is propagated as a common designation for all Bantu Kavirondo. The term 'Kavirondo', on the other hand, is generally rejected in these quarters as being of European origin.

In pre-European days the various sub-tribes of Bantu Kavirondo were, for their greater part, very loosely organized politically, each sub-tribe consisting of a number of more or less sovereign clans. Since British rule was established in the middle of the nineties they have been organized into chieftaincies. Since these sub-tribes did not possess any ruling clans with generally acknowledged clan-heads, suitable and deserving natives were appointed as chiefs by the British authorities. As a rule, such chiefs were chosen from the oldest and largest clan of the tribe. In a few cases, however, a different system, successfully employed in neighbouring Uganda, was resorted to: members of the ruling clan of the Wanga tribe—politically the most highly developed tribe of the district—were instituted as chiefs over other tribes.[2] The chief of the Wanga tribe who from the very beginning adopted a loyal attitude towards the British in which he

[1] Sir Harry Johnston, 1902, vol. ii, p. 722; cf. also N. Stam, 1919, p. 972: 'The early explorers are responsible for it, and they must have got it from the Swahili interpreters they had with them. Whether centuries ago a people lived here, called Kavirondo, we do not know; in any case none of the tribes out here, whether Bantu or Nilotic, know the word and only learnt it from the European official.' And furthermore, C. W. Hobley, 1903, p. 359: 'I have often made enquiries into the origin of the name of Kavirondo, and the Kisumu elders inform me that it is the name which the people of the south side of Kavirondo Gulf apply to the people of the north side; it is, however, a term used when they meet at a dance and smoke bhang and sing about old times. They call the people of the north side Kavirondo, because they were vanquished by the latter and driven across to the south side of the bay; it was thus, originally, more or less an epithet of reproach.' This would mean that the word 'Kavirondo' is of Nilotic origin.

[2] Cf. *N.A.D.A.R.*, 1929, p. 19: 'Briefly, the position is that in the early days the administration found a family of conquerers—the Wanga—in this District, very much superior to the indigenous tribes who were completely sunk in barbarism(!). As it was impossible to appoint chiefs from these indigenous people who could exercise any authority whatever, the practice was adopted of putting Wanga natives in charge of the different locations.'

THE PEOPLE

never wavered was, in the year 1909, given the official title of 'Paramount Chief' over the Bantu Kavirondo. His position, however, was and still is that of a mere figure-head, as he does not exercise any specific governmental or administrative functions beyond the limits of his own tribal area. In the course of time the chieftaincies which had been originally set up were, in a number of cases, subjected to alterations and corrections, a process which, to-day, seems to have been essentially concluded, even though in the various chieftaincies there are still a number of individual clans clamouring for political independence, i.e. for their recognition as separate chieftaincies.[1]

In 1937 the North Kavirondo District comprised the following twenty-two Bantu chieftaincies:

Name of chieftaincy[2]	Population[3]	Area in sq. miles	Density of population per sq. mile
1-2. North Wanga } South Wanga }	26,187	161	162·65
3. Mukulu	6,154	41	150·09
4. North Marama } 5. South Marama }	18,957	120	157·98
6. Buholo	8,667	34	255·50
7. Marach	14,864	99	150·14
8. Buhayo	16,816	146	115·18
9. South Kitosh	19,438	336	57·85
10. Malakisi	11,587	130	89·13
11. North Kitosh (Kimilili)	20,114	320	73·71
12. Kabras	10,829	200	54·15
13. Kakalelwa	4,859	55	88·35
14. Butsotso	8,457	77	109·83
15. Kisa	14,391	50	287·82
16. Idaxo	6,857	20	342·85
17. West Kakamega[4]	21,636	120	180·30
18. East Kakamega[4]	9,770	101	96·53
19. Tiriki	17,178	65	264·28
20. North Maragoli	25,451	43	591·88
21. South Maragoli	20,349	52	391·33
22. Bunyore	30,706	27	1,137·26
Total	312,787	2,197	..

[1] Cf. *N.A.D.A.R.*, 1935, p. 6 sq.: 'Now . . . each location is under a separate chief. But these chiefs seldom command the loyalty of their whole location; the habit of devolution has spread to the leading sub-clans and families who would scarcely be satisfied until every sub-clan had a puppet chief of its own. His Excellency the Governor reiterated his statement made in the previous year that Government would not consider the further splitting up of locations.' (There follows an enumeration of concrete claims raised by the various clans to be granted a chief of their own.)

[2] The following names are the official ones, laid down by the Administration.

[3] According to the census of 1932. [4] Tribal territory of the Isuxa.

INTRODUCTORY

The territories assigned to these various chieftaincies and their present-day boundaries (cf. map on p. 2) correspond, on the whole, to the areas actually occupied by the various tribal groups when British rule was first established. In several cases where more than one clan raised a claim for political leadership, what would be the tribal units from an ethnical and linguistic point of view were split up into several chieftaincies, e.g. North and South Wanga, North and South Kitosh, East and West Kakamega, North and South Maragoli. The official names given to the various chieftaincies are exclusively names of localities and, in the majority of cases, differ from the actual tribal names. The inhabitants of the three chieftaincies of North Kitosh, South Kitosh, and Malakisi, for example, are all called Vugusu; the people of Kakalelwa[1] and those of Kabras call themselves Nyala; those of East and West Kakamega, Isuxa, and those of Maragoli, Logoli. All the tribal names refer—as far as I was able to ascertain—to the personal name of the real or mythological founder of the respective tribal group. The different clans within each tribal group derive their origin from descendants of the tribal ancestor with the exception of those who, according to their clan traditions, joined the tribal unit to which they nowadays belong after it had been in existence. Among the Wanga, for instance, I compiled a list comprising 30 clans, of which 18 did *not* derive their origin from Omuwanga, the tribal ancestor. Having come from all directions, they have, one by one and at different times, joined the Wanga tribe where, however, they nowadays enjoy the same status as the original Wanga clans (cf. below, p. 66).

Although the various Bantu Kavirondo sub-tribes are *all* interrelated both ethnically and linguistically, they can be divided into a few major groups, each of which is characterized by common or very closely related dialects as well as by close political, social, and economic interrelations of its component tribal groups.

My notes taken on the origin and the migrations of the various tribes according to their tribal and clan traditions yield the following picture:

1. The *Vugusu*, who occupy the northern part of the district, have migrated to their present abode from the north-west. Muvugusu, the mythical tribal ancestor, is said to have lived at a place called Embai in Karamoja (Kirimodjo). Under the pressure of his enemies, the Tola (from the Teso tribe) and the Nyole (a Bantu tribe speaking a tongue closely resembling Luganda), Muvugusu together with his sons emigrated in a southerly direction, settling down again somewhere to the east of Mbale (between Mbale and Mount Elgon). His descendants again migrated from there towards the south, till they came to a hill to the north-east of Tororo, the so-called 'Vugusu Hill'. From there—again yielding to the pressure exercised by the Teso—they moved on in a south-easterly direction till they reached the country to the south of Mount Elgon, where they are still

[1] They deny, however, that they are related to the Nyala of Kabras.

living to-day. Upon their arrival at Kitosh the Vugusu found that the country was practically uninhabited, with the exception of such minor tribes as the Ngoma, Lago, and El Kony.[1] Only the Masai came occasionally from the east, raiding their villages and stealing their cattle.

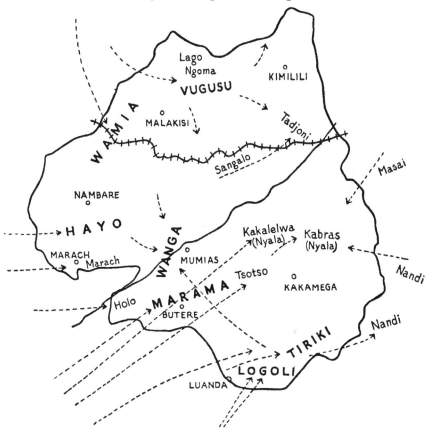

In the eastern part of Kitosh, along the upper reaches of the Nzoia River, live the *Tadjoni*, a small tribe which already in pre-European days maintained close marriage relations with the Vugusu and which to-day has been amalgamated into the chieftaincy of North Kitosh (Kimilili). According to the statements made by their old men, the Tadjoni formerly lived in the neighbourhood of Sangalo Hill (about 25 miles to the west of their present abode) until, under the pressure of the Teso and Wanga, they moved farther to the east. They say that their original home was in western Uganda, where they claim to have formed part of the Ziba tribe (nowadays living on the western shores of Lake Victoria to the north of Bukoba).

[1] Called Vakoyondjo by the Vugusu.

2. The *Wanga*, who nowadays inhabit the central part of the district along the middle reaches of the Nzoia River, call themselves after their tribal ancestor Omuwanga. According to the traditions of the ruling clan their history dates back far beyond Omuwanga (cf. vol. ii). They claim that their earliest ancestors lived in West Africa, at a place called Makatas. From there they moved towards the east till they came to Lake Albert, thence through Unyoro and Busoga until they reached the shores of Lake Victoria at the Kavirondo Gulf near Kisumu. There the tribe split up; one part migrated farther towards the south, while another part turned towards the north and north-east, settling down at a place called Elinde (in the present area of the Tiriki). It was here at Elinde that Wanga, the tribal ancestor, was born. After a quarrel with his brother Kaviakala he left Elinde and, after a longish period of roaming about, finally settled at Matungu (about 3 miles to the north-west of the present township of Mumias). The descendants of Omuwanga (the tribal genealogy lists ten generations from Omuwanga down to the present Chief Mumia) remained more or less at the same place. The Mukulu (meaning the upper ones, i.e. those living on the high ground) are part of the Wanga who have only recently split off to form a tribe of their own.

Like the Wanga, the *Marama*, *Tsotso*, and *Tiriki* also claim to have migrated into their present homes in North Kavirondo from the south-west, that is to say, from the neighbourhood of the Kavirondo Gulf and the eastern shores of Lake Victoria. Thus, the Marama say they have come from what is now the Luo chieftaincy of Alego in Central Kavirondo, while the Tsotso name a place called Mujiene on Lake Victoria as their original home.

The *Tiriki* say that their distant ancestors had migrated from Uganda to the Kavirondo Gulf whence they moved on to South Kavirondo like one section of the ancestors of the Wanga. Under the leadership of Lulidzi and his wife Aliowa they returned across the gulf and settled near Maseno, where Lulidzi died. His son Kisienya built a village at Hamasiri, a place situated on the border between the present-day chieftaincies of Bunyore and South Maragoli. The Tiriki elders claim that Kisienya and Wanga at first lived together. Later, when they separated, Omuwanga moved towards the north and Kisienya towards the east. Nandunda, Kisienya's son, is said to have begotten a large family, the various branches of which later separated at a place called Muluanyi.

The *Nyala* (*Kakalelwa*) migrated into North Kavirondo only a few generations ago, coming from Mumome and Olundu in Uganda. In the seventies of last century they still lived among the Wanga, under Chief Tomia (cf. vol. ii).

All I was able to learn about the *Kabras* was that they have come from the west. Only a few generations ago they lived in the territory that is now inhabited by the Tsotso. They appear to be closely related to the Tadjoni, with whom they frequently intermarry. A number of their clans claim to be of Nandi origin, the Nilo-Hamitic tribe adjoining them in the east.

THE PEOPLE 25

3. The *Hayo, Marach,* and *Holo* claim to have branched off the Soga in Uganda and to have only recently migrated to their present abodes. The Hayo have since then considerably mixed with their northern neighbours, the Nilotic Mia (Teso).

4. The *Logoli,* finally, say that they have come from the south, from the neighbourhood of Shirati on the eastern shores of Lake Victoria, immediately to the south of the Kenya–Tanganyika boundary.

'Mulogoli (the tribal ancestor)—so the tradition goes—moved with his people from Shirati towards the north and crossed the Kavirondo Gulf in boats. At first he settled near Maseno. Then (under the pressure of the Jaluo) he moved farther towards the east to Migono Hill (nowadays called Equator Hill), where he lies buried. Twice a year an old man who functions as tribal priest goes to Mulogoli's grave to pray there and to make an offering (*muŋoma*). The country to the east of Maseno and of Migono was uninhabited when Mulogoli arrived there; only elephants were grazing there. The Tiriki lived farther to the east (having thus, apparently, settled in their present abodes before the Logoli). The relatives of the Logoli who stayed behind in South Kavirondo call themselves Avasuva; they speak a similar tongue and observe the same customs.'

As these migratory accounts indicate, the greater part of the Bantu Kavirondo tribes has come from the west, with the exception of the Vugusu who claim to have come from the north or north-west, and the Logoli who have come from the south. It is, of course, possible that the Logoli, even if they *did* come from the south, have no connexion with the Bantu tribes living to the south-east of Lake Victoria (Shashi, Kulia, Nyamwezi), but rather belonged to that branch of the Wanga who, from their temporary abodes on the Kavirondo Gulf, moved farther to the south, while the immediate ancestors of the Wanga turned towards the north.

To judge by the genealogies of the ruling clans, most of the Bantu tribes of North Kavirondo have been in the district only for ten or fifteen generations, which would correspond to a period of between 200 and 350 years. Probably they had settled in Central Kavirondo (along the gulf) as well as in the western part of North Kavirondo before the southward migration of the Nilotic Jaluo began. Under the pressure of the Luo migration, which drove a sort of wedge from the north-west (between Lake Kioga and Mount Elgon) to the south-east, the Bantu advanced farther into uninhabited North Kavirondo as well as across the gulf and through the Nyando Valley to South Kavirondo.[1] After the southward migration

[1] According to entries in the district records at Kisii in South Kavirondo, the Avagusii (Kisii) formerly lived in the low-lying regions to the north and the east of the Kavirondo Gulf, viz. the Mugirangu in Uyoma and the Kitoto in Kano (in the Nyando Valley). Their southward migration was caused towards the end of the eighteenth century by the Jaluo coming from the north-west and pushing forward in a south-easterly direction. On the question of the migrations of Bantu and Nilotes in this area cf. also Macdonald, J. R. L., 'Notes on the Ethnology of Tribes

of the Nilotic Jaluo had come to an end, further Bantu possibly migrated from Busoga in an easterly direction towards North Kavirondo (the Hayo, Marach, and Holo). This assumption not only tallies with the traditions of these three tribes, but it also explains why a group of Bantu tribes lives between the Nilotic Jaluo in Central Kavirondo and the Nilotic Jopadhola (to the west of Tororo in the Budama District of the Eastern Province of Uganda).

A comparative survey of the different Bantu Kavirondo dialects is in full agreement with these migratory traditions. From the phonological point of view, the following four groups of dialects can be distinguished:

1. Luhanga (dialect spoken by the Wanga), Lutsotso, Lunyore, Lutiriki, Luisuxa, Luidaxo.
2. Luvugusu.
3. Lunyala (Kakalelwa), Lusamia.
4. Lurogoli.

English	Hanga	Vugusu	Logoli	Nyala (Kakalelwa)
(1) My wife	omuxasi wandje	ómuxasi wase	omukali wange	omuxasi wange
My wives	avaxasi vandje	váxasi vase	avakali vange	avaxasi vange
(2) My tree	omusala gwandje	gumurongoro gwase	omusala gwange	omusala gwange
My trees	emisala djiandje	gimirongoro giase	emisala djange	emisala gyange
(3) My thing	eʃindu ʃiandje	sísindu siase	ekindu kyange	esinyu siange
My things	eʃindu ʃiandje	vívindu viase	evindu vyange	evinyu viange
(4) My sheep	ligondi liandje	líxese liase	ligondi liange	ekondi liange
My sheep	amagondi gandje	kámaxese kase	amagondi gange	amakondi kange
(5) My cow	iŋombe yandje	éxafu yase	eŋombe yange	eŋombe yange
My cows	tsiŋombe tsiandje	tʃíxafu tʃase	edziŋombe dziange	eŋombe tjiange
(6) My tongue	olulimi luandje	lúlimi luase	olulimi luange	olulimi luange
My tongues	tsinimi tsiandje	tʃínimi tʃase	edzinimi dziange	enimi tjiange
(7) My flour	ovusie vuandje	vúvusi vwase	ovusi vwange	ovusie vuange
(8) My small hut	axasimba xandje	xásimba xase	akasimba kange	axasimba xange
My small huts	orusimba ruandje	rúsimba ruase	otusimba twange	otyusimba twange
(9) My big cow	ogugombe gwandje	kúxafu kwase	ogugombe gwange	okukombe kwange
My big cows	emigombe djiandje	kímixafu kiase	emigombe djange	emikombe kiange

As the above diagram shows, the plosives in Lurogoli correspond to fricatives or affricatives in Luhanga and Luvugusu. *ng* in Lurogoli is *ndj* (or *ntj*) or *s*; *k* becomes *x*, *s*, or *ʃ*; *t* becomes *r*. Luvugusu, which is practically identical with Lugishu, is furthermore characterized by double prefixes (*gumu-*, *gimi-*, *sisi-*, *vivi-*, &c.). Also from the semantic point of view it stands rather apart from the other Bantu Kavirondo dialects. Lunyala, which is almost identical with Lusamia, phonologically seems to occupy an

met with during Progress of the Juba Expedition of 1897–1909', *J.A.I.* vol. xxix, p. 242. The view expressed there that the 'Negro Nyifa' (Jaluo) lived in Kavirondo already before the Bantu who subsequently came into the country as conquerors seems, however, to contradict all the other evidence, as in the tribal traditions of the Bantu Kavirondo there is no talk of wars of conquest against the Jaluo, but only of a gradual recoiling from their pressure. Cf. Northcote, 1907, p. 58: 'They (the Jaluo) state that they came from the north-west under one big chief and that when they again became too numerous they split up into smaller chieftaincies.' See also Sir H. Johnston, 1902, vol. ii, p. 765; J. Roscoe, *The Northern Bantu*, p. 276; N. Stam, 1919, p. 968; C. W. Hobley, 1929, pp. 172–3, and 1903, vol. xxxiii, p. 328.

intermediary position between the Logoli and the Hanga dialects. It further differs from the other dialects in that the singular prefix of the fourth noun class (*li-*, *ma-*) is *e-* instead of *li-* and that the plural prefix of the fifth and the sixth classes is likewise *e-* instead of *edzi-* (or *tsi-*). Between the various sub-dialects of the Hanga group there are only minor phonological differences. Thus, Luhanga *d* frequently becomes *t* in Lutiriki; *v* becomes *f*, while Luhanga *i* becomes *yi* in Lunyole.

The political relations between the various tribes were formerly largely determined by the degree of their linguistic, ethnical, and genealogical relationship (cf. vol. ii). Although hostilities even between closely related neighbouring tribes seem to have been frequent enough, a clear distinction was made between tribes regarded as traditional enemies and those with whom one entered only into occasional feuds which then were not settled with sharp weapons but merely by the use of clubs and poles, although the old men insist that these latter weapons too were occasionally used to inflict fatal injuries.[1] Tribes that were on friendly terms with one another maintained regular marriage relations (even though the rule was to marry within the same tribe, cf. p. 393), while in the case of traditional enemy tribes it was customary to marry only women who had been captured as children, and who had then been brought up in accordance with the tribal pattern.

In the sense of this distinction, the Vugusu regarded the Gishu, Tadjoni, Kabras, and Kakalelwa as 'friendly neighbours', while they looked upon the Teso, Wanga, and Masai as their traditional enemies. The Idaxo maintained friendly relations with the Logoli and Tiriki and fought the Tsotso, Isuxa, Nandi, and Masai. The Tsotso again were essentially on good terms with the Marama, Wanga, Kisa, and Tiriki and hostile towards the Vugusu. The Logoli, finally, were friends with the Tiriki, Idaxo, and Nyole, but sworn enemies of the Nilotic Jaluo, Nyangori, and Nandi.

As regards their traditional culture, the general homogeneity prevailing throughout the district in all essential aspects of native custom is broken by certain local differences. These are due partly to indigenous local developments and, for the greater part, to influence issuing from neighbouring non-Bantu tribes. Such regional differences are most pronounced in the sphere of economic life. Whereas all Bantu Kavirondo are both pastoral and agricultural, cattle-keeping is far more important in the northern part of the district (among the Vugusu), while agriculture is more highly developed among the southern tribes, particularly among the Logoli, Nyole, Idaxo, and Tiriki.

As regards the development of their political institutions, the Wanga occupy a special place. The Nilotic influence is most pronounced in the southern and south-western parts of the district. It manifests itself, for instance, in the custom of knocking out the lower incisors, not practised in

[1] This distinction in the use of weapons was made by all my informants among the different tribes (Logoli, Tiriki, Nyole, Marama, Tsotso) so persistently and emphatically that it appears to be significant.

the northern part of the district; furthermore (among the tribes along the western border of North Kavirondo) in the absence or the sporadic or restricted practice of circumcision and initiation rites (cf. p. 336), and probably also in the manner of thatching the roofs of their huts which, among the Logoli and the Nyole, are terraced (as among most Nilotic tribes),[1] while among the remaining Bantu Kavirondo tribes the roofs are evenly thatched. In the eastern and north-eastern parts of the district, the clothing, ornaments, weapons, and style of hairdressing have been largely copied from the Masai and Nandi. Another obvious Nilo-Hamitic feature is the circumcision age-class system among the Vugusu which, in contrast to that prevailing among the other Bantu Kavirondo tribes, is subdivided into several sections and sub-sections for each age-class (cf. below, p. 375).

As regards their physical appearance, the Bantu Kavirondo are mostly tall and well proportioned, especially the men; the women frequently have very broad hips and short limbs. Individual natives attain a height of between 1·85 and 1·90 metres, the average height of the men being somewhere round 1·70 to 1·75; exact anthropological measurements of a major number of individuals, however, have so far not yet been taken.[2] The majority of the natives give the impression of being healthy and robust. With the exception of the aged, and especially of the old women, they are, as a rule, well nourished, even though obesity is a very rare exception which I have never been able to observe among married women and, as regards men, only in the case of a few wealthy chiefs and headmen. The prevailing colour of the skin is a dark chocolate-brown; occasionally, however, one also sees light-skinned individuals.

Head and face are moderately long, the back of the head often pronounced and pleasantly rounded; the nose is straight and only fairly broad and flat, and the lips, although full, are not very thick. The Nilotic Jaluo in their characteristic representatives are clearly distinguished from the prevailing Bantu type by much thicker lips which are seldom quite closed, so that the teeth usually show, furthermore by a squat nose with very broad nostrils and, on the whole, coarser though not uglier features. Occasionally this Nilotic type is also met with among the Bantu, particularly in the south-western part of the district where intermarriage between Bantu and Nilotes occurs more frequently. A second 'non-Bantu type', which I noticed particularly among the Isuxa and the Vugusu, is characterized by eyes lying deep in their sockets, a very flat nose especially at its root, broad nostrils, a protruding mouth and chin, a big mouth, and a long upper lip,

[1] Among the Jaluo, however, roofs are nowadays thatched evenly as among the majority of Bantu tribes. If the terraced roof encountered among the Logoli is actually due to Nilotic influence, this must date back to early times. Cf. also Sir Harry Johnston, 1902, vol. ii, p. 772.

[2] Cf. Sir Harry Johnston, 1902, vol. ii, pp. 496–7. The height of stature given there for 8 Kavirondo men (Bantu and Nilotes) amounts to an average of 175·6 cm., with a minimum of 168·7 and a maximum of 183·9 cm.

often convexly curved. Apart from this strikingly ugly and primitive type, one occasionally encounters natives with an Ethiopian strain which manifests itself in a narrow, longish face, a thin, slightly aquiline nose, and comparatively thin lips.

The general impression which the Bantu Kavirondo give by their physical appearance is summed up by Joseph Thomson[1] in the following words:

'The Wakavirondo are by no means attractive in their appearance and they contrast unfavourably with the Masai. Their heads are of a distinctly lower type, eyes dull and muddy, jaws somewhat prognathous, mouth unpleasantly large, and lips thick, projecting and everted—they are in fact true negroes. Their figures are better, though only among unmarried young women could they be said to be in any sense pleasing to look at. Among the married the abdomen is aggressively protuberant and roughly tattooed without betraying any attempt at ornamentation.'

Sir Harry Johnston arrives at a considerably more favourable judgement when he writes:[2]

'The Kavirondo proper (meaning the Bantu Kavirondo) . . . are, as a rule, a handsome race of negroes, exhibiting sometimes, especially among the men, really beautiful physical proportions and statuesque forms. Here and there, as throughout most of the negro races . . . there are reversions to an ugly and inferior type representing the Pygmy-Prognathous element which formed the first stratum of the human population in nearly all Negro Africa.'

Of these two judgements that of Thomson would appear to be rather unfriendly, but it must be taken into account that in returning his verdict on the physical appearance of the Bantu Kavirondo he was still under the impression of the Masai with whom, of course, they compare unfavourably. In characterizing the facial features of the Bantu Kavirondo, Thomson evidently had in mind the more inferior type which, however, would appear to me to be definitely in the minority.

To make a summary statement on the mental and moral qualities of the Bantu Kavirondo will be relevant only if based on a broad comparative knowledge of a large number of different tribes and not merely on contact with this one group. Hobley, who during a lifetime of administrative practice came to know practically all native tribes of Kenya, thus writes of the Bantu Kavirondo:[3]

'The great point about the Kavirondo (Bantu), however, was that they were men. Once they were beaten they readily made peace and, once they had made peace, it *was* peace, for within a few hours the women were in camp selling food, and one had no anxiety about a subsequent treacherous attack either at night or on the road. Under these circumstances mutual respect gradually supervened and we became great friends.'

---

[1] J. Thomson, *Through Masai Land*, p. 423.
[2] Sir H. Johnston, 1902, vol. ii, p. 726.
[3] C. W. Hobley, 1929, pp. 87–8.

30   INTRODUCTORY

This early verdict on the straightforwardness and reliability of the Bantu Kavirondo is borne out also by the reputation which they enjoy to-day among the white population of Kenya. In his book *Kenya Without Prejudice* Weller sums up this reputation with the following words:

'The Kavirondo goes everywhere in these days, and is worth his salt whatever he lays his hand to. He may be called the Sikh of Kenya, not theologically, because he is usually Christian; a good craftsman, a reliable constable, intelligent, and a quiet, hard-working fellow. There are two races of Kavirondo, the Bantu and the Jaluo, with different vernaculars; but in racial character, for practical purposes, they are one, and this character is high. It includes, moreover, a quality of independence which will have to be taken into consideration: they have been stirred up politically, by men who ought to know better, but have exhibited a surprising quality of thinking for themselves which has occasionally disconcerted their bear-leaders.... They have not only learned to read and to write but to burn bricks, work timber and build model villages to their own models. They are doing this for themselves, having been well started on the road.'

C. SURVEY OF THE HISTORY OF EUROPEAN PENETRATION AND OF THE PRESENT 'CONTACT SITUATION' IN KAVIRONDO

THE history of Kavirondo since the establishment of British rule—a period comprising less than fifty years—is characterized by a steady and on the whole undisturbed process of economic and educational development. The first European who set his foot on the soil of the present district of North Kavirondo was the Scotsman Joseph Thomson, who, in December 1883, coming from the Uasin-Gishu Plateau, crossed it from east to west and both on his way out and on his return journey stayed for about five weeks among the Bantu and the Jaluo.

As the northern and shortest trade-route leading from the coast to Uganda passed right through the centre of North Kavirondo, the Bantu Kavirondo had already for a long time maintained an occasional if indirect contact with the outside world. Probably this trade-route had been used already for centuries by Arab and Swahili traders. The chief traffic between the Coast and Uganda, however, followed the longer route around the southern tip of Lake Victoria, so as to avoid the territory controlled by the Masai.

In October 1885, two years after Thomson's visit, Bishop James Hannington passed through North Kavirondo on his way to Uganda where, shortly afterwards, he was murdered when travelling through Busoga. In 1889 Jackson and Gedge paid a visit to North Kavirondo to buy up ivory on behalf of the Imperial British East Africa Company. A little later, while Jackson and Gedge were climbing Mount Elgon, Carl Peters, the head of the German Emin Pasha expedition, came to Mumias, the Kwa Sundu of that time, where, in February 1890, he

SURVEY OF EUROPEAN PENETRATION

obtained possession of a document containing the famous plea for help sent out by Mwanga, the king of Buganda.[1]

In 1894 Sir H. Colville, the first commissioner of the new government of the Protectorate of Uganda,[2] founded an administrative sub-station at Mumias with a European (F. Spire) in charge and a garrison of fifty Sudanese. In February 1895 C. W. Hobley was sent to Mumias as sub-commissioner to open up an administration in North Kavirondo. In the same year occasional raids which the natives had made on trade caravans using the main route through Kavirondo as well as the repeated theft of rifles gave rise to several punitive expeditions against the Vugusu (Kitosh) and Nyala (Kakalelwa). Of these measures the expedition launched in 1895 against Kitosh in retaliation for the killing of 25 soldiers of the Sudanese garrison was a major action in which a company of Sudanese, 1,100 Ganda under Chief Kakunguru, 5,000 Bantu Kavirondo recruited from the tribal groups owing allegiance to Chief Mumia, 1,000 El Kony, and 600 Uasin-Gishu Masai (who after their expulsion from the Uasin-Gishu Plateau lived among the Bantu Kavirondo) participated under the command of two Europeans.[3] After several fortified Kitosh villages had been stormed, the Vugusu acknowledged British overrule, promising at the same time that in the future they would no longer settle in walled villages. Shortly afterwards—following a minor punitive expedition—peace was also made with the Nyala, who had to destroy their forest dwellings and settle in open country. In the following years several minor expeditions were carried out from Mumias for the suppression of cattle-stealing and tribal feuds; in 1899, for example, against the Nilo-Hamitic Ngoma and in 1890 against the Nyangori who border on the Logoli and the Tiriki in the southern part of the district. Since that time peace has reigned in Kavirondo, apart from occasional clan and border quarrels which, however, were always soon settled.[4]

For the mass of the natives the establishment of European rule began to make itself felt only with the introduction of taxation in the year 1899, when Sir Harry Johnston took office as Special Commissioner of Uganda. Taxes were levied at first in kind (timber, goats, iron hoes, chickens, crocodile eggs, &c.) or in the form of labour which every owner of a hut had to perform to an extent equivalent to the sum of 3 rupees per year. As Hobley writes, the idea of levying a tax was in the beginning 'to build up a will to pay something.... The principle was not foreign to the native mind... its payment was, therefore, an outward and visible sign that the particular section had definitely accepted Government control.'[5] To the extent to which in the subsequent years the traditional forms of currency (glass

---

[1] Cf. Carl Peters, *Die Deutsche Emin-Pascha-Expedition*, p. 301.
[2] The Protectorate was taken over by the British Government on 18 June 1894.
[3] According to statements contained in the district records. Cf. also Hobley, 1929, p. 82 sq.   [4] Cf., e.g., *N.A.D.A.R.*, 1928, 1930.
[5] Cf. Hobley, 1929, p. 124.

INTRODUCTORY

beads, cloth, brass wire, cowrie-shells) were replaced by money currency, the tax was gradually levied in the form of money. To-day it consists of a combined hut- and poll-tax, payable by every adult male of over 16 years of age, of 12/- shs. per year to which is added a local rate of 1 or 2/- shs., its exact amount being fixed every year by the Local Native Council (cf. vol. ii).

With the completion of the Uganda Railway which reached its terminus Kisumu in the year 1901, a larger number of Swahilis as well as the first Indians began to come to Kavirondo. Opening up their shops (dukas) even in the most remote corners of the district, they soon started a flourishing trade with the natives. A few years later, in 1905, the first mission stations were established.

The history of the North Kavirondo District from the beginning of the century up to the present is characterized by a steady process of westernization which, following a slow start, constantly gained in momentum and, especially after the First World War, transformed in many respects both the living conditions of its inhabitants and the outward appearance of the country. The successive stages of this development can be gleaned from the following time-table. Quoting mainly from the annual entries in the district books, it conveys an idea of the chief events of a political, economic, and cultural nature:

1883. Joseph Thomson visits North Kavirondo as the first European.
1890–5. A British administration is established in the North Kavirondo District (as part of the Eastern Province of the Uganda Protectorate). First British officials stationed at Mumias.
1895. Major military actions against Kitosh and Kakalelwa.
1896. The Slater Road, built for ox-carts, reaches Mumias from the East.
1898. Sudanese Mutiny (has no repercussions on the political life of the district).
1899. First taxes levied in kind.
1900. The task of suppressing wars and hostilities between the tribal groups largely accomplished.
1901. The Uganda Railway reaches Kisumu, its terminus on the Kavirondo Gulf.
1902. Kavirondo is separated from Uganda and added to Kenya Colony and Protectorate.
Appointment of tribal chiefs by Government.
Sorghum (Swahili: *Mtama*) the only agricultural produce which the natives can sell for money.
1903. First Indian shop (duka) opened at Fort Maxsted (Kakamega).
3,000 lb. of ivory brought in from Kitosh to Mumias for sale. Hut-tax paid in the form of trees, timber, goats, cattle, hoes, or work. 65 traders (Indians, Swahili, Arabs) living at Mumias.
Expedition against South Kitosh as a penal action for the theft of Masai cattle.
1904. Construction of a new road to Yala and extensive public works.
Small-pox epidemic. Many vaccinations.

SURVEY OF EUROPEAN PENETRATION

Attempts made to cultivate ground-nuts.
Much fighting between sub-tribes of Kavirondo.
Hut-tax collected by Swahilis. Chiefs receive 5 per cent. commission from the tax revenue.

1905. Establishment of the first mission stations in North Kavirondo.
Numerous Vugusu migrate in a northerly and north-westerly direction to escape the influence of Government. Consequence: up to 25 miles to the north of Mumias very scant native population.
Teso from Uganda undertake raids on Buhayo.
Natives of southern part of district sell their produce at Kisumu.
Unrest among the Tsotso, Vugusu, Nyala (Kabras). Police attacked. Amount of blood money paid for murder: ten head of cattle. Large gun-running trade in Mumias. Swahilis and Somalis sell arms to the Vugusu.

1906. Local opposition against the tax-collectors. Destruction of bridges across the Nzoia River. Slight famine. Natives, however, make little use of the opportunity to buy food from a European sent into the distressed area. Owing to the famine no collection of the hut-tax.

1907. Ivory trade closed at Mumias.
Completion of the prison at Mumias. Police force reduced from 73 to 65 heads.

1908. Border conflicts in Kitosh. Police patrols.

1909. Flourishing native market at Mumias. Indian shops opened at Yala, Marama, Malakisi, and Kakamega.
Issue of seed (ground-nuts, simsim, maize, and cotton) by Government.

1910. Introduction of the combined hut- and poll-tax (Hut- and Poll-Tax Ordinance).
Native market at Mumias spoiled by introduction of market fees.
Government experimental cotton plots started in Butsotso.
Natives begin to buy bicycles and clothes.
Rinderpest. 50 per cent. of the cattle lost in six months.
Large amount of labour done outside district.
Prestige of native councils renewed.
Experimental cotton farms abandoned.
Temporary hospital opened at Mumias.
Three Indian trading-centres surveyed.

1911. Setting up of Education Department.
Hundreds of miles of native roads for bicycles and mules constructed and ditched.
Prices of native Labour: In the sub-district: 4 rupees per month or 8/- shs. In the Uasin-Gishu area: 5 rupees per month or 10/- shs. On the Magadi Railway: 6 rupees per month or 12/- shs. plus blankets and posho (maize-flour). Fifty-five thousand head of cattle died of rinderpest in 1910–11.
Extensive illegal cultivation of bhang (Indian hemp) in Wamia, Kitosh, and Kabras.
Witchcraft prevalent. Swahili act as medicine-men and acquire influence over chiefs, notably Mumia.
Boundary disputes between the sub-tribes.

INTRODUCTORY

1912. Daily average of prisoners in District Prison: 38 natives.
Chiefs and other natives commence to use savings bank.
1913. Supervision of native tribunals. Fixing of court fees.
1914. Natives respond readily to the demand for labour.
Boundary disputes in Waholo, between Luo and Bantu.
1915. Efforts made to get the natives to agree to standardization of marriage price.
1916. Natives migrate from Kabras to avoid road work.
Agent of Singer Company arrives to start sewing schools in district.
Reduction made in the number of minor headmen in East and West Kakamega, as well as in the Wanga location.
Meeting between the District Commissioners of Mumias District and Eldoret *re* migration and squatters' question.
1918. Education Department begins to supervise native schools in the district.
Famine throughout Kavirondo.
Three thousand five hundred deaths caused by Spanish influenza.
1922. Health Officer of Government Hospital stationed in North Kavirondo.
Government Hospital at Kakamega starts work.
1923–5. Agricultural Department begins to give regular advice to natives.
1924–5. Setting up of Veterinary Station at Sangalo.
1924. The first three dispensaries in the district opened. Setting up of Local Native Council under the supervision of the District Commissioner (on the grounds of the Local Native Council Ordinance).
1924–5. Opening of the Jeanes School at Kabete near Nairobi.
1925. First financial support of mission schools by Government (grants-in-aid).
1926. Opening of the 'Alliance High School' in Kikuyu near Nairobi. Introduction of the system of paid *mlango*-headmen.
1926–7. Setting up of Native Appeal Tribunal at Kakamega.
Growing native demand for European agricultural implements.
1928. Erection of the first permanent native dispensaries.
1929. Ten native dispensaries in operation. Introduction of a regular ambulance service in the district.
1930. Permanent Sanitary Inspector stationed in district.
Permanent Agricultural Office set up in Kakamega.
Boundary disputes between tribes and clans.
'North Kavirondo Taxpayers' Welfare Association' founded under the lead of the Church Missionary Society.
1931. Opening up of Government School at Kakamega.
Beginning of a closer co-operation between Government and Mission in the field of native education.
Permanent Agricultural Officer stationed at Kakamega.
1931–2. Opening of Veterinary School at Sangalo.
Discovery of the Kakamega goldfields and beginning of gold-mining.
1932. Use of compulsory labour for public purposes abandoned.
1933. Supervision of the Court Fees Ordinance by Government.
1934. Setting up of 'District Education Board' with native members.

SURVEY OF EUROPEAN PENETRATION 35

Clashes over land issues between Bantu and Luo clans. In connexion herewith founding of a new native sect (Jo-Roho). Founding of the North Kavirondo Central Association, a political native organization.
1935. Increased native demand for the appointment of a paramount chief (as successor to the senile Mumia).
1936. Amalgamation of the twenty-four Tribal Courts of the District into six so-called 'Divisional Tribunals'.
Asiatic artisans are in a growing measure replaced by natives (e.g. marine workshops at Kisumu).
The Kisumu–Kakamega road made into an all-weather motor-road (daily load: 600 tons).
Paid *mlango*-headmen begin to be abolished and replaced by *olugongo*-headmen. Political agitation against chiefs in ten of the twenty-four chieftaincies of the district. Followers of the North Kavirondo Central Association increase to 300 persons.
1937. Fourteen dispensaries in North Kavirondo.

Mission Societies and Stations in North Kavirondo[1]

Society and Station	Founded in	Adherents
Friends' African Mission:		
Lirhanda (Isuxa)	1905	
Vihiga (South Maragoli)	1906	
Lugulu (Vugusu)	1914	31,000
Malava (Kabras)	1918	
Kaimosi (Tiriki)	1922	
Church Missionary Society:		
Maseno (Central Kavirondo)	1906	5,000
Butere (Wanga)	1927	
Church of God:		
Kima (Bunyore)	1905 (07)	
Ingotse (Butsotso)	1925 (?)	3,000
Kisa (Kisa)	1938	
Pentecostal Assembly:		
Nyangori (Central Kavirondo)	1924	2,000
Salvation Army:		
Malakisi (Vugusu)	1936	?
Mill Hill Mission:		
Mumias (Wanga)	1905	
Kakamega (Isuxa)	1906	
Eregi (Idaxo, North Maragoli)	1912	12,600
Nang'ina (Samia, Central Kavirondo)	1927	
Kibabi (Vugusu, South Kitosh)	1931	

The present contact situation, i.e. the level on which the 'old time' characterized by traditional native customs and institutions meets with the new era of colonial development, is chiefly determined by the following five factors: (1) The British Administration and the activities of the various Government Departments; (2) the work done by the missions; (3) gold-mining in the reserve; (4) the demand for native labour, both on farms and

[1] R. A. Phelp, *New Day in Kenya*.

plantations in the European highlands of Kenya and in the towns; and (5) the trade carried on by Indians and the opening up of the district by means of roads and railways. The extent to which each of these different factors is at present at work may be gauged from the following data:

1. The local administrative body which is stationed at Kakamega consists of the District Commissioner and several District Officers, a Magistrate, and a Police Officer. The District Commissioner administers the district under the system of 'Direct Rule', making, however, extensive use of so-called 'location chiefs' appointed and paid by Government and of sub-headmen or *milango*-chiefs, who are placed under the location chiefs and who, in the majority of cases, are territorial clan heads. Since 1936–7 the sub-headmen no longer receive any pay, being since that time styled *volugongo*; they remain, however, part of the system of native administration, their main duty being the political representation of the various clans. Besides, they have advisory functions in connexion with the administering of native customary law (cf. vol. ii).[1] The main duties of the location chiefs —apart from maintaining law and order in their respective locations—is to carry out the orders given by the District Commissioner and to collect taxes. Their competence and authority are defined in the Native Authority Ordinance (cf. vol. ii). Since the year 1924 there exists a Local Native Council, an organ of native self-administration aiming at the gradual development of an administrative system based on the principles of Indirect Rule. In addition to the District Commissioner as its chairman, the members of the Local Native Council comprise the location chiefs (*ex officio*) as well as a number of native representatives from each location who are appointed by the District Commissioner after previous consultation of local public opinion. The Local Native Council passes resolutions on matters of local significance and votes money to be spent on public expenditure as well as on educational grants-in-aid (cf. vol. ii). The Magistrate is in charge of the native tribunals. Formerly there were twenty-four such tribunals, composed of the location chief as chairman and the leading clan elders; since 1936–7 they have been reduced to six so-called Divisional Tribunals each of which consists of an annually appointed salaried native chairman and twelve advisory elders who change every month. Since 1936 the location chiefs no longer exercise any judicial functions. Besides, there exists a Native Appeal Tribunal under the chairmanship of a native, with six elders functioning as a jury. In accordance with the Native Tribunals Ordinance the law administered in the native tribunals is the local customary law, 'so far as it is not repugnant to justice and morality or

---

[1] Cf. *N.A.D.A.R.*, 1936, p. 7 sq.: 'It has been decided to remove the *mlangos* from the paid staff, and already effect to this decision has been made in five locations. The important functions that a family head group plays in the life of the tribe will not be forgotten, and their customary prominence as *liguru* or *jodong gweng* in matters connected with inheritance, marriage, and land management will be retained.'

SURVEY OF EUROPEAN PENETRATION

inconsistent with the provisions of any order of the King-in-Council or with any other law in force in the Colony'.

The Police Officer is in charge of the tribal police of sixty-seven men attached to the location chiefs as well as the police force of thirty-three men stationed at Kakamega, and of the District Prison at Kakamega (3rd-class prison) as well as the Detention Camp.

The following Government authorities and services are represented in the district:

(a) The Agricultural Department by a British official. Its institutions comprise an Agricultural School at Bukura (under the direction of a European), a seed-farm, and four experimental plots.

(b) The Veterinary Department by one British official. Institutions: a Veterinary School at Sangalo (under the direction of a European).

(c) The Medical Department by two Medical Officers, one Sanitation Officer, and several European nurses. Institutions: a native hospital and fourteen dispensaries scattered all over the district. In 1937 11,677 in- and out-patients received treatment in the hospital and 71,439 patients at the dispensaries.

(d) The Public Works Department by one European.

Each of these European officials is assisted by a staff of native assistants, such as medical orderlies, instructors, scouts, &c., whose task it is to carry out or supervise the execution in the native locations of the various measures passed by Government.

(e) The Education Department, finally, maintains a Government School at Kakamega with a European principal. Native education, however, is still chiefly entrusted to the various missions; the Government makes financial grants and exercises the control over the mission schools.

2. In 1938 a total of six mission societies, five Protestant and one Catholic, were working in the North Kavirondo District (cf. diagram on p. 35). In 1936 the number of Protestant Christians amounted to 41,011 and that of the Catholic Christians to 12,600, which makes a total of 53,611 or 15·6 per cent. of the entire population. In 1937 the various mission societies in North Kavirondo maintained a total of 547 schools, which are distributed as follows:

(a) Friends' African Mission	292	schools
(b) Church Missionary Society	103	,,
(c) Church of God Mission	78	,,
(d) Catholic Mill Hill Mission	41	,,
(e) Salvation Army	19	,,
(f) Pentecostal Assembly Mission	14	,,
	547	schools

Of these schools 491 belong to the type of bush or 'A' schools, 48 are so-called sector or elementary schools, 2 are primary schools, 5 are girls' schools, and 1 is a teachers' training school. The last-named three kinds of schools are boarding-schools. In addition to the evangelization and education of the natives, some of the mission societies are doing active work also in the medical and sanitary fields. The Friends' African Mission and the Church Missionary Society maintain a hospital and a maternity ward each at Kaimosi and Maseno[1] respectively and the Church of God Mission a maternity home at Kima.

3. In the North Kavirondo goldfields, which extend over an area of approximately 420 square miles,[2] 6,814 natives were employed in 1935 (4,515 of them Bantu Kavirondo, the remainder for the most part Jaluo). Of these 6,814 native miners, 4,756 were in the employment of six large companies with over 500 workers each. The number of Europeans engaged in gold-mining or prospecting for gold amounted to roughly 300 in the year 1935.[3]

Outside the district numerous Bantu Kavirondo work as wage-contract labourers in the service of Europeans, particularly on the maize and sisal farms in the neighbouring Uasin-Gishu and Trans-Nzoia Districts as well as in the farming areas of the Central Province and in the towns. Towards the end of 1937, according to the labour returns, a total of 31,078 Bantu Kavirondo were employed in the service of Europeans,[4] including those working in the Kakamega goldfields. This corresponds to 9 per cent. of the total population or to 44 per cent. of the male population between 15 and 40 years of age.[5] By far the greater part of these, however, had merely entered a six-month labour contract after the termination of which they returned home.

5. The native production of cash crops which is encouraged and promoted, not only by the Government and the missions, but also by the knowledge and experience which the native farm labourer gathers during his term of contract labour, is chiefly bought by Indian traders living in the reserve. At the same time they sell commodities of European or other foreign manufacture for which there is a growing demand on the part of the natives. In 1938 this trade in the North Kavirondo District was carried on by eleven Indian trading-centres, with an Indian population totalling 588 persons. In an additional 22 native markets there were, in 1937, about 200 native duka-keepers, partly agents of Indian firms and partly independent traders. In 1937 the value of the exports of agricultural and animal products (such as maize, cotton, simsim, pulses, hides, ghee, and cream) from the district totalled c. £149,185, and the value of the trade goods purchased by the natives in the reserve (clothing,

---

[1] Maseno is located in the District of Central Kavirondo, but so near the border of North Kavirondo that a great part of its patients come from the latter district.
[2] Cf. Sir Albert E. Kitson, 1932.
[3] According to the records at the District Office, Kakamega.
[4] N.A.D.A.R., 1935.
[5] Calculated on the basis of 20 per cent. of the entire population.

European foodstuffs, agricultural implements, bicycles, sewing-machines, cigarettes, soap, &c.) £92,000.

As regards communications, the North Kavirondo District, in addition to its two railway lines (Nakuru–Kampala and Nakuru–Kisumu–Butere) can boast of about 400 miles of motor-roads. The greater part of the roads is open for motor-traffic the whole year round, although the only all-weather road is the 30-mile highway leading from Kisumu to Kakamega. The fact that several of the main highways of Kenya and even of the whole of East Africa pass through the North Kavirondo District (e.g. the roads Nairobi–Kampala, Kitale/Eldoret–Kisumu, and during the rainy season also the road from Kisumu to Nairobi) establishes numerous links with the outer world, particularly with the adjoining Uasin-Gishu farming area and with Uganda, the great and advanced neighbour to the west. Conditions in the neighbouring Protectorate, with its well-developed self-administration under the system of Indirect Rule and its high economic standard of living, serve as a strong incentive for the progressively minded natives of North Kavirondo, who see in them the ideal they are anxious to attain for themselves.

These, in very broad outline, are the principal data that indicate the contact conditions under which the Bantu Kavirondo are living at present. In every sphere of life these conditions have brought about a significant and comprehensive change and released a number of drives either running parallel to, overlapping, or even clashing with one another. The ways in which the natives have so far reacted to these contact conditions and forces, the new tendencies which are developing under the various new influences, and the problems which result from them, I shall try to discuss following the description of their traditional forms of life.

PART II
ELEMENTS OF KINSHIP STRUCTURE
A. THE FAMILY

IN the whole of North Kavirondo the individual family constitutes the basic social group that co-operates most widely and intensely in the activities of everyday life. Although in the kinship terminology there exists no word which exclusively applies to the individual family,[1] it is, nevertheless, a clearly distinct group. It consists of husband, wife, and unmarried children. Married sons continue to live with their parents until they set up a family homestead of their own, which they usually do after the birth of one or several children. Until then—marriage being initially patrilocal—the young wife of a married son becomes, in a sense, a member of the family, her exact position in it being defined by formal rules of conduct with regard to each family member.

As a rule each individual family lives in an isolated homestead,[2] erected in the middle of the family gardens. The round living-hut (*enyumba* or *inzu*) is shared not only by the husband, his wife, and their small children, but usually also by the livestock. It has several partitions—in Maragoli[3] marked off by actual walls, in Kitosh only by the arrangement of objects—which, in spite of the smallness of the hut, keep the husband's and the wife's spheres quite distinct.[4] If the husband is wealthy there is a cattle enclosure (*olugaga*) at the side of the living-hut. Most homesteads, besides the storage space in the living-hut, have a few granaries that are grouped in a rough circle round a hard-trodden yard (*omugizi*). In those parts of Kavirondo where there is still some danger from leopards or where the owner of the homesteads wishes to protect himself against theft or sorcery, the homestead is surrounded by a hedge of thorn-bushes or euphorbia interplanted with various protective plants. It has a gate that can be closed at night by piling up a wall of logs placed horizontally between four posts. Narrow paths connect the various homesteads, winding through the fields or the banana-groves which, in Maragoli, are planted behind most homesteads.[5] They usually lead right across the yards of the homesteads which they pass, showing that no particular weight is attached to privacy.

Children of both sexes sleep in the house of their parents until they are about six years old. At that age their lower incisors are knocked out and

[1] The expression which comes nearest to it is *avényumba yange*, 'those of my house'.
[2] Until the establishment of intertribal peace the Kitosh lived in walled villages (*dzingova*) for protection against Masai raids, cf. p. 31.
[3] The word Maragoli denotes the country of the Logoli.
[4] For a full description of the hut and its sociology see vol. ii.
[5] In Kitosh bananas do not grow so well and are therefore planted only in valley bottoms or on the fertile sites of abandoned cattle kraals.

PLATE 3

A. Donera, an elder of South Maragoli

B. A woman in her traditional attire: South Kitosh

PLATE 4

A. *A Kitosh homestead*

B. *Maxeti, a Kitosh elder wearing a cowrie-shell cap*

THE FAMILY

they are thereby initiated into a second phase of childhood. They sleep now in the hut of a widowed grandparent, and a year or two later a son moves into the *esimba*, the bachelor hut of an elder brother or friend, while a daughter sleeps in the *ekegono*, the unmarried girls' hut. This is the hut of an old woman, the real or classificatory grandmother, who controls the girls' moral conduct and, at the same time, acts as a go-between in the arrangement of courtships and betrothals. Although they sleep away from home, both boys and girls continue to eat with their parents and are under their control during the greater part of the day.

Economically, the traditional family is essentially self-sufficient. Unless abnormal events, such as droughts, hailstorms, or prolonged sickness, upset the family economy, it does not depend upon outside help or trade for its food-supply. Although experts exist for every craft, the economic significance of such specialization has until recently remained very small. The traditional craftsman pursues his craft more as an avocation than as a profession. He neither depends on its proceeds for his family's food-supply, nor does he seem to increase his possessions substantially from it. The skill required being low, nearly every man or woman is an expert in one or two of the dozen traditional crafts, and knows something about the others. The number of customers of any one expert, therefore, naturally remains small and the profit negligible. Only magical and medical practitioners, whose occupations require a higher degree of skill, training, or personality, appear at times to derive substantial gain from their profession.

While thus outside the family we find little organized co-operation in economic production and no marked occupational differentiation, there is a clearly defined division of duties within the family group. It is a rule of custom (*elilago*) that 'a person cannot do the work that is on the side of the other person'. To quote further from a statement of a Logoli elder on the sexual division of labour:

'It is the wife's work to sweep, to grind, to cook, to build the fire, and to clean out the cattle partition. She carries the water from the spring, buys the cooking-pots and gathers firewood. She brings the salt (i.e. she burns the salt reeds in special pits and filters the ashes), cleans the walls of the house and the surface of the yard with cow-dung, beats the floor of the house (so that it becomes hard and level) and "knows" about the food on the food-shelf.'

In addition to this list of household duties the wife performs the greater and more strenuous part of garden labour, as hoeing is almost entirely woman's work.

The main duties of the husband, on the other hand, are

'to take care of his stool and beer-pipe, to sweep his yard (i.e. the *omugizi*), to look after the cattle, goats, and sheep, to know the place of digging and to cut the grass in the garden (thereby selecting that section of his lands which his wife is to till), to know when the roof of the house gets deteriorated and to pull the grass for thatching, to plait the string (for tying the grass) and to hand up the grass (to the thatcher who is always a specialist)'.

It is also the husband's concern to carry on kinship- and other transactions with his cattle and to exchange fowls for goats and sheep and these again for cattle. This is an involved business which, in view of the frequent legal complications that arise from partnerships in cattle and from the obligation to replace animals that have died even long after they had been transferred, takes up a great deal of a man's time and furnishes him with his chief worries and enjoyments. Both sexes, finally, join fairly equally in the tasks of planting, weeding, and harvesting (cf. vol. ii).

Children are trained at an early age to share the duties of family life. Soon after they have themselves learnt to walk properly, boys as well as girls are taught to carry about and generally 'nurse' their younger siblings, to run errands, and to make themselves useful in various little ways. At about the age of six boys begin to herd goats, then sheep, and later on cattle, a duty which they outgrow after they have been circumcised.[1] Girls assist their mothers in the daily work of carrying water, gathering firewood, wild roots, and vegetables and, above all, in the weary task of grinding eleusine or sorghum for the morning and evening meal. Whereas in Maragoli both boys and girls help their parents in the garden, in Kitosh, owing to the greater number of cattle, boys spend their whole time herding cattle while girls are given their own gardens at the age of fourteen. The crops raised by them are stored in a special granary which after their marriage is ceremonially 'opened' by their father-in-law and serves to give them a start in their own household.

The wife cooks for all members of the family, but they eat in two groups. The mother and her daughters—and sometimes small boys—eat together in the cooking-partition of the hut (*evuasi*), while the father and the older sons take their meals in the front partition. In Kitosh the husband frequently eats outside in the shade of a granary or on top of an ant-hill where formerly the men spent much of their time on the look-out for enemies.

The matrimonial relationship becomes fully established only after the birth of one or several children, as only then is the bond between husband and wife considered permanent. The pair now establish their own household; their hut, which previously served as their sleeping-quarters only, is furnished with cooking-stones, pots, and other utensils that are supplied by both the wife's and the husband's parents. From now on the pair are regarded as 'really' husband and wife, and no longer as 'boy' and 'girl'.[2] They can now receive visits from and offer hospitality to their parents and other persons of full married status who before would not have entered their house. In Kitosh, where this change in status is expressed in a more elaborate way than in Maragoli, husband and wife can now for the first time call each other by their ancestral names, i.e. by the names which they

---

[1] The notion that cattle-herding is below the dignity of adults is of recent origin, as formerly the danger from wild animals and enemies made cattle-herding a job which required the attention of full-grown men.

[2] *Omusaza* and *omukali*, and *omwana* and *omukana* respectively.

were given as small children and which, unlike the names which they received in later years from their playmates, may otherwise be used by near clansmen only. In a figurative sense the pair are now even regarded as *aviko*, a term which in its literal meaning distinguishes relatives by blood from the *avako*, the affinal relatives. Ceremonially their new relationship is enacted by the performance of the *sitexo*-rite, the main features of which are the ritual killing of an ox at the home of the wife's father as a sacrifice for her new status of motherhood and the cooking of the first porridge (*vusuma*) on her own cooking-stones. This porridge, as well as a piece of raw meat, husband and wife eat together, both dishes being ceremoniously handed to them by a younger brother of the husband. After they have eaten, they utter each other's clan-names and thus signify that they are now of 'the same flesh and blood'.[1]

The social valuation of parenthood, however, does not merely affect the status of husband and wife in the eyes of their tribesmen, but it also strongly influences the husband–wife relationship itself. A numerous offspring is desired by both parents. A prolific wife will command more respect from her husband and his kinsmen than a wife who is barren or who bears daughters only, a fate for which the wife alone is held responsible. Although neither of these two misfortunes is openly accepted as grounds for a divorce, they are often its real cause, especially if the husband is poor and cannot marry again without having first recovered the marriage cattle that he has given for his first wife. Before such an extreme step is taken, however, various magical rites and sacrifices are performed throughout a number of years. Their aim is to detect and remove the cause of barrenness, which is chiefly attributed to the anger of the ancestral spirits. Impotency of the husband, on the other hand, may disrupt a marriage for reasons of sex but hardly for reasons of procreation, as with the husband's tacit agreement one of his brothers steps into his place. In the frequent cases where old men marry young wives this is quite a customary arrangement which does not often seem to lead to divorce.

The respective sexual rights and duties of husband and wife among the Bantu Kavirondo, as in most Bantu societies, are ill balanced. The husband holds exclusive sexual rights over his wife.[2] Any extra-marital indulgence on her side is considered adulterous, and the husband can demand a cow as compensation both from the wife, i.e. her father, and the lover.[3] For repeated unfaithfulness husbands frequently divorce their wives and demand their bride-wealth back. The only exception to this rule is the custom that before the birth of the first child the brother of the husband

[1] The wife is not, however, adopted into the husband's clan but remains a member of her own clan. Cf. p. 57.

[2] Provided that the husband is not impotent.

[3] Such conduct is, however, considered adulterous only when engaged in with the intention of secrecy. A wife who openly leaves her husband to live with another man, with no intention to return, is considered divorced and merely the bride-wealth is returned; cf. p. 442.

may have occasional sex-relations with his wife which the husband is expected to tolerate. Even after he has children a husband cannot legally accuse his brother of adultery with his wife[1] but must try to secure his rights by the less drastic means of persuasion or by asking his father to intervene on the strength of his paternal authority. The wife, on the other hand, has no exclusive sexual rights to her husband, as, under the conditions of polygyny, any courtship that he might carry on with an unmarried woman would be regarded as possibly leading up to a second marriage. The only mutual right in their sexual relationship is the claim to sexual attention from the marriage partner. If either husband or wife persistently evades his or her marital duties, the dissatisfied partner may bring a complaint before the forum of the husband's or the wife's kin, as in any other matrimonial conflict.

The formal 'social' relationship between husband and wife is likewise ill balanced. The husband all along enjoys a superior status and expects formal obedience and certain outward signs of submission from his wife. This state of affairs is clearly reflected by the arrangement of the homestead and soon becomes apparent to the observer of the daily routine of family life. The front partition of the hut, with the main entrance and the front yard, is called the 'husband's side', while the rear partition, with the cooking-stones, the side door, and the back yard, is the 'wife's side' of the homestead. It is the husband's privilege to possess and sit on a stool (*endeve*), while women must sit on the ground. In the house, when men are assembled round the beer-pot from which they suck the beer through long hollow reeds, the wife must crawl along the ground to pass under the reeds, while men may freely step over them. Numerous other rules and customs of behaviour confirm this inferiority of the wife in the social life of the family. This does not mean, however, that wives are, as a rule, bullied by their husbands or generally show the behaviour one would expect in a typical master–servant relationship. The formal rules of conduct being taken for granted, there often prevails a congenial equality in the formal behaviour of husband and wife.[2] In actual life, as far as my observations go, the real master of the home tends to be the one who has the stronger personality or who knows how to exploit the strength of his position in his own kinship group. The share that a husband or wife contributes towards the economic maintenance of the family also strongly affects his or her social status. Where the husband possesses no cattle and depends entirely upon his wife's garden labour, not only for the family's food-supply but for all other economic necessities as well, his behaviour towards her tends to be meek even though his wife will still observe the formal rules of submission to him.

Both husband and wife maintain the social relations with their respective

---

[1] i.e. by bringing the matter before the judicial council of clan elders (*ekiruazo*); see below, p. 81.

[2] Some of my informants insist, however, that this is a new, although now general, development which sharply contrasts with conditions in pre-European days.

the marriage cattle given for a daughter accrue to the father, and, in the absence of sons, he can use them to marry a second wife or to increase his wealth in cattle.[1] The strong preference for male offspring must, therefore, be explained outside the structure of the individual family, and we must consider the problem again when we discuss the influence of the other social groups upon family life.

The economic advantages which parents derive from their grown children are reciprocated by the continued support which children are given by their parents. Apart from cattle-raiding, which in Maragoli has always been negligible in extent, there is under traditional conditions almost no other way in which a son can acquire cattle and found a family of his own than through the help of his father, who supplies him with the marriage cattle. During the first years of married life a son continues to eat the food cooked by his mother, to work in his mother's garden,[2] and to assist his father in the tasks of cattle-keeping, grass-cutting, and so forth. But even after the son has established his own household, the father continues to figure as an authority in his life. He gives him a 'cow for milk' and apportions to him a piece of his land which his daughter-in-law may till. As a sign that he is still the 'real' owner of this land, he continues every season to throw the first seeds in the son's cultivation. Where the personal relations between father and son are not strained, the latter will, out of filial respect, leave his own cattle at his father's place for many years after his marriage or even until his father's death.

A daughter, although she leaves the parental home on her marriage, continues to derive economic benefits from her parents in the form of frequent gifts which enhance her prestige in her own family and among her husband's kindred. Besides, she may at any time be forced to seek refuge and legal protection from her parents if conflicts arise in her own marriage relationship.

Thus the ties between parents and children tend to be strong, and parental authority as well as filial obedience and devotion continue far beyond the time of the children's physical maturity.

All sons ultimately receive an equal, or nearly equal, share in the father's legacy of cattle and land. Nevertheless, the relationship between parents and children differs according to the order in which the children were born. The eldest son (*omwana omukulundu*) is entitled to marry first, i.e. he has a preferential claim to the father's cattle for the purpose of paying bridewealth. When he establishes his own household he usually settles near the parental homestead and becomes 'like a brother to the father',[3] especially

---

[1] In Kitosh a man's obligation to pay marriage cattle is not limited to his own sons but extends to the 'sons' of his lineage-group. The above argument applies, therefore, primarily to Maragoli.

[2] i.e. the garden apportioned to his mother; cf. footnote 2 on p. 45.

[3] As an elder put it in a Logoli text: "The first-born (son) is who is helping his father dividing the things to those smaller (children). Because now he is as a brother to him (the father), and if he (the son) has a child (then) that son is a " 'husband (i.e. a married man of full status). He is saying things like a husband.' "

divided between father and husband. If the wife commits an offence against a 'third party', e.g. if she sets fire to a neighbour's house or injures someone else's child, her father and husband must jointly raise the fine. Conversely, if the wife is the victim of an offence, her father or husband must take legal action on her behalf, and the compensation paid usually goes to the one who has filed the case and paid the court dues.

If the wife commits adultery, her father must compensate the husband, as by acceptance of the marriage cattle he assumes responsibility for his daughter's marital conduct.[1]

The relationship between parents and children is characterized, as we have seen, by the strong desire for a numerous offspring. The reasons which conservative elders have given me for this attitude can be summed up under three headings: (1) A large family enhances a man's prestige, as through it his name becomes known to many people, who would accordingly respect him and listen to him. (2) A man with many children can obtain justice, as he would be feared by the people, who would not dare to take his cattle or other things away from him by force. (3) Where there are many children there will always be plenty of food. In Kitosh this last point was elaborated by the further statement that 'many sons would capture many cattle in war'. As we shall see later on, the truth of these assumptions is confirmed when they are viewed against the general economic structure of traditional tribal life.

However, a large family does not always produce the desired result of assuring the father's well-being, a fact which is emphasized by the saying, 'The father of many children dies in poverty.'[2] Rather than stating a general truth, this saying is meant to express the fact that filial ingratitude and feebleness of paternal authority may leave an aged father poor in spite of the obvious advantages of a numerous offspring.

As these reasons for favouring a large family imply, male and female children are not valued equally highly. Although a fairly even distribution of sons and daughters is appreciated, it is considered far less of a misfortune if a wife bears sons only than if she bears daughters only. This different valuation cannot be fully explained by the conditions in which the individual family lives. Before her marriage a daughter is at least as useful a member of the family household as a son. After she is married a daughter, it is true, sees her parents less frequently than a married son, but she continues during her regular visits to help her mother in the house and in the garden. As regards gift-making, it appears that a married couple on the whole consider their respective parents to an equal extent. Moreover,

---

[1] This is the traditional law, which in recent judicial practice is changing. According to customary law in Kitosh a woman carries the sole blame only when she commits adultery away from her hut, while her lover is also subject to a fine if he has entered her hut. In Maragoli the wife alone is considered the guilty party in all circumstances.

[2] *Omwivuli alikudzila kuvulavu*, 'the begetter will die on the public place'.

claim to anything in the house, except her own dress and personal ornaments. The husband's rights of ownership, on the other hand, are limited only by a number of kinship obligations within his lineage-group.

The low status of the wife with regard to property is paralleled by the fact that she has no rights over her children in her capacity as a mother.[1] If the marriage is dissolved, even if entirely owing to the husband's fault, the wife can under no circumstances claim any of her children, in the sense that she would have a right to take them with her to her father's house or to her new husband and there bring them up. If the divorced husband has no other wife and no near relatives in whose house his children can stay, he may temporarily let them go with his divorced wife. But he can fetch them back whenever he wants to do so, and in all circumstances he would receive the marriage cattle given for his daughters and have to furnish the same for his sons.

A father's authority over his children, on the other hand, is considerable, even though many fathers make little practical use of their rights, whether from parental devotion or because harsh treatment of their children would, in the long run, be reciprocated by an absence of filial love and devotion. Theoretically, however, a father has almost absolute rights over his children which are not curtailed by any actions which might be taken either by his own clan or by that of his wife. Formerly he could sell his uncircumcised sons in exchange for cattle or goats to another clan or tribe, and it is said that it was actually done in cases of serious famine.[2] Nowadays a father can still force his daughter to marry a man of his own choice, and he is also entitled to select a wife for his son without consulting the latter's opinion. If his son refuses to marry the girl he has assigned to him, he may disinherit him and drive him away.

If the husband dies, the widow has the option of being 'inherited' by one of her deceased husband's brothers (real or classificatory) or of marrying anyone she likes. In the latter case the marriage-cattle or some of them[3] must be returned to her husband's heirs.[4]

A necessary corollary to this lack of property status of the wife is the fact that she has no legal independence or individuality. That is to say, she herself cannot take legal action, nor does she bear any personal legal responsibility for her conduct. Before a woman marries, her father (or his substitute) is her legal guardian. After her marriage the guardianship is

---

[1] As distinct from her position as a wife and member of the household.

[2] A few years ago this custom was prohibited by an act of penal legislation passed by the British Government, of which, however, a number of violations have occurred.

[3] As a rule one cow is deducted for each child she has borne.

[4] Even in this case the deceased husband's brother or nearest classificatory brother legally steps into the father's place, and not the new husband. Thus in the case of daughters if they are raised at the mother's new husband's place (and not at the place of the husband's brother), he can claim one cow of the marriage cattle as compensation for the bringing up of the girl.

kin on an equal level. The wife can pay frequent and—especially during the first years of matrimony—extended visits to her parents. Although the husband must give his formal permission, he seldom prevents his wife from paying these visits. The husband's and the wife's relatives are usually shown an equal degree of hospitality in the family household. Although wife-beating occurs and is not considered a serious disgrace to the matrimonial relationship, there are safeguards against a husband's cruelty. The wife can always return to her parents or brothers, where she is given protection until some agreement has been reached or the marriage is formally dissolved by the return of the marriage cattle.[1]

As the wife grows old and becomes the mother of adult sons and daughters, her social position improves. Her husband and other people no longer call her *omukali* (wife) but *omukaye* (old woman), a term which implies respect and social standing. The relationship between husband and wife in old age tends to become more personal as they spend most of their time together, maintaining less strictly the segregation in work and recreation that prevailed in their former matrimonial life.

The legal—as distinct from the social—status of the wife is also inferior to that of the husband. Her position is characterized by the fact that she has no ownership status whatever. In her quality as the husband's wife she has a claim to be supplied by her husband with certain objects for her own and her children's use. The husband must build a hut for her, furnish her with a garden,[2] supply her with meat at reasonable intervals, and, if possible, with milk while her children are still small. Moreover, the crops planted by the wife are under her control in so far as she takes care of the stores[3] and is alone responsible for making an economical use of them in the interest of the family. But she has no rights of ownership to any of the objects which she handles. All material objects, whether they accrue to the family from without (i.e. through inheritance) or as a result of the family's combined economic effort, are owned by the husband, including even the various household utensils which are daily used by the wife. She has no right to dispose of any of these objects, unless she acts upon her husband's orders. Whatever she realizes through the sale or barter of any goods 'belonging' to the household or even produced by her (such as pots) comes under the husband's control. If the marriage becomes dissolved she has no

---

[1] Such protection, however, is given to the wife within limits only. As a rule the marriage cattle given for her have in the meantime been handed on as bride-wealth for another marriage and her brothers will, therefore, urge her to return to her husband. Cf. pp. 444 and 446.

[2] Both hut and garden are only apportioned to the wife by the husband, who remains the owner (*omwene*) of both, i.e. he retains the full rights of control and disposal. Cf. chapter on Land Tenure, vol. ii.

[3] A husband may not climb upon the storage shelf, an attic-like arrangement above the cooking- and sleeping-partitions of the Logoli hut, nor may he look into the granaries on the yard, unless he wants to take stock of the supplies or sell part of the crops.

as regards his relations with his younger siblings. After his father's death he inherits the *omulimi gwa guga*, the garden of the grandfather, i.e. that piece of land which his father was given by his own father when he established his household, as distinct from other lands that he might have acquired later on. The 'sons of the middle' (*avana va hagati*) usually settle farther away from the father's homestead, as the father apportions to them one of his more distant gardens. As a consequence they render less help to their parents than the eldest son. The last-born son (*omukógoti*) again remains more closely attached to his parental home. Often he will not yet have acquired full marital status when his father dies, and thus he inherits the house and takes care of his aged mother if she survives her mother's husband.

Brothers and sisters grow up in their parents' home under conditions of practical equality. When they reach the age where they begin to sleep in different huts (cf. above, p. 41) they likewise separate in their everyday activities, both in work and in play, and do so increasingly as they grow older. The brother seeks the company of other boys and the sister that of other girls. There are, however, no formal avoidances between brother and sister. A brother may even carry on a courtship and pay nightly visits to a girl who sleeps in the same hut as his sister. The danger that this might tempt him into incestuous relations with his sister is thought too remote to make prohibition of such visits necessary.

Although elder brothers exact a certain amount of obedience from their juniors, the privileged position of the eldest son becomes effective only after his marriage and, particularly, after his father's death when he may hold property in trust for his younger brothers. As these establish their households and attain full married status, the father's property is equally distributed among them and the authority of the elder brother gradually gives way to a status of equality among all brothers. The formal relationship between adult brothers and sisters, finally, is essentially characterized by the fact that the brother depends for his own marriage on the marriage cattle given for his sister. Where brothers and sisters are evenly distributed in number, each brother usually receives the marriage cattle of the sister corresponding to him in age. He then retains a closer relationship with her —in protecting her rights and interests—and with her children than the other brothers.

The polygamous family is structurally a social group made up of several individual families without any essential features of its own. It is, therefore, multiplied rather than transformed when it becomes polygynous through the husband's marriage of additional wives. Each wife in time establishes her own separate household and is allocated by her husband an individual plot of garden land and part of the banana-grove. The arrangement of the different households in the polygynous family is not subject to a definite plan but shows several variations. Frequently the huts and granaries of the different wives are grouped in an open circle round a common yard. Such a homestead is called *elidala* and known by the name of the husband as its owner. Sometimes, also, each wife lives in a detached homestead with a yard of her own, the different homesteads being grouped in an irregular fashion amidst the husband's gardens but usually within hearing distance. In its outer appearance this arrangement does not differ from the customary grouping of neighbouring homesteads. Sometimes, again, the different wives of a man do not all live in one *elidala* (a term which also refers to the loose grouping of detached homesteads), but are split up into three or four *amadala* which may be miles apart from one another. Obviously the relationships within the polygynous family must be affected by the differences in the residential arrangement. The following discussion refers primarily to the polygynous family living in one *elidala* (of the first or second type), which—under traditional conditions—is the most frequent form of grouping.[1]

The relationship between husband and wife in the polygynous family differs from that in the monogamous family mainly in that the 'plural wife' has to share her sexual and economic claims upon her husband with her co-wives.[2]

In theory the polygynous husband is supposed to devote an equal amount of sexual and economic attention to all his wives. In practice, however, this rule is observed within wide limits only, and the preference given by most husbands to a 'favoured wife' constitutes a frequent occasion for jealousy and strife among co-wives. Socially, the first or great wife (*omukali omunene*) enjoys a higher status. Her hut is usually the largest in the *elidala* and, where the homestead is surrounded by an enclosure, occupies the favoured position opposite the entrance gate. The husband keeps his personal belongings, his weapons, stool, and beer-pipe, as well as his medicines, in her house. He is also commonly supposed to eat no other food than that which has been cooked by the great wife as 'he fears to be poisoned by the other wives'. Even if this statement is hardly confirmed by the facts, it indicates that the husband is linked by a more stable and trustworthy bond to his first wife than to those whom he has married after-

[1] Taxation lists from South Maragoli and North Kitosh show the following data on polygyny:

	No. of wives							
	One	Two	Three	Four	Five	Six	Seven	Eight
N. Kitosh	4,404	746	150	32	3	2	1	1
S. Maragoli	5,356	314	25	3	..	..	2	..

This compilation requires two corrections: (*a*) The number of polygynous families is larger than indicated as plural wives are often not registered, for purposes of tax evasion. (*b*) The lists being compiled on the basis of local headmanships, a man with wives in two different headmanships is listed in each location separately, hence the number of people with more than two wives appears lower than it actually is.

[2] *Avahálikwa*, from *okuhálika*, to marry a second wife.

wards. The 'favoured wife', on the other hand, has no formal privileges as, in fact, her status is not permanent but dependent upon the changing likes and dislikes of the husband.

The great wife exercises a certain amount of authority over her co-wives, especially during the first year or two after a young wife's marriage, when the latter has not yet established a household of her own. If the husband's mother is dead or too old to maintain her own household, the great wife steps into her place and adopts a similar attitude towards her younger co-wife as the mother-in-law would have done towards her daughter-in-law, with the difference, however, that the young wife—for the first few months after her marriage—sleeps in the hut of the great wife and also eats in her company.[1] After the young wife has moved into her own hut and has been given her own garden and granary, the great wife's authority gradually diminishes. In all joint activities[2] of the co-wives, however, the great wife continues to take precedence, and her co-wives generally show her the respect due to a senior relative.

Children in the polygynous family are grouped with their mothers, the formal relationship between half-siblings differing in several respects from that between full siblings.[3] Half-siblings grow up in different huts. The children of each wife, as a rule, eat and—during their early childhood—sleep in the hut of their mother. They also share primarily in the house- and garden-work of their own mother's household. As regards the claims and duties that arise in connexion with the bride-wealth, in Maragoli the children of each wife form distinct groups, while in Kitosh the co-operation extends to an even wider group than the polygynous family, viz. the lineage-group. In Maragoli the claims to a girl's marriage cattle are primarily limited to her full brothers, while, likewise, chiefly full brothers assist one another in the payment of their bride-wealth. In the distribution of the father's cattle (cattle of the yard), on the other hand, the eldest son of the great wife occupies a preferential position over all sons as he becomes the sole guardian of the legacy if the father dies before all the sons have reached full married status. Accordingly, while the father is still alive, the 'cattle of the yard' are kept in the hut of the great wife only[4] and are not allocated to the huts of the different wives, although all wives have an equal claim to milk and meat. This different treatment of the 'cattle of the yard' and the cattle that accrue from the daughters' marriages incidentally shows that the

---

[1] The newly married wife who lives with her husband in the homestead of her father-in-law cannot sleep there as she has to avoid her father-in-law.

[2] Co-wives often cultivate their gardens jointly, beginning in the garden of the great wife.

[3] Also linguistically they are distinguished from full siblings: *amitu* (plur. *avamitu*) is the half-sibling of the same sex, i.e. a man's half-brother or a woman's half-sister, and *mbozua* (plur. *avavozua*) is the half-sibling of opposite sex, i.e. a man's half-sister or a woman's half-brother.

[4] If they are many they are kept in a cattle enclosure that adjoins the hut of the great wife.

transfer of the marriage cattle primarily serves as a regulator of marriages[1] and not as a means of increasing the father's wealth.

During the father's lifetime the sons show the same behaviour towards their father's co-wives as towards their mother, though a son of the great wife would show less formal respect towards his father's 'little wife' than a son of the latter towards the great wife. Even where the father's 'little wife' is younger than the eldest son—as often happens—there is no formal avoidance between the two. The discovery of sexual relations between them would, however, be strongly disapproved and punished by a curse pronounced by an elderly clansman, a fine for adultery being, of course, impossible in such a case. After the father's death the sons of a senior wife may 'inherit', i.e. marry, the junior wives.[2] This custom further adds to the authority of the great wife's sons over their junior half-brothers, as through the marriage of their father's widows they become their half-brothers' 'fathers'.

Summarizing this analysis of the traditional Bantu Kavirondo family we can distinguish the following principal features:

1. The family is an economically self-sufficient group. Each of its members contributes to the economic maintenance of the family group by performing those tasks which are assigned to him by the traditional rules of the division of labour. Co-operation within the family is maintained throughout the life of the parents, although in a modified form after the children have founded families of their own. Interdependence and co-operation within the household economy are direct, continuous, and personal.

2. A numerous offspring is strongly desired by both parents, a fact which finds expression in numerous matrimonial customs: (*a*) In the desire for polygynous marriage, especially if there is no issue from the first wife. (*b*) In the existence of elaborate magical rites and sacrifices which are performed as remedies against barrenness of the wife or impotency of the husband. (*c*) In socially condoned sexual access to a brother's wife, especially before the birth of the first child. (*d*) In the silent approval of extra-marital sex-relations of the wife in case of the impotency of the husband. (*e*) In the right of the husband to reclaim all or part of the bride-wealth, if his wife dies without leaving children. (*f*) In the remarriage of the widow to the deceased husband's brother, provided that she is not past the child-bearing age.

3. A strong preference is given to male over female offspring especially by the father and his kinsmen, despite the fact that daughters render the same amount of help to their parents as sons and, through the institution of the bride-wealth, add to the father's wealth in cattle, whereas sons for the same reason are an economic burden to the father.

---

[1] In a sense which will be discussed more fully in the chapter on Property Law; cf. vol. ii.

[2] The marriage of a senior wife by the son of a junior wife is not permitted, even if the difference in their age would not be too great to rule out their marriage under ordinary circumstances.

4. The father retains legal responsibility for his married daughters and lasting authority over his sons, as becomes apparent from: (*a*) the residential proximity of the eldest and youngest sons to the father's homestead, (*b*) the father's sustained rights of ownership over the lands apportioned to his sons, (*c*) his trusteeship over his sons' cattle, and (*d*) the compensation which he has to pay, in full or in part, for offences committed by his married daughters.

5. The eldest son commands authority over his younger brothers, especially after the father's death and until the father's legacy has been fully distributed.

6. In spite of close economic co-operation there is a social segregation and differentiation between the sexes within the family which finds expression in (*a*) the sexual division of labour, (*b*) eating customs, (*c*) the division of the hut and homestead into a husband's and a wife's section, and (*d*) general rules of social conduct.

7. The legal position of the wife is inferior to that of the husband with regard to her sexual and property rights as well as her claims to her children.

8. The status of sons and daughters differs with regard to the inheritance of family property as land and cattle are passed on in the sons' line only.[1]

B. CLAN AND LINEAGE

APART from being a member of the individual family, every native acquires by birth membership of another and larger social group, the clan. Among the Bantu Kavirondo the clan is a patrilineal, exogamous, territorial unit, i.e. it comprises all persons who trace their descent in paternal line to a common ancestor and who, on that ground, form a community of interests, refrain from intermarrying, and inhabit a common stretch of land. Every clan-unit clearly distinguishes itself from other such communities based on the same principle of classification. The emphasis laid on the patrilineal descent from a common ancestor or founder of the clan which connects all members of a clan with one another finds its chief outward expression in the common clan-name which—like the family name with us—is passed on from the father to his children of either sex. All persons bearing the same clan-name claim, accordingly, to have sprung from the same ancestor in paternal line, even if they are not in a position to trace their ancestry back to the founder of the clan, the real or hypothetical clan ancestor, by establishing an unbroken genealogical connexion with him. Such an unbroken tracing of the ancestral line is, as a rule, only possible to the members of younger clans who need only go back for seven or eight generations to arrive at their common clan ancestor. In several cases I received genealogical data, alleged to be complete, also from

---

[1] The preceding chapter merely aimed at giving a preliminary survey of the main structural features of the Bantu Kavirondo family. Their more detailed discussion will be found in their respective contexts in vol. ii.

members of older and larger clans, but, when the genealogical records given to me by several elders of the same clan and the same age-group were compared, there was, as a rule, a considerable discrepancy as regards the number of ancestors or generations respectively, a fact which indicates that at least some of the genealogies were not complete.

The common clan-name is, as a rule, the personal name of the founder of the clan; in a few cases—e.g. among the Idaxo and the Vugusu—clans have been named after the women whose sons seceded from their former clan and thus became the founders of a new clan. However, among the tribes mentioned, clans were named after women only if these happened to have been persons of unusual influence. In the subsequent reckoning of descent moreover, such clans were just as patrilineal as those named after a male ancestor.

Now, paternal descent is not only traced to the founder of any given clan (the clan ancestor), but back to the tribal ancestor from whose personal name—as has already been mentioned—the tribal names of most of the Bantu Kavirondo tribes and sub-tribes are derived. Accordingly, all clans of a tribal group tracing their descent to the tribal ancestor form a patrilineal descent group. Such a tribal group is formally distinguished from its subgroups, the various clans, merely by the fact that it no longer forms an exogamous community, having grown too big to maintain the laws of exogamy.

In every other respect, however, there is no sharp dividing-line between the tribal group (as a group of clans tracing their descent from a common ancestor) and the exogamous clan, a fact which, in the course of the further discussion of these two groups, will be confirmed also in other ways. In some cases a legendary or even a genealogical relationship is established between several tribal groups, e.g. if according to the tribal tradition the brother of the tribal ancestor became the founder of another tribe. Thus the tribal tradition of the Vugusu claims that the descendants of Muvugusu's brothers who did not join in the southward migration form to-day the tribe of the Masava or Gishu (cf. above, p. 23). Similarly, the tribal tradition of the Wanga extends beyond the tribal ancestor Omuwanga and establishes a genealogical connexion with the Tiriki which, again, is fully confirmed by the traditions of the Tiriki.

Just as the descendants of the tribal ancestor in the process of their biological increase have split up into exogamous clan-units, the individual clans, likewise, show the tendency to form sub-groups. Outwardly these sub-groups within the clan are marked by the name of the common ancestor who has founded the sub-group. As long as they have not yet detached themselves from the exogamous clan community to form a new exogamous unit, they do not constitute an independent clan but merely a subgroup within the clan which we shall call a 'lineage'. Such a lineage usually comprises the direct descendants of a common grandfather or great-grandfather and—as distinct from the larger clan-unit—its members can trace their mutual relationship genealogically. The chief characteristic of

CLAN AND LINEAGE

the clan is, therefore, the fact that it constitutes an exogamous unit; on the other hand, not all groups based on patrilineal descent are clans in the sense of our definition. They may comprise units that are larger than a clan, such as a tribe, or smaller ones such as the lineage.

The terminology used in the various native dialects fully corresponds to this state of affairs. In all Bantu Kavirondo dialects the exogamous clan unit is rendered by the word *oluhia* (plural *edzimbia*).[1] As a noun this word also has the meaning 'fire-place on a meadow'; and it is at this *oluhia* that the old men of the clan community meet every morning to warm themselves and to discuss the events and news of the day as well as to settle all important matters of the clan (cf. below, p. 78). In its verbal form the stem *hia* means 'to be hot', 'to burn', while the adjective *hia* has the meaning 'new' or 'fresh'. Apparently the adjective *hia* has nothing to do with the name *oluhia* 'clan', but this term is exclusively derived from the word *oluhia*, 'the fire-place as the centre of the public life of the clan'. Among the Tiriki the term *oluvamba* is occasionally used as an alternative for the word *oluhia*; I was, however, not able to learn anything about the etymology of this word.

Every larger group of clans which traces descent to a common ancestor but is no longer exogamous is in most dialects termed *ehili* (plural *edzihili*) (with the exception of the Nyole and the Vugusu). In the case of those tribes where *all* clans of the tribal group trace their descent to one common tribal ancestor, the term *ehili* is, accordingly, synonymous with tribe, and it is also used in this sense. Besides, it designates sub-groups of the tribe comprising several clans; it is, on the other hand, never used synonymously with *oluhia*. A term designating the tribe as a political unit, i.e. a group of clans both of common and of heterogeneous descent and forming a political unit under the authority of a chief, exists—as far as I could ascertain—only among the Wanga, who refer to the community of clans organized under the political rule of the Wanga chiefs as *lihanga*. Recently they have endeavoured to extend the meaning of this term so as to comprise all Bantu Kavirondo. In support of their argument they claim that Chief Mumia was appointed Paramount Chief over all Bantu Kavirondo by the British Government.

The lineage is either called *enyumba* (in Lurogoli) and *indzu* (in the other dialects), both words meaning 'house' or 'hut', or *ekilivwa* (*efilivwa*), which literally means 'gate' and, in particular, the gate of the enclosure surrounding a village or a homestead. As a *pars pro toto* it stands for the social group that lives together, referring primarily to that sub-group of the clan which dwelled within a common enclosure, viz. the lineage. In the northern half of the district the lineage appears to have formed a residential unit until well after the establishment of British administration. To-day, however, the *ekilivwa*-group no longer forms a residential unit within a common

[1] Luvugusu: *luyia*, *tʃimbia*. In the other dialects the prefixes are *tsi-*, *-edzi-*, &c. Cf. above, p. 26.

enclosure, but the residential differences which formerly existed between the north and the south still make themselves felt in the much more closely knit structure which characterizes the lineages in the north as compared with the same units in the south (cf. above, p. 31).

Within the area occupied by a tribe the various exogamous clans form territorial units, and all the land lying within the area occupied by a clan community is regarded as clan-land. Actually, however, the territorial unity of the clan is not completely unbroken. As long as land was still in abundance, the areas occupied by neighbouring clans were not rigidly delimited. Chiefly, however, the principle of the territorial unit of the clan was and still is infringed by the fact that clan-strangers (*avamenya*)[1] are permitted to settle on clan-lands. Such *avamenya* are mostly relatives of members of the clan, viz. in the order of their frequency: (1) so-called *avifwa* (sisters' sons), i.e. the sons of the married women of the clan and their offspring; (2) the husbands of the married women of the clan, in which cases matrimony is not patrilocal (as in the majority of cases) but matrilocal; (3) cross-cousins (*avasiala*), i.e. the sons of mothers' brothers; and (4) the brothers of the women married by members of the clan (i.e. brothers-in-law). Every clansman can grant the right of residence to relatives of this kind (in some cases also to more distant relatives or even friends) either at his own homestead or in his 'village' (the *lugova* of the Vugusu), and he even can allocate land to them on clan territory without having to ask anyone for permission.[2] According to the unanimous opinion of my different informants, it was customary also in pre-European days to give shelter to relatives and friends from other clans and to let them settle on clan-land; the various motives which helped to sustain this custom on either side we shall discuss more fully when describing the significance of clanship and kinship in the various spheres of life. In the majority of cases, however, the residence of clan-strangers on clan territory appears to have been only of a more or less temporary nature, for otherwise the clans would have completely ceased to be territorial units which, however, is not the case. In most parts of the North Kavirondo District the clans still form clearly distinguishable territorial units. Even in Maragoli, where the territorial alinement of clanship is rapidly breaking down, the percentage of persons residing in the territory of other clans (clan-strangers or *avamenya*) amounts only to approximately 37 per cent. (cf. vol. ii). By staying in the territory of another clan the *avamenya* do not, under any circumstances, become members of their host-clan. Even though they may live among it for several generations, their children and grandchildren retain their original clan affiliation and continue to be bound by its various rules of exogamy. Socially, of course, the status which they enjoy in the host-clan after a prolonged residence begins to resemble that of the clansmen, provided that they fit in with the life of the clan and

---

[1] From *okumenya*, to stay as a guest.
[2] Cf. chapter on Land Tenure, vol. ii.

CLAN AND LINEAGE

identify themselves with its interests (cf. below, p. 70). Adoption into the clan, in the proper sense of the word, seems to have been of very rare occurrence only, having been limited exclusively to stray orphans and young war-captives from other tribes who had lost all contact with their own clan. Such children were then raised together with the physical children of their foster-parents and, later, were tacitly considered as belonging to the clan of their foster-father without any special ceremony of adoption being performed for them. After a number of years they enjoyed the same social and legal status as real children. Among the Vugusu I was even told that foster-parents often treat their adopted children particularly well, so that the care and attention given to them sometimes arouses the envy and misgivings of their stepbrothers and sisters. Apart, however, from the adoption of war-captives, a change of clan-membership was not possible. One may, therefore, say that clan membership is practically determined by birth alone. Women, too, never change their clan affiliation upon marriage or at any subsequent stage of their matrimonial relationship, but throughout their lives remain members of the clan into which they were born.

The territorial unit of the clan was, formerly, curtailed also by the fact that various lineages split off the main clan and seceded from it, to settle either by themselves or within the territory occupied by another clan. As the traditions of several clans show, lineages that had separated themselves from the main clan sooner or later tended to become independent units, that is to say new clans, by forming an exogamous unit of their own, renouncing their former clan affiliations, and by adopting a new clan-name for themselves. After a lineage had in such a fashion asserted its independence, the principle of the territorial unit of the clan, or rather of the two clans, was re-established. If part of a clan, following a serious quarrel, emigrated from the territory not only of the clan but of the whole tribe to join a strong clan-unit in a neighbouring tribe, the emigrating sub-group frequently maintained its former clan-name, but considered itself socially and politically independent from the main part of the clan from which it had parted. Among the Tiriki, for instance, one encounters to-day a number of clan-names which are identical with clan-names found among the neighbouring Logoli. While in a number of cases this identity of names is explained by the fact that the founders of the two clans chanced to have the same names, in other cases the clan traditions in both tribes point to a common origin, although both clans to-day consider one another as completely separate units, even to such an extent that they may intermarry.

A third factor, finally, which interfered with the territorial alinement of the clan was the manner in which land conquered in war was distributed. If several clans combined to wage war against a neighbouring tribe and if, in the course of such an enterprise, they succeeded in driving the enemy from the territory formerly occupied by him, the conquered lands were shared out among the most deserving warriors of all the clans that had participated in the fighting. As a consequence of this procedure, newly conquered lands frequently were occupied by members of various clans.

Examining the data compiled by me, I shall now try to show of how many clans the various tribal groups are made up, in what way the different clans originated, and how, by the segregation of sub-groups (lineages), new clan-units have been and still are being set up.

In the chieftaincy (location) of South Maragoli (population in 1932: 20,349 heads) I compiled, in the course of time, the following list of clan-names:

1. Dámayi	12. Lógovo	23. Daŋa
2. Dindi	13. Málaha	24. Sali
3. Fúnami	14. Mavi	25. Salia
4. Gihayo	15. Menge	26. Sanga
5. Gímuhia	16. Mígangu	27. Sániaga
6. Gisindi	17. Mugezi	28. Témbuli
7. Gívagi	18. Muku	29. Tsátsala
8. Gonda	19. Muluga	30. Vígulu
9. Guga	20. Mutembe	31. Yonga
10. Kivuta	21. Ndega	32. Yose
11. Kuvera	22. Nondi	

All these thirty-two clans claim to be descendants of the tribal ancestor Mulogoli (*avana va* Mulogoli = children of Mulogoli). By far the largest and most important of these clans are the Mavi (14) and the Yonga (31). With these two clans rested essentially the leadership in warfare; they controlled the most extensive tracts of land and to each of them was affiliated a number of smaller clans which submitted to their leadership both in times of peace and of war (see below, p. 388). The Mavi and the clans politically attached to them inhabit the northern part of the chieftaincy, and the Yonga, together with the allied clans, the southern part. Of the two clans, the Mavi again surpass the Yonga both numerically and as regards the influence wielded by them. In their clan, for instance, was vested the hereditary office of the tribal priest who performed the semi-annual *ovwali*-sacrifice addressed to the Supreme Being and to the clan and tribal ancestors (cf. below, p. 290 sq.). The Mavi clan also supplied the majority of the leaders (cf. vol. ii) whose authority was recognized also by the other clans of the tribal community, as well as the present tribal chief nominated by the British Government. Of the remaining thirty clans some are as old as the Mavi and the Yonga, while others are sub-clans or lineages which became independent clans only at a later date by having split off the main clans. By combining and interpolating the information obtained from a number of leading elders of different clans,[1] the genealogical relations between the clans present themselves as follows.

[1] My chief informants were: (1) Wulule (Gímuhia), (2) Donera (Yonga), (3) Mutiva (Lógovo), (4) Oluŋafwa (Gihayo), (5) Paulo Agoi (Lógovo), (6) Christopher Mtiva (Yonga), (7) Lubanga (Yonga, Yose), (8) Jakobo Dovolosio (Fúnami), (9) Oluŋafu (Muku).

CLAN AND LINEAGE

Logoli, the tribal ancestor, had eight sons, two of them, Mavi and Kirima, by his first or great wife and the other six by his 'young wife'. They were Sali, the oldest one, Yonga, Kizungu, Muku, Daŋa, and Sániaga. Yonga had a quarrel with his brother Kizungu over the distribution of the marriage cattle received for one of their sisters. In the course of this quarrel Yonga killed his brother. To escape the revenge of Kizungu's sons, Yonga thereupon fled together with his sons to his elder half-brother Mavi who granted him shelter and support. The sons of Kizungu, after their father's death, left their former abode in the 'Bunyole Hills' and migrated in a north-easterly direction, crossing the Edzawa River until they came to what is to-day North Maragoli. Actually the Kizungu to-day form one of the major clans in the chieftaincy of North Maragoli. Later the Mavi and the Yonga fought together against the Kizungu who, on their part, entered into an alliance with their north-eastern neighbours, the Idaxo, for joint acts of warfare. Since the time of the quarrel between Yonga and Kizungu the Logoli tribe has been split up into the two sections which still exist to-day, viz. the two chieftaincies or locations of North Maragoli and South Maragoli. As a consequence of that early feud, no marriage relations appear to have existed between them in pre-European days; to-day, under mission influence, the two sections have begun to intermarry again. In dozens of widely ramified genealogies which I have recorded in South Maragoli I have on two occasions only come across clan-names from North Maragoli.

Kirima, the second son of Mulogoli's great wife, likewise had a quarrel with Mavi and with his younger half-brothers. He therefore followed Kizungu to North Maragoli, where to-day his descendants form a large clan.

Mavi, Mulogoli's eldest son, had four sons: Nondi, Lógovo, Gonda, and Mutembe. Their descendants form to-day the four 'great houses' (*edzinyumba dzinene*) or sub-clans of the Mavi. They are, however, not yet completely independent clans. On the grounds of their common descent from Mavi and the friendly relations always maintained between them, they constitute still to-day one large exogamous group, known by the name of their joint clan-ancestor Mavi. Another one of Mavi's sons by one of his younger wives was Témbuli. A son of Lógovo, again, was Málaha, whose issue was so numerous that the lineage named after him comprises to-day several hundred male persons.

Yonga, one of the sons of Mulogoli's young wife, had one son by each of his two wives. The son of his great wife was called Yose and that of his young wife Gímuhia. One of Yose's younger brothers was Gívagi (who, according to another version, was a son of Yose). To-day the Yose, Gímuhia, and Gívagi form sub-clans of the Yonga that do not intermarry.

It may be added that I was given three different versions concerning Yonga's descent, all of which, however, can be reconciled with one another. According to the view taken by most elders of the Yonga clan, Yonga was one of the sons of Logoli's young wife (as in the version given above).

Mutiva (of the Lógovo sub-clan of the Mavi), on the other hand, insisted that Logoli died when Yonga was still in his mother's womb. Thereupon Mavi, being Mulogoli's eldest son and chief heir, married his 'young mother' (Mulogoli's young wife), and so it happened that Yonga was born at Mavi's homestead. According to the information received by still another informant, Paulo Agoi, Yonga was one of Mavi's younger sons, but not one of the four sons of his great wife. The seeming contradiction between Agoi's version and that supplied by the majority of the elders of the Yonga clan thus finds an explanation in the information given by Mutiva. Mutiva's version is, further, supported by the fact that Yonga appealed for protection to Mavi instead of to one of his full brothers (e.g. Sali). Mavi, after all, was not only his elder half-brother but at the same time his stepfather.

The remaining names contained in the above list (p. 58) are those of sub-clans of more recent origin who, in the same way as the Yose and Gímuhia from the Yonga clan, have split off the older clans only two or three generations after Logoli. Although the members of some of these clans occasionally claim that their respective clan-ancestor was also one of Mulogoli's sons—e.g. my informant Jacobo Dovolosio of the Fúnami clan—this appears to be improbable, for nearly all my informants when asked to name the sons of Logoli mentioned with striking unanimity the eight names which I have quoted above. In the majority of cases the elders of the remaining sub-clans can merely say that their clan-ancestor has in some way descended from Logoli without, however, being able to state the exact genealogical relationship with him. In other cases I was told that the founder of the clan was related to the founder of this or that of the other sub-clans, but that the exact nature of the relationship had been forgotten. The Gihayo, for instance, claim to be related to the Mavi, and the Fúnami with the Yonga.

As has already been stated, nowadays all members of the Logoli tribe consider themselves to be *avana va* Mulogoli, 'children (i.e. descendants) of Mulogoli'. Nevertheless, this does not rule out the possibility that some of the smaller clans joined the Logoli tribe only at a later date, coming from neighbouring tribes such as the Nyole, Kisa, or Tiriki, but that they try to cover up that fact so as to be considered full-fledged members of the Logoli tribe.

In so far as the ancestral lists supplied by the elders of the various clans permit of any conclusions, it would appear that Logoli, the tribal ancestor, lived about seven or eight generations ago. According to the hut count of the year 1932, a total of 14,327 adult men were then living in the two chieftaincies of North and South Maragoli. Disregarding any outside groups that may have joined the Logoli in the course of their tribal history —on the assumption that such groups would keep the balance with Logoli groups which in turn, have left the tribal area to settle elsewhere—and taking all Logoli men living at present to be descendants of Mulogoli, the average number of sons in each family who married and begot children would range between three and four. As this number is obviously far too high, it must be assumed that the genealogies have been abridged. As the traditions relating to the immediate descendants of Logoli tally among the different clans even down to insignificant details, they would seem to correspond on the whole to the actual genealogical facts. But the names of some of the subsequent ancestors have apparently fallen into oblivion (especially those whose lives and personalities were inconspicuous), while the last five or six generations in each family are again in living memory.

A knowledge of their ancestors as well as of the traditions relating to the origin of their own clan and of the principal clans that have sprung from Logoli's immediate descendants is by no means possessed by all natives. In South Maragoli my informants included five elders who were looked upon as the chief receptacles of tribal tradition; the remaining four were natives of medium age who belonged to old and influential families and who already as children and young men had received instruction from their fathers as to the names of their ancestors and the history of their own as well as of the other major clans. Thus Lubanga told me that his father had once walked with him for several hours to show him the place where the quarrel between Yonga and his brother Kizungu is supposed to have taken place. But with few exceptions the knowledge even of the old men is limited to the principal events in the history of their own clan and, to a lesser extent, of their mother's clan, as well as to the knowledge of the sons of the tribal ancestors. When questioned about other clans, their knowledge is, as a rule, limited to their names and the place where they live and—if they have a relative or a good friend in a certain clan—to the name of the clan from which it has split off or of which it forms a sub-group. None of my informants was able to quote *ad hoc* the names of all the Logoli clans; on the average they could name between eighteen and twenty, so that a complete list of clans could be compiled only by combining the data given by quite a large number of informants belonging to many different clans, as well as those provided by genealogical charts. Discussing the complete list with my various informants, it turned out that they knew also the names of those clans which they had omitted in their own enumeration. But as they were small and distant clans not connected with them by any bonds of kinship or friendship, they had forgotten to mention them. There exists, accordingly, even in such a comparatively small tribal community as that of the Logoli, not a single native familiar enough with the entire clan-system of the tribe to be able to give a complete inventory of the clans and of their respective genealogical relation to the tribal ancestors.

In view of this state of affairs one might assume that the various informants would tend to exaggerate the importance of their own clan. As a rule, however, this was not so. The assertion, for instance, made by the members of the Mavi clan that as descendants of the eldest son of Mulogoli's great wife they were the most important clan in the tribe, was readily confirmed by the Yonga. These, in turn, never tried to make a secret of the fact that Yonga was merely a junior son of Mulogoli's second wife, nor of the fact that, following his quarrel with Kizungu, he fled to his elder half-brother Mavi to seek his protection. Similarly the Muku admitted to be but a small clan which a few generations ago had affiliated itself with the Yonga so as to benefit from the protection which this more powerful clan could grant them.

The genealogical knowledge of the average native of young or middle age is limited to the names of his own and his mother's clan, as well as to four or five ancestral names in the paternal and to two or three in the maternal line. Formerly it is said to have been a popular pastime among the young men when sitting round the nightly fire in their *esimba* to question one another about the names of their ancestors, the idea being to answer as quickly as possible and to continue the list of ancestors as far back as possible. The questions were asked and the answers given in the following standardized manner:

Question: *Dada wowo nivwaha?* Who is your father?
Answer: *Atonde.*
Question: *A Atonde?* (The father) of Atonde?
Answer: *Maɲule Ugwegwe.*
Question: *A Ugwegwe?*
Answer: *Ugwegwe Avayanza.*
Question: *A Avayanza?*
Answer: *Vayanza Vagavo.*
Question: *A Vagavo?* &c.

As this brief survey of the clan traditions of the Logoli shows, the prestige of a clan is determined, first of all, by its age and its genealogical relation to the tribal ancestor and, in the second place, by its numerical strength, i.e. its rate of growth. With the Mavi both factors are combined, thus securing for it a privileged position in the tribal community; while in the case of the Yonga it appears to be their fecundity and virility which caused them in the course of time to overtake and outgrow the Sali, Muku, Sániaga, &c., the founders of which clans, all of them being brothers of Yonga, were at least of equal importance to the latter.

Among the Tiriki (1932: 17,178 heads) who adjoin the Logoli in the east I compiled a list of thirty-four clans. A striking feature of this list is the large number of clan-names identical with those recorded among the Logoli (cf. above, p. 58):

1. Dura	9. Marama	17. Musali
2. Gisigi	10. Mavi	18. Rhimbuli
3. Gove	11. Mbo	19. Salia
4. Ixava	12. Mohia	20. Samia
5. Kisindi	13. Moli	21. Sanga
6. Loxova	14. Moniʃiri	22. Sianiaga
7. Luxombe	15. Mudede	23. Suva
8. Malava	16. Mugombero	24. Σidzudza

CLAN AND LINEAGE

25. Ʃiriga
26. Ʃirima
27. Ʃitsiola
28. Ʃivo
29. Vaiyi
30. Vala
31. Vuka
32. Xadiri
33. Xombwa
34. Xuvera

The two largest and most important of these clans are the Loxova and the Mbo; from their ranks the most influential clan-heads were formerly chosen. The clans of the Dura and Mudede are said to have come at a later date from Bunyole, while the Kisindi, Mavi, Rhimbuli, Salia, Sanga, and Ʃirima are supposed to have come from Maragoli. Apart from these clans which only subsequently joined the tribal community but which both in language and in custom have been completely assimilated by the Tiriki, all the other clans are said to have ultimately descended from Mudiriki. This tribal ancestor, however, appears to be of a more or less mythical nature. The ancestor who figured most frequently in the accounts of my various informants was Lulidzi, under whose lead the Tiriki left South Kavirondo, crossed the gulf, and migrated to North Kavirondo. Lulidzi's grandson, Nandunda, had a numerous offspring the different branches of which separated, thus becoming the founders of the present clans. Loxova, Mbo, &c., accordingly appear to have been sons of Nandunda.

Among the Idaxo (1932: 6,857 heads) I was given a list of nine clans (*tsimbia*) and a large number of lineages (*vilivwa*):

1. *Magambe*
    (a) Vwandia
    (b) Amasa
    (c) Sunditu
    (d) Ʃiasuli
    (e) Kwese
    (f) Sagala

2. *Manyiʃi*
    (a) Twehe
    (b) Ngose
    (c) Anyoma
    (d) Aʃiriga
    (e) Natanya
    (f) Nyundu
    (g) Aʃitsa

3. *Masava*
    (a) Navuli
    (b) Ʃimahatse
    (c) Anyonga
    (d) Amagole
    (e) Muʃitsyula
    (f) Mugare
    (g) Aʃilagaya
    (h) Muxuvi

4. *Muhali*
    (a) Igingwa
    (b) Amidede
    (c) Lusivwa
    (d) Tsalatsala
    (e) Isimbi
    (f) Adjisila

5. *Musali*
    (a) Mwaxa
    (b) Ʃinasimba
    (c) Ʃimega
    (d) Nambago
    (e) Lisalidza
    (f) Ligunda
    (g) Muyanzi
    (h) Vasie
    (i) Namugambi
    (j) Xanga
    (k) Lwidji
    (l) Mbuguli
    (m) Madali
    (n) Amugahya
    (o) Ndjeli

6. *Nyixu*
    (a) Kule
    (b) Huga
    (c) Malava

7. Σangala	8. Σigulu	9. Σumuli
(a) Ngove	(a) Amuhaga	(a) Anasie
(b) Ayemi	(b) Σilima	(b) Andaye
(c) Amwendwa	(c) Djengo	(c) Amulongo
(d) Amusembe	(d) Emuxu	(d) Amahera
(e) Asigunga		(e) Asere
(f) Ambale		(f) Kiduyi
(g) Amahani		(g) Asiligwa
(h) Amudaho		(h) Gasionami
(i) Avwaniʃili		(i) Amugondi
(j) Asilwa		(j) Amuvuga
(k) Amavusi		(k) Amusongu
(l) Axwaŋa		(l) Naxati
		(m) Vanuli
		(n) Visaho
		(o) Avuduxa
		(p) Adjihayo
		(q) Aluhove

Among the Tsotso (1932: 8,457 heads), collating the results of repeated inquiries, I recorded a total of twenty-two clans: Hobole, Kiviywa, Kovero, Mani, Manyulia, Matioli, Mukaya, Mweitjye, Mwende, Ngusi, Nyakwaka, Sumba, Σiambitsi, Σiamusingiri, Σianda, Σibo, Σibuli, Σirumba, Σisira, Σiveye, Tamanyini, and Uŋonya, four of which (the Matioli, Mweitjye, Tamanyini, and Uŋonya), however, seem to be considerably larger than the other ones.

Among the Marama (1932: 18,957 heads) I took down the names of fourteen major clans: Erekyeya, Ero, Lugoxo, Mahongoyo, Mumbia, Muxula, Suva, Σahanga, Σiemi, Σirotsa, Tahi, Tere, Tjenya, Tsetse, and of the largest of these clans, the Muxula, I listed again six sub-clans (in the order of their size): Mumbia, Ndulusia, Mutjelule, Mukolwe, Atsulu, Eyinda, who, however, do not intermarry. Among the Marama, minor clans who do not trace their descent from the common tribal ancestor but who have only later on joined the ranks of a larger tribe are referred to as *emikuru*, i.e. veranda-poles, because they support the big clan and lend additional strength to it in the same way as the veranda-poles of the circular native hut support the structure of the roof.

A list comprising a total of sixty clans I compiled among the Vugusu. In 1932 they numbered 51,079, including a few minor groups of alien extraction, such as the Tadjoni, the Ngoma, and others. The names of the Vugusu clans are:

1. Afu	7. Gitwika	13. Kuta
2. Alo	8. Itu	14. Lago
3. Embo	9. Kiavi	15. Leyi
4. Eŋere	10. Kimueyi	16. Lisa
5. Etjalo	11. Kiveti	17. Liuli
6. Gamkoŋi	12. Kunga	18. Lukulu

CLAN AND LINEAGE

19. Lunda	33. Refu	47. Tjemwile
20. Luondja	34. Sakali	48. Uma
21. Malidja	35. Sava	49. Vidjadji
22. Meme	36. Sefu	50. Vulo
23. Moyayo	37. Segese	51. Vuya
24. Muki	38. Senya	52. Xisa
25. Mukoya	39. Sime	53. Xoma
26. Muna	40. Simisi	54. Xondjo
27. Musomi	41. Sivadjuo	55. Xone
28. Mutiru	42. Sombi	56. Xuami
29. Muyonga	43. Songe	57. Xulalua
30. Mwaya	44. Taxwe	58. Yaya
31. Mweya	45. Tedjo	59. Yemba
32. Nayngali	46. Tjemayi	60. Yundo

All these sixty clans are independent exogamous groups. Only three of them—as far as I could discover—have, in turn, split into two sub-groups each. At present these are about to become independent clans and to intermarry. Members of these three clans refer to themselves by two names, that of the former joint clan-unit and that of the founder of the sub-group. These sub-groups are:

1. Of the clan of the Gitwika (7):
    (a) Gitwika va Kitanga
    (b) Gitwika va Kwangwa
2. Of the clan of Musomi (29):
    (a) Musomi vamae
    (b) Musomi vayasele
3. Of the clan of Vuya (51):
    (a) Vuya vaolo
    (b) Vuya vaxufwe

Although all these clans claim to have descended from Vugusu, none of the old men was able to state the exact genealogical relationship between his clan ancestor and Vugusu. All that seems to be known about Vugusu is that he had four sons and four daughters who are said to have married one another. The names of the four sons are: Maina (or Mayina), Mango, Malava, and Muŋoma. As to-day none of these four names occurs as a clan-name among the Vugusu, it appears that even the oldest of the now existing clans were established only by the descendants of these four sons.

In addition to these sixty Vugusu clans seventeen other clans are living in the three Vugusu chieftaincies (Kimilili, Malakisi, and South Kitosh). To-day these clans, too, form part of the Vugusu tribe:

1. Djemuluku	7. Meywa	13. Tjambayi
2. Kafisi	8. Muhongo	14. Vangadji
3. Kovolo	9. Samo	15. Viiya
4. Kuvuayi	10. Saŋalo	16. Wande
5. Matiri	11. Saniaga	17. Yumbu (from
6. Maxuli	12. Sioya	Kakalelwa)

Among the Wanga (1932: 26,187 heads), finally, only twelve clans of a total of thirty consider themselves as descendants of Omuwanga, whereas the remaining eighteen have immigrated at a later date and submitted to the political leadership of the Wanga clans.[1] The names of the twelve original Wanga clans are:

1. Xitsetse	6. Yundo	9. Mukalano
2. Murono	7. Mbatsa	(Mukalalu)
3. Tende	(Wambatsa)	10. Mboli
4. Munyafu	8. Muʃetjere	11. Sereme
5. Namaagwa		12. Tjitedji

According to the traditions concerning the Wanga chiefs (cf. vol. ii), the first seven of these twelve clans were founded by the sons of Omuwanga, while the remaining five are possibly the sons of one of Omuwanga's junior wives; Sereme is said to have been Omuwanga's youngest son. With the exception of the Murono (2) and Mbatsa (7), who form independent exogamous groups, all the other clans are sub-groups of the Xitsetse; they still consider one another as being too closely related for them to intermarry. Accordingly, they must either intermarry with the clans of the Murono or Mbatsa or with any of the immigrated clans. As to the latter, I have for the greater part been able to record not only their names but also the locality or the tribe from which they claim to have come:

1. Djero (it was their office to bury the Wanga chiefs).
2. Kalivo.
3. Kana (came from Alego in the Luo country but are Bantu).
4. Koluhi (came from Maragoli together with the Wanga, to-day a particularly wealthy clan).
5. Lega (came from Sangalo).
6. Madiru (came from Bugishu on the western slopes of Mount Elgon).
7. Manga (came from Malakisi).
8. Moira (came from Mbori).
9. Muende.
10. Mulembwa.
11. Nadziri (came from Sangalo).
12. Neʃieni (came from the north-west, lived formerly in Uganda).
13. Ngari (came from Samia and Marrach).
14. Sikava (came as servants of Omuwanga).
15. Tove.
16. Vuka.
17. Wesia (came from Uganda).
18. Xami (came from Ewali on the lower Malakisi River).

[1] Cf. K. R. Dundas, 1913. The list of Wanga clans quoted there by Dundas (which unfortunately I did not have with me when in the field) largely agrees with the information gathered by me. In addition to the clans listed by me it contains 4 sub-clans of the Xitsetse and 2 clans who joined the tribe later on, the Mwima and the Mwika. Of the 18 clans listed above, Dundas mentions the numbers 1, 2, 4, 5, 10, 12, 14, 15, 17, and 18 (some of them with a slightly different spelling); the other 8 clans are not contained in his list.

CLAN AND LINEAGE

As will be seen from the above data, a new clan can originate in a number of different ways. By far the most frequent cause which we encounter in the clan traditions is a quarrel between two brothers of the leading family of a clan, or even a serious clash between two ordinary clansmen leading to the formation of two parties within the clan community and, finally, to an open breach between them.

The weaker party or—as seems usually to be the case—both parties thereupon leave their former common domicile and migrate in opposite directions. From now on they form two separate clans which no longer call themselves after their former joint clan ancestor but usually after the man under whose leadership they migrated to their new abode. However, they do not adopt this new clan-name immediately after having severed their affiliations with the other half of the clan but only after one or even several generations have passed. For a time they retain the old name along with the new one, as in the case of the above-mentioned Vugusu sub-clans, the different sub-clans of the Logoli, &c. Gradually the old name falls into oblivion and so the common origin of the two sub-clans is no longer recognizable by any outward sign. As long as the feud between the two sections of the former clan continues, no relations of any kind are maintained between them (cf. below, p. 189 sq.). Every member of the one group observes a strict avoidance (Lurogoli: *omugiru*, Luvugusu: *gumusiru*) towards every member of the other group, the avoidance going so far that members of the two groups may not even talk together when they happen to meet at the homestead of a third party, nor may they both take part in a common meal (cf. below, p. 191). If the two new clans do not live at such a distance from one another that they have lost contact, a ritual reconciliation sooner or later takes place between them and therewith also a resumption of their mutual social relations (cf. below, p. 256 sq.). They continue, however, to live as two clearly distinct and independent groups. As long as the consciousness of their mutual relationship is kept alive by the memory of their common fathers or grandfathers, they will observe the rule of exogamy, i.e. they refrain from intermarrying even after they have terminated their feud (avoidance). Only after several generations, when the memory of their joint ancestors has begun to fade, would the bond of exogamy gradually be broken. The first step would be tacitly to condone the marriage with a 'sister's daughter' (Luvugusu: *omwiwana*) of the other section of the clan, i.e. a girl whose mother came from that clan. If such a marriage remains without evil consequences, both for those directly concerned and for the wider circle of clansmen on either side, such marriages are repeated. After another generation or two one would venture to go one step farther and enter into direct marital relations with the other clan. The number of generations which will pass until the two sub-groups of a clan, after having set up an independent existence, will begin to intermarry, seems entirely to depend on the strength of the clan traditions. In the case of politically leading clans that have kept their clan history alive so as to strengthen their prestige in the tribal community (as the clans that have sprung from the sons of Omuwanga, or the four sub-clans of the Mavi among the Logoli, cf. above, p. 59), the sub-clans still continue to form one exogamous unit, apparently because the authority of the common clan ancestor is still so strong and the memory of him so much alive that his descendants would not dare to ignore the fact of their common descent by infringing the laws of exogamy. Among the less tradition-minded clans, on the other hand, sub-groups that have come to live as territorial units will tend already after a few generations (i.e. after the last member of the former clan community has died) to establish their independence also with regard to the rules of exogamy by entering into marital relations with the other sub-groups of the main clan.

A characteristic example showing how, as a result of a quarrel between two brothers, a clan may split up into two new and independent sub-clans I have quoted already in connexion with the account of the Logoli clans when referring to the quarrel between Yonga and his brother Kizungu (cf. above, p. 59). In that case the quarrel even led to a prolonged blood-feud between the two groups concerned and, finally—the other clans taking sides—to a splitting up of the tribe into two parts. In a corresponding manner the two sub-clans of the Yonga, the Yose and the Gímuhia, have come into existence, viz. as a result of a quarrel which Yose and Gímuhia had with one another while they were drinking beer. Yose boasted to his younger half-brother of the fact that he was the son of Yonga's great wife and Gímuhia only that of his junior wife. And so they separated from one another. Yose and his family moved towards the west, and Gímuhia and his followers started off towards the east. To-day both clans have resumed friendly relations, but they still consider one another too closely related to intermarry.

An interesting account of a quarrel between two brothers which led to the origin of new clans and of the subsequent reconciliation between the two groups, I received among the Marama:

'Mukolue and Mumbia, two of the six sons of Muxula, had a quarrel with one another, in the course of which Mukolue destroyed Mumbia's village, killing many of the latter's children. Before Mumbia died he said that he did not wish to be buried in his own village but at Evulambalo, the village of his wife's kin, out of grief over the fact that his own brother had killed him (i.e. his offspring). After Mumbia's death, Mukolue's clan was virtually haunted by ill fortune, meeting with nothing but failure both in warfare and in elephant-hunting. So Mukolue consulted a diviner who advised him to have the bones of his deceased brother dug out again and to stage a big feast for him, such as is customary when somebody is installed as a clan-head. He gave orders for a young bull to be killed, and then anointed its hide and the excavated bones of his brother with fat. Then he appointed an old man who, armed with a spear, the headgear (*efimwata*) and the ivory armlet (*omukasa*) of a clan-head, went inside the hut and ceremonially placed these insignia of clan leadership beside Mumbia's bones which had been carefully spread out

CLAN AND LINEAGE

on the hide of the bull. Thereupon the bones were buried. Mutjelule, one of Mukolue's brothers, had never approved of the former's fight against Mumbia and had urged him to take the advice given him by the diviner. After the consecration and ritual burial of Mumbia's bones by Mukolue the Avamumbia and the Avakolue became friends again. Axuta, Mumbia's son, returned from his mother's clan and continued the clan of his father. To-day —so my informant added—when the old men of the Muxula clan quarrel with one another, the peaceably minded among them try to pacify the disputing parties by reminding them of the quarrel between Mukolue and Mumbia and the disastrous consequences it entailed.'

Among the Vugusu I was given an account of the splitting-up of a clan into three different sub-groups. The Mweya—so I was told—had formerly (when they still lived to the north-east of Tororo) formed one clan community. Then one 'son of the Mweya' whose mother belonged to the tribe of the Tadjoni migrated towards the east and joined the Tadjoni (then living near Sangalo), whose customs and dialect he adopted. As the Tadjoni could not pronounce his name properly, they called him Mumeywa, and so it came about that his descendants adopted this name for themselves. To-day this section of the Mweya clan is called Vamweya Vameywa. It forms only a small group of a few score of men who live among the Tadjoni.

Some time after the secession of this branch of the Mweya the other Mweya, who had remained behind at their former abode, staged a hunt. While on their way, a member of one of the 'junior houses' boasted that he was much quicker in climbing a tree than the sons of the senior house. A member of the senior house accepted the challenge, and so they held a contest in tree-climbing. The challenger, however, lost, and in his anger he speared his brother up in the tree. This led to a blood feud between the two houses of the Mweya and to their separation. The kinsmen of the challenger migrated to the low-lying regions of Kitosh, while those of the brother that had been speared moved off in an easterly direction. They finally arrived in the neighbourhood of Kimilili, where they settled on the high ground at the foot of Mount Elgon. To-day the two sub-groups are called Mweya *owa mwalo*, 'the lower Mweya', and Mweya *owa ngaki*, 'the upper Mweya'. At present the three sub-groups of the Mweya do not intermarry, because formerly they were one clan (*luyia*). However, as my informant assured me, the Mweya Vameywa (who live among the Tadjoni) are already beginning to marry the sisters' daughters of the two other groups of the Mweya, and it will not be long now before they establish themselves as a completely independent clan.

As these examples show, the motives leading to disputes between the members of a clan and consequently to its splitting up into two sub-groups can be of various kinds. Such disputes often arose on the occasion of beer-feasts as a result of contemptuous or slanderous remarks uttered under the influence of alcohol. Also on the occasion of funeral rites it was and still is customary for one group of kinsmen in the presence of all the mourners to accuse certain persons of having caused their clansman's death by the employment of harmful magic (cf. below, p. 495). The accused persons, who are often near kinsmen of the deceased, naturally resent the charges levelled against them, and so it easily comes to an outbreak of hostilities within the clan. Chief Mumia assured me that such accusations raised on the occasion of the funeral ceremonies have always been the chief cause for the splitting up of clans.

The above account of the origin of the Mweya Vameywa as an independent clan points to a second cause for the formation of new sub-clans, viz. the peaceful emigration of an individual clansman into his mother's clan or that of an affinal relative where he would then settle as a so-called *omumenya* (a clan-stranger). If he and his issue then permanently remained among the host-clan, they gradually lost contact with their original clan until they finally established themselves as an independent clan. Such a secession of an individual clansman is often due to persistent illness or economic failure in his family, to his fear of real or alleged evil magic practised by one of his neighbours, or else to the existence of particularly friendly relations with his maternal relatives, with those of his wife, or with the family of a married sister.

A third cause for the formation of new clans, finally, is the natural growth of the original clan and the tendency of its various lineages to become independent units. This tendency of the various lineages to establish their independence after having reached a certain numerical strength springs from a pride in their own strength and power and the resulting desire for a political status of their own (cf. below, p. 493). Moreover, as the number of clansmen increases, the cohesion of the clan-community is naturally weakened. The feeling of solidarity and the maintenance of the various rights and duties (which we shall discuss more fully in their respective contexts) no longer embrace the entire clan community but tend to be limited to the members of the different lineages which thereby automatically develop into sub-clans. From the evidence I have it appears that this tendency to become independent always begins in the political, legal, and economic spheres, whereas the various lineages and sub-groups of a clan continue for a much longer time to observe the laws of exogamy. Among the Logoli, for instance, the four sub-clans of the Mavi (the Nondi, Lógovo, Gonda, and Mutembe) still form one exogamous unit; in every other respect, however, they have become completely independent clans.

In some cases it may also happen that a lineage is, so to speak, compelled to establish its independence, because the other lineages of the same clan no longer wish to acknowledge the bonds of clanship even if there has been no open quarrel or conflict. Thus several old men of the Gívagi sub-clan of the Yose[1] told me that they themselves would prefer to form one clan together with the Yose from whom they have sprung. But the Yose

[1] The Yose are, in turn, a sub-clan of the Yonga.

decline to consider them any longer as part of their clan, refusing, for instance, to stand up for an Omugívagi and to help him when he had done wrong which had to be expiated. Unfortunately I have neglected to trace the causes for this peculiar attitude adopted by the Yose towards the Gívagi. It seems probable, however, that the Gívagi have a bad reputation with the Yose (as a sub-clan afflicted with *ovulogi* cf. below, p. 391 sq.), while, on the other hand, the Gívagi feel too weak to hold their own against the other, bigger clans.

As the preceding discussion will have made sufficiently clear, the origin of clans and sub-clans is in no way a completed development but a dynamic process which is still going on. It cannot, therefore, always be definitely stated whether a given group constitutes a sub-clan or an independent clan, whether merely a lineage or already a sub-clan. In this process two tendencies may be observed. The one is that small clans which do not feel strong enough to maintain their own independence seek affiliation with a larger clan (cf. below, p. 388), even if they are not linked with it by any bonds of kinship. The other, opposite, tendency is for large clans to split up into sub-groups which then tend to become independent, i.e. to form new clans. It is, accordingly, only a certain phase in the process of the development of a descent-group which offers the conditions suitable for the formation and maintenance of a clan community. Assuming that the above clan-lists are essentially complete, we can use them for making a rough estimate of the average size of the Bantu Kavirondo clans. Thus the Logoli (of South Maragoli), Tiriki, Idaxo, Vugusu, and Wanga whose population totals 121,650 have a total of 182 clans. This corresponds to an average of roughly 670 persons per clan or of 205 adult men (of over 16 years). This would appear to be the optimum size of a clan community. The different factors determining this 'optimum' we shall discuss in the second volume after we have become acquainted with the manifold functions of clanship in the various spheres of life.

Having discussed the various causes which lead to the formation and the splitting up of clans among the Bantu Kavirondo, we shall now turn again to the structural features of their clan organization. At the beginning of this chapter we stated that the feeling of solidarity between the members of a clan finds a clear outward expression in the common clan-name, in the prohibition of marrying within the group (clan exogamy), and in the principle—though broken by some marked departures—of forming a territorial unit and occupying a continuous stretch of land.

Although the clan-name is never used as a term of address, every native knows the clan affiliation not only of his near kinsmen but also of more distant relatives, neighbours, and friends. Joint clan-functions, weddings, birthrites, funerals, circumcision feasts, and other occasions on which the members of the clan assemble more or less in full number, offer frequent opportunities of getting to know all one's clansmen as well as the clan-strangers (*avamenya*) living within the clan community. If somebody comes to a village or a homestead where he is not known he will, immediately after having uttered the customary salute, state what clan he belongs to. Only then will he proceed to give an account of where he comes from and what the object of his visit is. Still to-day the clan-elders and the clan-heads are able to state not merely the personal names of all the *avamenya* living in their clan territory but their clan-affiliation as well even if there are hundreds of such clan-strangers.

Still more than in the joint clan-name the feeling of clan-solidarity or cohesion manifests itself in the classificatory use of kinship terms. As in all classificatory systems of kinship terminology, the terms for father, mother, brother, sister, son, daughter, father's sister, mother's brother, &c., refer not only to the physical relatives designated by these various terms in the English system of kinship terminology, but to all members of the clan community who by their sex and their generation correspond to the physical relations to whom the respective terms primarily apply. Thus the term *baba wange*, 'my father', is used with reference to all married men of the speaker's own clan who belong to the generation of his physical father, but he cannot use it with reference to married men of other clans. Sometimes people salute not only their 'clan-fathers' by the term *baba* but also their father-in-law or even unrelated men of other clans who belong to their father's generation, instead of using the customary term of address, *omukulundu* (elder). The term *baba* has, in these cases, the connotation of particular respect. When employed in talking to a man of another clan, however, it can never be used in connexion with the possessive pronoun *wange* (my). But even in such a loose way the term *baba* can never be used with reference to or when addressing one's mother's brother or any classificatory mother's brothers, who must always be addressed as *koza* (Luvugusu: *xotja*). If one wishes to distinguish linguistically between one's physical father and a classificatory one, one can do so by referring to the former as *baba wange* (my father) and to the latter as *baba wetu* (our father). By the differential use of the possessive pronoun it is, correspondingly, possible to distinguish a physical brother or a physical sister from a classificatory clan-brother or clan-sister. Furthermore, the Logoli use the term *amitu* indiscriminately both for a physical and for a clan-brother. But if they wish to make it clear that they refer to a physical brother, they use the term *amwavo* which designates only the full brother of a man or the full sister of a woman (cf. below, p. 87). Correspondingly, the term *mbozo* refers in the first place to the full sister of a man (or the full brother of a woman respectively), whereas the term *mbozua* refers primarily to a half- or clan-sister (or a clan-brother respectively).

In the Vugusu dialect the term *wanda yase* means 'my brother' or 'my sister' (used by both sexes); if, however, the Vugusu wish to stress that they talk about a half-brother (i.e. a son of one's father by another wife), they refer to him as *wanda yase owe xuluyia*, my brother of the yard (i.e. a brother who belongs to the homestead, but is not a son of his own mother).

CLAN AND LINEAGE

A full brother is referred to as *omwana wa mayi* (child of the mother), a half- or clan-brother, on the other hand, as *omwana wa papa* (child of the father).

Every clansman of one's own generation is, accordingly, addressed either as *wanda yase* or as *omwana wa papa*. If one speaks of a clansman of one's own generation, one calls him as a rule either *wanda yefwe* (our brother) or *omwana wefwe* (our child).

The terms for son and daughter (*omwana omuyai* and *omwana omukana* respectively) do not offer such possibilities of distinguishing between a physical and a classificatory child. But one would not salute a child or a young person of another clan as *omwana wange*.

The kinship terms referring to persons beyond the generations of the speaker's father or son respectively no longer reflect the notions of clanship. Thus the term *guga* refers both to one's paternal and to one's maternal grandfather, and likewise the term for grandchild (Lurogoli: *omisukulu*; Luvugusu: *omwitjuxulu*) is used with reference both to the children of one's son (belonging to one's own clan) and to the children of one's daughter (belonging to a different clan). If one wishes to distinguish terminologically between the father's father and the mother's father, one can do so only by using a descriptive circumlocution, e.g. (Luvugusu) *guga osala papa*, the grandfather who begot the father, or *guga osala mayi* and (Lurogoli) *guga yivuli baba*, or *mama* respectively.

In the course of this book we shall describe a large number of situations which will clearly demonstrate that the classificatory extensions of the kinship terms along clan-lines are not a mere formality but that the classificatory terminology is largely accompanied by a corresponding classificatory kinship behaviour. Towards every person whom one addresses by the same kinship term one displays, in principle, the same legal, economic, ritual, and social behaviour though, of course, graded in accordance with the degree of actual, i.e. genealogical relationship. This fact presents one of the most essential features of the clan organization among the Bantu Kavirondo. It ensures that the individual can never become socially or economically destitute. If his father dies, one of the father's brothers, being the nearest classificatory father, automatically steps into his place; if all full brothers of the father have died, the latter's half-brothers take over all his former rights and duties, after them the classificatory fathers of one's own lineage, &c. If somebody has no physical brothers of his own, he will adopt the same behaviour towards his classificatory brothers (i.e. his cousins of his own clan) which ordinarily he would observe towards his physical brothers. In matters of minor importance and as regards the general tenor of kinship behaviour the kinship relations between physical relatives and those between the corresponding classificatory ones are very much the same even while the physical relatives of a person are still alive. All that we have said in the preceding chapter about the typical relations between father and son, brother and brother, as well as brother and sister, applies in principle also to the relations between the corresponding classificatory kinsmen.

A further though very much less significant manifestation of clan solidarity is the observance of taboos (Luvugusu: *gimisilu*) on a clan-basis (see below, p. 200 sq.). Although the data which I was able to collect on such clan-taboos are limited to the Vugusu, they occur also, according to the accounts given by Hobley and Dundas, among the Wanga and the Nyala (Kabras).[1] But they are unknown among the Logoli and probably also among the Nyole and the Tiriki. Most of these taboos prohibit the consumption of certain plants, including some that ordinarily form part of the daily native diet, the meat of certain animals, or the milk of cows of a certain colour. In less frequent cases the prohibitions concern the utilization of certain tools and implements,[2] the wearing of certain kinds of ornaments (see below, p. 206), &c. Prohibitions to kill certain animals (e.g. the cobra, certain small birds, lizards, frogs, &c., cf. below, p. 198), on the other hand, apply to the entire tribal community and not merely to individual clans.

A violation of any of these taboos is generally believed to cause the offender's skin to 'turn pale' or to 'peel off' and to make his hair fall out.[3] As, however, the same sanctions apply to the infringement of any kind of ritual prohibition they stand in no particular relation to the clan-taboos. Among the Vugusu, most of the clans have not only one but several food taboos, and many different clans have one and the same prohibition. As these clans, however, do not regard themselves as related to one another, it would hardly seem that the origin of their common taboo dates back to a time when they still formed one joint clan. If this were so, the consciousness of a kinship bond between them would probably have been kept alive along with the common taboo. Besides, it would certainly manifest itself in a special attitude which such clans would still maintain towards one another. It seems rather that these clan-taboos, which do not bear any pronounced totemic features, originated in each case from a rule made by one of the more influential clan-ancestors. Having attributed a case of serious illness or an epidemic to the consumption of the particular food or dish (doing so probably on the strength of a diviner's diagnosis) he forbade his children and their offspring to eat of it. At the same time he imposed a curse upon anybody who might disobey his order. In cases where the taboo does not refer to a food but to some other kind of

---

[1] Cf. K. Dundas, 1913, pp. 30, 59 sq., and 65 sq.; furthermore, C. W. Hobley, 1903, p. 346 sq.

[2] Cf. K. Dundas, 1913, p. 66: 'Members of the Muhini clan . . . may not allow a *jembe* handle (their totem) to touch their sleeping skins. Should this occur, the handle, after detaching the *jembe*, must be taken outside the hut and burnt (it may not be burnt inside the hut); and a goat, a black one for preference, must immediately be slaughtered.'

[3] Cf. also Hobley, 1903, p. 347: '. . . the eating of a totem animal is not thought to be followed by death, but only by a severe skin eruption.'

object, this probably had been instrumental in causing an accident or some other kind of misfortune of particularly grave consequences.

This explanation is not only supported by the statements made by my native informants on the origin of their clan-taboos (cf. below, pp. 201 sq. and 206), but also by the fact that personal avoidances (which are also called *gimisilu*) are brought about in exactly the same manner even to-day (cf. below, p. 204). It is further in agreement with the method of association which prevails in all magico-religious notions entertained by the Bantu Kavirondo. If—so they would argue—a person after having consumed a certain dish (say the milk of a grey-spotted cow) falls violently ill and if, all circumstances of the case having been duly considered by the diviner, the illness cannot be explained as a result of evil magic or ancestral wrath, a dangerous relation must exist between the milk of cows of such a colour and the entire clan of the patient, and not merely between that particular milk and the particular individual who fell ill after having drunk of it. To escape this danger, all clansmen must henceforth avoid the milk of such cows.

Whether such a ritual prohibition is obeyed at all, how strictly it is observed, and for how many generations it is kept up, depends, of course, upon the influence wielded by the clan-elder who tabooed that particular dish (or whatever else it may have been), i.e. upon the power which his clansmen attribute to his curse. The stringency with which these taboos are observed varies greatly therefore among the different clans. Moreover, all such clan-taboos can be evaded or their violation rendered innocuous by certain ritual observances (cf. below, p. 201), resembling those by which a curse can be neutralized.

In this connexion we must also deal with the notion that the various clans possess certain qualities of character as well as peculiarities of a magico-religious, physical, and biological nature. A number of clans thus have the reputation of being greedy and insatiable, others of being easily irritable or quarrelsome, still others of possessing a cunning or underhand character. In most cases such attributes refer to qualities which become apparent in the mutual relations between the clans, in their economic, legal, and social dealings with one another. As regards the magico-religious sphere, a number of clans are reputed to own particular gifts, e.g. as rain-magicians, diviners, circumcision doctors, &c. (cf. below, p. 347). Perfection in these offices or arts cannot be acquired by instruction alone, but requires the presence of an inherited disposition which, having for generations remained latent, suddenly breaks forth again. The person to whom that happens is then possessed by the mysterious force that craves for its realization. He suffers from heavy dreams and nightmares brought about by visitations of his ancestral spirits; he is seized by fits in his arms and legs, suddenly begins to shake all over his body, to dance about wildly like a madman, to refuse any kind of food, &c. All these symptoms, however, stop immediately the victim receives instruction in the particular art the disposition for which he has inherited and which, in his particular case, has chosen to break forth (cf. below, p. 243).

The latent disposition for practising such arts is inherited not only in the direct male line but can be passed on also to a sister's son or a daughter's son. The ownership of these various arts is therefore not inseparably linked up with the clan in which they were originally developed.

Apart from such positively valued magical dispositions, a number of clans also have magical qualities attributed to them which are socially disapproved of. Thus among the Logoli the clans of the Lógovo and Gímuhia are reputed to be *avalogi* (witches). This does not mean that every member of these two clans is suspected of actively practising witchcraft, but merely that they all possess a latent disposition for witchcraft which at any time may break forth again. Ordinarily, their reputation of being *avalogi* does not seriously prejudice their relations with the other clans. In cases, however, where a father is suspected of practising witchcraft, his children will encounter considerable difficulties in finding a wife or a husband respectively. They are often compelled to marry into distant clans or even into a neighbouring tribe where no one has knowledge of the qualities attributed to their fathers (cf. below, p. 392).

As regards physical characteristics, finally, the natives distinguish between clans of tall stature and those of low stature, between strong and healthy clans and sickly ones, between prolific clans and unprolific ones. Even though it is known and acknowledged that physical characteristics are inherited in both lines of descent, the male line (strain) is considered to be the stronger one, and it is considered normal for sons chiefly to inherit the qualities of their paternal and, only in the second place, those of their maternal ancestors. Facial resemblances are recognized and commented upon within the family and also within the lineage but not between distantly related clansmen or even between all members of a clan.

The notions prevailing on these different points thus more or less correspond to what can empirically be observed, and it does not seem that —apart from the notions that have been mentioned—the strong sociological emphasis on the patrilineal line of descent and the feeling of solidarity between clansmen has given rise to any particular native theories on the existence of clan characteristics not based on empirical facts.

CLAN-HEAD AND CLAN-ELDERS

In the preceding discussion of the clan we have repeatedly talked of a clan-head or a clan-chief. Among the majority of the Bantu Kavirondo, however, this term does not denote a clearly defined office entailing explicit rights and duties. The status of a clan-head was, as a rule, tacitly assigned to that clan-elder who, by his personality as well as by a number of qualities which we shall presently discuss, stood out among his age-mates and who, in all matters and on all occasions where the interests of the clan community as a whole were concerned, proved himself capable of taking the lead. A general prerequisite, however, for obtaining leadership in the clan was advanced age which was socially marked by the institution of circumcision age-grades (cf. below, p. 373 sq.). The authority of seniors over their juniors, the principle of seniority, prevails in all social relations among the Bantu Kavirondo. Generally speaking, it is always the oldest member of a group of kinsmen whose opinion carries the greatest weight in matters concerning that group. Adult sons thus show more respect and obedience towards their father's oldest brother than towards their father himself, and after their father's death his authority is not immediately passed on to his eldest son but first to his eldest living brother. Consequently, with advancing age, a person's effective kinship relations and his membership of the various social groups increase both in number and in importance. The entry into every new phase of life thus implies a rise in social status, an increase in rights but also in duties. Owing to their widely ramified kinship-ties the old men are best suited to rise above the petty interests and jealousies of the smaller kin-groups and thus to use their influence for the solidarity of the clan community as a whole and for the maintenance of peaceful relations with the other clans.

The authority implied in old age is further strengthened by notions connected with the ancestor cult. One of these is that old age is regarded as a necessary condition for officiating at sacrifices (see below, p. 285). The other notion is that spirits remember the treatment afforded to them while they were still living persons and that they either haunt and trouble or spare and help their living relatives according to the treatment received. Old men, therefore, are more than others feared as potentially troublesome spirits, a fact which considerably adds to their authority. Their power of uttering a curse, and especially a dying curse, is an all-powerful sanction at their disposal.

If, however, among the old men of a clan there was no one whose qualities of leadership stood out noticeably from those of the average elders, there was no generally recognized head in such a clan but merely a council of clan-elders in which several of the influential old men jointly kept the balance. Such a clan community, however, was then particularly strongly exposed to the danger of splitting up into several sub-groups, for, according to the unanimous reports of my informants, one expected from a traditional clan-head above everything else that he showed himself capable of preserving the peace among the clansmen. Among the Vugusu the leading elders of a clan are called *avagasa*, i.e. 'men who talk gently and wisely and who can make the people listen and return to reason when they want to quarrel or fight'.[1] A son who, as a herd-boy, begins to show reason

---

[1] Such a willing and uncompromising submission of the natives to a strong personality, based apparently on the same kind of suggestibility, one encounters occasionally also in their attitude towards Europeans, even in those cases where the authority of the latter is not backed by any visible or tangible sanctions. Cf. also Hobley (1929, p. 120), who writes about the relations existing between a certain

and the ability to make his age-mates follow him in the various activities in which herd-boys indulge, is pointed out by the elders as a future *omugasa*. They welcome his presence when he comes to sit near them and listen to their stories of long ago. When he has become an old man he acts as an *omuseni*, i.e. he is called to speak to and comfort the people when they assemble after a funeral to distribute the property of the deceased, to decide who should inherit the widows, and to settle claims and debts. The death of each clansman is a critical moment for the preservation of peace within and between the clans, as it invariably leads to accusations of witchcraft or sorcery as being the cause of the death that has occurred. It is then the duty of the *omuseni* to forestall the effect of such accusations by pointing out that all people are born into this world to die and that people should not harbour grievances and accuse one another of sorcery, as such an attitude will merely increase the sorrow that has overcome them. The *omuseni* usually winds up his speech with a review of the great deeds of the clan and with exhortations to live up to that tradition and to forget petty quarrels for the sake of peace (cf. below, p. 492 sq.).

Similarly, the *omugasa* is expected to speak for unity when legal disputes are discussed before the elders of the *oluhia*. When homicide or murder has occurred and the kinsmen of both parties insult one another and show impatience to fight, he persuades them to give and accept compensation. The degree to which he succeeds in such efforts determines his recognition as a leader.

A further quality that in the past made for clan leadership was the reputation gained as a warrior. Both among the Vugusu and the Logoli the memory of the clan-heads of the past is closely associated with accounts of their deeds as warriors. Their respective successes were measured in terms of the number of enemies they had killed and the head of cattle raided by them or under their lead. The more somebody during his youth or in the prime of his life had excelled as a warrior, the more weight his opinion carried when later as a clan-elder he joined in the discussion as to whether a raid should be undertaken, a clan-feud terminated, or an alliance concluded

---

Government official and the natives of Kavirondo: 'He was one of those rare beings gifted with an uncanny influence over natives. . . . A man of few words, very reserved, even to his closest friends, his native interests absorbed him, and his power over those with whom he came in contact was immense. He never raised his voice, he gave orders almost in a whisper, and the recipient would immediately rush off to carry them out.' Referring to another European he writes: 'His manner was very repressed, he would listen patiently to a long story of some grievance, ask a question or two, and then mumble something in a rather whimsical way, and the natives would go off quite happy and do exactly as he directed. It was all the more remarkable as he was not a personage of striking mien, was generally untidy, grew an unkempt beard, his voice carried little conviction, and he was not a brilliant linguist; but there it was, he had the power of imposing his will upon all natives with whom he came in contact and without apparent effort on his part.' The authority of the traditional clan-heads, especially when acting as arbitrators, appears to be based on the possession of mental and moral qualities of a similar nature.

CLAN AND LINEAGE

with another clan or tribe. As long as he was still an active warrior he could act as a leader in actual warfare, but he did not yet enjoy any authority in the council of clan-elders. Actually, however, so I was told, the warriors did not always submit to the wishes and decisions of the old men, but at times engaged in raids and wars either without consulting the opinion of the elders or even against their express advice.

Another important function of the clan-head was (and still is) to officiate at all sacrifices offered to previous clan-heads (cf. below, p. 283). Moreover, on the occasion of important family sacrifices (cf. below, p. 277 sq.) the clan-head is summoned in addition to or in the place of the oldest living member of the family or lineage (cf. below, p. 285). Like the office of the *omuseni*, that of the *omusalisi* (sacrificial priest) requires particular qualities of character. The *omusalisi* must be known for his kindness and honesty (he must be a so-called *omuhotjya*); he must be past the age of sexual desire, and also the record of his former sex-life must have been beyond reproach (he must not, for example, have seduced any married women nor must he ever have been suspected of sexual perversions); he must always have observed the customs (*amalago*) and ritual prohibitions (*emigilu*) of the clan; he must never have been suspected of witchcraft (*ovulogi*) or even of sorcery (*ovuvila*). In short, he must be a person without *embala*, i.e. without any failures and blemishes in his past and present life, if his sacrifice is to be favourably accepted by the spirits. That elder in the clan who possesses these qualities to the highest degree is recognized as the *omusalisi munene* (the great sacrificer).

An indispensable condition for attaining a leading position in the clan is economic wealth. One who possesses a large herd of cattle, whose granaries are always filled, and who has several wives and retainers that can brew beer and wait on his hosts, will find enough people to sing his praise, and his homestead will become the favourite gathering-place of all clansmen, especially of the elders. It is expected of a wealthy man that he can at any time offer beer to his guests and at frequent intervals also meat, fowls, and other choice foods. In addition, a wealthy man can gain a more definite influence over certain of his clansmen by lending them a goat or a sheep for a sacrifice, a heifer for their marriage cattle, or basketsful of grain if they run short of food. The person who often receives such a support thereby assumes certain obligations towards his creditor. He must praise him whenever he has an opportunity to do so and render him small services. If he cannot return the loan he must do real work for his benefactor by herding his cattle, weeding his gardens, and keeping his huts in repair. The traditional type of 'retainer' or servant who is found in some wealthy homesteads has usually got into that position as a war-captive, as a widower without children, or as a debtor who could not return his debt. Moreover, by giving feasts on a clan scale, especially by killing the 'ox of splitting', a wealthy person has a means of gaining popularity among *all* his clansmen. Through his right of directing the distribution of meat, he can favour those who respect and honour him and who, at the discussion of clan matters, submit to his views. Finally, as elders of other clans are invited to these feasts, the wealthy persons also become, in a sense, the representatives of their clan. When elders of other clans kill the 'ox of splitting' they are invited in turn, or gifts of meat or beer are sent to them which they apportion to their own clansmen. They have thus an opportunity of gaining influence among their clansmen even when they are the recipients and not the givers of feasts.

It will be seen then that wealth, especially if wisely used, is a certain means of gaining prestige and influence within the clan community. The wealthy person, it is true, has the duty of being generous and helpful to the needy, but in return his homestead and thereby he himself become the centre of the social life of the neighbourhood or even of the entire clan community.

As this survey of the qualifications expected of a clan-head shows, his office combined the functions of a judge (or arbitrator) and of a priest with those of a political leader in the more narrow sense of the word. Although these various offices or functions were frequently vested in one and the same person, this was not necessarily the case. It could quite well happen that, of three or four leading clan-elders, one exercised the greatest judicial authority, a second one possessed the highest reputation as a sacrificial priest, and a third one, as a noted warrior, wielded the strongest influence over the younger age-grades and had the final decision in all matters concerning the political life of the clan, its relations towards other clans. Of the sacrificial priests of the Logoli who always belonged to the Nondi clan and who on behalf of the whole tribe offered a semi-annual sacrifice to the tribal ancestors and gods (cf. below, p. 291), the majority were known mainly for their qualities as sacrificial priests and not as warriors or judges. On the other hand, it is obvious that the ideal type of a clan-head should unite within himself as many of the above-mentioned qualities as possible. A man who is reputed as a courageous and successful warrior will be better able to command authority over his clansmen (especially among the younger people) as a judge, an arbitrator, or a peace-maker than somebody who has no such record. Similarly, that elder will be most welcome to the ancestral spirits as a sacrificial priest who in every respect is a worthy representative of the 'living section' of the clan community. The office of the clan-head is thus, at least in the theoretical conception of the natives, still undivided, even though in actual life not all of its functions are necessarily united in one and the same person.

The manifold qualities and functions of the clan-head, and at the same time the vague nature and scope of his office, are clearly reflected in the variety of names by which it is designated. Altogether I have encountered the following terms:

> *Eligutu* (*liguru*) *linene*, the great clan-elder (*eligutu* also means the supporting-post of a hut). Chiefly used among the Wanga, to-day also among the other tribes in the southern part of the district.

CLAN AND LINEAGE

Omumali wekiruazo, the one who 'finishes a meeting' (*omumali* from *okumala*, to terminate, to wind up, to settle; *ekiruazo* is the council of the clan-elders). Logoli.

Omugasa munene, the great arbitrator, the peace-maker, the wise man, &c. Vugusu, northern part of the district. Not used in the south.

Omulatji wamaxuva, the one who settles matters of public concern. Nyole.

Omusalisi munene, the great sacrificer. Logoli.

Omumali wemisango, the one who winds up the sacrifice. Logoli.

Omukulundu munene, the great elder. Logoli.

Omunene wetu, our great one. Logoli.

Omunene wovulwani, the great one of the war. Logoli.

Omundu mudúkilu, the important man (*kudukila*, to arrive at, to reach (the goal)). Logoli.

As the above account implies, the clan-head had no clearly defined rights and duties in relation to his 'subjects'. With the exception of the members of his own lineage he had no right to interfere with their 'personal' or family affairs (for instance, the question of their marriage, the settlement of their legacy, &c.). He could not demand any tribute from the people of his clan, nor was he entitled to employ their services for his personal benefit. Nor was the clan-head entitled to or given a share in the legacy of other clansmen, unless the deceased happened to be a close kinsman of his, in which case he would receive his share not *qua* clan-head but *qua* kinsman. It was, however, and still is customary voluntarily to send a piece of meat to the clan-head as well as to the other influential clan-elders whenever a ritual killing has been made, or a potful of beer whenever beer is brewed for one of the numerous ritual or ceremonial occasions which constantly arise in the normal run of life. Furthermore, the clan-head has the undisputed privilege to take part in every beer-feast, even if he has not been expressly invited to attend. On the other hand, no harvest dues or tributes are sent to the clan-head, not even by clan-strangers (*avamenya*) residing on clan-lands.

The voluntary making of gifts or the rendering of tribute to the clan-head serves the donor's own interests. By winning the favour of the clan-head and of the other influential clan-elders, a man can more readily rely on their help and sympathy if he should have a legal dispute with another clansman or if he needs the support of his own clansmen in dealings with his wife's relatives, &c. Economic wealth, accordingly, is not only a pre-requisite of political leadership but to a certain degree also a consequence thereof, for in a clan community of average size these voluntary gifts run into quite a considerable total.

Under traditional conditions the clan-head could on certain occasions summon the clansmen to accomplish such work as served the interests of the entire clan community. Among the Logoli, for instance, in case of a serious harvest failure caused by a drought, locusts, or a similar disaster, he could call upon all clansmen to clear and cultivate a strip of bushland or fallow. The crops yielded by such jointly cultivated fields, known by the name of *elilimilu*, were then distributed among all clansmen under the supervision of the clan-head (cf. vol. ii). After the first harvest the *elilimilu*-land was shared out to individual families and henceforth taken under individual control like other family lands (cf. chapter on land-tenure, in vol. ii).

Among the majority of tribes the clan-head was not formally appointed to or installed in his office. As his followers and supporters grew in number, he steadily gained in prestige until, finally, his authority in the clan community was taken for granted. An exception, however, appears to have been formed by the Nyole. Among them the *omulatji wamaxuwa*, 'the one who settles clan matters', was initiated into his office by having definite insignia bestowed upon him by the other clan-elders. Altogether there were three different graded insignia of rank: (1) A long club (*omutitjilo kwe lavusi*) which was sharpened at the end and provided with an iron point like a spear-shaft; (2) a leopard skin, and (3) a fur cap (*olusimbi*) adorned with cowrie-shells and the tail feathers of a certain small bird of rare occurrence. These insignia were handed to the *omulatji* in three successive years: first the club, then the leopard skin, and, as the highest insignium, the fur cap. They were either specially made for him or he inherited them from a former *omulatji*. If after the death of a clan-head there was nobody worthy enough to take his place, the insignia were kept in custody either by his eldest son or another close kinsman of his lineage. The bestowal of each of these insignia took place in a ceremonial manner. When the old men of the clan had agreed whom from their midst they wanted to appoint to the rank of an *omulatji*, they told the clansmen to collect large quantities of eleusine for brewing beer and cooking porridge. When everything was prepared, all clansmen assembled on the *oluhia*, the public meeting-ground of the clan. One of the old men handed the club to the *omulatji*, while another one admonished him 'to take good care of it, to look after his people, and to maintain the peace in the clan community'. Thereupon the *omulatji* together with six old men repaired to the hut of his great wife where, sitting in the *evwasi*-partition, they emptied a large pot of beer. The remaining clansmen drank their share of the beer either on the *oluhia* or on the yard of the *omulatji's* homestead.

Apart from the *omulatji* nobody in the clan was permitted to carry such a club or to wear an *olusimbi* fur cap. If an ordinary clansman had killed a leopard he could keep its hide in his hut, but he could not don it in public or appear with it on the *oluhia*.

Among the Logoli, only the most renowned warrior of the clan, the recognized leader (*omwémilili*) in warfare, was outwardly marked by having special insignia bestowed upon him. The chosen warrior was shaved and anointed with ghee in the presence of the clan-elders. Then an old warrior presented him with a head-dress made of cowrie-shells, a ribbon of colobus skin, and a cloak made of pieces of the skin of various animals. Besides lending distinction to the war-leader, this ceremony had a magic significance. Finger-rings, rare feathers, wristlets, ivory armlets, and spears are similar 'insignia' of this kind which were ceremonially given to a man recognized as a war-leader. They were kept by the person upon whom they had been bestowed, and when he had reached old age were passed on by him to his eldest son or to another worthy successor within the clan. Such insignia of leadership, however, seem to have been charms rather than proper regalia implying a clearly defined status, as they were not outwardly distinguished from similar ornaments worn by ordinary elders. They were neither limited in number nor clearly graded in importance.

C. MANIFESTATIONS OF KINSHIP

THE patrilineal clan organization of the Bantu Kavirondo is clearly reflected in their kinship structure. Not only do they distinguish terminologically between the various relatives on the father's side and those on the mother's side, but also the manifestations of the respective kinship relations differ from one another in a number of ways. However, despite the strong emphasis placed on patrilineal descent the group of relatives with whom the individual maintains effective relations shows a bilateral orientation. The maternal kin is by no means completely overshadowed by the group of paternal kinsmen. On the contrary, the maternal uncle plays a very considerable part in a person's life. On many occasions he fulfils ceremonial duties towards his nephew. But in economic and legal respects, too, there exist manifold relations between a mother's brother and a sister's son which we shall discuss in their respective contexts.

If the number of kinsmen whom a native can name and whose exact degree of relationship with him he can state may be said to indicate the extent of effective kinship relations, my inquiries have shown that the paternal and the maternal kin-groups are about of equal size (cf. the genealogical charts in vol. ii). As a rule, however, my informants were able to list their lineal relatives on the paternal side for two or three generations farther back than those on the mother's side. Moreover, where the lineage or the 'house' respectively is still an effective kin-group, as among the Vugusu, the greater emphasis rests with the paternal relatives, with the brothers and paternal cousins of one's father as members of one's own lineage. Elsewhere the question where the emphasis of a person's effective kinship relations is placed largely depends on whether he has spent his childhood and youth among his own clansmen (as would ordinarily be the case) or whether his parents live in his mother's clan or that of a relative-in-law. In the last two cases the relations with the members of his own clan are frequently neglected.

All blood-relations, kinship with whom one can trace genealogically, are denoted by the common term *aviko* (singular *omiko*). All affinal relatives, on the other hand, are classed as *avakó* (singular *omukó*).

Effective kinship relations manifest themselves in a number of different ways of which we can distinguish the following chief types:

1. The kinship term by which the specific relation between two kinsmen

is terminologically fixed. Some kinship terms are reciprocal, which raises the question whether in these cases the kinship behaviour between the persons concerned is also reciprocal. In a few cases the same kinship relation is rendered by several terms. One of these is then usually considered to be the 'proper term', while the others denote a specific aspect of the kinship bond.

2. The observance of definite forms of behaviour between certain kinds of kinsmen. They consist either in various forms of licence (e.g. joking relationships) or in the display of particular respect as well as in the mutual observance of permanent or temporary avoidances.

3. The one-sided or reciprocal fulfilment of ceremonial duties in connexion with the 'rites of passage' which mark the entry into the different phases of life (birth, initiation, marriage, parenthood, death), and on the occasion of ancestral sacrifices, &c.

4. One-sided or reciprocal gift obligations, likewise chiefly in connexion with the rites of passage. The nature and the value of the gift obligation is in all cases fixed by convention: it is mostly an animal (bullock, cow, heifer, ox, goat, sheep, or fowl) or a definite portion of a slaughtered animal, and less frequently a definite quantity of grain (eleusine or sorghum). Each of these gift obligations is known by a special name (e.g. *éxafu eye sitexo*, the cow of the cooking ceremony (cf. p. 43); *éxafu eye kumuoulo*, the cow which one owes to the son of one's father's brother as a counter gift for having received a share in the marriage cattle given for his sister; *éxafu eye sivexo*, the bull to which a maternal uncle has a claim in the case of his nephew's death, &c.). If the non-fulfilment of such gift obligations or their undue delay leads to disputes between the relatives concerned, the matter is taken for arbitration before the council of the clan-elders or, in lesser cases, before a group of relatives on either side.

5. The privilege extended to a blood-relative of a different clan and to in-laws to settle as *avamenya* on the land of their kinsman's clan.

6. Claims to inheritance and succession. The claims to inheritance extend (*a*) to the property of the deceased in livestock (cattle, goats, sheep), (*b*) in land, (*c*) in utensils of personal and domestic use (weapons, tools and implements, ornaments, &c.), and (*d*) to the rights which the deceased possessed in respect of his wife or wives (on the strength of having paid marriage cattle for them). These claims are intimately linked up with the gift obligations mentioned under (4). Gift obligations that have been fulfilled result in claims to a legacy and, on the other hand, the share in a legacy entails gift obligations towards the sons of the 'testator'. The principle of full reciprocity which prevails within a major group of persons both with regard to the gift obligations and to the claims to inheritance, and which extends over long periods of time, becomes therefore apparent only when the whole round of gift obligations and claims to inheritance is viewed in its full context.

The claims to succession extend to all 'offices' which cannot be practised at random by any ordinary member of the tribe but require instruction in esoteric knowledge as well as the transmission of special magico-religious faculties. The latter are frequently linked up with the possession of definite ritual objects which acquire their magical potency only if their former owner has handed them over to his successor of his own free will and in a ceremonial manner. Such offices include those of the rain-magician, the diviner, the circumcision operator, &c.

7. The paying of mutual visits and the willingness to render help in cases of economic distress (e.g. crop failure, &c.) as well as the granting of mutual support in the realization of legal claims.

The significance attached to the exchange of visits as an expression of an effective kinship relation is shown by the fact that my informants used to define the group of persons who maintain effective kinship relations as 'those who regularly visit one another'. This means, on the one hand, the frequent and informal granting and receiving of hospitality in the form of offering beer and food to one's visitors as well as of an exchange of minor gifts. In this connexion must also be mentioned the obligation to attend all rites and ceremonies performed on behalf of a member of one's own kin-group, even if one's presence at such functions does not involve any active participation in the ritual procedure. In the accounts given by my informants of the ritual observances which play such an important part in the social life of the Bantu Kavirondo, it is frequently stressed that a certain rite cannot be performed unless all blood-relatives (*aviko*) have assembled, as the absence of even a single one of them would frustrate the whole rite (cf., for example, below, p. 312). The summoning of all relatives in such cases is obviously based on the idea of strengthening the ritual status of the person concerned by making it apparent that he does not stand by himself but has the support of his whole kindred.

The avoidances between certain categories of relatives (referred to under (2)) form a conspicuous contrast to the exchange of regular visits as a typical manifestation of effective kinship relations.

The rendering of mutual assistance in the realization of legal claims extends, of course, chiefly to claims from which the wider kin-group draws direct or indirect advantages. The wider, therefore, the group of persons with whom an individual maintains effective kinship relations and the more firmly these bonds are tied, the more effective also will be the legal protection which he will get from them and the more securely established will be his place in the tribal society. If he has a claim against a member of his own kin-group, it will, of course, be backed only by that section of his kinsmen whose legal and economic interests are in some way linked up with the fulfilment of his claim. Since, however, the various categories of relatives (paternal, maternal, and in-laws) form different groups, each of which has its own specific legal and economic interests, the individual will in every contingency that may arise always be able to reckon on the effective support of at least one of these groups. Thus the kinship-bonds maintained with one's mother's clan (especially the maternal uncle) will strengthen a person's position in disputes with members of his own lineage (his half-brothers, the sons of his father's brothers, &c.), just as blood-relatives on both sides will lend active support in all property disputes with one's in-laws and vice versa. The reciprocal gift-obligations and claims to inheritance which serve to establish and maintain economic ties towards one's kinsmen on all sides thus create a network of joint legal interests (property interests) substantially assisting the individual in the realization of legal claims. The discussion of property law and of legal procedure (see vol. ii) will furnish ample evidence for this state of affairs.

8. A last manifestation of effective kinship relations is the special status which both consanguineous and affinal relatives have towards one another with regard to the tribal law of marriage. While a marriage between blood-relations (*aviko*) is under all circumstances prohibited, a marriage between in-laws is in some cases not only allowed but even particularly desired. In others it is prohibited or at least considered undesirable, although marriage-prohibitions between in-laws are based on other considerations than are those pertaining to blood-relations.

D. LIST OF KINSHIP TERMS

AMONG THE LOGOLI

(i) *Consanguineous Kin*

1. *Dada, avadada*, or *ise* (no plural): father, father's brother; in the classificatory sense: every clan-brother of the father.
2. *Mama, avamama*, or *nnya*: mother, mother's sister; classificatory extension: every clan-sister of the mother.
3. *Avivuli*: parents (derived from *okwívula*, to beget, to bear). *Omivuli*, father, begetter.
4. *Avenyumba yange*: my parents (literally, those of my house).
5. *Omwene, avene*: father, parents (literally, owners). In some contexts it also means 'clansmen', i.e. 'those to whom one belongs'.
6. *Omwana, avana*: child (of either sex). Refers primarily to one's own physical child. Classificatory extension: every member of the clan belonging to a younger generation than the speaker. The form *omwana wetu*, our child, is also used with reference to a clansman of the speaker's generation.
7. (*Omwana*) *omuyai, avana avayai*: son (male child).
8. (*Omwana*) *omukana, avana avakana*: daughter (female child).
9. *Omwana omukulundu*: first-born child (of either sex). When used as a term of address *omukulundu* means 'elder'. Other terms for the first-born child are: *omwana munene*, the 'great' child, and *omwana wokutanga*, the first child (literally, the child of the beginning).

10. *Omwana omuké*: the younger child. Refers to the second-born or any subsequent child with the exception of the last-born child.
11. *Omukógoti*: the last-born child.
12. *Amitu, avamitu*: (my) brother (of a man), (my) sister (of a woman).
13. *Amwavo, avámwavo*: (your) brother (contraction of *amitu wowo*?).
14. *Mbozo, avavozo*: sister of a man, brother of a woman.
15. *Mbozwa, avavozwa*: male parallel cousin of a woman, female parallel cousin of a man.
16. *Omusiala, avasiala*: cross-cousin. Refers primarily to the father's sister's child (of either sex). The mother's brother's child is usually called *omwana womifwa*.
17. *Omifwa, avifwa*: mother's brother, sister's child. (Term of reference.)
18. *Koza, avakoza*: mother's brother, sister's child. (Term of address.)
19. *Senge, avasenge*: father's sister.
20. *Guga, avaguga*: grandfather (paternal or maternal).
21. *Guku, avaguku*: grandmother (paternal or maternal).
22. *Omísukulu, avísukulu*: grandchild (of either sex).
23. *Ekisukulului, evisukulului*: great-grandfather (or mother), great-grandchild.

(ii) *Affinal Kin*
   (a) *Omusaza, ava-*: husband.
   (b) *Omukali, ava-*: wife.
   (c) *Omukaye*: great wife (the first wife). Respectful term of address for any aged woman.
   (d) *Omukali omunene*: big wife, chief wife (same as (c)).
   (e) *Omukali omuké*: young wife, plural wife.
   (f) *Muhálikwa, ava-*: co-wife (i.e. the woman with whom a wife shares the same husband).
   (g) *Mulamua, aválamua*: wife's sister, a woman's sister's husband, a man's brother's wife, husband's brother, husband's sister, a woman's brother's wife, wife's brother's wife, husband's sister's husband.
   (h) *Omukwasi, ava-*: wife's brother, and reciprocally, a man's sister's husband.
   (i) *Navizara, avanavizara*: parents-in-law, children-in-law. Refers to father- and mother-in-law of both husband and wife, and to a man's and a woman's son-in-law and daughter-in-law.
   (j) *Navana, avanavana*: mutual term of address used by the parents of a married couple.
   (k) *(Ovo)segwa, ava-*: wife's sister's husband. Husband's brother's wife.

AMONG THE VUGUSU

(i) *Consanguineous Kin*
   1. *Baba* or *papa*: father.
   2. *Ma(y)i*: mother.

3. *Vasasi*: parents (derived from *xusala*, to bear).
4. *Omwana, vavana*: child.
5. *Omusinde* or *omusoleli*: a son before he is circumcised.
6. *Omusani*: a circumcised son.
7. *Omuxana*: an unmarried daughter.
8. *Omugogo*: a married daughter.
9. *Omuvele*: first-born child (of either sex). Also: *omuvele omuxulu*.
10. *Omutua*: last-born child (of either sex). The other children are referred to by the descriptive term *vavana ve hagari*, 'children of the middle'. The terms *omuvele* and *omutua*, however, are only used as terms of address.
11. *Wanda yase*: my sibling (used by both sexes and always in connexion with the possessive pronoun). Means literally 'The one of my womb'. It refers, however, both to physical and to classificatory siblings. The term *omwana wa papa* refers always to a half-brother (same father, different mother), to the son of a father's brother, or to any other classificatory brother, but never to a full-brother, who is always designated as *omwana wa ma(y)i* (mother's son). Special terms distinguishing siblings according to their sex do not exist among the Vugusu. The English terms 'brother' and 'sister' can therefore only be rendered by circumlocutions such as *wanda yase omusoleli* or *omwana wefue owe soleli* (our child who is a boy) and *wanda yase omuxana* respectively.
12. *Xotja, va-*: mother's brother.
13. *Omwiwana, vavewana*: sister's child (of either sex).
14. *Senge, va-*: father's sister.
15. *Omwisengetjanwa, vavesengetjanwa*: woman's brother's child.
16. *Omwana wa xotja*: child of the mother's brother.
17. *Omwana wa senge*: child of the father's sister.
18. *Sianáɲina, va-*: child of the mother's sister.
19. *Guga, va-*: grandfather. The paternal grandfather can be distinguished terminologically from the maternal grandfather only by a circumlocution such as *guga osala papa*, 'the grandfather who begot the father', and *guga osala ma(y)i* respectively.
20. *Guxu, va-*: grandmother (paternal or maternal).
21. *Sísoni, vi-*: great-grandfather, -mother, -parents. No distinction according to sex or lineage. The term also refers to the great-grandchildren of either sex.
22. *Simila, vi-*: ancestor (of either sex) of the fourth generation.
23. *Sinamunda, vi-*: ancestor (of either sex) of the fifth generation.
24. *Omwítjuxulu*: grandchild (of either sex).

(ii) *Affinal Kin*

(a) *Ómusedja, va-*: husband.
(b) *Ómuxasi, va-*: wife. A person's first or great wife is called *ómuxasi*

omuxulu; his last or youngest wife, *ómuxasi omuro*; any other wife, *ómuxasi owe hagari* (the wife of the middle); the favoured wife, *ómuxasi omuxaye* (not necessarily the great wife or the youngest wife).
(c) *Wango yase*: my co-wife (literally, the one of my yard).
(d) *Mulamua, va-*: wife's sister.
(e) *Muxwasi, vamuxwasi*: wife's brother.
(f) *Masala, va-*: husband's mother-in-law, a woman's son-in-law. A wife calls her parents-in-law *baba* and *ma(y)i*; the husband calls his father-in-law *baba*, and he calls his son-in-law *musani wase* (cf. No. 6).
(g) *Vasagwa wase*: husband of wife's sister. The parents of a married couple also call one another *vasagwa*.

PART III

THE MAGICO-RELIGIOUS

A. INTRODUCTORY

THE wide range of magical and religious notions and practices that exist among the Bantu Kavirondo are interrelated in such a way that the nature of each will best be discerned by examining them jointly. The differences between them which, as we shall see, are quite subtle will then emerge far more clearly than if religion and magic were from the beginning treated as distinct spheres of spiritual and emotional life.

While in theoretical writings on religion and magic the definition of the two concepts has been made the subject of considerable controversy, most field-ethnographers, and particularly authors of books on Bantu cultures, have based their distinction between magic and religion upon the human *versus* the superhuman quality of the agent or force that is supposed to possess or wield mystical powers. The ideas relating to the spirits of the deceased, to other spirit-beings and to deities, and the practices linked with such ideas are thus generally ascribed to the sphere of religion, whereas all mystical power possessed and controlled by living human beings is assigned to the sphere of magic in the wider sense of the word, including witchcraft and sorcery. This formal distinction between magic and religion is based upon the assumption that there is a fundamental difference between the mystical power that is bound up with material objects, spells, and rites (*substanzgebundene Zauberkraft*) and the free mystical power with which spirits, demons, and gods are endowed (*freie Seelenkraft*). It is implied in this distinction that there must exist also a fundamental difference in the spiritual attitude and emotional response to these two types of powers.

However, the *a priori* classification of the magico-religious into two distinct types of beliefs and practices easily leads the investigator to stultify the analysis of his data, as from the outset they are coloured by having preconceived labels attached to them. When describing the various 'rites of passage' among the Bantu Kavirondo (birth, initiation, marriage, and death) we shall see that to them physical death does not mean the same decisive break it means to us. In their conception life after physical death goes on in a sense that is much more realistic and immediate than, for instance, the Christian idea of immortality. We shall see that the death-rites show numerous parallels with those connected with birth and circumcision, all of them being conceived as 'phases of transition' from one stage of existence to another. We would, therefore, hardly be justified in assuming that the Kavirondo make a fundamental distinction between the mystical powers wielded by the living and those wielded by the dead or by

INTRODUCTORY

other spirit-like agents. The following analysis will show that there are numerous traits which the mystical power controlled by human beings and that wielded by ancestral spirits and other spirit-like or demoniac beings have in common. There are close parallels between spell and prayer and between counter-magic and sacrifice. Further, the various types of divination serve to detect acts of evil magic issuing from a sorcerer as well as the misfortunes inflicted by ancestral spirits and demons. Hence the diviner is competent both for 'magical' and for 'religious' phenomena. It will, finally, appear that even the principle of homoeopathy—the notion that the force which has caused a certain condition to come about is, at the same time, the most appropriate means of counteracting it—is not only met with in the sphere of 'magic' (powers wielded by human beings) but in the cult of superhuman beings as well. The same may be said with regard to the principles of sympathy or analogy.

These few anticipatory remarks may suffice to justify the decision to discuss the magical and religious phenomena jointly as constituting one integral system of beliefs and practices.

To present my material it will be necessary to arrange it in a system. This involves the danger of introducing arbitrary principles of classification, of distinguishing types and categories of beliefs and practices that are irrelevant to the native mind or, worse still, of tearing apart what from his point of view forms an integral unit and vice versa. To avoid this danger I have endeavoured to adapt the system of presentation as closely as possible to the native manner of classifying the magico-religious phenomena.

Starting out from a 'neutral state of affairs' (i.e. a situation in which no mystical forces of any kind are in operation), from the zero point, as it were, the whole system of beliefs and practices is 'set in motion' by the agents and forces that are believed to wield mystical power affecting human welfare. Whether these agents are living human beings or spirits, whether they are ordinary people or specialists, whether they derive their powers from an inherited disposition or from the possession of medicines with particular virtues, whether they wield their power actively and intentionally or merely as the passive vehicles of an ulterior mystical force, whether they use it for beneficial or for destructive purposes, whether they are socially approved of or condemned: they all have in common that they affect human welfare in a mysterious way, that 'suprasensible qualities are attributed to them which, or part of which, are not derived from observation or cannot be logically inferred from it'.[1]

As they release certain energies which upset the neutral (or normal) ritual status and, accordingly, evoke a response, depending upon the nature of the effect produced by them, we shall label them 'releasing forces'. I shall begin the discussion of these releasing forces by dealing with the various human agents that are thought either actively to wield or to be the

[1] E. E. Evans-Pritchard, *Witchcraft, Oracles and Magic among the Azande*, Oxford, 1937, p. 12.

passive vehicles of mystical power. Next I shall describe the beliefs in ancestral spirits and in the various anthropomorphic spirit-beings. This will, finally, lead up to the conception of the High God or Supreme Being. The reason for following such a course is that the notions regarding ancestral and other spirit-beings are, in many ways, based on the notions held with regard to living persons, as the mystical qualities ascribed to different types of spirits merely appear as a transfer of the qualities ascribed to different types of living persons. By this I do not mean to assert that the cult of ancestral spirits and demoniac beings is more recent than the belief in the mystical powers of living human beings. Whether this is the case or not could, if at all, only be established by a broad comparative study of the two aspects of magico-religious notions. All I mean to imply by the proposed arrangement is that in the system of magico-religious ideas which we encounter among the Bantu Kavirondo to-day, the ancestor cult is coloured by the belief in magic and witchcraft to such an extent that it is profitable to discuss the latter belief first.

It follows from the nature of these aspects and the qualities attributed to them that they do not all possess the same degree of reality. The Supreme Being and the ancestral and other spirits exist merely in native belief. But also the human agents alleged to wield mystical power do not all of them necessarily exist in real life. People actually do practise promotive magic (garden-magic, love-making, &c.), utter curses and blessings, and feel convinced that, under certain circumstances, they are in a state of ritual impurity which is fraught with danger to themselves and to other people. But it is doubtful whether sorcerers (*avavila*) actually perform all the evil rites attributed to them. While definite individuals, on certain occasions, boast of being *avavila* (cf. below, p. 132), they would never openly confess to the evil practices attributed to them. The *avalogi* (witches) never admit any of their alleged practices. Although certain individuals and groups of persons are suspected of being *avalogi*, it is quite conceivable that the whole range of activities attributed to the latter are never actually practised, even though theoretically they would be in a position to do most of the things they are supposed to do.

From the native point of view the agents wielding mystical power are not differentiated into those who lead a real existence and those that exist merely in their belief. To illustrate the point, we may compare the 'releasing forces' with an iceberg. The five-sixths of it which are submerged under the water correspond to the part that merely exists in native belief, while the remaining portion that protrudes from the water corresponds to the part which, like promotive magic, curses, and blessings, &c., is actually practised. From the European point of view, on the other hand, there is a great difference between the two, as in the one case we deal with magico-religious *practices* and in the other with mere *beliefs*. This example clearly shows how misleading it would be if one were to impose European principles of classification upon the native notions.

INTRODUCTORY

Now the (real or alleged) activities of the 'releasing forces' evoke a response aiming at their control. This second type of forces we shall label the 'controlling forces'. In so far as the 'releasing forces' are deemed to promote human welfare, the response consists of their invocation, and in so far as they are held to be harmful or destructive, it consists of evading or combating them. Since, as we shall see, the agents wielding mystical power are chiefly thought to bring harm rather than to do good, the element of invoking their help is completely overshadowed by that of dodging, combating, or reconciling them.

To avert misfortune threatening from the 'releasing forces', people resort to protective and preventive measures. These consist of such practices as the observation of signs and omens, the interpretation of dreams, the acquisition and handling of protective medicines and charms, and the observance of avoidances and ritual prohibitions. On the other hand, the harmful activities of the 'releasing forces' call for means of counteracting them *after* they have come into action. The need for such 'cure after the event' leads to the various forms of propitiatory sacrifice, prayer, counter-magic (or anti-witchcraft), and reconciliation with the agent from whom the evil action has issued.

The idea, finally, that counter-measures against the operation of mystical forces can only be taken if, in any given case, the particular cause of the misfortune has been detected, leads to the various practices of divination.

The practices aiming at a control of the 'releasing forces' (in so far as they are held to be negative) may thus be classed in three categories: (1) prevention and protection, (2) detection (or divination), and (3) cure or counteraction.

It must be added that the various magico-religious practices do not always fall precisely within the limits of one of the different categories that we have distinguished. Thus the sacrifices offered to the ancestral spirits and the Supreme Being, although predominantly undertaken when a particular misfortune has occurred, serve at the same time to ward off future hostile actions against the living. Similarly, most ancestral sacrifices combine the two elements of placating ancestral wrath and of invoking the positive help of the benevolent spirits. They are, therefore, at the same time measures of protection and counteraction, and of reconciliation and invocation respectively. The degree of overlapping, however, is not marked enough to render the system of classifying the various practices unworkable.

Throughout the preceding pages I have used the term 'mystical' to render the particular quality that is attributed to all forces or agents of the magico-religious sphere. Evans-Pritchard, who has used this term in his admirable study of Zande magic and witchcraft, defines it in the following manner: 'Mystical notions are patterns of thought that attribute to phenomena supra-sensible qualities which, or part of which, are not derived from observation or cannot be logically inferred from it, and which they do not possess.' These he contrasts with what he calls common-sense notions which he thus defines: "These (i.e. the common-sense notions) are patterns of thought that attribute to phenomena only what men observe in them or what can logically be inferred from observation. So long as a notion does not assert something which has not been observed, it is not classed as mystical even though it is mistaken on account of incomplete observation. It still differs from mystical notions in which supra-sensible forces are always posited."[1]

As these definitions of the mystical and common-sense notions render exactly the relation between the magico-religious and the empirical among the Bantu Kavirondo, I propose to adopt the term 'mystical' and use it in preference to such terms as 'supernatural' or 'praeternatural'. To a much greater extent than the word 'mystical' these latter terms posit a duality of phenomena. Now the concept of the 'natural', and hence the recognition of a duality of natural and supernatural phenomena, arises only where causal connexions based on empirical observation attract the attention of the intellect and, as the result of such attention, are felt to present a different type of reality than causal connexions which are derived from the alleged qualities of imaginary phenomena not supported by empirical observation. From all the evidence I have it appears, however, that among the Bantu Kavirondo there exists no notion of such a duality of 'natural' and 'supernatural' phenomena as mutually exclusive types of reality. For them the empirical and the mystical are rather two aspects of one and the same reality. They are not mutually exclusive, but they supplement one another like the external and the internal aspects of a process. Their notion of the relation between the empirical and the mystical may, in fact, be compared with the distinction that we make between an immediate cause and the ultimate force behind it. Thus it would be futile to attempt the classification of the phenomena and events of native life into those which would be fully explained by empirical observation and those which would be ascribed to the working of mystical power. In the initial stages of my fieldwork I made such an attempt, assuming that certain phenomena, the causes of which would appear to us to be completely laid bare by the facts of empirical observation, would also to the native leave no room for any other explanation than one in terms of empirical facts. I soon found out, however, that every phenomenon, no matter how apparently fully 'accounted for' by empirical facts, may be explained by the Bantu Kavirondo both in terms of empirical observation *and* in terms of mystical notions. Thus the burns suffered by a small child who falls into a tray of boiling porridge are 'explained' both by the carelessness of the child and the heat of the porridge which, as everyone knows, causes blisters if it comes into contact with human skin, and by the working of a mystical power which has singled out this particular child to receive injuries of this kind and prevented its mother or nurse from guarding it

[1] See E. E. Evans-Pritchard, op. cit., p. 12.

just at the crucial moment. Even an act of suicide committed by an adult person is accounted for in terms of such 'double causation'.

The relative degree of attention which in any given case is paid to the empirical facts and to the mystical power behind a phenomenon or an event varies with the strength of the emotional reaction to it. If an aged person dies from what we would call the infirmity of old age, his death is attributed by the natives to his old age as well as to an act of sorcery practised by someone who desired his death. Accordingly, in the course of the funeral rites, and particularly at the hair-shaving ceremony which follows them, accusations are levelled against the alleged sorcerer. I have heard of this being done even after the death of one of my oldest informants (Mtiva), who had been so infirm that people had expected him to die for a long time. However, since in his case death did not occur unexpectedly and since it did not cause any social or economic disruption among his relatives but, on the contrary, rather a relief from a burden, the accusations of sorcery were soon dispelled by the speech of the 'comforter', whose task it is to remind the bereaved ones that 'from long ago people have always died' and that they should not let their grief over the death of the old man of their clan induce them to commit acts of revenge, merely causing the strength and unity of their clan to be weakened by another death. If, on the other hand, a person dies who is still in the prime of life or if somebody becomes the victim of repeated misfortunes, the empirically observed causes of such misfortunes are almost entirely disregarded. All attention is concentrated upon the deeper mystical causes and upon the attempt to counteract or destroy the force that is held responsible for what has happened.

In the course of the following analysis numerous examples will be given which will further demonstrate how this double causation behind all phenomena and events works in actual situations.

B. AGENTS AND FORCES BELIEVED TO EXERCISE A MYSTICAL INFLUENCE OVER HUMAN WELFARE

MOST of the various agents which, according to native belief, wield mystical power that positively or negatively affects human welfare— one's personal health as well as one's material well-being and the outcome of undertakings of all kinds—are living human beings. Among these we can, for the purposes of preliminary classification, distinguish three major groups, each of which is marked by some outstanding characteristics.

First of all there is the wide category of ordinary people possessing and handling magical substances of an active but generally harmless nature and being able to utter curses or pronounce blessings.

The second category comprises people who are regarded as passive vehicles of a dangerous mystical power, because they have temporarily fallen into a state of ritual impurity. This state is brought about in many different ways, e.g. by having broken a rule of avoidance or taboo, by having done something that is contrary to the customary forms of behaviour, by having committed a bloody crime or having in other ways become associated with blood, by being actively or passively involved in some unusual and ritually alarming event or phenomenon, and by being closely associated with such decisive crises of life as birth or death. According to their causes, several types of such a state of ritual impurity are distinguished, all of which differ to some extent as regards the nature and scope of the dangerousness which emanates from the person thus afflicted. All these types of ritual impurity, however, have certain essential features in common. (a) They involve dangers of a mystical nature, either to the person afflicted or to others who come in contact with him, or to both; (b) they overcome their victim as an automatic consequence of the act which he has committed or in which he is passively involved regardless of his volition; (c) the state of impurity is only temporary and wears off either after an appropriate purification ceremony has been performed or after a certain period of time has elapsed; (d) finally, although a person who goes through such a state of ritual impurity is feared and avoided, he is not blamed for his condition (although he may be blamed for having committed an act which is regarded as instrumental in causing his condition), nor is it thought that he will intentionally make use of his state of dangerousness to inflict harm upon his fellow beings.

Thirdly, there is the important category of specialists or experts in wielding active mystical power. It comprises the various types of sorcerers and witches as well as the rain-magicians. They all have in common (a) that they wield their powers permanently, (b) that to practise their art they require either an inherited disposition or a special training or both, and (c) that their knowledge and the techniques used by them are esoteric. These features clearly distinguish them from ordinary people possessing and handling public magic as well as from the people who are in a temporary state of ritual impurity.

I shall now discuss *seriatim* the beliefs and notions concerning each of these three major categories of human agents. As a result of this discussion, finer distinctions and a number of principles of classification will emerge.

(1) ORDINARY PEOPLE POSSESSING AND HANDLING PUBLIC ACTIVE MAGIC

The Bantu Kavirondo believe that ordinary persons—as distinct from specialists—can exercise an active mystical influence over their own welfare or that of their fellow beings, either by using certain commonly known plants or other objects alleged to possess magical qualities, or by pronouncing curses or blessings.

(a) *Promotive Magic*

The application of commonly known or public magic substances is not bound up with particular personal qualifications, such as inherited and acquired dispositions, nor with age or sex. Anyone can gather such substances if he knows where to find them or acquire them from anyone who is willing to sell or give them away. Such public magic, known as *olunyasi* or *amasambu*, is linguistically not distinguished from substances that have therapeutic qualities (medicines), and it is only the use to which they are put and the effect which they are alleged to have that enables the European observer to distinguish them from the latter. Nor—as far as native classifications are concerned—can a clear line of distinction be drawn between magic that promotes one's aims and desires and thus works as an active force, and magic that is merely used for the purpose of preventing, or protecting one from, various misfortunes and failures. Inasmuch as preventive and protective magic does not work as an active force and is, therefore, not intended to produce any 'positive' results, we are justified in distinguishing it from promotive magic and in discussing it (separately from the latter) along with other practices that serve to combat the effects of active mystical powers. From the native point of view, however, promotive as well as preventive and protective magic help to secure the attainment of a desired aim, and it is therefore not always easy to decide whether a particular type of magical substance merely serves the purpose of protecting a person, an object, or an undertaking from destructive influences, or whether it is at the same time supposed to possess the positive quality of actively producing or fostering the desired result. The making of such a distinction leads right up to one of the central problems of the present chapter on the magico-religious, viz. the question as to the native conception of the motivating powers in life. Anticipating some of the results of the present analysis, we may state that on the whole it appears that physical health, material well-being, and success in various undertakings are regarded as the normal state of affairs, which will prevail as long as no force of an adverse nature interferes with the ordinary course of events. From this basic attitude it follows that health and prosperity will be less accounted for by the positive influence of sustaining and promotive mystical powers than by the absence of negative, i.e. destructive power. This explains why promotive magic is of far less importance than protective and preventive magic and other means of combating destructive mystical power.

If we now examine the various occasions where we might expect promotive magic to be employed by the Bantu Kavirondo we find that in the activities of hunting and raiding cattle there is a complete absence of it. Although I have persistently searched for such magic, all my inquiries in that direction have yielded only negative results. As regards the cultivation of the land, there likewise exists no commonly known magical substance which is thought to increase the fertility of the soil or in a general way to promote the growth and yield of crops. However, when planting eleusine, the most highly valued crop, certain magical observances are followed that, to some extent at least, appear to be of a promotive nature. Thus among the Vugusu the women who intend to plant their gardens jointly (either the co-wives of a polygynous husband or the women of several neighbouring homesteads) brew the so-called *gamalua gamaravula*, 'the beer of the shadows'. It is called by this name because the women drink it while sitting round the centre post of the hut which is considered one of the abodes of the ancestral spirits or shadows. With this beer, the sorghum for which is supplied by the oldest woman in the planting group, they eat eleusine porridge and a mush of sesame seeds as a relish but no meat. Although no special offering is made to the spirits on that occasion and no prayer or invocation is addressed to them, I was assured that the idea of this beer drink is to secure the goodwill and blessing of the spirits for the proper growth of the crops that are about to be planted.

On the eve of the day on which they begin planting the eleusine, every woman places her basket of seeds at the base of the centre post, putting a harvesting-knife, a raw chicken egg, and some tobacco kneaded into a hard lump on top of the seeds. The basket containing the seeds and these various objects 'sleeps' (as they say) for one night at the centre post where it is blessed by the ancestral spirits. As regards the meaning of these objects I was told that the placing of the harvesting-knife on top of the seeds 'would help to produce an ample harvest'. After the planting it is taken home again in the empty basket and no further ritual attention is paid to it. The raw egg becomes the temporary abode of the ancestral spirits who enter it during the night. It is left in the basket while the planting is going on and is afterwards thrown out into the bush by the male owner of the garden, 'as it is now empty, for the spirits have left it and gone into the soil of the planted field'.[1] The tobacco, finally, is smoked by the woman while she plants. This likewise has a magical significance, for 'the smoke that rises from her pipe will attract the rain to fall soon' so that the seeds will germinate. The same observances are followed among the neighbouring Tadjoni, with the difference that they do not place the seed-basket with the other paraphernalia at the base of the centre post but in the entrance of the sacrificial hut, where they leave it from sunrise until about nine o'clock when they go out planting.[2]

It is obvious that the placing of the harvesting-knife on top of the seeds and the smoking of tobacco that has been blessed by the ancestral spirits are true examples of promotive magic that work in accordance with the common principle of sympathy. As regards the part attributed to the ancestral spirits in these observances I cannot say with certainty whether the idea is merely to appease them, and thus to keep them from negatively interfering with the growth of the crops, or whether they are believed to be capable of actively promoting the growth of the crops. It may be signi-

---

[1] For the significance of eggs in other magical situations cf. p. 115.

[2] A possible reason for placing it there at sunrise only and not for a whole night seems to be the idea that it might otherwise be tampered with by the evil spirits who would not dare to come in the daytime. I have, however, no direct or indirect evidence to support this explanation.

ficant to mention in this connexion that among both the Vugusu and the Logoli it is the privilege of the owner of the garden to throw the first seeds and that a father still retains this right after he has divided his garden among his married sons and thereby gives expression to his rights of ownership over such gardens. It seems then that by placing an egg which has become the temporary abode of the ancestral spirits on top of the seeds while planting, this right of throwing the first seeds is still accorded to the ancestors as the original owners of the land. If this interpretation is correct, the significance of this custom would lie in the idea of propitiating the spirits who can no longer exercise their rights of ownership themselves rather than in the belief that they are capable of actively promoting the growth of the crops. This view is also corroborated by Xasoa's statement that 'the spirits do not make the crops grow but the rain, and the rain is sent by God (Wele)'. The point raised here, however, remains a moot one which we shall have to discuss again at various other junctures of this chapter.

Among the Logoli, no magical observances accompany the planting of eleusine, but promotive magic is administered over it in the early stages of its growth. In February, when the eleusine plants are about 6 or 7 inches high and the first rains have set in, the *omukingi womulimi* (magician of the garden) on his own account makes a round through all the gardens of the neighbourhood. He carries with him a pot filled with a liquid (dried and pounded leaves of a certain herb steeped in water) and, dipping some leaves into it, sprinkles it over the tops of the plants as he walks along. Before he does so he cuts a straight stick from a tree (any tree) and ties a bundle of a certain grass to it. This object, called *esalu*, he places in the fork of a tree standing in the midst of the fields, where he leaves it until after harvest. Then he takes it down from the tree, ties it for a few days to the fence of his homestead, and then burns it in the fire-place of his yard. As a result of this procedure and the sprinkling of medicine, the millet is supposed to grow faster and to yield a richer harvest; it is expressly denied that it is administered against a plant disease or any other destructive force. Unfortunately, although I have on one occasion met and photographed a garden-magician while he was sprinkling the fields, I could not persuade him to show or give me a specimen of the herb he used. The garden-magician does not ask for a payment before or immediately after he has administered his magic, but he waits until after the harvest, and if the yield has been satisfactory he is given a small measuring-basket (*enavodo*) full of eleusine from each person whose garden he has sprinkled.

The belief in the efficacy of promotive magic is most clearly developed in the sphere of human relationships, particularly in the realm of sexual love. It is thought possible by the application of certain magical substances to produce or increase in another person a feeling of sympathy or sexual attraction towards oneself. The most common method employed for this end is to wear talismans tied to necklaces or wristlets, or suspended from one's belt, which consist of the branches, leaves, or roots of certain plants. Such talismans are not necessarily supposed to have a specific effect upon a definite person or in a particular situation, but they are worn permanently and are thought to promote one's success and good luck in a good many ways. The most important of these which I have listed are: to make one sexually desirable in the eyes of women (or men respectively), to make one hospitably received when visiting people, to help one get the support of the elders when carrying on litigation in the tribal court, to come off best in family quarrels, and to gain the favour of a wealthy and important tribesman or, nowadays, of one's European employer. In all these cases, it will be noted, the talisman exercises an influence over another *person*, even where the ultimate aim of wearing it is to gain some material benefit (as in a lawsuit or in anticipation of hospitality) and not merely the sympathy of another person towards oneself. This is significant as it shows that the efficacy of promotive talismans is restricted to their influence over living persons and does not extend to material objects. People do not wear talismans to increase their wealth in cattle or their stores of grain or to exercise some other direct influence over any other but human beings.

The objects used as talismans for exercising a favourable influence over another person comprise a wide range of plants and herbs. Some of them are used for other purposes as well (e.g. as protective magic), and new ones constantly come into fashion, especially as people nowadays travel a great deal between the different areas and thus get a wider knowledge of such objects.[1] There exists no general notion which explains the source from which these objects derive their potency. In some cases it is a particular scent or another outward characteristic of a plant which accounts for its alleged magical virtues. In other cases the mere distance of its place of origin or the apparent success of its application which the vendor can demonstrate or vouch for are the only indications of its mystical qualities. Among the Logoli, the three major ones are the leaves, roots, or branches of the *ekisugi*-tree, the *ekigundu*-grass which is tied round one's wrist or stuck into one's belt, and roots of the *ekyeywi*-plant which have the colour and texture of cork and for a long time retain a pleasant, earthy smell.[2] They are cut into pieces and lined up on a length of string to form a necklace. In the case of these roots it is evidently the scent which accounts for their use as a talisman; as regards the other two plants I have not been able to discover to what particular qualities they owed their reputation. In addition to the wearing of talismans, there are also specific means of gaining the favours of particular persons on definite occasions. To make himself

[1] During the trial of a young man accused at the Logoli tribal court for practising sorcery his pockets were searched and a large number of dried-up roots and leaves were found. When questioned by the elders as to their meaning he described the alleged qualities of each and mentioned the places where he had obtained them.

[2] One of my Vugusu informants (Nandoli) called it the native equivalent of 'Yardley's lavender powder' which is now generally coming into use as one of the toilet requisites of native women.

AGENTS AND FORCES

sexually attractive to a girl a man, in the morning, chews the roots of the *keŋereŋani*-plant if he expects to meet the girl that day, and it is said that the smell of his breath will then cause the girl to like him. Or he burns the branches of the same plant or of a herb called *ekyeyui* to charcoal and rubs it between the palms of his hands before he salutes the girl; or again he secretly puts small pieces of it into her pipe or throws them into a fire while he talks to the girl, so that she will inhale its scent. Roots of the *kidumusi*-tree are chewed for the same purpose, but they are not used in the other two ways. To induce a girl who resists a man's sexual approaches to change her mind the lover must chew a piece of bark of the *kivinu*-tree and spit tiny bits of it into her ears while he embraces her and implores her with such words as: '*o'makuvugane nive!*', 'oh, may I join with you?', (i.e. may I sleep with you?). The same effect is attained if one mixes the pounded leaves of the *kivinu*-plant with porridge and invites the girl to one's sister's place to eat of that porridge.

Among the Vugusu, if somebody has a case pending in the tribal court he pounds the dried leaves of a certain herb before he goes to the hearing of the case. He then licks the powder and rubs some of it on his thighs. If he is the defendant he puts some of this powder on the back of his hands and, quickly raising his hands, throws it back over his shoulders, which means that he will be able to throw the accusations back to the plaintiff.

Branches of the *kivinu*-plant are also burnt as incense in the fire of the hearth to win the favour of a visitor or in the fire that is kindled at the base of the centre post after a sacrifice has been offered to the ancestral spirits.

To cut out a rival in a courtship, a lover makes use of the pounded leaves of the *ekisávasavi*-tree or, if that fails, of the *ekisuga*-tree which is supposed to have a stronger and more lasting effect. To administer this medicine he invites his rival for a common meal of porridge and tells his mother to prepare the dish in such a way that only one half of it will contain the pounded leaves. He then offers the dish to his rival in such a way that the latter will eat of the prepared half while he himself eats of the other half. Having eaten of the porridge that contained the medicine his rival will become dull and unattractive to the girl but otherwise will suffer no harm. When the lover has attained his purpose, he can later undo the effects of his magic upon his rival by performing an appropriate rite over him. The same two plants are used in the same way by women who are jealous of their co-wives or of other girls. They bear, therefore, no relation to the sex of the victim.

All these types of promotive magic have in common that to be effective they require no spells or formal details of ritual behaviour. They can be handled by anyone, and their possession and application do not involve social disapproval nor, on the other hand, lend prestige.

(b) Curses and Blessings

Apart from the handling of substances with alleged mystical qualities, ordinary people can exercise a mystical influence over their fellow beings by uttering curses or pronouncing blessings over them. As regards curses, two major categories may be distinguished, viz. (1) those directed against definite persons and uttered in their presence,[1] and (2) those directed against unknown offenders.[2] Although both kinds of curses are the same in effect, they differ in several respects. Theoretically, every person is in a position to utter curses, but as real efficacy is attributed only to curses and blessings spoken by elderly persons, young or even middle-aged people would seldom curse or bless in earnest and nobody would pay serious attention to them if they did so. There is, however, no idea of a definite age-limit beyond which a person's spoken words under certain conditions suddenly acquire a mystical potency. It appears rather that, as the amount of respect and authority which people command increases with their age, so does the power attributed to their curses or blessings. Unlike respect and authority, however, the strength of a curse is not closely linked with the social status, wealth, or political leadership of the person who utters it. It appears on the contrary that curses are predominantly the spiritual weapons of persons who are not in a position to impose their will by more tangible means, because they are poor, old, or physically weak. Accordingly, old women are usually mentioned first when the subject of curses is brought up, as their status when they become widowed and unable to provide their own food is economically less secure than that of old men who retain their rights of ownership until they die. If other people, who command wealth and authority, utter curses they do so mainly on occasions where the circumstances of the offence that has incited their anger are such that no other retaliation is possible, e.g. if the offender is not known or if he is a close relative, so that compensation by the payment of a fine is ruled out. As the utterance of a curse is considered a serious matter it is resorted to only in cases where the offence was weighty, at least if the victim of the curse is a definite person. Where, on the other hand, a curse is addressed to an unkown person, even a rather trivial offence may incite the person who has suffered it to pronounce the most devastating curse. In these cases, however it chiefly serves as a threat to the offender, who can easily escape its consequences by confessing his guilt and repairing the damage he has done. The main offences that give rise to a curse are acts of theft, encroachments upon one's sexual privileges, e.g. the discovery of sexual relations of a son with his father's junior wives, incest, and all forms of gross neglect of parents by their children or of disobedience to their parents' wishes.

The victim of a curse, as has already been implicitly stated, may be either a definite person in whose presence the curse is uttered, or an unknown offender who then is cursed *in absentia*. In both cases the curse is supposed to be equally powerful, but if the offender is cursed *in absentia*, care is always taken that a few persons are present as witnesses while it is

[1] Called *okutjena* or *okulomolela* (Lurogoli).
[2] Called *okulama* (Lurogoli), *xulama* (Luvugusu).

uttered, if possible those persons who are suspected of having committed the offence. This indicates that a curse, to become efficacious, should be made known to its victim. Thus Xasoa, an old woman who had frequently served as my informant, one day missed the money which she had received from me in the course of our work. She suspected one of four young lads who were sleeping in her hut of stealing the money, as they were the only ones who could possibly have known the place where she had been hiding it. However, when each of them denied the theft she cursed the unknown thief in the presence of all four of them, saying: 'Whoever has taken my money, may his feet swell till he dies!' Actually in this case the money was secretly returned to the place from which it had been taken less than a week after Xasoa had uttered the curse.

Curses that are addressed to definite persons can only be levelled against members of one's own clan or other near relatives by blood, such as nephews or grandchildren. Also, the victim of the curse must always be junior to the person who utters it. It seems, therefore, that the belief in the potency of a personal curse is derived from the notion of a kinship tie (implying the notion of ownership or control) which connects the person who pronounces the curse with his victim and which lends him a particular power over the latter. The most common types of curses are those pronounced by parents over their children (of either sex), and here, obviously, the potency of the curse should be greatest, as the father, being their begetter, retains power over his children.

If, as it seems, this notion of a latent but persistent power of parents over their offspring is the source from which the potency of the parental curse (and its extension to other near kinsmen and clansmen) is derived, then this type of curse would appear to belong to quite a different category from the curses pronounced over unknown offenders. The potency of this latter type of curse is then not based on any direct bond between the pronouncer of the curse and its victim but rather on a bond of ownership with the particular object which the offender has stolen. It is significant in this context that curses against unknown persons are uttered only for such offences as theft or adultery with one's wife, but not in cases where no connexion can be established with the offender through an object.

The manner in which a curse is spoken differs for both types of curses. If addressed to a definite person it is uttered spontaneously and, as a rule, in a state of violent anger and resentment. The wording of the curse, in that case, is not bound to a fixed formula, nor are any accompanying rites deemed necessary to lend it potency. Nevertheless, the utterance of the curse is often accompanied by gestures, such as the showing of the palms of one's hands or the indecent exposure of one's buttocks or sex-organs to the person to whom the curse is addressed. Such gestures—although made spontaneously—are not merely expressions of contempt accompanying the curse, but are in themselves an integral part of the curse and just as efficacious as the spoken words. Even if made without words, such gestures are feared as a kind of silent curse.[1] Other gestures or pantomimic acts which by themselves have the power of curses are the throwing of a handful of soil from a freshly dug grave at a person or the cutting of a line of notches in the door-posts of a hut.

If, on the other hand, the curse is addressed to an unknown offender, it bears the character of a magical rite which must follow a definite procedure depending upon the kind of punishment that the curse aims at. The following are examples of typical situations in which curses against unknown offenders are employed and of the manner in which they are uttered:

1. If a person discovers that somebody has stolen, e.g. a fowl or a hoe from him and he cannot retrieve the object by asking for it among his neighbours, he goes to borrow a small drum (*esugudi*) from a person who possesses one. With this drum he enters his house and says: 'Now I want to curse (*okulama*) this homestead, because somebody has stolen something from here.' Then he takes a hoe and digs grooves across the paths leading to his house. Having done so he takes the drum and, while beating it, utters the following curse:

> *Ah, yive vwoli,*
> *omundu wahila engoko yange*
> *nuvimba vilenge nuvimba,*
> *nuvimba amalu nuvimba*
> *yengoko yange vudzwa*
> *ma wahilanga vudzwa*
> *ah, yive vwoli!*

> 'Ah, you be cursed!
> (You) person who took my fowl.
> You swell, the feet, you swell;
> You swell, the knees, you swell.
> My fowl only.
> Then you were taking my fowl for nothing,
> Ah, you be cursed!'

The digging of grooves across the paths leading to the homestead and the curse are thought to have a twofold effect. The curse will cause the thief to suffer from swollen feet and knees and the grooves will cause him to die should he try to return to the house to commit another theft. The curse, however, is not expected to take effect immediately but only within a year or two.

2. If somebody—by intention or accident—has killed a cow, a goat, or

---

[1] Thus it is stated in a text: 'If you quarrel with your father and he shows you his hands (*yakumannya amakòno gege*) or turns aside his hide (*yakunula enguvu yeye*) which he wears and he does not later reconcile you to him, then you cannot beget (any children) at all.' According to my informants the display of his wrinkled palms and his sex-organs transmits the impotency of his old age to the person for whom the gestures are meant.

a sheep belonging to another person while nobody watched it, and he fails to report what he has done, the owner of the dead beast has recourse to a curse. He skins the dead beast and, tapping[1] its stomach or its head, he speaks the following words:

Niva wali kwita numundu alatavagirange mukifu kitjye kuli yive uvimbi kifu kitjyo ndi.

'If you have been killed by someone, may his stomach boil like your stomach is swelling (thus).'

He then divides the meat among his neighbours and only keeps the skull (over which he has spoken the curse), which he carefully hides away, as the power of the curse now resides in it (cf. below, p. 255).

3. If a man has placed a honey-barrel in a tree and later when he opens it to collect the honey discovers that it has been taken out already, he curses the thief in the following manner: he takes one bee, cuts off its head, and throws its mutilated body (which is still humming) back into the hive. While doing so he says:

Yive ulayingange naŋana endzuki yiyi, ngutagika, ulayingange.

'You, may you be wandering about aimlessly like this bee, I did not place the barrel with you,[2] you may be wandering about.'

4. If someone has trespassed in another person's garden while it rained and later does not admit having done so, the owner curses him. He takes a knife (*olugembe*) and cuts through the footprints made by the trespasser. While doing so he says:

Nguheye amalenge kuvimba, a'omulimi gwange, yive vwoli!

'I may give you the feet to swell, oh my garden, you be cursed!'

5. If through carelessness somebody lets his cattle eat the crops growing in a neighbour's garden and fails to tell him of the damage he has caused him, the owner of the garden curses him in the same manner as above. The kinds of misfortune called down upon their victims by curses are more or less standardized for the different types of offences. Thus, thieves are usually cursed by wishing that their feet may swell. This wish is apparently based on the idea that the light and quick feet of the thief have played a substantial part in permitting him to commit his misdeed without being caught. Sometimes also the object that has been stolen is invoked to bring misfortune on the thief. This is also done before an object has been stolen, especially if it has to be left unguarded like a beehive or a trap and thus may tempt a thief. In this case the curse really becomes a form of preventive magic, although it retains all the proper features of a curse. If parents inflict a curse upon their children, they usually wish them to remain poor throughout their life or to be stricken with sexual impotence or barrenness respectively. For minor offences, such as

[1] *Kukóŋonda.*   [2] i.e. we did not join in the ownership of the barrel.

disobedience, fathers would often 'curse' their sons by wishing that their penis may bleed excessively when they are circumcised. For a very grave offence, such as a violation of rules of sexual avoidance or physical assault of one's parents, a father may curse his son to become a half-wit or to be afflicted with a disgusting and painful disease 'which will always make him think of his father'. Parents would, however, never curse their children to die, and even if they did so, a curse is not thought powerful enough to kill a person unless it is linked with an act of sorcery.

A person who has pronounced a curse, either over an unknown offender or over a kinsman, does not meet with public disapproval for his action, nor would the victim of the curse ever try to combat the effect of the curse by practising counter-magic directed against its originator. This does not mean, however, that once a curse has been uttered the consequences that arise from it are irrevocable. A curse pronounced against an unknown thief is automatically rendered void as soon as the stolen object has been returned to its owner; other curses can, likewise, be lifted if their originator can be persuaded to forgive the offender and to join with him in a ceremony of appeasement (*okuhóliza*).[1]

Blessings (*okugasidza*, to pronounce a blessing) are the positive counterpart of curses. In particular they correspond to the curses uttered against definite persons, for like these they are potent only within one's clan-group and that of other near kinsmen. They are spoken by the father or other senior relative on such occasions as the name-giving rite, a boy's initiation, the dedication of a new hut, and, sometimes, at marriage. Their aim is to promote the healthy growth of a child and to assure for him material wellbeing and numerous offspring.

(2) PERSONS AND ANIMALS IN A STATE OF RITUAL IMPURITY

The term 'ritual impurity' is an abstraction of a number of closely related notions and in the sense in which it will be used here covers a wide range of phenomena. They all, however, have certain essential features in common: (1) They involve dangers of a mystical nature, either to the person afflicted or to others who come in contact with him, or to both. (2) These dangers of ritual impurity threaten their victim as an automatic consequence of an act which he has committed on purpose or in which he is passively involved without his volition. (3) The actual state of impurity—although its underlying causes may have been latent throughout the victim's life— is only temporary and subsides again either after an appropriate purification ceremony (cf. below, p. 246 sq.) has been performed or after a certain period of time has elapsed. Finally, although a person who passes through such a state of ritual impurity is feared and avoided (cf. below, p. 191 sq.), he is not blamed for his condition, nor is it thought that he will intentionally make use of his dangerousness to inflict harm upon his fellow beings.

[1] See below, p. 256.

AGENTS AND FORCES

Having thus anticipated the common characteristics of the concept of ritual impurity among the Bantu Kavirondo, we can now turn to a discussion of its different types and variants. The most important of these is a state called *luswa* or *kiragi*, the former term referring to persons (and certain animals thought of as persons) and the latter to animals. Accordingly one speaks of *kugwá luswa*, 'to fall *luswa*', and of *kugwá kiragi* respectively. It is a form of ritual pollution known all over Bantu Kavirondo and manifesting itself in a great variety of ways. The following is a list of the more common modes of active and passive behaviour which are regarded as manifestations of *luswa*:

1. If an infant cuts its upper teeth first.
2. If a small child cries excessively without having any apparent reason for doing so. The child's behaviour is then regarded as an expression of its desire to kill its parents. To feel such a desire is expressed by the verb *xusutja* (Vugusu).
3. If at a boy's circumcision his blood 'gushes' out of his wound as if under pressure.
4. If a circumcised person rides on the back of an ox or a cow (as small boys sometimes do when they are herding cattle). To do so before being circumcised is quite normal; afterwards it is a sign of having fallen *luswa*.
5. If a woman climbs upon the roof of a hut. A woman must strictly avoid doing so, as it would be interpreted as an expression of her desire to kill her husband, a desire which is likewise referred to by the verb *xusutja* (see above under (2)). The making and repairing of roofs is, accordingly, exclusively done by male persons. The custom of placing the *ekisuli*-rod on the apex of the roof as a symbol of the male owner of the hut is an expression of the same notion that the roof of a hut is in some mystical way associated with the male sex.
6. All forms of ritually prohibited and incestuous sexual intercourse are regarded as manifestations of *luswa*. In the approximate order of their gravity such offences are: sexual relations between mother and son, father and daughter, a husband and his mother-in-law, a wife and her father-in-law, and a brother and his real or classificatory sister.[1]
7. If a man sees a widow or his mother-in-law in the nude, e.g. while she is bathing in a stream.
8. If a person performs acts of indecency in the presence of a person of opposite sex, e.g. if a husband points his buttocks at his wife while they are quarrelling. Loose talk without any accompanying indecent gestures is regarded as bad manners but not as a sign of having fallen *luswa*.
9. If a beard grows on a woman's chin.

[1] Cf. below, p. 383 sq.

10. If either men or women indulge in homosexual practices.
11. If a man has sexual intercourse with a cow or a sheep.
12. If a hen crows like a cock or alights on the roof of a hut or granary it is regarded as *kiragi*.
13. If a certain bird called *efurusi* drops its excreta upon a person the bird becomes *kiragi*.
14. If a cow twists its tail round the trunk of a tree the cow becomes *luswa* or *kiragi*.
15. If a person passes the garden of a stranger and eats of the crops growing there without asking the owner and it so happens that the owner has not yet eaten of that crop (Maragoli).
16. If a woman has borne twins, the ashes of the fire on which her first meal after delivery has been cooked are dangerous. If she throws these ashes into a stream and a man bathes in the water thus polluted he becomes *luswa*.
17. If a bull-calf jumps on the back of a person.

As these examples show, the active or passive offence which is regarded as a manifestation of *luswa* is, in most cases, a form of direct or indirect sexual perversion or of some other abnormality, as in the case of infants whose upper incisors cut before the lower ones. From the native point of view no distinction is made between those cases of *luswa* that arise from active forms of behaviour such as incest, and those arising from physical peculiarities, such as the growth of a beard on a woman's chin, or from a coincidence, such as the droppings of a bird falling upon a person or the case of a man accidentally seeing his mother-in-law in the nude. In all these cases the person or animal that becomes *luswa* (or *kiragi* respectively) is regarded as the victim of a mystical force[1] acting inside him (or it) and producing one of the various manifestations that have been mentioned. Generally, the consequences of falling into a state of *luswa* are disastrous, both to its immediate victim and to persons who came into contact with him. Unless a purification rite is performed without delay, the person who has 'fallen' *luswa* will rapidly become lean and weak and will finally die by a sudden collapse. Where two people are involved, as in the case of incestuous intercourse, both will suffer the same fate. Of those who come into contact with a person who has fallen *luswa*, the ones in greatest danger are the wife or husband and his (or her) children. They may even die first, for if a person's wives or children die in rapid succession he is suspected of being afflicted with *luswa*. The consequences of falling *luswa* are, however, not always the same. Thus, incestuous relations between siblings will not kill the offenders but 'destroy' the clan; sexual intercourse with animals is supposed to cause the offender to go crazy, while homosexual practices, although they are also classed as manifestations of *luswa*, have no mystical sanction at all. If a cow falls *luswa* (or *kiragi*) it is thought to endanger the lives of all the

[1] Cf. above, p. 94.

people who live on the homestead where it is kept. The same is true, although to a lesser extent, if a chicken becomes a victim of *luswa*. Over such an infected animal, however, no purification rite is performed but it is slaughtered and eaten. Apparently the *luswa* is thought to leave the animal once it is dead, for its meat may be eaten without any ritual precautions having to be taken over it.

Although the force of *luswa* is dangerous only when it becomes manifest in one of the different ways I have enumerated, it does not arise suddenly and from nowhere, but the persons or animals that are overcome by it are thought to have an inherited disposition towards it. This disposition is passed on either in the paternal or the maternal line, but as long as the *luswa* remains latent it does not involve any dangers. Among the Vugusu this disposition towards falling *luswa* is said to reside in the blood, but as such blood differs neither in colour, thickness, nor temperature from normal blood, the disposition as such cannot be detected. I assumed at first that to observe whether the blood that flows from the circumcision wound 'gushes out' would offer such a means of detecting a person's disposition towards falling *luswa*, but my informants maintained that the blood gushes forth only when the *luswa* happens to 'wake up' or 'stand up'[1] on that occasion. Thus, even a lad whose blood behaves in quite a normal way while he is being circumcised may yet have a disposition towards falling *luswa*.

Some of my Vugusu informants claimed that the disposition towards becoming *luswa* does not merely reside in the blood but that it actually can be recognized by a growth of so-called *gamadjumi*. These are folds of skin which look like the labia of the female pudendum (*gamafuli*) and which are said to grow round the anus of persons who have a disposition towards falling *luswa*. Thus, if a person falls *luswa* by committing incest or by indulging in homosexual intercourse or other sexual perversions, it is said that 'it is the *gamadjumi* which have caused him to act like that'. Both men and women can be afflicted with these *gamadjumi*, and in both sexes they are said to cause the same types of abnormal sexual behaviour. When a man is afflicted with them and his children die one after the other, he may call one of his joking relatives (*omukulo*), who will excise them on the public ground, the *oluhia*. In the case of women they were formerly operated when they were circumcised. Such an operation is said 'to finish' the *luswa* and to restore the patient to a normal ritual status.

Next to the state of falling *luswa*, the most important types of ritual impurity or contamination are those known by the terms *vuxútjakáli* (Lurogolis: *vukunzakáli*) and *vusixu*. Both states produce the same kind of dangerousness, but they are derived from different sources. *Vuxútjakáli* is caused by the breath of a dying person and, accordingly, it afflicts everyone who has been in close contact with a dying person, especially a wife

[1] Luvugusu: *luswa lwaminyoxe* (from *xuxwinyoxo*, to wake up or stand up from a lying position).

who has attended to her husband, but also his children and, in the case of a wife's death, her husband, though to a lesser extent only. It is definitely the breath of a dying person and not association with death as such which is thought to produce the state of *vuxútjakāli*, for people do not fear to approach or touch a corpse and no ritual observances are necessary before or after one has done so. *Vuxútjakāli* also afflicts a murderer and a warrior who has slain his first enemy, but in these cases the state of pollution caused by the breath of the dying person is coupled with *vusixu*, the impurity that is caused by association with blood. The *vuxútjakāli*, however, seems to predominate, for a warrior who for the first time has killed an enemy is called *omukāli* and his condition *ovukāli*, a word that is obviously derived from the same root as *vuxútjakāli*.

The common element in all cases that are grouped under the *vusixu* type of ritual impurity is the pollution of a person with human blood, either his own or that of another person. Thus a mother who has given birth and her child are afflicted with it, further, a boy who has just been circumcised as well as the operator and, finally, any person who has inflicted an open wound upon someone else, whether it be fatal or not. The knife or spear employed is likewise polluted and has to be ritually cleansed to become neutral again.

On the other hand, contact with blood originating from a self-inflicted wound (by intention or accident) or from one caused by the bite of an animal, as well as contact with menstrual blood or the bloody discharge from an ulcer or some other inflammation, is not thought to produce *vusixu* or any other type of ritual impurity. It is therefore possible that the ritual impurity from which a new-born child and its mother suffer is not actually caused by *vusixu* but by the so-called *vwivu* smell with which an infant is supposed to be afflicted for the first month or so after its birth and which is likewise considered to be a source of ritual impurity. If this is so, it would appear that the situation of *vusixu* arises only when blood flows as a result of an injury inflicted upon another person but regardless of the motive.

The particular danger attributed to all these conditions of *vuxútjakāli* (*vukunzakāli*), *ovukāli*, *vusixu*, and *vwivu* is that the persons immediately affected and those who come into contact with them will turn pale. Their skin will adopt the yellowish colour of a ripe banana, it will persistently itch, and finally decay like a rotten banana. At the same time these people will become emaciated and gradually lose their physical strength. To prevent this from happening, persons afflicted with these conditions must undergo a number of purification or lustration rites which will be discussed in a subsequent chapter. Besides, while their state of impurity lasts they must be isolated from other people and avoided by them (cf. p. 192).

Related to the *vwivu*-smell which emanates from a new-born child is the condition of *vuxwana*, 'twinship', with which twins are afflicted during the early years of their life. This *vuxwana* is fraught with danger not only to

AGENTS AND FORCES

the twins themselves but also to their parents and siblings and to anyone who directly or indirectly comes into contact with them. It causes the eyelashes to fall out and produces blear-eyes and other eye-diseases. To counteract its force, a number of elaborate ritual precautions have to be taken and maintained throughout the first three or four years of the twins' life. In connexion with these different states of ritual impurity I may, finally, mention the condition that is brought about by the violation of the various food taboos which the members of each clan have imposed upon themselves.[1] Besides causing the offender to vomit and suffer from indigestion it makes his hair fall out and his skin come off in patches. These effects, however, are restricted to the person who has broken the taboo and do not extend to any other persons.

(3) SPECIALISTS

Among the different kinds of specialists that by wielding active mystical power affect the lives and material welfare of their fellow beings, two major categories can be distinguished: the *avalogi* (Luvugusu: *valosi*) and the *avavila*. These two categories of specialists differ chiefly in one important point. Whereas the activities of the *avavila* are socially approved of, even though they are thought occasionally to abuse their power and to inflict harm upon innocent people, the *avalogi* are socially condemned and their activities are always classed as morally bad.[2] This means that the latter never act with the overt or tacit approval of public opinion but always and exclusively against it. I shall now discuss each of these two categories of specialists in turn: the methods employed by them and the (real or alleged) effects produced, the sources from which they derive their powers and the motives which stand behind their actions and, finally, the social attitude that is taken towards them and their magic.

(a) *Avalogi*

Owing to the anti-social nature of their magic, the real or alleged activities of the *avalogi* are always carried on in secrecy. No person would ever publicly admit to being an *omulogi*, and to call somebody by this name is one of the greatest insults one can level against him. It would provoke either

---

[1] cf. below, p. 201.

[2] The same distinction is made, for instance, by E. E. Evans-Pritchard (in an article entitled 'Witchcraft' in *Africa*, vol. viii, p. 417 sq.) and by Raymond Firth. Firth (Modern Discussion Books, vol. ii: *Human Types*) gives the following definitions of the concepts of 'sorcery' and 'witchcraft': (1) 'Sorcery: Performed either by private individuals for themselves or by specialist magicians for others or the community as a whole. Sometimes socially approved, sometimes disapproved. Often a force of social control.' (2) 'Witchcraft: Sometimes attempted, often doubtful if actually performed, and sometimes of imaginary occurrence. Classed as morally bad. Provides a native theory of failure, misfortune, and death.'

a fight or a quarrel, and the person thus insulted would not rest content until he had vindicated himself by swearing an oath or by submitting, together with the accuser, to an ordeal. Nowadays the offence of having called somebody an *omulogi* is frequently brought before the tribal court, and if the offender has no convincing evidence to substantiate his insulting remark a fine is imposed upon him.

Their activities being always carried on in secrecy, a study of the *avalogi* means in practice a study of the various forms of behaviour attributed to them and it is, therefore, impossible to say to what extent these alleged activities are ever actually carried out and how far they are mere products of the imagination. My informants, including even baptized Christians of long standing, assured me with the same unshaken sense of conviction that *avalogi* have the habit of keeping grown leopards as pets in the lofts of their huts, that they try to make people ill by performing magical rites over certain poisonous medicines and uttering evil spells against them, or that they reduce the pile of grain crops heaped up in the yard of a homestead to a small fraction of its former size merely by casting the evil eye on it. The native attitude towards the reality of the practices of *avalogi* is thus not graded according to what can and what cannot be substantiated by observed or observable behaviour, and it seems futile to base any classification of the different types of *avalogi* on the criterion of the relative possibility or impossibility of the qualities and activities ascribed to them. There are, however, a number of other respects in which the various *avalogi* differ from one another, such as the motives and incentives for their practices, the sources from which their powers are derived, the methods and techniques employed by them, and the relative potency of their power as well as the kinds of effects produced by it. After we have examined all these points we shall be able to find a basis for a classification of *avalogi* into different types. As the beliefs that are held with regard to the *avalogi* differ to some extent in the different sub-areas of Kavirondo I shall, for reasons of clarity, deal with them separately and begin with the tribe of the Vugusu.

Vulosi, an abstract Vugusu noun referring collectively to the activities of *valosi*, can be practised by both male and female persons. Each of the two sexes, however, has specialized in a number of different techniques, and different kinds of misfortunes are attributed to each of them. According to these techniques, the following specialists are distinguished in the native terminology:

Male *valosi*	Female *valosi*
(1) *ovinásitjula* (who dances naked)	(1) *ómuvini* (the dancer)
(2) *omurori* (the collector)	(2) *omurori* (the collector)
(3) *omusindixilisi* (the one who causes one to run into danger)	(3) *ómuxupi owè vílasila* (the thrower of *vílasila*)

(4) *omuxingi*
   (the one who hides deadly medicines)

(4) *omufúndilili*
   (the one who infects the food of others)

(5) *omuxondoli*
   (evil eye)

The specialists known by these terms are not necessarily different persons, but one and the same person may practise several techniques. He is most likely to do so if he has practised his art for a long time and if, through repeated successes, the confidence in his power has become firmly established. As will be seen from the above list, the 'dancers' and the 'collectors' may be either men or women, while the *vasíndixilisi* and the *vaxingi* are always men and the *váxupi* and the *vafúndilili* always women.

The *ovinásitjula*. When one asks a casual informant what an *omulosi* is he will, as a rule, begin to give an account of the activities of an *ovinásitjula* and then add that *valosi* also practise various other techniques. As I have found the same to be true among the Logoli and the other tribes I have visited, it appears that the *ovinásitjula* is the prototype of an *omulosi*.[1] He is said to leave his hut in the middle of the night when there is no moon and the people are fast asleep in their huts. He goes completely naked, so as to avoid any unnecessary noise which his clothes or ornaments might make while he moves about. To make his skin dull, he rubs ashes from his wife's fire-place all over his body. Thus he proceeds to the homestead of his victim and dances about in his yard, jumping up and down and suddenly pointing his buttocks at the door of his victim's hut or banging against it just before running off again. If his antics awaken the inhabitants of the house and they come out, he will not put up a fight but dash away as quickly as he can.

As a result of his dance the inmates of the hut, and in particular the person to whom the dance is addressed, will get ill, suffering from headaches and pain in their muscles. If the owner of the hut happens to be away, the *ovinásitjula* will try to enter it and throw some of his own or his children's excreta into the hut, either on the floor or into one of the pots. When the owner comes home and notices the smell he knows that his house has been visited by an *ovinásitjula* and he will then soon begin to suffer from the same symptoms as if he had been at home. By dancing in the same fashion in front of a cattle kraal, the *ovinásitjula* can also cause cattle to become sick. While performing these dances he does not utter a spell, but he may in a low voice hum a song, such as this one:

> *Xane yona namwe nonaka*,
> 'Perhaps I do well, or I do badly',

i.e. perhaps my dance will make my victim ill, perhaps it will be in vain. The dancing and singing, however, are not in themselves capable of pro-

[1] Cf. also accounts of the *omulosi* in other parts of Bantu Africa (Blohm, Smith, Junod, Hunter).

ducing the desired result, but they must be coupled with the power that emanates from the *gamalogo*, i.e. roots or small pieces of bark which the *omulosi* keeps in his house and over which he uttered a spell while he ritually tied them into a small bundle. The *gamalogo* and the dancing at the victim's homestead thus act together to produce the illness.

To protect him from being caught while he performs his antics, the *ovinásitjula's* wife must stay home and roast a single sesame seed in a broken potsherd, turning it continually with her right index-finger to prevent its being burnt.

During the daytime the *ovinásitjula* behaves in the same way as ordinary people and only his tired look may cause people to suspect him of having been out all night, but this furnishes no certain evidence against him.

A female *ovinásitjula* or *omuvini* also dances naked, but while she does so she holds a chick (male or female) to her chest. The suppressed gobbling of this chick is said to increase the effect of her dance and of the *gamalogo* which she has 'tied'. While dancing about, she sings in a low voice:

Ese omulosi namagangala orindoka vari saloga,

'I am an *omulosi*, I am Magangala; if I bewitch they say I do not bewitch.'

Which means: Although I am a witch and dance about, the people do not know what I am doing. The victims of a female *ovinásitjula* are said to be children only and never adult persons.

The *omurori*. A second method employed by *valosi* is to procure objects associated with their intended victim such as remains of food they have eaten, parts of their clothing or ornaments, hair, nails, excreta, or soil taken from their footprints. Such objects are secretly collected by the *omulosi*, whence he is called *omurori* (from *xurora*, to collect). To use them for his evil purposes, he must tie them together with certain poisonous or magically destructive roots (*gamalesi*) which he either collects afresh each time or of which he hides a small store somewhere near his house where nobody will find them. The destructive powers of these roots will then affect the objects, and being associated with the victim their destruction will by sympathy destroy him. When he has tied the two objects in a small bundle he 'traps' the bundle in a tiny gourd, in a section of reed-grass, or in a beer-strainer, so that no other force will be able to interfere with it. While doing so he utters a destructive spell over the bundle, saying:

> *Wanangali kuno gwamenya ano*
> *ne kurakara kila*
> *ano gwalexa ewavwe kuxoya*
> *gwafwa!*

> 'The bad person may stay here,
> he still walks briskly;
> he will leave the place where he is,
> he must die!'

The *omurori* must utter this spell at night and in the privacy of his hut, and only his wife may know what he is doing. Then he takes the 'trapped' *gamalogo* and hides them either under the roof or outside in a hollow tree or in a pit which he digs near a stream. As soon as the objects procured from his victim begin to decay, the latter will fall ill and suffer from headaches, perspiration, and pains in his joints. If the *omurori* has collected a person's faeces and hidden them in the damp soil near a stream, the victim will suffer from diarrhoea. Like the illness caused by the *ovinásitjula*, that brought about by the *omurori* will not manifest itself in a sudden and violent outbreak but in a slow wasting away of the victim's health.

Female *varori* employ the same methods as their male counterparts. When married the two often work together, the husband gathering the destructive roots and the wife procuring the objects associated with the victim. Women are thought to be particularly apt to practise *vurori*, as they have better opportunities than men of entering other peoples' homes and of collecting the desired objects.

The *omusíndixilisi*. A third method of inflicting harm upon other persons is employed by male *valosi* called *avasíndixilisi*. This term is derived from the verb *xusindixilisia*, 'to cause to fall on', because the expert who wields this type of evil magic is supposed to cause people to fall victims to sudden accidents or mishaps. The accidents for which *vasindixilisi* are most frequently held responsible are snake-bites, attacks by wild animals, especially while hunting, drowning while fording a stream, or falling from a tree and breaking one's limbs. Nowadays accidents with motor-cars or bicycles are exclusively attributed to the evil intentions of an *omusíndixilisi*. Serious quarrels that lead to fighting as well as suicides are also attributed to his magic, which will affect the minds of his victims in such a way that they will provoke a fight or kill themselves.

The technique employed by the *omusíndixilisi* is to kill a special kind of lizard or to procure a chicken-egg from his intended victim's homestead. These objects he must cut open and put some of his poisonous roots (*gamalesi*) inside. Then, without tying it, he hides the object at a place near which the intended victim will pass or over which he will step. While burying it there he mutters a spell, specifying the kind of accident or death which he desires his victim to meet with, e.g. *ese ngana leve afwe, endemu emulume*, 'I want So-and-so may die, a snake may bite him.' The power emanating from the hidden substance over which the spell has been uttered will then cause the intended victim of his magic to meet with the kind of accident specified by the spell. The efficacy of *vusíndixilisi* magic consists in influencing the victim's mind in such a way that he exposes himself to danger or fails to save himself when he suddenly confronts a dangerous situation. Thus the *omusíndixilisi* is not thought to be capable of controlling the force which kills the victim, i.e. he has no influence over the snake, the crocodile, the falling tree, or whatever else may be the immediate cause of the victim's death. Nor does the *omusíndixilisi* have any prescience as to the movements of the animals, &c., that would permit him to direct his victim towards them; all he can do is to influence his victim's mind so that it will dispense with the usual caution and alertness when it suddenly meets with a dangerous situation. This fact is significant, as it shows that the power attributed to the *omusíndixilisi* is far more limited than might be expected from a mere account of the effects of his magic.

There are no restrictions as to the potential victims of an *omusíndixilisi*. While only men practise *vusíndixilisi*,[1] they can employ their magic against persons of either sex and against strangers as well as close relatives, although they never direct it against their wives and children. They are said to favour their own brothers as victims of *vusíndixilisi*-magic, so that they may inherit the latters' wives or get a larger share in their father's legacy. A person would be suspected of having practised *vusíndixilisi* if he had quarrelled with or threatened somebody who a few days afterwards fell victim to an accident.

The *omuxingi*. By far the most dangerous type of *omulosi* is the specialist known as *omuxingi*. Like the *omusíndixilisi*, he is always a man and his technique consists in hiding poisonous objects (*gímisala*) at a spot over which his victim will pass. But these *gímisala* are supposed to be so powerful that their lethal effect is assured merely by placing them in the gateway or under the path of the victim's homestead. No spells need to be uttered over them and no magical preparations, such as tying them into a bundle together with objects procured from the victim, are required to render them efficacious. However, being so powerful that they will kill a person within a few hours merely by emanating their poison through the air, their occurrence is extremely rare and even more so are the *avalosi* who have a knowledge of these *gímisala* and who can handle them with impunity.

The *ómuxupi owe vílasila* and the *omuxondoli*. Of the exclusively female *valosi* the most conspicuous type among the Vugusu is the *ómuxupi owe vílasila*, the 'thrower of *vílasila*'. These *vílasila* are tiny objects, such as hairs, bits of grass, beans, splinters of bones, &c., which in a mysterious way are transmitted from the *ómuxupi owe vílasila* into the body of her victim. When these objects have entered the victim's body they cause acute sickness, a swollen stomach, and cramps accompanied by vomiting, an intense headache, hot temples, and a generally feverish condition. In short, all the symptoms of acute food-poisoning are regarded as an indication of the presence of *vílasila* particles in one's body.

These *vílasila* are thought to emanate from the eyes of the *ómuxupi* while she winks at her victim or casts a quick glance at him sideways. To be efficacious her glance must be accompanied by an evil wish addressed to the victim, but no actual spell needs to be uttered by her. To increase the power of their evil eye some *avaxupi* are said to rub or wash their eyes with a certain medicine prepared by them for that purpose.

---

[1] The prefix *vu*- denotes the activity practised by the *omusíndixilisi*.

While the *vilasila* emerge from the *ómuxupi*'s eyes and fly through the air they are 'like shadows', but once they have entered the victim's body they become solid substances again. Although emitted exclusively from the *ómuxupi*'s eyes, they may enter the victim's body anywhere and not necessarily through its eyes. It is, therefore, not necessary to look into the eyes of an *ómuxupi owe vilasila* in order to fall a victim to her magic.

The peculiar power with which the *ómuxupi owe vilasila* is endowed is exclusively passed on by inheritance from mother to daughter. It cannot be acquired by purchase, nor can it be taught to someone who has not inherited the disposition for it from her mother. A woman's power to transmit *vilasila* reaches its peak at middle age, although she may begin to practise her art when she is still an unmarried girl. An *ómuxupi owe vilasila* is particularly active in the early stages of her pregnancy, and the more children she has killed or made ill during her pregnancy, the better will her own child thrive and grow. As she gets past childbearing her power of transmitting *vilasila* gradually decreases until finally it entirely expires. Thus, unlike the power of uttering curses which increases with age, the power of the evil eye is associated with the prime of life and with sexual fecundity.

The *ómuxupi owe vilasila* chooses for her victims mainly the children of women whom she dislikes or who have quarrelled with her, but she may also direct her magic against men and adult women. Although the driving force behind her activities is an inherited disposition, the *ómuxupi owe vilasila* is not just a passive vehicle of that force, but employs her powers consciously and with the clear intention of inflicting harm upon a definite victim.

Besides human beings she can also transmit the *vilasila* to calves which will then refuse to suck and consequently grow lean.

A similar effect is produced by yet another type of female *omulosi*, the so-called *omuxondoli*. Her magic is based exclusively upon the power of her evil eye. By means of it she threatens particularly the eleusine crop when it has been piled up in the yard of the homestead to dry. As the result of her evil eye the heap of millet is suddenly reduced to a fraction of its former bulk. Strangely, an *omuxondoli* can inflict no harm to the crops while they are still growing in the field.

Another type of female *omulosi*, finally, is the *omufúndilili*. Her technique consists in secretly putting certain particles, alleged to cause stomach pain and vomiting, into the milking-gourd, &c., of her victims. These particles or substances (*vifúndilila*) vary in their efficacy. Some, like the hair of a dead fox or a hair pulled from her private parts, cause the victim to get ill, while others, like the dung of a hyena, will kill it within a few hours. Like the *gimisala* employed by her male counterpart, the *omuxingi*, the *vifúndilila* act on their own account without being accompanied by a spell or having to be handled in a ritual manner. The *omufúndilili* acts from the same motives as the *ómuxupi owe vilasila* and her victims are, likewise, mainly children. She acquires her knowledge by being taught by her mother or paternal aunt (*senge*), but no particular inherited disposition is required for practising *ovufúndilili* magic.

Having discussed the various techniques used by the different types of male and female *valosi* and the effects which their alleged destructive activities are supposed to have on their fellow beings, we can now turn to the question of the motives and incentives which are thought to account for the anti-social behaviour common to all types of *valosi*.

The question of the motive behind the activities of an *omulosi* is closely linked up with that of the acquisition of the particular knowledge and disposition which the *omulosi* must possess to be able to practise his evil magic. We have already stated that in each of the different types of magic employed by the *avalosi* it is not merely the inherent virtue of the magical substance which produces the desired effect but the combination of several factors or conditions, such as the contact of an object procured from the victim with a strong poisonous root, both being tied into a bundle in a ritual manner while a spell is uttered over it. The most important of these conditions, which applies to all forms of *ovulosi* magic, is that the person who handles the magical substance *must* be an *omulosi*. This means that over and above the proper handling of medicine, spell, magical gestures, and rites, the wielder of *vulosi* must be a man 'entitled'[1] to the possession of these things and endowed with the mystical power of handling the destructive and poisonous objects and implements of his craft with impunity. Should an ordinary person, a man free from *vulosi*, come into the possession of the various objects and medicines used by an *omulosi* and should he even acquire a knowledge of the appropriate spells and the manner of handling the objects by secretly observing an *omulosi* at work, he still could not succeed in inflicting harm upon another person, as he lacked the chief prerequisite, viz. the quality of being an *omulosi*. He would merely run the risk of himself falling a victim to the destructive substances which he has handled without being entitled to do so.

How then does a person acquire this particular quality of being an *omulosi*? Among the Vugusu there is only one way of becoming an *omulosi*, viz. by inheriting an intrinsic disposition, in addition to which special knowledge and skill must be acquired. The disposition for becoming an *omulosi* can be passed on both in male and in female line, and is inherited either directly from one's father or mother or indirectly from one's maternal uncle or paternal aunt respectively. An *omusíndixilisi*, for example, may have inherited his disposition either from his father or from his mother's brother, even if his mother herself did not practise any type of *vulosi*, and, correspondingly, an *ómuxupi owe vílasila* may have inherited the evil eye either from her mother or from her father's sister (*senge*)

---

[1] The expression 'entitled' refers in this connexion only to the laws inherent in the notions of witchcraft and sorcery and has, of course, nothing to do with any approval of these practices by the community.

irrespective of her father's knowledge of *ovulosi*. However, what is inherited is merely the latent disposition for becoming an *omulosi*, and unless this is supplemented by teaching and training, it will remain inoperative throughout a person's life.

It is doubtful whether the disposition towards practising *ovulosi* is thought to have a material basis or seat in the body or whether it is regarded merely as a trait of character. None of my informants ever mentioned an organ as the seat of *ovulosi* (excepting, of course, the eye in the case of the *ómuxupi owe vílasila*), but some insisted that it is a disposition of the blood which prompts the *valosi* to leave their hut in the middle of the night to dance.

The first person who is said to have introduced and practised *ovulosi* among the Vugusu is Maina, the eldest son of Muvugusu, the tribal ancestor. According to the tribal tradition, Maina acquired both the general disposition towards practising *ovulosi* magic and the particular knowledge of it from his maternal uncle who was a Mumasava (a Mugishu) and at whose place he spent some years of his childhood. When he returned from there to his father's place he began to frighten cattle by shooing at them. Although his father, Muvugusu, scolded him for his behaviour, he continued to practise those things which his maternal uncle had taught him and to collect the various *gamalesi* (poisonous roots) with which he caused other people to die. Having inherited Maina's knowledge and disposition and having succeeded him in his evil practices, members of the clan that descended from him, the Vakitwika, have become the foremost *valosi* in the whole tribe. Other clans, like the Valiuli and Navuya, acquired the possession of *ovulosi* later on by intermarrying both with the Vakitwika and with clans of other tribes, such as the Kakalelwa, who are reputed for their knowledge of *ovulosi*. Nowadays some *avalosi* are supposed to live in every clan, but in each case it would theoretically be possible to trace the presence of an *omulosi* to a previous *omulosi* in his paternal or maternal line of ancestors. In practice I could, of course, never check this allegation as it would be quite impossible to go to a suspected *omulosi* and ask him from which one of his ancestors he had inherited his powers.

As has already been stated, the mere disposition for becoming an *omulosi* does not suffice to practise *ovulosi*, nor does it render the person immune against the magic wielded by other *valosi*. To become operative the latent disposition must 'break forth'. In the case of a prospective *ovinásitjula*, for example, this breaking forth of the power of *ovulosi* takes the form of an irresistible desire to go out at night and dance, in harbouring ill will and unfounded grudges against other people, and in a tendency to use rough and uncouth language, making frequent use of the derogatory prefix *gu-* instead of *omu-*. In addition, the novice requires special knowledge before he can begin to engage in his evil practices. This knowledge can be imparted to him either by teaching and training or by visions or dreams revealing to him all the required knowledge in the form of visions.

The process of teaching a child to become an *omulosi* is quite elaborate and takes a long time. Thus, a father (who is himself an *omulosi*) would begin by teaching his son to frighten the cattle of other people by hiding in the bush and suddenly jumping at them when they are driven past. Next, he would show him where to find poisonous roots (*gamalesi*) and how to handle and preserve them. Only at an advanced stage would he instruct him how to procure personal objects from other people and carry them home between the fingers of his hands, giving the impression that his hands are quite empty. Finally, he will teach him how to tie the personal objects procured and the *gamalesi* into a bundle and what spells to utter over them while doing so. However, a father or uncle will never transmit his entire knowledge to his son or nephew, thus making sure that he will always remain more powerful than his pupil and preventing the latter from turning the knowledge that he has gained against his own teacher. Besides, there appears to exist a notion that an *omulosi* gains immunity from the objects, spells, and rites which he handles, so that there is no danger that—in ordinary circumstances—an *omulosi* may come to grief by having his own magic turned against him.

The second method of 'bringing out' the disposition for becoming an *omulosi*, that of appearing to the chosen person in a dream, is said to be used by the spirits of deceased *avalosi* who have neglected to pass on their knowledge while they were still alive. Thus, they appear to their chosen successor in a single or in repeated dreams and impart to him all the knowledge which he requires to practise *ovulosi* of one kind or another. They are said to appear to the novice either as the persons they were in actual life or in the form of animals, particularly cats.

My Vugusu informants insisted very firmly that the knowledge of *ovulosi*, whether acquired by means of instruction or through dreams, can be handed on exclusively to those persons who, owing to their direct or indirect descent from an *omulosi* in male or female line, are endowed with the disposition for becoming an *omulosi*. Thus no *omulosi* can ever teach an *omuravola*, i.e. a person free from *ovulosi*, for payment, no matter how much the latter offers him or how much the former likes his would-be pupil. Even if he did teach him, his pupil would never be able successfully to practise *ovulosi*, as he would lack the inherited disposition for it. Succession to the practice of *ovulosi* is further restricted by the fact that its knowledge can only be passed on from a member of a senior generation to one of a junior generation. Thus, a father can teach his son or an uncle his nephew, but a brother can never teach his brother or a sister her sister. A father is said to choose only one or two out of four or five sons to succeed him as *valosi*, and he does so secretly without letting his other sons know. If a person has reason to suspect his brother of having acquired the knowledge of *ovulosi* either from his father or maternal uncle, he would fear and avoid him and, if possible, move away, as it is generally thought that a person will make use of his newly acquired knowledge to kill his brothers, so that he may inherit their wives and their cattle or claims to cattle.

An *omulosi* will, as a rule, marry a woman who is herself a specialist in the female branches of *ovulosi*, partly because the two can then work together, and partly because it will be difficult for a notorious *omulosi* to obtain a wife who is 'free from *ovulosi*' (i.e. an *omuravola*), and vice versa. However, should he escape being suspected of practising *ovulosi* and marry a woman who is unaware of his secret activities, he will nevertheless confide in her, for he cannot practise his craft without his wife's knowledge and help. He can then train his wife to become a kind of assistant to him, but this does not enable her to practise *ovulosi* herself, unless she has an inherited disposition for it.

Stories are frequently told, and even cases brought before the tribal courts, of newly married women who had run away from their husbands because they had found out that the latter were practising *ovulosi*, and also of men who after their marriage had discovered that their wives were *avaxupi owe vilasila* or *avafúndilili*. If a husband frequently beats his wife in his hut without apparent reason, people say that he tries to show her his technique of killing people by *ovulosi* and that she refuses to be taught. If she runs off to her parents or brothers to complain of her husband's secret activities they will, as a rule, send her back and ask her to keep quiet, as otherwise her husband might try to kill her and them as well.

We see then that according to the native theory a person does not become an *omulosi* and practise his evil art according to his own free will, but as a result of having inherited a disposition towards it and of having been singled out and instructed in the special knowledge of *ovulosi* by one of his senior relatives. Nevertheless, an *omulosi* is not thought to act altogether wantonly, harming or killing people indiscriminately by his magic, but in each particular case he acts from a more or less clearly defined motive. He is said to choose his victims from among those people who have quarrelled with him or who show that they despise him, and generally he prefers to direct his magic against people who are wealthy (in cattle, women, or children) rather than against people who are poor and lead inconspicuous lives. The *omulosi* thus acts out of a feeling of envy and inferiority and hopes that as a result of his evil practices his own good luck and prosperity will increase. This is especially apparent in the case of the female *omulosi* who is alleged to be most strongly bent upon inflicting harm on other people during her state of pregnancy, as the illness or even death of other children are necessary to make her own child grow in her womb. The same idea, even if slightly less pronounced, applies to the male *omulosi*. If a wife were to complain to her husband about his evil practices and implore him to leave off sending disease and death to other people he would reply to her: 'How can I leave off doing what is my custom? If

I were to stop practising *ovulosi* we would get weak and lean, our children would die and our possessions would dwindle!' The *valosi* among the Vugusu are thus conceived of as a sort of vampire who for their own welfare and prosperity depend upon the misfortune and death of their fellow beings. In each particular case where they employ their destructive powers they do so consciously and deliberately, but on the whole they practise their magic under the impulse of the peculiar force which by inheritance and teaching has been implanted in their personalities and which they cannot renounce without coming to grief themselves. One therefore says of a person who practises *ovulosi*: 'Once an *omulosi* always an *omulosi*', and thinks that it is quite impossible for an *omulosi* to give up his practices altogether, even if he has been converted to Christianity and pledged himself to lead a new life.[1]

Apart from the vampire-like urge to practise *ovulosi*, the prospect of material gain by taking orders from clients appears only as a secondary incentive for the *omulosi*. *Valosi*, especially those who work as *vasindixilisi* and *vaxingi*, are said to undertake killing people by their magic on behalf of a client in return for the initial payment of a bull or a heifer and another bull after the job has been done. However, as an *omulosi* never advertises his special knowledge and, on the contrary, strongly rejects any suggestion that he might be an *omulosi*, even towards his near relatives, such clients can only be very intimate friends.

This, finally, leads to the question of the general attitude which the Vugusu take towards the whole phenomenon of *ovulosi* and towards the personality of the *omulosi*. Do they regard *ovulosi* as a pest that devastates their lives, and the different kinds of *valosi* as criminals or dangerous lunatics that must be hunted down and stamped out, or do they regard both as phenomena that must be taken for granted and endured? From numerous conversations on this subject I have come to the conclusion that the Vugusu take the existence of *valosi* for granted and that it does not occur to them to take concerted and wholesale action against them. (There are no anti-witchcraft drives among the Vugusu such as have been reported from other parts of Africa.)[2] When I inquired into the existence of any organized methods of combating or stamping out *ovulosi* I was told that 'people cannot do anything against it as it started long ago'. Although the number of people believed to be actively engaged in practising *ovulosi* appears to be relatively small (estimates by my informants varied between one and five in a hundred), a much greater number of people is, as we have seen, supposed to have an inherited disposition towards becoming *valosi*, and their latent qualities might 'come out' if the active practitioners were concertedly attacked and decimated. Thus, as a potential force *vulosi*

---

[1] The actual words in which this idea was expressed to me were: *owe kumwina gwewe salexa xukuxola*, 'of his custom he cannot leave doing it'.

[2] Cf. Audrey Richards, 'A Modern Movement of Witch-finders', *Africa*, 1935, pp. 448–61.

is overwhelming and almost ubiquitous, and the belief in the existence of this vast reservoir of potential *vulosi* makes it appear much too formidable a power to encourage any attempts at its wholesale destruction. People therefore put up with it, and the idea seems to prevail that since their forefathers had to endure *vulosi*, the present generation must endure it as well. When a person has actually died and emotions run high, the *omuseni*, the public comforter, points out to the mourners that 'people have died from long ago and that they should not harbour any feelings of revenge'. Since the great majority of deaths are attributed to the evil work of *valosi*, this consolation implicitly asks the bereaved passively to accept the destructive activities of the *valosi* and to refrain from revolting against them, as this would merely increase the misfortune which has overtaken them.

But although the existence of *ovulosi* as such is taken for granted, people are by no means indifferent towards the dangers which, in their opinion, are constantly threatening them from this mysterious power. Individually, they try to protect themselves by various types of magic which we shall discuss below (p. 182 sq.). Besides, people try to avoid arousing the envy or hatred of potential *valosi* by refraining from boasting of their health or wealth or doing anything which deviates very noticeably from the ordinary life that all people lead. The universal reluctance of the natives to reveal their exact wealth in cattle, land, or stored grain, their unwillingness to admit having many children, and their insistence on being in a poor state of health when actually they are quite fit, are all matter-of-fact or routine precautions against being singled out as a victim of an envious and evil-wishing *omulosi*.

But there is also a collective response to danger from *ovulosi*. If within a limited area a number of deaths occur in rapid succession this is regarded as a sign that *vulosi* is rampant there. Consequently even those families not directly affected will leave their homesteads, hoping thereby to escape the threatening danger. In some of the genealogies I have taken down, movements of sections of a lineage were accounted for by such motives. Some of my informants even claimed that the eastward migration of the Vugusu during the past fifty years was largely undertaken by people who wanted to get away from the threatening dangers of *vulosi*. This statement is supported by the fact that a far greater number of diviners and other specialists practising anti-witchcraft live in the western and southern part of the Vugusu country (South Kitosh) than in the more recently settled eastern part.

The Logoli even have a special term, *eliamwama*, which designates a cluster of homesteads that have been abandoned because they are thought to be infested with destructive magic. Although it is extremely difficult to obtain precise and reliable data on this subject, the frequency and regularity with which my informants in all parts of Bantu Kavirondo mentioned fear of witchcraft as one of the prime causes of migration leads me to believe that this is indeed a factor of wide importance which should be taken into consideration along with such motives as search for better pasture or richer soil for cultivation or the retreat from the raids of a more powerful neighbouring tribe.[1]

It will be seen that all these different ways of responding to the dangers of *vulosi* are passive and defensive rather than aggressive. While this is true in a general way it is also true of the specific attitude displayed towards a particular person who is suspected of practising *ovulosi*. As long as the suspicion remains only vague and is based upon peculiarities in his behaviour and appearance rather than upon actual cases of disease or death for which he is held responsible, his neighbours will maintain the same social relations with him as with any other person. This behaviour, however, is not due so much to indifference as to the fear of provoking resentment on the part of the suspected *omulosi*. An *omulosi* is thus a person who must be treated with circumspection and this, in fact, raises his status and influence in the community. Nevertheless, he can never overtly make use of this instrument of gaining prestige, for publicly he must disclaim all knowledge of *ovulosi* and give the impression that he despises it just as much as anybody else. At the same time, the actual influence which a person wields over his fellow beings by having the reputation of being an *omulosi* explains why *valosi* in many little ways betray their true character, e.g. by using rough language, by uttering ambiguous threats to persons whom they dislike, &c. If it were altogether to their disadvantage to be suspected of practising *ovulosi* one would expect them to avoid any forms of behaviour which might give them away. But since a vague suspicion increases their influence it becomes clear why they indulge in giving hints of what they are without, however, giving any real evidence away.

If a person harbours a very definite suspicion against an *omulosi* and especially if he fears that his own relations with him are strained, he will avoid him as much as possible so as to prevent him from procuring objects closely associated with his body or from poisoning his food. When visiting his house he will, if possible, refuse to accept food, and if he cannot do so without offending his host he will see to it that his host eats first to prove that the food is not poisoned. To save one's guest this predicament it is a rule of etiquette for the host always to taste first of any food or drink that he offers to his guest.

If it appears necessary to take action against a suspected *omulosi* this is seldom done in the form of a straightforward accusation of the suspected person, for few people dare publicly to challenge an *omulosi* in this way. The various methods of counteracting his magic which will be discussed below (see pp. 257–77) likewise show that *valosi* are, as a rule, not fought openly but in a carefully guarded way which avoids any direct action

[1] It is even said among the Vugusu that ordinary people who covet their neighbour's land try to induce them to move away by placing eggs or drops of blood near their door, hoping that in their fear of being haunted by an *omulosi* they will migrate to another place.

against a definite person and which exposes his opponent as little as possible to the *omulosi*'s revenge. It seems that only in very exceptional circumstances have *valosi* ever been put to death. Even then they were not executed after the elders had passed a judgement over them in cold blood, but were lynched by as large a group of persons as possible brought into a state of frenzied fear and rage after a rapid succession of fatal diseases or misfortunes among their kinsmen. The idea then was that by splitting up the responsibility for the *omulosi*'s death among a large number of persons each of them had little to fear from the *omulosi*'s revenge.

Having discussed the different types of specialists wielding mystical power among the Vugusu I shall now turn to the Logoli and examine in what respects the beliefs held by them differ from those of the former. Among the Logoli the notion of *ovulogi*, as it is called by them, likewise exists and essentially the same techniques and the same powers are attributed by them to the various types of *avalogi*.

The *omulogi* proper is nearly always a male person and he corresponds in his activities to the *ovinásitjula* of the Vugusu. My informants in fact knew only one woman who used to dance like the male *avalogi*, and she is said to have been found out and killed by the people many years ago. As among the Vugusu, the *omulogi* dances in the yard of other people's homesteads at night, bangs at their doors, and frightens their cattle. He is also said to waylay people at night when they return from a journey or from a beer drink and choke them to death. As well as dancing at night and assaulting people he also prepares evil medicines (*amalogo*) consisting of bundles in which poisonous roots or herbs and objects procured from the victim of his magic are tied together. But the same person never procures objects and concocts the medicine as is the case among the Vugusu. The task of collecting is, among the Logoli, attributed to the *omukingi*, who also hides the medicine concocted by the *omulogi* under the doorway or near the path leading to the intended victim's homestead. The *omukingi* is thus a kind of assistant to the *omulogi* and the two always work hand in hand. If he is skilful he may later be taught by his master how and where to collect roots and herbs and how to concoct them into the destructive *amalogo*, but once he has learnt this art he does not practise *ovukingi* any longer. The *omukingi* of the Logoli is thus a far less important specialist than the *omuxingi* of the Vugusu and the only characteristic that the two have in common is that they both place destructive magic in the path of their victims.

The Logoli counterpart of the *omusíndixilisi* is the *omusíndiki*: he likewise causes people to commit suicide or meet with accidents, but he does not make use of any magical substances for this end but merely of bad words, *emiŋana miví*. He is therefore also called *ogunua guví*,[1] 'the bad mouth', and his death-spells are always uttered in a harsh and rasping

---

[1] The prefix *ogu-* (taking the place of *omu-*) implies contempt and disgust (it expresses the notions of 'big, old, ugly').

voice. The wording of his spells is not fixed and they may even sound quite harmless. But they are actual spells in the sense that their magical virtue lies in the words uttered and not in a material substance or a rite performed along with the utterance of words. As among the Vugusu, the *omusindiki* is always a man.

There exists, of course, no *omurori* among the Logoli as his functions are performed by the *omukingi* who both collects and hides the objects associated with the victim and used in the manufacture of the destructive bundles.

Of the female *avalogi* the Logoli counterpart to the *ómuxupi owe vílasila* is the *omulasi wevikoko*, 'the thrower or shooter of *evikoko*'. *Evikoko* are the same small objects which among the Vugusu are called *vílasila*. The methods employed by her and the effects produced have been described to me in the following text:

'There exists an *omulogi* of *evikoko* and that is always a female person. The *elilogo* (evil medicine) of this woman is that which is called *evikoko*. This *ovulogi* which causes colic (*ovusula*) comes from (i.e. emanates from) the eyes (of the woman); she can shoot it into the eyes of another person and she can bewitch (*okuloga*) anybody. If she meets a child or an old man or another woman she does not choose and think: "This is a person whom I cannot bewitch." Then she bewitches everyone indeed (i.e. she does not discriminate in the choice of her victims). She begins to bewitch people on the day she wants to conceive; then now she begins to bewitch when she meets with another woman. She looks at her when they meet on the path; then when the woman whom she has met arrives home or wherever she was going she can say, "I have met another woman on the road, it must be on account of her that I am sick indeed, the eye (i.e. the evil glance of the *omulasi wevikoko*) will kill me; perhaps she has splashed much *ovusula* into my eyes." It is the *evikoko* in the belly (which cause the sickness). It is also difficult for a woman who is an *omulogi* to pass near the place where they are threshing the grain, near the threshing floor or the yard, or even anywhere near the house.'

As this text shows, the *omulasi wevikoko* corresponds in all essentials to the *owe vílasila*.[1] However, while the *owe vílasila*—according to the information I have—by casting her evil glance transmits purely imaginary objects into her victim's body, the *wevikoko*[2] must first gather her objects (the *evikoko*) from the people whom she wants to harm. She thus employs the same technique as the *omurori* or the *omukingi*. At her home she keeps the *evikoko* (which she has procured from her intended victims) hidden away in a pot. Before starting off to send forth her magic she mixes them with ashes of the *ekisugi* and *kisongulwa* plants. I could not discover for certain whether she is supposed to utter a spell while doing so or not. Then she grinds the mixture in a mortar, and the powder thus obtained she carries with her in a small bag (*akamuya* or *akadígolo*) which she hides underneath her clothes. What actually happens when she meets her

[1] The one of the *vílasila*, abridged for *ómuxupi owe vílasila*.
[2] Abridged form of *omulasi wevikoko*.

intended victim is that by looking or winking at him she transmits the *evikoko* from inside her little bag into the other person's body. Her evil eye is thus merely instrumental in making her magic work, but it does not in itself produce the disease which is brought about by the same type of magic as that employed by the male *omulogi* in conjunction with the *omukingi*. An object is procured that is closely associated with the victim, and after having been magically infested by mixing or tying it with poisonous matter, it is again brought into material or mystical contact with its owner.

Besides the *omulasi wevikoko* the Logoli recognize another specialist who employs the evil eye or the eyil look (*emoni embi* or *elihenza livi*), the so-called *omusohi*. Whereas the *wevikoko* must always be a woman, the *avasohi* may occasionally also be male persons. They use no medicines of any kind and no spells, but work exclusively through the power of their eyes. Before or while they cast their evil eye upon their victim they are supposed to address it in a flattering manner, greeting it, for example, with a friendly 'oh, look! what a nice and healthy child you are'. These words by themselves are not thought to have any magical potency; but they are uttered by the *avasohi* merely to instil confidence into their victim and to induce it to look at them. People say that they can recognize the *avasohi* by their piercing glance and the reddish colour of their eyes, but these criteria are not sufficiently conclusive to permit taking action against them. Like the *avalasi vevikoko*, the *avasohi* cast the evil eye (*okusoha*) indiscriminately upon men, women, or children, and like the former they can control their power and look at people without inflicting any harm upon them.[1] Their chief victims, however, are calves and various material objects rather than human beings. As a consequence of having been looked at by the *omusohi* the objects shrink in size or quantity and deteriorate in quality. The following are typical examples of the effects produced by the evil eye of an *omusohi*: (1) if she looks on while a cow is milked or if she does the milking herself the milk will dry up in the cow's udder; (2) if she looks at food while it is cooking it will not get done, no matter how long it is kept on the fire; (3) if she casts her evil eye upon gourds growing in a garden they will crack.

A last type of female *omulogi* among the Logoli is supposed to be capable of making children ill by capturing their souls and keeping them trapped at the base of her cooking-stones where she also keeps her medicines (*amalogo*). To aggravate the condition of her alleged victim the *omulogi* utters secret spells over the entrapped shadow while she cooks. The procedure adopted by this type of female *omulogi* is described in the following text:

'And also there are female *avalogi* like these: a woman can be an *omulogi* and others know her from long ago: This one is an *omulogi*, she bewitches

[1] Cf., however, the following passage from a text: 'Many *avasohi* cast their evil eye without intention; it is a quality with which they are afflicted against their will. Some also may do so on purpose.'

other people or the children of other women, because they know that she has done so. She can pass near the home of another person and his child. If the child has been there, it soon falls ill. Even if the parents have given bad food (*viokulia vitaduki*) to the child and it gets sick they will say, "Alas, the wife of So-and-so has passed here and bewitched our child".[1] They call this "to take the child and to keep it". "The *omulogi* has been passing only near where the child was playing and then it fell ill like this: It began to suffer from diarrhoea indeed." Then the parents wonder about their child and say: "Ah, ah, how the child was!" (i.e. a little while ago it was still playing and now it is ill). Then they say: "Let us go to the diviner (lit., into the divination)."[2] When the child's father has arrived at the diviner's he can say to him: "I have come here on account of the sickness of our child, it is suffering very badly indeed." Then the diviner begins to divine and when he has finished he says to the child's father: "It is a female person who has taken your child; she has taken it to the base of her cooking-stones."[3] Thus the mother of the sick child will get to know that it is the wife of So-and-so who is killing her child by putting it under the hearth-stones in her house.'

Summing up, we can distinguish the following different types of *avalogi* among the Logoli:

Male *avalogi*

1. *Omulogi* proper or *omuvini*: the one who dances at night.
2. *Omukingi*: procures objects associated with his victim and, after they have been prepared by the *omulogi* proper, hides them near the victim's homestead. Works as assistant and in conjunction with the *omulogi*.
3. *Omusindiki*: drives his victims to commit suicide or to succumb to an accident.
4. *Omusohi* (only rarely a man): employs exclusively the evil eye.

Female *avalogi*

1. *Omulogi* proper or *omuvini*: the one who dances at night. Only very rarely a woman.
2. *Omulasi wevikoko*: procures and prepares objects associated with her victim; transmits them by means of the evil eye.
3. *Omusohi*: works exclusively through the power of the evil eye. Chiefly directs her magic against animals and material objects.
4. *Omukali omulogi* (no special name): takes the soul of a child away and traps it together with her *amalogo* underneath her hearth-stones.

Among the Logoli the disposition necessary for becoming an *omulogi* is, as in Kitosh, passed on by inheritance in the paternal or maternal line. Although, unless receiving a further stimulus, this disposition may remain

---

[1] Apparently the narrator of this story is sceptical of the real existence of this type of magic and would rather attribute its alleged effects to bad food.

[2] Instead of saying 'to go to the diviner' one frequently says 'to go into the divination' (*okudzia muvukumu*) or 'to go to the skins of the diviner' (*okudzia kuvisero vyomukumu* cf. below, p. 226).

[3] The base of the cooking-stones is regarded as a favourite place for a woman to keep *amalogo* (evil medicines), because no strangers and not even members of her family are supposed to come near the hearth.

latent throughout a person's life, the Logoli seem to put more weight on this alleged disposition and less on the additional teaching and training. The notion that the faculties required by an *omulogi* are inherited is carried by them to the point that they consider *all* members of certain clans as potential *avalogi*, because the founders of those clans were *avalogi* or married the daughters of *avalogi*. Such clans, for instance, are the Gímuhia, a sub-clan of the Yonga, and the Lógovo, a sub-clan of the Mavi. The inheritance of most types of *ovulogi* is not bound up with sex; i.e. a person of either sex can inherit the faculty for practising *ovulogi* from his father as well as from his mother, his maternal uncle, or his paternal aunt. Only the evil eye is inherited exclusively in the female line (i.e. from mother to daughter).

However, among the Logoli the disposition for practising *ovulogi* is not passed on by inheritance only but also in a number of other ways: thus an *omulogi* can transmit his powers to another person by lending him tobacco which he has mixed with *amalogo*. Having smoked of such tobacco the infected person will dream that he himself has become an *omulogi*. When he wakes up he will feel like dancing at night and doing all the other things *avalogi* are supposed to do. Other favourite methods of transmitting *ovulogi*, are to induce a person to wear the clothes of an *omulogi* or to offer him food or drink which has been magically prepared. In all these cases the person affected must take immediate action if he wants to escape the fate of becoming an *omulogi* himself.

The general attitude adopted towards *avalogi* by the people who are free from witchcraft (the so-called *avilongo*) is the same as among the Vugusu. They are feared and despised but seldom openly accused. But while the Vugusu actually avoid them only if they suspect them of having committed a definite and recent offence, among the Logoli their segregation from other people appears to be much more pronounced. People who are free from *ovulogi*, the *avilongo*, avoid intermarriage with clans that are alleged to be infected with *ovulogi*. The members of such clans are thus forced to intermarry with clans of a similar reputation or to look for their marriage partners in distant clans where nobody would suspect them of being *avalogi*. In a text which I have taken down on *ovulogi* this aversion from marrying the daughter of an *omulogi* finds the following expression:

'Also when you know for certain "this man is an *omulogi*" and he has a daughter, and you are a person whom they are calling a *milongo* (a person free from witchcraft), then you cannot like to marry the daughter of that man. You must fear to marry her, because he is an *omulogi*. And if you have already married a girl and then you hear that there is an *omulogi* at the girl's place, then you refuse indeed, for nobody wants to marry the daughter of an *omulogi*.'

That considerations of this kind actually *do* have an influence on the choice of the marriage partner is borne out by two cases which I verified myself. One of them which I shall discuss in detail in the chapter on marriage (cf. below, p. 392) concerns the family of a wealthy Gímuhia elder with four grown-up daughters. Owing to their father's reputation as an *omulogi* none of them married within the tribal community, although, as a rule, the Logoli have a strong aversion from marrying their daughters off to members of other tribes.

The second case concerned a Christian called Petro Elidundu who, in 1932, married a girl from the Lógovo clan. Actually, among the Logoli all members of the Lógovo clan are suspected of being *avalogi*, but this particular girl had for several years lived with relatives at Kitulu, a place in the territory of the Mavi clan, and thus had made her husband believe that she was 'a daughter of that clan'. About a week after their wedding the wife is said to have returned from a visit to her parents bringing a young leopard with her as a pet. Petro then knew that he had married an *omulogi*, for it is supposed to be the custom of a female *omulogi* to keep a leopard in the loft of her hut and to make it sleep on the same skin with her, as otherwise she would not conceive. After having made his discovery, he implored the senior missionary of the Friends' African Mission to which he belonged to grant him a divorce. His request, however, was rejected as being based on mere superstition. About a year later he confessed in the church that under his wife's influence he had become an *omulogi* and had danced at other people's homesteads at night. Since then he is said to have gone 'quite mad'.

Not only do the Logoli refrain from intermarriage with a clan or family of suspected *avalogi*, but the precautions taken against them go so far that people steer clear of them as much as possible, especially at night-time. To quote a further passage from the text on *ovulogi*:

'And who is an *omulogi* he lives like the others, but all people must know: "Indeed, this one is an *omulogi*." The people know him to be an *omulogi* because he has been found outside at night without wearing any clothes. You must fear him very much and you cannot talk with him; only in the daytime you can stand together with an *omulogi* but not when it is dark. You must fear him because since long ago a person who has become an *omulogi* cannot walk together with his friends; nor can he offer you food without eating of it himself. Only after he has eaten first, then you can begin to help him eating. You must watch everything carefully, lest he might give you food like grain. If he has given you something (and you have not yet touched it) you must wait until he is not there. Then you must call a woman and she must touch (what he has given you) with her hand. Then now you may begin to eat or touch the thing which the *omulogi* has given to you.'

The extreme precautions taken by the Logoli in their intercourse with *avalogi* appear to be dictated by the notion that the power of *ovulogi* can also be transmitted by contact with infected objects and not merely by inheritance, as is the belief among the Vugusu. As distinct from the inherited faculty or disposition for practising *ovulogi*, the transmission of *ovulogi* by contact is closely associated with sex, as can be gleaned from the above text. Thus *ovulogi* can be passed on only between persons of the same sex and even then only if the transmission is direct, i.e. without any interference by a person of opposite sex. If a woman touches an object 'charged' with the *ovulogi* of a man it is thereby neutralized and rendered ineffective. Conversely, the current of *ovulogi* intended to flow from one female to another can be interrupted and rendered void by being tapped by a male person. The principle implied in this notion appears to be that the person who interrupts the current absorbs its potential energies without himself being affected by them.

Among the Logoli the *omulogi* never turns his possession of magical power to any material advantage, for he does not perform his evil magic in the service or on behalf of other people who would approach him as clients, as the *omulosi* occasionally does among the Vugusu. The only motive for engaging in his evil practices lies in his inherited or acquired disposition. It causes him to hate and envy other people, and it fills him with an inner urge to make use of his destructive powers. Among the Marama, whose ideas concerning *ovulogi* appear to be practically identical with those held among the Logoli, I was told that the *avalogi* go out and dance at night, 'because they are wrong in their bodies. Their blood "melts"[1] while they sleep, and so they have to go out and dance to make their blood cool off again.' The idea that by inflicting misfortune and disease upon other people the *omulogi* assures and enhances his own welfare and that of his family is also found among the Logoli, but it is not emphasized as much by them as by the Vugusu. Persons suspected of being *avalogi* usually are not conspicuous by their wealth or by the possession of many children. On the contrary, they are frequently individuals who suffer from all sorts of disabilities and are, therefore, discontented. They give little cause for others to envy or respect them. People merely fear and despise them, and even though they do not think that his peculiar disposition or craving causes the *omulogi* any actual suffering, they dread the idea of becoming *avalogi* themselves. In a text that I have taken down on the transmission of *ovulogi* (see p. 266) the person who has dreamt that he was afflicted with *ovulogi* is in a state of great alarm and dismay and immediately tries to undo what has been done to him. Reports on actual cases confirm this attitude. In 1922 a member of the Yose sub-clan went so far as to accuse a Gimuhia before the tribal court, because after having borrowed the latter's pipe he had dreamt that he was infected with *ovulogi*. The elders apparently accepted his evidence, for the alleged *omulogi* is said to have been fined a goat for having attempted to pass on his *ovulogi*. My informants remembered another case from the year 1928, where fear of having become an *omulogi* even led a youth of the Mavi clan to take his life. A Gimuhia boy with whom he had become acquainted while both were working on a farm had lent him his shirt, pretending that he wished

[1] *Amatsahi gayaka.* It means that their blood starts boiling and bubbling like molten butter.

to make friends with him. Only later he heard that his new friend belonged to the Gímuhia clan and was therefore likely to be an *omulogi*. Then he dreamt that the shirt had been infected with *amalogo*. As he had already worn it a number of times he thought that there was no hope of escaping the fate of becoming an *omulogi* himself. Besides, he was far away from home and could not get hold of a senior kinsman to perform a purification rite for him. So he committed suicide, preferring death to the prospect of having to lead the life of an *omulogi*.

(b) Avavila

AT the beginning of the present chapter we distinguished two major categories of specialists, *avalogi* (*avalosi*) and *avavila*. Having discussed the former, we can now turn to the latter type of experts. As has already been stated, the most obvious difference between them which permits their classification into separate groups, even without a detailed analysis of their activities, is that the *avalogi* use their powers exclusively for anti-social or criminal purposes whereas the *avavila* are supposed to wield their magic—at least predominantly—for legitimate ends.

The belief in the existence and powers of *avavila* (sing. *ombila*) is not common to all tribes of Bantu Kavirondo.

The Idaxo and Isuxa (Kakamega) are reputed to possess the most powerful *avavila*, but a belief in them is general among all the tribes living to the south of the Nzoia River. The Vugusu until very recently completely lacked the belief in *avavila*. But as a consequence of their more frequent contacts with the neighbouring tribes to the south it is now gradually spreading among them too. Most of my information on the *avavila* I obtained among the Logoli whose notions regarding them appear to be typical for the whole area. Shorter surveys among the Marama and Tsotso (where they are called *avafila*, singular: *omufila*) have revealed very much the same beliefs as those I found among the Logoli.

Among the Gusii (Kisii) of South Kavirondo the specialist who corresponds to the *ombila* of the Logoli is the *omunyamusira*; he employs a magical substance called *omusira*. According to the short notes which I took among the Gusii during a rapid visit to their country it appears that the contrast between the *omulogi* and the *omunyamusira* (*ombila*) is more pronounced and more clearly formulated by them than by any of the tribes of North Kavirondo. Thus I was told:

'The *omulogi* comes at night and dances in front of your house and he also buries evil magic which causes you to get ill. While on his way he carries a mysterious light which he flashes at times to frighten the people whom he meets. His power (*ovulogi*) can be transmitted to other people, but nobody likes to become an *omulogi*. It is like being cursed. But the victim must either accept it or die. The *omunyamusira* is more powerful than the *omulogi*. He has the power to kill anyone at any time. Only a few people possess the medicine which lends them such power and they sell it for many head of cattle only. They boast of being able to kill people outright. But they are liked by the people, because they use their medicine to kill only those people who have done something bad. In particular they kill the *avalogi* if they fail to die from your counter-magic. Thus they save people from being bewitched. An *omulogi* will never go to the village of an *omunyamusira* because he fears him. If an *omunyamusira* wishes to do so he can also kill people out of spite.'

This brief account clearly brings out the anti-social nature of the *omulogi* and the essentially beneficent character of the *omunyamusira* who is regarded as the *omulogi*'s stronger opponent and as the protector of the people against *ovulogi*. The difference is not quite as marked among the tribes of North Kavirondo, but it is still clearly there. It is significant in this connexion to note the fact that the Logoli believe themselves to have originally formed one tribe together with the Gusii and to have come to their present habitation from the south (cf. p. 25). One would, therefore, have a good reason to believe that the same clear distinction between *ovulogi* and *ovuvila* which is still found among the Gusii was formerly also shared by the Logoli.

Avavila are nowadays always men, but female *avavila* are said to have lived in former times. As distinct from the *omulogi*, the objects of the *ombila*'s magic are exclusively human beings and neither animals nor material possessions. Within this wide category of human beings, however, there are no further limitations as regards the *ombila*'s potential victims or patients. They can be of either sex and of any age (although he rarely kills children), and they may be people of his own clan or kin-group as well as strangers.

The methods or techniques employed by the *ombila* comprise two distinct types: those of curing or protecting and those of killing people. As his curative activities are considered less important than his lethal ones and as, moreover, the cure or protection afforded by him serves primarily to counteract previous acts of destruction, I shall begin with a discussion of the latter.

As in the case of *ovulogi* the destructive power of the *ombila*'s magic does not reside in the medicine alone nor exclusively in the rite or in the spell, but in the combination of two or of all three of these elements and, in addition, in his intrinsic power of being an *ombila*. By combining these different elements in different ways the *ombila* can command a variety of techniques between which he may choose according to his liking.

His lethal medicines are exclusively herbs or roots which collectively are called *ovuvila*. The magical virtue of these plants consists in their capacity under certain conditions to kill people by sending forth a lethal power usually in the form of a smell. This affects anyone who comes near them, but it cannot always be perceived through one's senses. The *ombila*, who himself is immune from the effects of these plants, collects them himself. As they are of very rare occurrence he often has to search for many days to replenish his supplies. *Avavila* living in Maragoli are said to undertake longish journeys not only to the adjoining Luo country but also to Kitosh which is some sixty miles away, and even to distant Uganda solely for the purpose of collecting rare specimens of *ovuvila* and of buying them from other *avavila*. Besides, every *ombila* plants his own small garden, choosing for the purpose a remote hill-side (*ekigulu kyovovila*) which nobody is likely to visit. At the same place where he plants his garden he also mixes and cooks his medicines. This he must do in special pots (*edzinyingu dziovovila*) which he never takes home but keeps at a secret place in the hills. It is essential that he prepares his medicines in absolute solitude, not because he fears that other people might know about his activities, but because the potency of his medicines would be spoilt if anyone came near while they are being prepared. Furthermore, he must choose the late afternoon of a rainless and cloudless day, and the actual mixing and cooking of his medicines must be done just before sunset. While engaged in this work he must be quite naked, only wearing his side-bag (*emuya*) in which he keeps his medicines. As far as I could discover, he does not have to observe any rules as regards food or sexual intercourse.

Having prepared, i.e. ground, dried, mixed, burnt, or cooked his medicines he puts each kind into a small container, called *liveye*. A *liveye* is a round, hard-shelled fruit growing on trees. To make this fruit serve his purpose the *ombila* hollows it out like a gourd. The *liveye* itself does not possess any magical virtues, but merely serves as a container that prevents the *ovuvila* from evaporating and thus losing its potency.

When the *ombila* goes out to kill people he takes his side-bag with an assortment of *amaveye*[1] with him, each containing a different powder or a different concoction of herbs. As I have not been able to compile a list of these various medicines and of their alleged virtues, I cannot say according to what principles they are classified, nor owing to what characteristics each plant has its particular magical quality attributed to it. The majority of them appear to be poisonous plants and parasitic creepers of which numerous varieties are found in Kitosh. In contrast to the practices of an *omulogi*, an *ombila* never procures and uses objects associated with his intended victim (hair, nails, &c.) as part of his magic.

The most common technique employed by the *ombila* is to point a *liveye* filled with *ovuvila* at his intended victim, so that the opening of the *liveye* is directed towards him; at the same time he casts a 'bad look' (*lihenza livi*) at him. The person at whom he has pointed the evil medicine only knows that he has met with someone who has cast a weird look at him and has pointed at him. He never sees the *liveye* itself, as the *ombila* always hides it in his fist. If then after a few hours he gets violently ill he knows that he has met with an *ombila* who is trying to kill him. He will feel severe pain in his head and limbs and that side of his body on which the *ombila* has passed him will begin to ache.

A similar method frequently used by *avavila* is to utter a death-threat, usually following a quarrel, and at the same time to point at his victim,

[1] Plural of *liveye*.

again hiding a *liveye* in his hand. The death-threat in this case has the effect of a spell. Its wording may vary from case to case and it is never very explicit, but the person addressed always knows what it means. A typical threat of this kind runs: 'If you still see the next harvest you will be lucky', i.e. you will be dead before the crops that are growing are harvested. Or, after a quarrel over a piece of land: *'yive olazara sinuvulie muhiga gunu mba'* ('You are proud, you may not eat it (the eleusine) this year').

During my stay in Kavirondo numerous deaths occurred which were attributed to such threats and the accompanying effect of the *ovuvila* pointed at the victim. The two following cases were particularly striking, as the suspicions were directed against definite persons while the patients were still alive and as in both cases I had seen the patients in a state of apparent fitness only a few days before they succumbed to their illness.

In the first case the alleged victim of *ovuvila* was a man called Elikoti who held the office of a headman (*mlango*) under Chief Shimoli in East Tiriki. I had paid him a courtesy visit and a few days later heard that he was seriously ill. When inquiring about the nature of his complaint I was told that it had probably been caused by an *ombila* and that his brother was going to accuse the person whom he suspected before the tribal court. So I attended the next sitting of Chief Shimoli's court and witnessed the following procedure. The sitting took place on 29 July 1935:

Elikoti's brother, the plaintiff, began to plead his case in the following words: 'I want to tell you elders that my brother, the headman Elikoti, has suddenly fallen very ill. I went to fetch an *ombila*, called Ogada, to cure him, but after having visited my brother once he refused to come again. The reason why he does not come again is that Kisanyanya (the accused) has warned him while they were drinking together not to go and administer medicines (*amasambu*) to my brother. I have come, therefore, to accuse Kisanyanya, because it is obvious that he wants my brother to die.' Kisanyanya interrupted him and asked: 'Who has heard that I said to Ogada not to go and cure your brother? I should like to see the witness who has heard me say such a thing.' The plaintiff replied that an elder called Ludjendja could act as a witness. Ludjendja then stated that Kisanyanya had in fact warned Ogada not to administer medicines to Elikoti. His testimony was supported by another elder who had also taken part in the beer drink and who said that he had heard Kisanyanya say to Ogada: 'Don't go and visit Elikoti, let them take him to the mission hospital.' The elder added that he then knew that Kisanyanya had made the headman ill and wanted him to die. As a third witness an askari (native policeman) stepped forward and volunteered that at the beer drink in question he was sitting next to Ludjendja and heard Kisanyanya say to Ogada: 'Why are you taking medicines to the headman, do you think you are a greater *ombila* than I am (*uvere mukali xumbila*)?' i.e. do you think you can undo what I have done to him?

Having obtained all this evidence, the presiding elder turned to the accused: 'Kisanyanya, do you admit the truth of what the witnesses have said? If you have a grudge against us you can tell us what it is and we shall pay you a cow or a goat. But why do you want to kill the headman? He has not done anything to you!' Whereupon Kisanyanya replied: 'I bear no grudge against anyone of you or against Elikoti; he has not taken anything away from me, so why should I want to kill him?' Here one of the witnesses interrupted the accused, asking him: 'Didn't you boast to me how many people were in here who had been ill and whom you then had cured again? Didn't you say that?' The implication was that Kisanyanya had not only cured them but that he had also caused them to get ill in the first place. Kisanyanya, however, denied having said anything of the sort. But another witness confirmed what the first witness had said.

Now the accused defended himself by attacking the witnesses: 'You are all kinsmen of Elikoti, and it is you yourselves who are killing him. You just say that I am killing him so that the people will not suspect you.' To that the first witness replied: 'Didn't you tell me some time ago that you would kill me (by *ovuvila*) if I called you an *omulogi*? Didn't you say that the old man Kikuyu is dead now because he always quarrelled with you?' Kisanyanya did not reply to these allegations but stressed his friendly relations with the headman: 'Did you ever see me quarrelling with the headman Elikoti? Didn't I always walk in his company and drink beer with him? So you see that I have nothing against him.' This time the askari replied to Kisanyanya's statement, addressing the elders: 'One day this court fined Kisanyanya 150/- shs. because he had committed adultery with another man's wife. When the headman and I took him to the chief he (the chief) handed us a rope and we tied his hands. Then Kisanyanya said to us: "Now you are troubling me, but you know how many people have already died who have troubled me." Later, when we were taking him to the Kakamega Prison and we reached the Yala River, Kisanyanya wanted to tear himself loose and jump into the water because, he said, he did not want to go to prison. We held him firmly and then he said to me: "When I return from jail I shall *okuvila* the headman (i.e. kill him by employing *ovuvila* magic against him)."'

The presiding elder then asked the accused if he would now admit having caused the headman's sickness by having uttered a threat against him and pointed *ovuvila* at him. If so he should go and cure the headman, otherwise they would send him to prison. The assistant chairman endorsed this preliminary judgement, but a young man remarked: 'I think if you send Kisanyanya by force to cure Elikoti he will not help him but give him medicine which is no good (*olunyasi olutali ululahi*).' The court clerk then suggested that it would be good to send two *avavila* to cure him and said that Kisanyanya and Ogada should go together. Kisanyanya accepted this suggestion and promised to go together with Ogada. However, when I visited the headman again a few days later he was still very ill and neither of the two *avavila* had as yet come to see him. Even two weeks later they still refused to come, but no further action was taken against them. Eventually the headman recovered from his illness.

The second case arose in connexion with the sudden severe illness and death of Vigeti, a leading elder of the Tadjoni tribe and a member of Chief Amutala's tribal court at Kimilili. When I saw Vigeti at a sitting of the tribal court he was in perfect health and in spite of his advanced age he regularly attended the meetings twice a week, although this meant a walk of twelve miles each way. Suddenly he fell ill and within a few days he died.

At the hair-shaving ceremony which followed his funeral the following explanation of his death was given by one of his classificatory maternal uncles. Addressing the crowd of kinsmen and mourners that had assembled for the occasion he said: 'I came to see Vigeti on the sickbed and he told me this: "*Xotja* (maternal uncle), I know I am leaving the country but who has killed me[1] is Kavudjanga."' Then the maternal uncle gave an account of the events that led to Vigeti's sickness. 'Six months ago Vigeti bought a sheep from Kavudjanga which he required for a sacrifice, for the diviner had told him to slaughter a sheep of a certain size and certain colour and he didn't find anybody but Kavudjanga to sell him such a sheep. He came to an agreement with Kavudjanga that he would pay him 3/- shs. Last week Vigeti met Kavudjanga at the *baraza* (the tribal court) and Kavudjanga very harshly demanded the 3/- shs. from him. Vigeti replied that he did not have any money with him but that he would give it to him later. Kavudjanga acted very impatiently and told Vigeti that unless he could give him the 3/- shs. right away he did not want to have the money at all. Seeing Kavudjanga in such a mood, Vigeti borrowed the 3/- shs. from another headman, but when he wanted to give it to Kavudjanga he violently refused to take it. Vigeti then called other people to help him talk sense to Kavudjanga, but he still refused to take the money and finally uttered a death-threat against Vigeti, saying: "*nomenya omwesi gundi gwalavuxa eva wumusadja*" (lit., "If you live another moon will be bright again it will be of a man", i.e. if you live until the next full moon you will be a real man). All the people standing round them heard Kavudjanga say that and they immediately blamed him for using such bad words.

'When Vigeti came home that day he had a bad headache and had to lie down. Next day Kavudjanga was called to administer medicine to Vigeti. He came and did so, but after having taken Kavudjanga's medicine Vigeti felt even worse. Two days later he died. Kavudjanga then came to Vigeti's funeral to wail, but one of his kinsmen wanted to spear him in revenge for Vigeti's death and so he ran away. Now Kavudjanga is threatening to accuse the man who wanted to spear him.'

Winding up his speech the maternal uncle added that this was already the second obvious offence of employing *ovuvila* magic which Kavudjanga had committed. On a previous occasion he had wanted to seduce a woman but she had refused him because of the disfiguring scars on his face. Then he made her ill with *ovuvila* and soon after she died. After she was buried her husband watched the grave every night from a secret look-out and one night Kavudjanga came indeed carrying a long pole which he thrust into the grave as deeply as he could just where the head of the deceased woman was. Then he poured hot water from a gourd into the hole he had made (to burn the spirit of the woman and thus to prevent it from taking revenge on him). When he left the grave the husband tried to catch him and kill him, but fearing the Government he refrained from spearing him. Kavudjanga then ran away to a European farm and when he was accused before the tribal court for having interfered with the woman's grave he claimed to have stayed at the European's farm all the time.

[1] The natives always speak of a person who is dangerously ill as if he has already died.

The crowd listened attentively to this indictment but no further comments were made and, as I heard later on, no legal action was taken against Kavudjanga.

These two cases clearly show the type of behaviour that causes a man to be suspected of abusing his powers as an *ombila* and, at the same time, the degree of circumspection with which an *ombila* is treated. Apart from the people who are emotionally so deeply shocked by the death or illness of their kinsman that they are willing to risk their own safety, nobody dares to attack him outright and the judging elders in particular have recourse to friendly persuasion rather than to threats and actual convictions. The *ombila* himself, while sternly denying the specific act of which he is accused, appears to enjoy the reputation in which he is held and, as will have been noted, never denies his power to kill other people by magic but merely his having done so in the particular case that is under discussion.

A third method of killing people which is said to be employed by an *ombila* is to plant seeds or seedlings of *ovovila* near the homestead of his intended victim. To avoid being seen by the owner of the homestead he plants the *ovovila* in the middle of the night when everybody is asleep, and only during nights where there is no moon. He always plants two seeds or seedlings close together, one to sprout and one to decay. Having done so, he mentions the day on which the two plants will blossom and decay respectively. On that day the victim is supposed to die. The first symptoms of his approaching death are a terrific headache, vomiting, and a lame feeling in his legs. Death usually takes place very rapidly, at the longest after four days. Although the *ovovila* thus planted primarily affects the particular person whom the *ombila* wishes to kill, everyone is afraid to touch or pull out such plants if he is aware of their evil nature.

In 1935 a case was brought before the tribal court in Maragoli in which an old man, Lotjo, was accused by the headman of his location (Thomas) of having planted deadly *ovuvila* in his garden. Attention had been drawn to these plants by a visiting Luo who knew their lethal qualities as they also grow in his own country. All Lotjo's neighbours were alarmed at the news that such plants were allowed to grow in their midst. They reported the matter to the headman (not daring to approach Lotjo directly) and he, being afraid of inspecting the garden himself, ordered his askari to have a look at the plants. The askari confirmed that they were of a dangerous nature but did not pluck a sample, as he likewise feared to touch them. When the matter came before the tribal court the elders appointed another *ombila*, Elijah, to inspect the plants and then to report on them. Lotjo was very indignant about the whole affair and threatened to bring a charge of slander against the youth who had first reported him to the headman. After Elijah had been appointed to make a statement as an expert the case was adjourned indefinitely and nothing was ever heard of it again.

Apart from his destructive magic the *ombila*—as has been stated—also employs magic to cure and protect people. The substances used by him for these two latter purposes are referred to either as *olohólizo* or *elihonya*. The first of these two words is derived from *okuhóliza*, which in different contexts means: to end a quarrel, to reconcile, to forgive, to lift a curse, to apply counter-magic, and to make thrive, fat, prosperous. It here refers to those activities of the *ombila* by which he undoes what he himself has done before, i.e. he administers medicines to the patient which counteract the effects of the destructive magic which he had previously employed against him. The second word, *elihonya*, is derived from *okuhonya*, to cure, and refers to his efforts to cure the patient of ills with which he has been afflicted by the evil magic of other persons, either other *avavila* or, less frequently, *avalogi*. Magic of protection the *ombila* either sells to his clients or plants for them round their homesteads to render them immune from the evil magic of other *avavila* or *avalogi*. The details of the *ombila*'s curative and protective magic I shall discuss in conjunction with the various other kinds of protective magic and counter magic (see below, p. 264 sq.).

What then are the motives which lead the *avavila* to employ their magic, be it for destructive or for curative and protective ends? As a preliminary to answering this question we must first examine the way in which they acquire their particular powers, as this will determine to what extent they act as responsible persons and how far they are incited to action by forces outside their own personal control or volition. Among the Logoli a person becomes an *ombila* either by being taught by his father or by starting as the apprentice of another *ombila* (who may or may not be related to him). In either case the essential element in the transmission of *ovuvila* from one person to another is the teaching of the special knowledge and manipulations required, and not the passing on of a mystical disposition (as in the case of *ovulogi*). A person can therefore never become an *ombila* all of a sudden, as by mere contact or by a dream, but only gradually and by a persistent effort as is the case with the mastering of any craft that requires skill and knowledge. Although an *ombila* always teaches his eldest and sometimes also his last-born son (the *omukógoti*) to become his successor, such instruction is not additional to an inherited disposition, but it is the whole thing. Those sons whom a father has not chosen to become *avavila* do not have any latent disposition towards it or qualifications for it, as is the case with the children of an *omulogi*. *Ovuvila* is thus clearly not based on any inherited or mystically acquired organic or psychical substratum working as an inner force that urges the person in whom it resides towards action. Hence, *ovovila* is not associated with certain clans or lineages but *avavila* are said to be fairly evenly distributed over the whole tribe. The absence of such a substratum does not, of course, preclude the notion that every *ombila* in the course of time enters into such an intimate relationship with the magic wielded by him that his whole personality is pervaded by it and thus participates in producing the desired effect.

If an *ombila* chooses his son to succeed him he begins to teach him the knowledge of secret plants and the preparation of *ovovila* only after the latter has married, begotten children, and founded a homestead of his own. Later he sends him to stay with other *avavila*, so that he may improve and widen his knowledge. However, a son never actively practises *ovovila* magic while his father is still alive, and even after his death he waits for several years before becoming an active *ombila*. He always begins his career by killing his wife or one or two of his children with his magic. It is said that unless he does so he will not be successful in his efforts to kill other people. Afterwards he marries again and his second wife and her offspring are then immune from the dangers of his craft. One would expect that the prospect of becoming the first victim of his lethal magic would deter a girl from being married to the eldest son of an *ombila* and her father from agreeing to such a marriage. However, I could not discover any evidence showing this to be the case, notwithstanding the numerous stories that circulate to prove that wives or children of *avavila* have died under mysterious circumstances in the early stages of their husband's or father's career as an *ombila*.[1]

A person can become the pupil or apprentice of any *ombila* who is willing to instruct him. He must make him an initial payment of two head of cattle, adding further animals whenever he has reached a new stage in the process of learning. After his first successful 'kill' he must render a final payment of another two cows. Only then can he practise independently of his master.

In the absence of any mystical disposition of mind or body for practising *ovovila* magic the motives prompting an *ombila* lie exclusively within the sphere of his own conscious and controllable intentions. The main incentive that drives persons to acquire the knowledge of *ovovila*, and later to make use of it, is the craving for the power and respect (mingled with fear) that are commonly enjoyed by an *ombila*. The two cases of Kisanyanya and Kavudjanga that have been quoted above clearly show the circumspection with which a reputed *ombila* is treated. To be an *ombila* appeals particularly to people of a vain, boastful, and assertive character, and the people who have been pointed out to me as *avavila* always seemed to have these traits of character—rather commonly found among the Bantu Kavirondo—to a particularly marked degree. When an *ombila* is thought to have used his powers for *killing* a person it is usually following a quarrel, an insult, or a challenge of his authority, but seldom out of mere spite or envy, as in the case of *avalogi*. Moreover, he predominantly employs his magic in a professional way, both curing and killing in the name of his clients, and as his fees are high his practices are a source of substantial income to him. When he is called to cure a person he asks for an initial payment of

---

[1] Among the Yonga, for instance, the case of a reputed *ombila*, Kivia, is always quoted. He is said to have killed his wife and several children, sparing only one boy and one girl.

a goat or young bull-calf and a similar payment must be made again when his patient has recovered. When he takes orders to kill a person he even charges the price of a heifer to begin with and of a second one after he has done his job. *Avavila* of great repute are said to take even higher fees. Accordingly, they are always wealthy persons, just as only wealthy persons can afford the comparatively high fees which they have to pay to be instructed in the knowledge of *ovovila*. The prospect of material gain appears therefore as a second incentive for becoming an *ombila*.

Only those of an *ombila*'s activities which are socially beneficial are openly admitted by him; they comprise his efforts to cure people who have been made ill by another *ombila*, to sell protective medicines (*amanyasi gokwélinda*), and to employ destructive magic against *avalogi*. However, as it is always a moot point to decide exactly who is an *omulogi* and therefore deserves to be put to death by lethal magic, the *ombila* prefers to wield his destructive magic under a veil of semi-secrecy, whether he employs it for socially approved of or definitely criminal purposes. This means that although the *ombila* gives some hints of what he is doing by uttering the threat and seeking a quarrel with his intended victim, he will always deny that he had any intention to kill the person concerned when the matter is brought before the council of elders or some other forum. Or again he will betray his real intentions by refusing to come to the aid of a sick person, thereby implicitly admitting that he prefers to see him die and that either he or another *ombila* with whom he is collaborating has caused his illness. But when openly challenged for his unfriendly behaviour he will try to find plausible excuses for his refusal and deny that he harbours any evil intentions against the person in question. Thus, as Christopher Mtiva put it, the *ombila* always works half in the open and half in the dark. He both helps and harms people, and when he sends them illness or death he does so partly for legitimate reasons, killing people who have merited no better fate and whom public opinion likes to see put out of the way without daring to persecute them openly (such as *avalogi*), and partly for selfish and criminal reasons, killing people for his personal dislike or merely to boast of his powers. Owing to the ambiguous nature of his activities the *ombila*, on the one hand, enjoys prestige and respect and, on the other, is the object of fear and hatred. He is commonly known to all people and they refer to him as an *ombila*, but they would not dare to address him by that term (unless they want to challenge him), as the term *ombila* signifies his destructive and not his curative or protective activities. However, they would not address him as a *wolunyasi* either, because he would consider it below his dignity to be called a mere 'dispenser of therapeutic herbs'. As far as I could discover, people do not address him by any particular term at all but merely call him by his name.

The ambiguous nature of the *ombila*'s magic is brought out very clearly in the following narrative that gives an account of what can happen to a client who approaches an *ombila* with the request to plant protective magic for him:

A person has been suffering from sickness for many years without a rest. Finally he has recovered and he says to himself: 'Now I have recovered from my illness, I must go to find an *ombila*. He may give me medicines with which to protect myself at this my home, because I have always been ill indeed.' Then he goes to the *ombila* and tells him: 'I have come here because I want medicines of protecting myself at my home.' And the *ombila* asks him: 'Do you want medicines of protecting yourself or those with which to kill a person?' And his client replies: 'No, I am wanting those of protecting myself only, because people are always casting the evil eye at me.' Then the *ombila* tells him: 'You may go and bring all the people of your house; they may all come here and I may look at them and then they may all be given medicines (*amasambu*). Then we may talk together about the matters which you have mentioned.'

Now when they have come to the *ombila*'s home they get the medicine (*olunyasi*) which they call *amasambu*, and when they begin to go there they must go secretly; nobody must know (about their visit). They must go at a time of the day when it is still dark indeed, because they do not want to be seen. Also they must go to a person who is living very far away, e.g. to an *ombila* who lives in the Luo country if the person who wants the *ovovila* is an Omulogoli, because otherwise he might be seen when he leaves the home of that *ombila*. This is the reason why they are going so far.

When the *ombila* has come to terms with his client he tells him: 'Now you can pay me a bull,' and when he has paid him then the *ombila* thinks how he may begin to do (i.e. how to plant the *ovovila*) at his client's house. First he takes medicine (*olunyasi*) and makes his client's children lick it. When starting off (to go to his client's house) he must leave his home at night, because if he leaves in the day-time the people can see him and say: 'Why, this one may be taking the *ovovila* for killing other people?' Then the *ombila* must hide himself, and when he has arrived at the home of the person who wants the *ovovila* he must ask the owner of that home: 'Where can we plant?' and the owner replies to him: 'Come, I will show you where we can plant this *ovovila*.' They themselves cannot call it '*ovovila*', they must call it '*musala gwetu ogwokwelinda*' (our medicine of protecting oneself), lest a person might kill with the *ovovila*.

When they have finished planting the *ovovila* the owner of the homestead brings food. When the *ombila* has finished eating, the owner of the home can add a fowl (for the *ombila* to take home) as is the custom of long ago. Nowadays you can give the *ombila* 2/- shs. which he takes home with him. Now when the *ombila* has arrived back home he cannot have another matter. He is staying home and the client always visits his friend (the *ombila*). Then when the *ovuvila* sprouts and begins to ripen then it begins to *okufunya*[1] at the home (of the client), it begins to 'broadcast' (the poison) indeed, then it begins to kill a child living there. If the first child that it kills happens to be a girl then only few people will die, but if it begins by killing a boy then they must

---

[1] *Okufunya* in this context means 'to emit poison' and not to smell, for the emanations or radiations of the *vila*-plants are not marked by a noticeable smell.

AGENTS AND FORCES

all die. And their father must hide (the reason), he cannot warn them against that matter of *ovuvila*. Now when it begins to kill his wife, then the husband may think: 'Perhaps it is the *ovuvila* which I have planted at the back-door, then it has caused my wife to die indeed.' If he sees this happening he does not want (or dare) to tell the people, but he goes to the diviner (*omukumu*) and tells him: 'The people of my home have all died,' and the diviner says: 'Perhaps there is a medicine (*musala*) at your home which somebody has brought to bewitch (*kukinga*) you all, now you may all die indeed.' The person who went to the diviner must fear to admit: 'I brought the medicine of protection to my home.' Then the diviner looks at his oracles but he cannot see a thing. Then he asks his client 'hard' and says to him: 'You may tell me if you were thinking to bring the medicine (*musala*), you may say so! And also you may go and call an *ombila*; he may come and pull the *ovuvila*. And the person who must pull that *ovuvila* is not the one who has planted it, it must be another one.'

The beliefs held concerning the qualities and activities of the *avavila* among the Logoli appear to apply with minor variations to all the tribes south of the Nzoia River. Among the Marama (a tribe closely related to the Wanga) the specialist that corresponds to the *ombila* is called *omufira* and his magic *ovufira*. The following account of his activities was given to me:

Whereas the *omulosi* is an enemy of man the *omufira* is respected. He is a well-known person. People are afraid of him and they keep on good terms with him, as otherwise he might kill them. People consult the *omufira* to come and kill somebody for them. They also call him when people are sick so that he may give them medicine (*olunyasi*). This will work against the poison in the person's body. The *ovofira*, on the other hand, is the secret medicine employed to send sickness or death. The *omufira* possesses both kinds of medicines. When people go to consult an *omufira* they visit him either openly or secretly, depending upon whether they want him to employ *ovufira* or *olunyasi*. In both cases they must pay him a fee, either goats or cattle. But they never address him as *omufira*; if they did so he would be angry.

The *omufira* of the Marama and Wanga differs from the *ombila* of the Logoli in that he employs a greater variety of methods, some of which are, among the Logoli, only employed by *avalogi*. Thus he does the following things in order of their frequency: (1) He passes a person without saluting him, then he looks at the victim's shadow and points *ovufira* at it. (2) He goes to his intended victim's homestead at night and plants *ovufira* all around it. When the plants are in full bloom all the people living there will die. (3) He digs a hole into a man's foot-prints and places *ovufira* in it. (4) He takes his victim's excreta and mixes them with *ovufira*. (5) He infects a public spring with *ovufira* and utters a spell while doing so, thereby killing all the people who drink water from this spring. (6) He utters curses like any ordinary old man or woman.

(c) The Rain-magician

(i) *The importance attached to rain-magic*

The widespread African belief that magical powers possessed by human beings extend to the control of precipitation is also generally held by the various tribes of Bantu Kavirondo. The 'rain-magician' (*omugimba*) among them is an influential person whose reputation often extends beyond the boundaries of his own tribe. His alleged foreknowledge and power of controlling the rainfall give rise to organized co-operation among his clients for the purpose of sending petitions and paying tribute to him on a scale that, except for a major religious ceremony addressed to the Supreme Being, is quite unparalleled in the social life of the Bantu Kavirondo.

That rain-magic should occupy a prominent position in an area such as Kavirondo seems somewhat surprising, for meteorological observations over a number of years and at several stations have shown that the rainfall is not only heavy but also quite regular and well distributed. Serious droughts appear to be of very rare occurrence, the only one in recent times which caused a severe famine being that of 1918. It is true that in the economic life of the people a great deal does depend on the rains breaking at the proper time after the dry season and that a delay of the rains for a week or two may substantially impede the growth and reduce the yield of the crops. Thus, although it would seem that the office of the rain-maker must have developed under meteorological conditions that made the cultivation of the soil a more hazardous undertaking than it is in present-day Kavirondo, an ample and evenly distributed precipitation is a vital enough matter among them to keep the belief and interest in rain-magic going once it was there.

Like other specialists, the rain-magician owes his reputation to the belief that he is in the possession of secret knowledge and carefully guarded medicines that together enable him to work his particular magic of controlling the rainfall. As distinct from other specialists, however, the *omugimba* seldom employs his magic against or for the benefit of single individuals, but it is as a rule whole communities that suffer from or benefit by the manner in which he wields his power. Accordingly he is, as a rule, not approached privately by single individuals, but publicly by a whole community or its representatives. This fact alone, with all that it entails, places the rain-maker in a class by himself and clearly distinguishes him, not only by the aim and technique of his magic but also by his social position, from the specialists of the *logi* and *vila* types.

The number of rain-makers that practise in Kavirondo is far smaller than that of other specialists. This appears to be an indication of their high social status and of the extreme jealousy with which they guard their privileges rather than a sign that rain-magic is regarded a matter of minor importance only. The ample tribute paid to the rain-magicians and the unusually high fees that they charge for passing on their knowledge (if they are willing do so at all) definitely rule out the latter interpretation of the small number of rain-magicians. In the southern part of the North Kavirondo District there is only one family of reputed rain-makers which belongs to the Nyole tribe. The sphere of their influence is not restricted to the Nyole but extends to the Logoli, Tiriki, Kisa, Idaxo, Isuxa, and some of the Nilotic Luo as well. Delegations from all these tribes come to consult the Nyole rain-magician if they are in need of rain. In the central part of North Kavirondo, one rain-magician practises among the Samia, two minor ones in Marama, one in Butsotso (in the Mwende clan), and one in Kakalelwa. The Wanga, in spite of their political leadership over the neighbouring tribes, do not boast a rain-magician of their own but consult either those of Marama or Butsotso. In the northern part of the district (to the north of the Nzoia River) there is only one reputed family of rain-magicians in the easternmost part of North Kitosh. Thus, in an area populated by a third of a million people there are only seven or eight rain-magicians each of whom is consulted by people living as much as thirty or forty miles away and belonging to different and (formerly) even hostile tribes. It is possible that, in addition, there are a few other rain-magicians of a lesser and purely local reputation, but they are never publicly approached. The Nyole family of rain-magicians enjoys by far the highest reputation in the whole of Bantu Kavirondo. I was told about them even among such distant tribes as the Wanga and the Vugusu who acknowledge the superior powers of the former as compared with their own rain-magicians or those living in Marama and Butsotso, but who do not consult them, as they live too far away to be able to control the rain over such a wide area. According to my informants, the Nyole rain-magician owes his high reputation to the fact that he has repeatedly given startling proof of his ability both to cause the rain to fall and to withhold it, making it quite clear in each case what he intended to do. Of the lesser *avagimba* of Butsotso, Kitosh, &c., on the other hand, it is said that their magic often fails them and that they have to consult the diviner to find out why their magic does not produce the desired result. To the European observer the superior reputation of the Nyole family of rain-magicians would find a possible explanation in the fact that Bunyole is the most fertile part of North Kavirondo and also appears to have the most regular rainfall, so that an *omugimba* practising there would, in fact, stand a better chance than elsewhere to have his forecasts come true.

There is no co-operation between the different rain-magicians of North Kavirondo, nor do they compete with one another to any pronounced degree. It is thought possible, however, that their different activities come into conflict with one another, cancelling each others' efforts. This, in fact, is used as an excuse by some of the lesser rain-magicians (cf. below, p. 158), if their magic fails to produce the desired result. Otherwise each rain-magician works quite independently in his own area or even on behalf of a limited group of people within that area. As rain- and hail-showers are often very local—when driving along a road one notices completely dry and soaked patches alternating every few miles—this spatial limitation of the rain-magician's influence is not seriously contradicted by the facts of empirical observation.

(ii) *The technique of rain-control*

The rain-magicians practise their art in strictly guarded privacy. Accordingly, the methods and techniques employed by them are known only by hearsay. To maintain the public's confidence in their magic they must, of course, give some indication of what they are doing. Thus, they permit the senior clan-elders who come to consult them as representatives of their people to inspect their paraphernalia, but they do not permit them to be present when they actually perform their magical rites. In spite of this secrecy the accounts which I obtained from elders in the various parts of Kavirondo tally to a considerable degree and give a fairly clear idea of the main features of Kavirondo rain-magic—at least as it exists in the minds of the people. I shall, in the following, quote seriatim the techniques as they have been described to me in the different parts of the district:

Bunyole. The *omugimba* has four pots (of the *oluvindi* type), two small ones and two large ones. When he wants the rains to come he fills the two small pots with water from a stream, making them about three-quarters full. Then he hides them in a secret grove, called *ovugimba*, and places the two larger pots on the smaller ones like lids. He goes every day and inspects the level of the water in the pots. If it has kept steady, he knows that the rain is coming soon; if the level is gradually sinking this is a sign that the rain is still far away, and to make it come quickly he adds more water to the pots. If the water has sunk very low, he knows that a hail-storm is imminent. To ward it off, he must pour out the remaining water and fill the pots up again with fresh water. If he wants to prevent the rains from coming altogether he must turn all the four pots upside down. On the other hand, if the level of the water is rising and the pots are nearly brimfull this is a sign that 'bad rains' (i.e. cloud-bursts) are about to come. To counteract this he must pour out all the water and fill the pots again to the normal level.

This account, which was given to me by Donela, a Logoli elder, was confirmed in all its essentials by other elders both in Maragoli and in Bunyole. According to another Logoli version, the *omugimba* has not only four but a great number of pots, some of which he keeps in his house, some in a forest, and some on a hill. Although the pots are not distinguished by any particular shape or design, the *omugimba* must use only pots which have been given to him as presents: 'The pots which he is using he gets from the hills,[1] and those are the pots which the people take to him so that he may bring the rain, because they say that he cannot buy them.' Thus the pots appear to possess a magic virtue which is essential both to make them work as forecasts of the weather and to lend them the power of controlling the kind and quantity of precipitation.

[1] i.e. the pots which he does not need he hides in the hills.

AGENTS AND FORCES

In addition to the rain-pots, the *omugimba* has four kinds of horns which enable him to produce different kinds of precipitation. To produce a soft, gentle rain that will make the crops grow, he uses the horn of a small antelope (*kisusu*), to make it rain heavily the horn of a deer (*indja*), to attract a hail-storm the horn of a bush-buck (*embongo*), and to cause a thunder-storm the horn of a buffalo (*embogo*). In each case he employs the same technique: he pours a small amount of water into the respective horn and, tilting it slightly, points it in the direction where he wants it to drizzle, hail, or thunder respectively. Into the buffalo horn with which he produces thunder-storms he puts in addition some red-hot charcoals which sizzle when they drop into the water and thus cause the rain 'to boil', i.e. they cause the roaring of the storm.

The *omugimba* can also handle the horns in such a way that they prevent the rain from falling, as is explained in the following text:

The *omugimba* may refuse the petition for rain, so that it will not rain quickly. (To do so) he must not tilt the horns which he possesses. He has dozens (lit., tens) of horns, so many that you cannot count them, and of all these horns he must not tilt a single one when water is in it. He must take great care, for he fears: 'If I tilt a horn then the rain will fall right away.' And the rain will fall right away when he has tilted the horns. Besides, he must observe a (negative) rule when he drinks beer, not to pour (or add) water into the beer which he is drinking. He must think, 'If I pour water into the beer, the rain will fall everywhere'.

Marama. The ritual paraphernalia of the Marama rain-maker (*omutjimba*) are two horns and two pots, all of which he keeps in his hut. When he wants the rain to fall, he must obtain some herb medicine (*olunyasi*) which he collects and pounds in strictest privacy at a secluded spot in the bush. The pounded medicine he puts into the pots and on top of it he pours water which must be obtained from a spring. Then he places the pots on a fire and boils the water with the medicine. When boiling he blows into it through a hollow reed (*ligada*) until the concoction begins to foam like soap. When it foams properly, the rains will come in a day or two and no further attention is given to the pots. Both pots are treated in the same way, and it is not clear why two pots must be employed. They are both of the same size and, as far as my informants[1] knew, they do not differ as regards their functions. If this technique of producing rain remains ineffective, the *omutjimba* gathers new medicine which he pounds and mixes with ghee. He then puts the mixture on a wooden tray which he places on the roof of his hut. If the ghee melts in the sun, it is a sign that the rain will come the same afternoon. The *omutjimba* then pours the molten medicine into the two horns which are called husband and wife. According to one of the elders, different medicines are put into each of the two horns, which would suggest that the two pots also contain different medicines and that they, perhaps, are likewise thought to be of opposite

[1] Chief Mumia and his elders.

sexes. They are usually horns of cattle (of male animals only), but horns of wild animals may also be taken. The kind of horn used does not have any bearing on the kind of precipitation as is the case with the horns used by the Nyole rain-magician. The *omutjimba* sticks them into the edge of the roof, the 'husband' and the 'wife' close together, and tilts them in the direction in which he wants the rain to fall. When it is about to rain, the *omutjimba* takes the two horns off the roof as they must not get wet.

As far as I could discover the Marama rain-magicians do not employ different techniques for producing different kinds of precipitation, such as gentle rain, violent showers, storms, or hail. The technique of the rain-magicians in Marrach and Samia is said to be the same as that employed in Marama, with the difference that the rain-magician in Marrach uses only one pot (and presumably only one horn).

Butsotso. The account which I obtained from a Tsotso elder of the rain-magic practised by the Tsotso rain-magician is almost identical with that given by Chief Mumia and his elders of Marama rain-magic. As in Marrach, the Tsotso rain-magician (*omukyimba*) has only one horn (of a male or female animal) and a pot of the size of a small calabash, called *lifuvgyilo liefula*. When he wishes to attract the rain he puts pounded medicines (*dzinyasi*) into the pot and pours water on top of them. The concoction then foams up without being boiled. To augment the foaming the *omukyimba* stirs the mixture or blows into it through a hollow reed until the froth runs down the sides of the pot. If it fails to do so, his medicine is not potent enough or some other magic interferes with his own, and he must gather fresh herbs and repeat the whole procedure. The horn—according to my informant—he merely uses as an instrument of divination by looking into it in meditation. 'It gives him advice (*ovugyesi*) and tells him whether his attempts to produce rain will be successful or not.' It also tells him whether the rain-magic of the rain-magicians of Kakalelwa or Bunyole will interfere with his own efforts, in which case he must add other herbs to his concoction which will counteract those outside influences.

Kitosh. The only paraphernalia which the *omugimba* of North Kitosh employs in his rain-magic are a pot and two kinds of medicines, one for attracting the rain and one for keeping it away. Both medicines he gathers in the forest belt on the slopes of Mount Elgon and hides them carefully in his house, not even showing them to his own wives. To perform his rain-magic he takes his paraphernalia to a secret spot in the forest where he builds a small arbour. If he wants to attract the rain, he kindles a fire under the arbour and boils the first medicine in water drawn from a clean spring. The vapour then rises in big white clouds, forming a nucleus round which the rain-clouds are supposed to gather. While the medicine-water boils, the *omugimba* mentions the names of the people in whose gardens he wants the rain to fall. If, on the other hand, he wants to prevent the rain from falling, he merely pours water over the preventive medicine without boiling it. By doing so he 'ties' the rain. At the same time he utters the names of the people whose gardens he wants to suffer from drought.[1]

The rain-magicians of South Kitosh use both a pot and a horn like those of Butsotso, but the manner in which these two objects are handled is slightly different. To attract the rain at the end of the dry season, the *vagimba* fill the pot with water from a stream and towards evening put the pounded leaves of a certain herb into it and then blow into the pot through a hollow reed. The bubbling noise which resembles that of falling rain is then supposed to attract the rain. The pot filled with the medicine-water is thereupon placed in the fork of a tree at a lonely spot in the bush or at the back of the *omugimba*'s house. While he carries the pot out into the bush nobody must meet him, let alone talk to him. Should a child meet him on his way and ask him what he is carrying in the pot, he would put it down and ask the child's father to pay him a fowl before he proceeds with it. An adult person would make a wide detour round the *omugimba* when he meets him carrying a pot. Similarly, if anyone accidentally comes across the *omugimba* while he concocts his medicines he must pay the heavy fine of two bulls or even heifers, as otherwise the *omugimba* would threaten to withhold the rain indefinitely. My informants unanimously insisted that the rain-magician would experience no difficulty in collecting such fines, as the village elders and the public would press the offender to pay lest they should all suffer from the *omugimba*'s drought magic.

The horn (*luluika*) is used by the rain-magicians of South Kitosh primarily to control the wind and thus indirectly the rain, for it is realized that wind and rain seldom go together. When a strong wind is blowing from the east, as is usually the case towards the end of the dry season, the *omugimba* holds his horn with the opening turned towards the east as if to let the wind enter. Then he quickly shuts it by smearing the opening of the horn with clay and anoints it all over with ghee. By this procedure he 'traps' the wind in the horn, thus permitting the rain to fall. Apparently, this procedure is preliminary to the boiling of the rain-medicine, although I am not certain on this point. To cause the wind to blow again—and thereby to stop the rain—the *omugimba* pierces a hole in the clay lid and holds the horn with its opening towards the east, thus releasing the wind.

This type of rain-magic, or rather wind-magic, corresponds to the general notion which the Vugusu hold with regard to the origin of the wind. They say that the wind has its home at a distant place in the east whence it comes out of the earth through small openings looking like the tiny holes made by white ants. By trapping the wind in his horn the *omugimba*, in a mystical way, shuts the wind-holes in the east and, conversely, opens them again by piercing the clay cover of his horn. An alternative method of preventing the rain from falling, which the *omugimba* employs if he wants a particular person only to suffer from drought, is to plant preventive

[1] My informants (Maxeti and Wefwafwa) did not know whether he covers the pot with a lid as well or uses some other additional means of 'trapping' the rain.

medicine round that person's garden. These plants will cause the rain to pass over the garden and come down beyond it or to fall just short of it.

These accounts of the different methods of controlling precipitation can be reduced to a few basic features. There are two general elements which are common to all these types of rain-magic. The first is the ritual handling of water in a pot with the aim of producing something which is analogous to rain, either by its visual appearance (steaming clouds or white foam) or by its sound (the bubbling or hissing sound of the water caused by blowing into it). The primary idea in Kavirondo rain-magic thus appears to be the positive production of rain by employing a technique that rests on the principle of analogy. Among most tribes, moreover (everywhere except in Bunyole), the rite of analogy is linked with the use of a herb with magical virtues. This corresponds to the common pattern of Kavirondo magic, according to which a rite is nearly always linked with the use of a magical substance which lends potency to or at least strengthens the efficacy of the rite. Besides, the medicine seems to be necessary for producing the foam or the steam respectively, i.e. it forms an essential part of the rite of analogy. Owing to the extreme secrecy with which the rain-magicians are said to guard their medicines I could, unfortunately, obtain no information on the nature of the herbs and therefore cannot explain for what qualities they are chosen; one might expect that plants with succulent stems or leaves are chosen, but my informants did not appear to hold any definite views on that point. The spell as another feature lending potency to the magical procedure does not seem to be of great importance; in most cases my inquiries into the nature of the spell merely evoked the reply that nobody could know whether the *omugimba* uttered a magical formula while performing his rite or not, as nobody had ever watched him at work.

The second element in Kavirondo rain-magic that occurs in all accounts but one (North Kitosh) is the use of a horn or a variety of horns. Whereas the rites performed with the rain-pot merely produce (or attract) rain as such, the magical virtue of the horns consists in their power to direct the rain to certain locations (as in Bunyole, Marama), to control the kind and quantity of precipitation (Bunyole), or to control the wind (Kitosh). As a control both of the direction in which the rain shall move and of the kind of rain which shall fall (a gentle, drizzling rain, a hard rain, a rain-storm, and a rain-storm accompanied by thunder) implies a control of the wind, it appears that the basic significance of the horn in Kavirondo rain-magic is its power to control the wind.

Thus the two main objects employed, the pot and the horn, serve the two different purposes (1) of producing rain or moisture in the air as such, and (2) of making it come down at the desired places and in the desired form and quantity. In the first case, the magical procedure rests on the principle of analogy and, in the second case, on that of sympathy. The two procedures, accordingly, clearly fit into the general pattern of productive or active magic.

The withholding of rain when it is due to come or its premature termination clearly appear to be secondary features of rain control, as the techniques employed for these purposes mainly consist in undoing the effects of positive rain-magic, be it by pouring out the water and turning the pots upside down or by releasing the wind again after it has first been trapped.

To judge by the technique of his procedure, the magic of the *omugimba* is, therefore, primarily productive and beneficial to the people but, like most magical experts, he has the power of using his magic both ways, to stop and prevent as well as to produce. It seems significant to note that in those areas where the rain-magicians enjoy but a minor reputation (as in Marama and Butsotso), I obtained an account only of their positive efforts to produce rain while the absence of rain is explained by the weakness of their magic. It thus appears that only the highly reputed rain-magician dares to turn his magic against the interests of the people and to use this method for extracting higher payments and for increasing his prestige. This attitude is closely analogous to that displayed by the *ombila*, who more or less openly boasts of the abuses of his magic only if his reputation is great enough to render him immune from the revenge of other people.

The remaining features of Kavirondo rain-magic appear to be merely local elaborations of the two basic ideas of producing and controlling precipitation, or adaptations to other types of magical procedure. We have seen that both pots and horns are often used in pairs. This suggests the idea of the sexual significance of the objects used. Thus the two horns employed in Marama rain-magic are actually called husband and wife. Similarly the two pots used in the same manner by the Nyole rain-magician or the pair of pots (one being used to cover the other) may possibly represent a male and a female element, although I could not obtain any evidence to confirm this point. To judge by their shape, the pot and the horn likewise suggest a sexual symbolism in their relation to one another; there is, however, nothing in the ritual procedure which would justify the conclusion that such symbolism is a living element in the present-day form of Kavirondo rain-magic.

Charcoal and ghee are employed also in numerous other magical rites, and they must be considered as objects of a general magical virtue with no specific meaning. The significance of the horn in Tsotso rain-magic as a source from which the *omukyimba* derives inspiration is obviously an adaptation to divinatory practices where small antelope horns are used together with pebbles for detecting unknown causes. The observation of the varying levels of water in the different pots and the interpretation of these levels as weather forecasts, finally, appear as a local development from the more common technique of concocting a rain-producing medicine. It is the only feature in Kavirondo rain-magic which may possibly be the outcome of empirical meteorological observation, since it takes cognizance of the fact that a greater amount of water evaporates when the air is dry than when the humidity of the air is high and rainfall is imminent.

The variations in the technique of rain-magic also appear to show some correlation to local differences in the prevailing weather conditions and thus the influence of environment upon the details of ritual. In the open plains of South Kitosh where very strong and regular easterly winds blow throughout the dry season the significance of the horn is exclusively that of controlling the wind. In the more hilly Bunyole District, on the other hand, where high winds are rare but hail-storms, violent thunder-storms, and cloud-bursts are frequent and more pernicious to the economic well-being of the people than they would be in the more pastoral north, the horns serve to control the different kinds of precipitation without having any direct bearing on the wind.

(iii) *The origin of rain-magic according to the local tradition*

The preceding analysis of the technique of rain-making has not revealed any features which are fundamentally different from other types of magical procedure. Like such other types, rain-magic consists in the combination of a rite, a spell, and a substance with magical virtues employed by a person who is entitled to perform the magic. Nevertheless, the rain-magicians enjoy a higher prestige and derive greater material gain from their profession than other specialists. Although one would expect this fact to attract many people to become rain-magicians, there is only a very small number of them who hold a sort of monopoly in wielding their magic. While individual fees paid to the rain maker are comparatively small, the combined payments offered by whole communities are very considerable. In fact, the more noted rain-makers are said to be by far the wealthiest persons in the country. Of the Nyole rain-maker it is said that 'he has so many wives that one cannot count them', and even the lesser rain-maker of Butsotso has three separate villages in which he resides in turn and in each of which he keeps a number of wives. This state of affairs raises the question how the rain-makers came to acquire their privileged position and how they succeed in upholding their monopoly and in preventing competitors from taking away their trade.

In Bunyole, Butsotso, and Kitosh, where I have made inquiries into the supposed origin of rain-magic, I was told that the art of making rain started many generations ago and has since been handed down from ancestor to ancestor, remaining always in the same families. In South Kitosh rain-making is said to have been practised first by the founder of the Lunda clan, the senior line of which is still the present 'owner of the rain'. I could, however, obtain no story relating the manner in which Omulunda first obtained his magic. Among the Tsotso, likewise, I was merely told that the ancestors of the Vamwende (a clan living near Bukura) first practised rain-magic, but nothing seems to be known about the way in which they came to do so. Only about the family of Nyole rain-makers there exists an elaborate origin story. It is fairly common knowledge both among the Nyole and the Logoli and explains why the first rain-maker—a woman who

PLATE 5

A garden magician: South Maragoli

PLATE 6

Inspection of entrails: South Kitosh

AGENTS AND FORCES

originally came from another tribe to the East, presumably the Nandi[1]—settled among the Nyole and thus rendered it necessary for the Logoli to go all the way to Bunyole if they want the rain either to fall or to stop.

The following is the most complete version of this origin-story which I obtained among the Logoli:

'In the beginning of this country, very long ago indeed, it was like this with the rain: The people saw the rain falling and wondered only; they did not know where it came from, nor did they know if there was somebody who was the owner of the rain. Thus the rain could either stop or it could go on raining all the time. The name "rain" (*embula*) was there from long ago.

'Then there was one woman who had been lost to her clan. She wandered about and finally arrived at the place of a man called Agayenga. This man was a Logoli and the woman came to stay at his place and became his wife. One day she said to her husband: "My old man, do you know the matter of making the rain to fall; may I show you something about this knowledge?"[2] Agayenga replied: "Yes, try to do it, then I may see." The woman waited till evening time and then she said: "It is good that I may begin now." She took pots (*dzinyingu*) and put them down at the place of making the rain (*ahukugimbiliza*); then she began to bring thunder and lightning[3] into the house. When Agayenga heard the noise and the roar he said: "*A*', *a*', *zai, zai,* she is not a person whom one may keep, it is better that she should go away; she is a loafer only, we cannot live here together with her. She must return to the place she has come from; she cannot remain here because she is a woman who might kill other people." Agayenga then drove her away and told her: "I do not like you, because I see that you are doing things which scare the people and which will make all the people of the clan wonder. I do not want all the clanspeople to call me 'something' " (i.e. an *omulogi*, a witch).

'Then that woman went away again but she had no place where to go; so she left Agayenga's place and roamed about in the open (i.e. aimlessly) until she came to a place called Enameza Edivwongo. Near the home of a certain man called Ambula she found a person who belonged to the Nyole people. She followed him and said to him: "I am roaming about only" (i.e. do you want to take me with you?) And that woman was an old woman indeed; perhaps at the place she had come from she had been living with a husband who was called a rain-maker, but why she came to the country of the Logoli they do not know well.

'When she arrived at Ambula's place she entered the house and sat down and rested awhile. Then the people who were in the house began to wonder and said: "Who is she?" And while they were still saying so, they suddenly saw poisonous snakes (*amahili*) and other snakes entering the house and then all the other creatures that crawl were coming into the house. Then Ambula

[1] According to Ludjenda, a Tiriki elder, the knowledge of rain-magic came to Kavirondo from the Elgeyo people who live to the north-east of the Nandi.
[2] ... *yive umanyi liŋana lyokulete embula kuduka akuba ugumanyie kuvugeli zana yivu?* lit. do you know the matter of to bring the rain till it falls, may I show you of that knowledge?
[3] *Dzinguba kandi oluheni.* In Lurogoli the thundering is always put first and the lightning second.

himself said: "*A*', *a*', is this a person who can be kept here?" Finally the woman said to Ambula: "Let me stay here, then I will show you the knowledge of the rain, so that you can let the rain fall." The old woman then began indeed to do as she had said and to let the rain come. When she had finished, they heard a great noise and much thundering and lightning. Then Ambula said: "*Ai, ai*, this is not a person who can stay here, she must go back where she has come from." Finally Ambula drove her away, and the old woman went on till she came to the side of Bunyole. And she arrived at a place near Kima which they call Emuhaya. There she found a person who became her husband and his name was Nganyi of Bunyole. They lived together and began to build their house, then they found near their place some bushland (*vulimu*). They prevented (*vasola*) other people from going there and it became like a forest. Then that old woman lived together with Nganyi and showed him the knowledge of making the rain fall. Nganyi did not understand quickly, but the old woman said: "You may look on only and I myself will make the rain." While they were living at Emuhaya the old woman said: "Nganyi, we better go near the hill, there we might find a chance of making the rain." Then they went to a place which they call Evutjigwi and there they found a place where they could live. When they had settled there, they began to think how they wanted to make the rain.[1] The first one to be clever (in making rain) was that old woman. She began to make the rain, and Nganyi learnt from her until he knew the work of how to make the rain fall.

'When the old woman was still making the rain she did not get presents right away. What she did was not known to all the countries, then (later) when the people knew there is a person who is making the water which is falling from the sky they said: "Now this may be why it is that the rain passes over us for many days and it is very hot, perhaps the rain-maker is refusing to send the rain." Then they send the elders of the clans and they say "now we may go to find out the reason why we do not see the rain". They find the rain-maker saying to them: "I cannot give the rain for nothing, without being given payments (*amadanyi*); I want you to bring presents, then I may think what I can do indeed." Those people then leave the place of the rain-maker and return home to tell their clansmen (*avaluhia*): "Nganyi wants you to take presents to him." Then the "big one" (*omunene*) of every clan calls those who are called the "elders" (*amagutu*), and they sit down for a council (*ekiruazo*). Then they hold council and the big one says: "You went to look and see what the rain-maker has asked for, he wants presents. I am speaking to all you elders, you may send words to all people that they may collect grain." Then they begin to collect grain throughout the country (i.e. in the whole of Maragoli); they take it to the big one of their clan and he appoints people who will carry it. Then they carry the grain there, and when they have arrived at the rain-maker's place they give him all the food. Then the rain-maker says to them: "You may go home and sleep three nights (lit., sticks) and then you will see the rain beating down, then it will rain indeed." And the people believe him and say: "Perhaps it is true, this one knows indeed" (*ngani nageligali uyu yamanya ligali*). Now when we hear the rain roaring we know that the rain is about to beat down; we call this "*embula ehizanga*"

[1] Literally, the customs of the rain.

(the rain is boiling), then it is falling (*ekubanga*), and when it leaves off we say: "*egaduka*" (it ceases).

'Agayenga, the husband of the woman who was the owner of the rain at the place to which she came first, is now called Ambula, because he is the owner of the rain (*embula*). And they do not know from which clan that woman came, so they are saying that she came from the country of the Nandi. But they did not listen to her when they saw the lightning and the roaring of the rain. Then Agayenga said: "This person may not stay on here." He said: "The house may burn down, I do not like her." After a few years they heard that the Nyole had a clever old woman who came to them from the side of the Logoli and that she was making the rain till it rained indeed and also the lightning and the roaring. Then the people of Agayenga and the people of the whole country heard that it was their old woman who had gone to the people of Nganyi at Vudjigwi where she now was making the rain. Then all the clansmen said: "Oh, oh, alas, why did we drive away a good person; alas, if we had let her stay here perhaps it would be ourselves who would be making these matters (i.e. rain), perhaps we would be finding this wealth now." They said: "Now we cannot do so, but if there will be fighting perhaps we can take her back here." '

According to another version of the same story which I obtained from an elder of the Mavi clan in Maragoli, the old woman said to Agayenga: ' "Bring me two trays (*vidavo*)." He brought them and placed them in front of her. Then that old woman took a little water and poured it into those trays. Right away there was thunder, lightning, and an earthquake; it seemed as if the house was tumbling over.'

Thus the first rain-woman used essentially the same technique of filling pots with water which is employed by the present rain-makers. Furthermore, this second version stresses even more emphatically than the first one that the first rain-maker acquired the knowledge of making the rain because he was a fearless person who successfully withstood all the attempts of the old woman to scare him. Thus it runs:

'... The old woman finally arrived in the country of the Nyole where she came to the house of Lugiriki of the Tjigwi clan. She entered the hut and, sitting down in the front partition, she said: "Ah, my son, will you look at me, perhaps I can show you a medicine from which you may profit." Then Lugiriki said: "Enter!" Lugiriki took a castrated goat and killed it and gave it to that old woman to eat. When the old woman had eaten and was satisfied she said to Lugiriki: "Bring the dishes and put them down inside the door here." Lugiriki then brought the dishes and put them down inside the door. The old woman then said to Lugiriki: "Will you also be afraid as Agayenga was?" But Lugiriki replied: "No, I am not a young one. Never mind, I may see for myself." Then as soon as the old woman poured the water into the small pot it began its work: Thunder, lightning, snakes, all birds of the bush and all other bad things of the wilderness arrived in Lugiriki's house and licked his body, so that they might see if he was afraid. In that case she would not give him her medicine. But because Lugiriki was no coward she finally told him: "You are really a full-grown person, you may be given the medicine and profit by it." The things which she took and gave to him are these: The horn of the *kisusu*-antelope which shows him how to make the rain fall with good water; then she gave him the horn of an *indja*-antelope which shows him the rain that can pour down heavily. Then she showed him the horn of a big animal which brings the rain of the hail-stones and also the storm which destroys what has been planted. Then she also told him to keep a little water in those pots: One little pot under the eaves of the south and another one under the eaves of the east. And his eyes must be looking towards the east (the direction from which the rain usually comes). Into these pots he must not pour much water. If he keeps much water in them the rain can beat down the whole day from early in the morning until the time when the chickens come home. And she also told him to build a small hut in the bush where he must keep those pots, and they must not be taken away from that bush.'

These two versions of the origin-myth of rain-making not merely explain how the family of Nyole rain-magicians came to wield the power of controlling the rainfall, but the common knowledge of this myth provides this family with a charter for holding the exclusive privilege of rain-magic. When I asked some Logoli elders why none of their own tribesmen ever tried to make rain, they replied that they could not do so as they did not possess the knowledge which the old woman had passed on to the Nyole. If they were to try and copy the rain-maker he would be angry and withhold the rain altogether.

(iv) *Succession to the office of rain-magician*

Although the Nyole rain-magician originally obtained his power of controlling the rainfall from a woman, the office of *omugimba* has since been handed down from father to son only, so that there have been no more female rain-makers.

Among the Nyole it is left to the father's choice which one of his sons he wants to appoint for his successor. If he wishes to do so, he may also split up the office of rain-making between two of his sons:

'When the rain-maker dies he can take all the rules which are good and give them to the son whom he likes best. To him he can give these objects: The horn of the little rain and the horn of the heavy rain. And to the son whom he does not like well he can give the horn of the rain of hailstones and that of the wind-storms. No person who comes from another clan can become a rain-maker.'

Among the Vugusu, on the other hand, it is not left to the father's personal choice which of his sons will succeed him, but—as is the case with most ritual offices—the successor is pointed out by the ancestral spirit of a previous rain-maker. This spirit indicates his choice by causing the candidate to suffer from a variety of symptoms. Thus he would make him shiver and tremble violently whenever his father performs his magic, or he would make him act like a crazy person; he would afflict him with an eye disease and nearly make him blind, or, finally, cause the death of all his children. To ascertain the precise meaning of these different symptoms, the father consults a diviner. If he interprets them as indications of a spirit's choice of a successor, the present rain-maker promises his son to teach him the knowledge of rain-making when he himself gets old. In South Kitosh he confirms this decision by blowing through his reed-stalk into the rain-pot which he keeps behind his house, a rite which apparently has the significance of a vow.

To prevent his sons from competing with him while he is still alive and to safeguard the full privacy of his office, the rain-maker performs his magic all by himself, without the assistance even of that one of his sons who will eventually succeed him. He entrusts his knowledge to his successor only when he is near death. Among the Vugusu of North Kitosh and in Butsotso where the rain-makers have a minor reputation only, their office may be handed on both in the male and the female line (mother's brother to sister's son). If the rain-maker has an intimate friend, he may even sell him the knowledge of *vugimba* for the comparatively high price of four head of cattle. Moreover, before receiving any instruction, the friend must stage a meat feast for all the relatives of the rain-maker at which he must slaughter two more animals.

(v) *Tribute paid to the rain-magician*

Corresponding to the unequal prestige of the rain-makers, the quality and quantity of the tribute taken to them vary considerably in the different parts of Bantu Kavirondo. The Nyole rain-maker who enjoys by far the greatest reputation, receives also the most substantial tribute or presents. He cannot be approached privately by ordinary people but only publicly by a delegation of the highest clan-heads of the tribe. The manner in which the tribute is taken to him is described in the following text:

The people go to the rain-maker once every season. They take presents to him because the heat is very great, and they call that time *ekimiyu* (the major hot season) and this is at the end of the (European) year in the month of December. At that time they dig for eleusine and sorghum. In the fields from which they have harvested beans and maize they must now plant eleusine, and this we call *egudu* (the eleusine season). Then the big elder of the clan sends for a pot to the hill where the person lives who is pottering the pots; he must make a very big one indeed and they also prepare tobacco which they take to the rain-maker. Then they take both the pot and the tobacco to the rain-maker's place where he lives at Vudjigwi. He who is taking these things to the rain-maker is an old man called Amambia, and he is a chief (*omwami*) in the country of the Logoli. He must go with three of his people only, and when they have arrived there they may sleep at the place of the rain-maker, because Amambia is a big person in the country. Amambia is one of the rich people like the rain-maker. If he were to send his elders they would not get there a thing (i.e. they would not get any rain for their people). Then they leave again, for the rain-maker cannot take them to see the place where he is making (*alombelanga*) the rain.

Moreover, it is said that formerly people would never have dared to challenge the *omugimba* for withholding the rain, but they would have increased the number of their petitions and the value of their tribute:

'When they had taken their things to him and the rain did not fall, he would cheat them and tell them, "the things which you have brought to me are not enough. If you add more I will make the rain fall for you." When he said so those people who had not yet paid anything would add more. If the rain still did not fall they would take things there every day until the rain-maker had collected a great amount of tobacco.'

Apparently the tribute increased in value as the reputation of the rain-maker grew. Thus one elder relates in a narrative:

'One day a man from another clan went to the rain-maker and said to him: "Ah, *omugimba*, you are like a chief who is watching the earth and the sky! Why do you permit the people to bring you tobacco only? You are indeed a person who ought to be given cows and goats!" From then on the people began to fatten the goats and for a few years they brought him the goats. Then again when they saw that the rain did not fall all the days they thought, perhaps the rain-maker refuses to let the rain fall because we are not giving him cattle. Then they began to fatten cattle.'

The lesser rain-makers, on the other hand, perform their magic much like other departmental specialists. Thus the chief of the Wanga tribe told me that he calls the Marama rain-makers to come to his village when he is in need of rain. They bring their paraphernalia along with them and perform their magic at his place, although they, too, insist on doing so in privacy. In Kitosh, the rain-magician is likewise called to the village (*lugova*) which is in need of rain and he collects his presents before he goes home to perform his magic. If then, in spite of having received his payment, he fails to procure rain, the people of the *lugova* will go to the rain-maker's home early in the morning and give him a good beating for withholding the rain. Thus in January 1933 when the sky cleared again after it had looked for a few days as if the rains were about to break, the people went to the rain-maker of North Kitosh to remind him of his duties. As he himself had escaped (to Chief Sudi's country), they caught his two sons and made them lie flat on their backs in the hot sun beating them with sticks.[1] Nandoli, who shortly afterwards slept in the same hut with one of them, told me that he had asked him why they had not simply denied that they had the power of making rain and said that it was only God who made the rain. But he had replied that he would rather suffer an occasional beating than let his profit go.[2] Among the Vugusu, the rain-

[1] Among the Vugusu such a procedure is merely a punishment and has no magical significance as is the case among the Azande where an obstinate rain-maker is thrown into the water and where the idea seems to be that the rain-maker's contact with water will in itself produce rain. Cf. E. E. Evans-Pritchard, *Witchcraft, Oracles and Magic among the Azande*, Oxford, 1937, p. 471.

[2] In the year 1927 the rain-maker among the Nyole was likewise blamed for his

makers are also approached privately by ordinary people. Apart from being asked to bring rain in times of drought (i.e. at the time when the rains should come again), they are mainly employed by their clients to withhold the rain from the gardens of people who have refused to return a debt. This method of securing the payment of a debt appears to be very commonly used, for it was always mentioned in the first place whenever I inquired into the sanctions by which people enforced their claims to property. It is said that usually the mere threat to go to the rain-maker is sufficient to make a person pay his debt. This sanction is all the more powerful as it affects not only the debtor himself but his neighbours as well, so that they will bring pressure to bear on him to settle his debt without delay.

In spite of the greater or lesser prestige which the rain-maker enjoys everywhere among the Bantu Kavirondo, his status has remained that of a departmental expert and has not been linked with that of a 'chief' exercising political authority. That is to say, his advice is not sought in any other matter than that of procuring rain, and the group of people or even tribes who render tribute to him are not united under him as under a common ruler. He has nothing to do with the maintenance of law and order (apart from being used as an instrument in enforcing the payment of debts), nor does he, in his capacity as a rain-maker, assume any leadership in the organization of warfare or of religious ceremonies.

(4) THE SPIRITS OF THE DEAD

The second great category of agents that wield mystical power affecting human welfare are the spirits of deceased persons. As regards the effects produced by them upon the living, the spirits of the dead and the various kinds of human agents have much in common, so much in fact that in many cases a particular event that has occurred may be attributed either to a spirit or to one type or other of human specialists. It seems proper therefore to discuss the various notions concerning the spirits of the dead under the same major heading as those regarding human agents.

As the spirits of the dead have originated from living human beings, the best approach to an understanding of the nature of these spirits is obviously to analyse the native conception of life—i.e. the essential qualities attributed to living human beings—and then to examine in what particular way these characteristic features of a living human being are thought to become transformed into those of a spirit being.

When inquiring into the native ideas as to what constitutes the essence of life one meets with three distinct concepts, viz. body, heart, and shadow.

alleged refusal to bring the rain, although he had received ample tribute, and a complaint about him was lodged by the natives with the D.O. at Kisumu. He was thereupon arrested and forbidden to accept any further tribute. Although the public collection of tribute for the Nyole rain-maker has been stopped since that time, all my informants agreed that in times of drought secret presents are still taken to him (or to his successor).

The *body* of the living (*ombili*) is looked upon as a material substance, which in some vague way is the 'seat' or 'substratum' of the heart and the shadow. Thus the Bantu Kavirondo talk about the *ombili* much in the same way as we talk about the human body: 'The *ombili* is the flesh and bones of a person which one can see and feel. Both men and animals have an *ombili*.' But the *ombili* is distinguished from mere material substance by being filled with the life of the living: when a person dies his body is no longer called *ombili*, but *omukuzu*. The *omukuzu* decays 'and becomes like earth', but it still differs from inanimate objects in a way which will be discussed later on. The *ombili* as the material substratum of living beings still forms an undifferentiated whole. The various parts of the body are merely labelled by descriptive terms, the different units being distinguished according to their anatomical structure and—as far as the outer organs are concerned—by the use to which they are put.

The second concept, 'heart' (*omwoyo*), refers both to the bodily organ and to a quality of living man which might be termed his 'consciousness of being alive' or his 'soul'. As linguistic usage indicates, the heart is held responsible for the acts of feeling and thinking (of a person). Thus one says: 'My heart fears', *omwoyo gwange gutia*; 'my heart is glad', *omwoyo gwange gusalama*; 'the sorrow of the heart', *ekeverera kyomwoyo*, &c. If a person has a dream, one says that 'the heart makes him dream'. According to some of my informants the heart can leave a person's body while he is dreaming. It then visits the various places which he sees in his dream. Likewise the heart of another person can come and visit one in a dream. The *omwoyo*, however, always returns to the body as soon as one wakes up (or rather one wakes up as soon as the heart has returned). It thus either is or parallels consciousness which also returns to the body as soon as one wakes up from sleep. The *omwoyo* is also regarded as the essence of being alive as a human being; the expression *ali mwoyo*, literally 'he is heart', therefore means as much as 'he is alive', and the word 'life' itself can be rendered by the expression *eliva liomwoyo*, which literally means 'the being of the heart'.

The term for shadow, finally, which is *ekilili* in Lurogoli and *sisinini* in Luvugusu, stands both for the visible shadow of a person and for a quality of living man which might be termed his physical energy, for the bodily strength itself is rendered by the term *engulu*. Of a person who is healthy and in the full possession of his physical strength one says that all his shadows are with him, for it is believed that a person has not only one but several shadows. Like the heart, the possession of the shadow is an essential condition of being alive (as a human being). Thus, if a person dies, one says that his shadow (i.e. the sum total of his shadows) has left him or escaped from him (*ekilili kwiluka*). When a person sleeps, his shadows are also asleep, but they do not dream like his heart. This corresponds to a person's physical energy which rests during his sleep without taking any part in his dream consciousness. It may also happen that some of the shadows which a person possesses leave him while he is asleep, because they have been taken away by other powers, particularly the spirits of the dead. It is thought that the spirits of the dead like the occasional company of the living and that they can obtain it by temporarily taking the shadows of the living with them. Such a temporary absence of one's shadows and the things which they experience while they are away do not, however, enter into the consciousness of the person concerned. For this reason nobody can make any definite statements about the land of the dead or any other adventures which his shadows might have met with while they were in the company of the spirits. The fact that his shadows have been temporarily taken away by a spirit becomes evident only from a feeling of tiredness upon wakening. The shadows, instead of having rested and thereby restored the physical strength of their 'owner' as they normally would have done, have used up their strength during their absence from the body. If some of them have not yet returned upon waking, their 'owner' suffers from a severe headache and pain in his limbs; his blood flows heavily and slowly and he is unable to do any work; in short, the absence of his shadows lowers his physical energy.

As regards the normal activities of the shadow, one says that its activities parallel those of the body. If the body raises his arm, the shadow also raises his arm, if the body smokes a pipe, the shadow also smokes a pipe. This confirms our interpretation of the *ekilili* or *sisinini* as the source of physical energy, for behind every bodily function there must obviously be an actuating force. To conceive of this force as a double requires the least amount of abstraction.

It appears, therefore, that his notion of a parallelism between the source of physical energy and human action has given rise to the interpretation of the visible shadow as a manifestation of the *ekilili* concept, rather than that the whole concept is merely an 'explanation' of the visible shadow. This conclusion is based on the fact that there are no other instances where natural phenomena are 'explained' merely to satisfy intellectual curiosity. It would, therefore, be quite unparalleled if a phenomenon like the visible shadow should give rise to such an elaborate theory as the one which has been discussed. The functions of the human body, on the other hand, become a matter of practical interest because experience shows that these functions occasionally fail to work properly (in the case of sickness or physical injury) or that they stop entirely (in the case of death). The desire to control the functions of the body would then give rise to the notion that there must be a particular force behind them. The idea of identifying the visible shadow with this force would easily suggest itself owing to the parallelism between the movements of the body and those of the shadow.

Body, heart, and shadow are thus the three elements which together constitute the essence of being alive as a human being. Now when a person dies, i.e. when his body ceases to function, the personality of the living becomes transformed into the spirit of the deceased. The general terms for this spirit are *ekigingi* among the Logoli and *musambwa*[1] among the Vugusu. The etymology of both words is not clear; it is possible, however, that the word *musambwa* is derived from the passive verb form *oxusambwa*, 'to be burnt', which might then mean as much as 'the burnt one' or 'the one who has turned to smoke'.

There do not seem to exist any clearly conceived ideas in the minds of the natives as to the exact manner in which this process of transformation from a living human being to a spirit takes place.

The only point on which there was general agreement among my informants was that at the moment of physical death 'heart' and 'shadow' leave the body, which thereby loses both its consciousness and its strength and thus 'dies' (*kukuza*). The body now becomes an *omukuzu*, a corpse. As to the manner in which the heart leaves the body, contradictory views are held. Some informants claim that it emerges through the crown of the head, others that it escapes as breath through the mouth.[2] According to either view, it is not the physical organ which leaves the body but the spiritual power which somehow resides in the heart of the living. Analogously, the *ekilili* or *sisinini* which leaves the body is not the visible shadow but the power that during a person's life resides in his shadow. When natives claim, therefore, that an *omukuzu* has no *ekilili*, they do not mean that he has no visible shadow, a statement which would obviously be contradicted by experience; they rather mean that his shadow has lost its power, its ability to actuate the movements of the body. This again confirms our interpretation that the visible shadow is merely the shell or container of a force which resides in it.

Contradictory views are also held concerning the relative share which 'heart' and 'shadow' have in the formation of the *ekigingi* or *musambwa*. Some people identify the spirit and the shadow, saying that the heart goes up to God, while the shadow stays near the people and comes back to trouble them (as spirits do). Others say that heart and shadow join together and become the spirit. It remains doubtful whether any definite views are held on the subject at all. The qualities which are attributed to the spirit agree better with the second view (that heart and shadow jointly become the spirit), for the spirit of the deceased is thought to possess all the qualities of the living. He can think, feel, and act like a living person; he has thus retained the complete personality of the living detached from his bodily substratum. In his outer appearance he is said to be a weak outline of his former self: 'When you see him he looks like smoke; you can see right through him and when you touch him he disappears.' However, in spite of the immaterial nature of the spirit, his association with the material remains of the body

---

[1] Apart from this name which is used as a term of address in prayers and sacrifices they are also referred to as *vamagombe*, a term which implies their hostile attitude towards the living and seems to be derogatory.

[2] An analysis of the death rites—as far as I have been able to observe and record them—does not throw any light upon this problem.

is not completely severed. Not only does the spirit demand a proper handling and burial of the body, but for many years he is sensitive to any harm which his bodily remains may have to suffer.[1]

In addition to the qualities of his former personality as a living human being the spirit of the deceased possesses an increased power to exercise an active influence over the welfare of his living relatives and descendants. This alleged power is the chief characteristic of a spirit which causes the living to concern themselves with him and to do everything in their power to establish good relations between the spirit and themselves. The belief in the mystical powers of spirits is thus the pivot of the whole complex of beliefs that are held with regard to them.

The spirit of a dead person does not enter into his last and final stage immediately after physical death has taken place, but—much like a living human being—he passes through various successive phases. For the first few days he is still in the vicinity of the corpse and watches the funeral of his bodily remains. Thus the Logoli say that he sits under the eaves of the hut, on the roof of a granary, or in the branches of a nearby tree from where he can have a full view of the funeral proceedings and of all the persons who have come to mourn for him. If the funeral is staged in the proper manner with pantomimic performances of his former activities, a cattle-drive, and a large dance (cf. p. 451 sq.), he will be pleased, while otherwise he will be unhappy and full of resentment against the living whose daily company he has been forced to part from. Among the Vugusu it is believed that during the first two or three months after death the spirit is still infected with the smell of the living (*omuya*). This smell is resented by the spirits of those people who died long ago and they refuse to accept him in their company. A similar idea prevails among the Nyole, where the spirit of one recently dead is referred to by the same term as a new-born child for which no sacrifice has yet been performed and which has not yet been 'presented' to its relatives and accepted into their community. During this intermediate stage the spirit is thought to be in a very unfortunate state. Expelled from the company of the living and rejected by the community of the spirits, he feels lonely and restless and harbours feelings of revenge against those whom he thinks have caused his death.

The permanent abode of the ancestral spirits is usually referred to by the general term *hasi*, 'down', 'underneath the earth'. However, while it is thought that the spirits of those who have recently died stay by themselves in the grave of the corpse, the older spirits are said to live together in a sort of spirit-land[2] which is likewise located under the earth somewhere in the west. The mode of existence which the spirits lead in this land of the dead is thought to be similar to the life of the living. They have wives and children,[3] they own cattle and make the same social distinctions as

---

[1] Cf. the burning of the bones to frighten the spirit of a dead person; p. 288.
[2] *Emagombe* in the Vugusu dialect and *muvakuzu* in the Logoli dialect.
[3] i.e. their wives and children join them after they have died.

the living people. Apart from such general notions, however, the living do not seem to devote a great deal of thought to this land of the dead. This becomes evident from a number of contradictions in the various statements that are made regarding it. Thus, on the one hand, one persuades a patient who is seriously ill to take food by telling him that 'there are no gardens in the *emagombe*', meaning thereby that he should not miss what might be his last opportunity to provide himself with food. On the other hand, the absence of vegetable-food offerings to the spirits of the dead was explained to me by the statement that the women in the spirit-land were able to cook their own eleusine porridge for their families, but that the male spirits could not obtain their own meat. This explanation again hardly tallies with the prevailing view that the spirits possess cattle and other livestock. When I attempted to probe into these contradictions my informants merely shrugged their shoulders and insisted that nobody really knew what sort of existence the spirits *were* leading in the spirit-land.

From their subterranean abode—whether this be in the grave or in the land of the dead—the spirits are thought to visit their living kinsmen and to appear to them in a variety of ways. Most commonly they appear to the living in the form of dreams, but occasionally—and especially to older people—their presence makes itself felt also in the form of hallucinations or auditions. Thus some old men among the Logoli told me that on a windless day they can hear the spirits moving about in the foliage of the banana-grove; other people claim to see them in vague outline in the roof of the hut or on the storage shelf which forms a sort of attic or loft in many Maragoli huts. At night, when a person cannot sleep and is tossing about restlessly, he is liable to be visited by a spirit. The spirit then softly taps his victim's shoulder, scratches him, or even shakes him violently, but any attempts to seize the spirit are said to be useless, for he vanishes as soon as one tries to touch him. It is regarded a symptom of such a visitation by a spirit if a person talks in his sleep or if he suddenly throws himself about as if fighting an invisible opponent.

As a rule, a person who has had such a visitation from a spirit is frightened and if they occur repeatedly, especially by the same spirit, his health deteriorates; he becomes weak and emaciated and ultimately dies, unless it is possible to restore his energies by persuading the spirit to spare him, i.e. to cease troubling him with his visitations. Although in the majority of cases the illness which is caused by a spirit is preceded by such a consciously experienced visitation, a spirit can also send illness and adverse luck to a person without appearing to him. It is regarded as a common characteristic of the illness sent by ancestral spirits that it does not take the form of a sudden, violent outbreak but rather of a slow, creeping disease, of an all-round lessening of vitality and of one's power of resistance. A quick and unexpected death is therefore only seldom[1] attributed to the spirits of the dead but mostly to human agents such as the sorcerers of the

[1] Cf. below, p. 492.

logi or the *vila* type. In the same way, if the alleged powers of the spirits are directed against the material welfare of the living, they do not involve sudden destruction but disappointment and frustration in every undertaking: a small yield of crops, disease among one's livestock, a succumbing to one's opponent when carrying on litigation, &c. The misfortunes caused by the spirits of the dead thus consist in a lowering of one's vitality and energy, i.e. in a weakening of one's *ekilili* or *sisinini*.

The range of the negative power which the spirits of the dead can wield is, however, limited in several ways, first of all in time. Thus it is thought that their desire to inflict illness and misfortune upon the living is at its peak during the first few months after physical death. Gradually their 'fierceness' (*ovululu*)[1] subsides, and after four or five years have passed, it is said that the spirit has become 'tame' (*okukuba amasinde*) or that he has 'cooled off' (*okukinda*). This, however, does not mean that the spirit now ultimately 'dies' or that he loses his power. It rather means that he has now fully accustomed himself to his existence as a spirit and that he has lost his former desire to inflict harm upon the living. From the psychological point of view one might say that the time when the spirit is thought to have cooled off has come when the living no longer fear him, because their memory of him has become so weak that they cease to think and dream of him. As the remembrance of an old and well-known person would naturally remain alive for a longer period of time than that of a younger and less important person, it is quite logical that the spirits of the former are thought to cool off more slowly than those of the latter.

Apart from this limitation in time the power of the spirits is also restricted as regards the kind of people against whom it can be directed. Thus, as a rule, a male spirit can only harm a male person, and a female spirit only a female person. Exceptions to this rule are the spirit of a husband who can harm his former wife and vice versa, and the spirits of parents who occasionally may harm their children of either sex, especially if they have uttered a dying curse against them. Furthermore, the kinds of spirits which one has to fear are mainly those of relatives by blood, i.e. one's own ancestors, and particularly those with whom one has been affiliated by close economic and legal ties. The spirit of a mere neighbour or friend can never harm one, even if one has been in close social contact with him throughout his life.

Spatially, on the other hand, the range of power of the ancestral spirits is unlimited. As one of my informants said: 'They are like wind and can travel anywhere and enter anything, but they cannot penetrate a solid substance.'[2] As they are not bound to remain at a definite abode, they can follow the living wherever they go, so that these have no chance of escaping from them.[3]

---

[1] The same expression refers to wild and ferocious animals.

[2] Cf. below, p. 289.

[3] The sister of one of my informants (Christopher Mtiva) had an illegitimate

What motives, then, does one ascribe to the ancestral spirits for their hostile attitude towards the living? It has been stated that shortly after a person's death his spirit feels restless and lonely, as he has had to leave his body and thus to give up his former life without as yet having been accepted into the community of the other spirits and having become accustomed to his new mode of existence. Accordingly it is thought that the life of the dead means—especially at first—a decided change for the worse as compared with the life of the living. This change for the worse causes the spirits, on the one hand, to harbour feelings of envy towards the living; on the other hand, it creates in them the desire to visit the living or to fetch them to their own abode so that they may have the benefit of their company.

A second motive which accounts for the hostility of the ancestral spirits is their wish to revenge themselves for the fate that has overtaken them as well as for any evil treatment which they had been made to suffer while they were still alive as human beings. Since every death, apart from its immediate cause, is attributed to the death-spell or evil rite of another human being, this desire for revenge is directed in the first place against the person who is supposed to have caused the death. In addition, it is directed against every relative who had ill-treated or neglected the spirit while he was still a living person, especially against his children and grand-children if they failed to care for him properly when he was old and helpless.

A third explanation of the hostility of the ancestral spirits appears to be the mere continuation of the bad deeds which they used to commit during their lifetime. Thus it is thought that quarrelsome and evil-minded persons as well as sorcerers retain their bad qualities even after they have turned into spirits and that they abuse the power which they now wield as spirits to send illness and misfortune to the living, even if they have never suffered any harm from them.

It will be seen that the first of these three motives, the desire of the spirits to share the company of the living, entails a negative attitude towards the latter in its effect rather than in its intention. Visitations of the spirits are feared, because they have the undesirable effect of weakening one's physical energies, of sapping the strength of one's shadow, and thus, ultimately, of endangering one's life. In this sense any contact between the dead and the living is considered dangerous and unwelcome to the latter. Otherwise the attitude of the spirits who wish to share the company of their living relatives is quite positive: they want to continue their former relations with them, they desire to be near them, but they are not bent upon their destruction.

child which frequently suffered from fits. These were interpreted as visitations from the spirit of the child's maternal grandfather who had been a farm-labourer at Thika (about 250 miles away from Maragoli) where he is buried. His spirit was thought to feel hostile towards his grandchild for having been born out of wedlock.

This idea, it seems to me, explains why, under certain conditions, the spirits of the dead are not regarded as antagonists but as friends and helpers of the living. These conditions are given when the spirits cease their attempts to fetch the living to their own abodes in the spirit-land.

Now, as has been stated, the spirit of a dead person is thought to 'become tame' or to 'cool off' after a number of years, i.e. to acquiesce in his fate of being a spirit. When this has happened, it is no longer thought to be dangerous to have a visitation from him. His existence in the spirit-land having become firmly rooted, the ever-present positive element in his attitude towards the living can manifest itself, for he no longer envies the living and therefore has no reason to kill them (i.e. to fetch them to the spirit-land). On the contrary, his visitations may now be invoked and turned to the advantage of the living, as he is now thought to be willing to help the living, just as during his lifetime he used to care for the well-being of his children and grandchildren and to protect them from dangers.

The seemingly ambivalent attitude displayed by the ancestral spirits towards the living—their hostility on the one hand and their friendship on the other—is thus derived from the same basic idea, viz. that 'life' does not end with physical death but is continued in a different way and that the transition from the 'life of the living' to the 'life of the dead' means a change for the worse to which the spirits can only gradually accustom themselves. This has two consequences. On the one hand, it entails the notion of a lasting bond between the living and the dead, much of the same nature as that which exists between living relatives. On the other hand, it gives rise to the thought that physical death causes a dangerous tension between the deceased and the survivors which results partly from a feeling of envy towards the latter and partly from a desire for revenge. The motives which one ascribes to the spirits of the dead for their varying attitude towards the living are thus the same as those which one knows as motives behind the actions of living people. Likewise, the nature and the range of their power are entirely conceived of in terms of their former existence as living human beings. Although endowed with superior powers, they are still essentially the same as human beings.

(5) THE SUPREME BEING

In addition to the belief in ancestral spirits there exists among the Bantu Kavirondo the notion of a Supreme Being or 'High God', as well as of a number of minor spirit-beings. The clarity with which this notion can be defined and elaborated, however, differs greatly among the various sub-tribes. Partly at least this appears to be due to the fact that Christianity has affected the different tribes to a very unequal degree. In those parts of Kavirondo where missions have been at work for the longest period of time and in the most intense manner I have failed to elicit any coherent set of ideas regarding the belief in a Supreme Being or even a vestige of ritual or prayer which would throw any light on the presence of such a belief. Thus among the Logoli I could not even discover with certainty whether in the pre-Christian era they had a commonly employed name for a Supreme Being and what that name was. Nowadays the term 'Nyasai'[1] is in general use among them. But it is uncertain whether this term, which is also shared by the Luo, has been introduced only since the advent of missionaries or whether—in a similar form—it was employed also in pre-European days.[2] Frequent conversations on this subject with the pagan elders in Maragoli yielded nothing but vague and contradictory information. According to some the Supreme Being was formerly called Asai or Isahi, according to others Emungu, but in no case was I able to obtain any reliable details on the belief in the Supreme Being which would throw any light on the qualities ascribed to him. It was frequently stated by my informants that the semi-annual sacrifice performed by Logoli on a tribal scale was addressed to Asai, but—as we shall see later on—there is no evidence in the ritual procedure, in the songs sung, or the prayers spoken on that occasion which would confirm this view. The term Emungu seems occasionally to be used as a label for something that is marvellous, out of the ordinary, or simply unknown. The concept of the Supreme Being is much more elaborate among the Vugusu where it is called Wele. The same term is also employed by the Gishu, Wanga, Kakalelwa, and Kabras. Although Christian influence started among the Vugusu at a much later date than among the Logoli it seems that their traditional concept of the Supreme Being has not only been better preserved but that it was much more fully developed than among the latter tribe. For it appears most unlikely that if the Logoli had had such a definite notion of the Supreme Being as the Vugusu still have to-day, every trace of that belief would have vanished within the thirty years during which they have been evangelized. The following analysis will deal exclusively with the concept of Wele as I have found it to exist among the Vugusu. The foremost quality ascribed to Wele is that of the creator of the world and of man. Although the way in which the world was made by him is not laid down in a myth, his role as a creator becomes evident from the stereotyped formula by which he is addressed in prayer:

Wele ewe waxuŋona xugende xusivala siowo.

'Wele, you who made us (so that) we may walk on your earth.'

[1] The same term (with minor deviations) is used also among the Nyole, Kisa, Tiriki, Isuxa, and Idaxo.

[2] J. Rees, the first missionary who worked among the Logoli, states in his (unpublished) vocabulary of the Logoli dialect that the word 'Nyasai' is not a Lurogoli word but that it originated from missionary use. He gives no Lurogoli word for the Supreme Being. Cf. Pater N. Stam, 1910, p. 360: 'Though entirely different in origin and language, the religious beliefs of the two races (Nilotes and Bantu) are very similar, differing only in minor points of ritual. Both the Nilotic and the Bantu Kavirondo have a distinct idea of God, the Supreme Being. The first call him Nyasaye (from *sayo*, to adore), and the latter Nasaye (from *kusaya*, to beseech). He is considered to be the creator or originator of all things.'

Waŋona tjixafu nevivindu vilimo.
'You who made the cattle and the things which are on it.'

Following this preamble the actual prayer is spoken. It is also said that when Wele had created both the world and the people on it he said to himself:

> *Ese ngona vavandu;*
> *niongánile áxula*
> *ne nio endo vila áfua.*
>
> 'It is I who made the people;
> whom I like he (shall) grow
> and whom I refuse he (shall) die.'

Thus Wele, having created human beings, is also thought to have retained control over their welfare, the power to make them prosper or die according to his will. It is generally stated that the first person whom Wele made was a man, called Umugoma. This Umugoma is also referred to as Umugoma wa Nasioka. According to present linguistic usage this addition to his name would indicate that he was the son of Nasioka. As the name Nasioka is not used synonymously with Wele, his very name, Umugoma wa Nasioka, seems to belie the claim that he was the first person whom Wele had made.

My informants, however, did not see any problem in this apparent contradiction and simply explained it by saying that Umugoma may not actually have been the first person who lived on earth but he was the first person to become famous and therefore the first one to be remembered. Later on Wele also made a woman, who was called Malava. While there exists no creation myth among the Vugusu, they have some other 'origin stories'. Of the first human pair, Umugoma and Malava, it is said that for a long time they did not know how to have sexual intercourse and thus to reproduce themselves. When Umugoma wished to embrace Malava he inserted his penis into her arm-pit and, accordingly, they remained without children. This went on until one day Umugoma, who was resting in the shade of a granary, saw Malava climb into the granary to take out some millet. As she did so he noticed her sex-organs and suddenly felt the desire to have intercourse with her in the proper way. When night came he tried to do so, but Malava refused him, pretending that what he had seen was an ulcer. In the end, however, she yielded to Umugoma and at first suffered much pain. A month later she conceived. Thus people began to increase.

A second 'origin story' relates how people came to die, for it is thought that long ago the people were blessed with eternal life.[1] It is the story of the chameleon as the bringer of death which is so widely known throughout Bantu Africa. According to the Vugusu version of this story the chameleon

---

[1] According to one informant people died even long ago but they came back to life again after four days, breaking through the grave.

one day came to the homestead of a certain man who was one of the sons of Maina. He was just sitting in front of his hut eating his evening meal. So the chameleon begged him for some food, but the son of Maina refused. The chameleon kept on asking until he got angry and drove it away. Then the chameleon cursed him and all other people, saying:

Nono neuma hano. Enyue mwesi mufwitjenge.
'Now I am leaving this place. You may all be dying.'

When the chameleon had spoken its curse the people began to breathe the air, to get sick and to die. Next the chameleon went to pay a visit to the snake. When it arrived at the snake's place the latter was just feeding, so the chameleon in turn begged it for some food. The snake then shared its meal with the chameleon, and as a blessing for its friendliness the chameleon told the snake that it should live on for ever and merely cast its skin when getting old instead of dying. For that reason even nowadays snakes do not die naturally but only when they are killed.

In addition to his quality as creator Wele is conceived of as the maintainer and promoter of all forces and things which are good and helpful to men. Accordingly, he is not only the one-time creator, the otiose god, who has retired after the act of creation and left the world with everything on it to look after itself, but he is an ever-present and ever-effective force working exclusively for the well-being of his creation. This quality of Wele finds expression in numerous sayings and prayers: if someone starts out for a journey one says to him: 'May Wele protect you' (*Wele axulinde*) or 'May Wele make (your) feet light' (*Wele axwanguyie vigele*). If a person is favoured by exceptionally good luck[1] in everything he does, one says of him 'this person has his Wele' (*mundu uyu na Wele wewe*). Similarly, it is said that unexpected but beneficial happenings have been caused by Wele and should be appreciated as a token of his goodwill. If a person comes across a dead animal or other useful thing while walking along a path, he should pick it up and make the best possible use of it, for 'what Wele offers you with one hand you should take with both hands' (*Wele axuela gumuxono mulala waganila gombi*).

This idea assumes what appears to be an ethical connotation when people are warned not to despise what Wele has given them, even if at the moment they do not care for it. Thus a man who has impregnated a girl and refuses to marry her is told 'what Wele gives you is what you should eat' (*Wele axua nio walia*, or *nisio Wele axuele nisio lia*), i.e. you should not refuse a gift that Wele has bestowed upon you. The same is said to a man who has tired of his wife and wishes to drive her away, or to a husband who scolds his wife for having borne a daughter instead of a son.

In prayers Wele is invoked for help and for lending success to an under-

---

[1] The word *exavi*, 'luck', is said, however, to be a new word.

taking: while sharpening his sword or spear before going to war a warrior prays:

> *Ndixo mbagala embalu,*
> *Wele, nosima gane wuumbe nisio oganile.*
> *sixangwile evweni evawasimbele*
> *noxambele tawe*
> *eva sexasinyole tá.*

> 'I am sharpening the sword,
> Wele, if you like you may give me what you may like.
> What shall fall in front of me is what you will give me;
> if you should not give it to me
> I cannot find it.'

Similarly, before going on a hunt one prays:

> *Wele nentjia ndi*
> *xava wandangilila nanyola nyama,*
> *gunumyu gulindjira*
> *namwe gumutambo gulindjira.*

> 'Wele, I am going thus,
> if you will lead me I shall find the animal,
> (otherwise) the salt will kill me
> or the poverty will kill me.'

The expression 'the salt will kill me' means in this connexion that if Wele does not lend success to his hunt he will have to eat his food with salt as his only relish instead of with meat, and that the salt alone will not keep him alive.

Wele can also warn people to refrain from committing a bad deed which they are contemplating. Thus, when several people conspire to kill a person or to commit a theft and one of them sneezes repeatedly this is considered a sign of warning sent to him by his Wele.[1] They also say that Wele has sent them an *engani* (prohibition) against doing what they had planned to do.

Although Wele has the power to kill people and is also said occasionally to do so because he wants them to live with him, all my informants insisted emphatically that he never punishes people for bad deeds committed by them. There is, however, one situation where Wele's interference with the fate of human beings does seem to be in the nature of a punishment. If a woman who has borne several children commits adultery and her children die soon afterwards, their death is commonly attributed to Wele. Wele is then supposed to appear to the woman in a dream and to say to her: 'I have given you these children from your husband. Why have you left him and joined another thigh? Now I shall take these children back to me.' Strangely, this sanction for a woman's adultery is said to apply

---

[1] See below, p. 208. Such a sneeze has the meaning of a warning by Wele only in the case of people who were born in the day-time. For people born at night it is without significance.

only in the case of women who begin to have a lover *after* they have borne several children. If a woman is unfaithful to her husband and later she bears children it is not thought that they will die, and if they did their death would not be attributed to Wele, even if the woman has continued her adulterous conduct. It appears, therefore, that this one case in which the role of moral judge and punisher is ascribed to Wele forms a singular exception which does not invalidate the prevailing idea that Wele is indifferent to the moral conduct of man.

From all these statements it appears that the conception of Wele has many anthropomorphic features. One prays to him and talks to him as to a human being. Furthermore, on the same occasions on which sacrifices are made to the ancestral spirits meat offerings are also made to Wele. As regards the abode of Wele, it is said that in contrast to that of the spirits of the dead it is 'above' (*yigulu*), i.e. in the sky. On the other hand, however, it is stressed that Wele is not bound to any particular abode, but that he is like air or smoke and, therefore, can penetrate everywhere. As far as a definite sex is ascribed to Wele at all he is regarded as a male being. His personification, however, does not extend so far that one bestows upon him definite external features—except the attribute white. Whenever I inquired into this matter I was given the same reply, viz. 'nobody knows what Wele looks like for no one has ever seen him, but who sees Wele must die'. There is no identification between Wele and the sun, *liuwa*. This, besides being an obvious consequence of the statement that no one has ever seen Wele, becomes evident from the fact that the sun and the moon are regarded as having been created by Wele along with the rest of the world.[1] Although the Vugusu greet daybreak with a short ceremony and a prayer, this is not actually addressed to the sun but to Wele. Thus all adult persons, male and female, when leaving the hut look first towards the east and spit once, then they look towards the west and spit again. Having done so they say:

> *Po, Wele, wasiele vulai*
> *oxufutjexo gamanyasi*
> *xugende vulai.*

> 'Po! Wele, may the day dawn well;
> may you spit upon us the medicine
> so that we may walk well!'

---

[1] In his article, 1910, vol. v, p. 360, Pater N. Stam writes: 'As, however, no external worship is given to the Creator, it would seem to the ordinary observer that the Sun is their principal deity and the Moon their second, whilst the spirits of their forefathers rank as minor spirits.' In a subsequent publication, 1919–20, however, he expresses a different view. 'If one asks a native here (viz. one of the Bantu) or a Nilotic whether he thinks the Sun to be God, they will decidedly answer in the negative, that God uses the Sun, etc. as a means to give us food and health. . . . Their idea about God (Wele) is naturally a poor one, but his main attributes are known to them. He is almighty, creator, lifegiver, omnipresent, and good.'

It is significant that one does not delay this morning prayer until the sun has risen but that one utters it at the first dawn of the day. It is thus a prayer imploring Wele to let the sun rise as always, to let all things take their usual course, and to bless the people in their daily tasks by spitting his all-powerful medicine upon them.

In the only two sun-myths which I have encountered among the Bantu Kavirondo the sun is likewise not identified with Wele, although in one of them it is, like Wele, considered to be a bringer of wealth. It runs as follows:

'Once there was a girl who disliked having courtships with boys and always refused them when they wanted to marry her. Finally, one of her suitors paid the marriage-cattle to her father and he took it, because he wanted to marry off his daughter by force. The girl, however, disliked the would-be husband and so she secretly ran away from her father's homestead until she came to a place about twelve miles away from her home. There she found a rope hanging down from the sky. She grasped the rope with her hands and looked upwards along it into the sky. While she did so the rope suddenly went up into the air and lifted her up so quickly that she was high up in the air before she realized what had happened.

'After a while she arrived in the sky, but the place where she found herself was the *sigoxe* (the place behind the hut where rubbish and the ashes are dumped down). As soon as the girl had reached the sky the sun stopped shining and it was dark on earth. While the girl was still at the *sigoxe* the mother of the Sun came there to pour out the rubbish. Then she noticed the girl sitting there and asked: "Who are you?" The girl replied: "I have just come to this country, I have no mother or father." Then the mother of the Sun said to her: "I want you to stay with me and help me, but my son is a chief (*omwami*)." The girl agreed and the woman continued: "My son will want to marry you," whereupon the girl replied: "But I am rubbish only, how can I marry a chief?" But the mother of the Sun encouraged her: "Never mind, you will become the favourite wife of my son." Then the girl agreed and they went into the house. There the woman gave food and milk to the girl, but she was shy and ate only very little. Next the mother began to teach her the customs of her son. She said to her: "My son is away in the garden working with others but soon he will come back. When you see something in the village that looks very bright and red don't cry." This was all she told the girl. Then they waited for the Sun to come. As soon as the Sun returned to the village everything looked very red and shiny like lightning. When the girl saw this she began to be afraid and lay down hiding her face. The Sun passed by and together with his people went into another house where he sat down to have his evening meal. When he had eaten, all his wives told him that their mother-in-law had brought him a new wife and he went to see her. He saluted her, saying, "*mulembe*", but the girl did not reply; as is the custom for a bride she was just humble and cast her eyes down. Three times the Sun tried to talk to her, but finally he went back to his house without having got a reply from the girl. Then he sent his biggest servant, the Moon, to salute her, but again she did not reply. Then the Sun sent a second, a third, a fourth, a fifth, and finally a sixth servant to speak to the girl, but they all came back without getting a reply from her. Then the Sun held council with his servants and they talked the matter over. They agreed that they had made a mistake, because they had not yet sent a present to the girl. So the Sun sent her some eleusine and sorghum and everything that grows in the country. However, the girl refused to reply to his salute.

'Finally, the chief (i.e. the Sun) decided to send her his *kumumu* (the sun-rays) and gave them to the bride himself, again saluting her by saying "*mulembe*". Now the bride in a high and thin voice replied, "*mulembe*". The Sun returned to his house and told all his servants that the girl had at last saluted him. Then the Moon went to talk to her again to see whether she was a good girl or not. The bride also replied "*mulembe*" to his greeting but in a very low voice. Then the other servants came and saluted her. When they had all done so they brought the ghee to anoint the bride.

'Now the girl joined the Sun and the first child that she bore him was a boy. Then she gave birth to another son, and then again to a third child who was also a boy. All that time the rays of the Sun were not (yet) shining down upon the earth, but they were still tied to the pot which the Sun had given to his bride as a present. Now the wife asked the Sun for permission to return to the earth, so that she might visit her father and mother. She said that she needed the servants to carry the things which she wanted to take along as presents for her mother. The Sun agreed and told his servants to go with his wife.

'Then they all went to a certain place from where the Sun let down a rope to the earth and they all climbed down that rope, one after the other.

'When they arrived at the homestead of the girl's father all her relatives were very much surprised, because they thought that she had died in the bush or been drowned in the water. Then both her mother and her father came out of the hut and looked at her. They said: "Before we can salute her we must kill a cow for her."[1] Then they drove the whole herd of cattle across the yard of the father's homestead, so that they might choose an ox with a nice colour. First they chose a black one, but their daughter shook her head. Then they chose animals of various other colours, but every time she shook her head. Only when they tapped the back of a white ox she agreed by nodding her head.

'The wife of the Sun was accompanied by her three sons and the servants. Then her father killed the white ox and gave all the people to eat who had come along with her. When they had eaten they saluted one another, falling round each others' necks. On the following day the father killed two more white oxen for his daughter's servants to take back to the sky. All that time the rays of the sun were not yet shining. On the third day the visitors began to return to the sky, the parents accompanying their daughter until they came to the place where the rope was hanging down from the sky. Then all at once their daughter with her children and servants grasped the rope and went up to the sky so quickly that they could not even shake hands with the parents.

'When they had arrived at the chief's (i.e. the Sun's) place the wife began to open the pot with the rays, so that they were shining upon the earth. There were many cows in the rays and they all fell down on her father's homestead. And the whole earth was warmed by the rays of the Sun and things began to grow well. Now all people could live well and in plenty.

[1] As a rite of lustration; cf. below, p. 247.

'Then the Sun also told his wife that from now on his big servant, the Moon, should shine for the people at night. Then the Moon began to shine during the night. Before that she was only a servant of the Sun but she did not shine.'

Xasoa, the old woman who told me this story, added: 'The poor people must always marry their daughters to a chief; then he will give them many things in return.'

The second sun-myth explains why the sun looks bright and the moon dull:

'The Sun and the Moon were *valeve* (i.e. they belonged to one clan). One day when they were still children they went to herd cattle. When they had driven the cattle down to a stream to drink water they began to quarrel who should water his cattle first. They wrestled with each other and the Moon threw the Sun into the mud. Then the Sun in turn threw the Moon down. When both had been thrown down once the Sun said to the Moon: "Now we are even, you have thrown me once and I have thrown you once." And the Moon agreed. Now where they had been wrestling it had been very muddy, so their bodies were covered all over with mud. Then the Sun said to the Moon: "Now you must wash me; you have thrown me down first, so you must wash me first." Then the Moon began to wash the Sun and made him shiny and bright again. Now the Moon asked the Sun to wash her in turn. But the Sun refused to wash the Moon and went away. So it came about that the sun is shiny and the moon dull. The Moon then felt ashamed of her dullness and therefore she hides during the day-time and only shines at night.'

Now what relation is thought to exist between Wele as the creator, maintainer, and promoter of all good things and the hostile and destructive powers, such as are wielded by the evil sorcerers? For the sake of brevity and clarity I have so far used the term Wele only with reference to the Supreme Being. Actually, however, the Vugusu apply the name Wele to a whole range of spirit-like beings. There is, accordingly, not only one Wele but a plurality of *weles*. Among these, however, the proper Wele (whom we might spell with a capital W) is clearly distinguished as the High God, and to mark this distinction he is also referred to as *Wele ómuwanga*, the White God. He is clearly conceived of as a single being and, in spite of the plurality of *weles*, all my informants emphatically agreed that there is one *Wele ómuwanga* only.

His most important opponent or counter-force is the *wele gumali*[1] or *wele evimbi*, the black or the evil god. It is said of this black god either that he is the younger twin brother of the White God or that the White God created him along with the rest of the world. According to both versions the White God had later driven the black god away when he noticed that the black god was evil-minded and only bent upon killing people. Since that time the black god is said to live in lonely or deserted

---

[1] The prefix *gu-* has a derogatory connotation.

places, preferably in dense bush or in caves from where he pays occasional visits to the people to trouble them and bring them illness. The White God is clearly regarded as the more powerful of the two. He can prevent the black god from carrying out his evil plans, but occasionally it happens that the black god wields his evil powers and causes mischief before the White God has intervened. Once a person has been killed by the black god the White God cannot undo what the former has done, but as long as the patient is still alive he can save him by fighting the black god and overpowering him. Thus if a person who is seriously ill loses consciousness for a few hours and then recovers again and gathers strength it is said that the White God and the black god have fought together and that the latter has ultimately been defeated by the White God and put into the fire. To invoke the help of the White God against the black one people pray to him in words like the following:[1]

> *Wele ewe waxuŋona xugende xusivala siowo*
> *waŋona tjixafu nevivindu vilimo*
> *ewe wamwene ofudje xumundu wowo gamasuswa*
> *aone agende vuluai*
> *axole gimilimo gyeve*
> *one wele gumali*
> *gurule xumundu wowo*
> *gwisende mundemu*
> *nemumagunda*
> *gurule muntju djefwé.*

'Wele, you who made us walk in your country,
you who made the cattle and the things which are in it,
you yourself may spit the medicine on your person,
he may recover and walk well,
he may do (i.e. plant) his gardens!
Drive away the black god;
he may have your person,
he may move into the snake
and into the abandoned homestead;
he may leave our house!'

Besides the *Wele ómuwanga* and the *wele gumali* the Vugusu recognize a third spirit-like being of major importance which they call *Emongo*. I could not discover, however, in what exact relation the *Emongo* is supposed to stand to either of the two *weles*. When a person has done something bad and then meets with an accident they say: *Emongo emúlile*,

---

[1] The prayer quoted here was spoken by the father of Nandoli when the latter was seriously ill in 1921. Before uttering the prayer he killed a red sheep, suffocating it with a rope. Then he took it by its front and hind legs and, slowly going round the hut and beating the back of the sheep on the ground (especially near the doorway), he spoke the prayer in a subdued but quite penetrating voice. Then he suspended the sheep from the top of the doorway.

Emongo ate him, i.e. *Emongo* has punished him by sending him the accident. Like the black god, *Emongo* only harms people, but he (or it) never does so out of spite (as does the black god) but always in retaliation for a bad and anti-social deed.

Now both the white and the black god have a number of helpers or servants (*visumba*) who are likewise called *wele*. The servants of the black god are the so-called *visieno*, i.e. evil-minded spirits whose exclusive aim it is to send misfortune, sickness, and death to the living. They are the spirits of those people who during their lifetime were witches and sorcerers of one type or another. The servants of the White God, on the other hand, are the spirits of those persons who died long ago and who, having reconciled themselves to their fate, are acting now as guardian spirits of single individuals and families. Among these minor *weles* there are particularly two who are known by name and to whom special sacrifices are made, viz. the *wele muxove* and the *wele muŋoma*. They are the two ancestral spirits who come nearest in rank to the White God. Apart, however, from being considered a kind of messengers and executives of the divine will they have no particular functions ascribed to them. Their elevated status among the ancestral spirits seems to be derived from the fact that they are regarded as the spirits of the first two men who lived on earth. The tribal ancestor, Muvugusu, is said to have lived only much later. This tallies with the tribal tradition according to which the Vugusu formed part of the Gishu tribe before they became a separate tribe by the secession of Muvugusu and his followers.

The Supreme Being, the White God, thus forms the apex of a kind of hierarchy of ancestral spirits who, like Wele himself, are favourably inclined towards the living and act essentially as their helpers and protectors. Opposite to them is the black god with his helpers, the evil-minded spirits. Although the black god also owes his existence to the White God, he was not created by him as the bringer of death and misfortune, but embarked upon these evil practices on his own account and was subsequently driven away by the White God. The White God, accordingly, does not bear any responsibility for the evil forces in the world. On the contrary, these forces act against him and although they are weaker than the powers commanded by the White God they are independent of him. Having no control over the bad forces, the White God is not regarded as a moral judge who punishes people for bad deeds by sending them death and destruction, but he acts essentially as the bringer and promoter of all that is good and pleasant and helpful. Thus the *Wele ómuwanga* is indeed the Supreme Being, for he is more powerful than all the ancestral spirits including the black god and his helpers. He is, however, not omnipotent, for he exercises no control over the powers of the black god who stands apart from him as a counter-force. The concept of the Supreme Being among the Vugusu is thus still dualistic, since it reaches its climax in the two *quasi*-personified principles of Good and Evil.

C. MEASURES OF PROTECTION AND PREVENTION

(1) INTRODUCTORY

THE preceding analysis has revealed a wide range of magico-religious notions. In nearly all his activities—in the routine of everyday life as well as in particular enterprises—man is confronted by invisible and yet real forces. They intervene in the course of events, frustrate his endeavours and send him illness and unrest or even death. Or again they are favourable to him and promote his health and material welfare. Ordinary people, experts or specialists, the spirits of the dead, the Supreme Being, and a number of minor spirits—they all can be agencies of mystical power, either wielding it actively and consciously or serving merely as passive vehicles in whom such power resides independent of their own volition.

The belief in these powers and in the variety of agents who wield them must naturally be coupled with a desire to exercise an influence or control over them, i.e. to invoke them in so far as they are thought to be helpful and to combat them and banish them in so far as they are deemed to be hostile. It will be the task of the following chapters to discuss the different ways in which such a control is sought to be attained.

The first part of our investigation has shown the sphere of the 'releasing forces' to be a well-organized system of clearly conceived beliefs and practices. The particular qualities ascribed to each kind of power, its range of efficacy, the conditions in which it operates, the agents by whom it is wielded, and the manner in which this is done are all well defined. Correspondingly, the manner of controlling these various forces does not consist in arbitrary and haphazard individual devices but likewise in a well-organized system of activities.

The practices and observances that aim at a control[1] of the active magico-religious forces and agents may be classified in two major categories: (1) those that are primarily of a protective and preventive nature, and (2) those that aim at the restitution of the normal state after an event has happened or while it is in progress. Such a restitution may be achieved either by propitiating or invoking the help of a spiritual agency or by performing rites that counteract the original magic power. The distinction of these two categories of practices is, of course, only one of several possible distinctions. For the purpose of presenting the material its chief merit is that it is based on a merely external feature—the chronological sequence of events. It does not imply any theoretical interpretation of the nature of the practices performed. Besides, the distinction is marked by a significant break in the sequence of events. Whereas the protective and preventive measures can be taken by anyone at any time, the practices of restitution in most cases require as a preliminary the consultation of the diviner.

---

[1] This term is here used in the widest possible sense, including the invocation and propitiation of spirit-beings.

MEASURES OF PROTECTION AND PREVENTION

Within the sphere of protective and preventive magic we can again distinguish several types of practices and observances. In the first place there is the employment of medicines and positive rites for the purpose of warding off danger, i.e. protective magic in the narrow sense of the word. Secondly, there is the observance of avoidances or 'taboos'. They likewise protect a person from threatening dangers, but the protection in this case is achieved by a 'negative' ritual behaviour that evades the danger instead of keeping it at bay. Thirdly, there is the observance of signs and omens. It enables a person to determine whether an activity in which he is engaged or which he contemplates is auspicious or not. Like the observance of taboos, it permits him to steer clear of threatening dangers by abstaining from an undertaking if the omens are unfavourable. These three types of protective and preventive measures are alike in that they do not attempt to influence the sway of mystical forces by active control or supplication but merely by passive resistance and by evasion, by defensive rather than by aggressive means.

Before discussing these three types of protective and preventive magic—or passive magic as they may also be styled—I shall first briefly survey those protective measures which are of a non-magical order. This will help to define more precisely the conditions and circumstances in which magical practices and observances are resorted to.

(2) ORDINARY PRECAUTIONS AGAINST DISEASE AND MISFORTUNE

Although the Bantu Kavirondo, as we have seen, are wont to ascribe disease and misfortune to the influence of supernatural powers, this notion does not militate against an insight into empirical causes and effects as far as such insight is accessible to them, having regard to the level of their knowledge and observation of nature. Just as they would not dispense with skill and effort in cultivating their gardens because they employ magic to promote the growth of their crops, neither would they discard empirical knowledge when protecting themselves from contracting a disease or meeting with an accident because they believe that diseases and accidents are sent by spirits or sorcerers. The magico-religious notions nowhere appear to have led them to rely on magic alone and, for the rest, to take a fatalistic outlook and thus to behave unreasonably. On the contrary, these notions merely serve to fill the gap between their actual command of nature based on empirical knowledge and their desire for a more effective command.[1] Inasmuch as the magico-religious notions succeed in filling this gap to their own satisfaction, they may indeed prevent the *widening* of empirical knowledge but they never clash with it.

It need hardly be said that in the face of immediate danger the natives use their senses as well as Europeans or even better. But they also use foresight in avoiding dangers so far as they perceive their causes. Knowing that their huts easily catch fire, they are very careful with it. The burning

[1] Cf. Malinowski.

down of huts is, in fact, a far less frequent event than one might expect, in view of the open construction of the fire-places and the inflammable material of which the roofs are made. It happens more frequently that small children get scalded from boiling water or gruel or that they are burnt by falling into the fire. However, such accidents occur in spite of constant warnings given to them and not because parents take no care, thinking that an amulet hung round the child's neck will give it automatic protection from accidents and relieve them of their duty to watch their small children. Nevertheless, accidents of this and other kinds are commonly attributed to the evil magic of a sorcerer.

When preparing food the natives likewise take all the precautions that experience has taught them to safeguard themselves against eating bad or poisoned foodstuffs. It would not occur to them to employ protective magic in a wholesale manner and then expect it to 'work miracles', i.e. to render them immune from dangers which they know to be inherent in the consumption of poisonous roots or herbs, of decayed fish or of meat that has gone bad. Should someone find the carcass of a wild animal or should one of his cows, goats, or sheep die from a disease, the meat of such a beast is only consumed after special precautions have been taken with it. It is dried over the fire for a considerable time and then boiled repeatedly. The first broth is poured away and only the second and the third are drunk and the meat then eaten with plenty of vegetable salt which is supposed to make it more easily digestible.

In a subsequent chapter we shall describe various methods of preserving food—meat, milk, fat, &c.—which all go to show that observation and experience have been utilized to gather practical knowledge and that within the scope of such knowledge protective magic has no place.

In the efforts which the natives make in warding off disease, protective and preventive magic, likewise, do not rule the entire field. As far as 'primary' causes of diseases are known, the preventive measures taken are in full accordance with such knowledge, i.e. they are of an empirical and not of a magical order. Thus it is clearly realized that certain diseases are contagious (Lurogoli: *kuhámbizana*, to catch one another) and people who suffer from them are isolated from their fellow beings in varying degrees, depending upon the strength of the danger of contagion. People afflicted with harmless but contagious skin-diseases (such as certain itching sores, *amasisa*) or those who suffer from colds are either not permitted to join in a beer drink or they are given a drinking-vessel to themselves. Similarly, people with bad ulcers must not come into direct contact with objects used by other people, although otherwise they may move about freely. People afflicted with yaws (*evitimba*) or gonorrhoea (*kisununu*) must particularly avoid sitting on stools or hides used by healthy people, eating out of the same dishes, and sleeping near them. But it is not thought dangerous merely to be in their presence. Other diseases again, like leprosy (*ovogere*), bubonic plague (*olukuzu lwelivumba*, disease of swelling), sleep-

MEASURES OF PROTECTION AND PREVENTION

ing-sickness (*olukuzu lwedzindolo*), smallpox (*enyundu*) and chicken-pox (*ekihéregete*), dysentery (*elikenyi*), and tuberculosis (*kihera*), are deemed to be infectious by the mere presence of the patient. People suffering from these diseases are, accordingly, left alone in their huts and are attended to by one and the same person (*omulindi womuluai*, the caretaker of the sick one). He, too, avoids the patient as much as possible, and if the latter dies he bathes frequently and stays away from other people for several weeks to make sure that he has not caught the disease. The most thorough precautions are taken with lepers. Formerly[1] special huts were built for them in the bush as far removed from other homesteads as possible. The path leading to the hut of a leper was marked so that strangers would be warned against using it. When food was brought to him it was placed a few hundred yards from his hut as no one dared to go near him. No object that a leper had touched was used by other people, and he was strictly forbidden to leave the immediate neighbourhood of his hut in the bush (*ekizimi* or *tjagalangwi*). When a leper died his corpse, the hut in which he lived, and the bush surrounding it were burnt and nobody went near the place for several years.

We see then that experience and observation are made use of in the taking of protective measures and that these are taken independently of magical notions. There is not merely a vague realization that disease involves danger to others and accordingly a vague fear of sick people, but diseases are clearly distinguished according to the particular kind of danger that they involve and the kind of precautionary measures taken are appropriate to such knowledge. Thus, in the case of the diseases we have mentioned we find varying degrees of isolation which roughly correspond to our distinction between merely contagious diseases and infectious ones. It is true that native observation is often incomplete and faulty, a fact which occasionally leads them to take either unnecessary or else inadequate precautions. Thus the Bantu Kavirondo commonly think that epilepsy (*endulumi*) is a contagious disease and insist on isolating a person who suffers from it.[2] Their attitude towards epilepsy, however, could hardly on that account be called magical.

(3) PROTECTIVE MEASURES BASED ON THE EMPLOYMENT OF CHARMS AND MEDICINES

The fact that protective magic is employed over and above the taking of ordinary precautions does not require any further explanation in view of the fact that, apart from its immediate causes, all human illness and misfortune is ultimately ascribed to mystical forces. The unformulated though

[1] Nowadays a leper camp for the whole district has been provided by the Government's Health Service and every case of leprosy must be immediately reported to the health authorities.

[2] This attitude still prevails among the patients attending Mission hospitals, as the European doctor in charge of the F.A.M. Hospital at Kaimosi informed me that his patients refuse to be put into the same room with a person suffering from epilepsy.

clearly evident notion of the double causation of all happenings[1] must thus obviously entail a twofold manner of reacting towards them.

As protective magic is mainly directed against the ultimate, mystical causes of illness and misfortune, its various practices can, with few exceptions, not be classified according to the kind of illness or accident from which they protect their owner but rather according to the different types of mystical agents against whom they are directed. Protective magic is chiefly employed against human agents, such as the various kinds of *avalogi*, and against *avavila*. In warding off the evil practices of witches and sorcerers it offers protection at the same time against all diseases and misfortunes that are supposed to be wielded by them. Other kinds of protective magic are employed against the bad intentions or actions of ordinary people, e.g. against theft, intrigue, the ill temper of chiefs, and, nowadays, of the European employer or Government official. Only in a few cases is protective magic employed against specific dangers instead of against the agent controlling the danger.[2] Thus there exists particular magic against being struck by lightning, against the devastation of one's fields by hail-storms, and against the various dangers inherent in travelling. Protective magic is never employed against the powers wielded by ancestral spirits, a point on which all my informants were emphatically agreed. A seeming exception to this rule is a ceremony performed over a new-born child whose siblings have died, for the apparent idea behind this ceremony is to deceive the spirits about the origin of the child and thus to prevent them from harming it (see p. 330). Although the rite serves to protect the child it can hardly be classed as magic, for it does not involve the handling of any protective power which is set against that wielded by the spirits, but is merely a trick or deception such as one might play on any ordinary person. Protective magic consists, for the most part, of amulets or medicines. Their magical virtue is thought to reside entirely in the material object as such, so that the mere possession and physical presence of the amulet suffices to make it serve its purpose. Its potency is therefore independent of its owner. It lasts continuously—as long as it retains its strength —and no rites or spells need be performed over it to ensure its action when this is required. As protective magic cannot be used for any other but protective purposes it is, as a rule, acquired and handled quite openly. If the owners conceal it they do so to prevent its being stolen or tampered with and not because they fear the disapproval of other people for possessing it. A person, however, who displays an unusual concern over protective magic and goes out of his way to acquire rare and powerful medicines is often suspected of practising evil magic as well, as it is thought that bad sorcerers are in particular need of possessing medicines to defend themselves against all those people whose revenge they have to fear.

[1] Cf. above, p. 95.
[2] My material does not suggest any explanation as regards the relation between these two kinds of protective magic.

MEASURES OF PROTECTION AND PREVENTION

Wealthy and influential people also are supposed to be in greater need of protective magic than ordinary people, as they are likely to arouse the envy and misgivings of their less fortunate fellow-beings and thus to be singled out as the victims of bad magic.

The more usual types of protective magic consist of objects that are commonly known and that can be collected by ordinary persons. The rarer—and accordingly more powerful—medicines are purchased from diviners (*avakumu*) or from herbalists (*omwahi wolunyasi*) who either deal exclusively with protective magic (*olunyasi lukwelinda*, medicine of guarding oneself) or sell both protective and curative medicines. As it is thought that the efficacy of an amulet or a medicine increases with the distance of the place whence it has been obtained, the herbalists are usually widely travelled people or they maintain friendly relations with herbalists from neighbouring tribes from whom they purchase their medicines. Among the Logoli the more highly appreciated medicines are usually purchased from the Luo or collected in the forest of the Kakalelwa tribe, on the plains of Kitosh or even in Uganda. Protective medicines are also bought from ordinary people if they can make it appear that a particular medicine has done them a great deal of good. Thus a person who is always in good health or who has conspicuous success in all his undertakings will have no difficulty in finding a customer if he is willing to sell the object to which he ascribes his success.

The prices paid for amulets and protective medicines range from small quantities of tobacco or grain to a goat or even a cow. A cow, for instance, is said to be paid by a rich elder for the knowledge of a rare plant which, when planted along the enclosure of his homestead, will protect him and his family from the deadly magic of an *ombila*.

To compile a complete list of the various kinds of protective amulets and medicines would hardly be possible, as the faith in particular roots or herbs differs from location to location and new devices are constantly tried out, come into fashion, and are abandoned again. The following list, therefore, merely purports to give a few examples of the more commonly employed amulets and medicines and the agents against whom they are supposed to be effective:

1. To protect themselves against the death-spell of an *ombila* people lick the ashes of the fruit of the *endovo* bush. This is a red fruit with a thick rind that grows on a thorny bush and has a bitter but otherwise pleasant taste. Another protective medicine against *avavila* is the bone of the *ekihungu* bird which is burnt and pulverized and then licked. The *ekihungu* is a bird that lives near forests and is extremely difficult to kill as it rises quickly and almost straight into the air. It is the size of a hen, has a slightly curved bill, and its plumage is bluish on the breast, white on the sides, and between brown and grey on the back. The magical virtue of its bones is obviously based on its rapid flight and its successful resistance against being hunted with arrows. Against the effects of evil plants (*ovovila*) which the

avavila are alleged to plant at night in the immediate neighbourhood of their intended victim's homestead, people either plant *elineke* (a kind of saxifraga), *ekisungulua* or *ekinazogi*, or a short grass called *ekigundu* round their houses. As a protection against the evil glance of an *ombila* people also wear iron armlets, either round their left wrist or hidden under their cow- or goatskin. To be efficacious, however, it must have been purchased from an omuahi *wedzinyasi* (herbalist) who has rubbed it with particular medicines.[1]

2. To render themselves immune from the *elilogo* of a witch people tie the fruit of the *endovo*-bush to an iron necklace and wear it as an amulet.

3. Against the evil eye of a *wevikoko* or *omusohi* children are protected by wearing the beak of a hen that was killed at the first sacrifice performed after their birth. It is tied to a string of banana-fibre and hung round their necks. Often an *engombo*, the tip of a gourd neck, is added to it, filled with ghee (*amaguta*) and the pulverized blades of the *ekidúmusi*-grass. This is a tall grass which is also used in the preparation of medicine for taming unmanageable cattle. Another amulet against the evil eye is a necklace made from the roots of the *ekisugi*-plant which is chiefly worn by children. Adults also use the *ekisugi*-plant for the same purpose, but they make it into a paste by pounding its roots and branches and then anoint their iron armlets with it.

4. Branches of the *ekisimwa*-tree are used as protective magic against being killed by lightning[2] and against the various dangers one might meet with while travelling. The branches are burnt and pounded and then rubbed on one's belt and round one's waist and wrists. The same device is said nowadays to be used by persons in the employment of Europeans to protect them from outbursts of ill temper on the part of their masters. Tiny pieces of a lion's heart or of the skin of wild pigs which people claim to have purchased from the Masai or Kikuyu are said to serve the same purpose when carried in one's pocket tied into a small parcel.

Besides these amulets and medicines which are worn more or less permanently, there are other kinds of protective magic that are employed only in particular situations. Thus chiefs and other leading and influential persons, who know that they have rivals who covet their positions, are said to possess specially potent amulets which they wear when they enter the houses of other persons. Should the rules of etiquette oblige them to accept food from a host whom they do not trust, they lick the ashes of the *ekisugi*-plant which is said to protect them from getting ill after having eaten poisoned food. Moreover, they take great care to obliterate their traces upon leaving a place where they have stayed so as to prevent their personal

---

[1] One of these is said to be made from the leaves, roots, or branches of *ekisugi*-plants which were growing near the *ovovila* of an *ombila*'s garden. They owe their protective virtues to the fact that they have been near the poisonous *ovovila*.

[2] This is said to be used only when lightning has struck near the hut where one lives or when there has been a series of unusually heavy thunder-storms.

enemies from securing objects associated with them (*xurora*, cf. p. 114) and using them for practising sorcery against them. Some people even go so far as never to spend a night away from their own homestead, as only in their own villages are they equipped with protective plants, &c., which give them the feeling of a sufficient defence against the various magical dangers threatening them during the night-time. I was told that Chief Sudi of South Kitosh, when he had to pay a formal visit to Chief Amutala of North Kitosh in 1934, insisted on spending the night in an improvised grass hut which he made his own retainers put up for him. Next morning, before his departure, he ordered the hut to be burnt down for fear that someone might 'take' his footprints or some object that he had touched and perform bad magic over it.

When attending one of the quarterly meetings of the Local Native Council which are held at a central place in the District and last several days, I noticed that a number of chiefs returned to their homes at night to come again on the following morning, although quite comfortable sleeping accommodation exists for them at the Council Hall. One of them had to cycle a distance of over thirty-five miles each way over muddy roads. His behaviour puzzled me at the time, but he evaded my requests for an explanation. Only after several months, when discussing protective magic with one of my informants, did I learn that the chief's behaviour was merely a measure of precaution against evil magic.

In the round of agricultural activities protective magic is employed both against the danger of hail-storms and that of the evil eye. Among the Logoli it is one of the tasks of the *omukingi womulimi*[1] to recite a spell during the times when hail-storms are expected and would cause damage to the crops. When a hail-storm appears to be imminent the *omukingi womulimi* is summoned by the clan-head and after a meeting has been held by all the elders of the clan he is sent forth to perform his magic. Armed with a stick to which a particular preventive medicine (a species of grass, *olunyasi*, which is his secret knowledge) has been attached, he walks through the gardens and in a loud voice recites the following spell:

Amagina gahere gatakuba mba, galononye milimi.

'The hail-storms may vanish, they do not fall down (lest) they will destroy the gardens.'[2]

To render the hail-storm magic effective all work must be stopped in the gardens while the *omukingi womulimi* recites his spell and it must not be resumed until the third day.[3] After he has performed his magic he goes in turn to all the people through whose gardens he has walked and asks them for a small basketful of eleusine or sorghum as payment for his magic.

[1] Cf. above, p. 99.
[2] According to one informant he winds up the spell with the words: '*Nyasai siangonya*, God may help me!'; I could not find out for certain whether this is a recent addition or part of the traditional wording. The first part, however, is worded like a typical spell and not like a prayer. [3] Cf. below, p. 292.

From the grain collected in this way he brews beer, and when it is ready for consumption he invites all the elders of the neighbourhood for a beer-feast.

According to my informants, in the past the faith in hail-storm magic was not shaken if, in spite of the magic having been performed, a hail-storm did come and devastate the gardens concerned. Nowadays, however, there seems to prevail a feeling of scepticism towards the efficacy of this kind of magic, and since the incident with the Nyole rain-maker in 1927[1] the prestige of the *omukingi* seems to have sunk along with that of the rain-maker. He is no longer summoned to perform his magic on behalf of whole communities, but his services are engaged *sub rosa* and privately by pagan elders.[2]

The Vugusu, likewise, employ magic to protect their gardens from hail-storms. Like the Logoli, they engage specialists for that purpose who are called *vaxingi ve gamararara*. These are mostly men (although a woman may occasionally learn how to *xuxinga*)[3] who have either inherited their knowledge from their father or maternal uncle or have purchased it from the rain-maker or from another *omuxingi*. They are summoned individually by anyone who wants to have his garden protected, and if several *vaxingi* live close together they compete with one another in offering their services. The technique employed by them differs slightly from that of the Logoli. An integral part of their magic is the knowledge of certain roots to which is attributed the power of diverting the hail. When they have collected these roots they pound them into pulp and thoroughly knead them with mud obtained from the banks of a running stream. Some of the paste which results the *omuxingi* then places in a hollow tree. The remainder he puts into a basket which he leaves at the base of the centre post of his hut to 'sleep' there for one night. The ancestral spirits are then supposed to bless the medicine and thus to make it more powerful. They do not, however, join the medicine basket and accompany it when, on the following day, the *omuxingi* walks through the fields to strew tiny bits of his medicine round the edges of the gardens which he wishes to protect from hail-storms. The spirits are thus invoked to increase the potency of the magic, but its efficacy lies primarily in the magic virtues of the roots, in the mixing of the roots with the mud, in the rite of placing part of the medicine in a hollow tree, and, finally, in the spell.

While walking through the fields and scattering his medicine the *omuxingi* recites the following spell:

Pó xusava
gamedji goŋene nigo xusavile
sexusavile vilasila tawe
otjiá mumbo munyandja.

[1] Cf. above, p. 158, footnote 2.

[2] The public performance of hail-storm magic and the collection of payment is an offence under British law and must be reported by local headmen.

[3] Thus one of my chief informants among the Vugusu, the old woman Xasoa, claims to have learnt how to *xuxinga* from her father who always sent her to fetch the medicines which he required for performing his magic.

PLATE 7

Diviner consulting the pebble oracle: Butsotso

PLATE 8

Diviner consulting the rubbing-board oracle: South Kitosh

'Po! I beg you,
water is only what I beg from you.
I do not beg you for evil stuff,
go on down west into the lake!'

The wording of the spell seems to suggest that a personal being is addressed by it, but according to my informants it is merely the clouds to which the *omuxingi* speaks and not a spirit or even Wele.

Besides asking the hail to pass by the *omuxingi* can also attract it if he wishes to do so. This he would do, for example, if, after the harvest, one of his clients had refused to send him the customary bundle (*sinywa*) of eleusine or sorghum as a payment for his magic. During the following season he would then secretly change the wording of his spell, thereby causing his medicines to have the opposite effect. Thus he would say:

*Omwene gaxanga xundunga
nono newidja wilungixa omwene yeŋene.
Eva vandi ova gamedji goŋene.*

'The owner (of this field) he refused to pay me,
now if you (addressing the hail) come, come right here to the owner only.
To the others give water only.'

The notion that the hail-storm magician has the power both of preventing and of attracting hail-storms thus at the same time helps him to get his payment and furnishes an explanation for what would otherwise appear as a failure of his magic.

Protective magic against the evil eye of one of the types mentioned above is also administered to the growing crops, but the dangers threatening the crops from the evil eye are mainly feared during and after the harvest.

When harvesting eleusine the crops are protected from shrinking under the influence of the evil eye of an *omusohi* by placing a wreath (*engata*) woven of the *etiri* plant (a papilionaceous plant) on top of each heap of grain. The same precaution is used by women who carry bundles of bananas on their heads. Among the Vugusu more elaborate precautions are taken to protect the eleusine crop from the evil eye of the *omuxondoli*. Before beginning to reap the harvest the owner of the crops gathers certain roots and puts them on the floor of his hut near the centre post where they 'sleep' for one night, so that they may be blessed by the spirits. Next morning he goes into his garden and cuts three bundles of eleusine. To each of these bundles he ties some of the roots he has gathered and then puts the bundles down in the yard of his homestead, placing one in the middle and the other two on each side. The entire millet crop is then piled on top of these three bundles where it is now safely protected from shrinkage, should an *omuxondoli* pass by and cast an evil eye at it.

Magic is also used to protect cattle from various dangers. Small calves which are thought to be particularly prone to suffer harm from the evil eye of an *omusohi* have *evisugi* necklaces hung round their necks like children. Moreover, they are kept as much as possible in the *ekego*, the cattle-partition of the living-hut, so that an *omusohi* has no opportunity to look at them.

Among the Logoli elaborate precautions are taken with pregnant cows to protect them from the evil magic of an *omulogi*. When a bull has joined a cow its owner first strikes its back with a switch of the *elisazi*-tree to ensure thereby that pregnancy will follow. Then he drives the cow back to his hut, and after it has entered through the main door he sticks the *elisazi*-switch into the wall above the door so that it protrudes into the front partition like a flag-pole, its end pointing towards the *ekego*. It remains there until the cow has calved and is then burnt in the fire-place of the hut. The ashes are then gathered together and rubbed into the back of the cow. Before it is driven out to the pasture again its owner ties the fruit of an *endovo*-bush round its neck to protect it from being afflicted with *elilogo* while grazing. To prevent *avalogi* from coming near the hut during the night he places two *dzindovo*-fruits above the front and the back doors. After about a month he takes off these *dzindovo*-fruits, pounds them, and mixes them with *ovosé* (the stomach content of a sacrificial sheep; cf. below, p. 282) and with the blood of a hen killed on that occasion. Some of this mixture (which is now called *ovukíngilu*) he then feeds to the cow and some he scatters over the pasture round the house, especially near those spots where the cow is tethered when grazing. This lends it further protection against any attempts by an *omulogi* to make it sick. The remainder of the mixture is kept in store as medicine to be used in an ordeal which would be administered to the suspected *omulogi* should the cow get ill in the future (cf. below, p. 272 sq.). As a further protection of their cattle against the evil intentions of an *omulogi* people tie small sticks (*evisala*) of the *ekikuvati*-bush into plaited strings (*emidindi*) or ribbons of leather which they tie round their cows' necks. To lend magic potency to these sticks they must be hardened in the fire and cut to their proper length by the herbalist from whom they are purchased.

Finally, protective magic is employed against the theft of cattle. Among the Vugusu the owner of a herd concocts a medicine from a leafy plant (the place where it is found is kept secret by the herbalist who offers it for sale) and either feeds the liquid to his cows or sprinkles it over their backs. Should a thief or enemies engaged in a cattle-raid try to steal cattle to which such anti-theft medicine has been administered, the animals will lie down on the spot, and no amount of beating will induce them to get up and allow themselves to be driven away. It is said that this magic is occasionally also resorted to by people who have had the payment of a cow imposed on them as a fine or in fulfilment of a kinship obligation. When the person to whom the cow is due comes to claim it, it either refuses to be led away or it returns to its former owner as soon as it is driven out on the pasture. While staying in Kimilili I heard about the case of a certain man called Mayu who had a claim to another man's cow in repayment for a heifer he had formerly

MEASURES OF PROTECTION AND PREVENTION 189

lent him. The debtor offered Mayu a cow which he did not like, and so he chose another one instead which the debtor hated to part with. Mayu, however, insisted on having this particular animal. When he had driven it for half a mile it kicked, lay down, and refused to move; so Mayu kept on beating it till it finally died. He then sued the debtor before the tribal court for another cow as he had performed magic over the first one.[1] Unfortunately, I did not stay to learn how the case was finally decided by the elders.

Protective magic is conspicuously absent in warfare and hunting. The various observances of a magical nature which we shall describe in the chapter on warfare are intended to lend courage and perseverance to the warrior, but I could not discover any specific magic against being wounded or killed in battle. This fact appears to be significant, for it is in accordance with the general tendency we have noted, viz. that protective magic is predominantly directed against the ultimate, magical causes of death and misfortune and not against such immediate and apparent causes as the spear or arrow of the attacking enemy or the fury of a wounded or hunted animal. Where the risk to one's life is as obvious as in warfare, and where everything depends upon the skill and courage of the warrior, apparently little need is felt to assume the interference of magical powers and to resort to protective magic.

(4) AVOIDANCES AND OTHER RITUAL PROHIBITIONS

The observance of ritual avoidances and other kinds of ritual prohibitions appears to be derived from two principal notions. One of them is that the mystical dangers which confront man in his various undertakings can to a large extent be averted by steering clear of persons and objects that are regarded as agents or wielders of dangerous magical powers. In so far as it is based on this notion the observance of avoidances is primarily a measure of protection and prevention. It pursues the same aim as the employment of amulets and medicines or the performance of protective rites, and differs merely by its method. Instead of putting up a defence which acts, so to speak, as a shield behind which ordinary activities can be carried on, the danger is evaded and an attitude of resignation is adopted. The scope of ritual avoidances and prohibitions must therefore be restricted to situations where evasion or resignation is possible without seriously interfering with vital needs for positive action.

The second notion from which ritual avoidances and prohibitions are derived is that of lending a mystical sanction to types of conduct that have their original motive in emotional attitudes or pragmatic considerations, such as the protection of the rights and privileges of certain persons

[1] To ensure that a cow which is separated from a herd and handed to another person gives no trouble to him the former owner must throw earth over the backs of his own cows (*xuanya lilova muxafu*). Among the Logoli he must strike the parting cow on its back with a stick; see vol. ii.

or groups of persons against their infringement by others. Thus the ritual avoidance between two clans that have had a serious quarrel[1] with one another serves as a means of enforcing their separation which originated from a state of emotional tension between the two groups, and the various ritual prohibitions that affect social intercourse between relatives-in-law serve to organize and regularize the conduct and status of a group of persons who, by marriage, have entered into a particular relation with one another, involving definite rights and duties.

These two notions have thus given rise to two widely different categories of ritual avoidances and prohibitions. In the first case, the fear of mystical dangers lies at the root of the avoidance, while, in the second case, it furnishes a useful instrument for enforcing an avoidance or prohibition. It is, however, not always easy to decide from what motive a particular rule of avoidance has arisen. In some cases the answer seems to suggest itself by asking what would happen if the avoidance did not exist, but even where this question yields a definite answer, and where, accordingly, the avoidance or prohibition appears to fulfil an obvious function, it can hardly be determined with certainty whether such a function is identical with the original cause of the avoidance, or whether it is merely a secondary feature, a 'by-product'. Even in cases where the native can furnish a plausible explanation for a rule of avoidance or prohibition it will be difficult to decide whether this is a rationalization of an existing rule or whether it is due to an insight into its actual causes.

We shall therefore deal with ritual avoidances and prohibitions under a joint heading regardless of the ultimate causes or motives behind them. The common characteristic of all of them is that they are thought to be sanctioned in a mystical way. Their violation is automatically followed by dangers to the health or life either of the offender himself or of the person involved by the offence or of both of them. The particular kind of danger varies according to the kind of avoidance or prohibition, but it always arises automatically and in a mystical way and not from interference by other persons. This also distinguishes 'ritual' from 'ordinary' prohibitions or negative laws as well as from restrictions on conduct imposed by the rules of etiquette or good manners. These latter are sanctioned by physical punishment or fines, by retaliation or ridicule, but not by consequences of a mystical order.

(a) Avoidances between Persons

(i) Following a quarrel or a curse

Avoidances[2] between persons, as well as one-sided avoidances of certain persons, result from a number of different situations, the nature and extent of the avoidance varying accordingly. An 'all-out' avoidance is observed between two persons or, more frequently, two groups of persons who carry

---

[1] Cf. above, p. 67. [2] *Emigiru* in Lurogoli, *gimisiru* in Luvugusu.

on a blood feud following a case of murder or manslaughter, or who have had a serious quarrel in the course of which a curse was pronounced. Such curses are usually provoked by the public denunciation of a member of one group for having performed evil magic against a member of another group. While such an avoidance prevails between two groups they break off all social and economic relations with one another. They do not salute one another when meeting on the road but turn their heads away; they do not grant one another hospitality, and if they meet at a third person's place they only accept food or beer when served to each of them separately.[1] If they are formerly friendly clans who used to intermarry, they break off all further marriage relations (although they would not send away the women of the avoided clan whom they had married before the avoidance began). It is claimed that if they were to relax the avoidance without previously performing a rite of reconciliation they would die or become insane. The rule of avoidance extends even to small children of the two groups concerned. Thus a Logoli narrative on an avoidance of this kind states:

'It is very serious for a child if it eats food with the people whom they (i.e. its clansmen) avoid (*vagirana*). The child must become a fool (*kuyinga*) or even turn insane (*kugwa mulalu*). Its head becomes sick, and the relatives of that child begin to die. Then they know, alas, this child went to eat with the people whom we avoid.'

(ii) *Avoidance of persons in a state of ritual impurity*

While in the case of avoidances that follow a quarrel the ritual element is linked with a feeling of actual hostility, a purely ritual avoidance is observed towards people who are deemed to be in a temporary state of ritual impurity. In a previous chapter (cf. above, p. 106 sq.) the various types of such ritual impurity have already been discussed, viz. the state of being *luswa* and the various conditions caused by contact with death and with human blood. The persons thought to be particularly afflicted with these states of impurity are the near relatives and attendants of a person who has just died, particularly widows, warriors who have killed an enemy, murderers, and people who have committed manslaughter. Furthermore, young mothers with their new-born children, especially twins, and youths that have just been circumcised as well as the circumcision operators. A common characteristic of all these people is that their state of ritual pollution is fraught with dangers, not only to themselves but also to other people who come into contact with them, and sometimes only to those other people. Their impurity is, so to speak, contagious or infectious: in some cases it can be transmitted by mere proximity to them or by looking at them, in

---

[1] Cf. the following statement in a Nyole text on beer-feasts: *avasilana navandi emisilo nali nakavwe musivera, nava nalexa hareyue atsie musireve siavandi anyala xupakwa*, 'Those who have an avoidance with others get theirs (the beer) in the ashplace (behind the cooking-stones), and if he left where he was put so that he may go to the sitting place of the others he must be beaten.'

others by direct physical contact with them or with objects that they have used or that are otherwise associated with them. The avoidances and other ritual prohibitions observed towards them are thus determined by the particular danger emanating from them.

In the case of widows it is primarily the objects used by or associated with them that have to be avoided. The ritual dangers inherent in their mere physical presence are guarded against by administering a certain medical concoction (*edzinyasi dziokunwa*). 'Should they fail to give this to her, then the people with whom she walks together must turn pale on their bodies.' Nevertheless, a widow, from the time of her husband's death until a purification rite has been performed for her, is confined to her hut except for the performance of certain ceremonial observances. She may not visit other people and must refrain from working in her gardens. Her food[1] is prepared and cooked for her by certain relatives or neighbours (so-called *avadili*) specially appointed to attend on her. They must also remove the rubbish from her hut and the ashes from her fire-place in such a manner that nobody will accidentally come across them and thereby become contaminated by them. She does not sleep on a skin, but on layers of banana-leaves which are destroyed when her period of mourning comes to an end. Her shadow must be carefully avoided by other persons, especially by children, whose skin is said to turn pale and to decay if they step on it by accident. She must avoid bathing in the presence of other women or even at the same place where other people bathe or wash themselves, as the water used by her becomes polluted and thereby dangerous to other people. A special, narrow path is therefore made for her which leads to an unfrequented part of a stream so that she may bathe without being seen by anyone. Particular danger is attached to her faeces and urine, which she must deposit at a secluded spot which nobody may approach. Needless to say, she must practise continence even if the question of her remarriage has already been decided upon, as any intimate contact with her would be fatal to her new husband. Among the Vugusu, if the widow is to be remarried to her former husband's brother or clansman, the ordinary purification rites which are performed over her at the end of the period of mourning are not regarded as sufficient to make it safe for her new husband to have sexual intercourse with her and thus to step into the place of his deceased kinsman. The widow must therefore go to a distant place and try to induce a stranger to have sexual intercourse with her, pretending that she intends to stay at his place and that she wants him to marry her. He must be a person with whom neither her deceased husband nor his kinsmen have maintained any bonds of kinship or neighbourhood (such as sharing meals together or exchanging gifts with one another), otherwise he would suffer harm as well. If a widow did not take this precaution

[1] The first meal which is cooked for her after her husband's death is handed to her on potsherds and ceremonially eaten by her while sitting under the eaves of the hut. Even afterwards she must eat by herself and from special dishes.

MEASURES OF PROTECTION AND PREVENTION 193

of having ritual intercourse with a stranger before being remarried to her former husband's brother or clansman, the latter would die.

Very similar avoidances and ritual prohibitions apply to warriors who have killed their first enemy in battle, the so-called *avakāli*. As in the case of widows, their presence would cause all other people 'to turn pale'. They may, therefore, not return to their homes but—after having ceremonially cleansed their blood-stained spears—must spend a period of over three months in an old and deserted hut that had previously been occupied by an old woman and that no ordinary person may approach. The food brought to them by their wives or mothers must be set down at a distance from the hut or given to their attendant (the *omudili*). This must be a person who has already killed an enemy on a previous occasion and who is therefore immune from the danger of *ovukāli*, as their particular kind of ritual impurity is called. Before they are purified the *avakāli* must particularly observe the rule of continence and avoid meeting children, as it would be dangerous for them to step on their shadows. Before they may cohabit with their wives again they must seek to have sexual intercourse with the wife of a stranger, 'so that they may leave their bad blood with another woman'. If a warrior has difficulty in finding a woman who will yield to him he must roam about the country until he has succeeded in doing so. Otherwise he would bring sickness to his own family. Further ritual prohibitions apply to the life of the *avakāli* in the hut of seclusion. They must not wear a skin while walking about but go absolutely naked, they must not wash their hands until they have been given permission to do so, and when drinking water from a stream they must not draw it with their hands but bend down and drink 'like cattle'.

The avoidances and prohibitions which the *avakāli* must observe thus correspond in almost every detail to those applying to widows, a fact which is not merely revealed by a comparison of the ritual behaviour of the two but which is realized by the natives themselves.[1] A further parallel with the behaviour shown by widowed persons and warriors is found in the conduct of the lads (*avakulu*) who have just been circumcised. Their ritual confinement in the *etumbi* hut and the various prohibitions that govern their daily life during the period of seclusion correspond point by point to the behaviour enjoined on the unclean warriors.[2] The only difference in the ritual situation as compared with warriors and widows is that if they are seen by other persons it is not dangerous to those who see them but to the *avakulu* themselves.[3] To protect themselves from this danger they must, therefore, wear the grass dresses which cover their heads

---

[1] In a narrative on the rites observed by returning warriors there is the following passage: '(While the *omukāli* stays in the hut of seclusion) his wife is filled with fear towards her husband. And she says, "This my husband is like a widower; I must avoid him lest I turn pale".'

[2] See p. 353 sq.

[3] The particular nature of the danger is referred to by the verb *xuvenyexa* (Lwidaxo).

O

and bodies whenever they leave the immediate neighbourhood of the hut of seclusion.

The avoidance observed towards young mothers resembles that adopted towards widows. During her period of confinement a young mother must remain in the sleeping-partition of her hut. If she wants to leave the hut she must use a private path specially made for her, for if other people should catch sight of her they would 'turn pale'. The bedspread of banana-leaves used by her as well as the rubbish and the ashes from her hut must be hidden away in the bush where nobody will find them. When eating she must not touch the food with her hands. As wooden or earthenware dishes would become polluted and unfit for further use if she ate from them, her meals are served to her on leaves which, later, are thrown away. After a few days, when she and her child have undergone a purification rite, most of these prohibitions are relaxed, except the rule of continence, which applies for about four weeks after her delivery and is dropped only after some further ritual observances. In the case of twins the additional ritual danger of *ovuxwana* (twinship), which causes anyone who looks at them to be afflicted with blear-eyes and other eye diseases, gives rise to a prolonged avoidance and to the ritual seclusion of the twins in their mother's hut for several years.[1]

People who have committed an offence or met with a situation that has rendered them *luswa* are avoided until they have been restored to their normal ritual status by the performance of a purification ceremony or other ritual observance. As this is usually done immediately after the condition of *luswa* has been discovered, the avoidance is kept up only for a short time. However, in the case of a girl who has conceived a child as the result of incestuous intercourse, the purification ceremony which terminates the avoidance observed towards her is only performed either after a successful abortion has been brought about or after her child has been born and killed. In the meantime she must eat from separate dishes, and other people avoid her company as much as possible. The man responsible for her condition is likewise avoided during that time; in particular he must not come near the clan-elders when they sit together on the *oluhya*. If the state of *luswa* has been caused by the abnormal behaviour of an animal (cf. above, p. 108, examples 12, 13, 14, 17), the animal is either killed or— e.g. in the case of a cow—the owner refrains from drinking the milk or blood of such a cow. Similarly, if a person has committed an offence while drunk that has rendered him *luswa*, he will henceforth refrain from touching beer again, especially if it was a serious offence such as a violation of the mother-in-law avoidance, an act of incestuous intercourse, &c. The same kind of temporary avoidance that is observed towards persons who are in a state of *luswa* applies also to certain 'specialists', who, by performing their magical or ceremonial duties, become ritually contaminated. Thus the circumcision operator may not wash his hands or

[1] Cf. the chapter on ceremonies performed over twins, p. 323.

eat in the presence of, or from the same dishes as, other ritually clean people until he has circumcised all the boys in the tribe and undergone a rite of purification (cf. circumcision, p. 353). Similarly the *omuliuli* (the specialist who searches the homestead of a suspected sorcerer for evil magic) must not join the company of other people after he has touched the harmful substances. Owing to his protective medicines he himself is thought to be immune from the dangers emanating from those substances, but if unprotected people came into contact with him they would die. The same applies to the man who is engaged by other people to dig out and burn the bones of a dead person whose spirit incessantly troubles them.

(iii) *Avoidances between in-law relations*

Yet a different type of avoidance is maintained between persons related by marriage. Such avoidances between affinal kinsmen are sometimes difficult to distinguish from mere formality or constraint in their kinship behaviour. They are always strictly mutual, and they are determined by the particular nature of the relationship that has been established between the two persons involved and not by any personal qualities possessed by them. The avoidance is most pronounced and most rigidly enforced between mother-in-law and son-in-law, but to a lesser extent it applies also to the relationship between a woman and her father-in-law and, for the first few days after marriage, to that between a woman and her husband's mother as well as that between a man and his wife's father. The avoidance observed between these persons is said to be due to 'fear' (Lurogoli: *ovuti*; Luvugusu: *vuxwe*) or 'shame' (*esoni, tjisoni*). Although this shame is obviously a conditioned emotional attitude, i.e. determined by convention, it seems to be aroused quite genuinely whenever a situation arises which demands its display. The avoidances are observed not merely because custom demands them or because specific sanctions are expected to follow their violation, but because the persons concerned actually feel fear or shame towards one another. This became evident, not only from the behaviour of the people as I have actually observed it, but also from a number of statements made by my informants of which I shall make mention when discussing the various forms in which the avoidances manifest themselves. In spite of their emotional immediacy, the avoidances have their 'magical sanctions' as well, for it is thought that the *esoni* or *vuxwe* would 'burn' the persons, i.e. cause them to become insane or even to die if they were to disregard the avoidances. In this case, the spontaneous emotional inhibition and the conscious fear of supernatural punishment are merged so completely that it is hardly possible to keep them apart as distinct motivating forces behind the avoidances.

The mutual avoidance between a man and his mother-in-law begins with the man's betrothal, so that even before the marriage is consummated the prospective husband must not come to the homestead of his future wife's parents and accept food there. Vice versa, the wife's mother must refrain from visiting her daughter as she must not enter her son-in-law's house. Only in exceptional cases—e.g. if her daughter is seriously ill—she may do so, but she must then first make sure that her son-in-law is not present. If mother-in-law and son-in-law meet on the road they must make a detour round each other or at least turn their heads away should they suddenly find themselves 'face to face'. Among the Vugusu, they may greet one another from a distance with a brief and formal salutation (such as *milembe mayi*), but they may not stop to exchange any news or gossip. A man must also avoid mentioning the name of his mother-in-law, not only when addressing her but even when referring to her. Some of my informants who had been married for a number of years even claimed that they did not know the names of their mothers-in-law, although that may have been merely a pretext to avoid mentioning them.

The mutual avoidance between father-in-law and daughter-in-law is less stringent but essentially of the same nature. They may formally salute one another when they meet and briefly exchange important news, but they must not start a real conversation. The initiative in any conversation between the two always rests with the father-in-law, and the daughter-in-law may only shyly reply, not using more words than are necessary to answer the questions put to her. She cannot enter her father-in-law's house while he is there nor any other house in which he happens to be present. Correspondingly, if the father-in-law wants to visit his son's house he must remain on the veranda or sit down by the side of the door. Even then he may stay only for a short time and without accepting food from his son's wife.

Between a young wife and her mother-in-law no real avoidance is observed, but the former must refrain from entering the cooking-partition of the latter's hut. All the housework which a young wife does for her mother-in-law (such as grinding, cleaning pots, peeling cassava, &c.) she must do in the front partition of the hut or outside under the eaves. Although she eats the food cooked by her mother-in-law, she must not take her meals in her presence but either by herself or in the company of her sister-in-law. The reason for doing so is, however, not the same ritual fear or shame (*esoni*) which prevails between mother-in-law and son-in-law but rather an initial shyness which the young wife feels in the presence of her husband's mother. As one of my informants put it: 'The newly married wife fears that she might not eat the food properly and gulp it down or belch on account of her embarrassment in being exposed to the critical eyes of her mother-in-law. Owing to her fear that she might make a bad impression upon her she would not eat sufficiently.'

Between a man and his father-in-law the avoidance lasts only from the time of betrothal (the proposal, the payment of the bride-wealth and all the other arrangements are made by the future husband's mother and brother) until shortly after the wedding. To terminate the avoidance the young husband pays a visit to his father-in-law's house and makes him a present of a goat or of an expensive blanket,[1] saluting him at the same time in the customary manner. The father-in-law thanks him in reply and speaks to him, 'Our shame is over now' (*ulufweye, edzisoni dzivoli ho*, it[2] is finished, the shame is no more). He then brings a stool for his son-in-law and asks him to sit down in the front yard, offering him beer to drink or ripe bananas to eat. He would not, of course, invite his son-in-law to enter the house, as he might then see his mother-in-law. However, even if she were not present he would not like his son-in-law to come inside the house, particularly if the things in the house are not kept as well by his wife as they ought to be, e.g. if the floor is not smooth and clean or the walls not properly smeared with cow-dung. A man is thus anxious to make a good impression upon his son-in-law and to avoid anything which might lessen the latter's respect for his own family and especially for his wife.

It is a characteristic feature of all the avoidances observed between relatives-in-law that they are kept most rigidly immediately after the relationship has been established. After a number of years they are eased or even entirely lifted. Among the Vugusu, the *sitexo*-rite[3] is usually made the occasion for terminating the partial avoidance between a wife and her parents-in-law. The wife then establishes her own household and from now on both her mother- and her father-in-law may come to her house informally and accept food that she offers them. Vice versa, the wife may now freely enter her mother-in-law's house, including the cooking-partition, and may even help her to cook on her hearth.

The avoidance between mother-in-law and son-in-law is terminated after the first child has been borne by her daughter. She then comes for her first formal visit to her son-in-law's house, bringing elaborate gifts along with her, and her son-in-law later returns her visit and likewise makes her a present. After that a mother-in-law and a son-in-law can attend the same feasts and talk together more freely, but they never become really familiar with one another.

Although the avoidances between relatives-in-law apply primarily to the individual persons between whom the relationship has been established, they are up to a point extended along classificatory lines. A man shows a restrained behaviour not only in the presence of his own mother-in-law but in that of her co-wives and sisters as well, and a young wife extends the respect shown towards her father-in-law to his real and classificatory brothers.

(iv) *Ritual Prohibitions between Kinsmen*

Partial avoidances or rather ritual prohibitions are observed also in the relations between parents and children. Thus a man must not sleep on or

---

[1] Whereas kinship obligations and presents are nowadays usually paid in money, it would be considered bad manners in this case if he were to offer money to his father-in-law.
[2] The pronoun *lu* (it) refers to *olukuzu*, 'deadly danger'.   [3] Cf. p. 43.

step over the bedspread (*vugono*) of his child (male or female) or any person whom he calls child (i.e. any classifactory child) unless he is past the age when he can beget children. If he were to infringe this prohibition either he himself could beget no further children or any children which his son or daughter might have would die. Analogously, a married daughter or a circumcised son must not step over the bedspread or sleeping-skin of their mother as long as she is still bearing children.[1] The sanction behind this prohibition is of the same kind as in the previous case: any further children that the mother might bear would die and the same would happen to her grandchildren. In both cases these evil consequences of a violation of the rule can only be averted by the performance of a purification rite.[2]

In this connexion, finally, may be mentioned the laws of exogamy as well as the marriage prohibitions between unrelated but friendly clans that have ceremonially pledged their mutual support in fighting.[3] From the native point of view they are classed as *emigilu* (avoidances), and the sanctions behind them—besides social ostracism or even physical punishment by the clansmen of the offender—are thought to be of the same kind as those behind other avoidances: the offspring resulting from an incestuous or forbidden union will be weak or likely to die, or it will be afflicted with the curse of insanity or physical abnormalities and deficiencies.

(b) *Other Avoidances and Ritual Prohibitions*

Besides avoidances of or between persons, most of the Bantu Kavirondo tribes observe ritual prohibitions that refer to animals or objects or to certain modes of behaviour. In all these cases the common idea is to evade dangers of a magical nature which would threaten if the prohibition were disregarded.

(i) *Prohibition against killing certain Animals*

As far as I could discover, prohibitions against killing apply to very few animals, viz. to the cobra, the python (*evaga*), and other large snakes[4] (but not to small ones) and to certain small birds (*amadudu*) that build their nests under the eaves of the hut. Among the Logoli, if somebody kills a python (*evaga*), even in self-defence, it is feared that he will subsequently suffer from impotence or that he will not beget any children, even if many years have passed between the act of killing the snake and his marriage.

---

[1] Cf. chapter on circumcision, p. 358.

[2] Unfortunately I failed to ascertain (*a*) whether a father must avoid his son's or daughter's sleeping-place only after they are circumcised or married respectively or even during their childhood, (*b*) whether the prohibition applies also to the children who would have to avoid their father's sleeping-place, and (*c*) whether a mother must also avoid sleeping on or stepping over her adult children's sleeping-place.

[3] Cf. chapter on marriage, p. 388.

[4] It seems that the name *evaga* refers to any large and poisonous snake. Mr. Rees translates the word as 'python', but the description which I was given also fitted a cobra. The generic term for a snake is *enzoka*.

MEASURES OF PROTECTION AND PREVENTION

To prevent this from happening a rite of purification must be performed for him either immediately after the killing or later when the above-mentioned symptoms begin to show and the diviner has detected the killing of the *evaga* snake as the probable cause of his complaint.[1] Among the Vugusu a similar belief is held. If a man kills a cobra (*mugóyovaka*) during his wife's pregnancy or if the wife herself accidentally crosses its path or visits the place where it has died it is feared that the child will not develop properly but will remain weak and sickly.[2]

The prohibition against killing the *amadudu* birds applies primarily to uncircumcised boys and seems to be connected with the belief that these birds become the occasional abodes (but not reincarnations) of ancestral spirits. For the same reason people also fear to kill large bulls, and if they do so the owner of the animal is never present when the bull is killed. Later he expresses his surprise and dismay, pretending that the bull has been killed without his knowledge and permission so that the ancestral spirit that resided in the bull may not be angry with him.

Large fig-trees (*omukuyu*) and other shady trees with a big crown and rich foliage are also considered to be the occasional abodes and meeting-places of the ancestral spirits and therefore must not be cut down.

Among the Vugusu, people also avoid killing frogs,[3] and when a big frog happens to stay near their homestead they build a small shrine (*namwima*) under the eaves of the hut for the frog to live in.[4] If the frog occasionally stays in this little hut or returns to it, this is thought to bring luck to the homestead in a general way. In explanation of this peculiar attitude towards frogs I was told the following story:

'One day in the distant past a woman took a basketful of eleusine to the market (*mwikandjo*) to barter it for some meat. When she received the meat, a small piece was added to the big chunk as *etaso*.[5] Then she went home again and on her way back met with a big frog called Namaganda. Namaganda begged the woman for the small piece of meat which she had been given as *etaso*. Being kind-hearted, she gave the meat to the frog. When she came home her husband asked her for the *etaso*, saying that he wanted to roast it for himself. So when his wife told him that she had given it to a frog she had met by the roadside, her husband at first disbelieved her and then became very angry and scolded her for her foolishness. He took a club and asked his wife to lead him to the place where she had seen the frog. When they arrived there Namaganda was still there and the woman asked him: "Did I not give you a piece of meat?" The frog merely replied: "*e.*" Then the wife stood aside, and the husband quarrelled with the frog: "Why did you ask my wife to give you the meat?" The frog just listened and the

[1] Cf. the life-story of Christopher Mtiva, vol. iii.
[2] Cf. chapter on birth, p. 331.
[3] There is, however, no particular sanction behind this rule.
[4] Such a shrine is also called *muravula*.
[5] From *xutasa*, to add to. It is a common practice among the Bantu Kavirondo when making a purchase to get a small amount over and above the quantity that the customer can claim. Nowadays this extra bit (*etaso*) is also referred to as baksheesh.

man went on: "Was it my millet for which the meat was bought or yours?" The frog replied: "It was the millet from your garden." The husband went on scolding: "Did I dig the garden for myself or for you?" Then he took his club and poked the frog under its legs where the soft spots are. Namaganda did not reply and the man went on beating it severely until it was nearly dead. Then Namaganda said: "I am dying now because you have beaten me, but from now on the people shall all die from the illness of the chest." '

According to some people Namaganda was the wife of the tribal ancestor Muvugusu.

(ii) *Food Avoidances*

Far more common than the prohibition against killing animals are the rules prohibiting people from eating certain animals as well as other foodstuffs. These prohibitions not only cover a large variety of foods but also differ as regards the categories of persons to whom they apply, the length of time during which they must be observed, the kind of other ritual observances linked with them, &c. Taking these factors into account, the following six kinds of food avoidances or prohibitions can be distinguished among the Bantu Kavirondo: (1) The avoidance of animal and vegetable foodstuffs along clan lines; (2) food prohibitions on a sexual basis; (3) avoidance of milk by unmarried girls and young wives; (4) temporary food avoidances observed by pregnant women; (5) personal food avoidances; and (6) abstention from foodstuffs on certain occasions. Although the motives from which these different food avoidances have sprung differ widely, they all have in common that any infringement of the prohibition is thought to be followed by evil consequences of a mystical order which—once the infringement has taken place—can only be averted by the speedy performance of a lustration rite.

1. Food avoidances along clan lines are not observed by all Bantu Kavirondo, but only by certain sub-tribes. They are quite unknown among the Logoli, although the latter are aware of their existence among other tribes. In the existing literature[1] on the Bantu Kavirondo some of these

[1] Cf. K. Dundas, 1913, p. 30: 'The clans are exogamous, children taking the totem of their father.' On p. 59 Dundas gives a list of totems together with a list of clans. To 7 of 17 Wanga clans that he lists he ascribes the 'bushbuck' as totem animal. He does not add any explanation to the bare statement that these are the 'totems' of the respective clans. For one clan he lists as the totem 'a new pot', adding in a footnote that the members of that clan may not eat food cooked in a new pot. Other such 'totems' listed by him are 'roasted *mwimbi*' (eleusine), a milk pot (the members of the respective clan may not drink out of a milk gourd), 'two water jars' (if members of this clan meet a person coming from the river with two water jars it is considered a sign of ill luck and the person concerned must kill a goat or a fowl as a lustration rite), a species of small bird (*khatietie*), &c. These so-called totems are obviously the same clan avoidances that will be discussed below on p. 206. Cf. also Hobley, 1903, p. 346 sq. Hobley translates the word *muziro* (Logoli: *omugilu*, Vugusu: *gumusilu*) as 'totem'. The term which is frequently used and also occurs in numerous texts that I have collected refers, however, to any avoidance or ritual prohibition that is sanctioned in a magico-religious way.

MEASURES OF PROTECTION AND PREVENTION

prohibitions are labelled 'totemism', but this term is hardly justified as the various prohibitions against killing and eating animals or other objects are—with one exception—nowhere linked with the belief in a descent from or relationship to the objects concerned. Among the Vugusu, each clan has at least one food taboo and often two or three, but the stringency with which such taboos are kept varies considerably among the different clans. The members of the Gwangwa[1] clan have three different taboos: they must avoid (*xusila*) the meat of the reed-buck (*esunu*), the meat of cows which have a certain colour called *eŋenda* (a chequered design of brown and yellow) and, thirdly, eleusine grain, except in the form of beer. These avoidances must be observed by both sexes, but they are not rigidly enforced in the case of children until they reach an age of about eight or ten years. Married Gwangwa women may cook eleusine porridge as well as the meat of the *esunu* and of cows of the *eŋenda* colour for their husbands and children, but they must refrain from eating these things themselves. Women married to Gwangwa men, on the other hand, are not affected by the Gwangwa food taboos, but they must not give the prohibited foods to their children. The prohibitions are thus clearly limited to the members of the clan. The avoidance applies to the act of eating alone and is not linked with a prohibition against killing the animals concerned or with a taboo on growing and possessing eleusine. The members of the Gwangwa clan claim that if they were to eat eleusine or the meat of a reed-buck they would have to vomit and then get severely ill. As, however—eleusine being one of their staple foods—it would mean a serious curtailment of their diet if they were to abstain from it altogether, they can evade the prohibition by cooking the eleusine together with a certain medicine which neutralizes its harmful effects.[2] I was assured, however, that this is only done by the women and not by the elders of the clan.

The people of the Yundo clan—to mention a second example—refrain from eating a certain kind of black pea, called *tjivalayo*. If they were to disregard this rule, large spots would show on their skin, their hair would fall out and, finally, their skin would peel off.[3] As in the case of the Gwangwa, the prohibition applies only to the actual members of the Yundo clan, and the bad effects of its violation can, likewise, be averted by putting a certain medicine into the pot when cooking the peas. The origin of the avoidance of black peas by the Yundo clan is accounted for by the following story:

'Long ago the people of the Yundo clan were eating black peas as the other

[1] A sub-clan of the Gitwika, cf. p. 65, where it is referred to as 'Gitwika va Kwangwa'.

[2] Cf. also Hobley (1903), p. 347: '... if, by any mishap, the meat of the totem is eaten, the evil consequences referred to can be averted by making a medicine "dawa", extracted from certain herbs, and this extract is mixed with the fat of a black ox and rubbed all over the body of the patient.'

[3] Cf. Hobley (1903), p. 347: '... the eating of a totem animal is not thought to be followed by death, but only by a severe skin eruption.'

clans are still doing to-day. At one time, however, they all got ill, suffering from a skin disease similar to mange. Then one elder, called Kilovene, decided to stop eating black peas, and he soon recovered from his illness, while all the others continued to suffer from it. He then knew that his health had improved because he had refused to eat those peas. So he ordered his children to do the same, threatening to curse them if they should disobey his order. Kilovene's children did as he had told them and they likewise recovered. From then on the whole clan refused to eat black peas.'

People also swear by the food avoidances observed by their own clan. Thus, a Yundo, if someone were to doubt a statement that he had made in a legal dispute, would say: 'If I have told you a lie, may I eat black peas.' Other common food avoidances on a clan basis are elephant meat (it is feared that an infringement of this prohibition would cause the offender to suffer from elephantiasis), various kinds of antelope, cows of certain colours, wild-growing vegetables and fruits, different kinds of fish, and so on.[1] The food taboos are not exclusive, i.e. several clans may have the same avoidance without, therefore, being or considering themselves related to one another. The people of the Mweya clan, for example, avoid the meat of the *esunu*, but they do not consider themselves in any way related to the Gwangwa who have the same avoidance. The stringency with which these food avoidances are observed differs not only among the various clans but also among the different members of the same clan. Many of the younger people pay no attention to them at all and even have to ask the elders of their clan to find out what their clan avoidance is. The main force keeping the food avoidances alive seems to be the diviners who will often blame the violation of a food taboo as the cause of a disease when the relatives of a sick person come to consult them (see below, p. 229). If, in such a case, the patient recovers he will henceforth observe the prohibition more strictly and also enforce it among the junior people of his lineage.

If a sub-clan splits off a main clan (cf. above, p. 57) the former food taboo is usually adhered to for one or a few generations until it gradually lapses into oblivion as the independence of the new sub-clan becomes more firmly established or until it is replaced by other avoidances.

2. *Food prohibitions on a sexual basis.* Throughout Kavirondo women must refrain from eating fowls and eggs. Small girls up to an age of about ten years may eat both when they can get them, but then they are taught by their father and mother that it is a disgusting and shameful thing for a woman to eat these things. Several women whom I questioned on this subject emphatically insisted that if they were to eat eggs or fowls they would have to vomit and that they observed the avoidance not merely because custom enjoined them to do so, but because it was actually

---

[1] According to Hobley (1903), p. 347, many Vugusu clans have a stork as their common 'totem': 'In Kitosh there are several totems, according to the clan, but over a large portion the special totem is *makuyi*, a large black and white stork which appears in large flocks about November; it eats locusts.'

a repulsive thought to them to touch these foods. This attitude is confirmed by the fact that even women in Christian families can only with difficulty be persuaded to disregard the prohibition, although their husbands no longer insist on it or even scoff at the idea of observing such avoidances. Among the Logoli, where the mission has endeavoured to break down the avoidance, a few female members of the Christian community now eat fowls, but they still refuse eggs. If a pagan husband discovers on repeated occasions that his wife has secretly eaten chicken meat, he may drive her away and demand his marriage-cattle back, but no purification ceremony has to be performed for the wife in such a case.

Whatever may have been the original motive for imposing such food prohibitions on a sexual basis, they clearly have the effect of securing the choicer items on the native bill of fare for the male members of the household. As men are often away from their homesteads for longish periods of time, and as it is one of the women's duties to look after the fowls, the female members of the household might easily get the better of the men if they were permitted to eat fowls and eggs. Among the Vugusu, an explanation for these taboos was volunteered to me which points in that direction. A long time ago, so my informant said, the men had a grudge against their wives for always getting the best morsels of food. So when sitting round the beer-pot they sang mock songs, comparing the women to dogs or foxes which always steal the choicest bits of food. One of these songs ran:

> *Mbolele nioyáona nase ndjeyo*
> *vaxana valia tjimbigo*
> *vafuana exutu.*

> 'Tell me where the remainder[1] is, then I may go there.
> The girls eat the kidneys,[2]
> They resemble a tortoise.'[3]

The women, of course, resented being the targets of such ridicule and abuse and henceforth refused to eat both fowls and eggs.

Even though this story will hardly be accepted as an explanation of the 'origin' of the food taboos for women, it appears that the men's fear of being cheated and outwitted by their wives has something to do with them.

3. *Avoidances of milk by unmarried girls and young wives.* From puberty on, unmarried girls (*avagima*, virgins) must refuse to drink milk, as it is feared that otherwise their fathers would not be able to marry their daughters off for cattle but that they would elope with a boy. This rule

---

[1] 'The remainder' refers to the Vugusu cattle that have been raided by the Masai or that died from disease.

[2] The word *tjimbigo*, 'kidneys', stands for choice and pleasant foods.

[3] The *exutu* (tortoise) is a despised animal and to apply this epithet to a girl is a grave insult. The song means: 'Let us go and get our cattle back by fighting for it, so that we may have beef to give our women lest they eat all our best things and let us go empty.'

of avoidance, however, is said to be observed by the girls on their own account without being enforced by their parents. 'If a girl were to be seen drinking milk her age mates would ridicule her and she would feel much ashamed.' After her betrothal a girl may drink milk if she is by herself but not in the presence of her mother and even less of her mother-in-law, 'as she must fear their eyes'.[1] If she were to drink the milk from the cows that her father has received as marriage-cattle for her she would thereby show that she refuses to be married.[2] These milk avoidances are maintained by a girl until after her marriage. Only when her husband has a cow of his own to milk may she drink of this milk in the presence of other people.

4. *Observance of temporary food-taboos by pregnant women.* During pregnancy women must avoid eating meat from the ribs and back as well as from the heart of a cow, as otherwise they would have difficulties at the time of delivery. Among the Vugusu women, during the last three months of pregnancy, must also refrain from drinking milk and eating ripe bananas to keep the foetus from growing too big. Many women also observe personal food-taboos during the time of pregnancy.[3]

5. *Personal food-avoidances.* Besides food taboos observed by individuals on a basis of clanship, sex, age, &c., some people—in particular elderly men—have personal food avoidances or dislikes (Lurugoli: *okuyera*, to abstain from certain foods for personal reasons as distinct from *okugila*). There may be many different reasons for starting an avoidance of this kind, but usually it is an unfortunate event that has happened in connexion with the handling or following the consumption of a certain food which is then held responsible for the unfortunate event. Thus among the Logoli I heard of a person who refused to drink milk because he had once accidentally killed a cow that was in milk; another person in Kitosh refused to drink milk because in an angry mood he had once broken a milk-gourd and thrown it at his wife because she had left nothing over for him when he came back from a journey. Also people who have once got frightfully drunk and committed an offence or made a fool of themselves would give a pledge never to touch beer again. Similarly, if a person became severely ill after the consumption of a certain food he might henceforth avoid eating it. It will be seen from these examples that such personal food-taboos may easily become clan-taboos if the person who imposes them is a leading clan-elder and if he has the notion that the dangers which he attributes to a certain foodstuff not only affect him personally but all the people who are of his 'blood'.

6. *Abstention from foodstuffs on certain occasions.* Fasting, or the abstention from certain foods as a preparatory or accompanying feature in the performance of rites, is not practised to any noteworthy extent among the Bantu Kavirondo. Neither the various specialists that wield active magical powers, nor the diviners or priests that detect or combat these powers, have

[1] *Anyala kutia mudzimoni dziavo.*
[2] Cf. chapter on marriage, p. 408.
[3] Cf. chapter on birth, p. 299.

to observe any particular food-customs before or while they are engaged in their respective tasks. Likewise, purification rites (see below, p. 245) do not involve fasting but, on the contrary, the ritual eating of certain foods. The only case of ritual fasting that I have noticed is the abstention from food observed by the circumcision candidates among the Logoli during the day preceding the operation. But even in this case the idea does not seem to be to lend the candidates the proper *ritual* status or condition, but rather to test their discipline and to enable them to bear the pain of the operation.

Among the Logoli, however, a food avoidance of a particular nature must be observed in connexion with the performance of the first-fruit rites. Before the eleusine crops cultivated by the members of a household group have been harvested and before the first meal cooked from the new crops has been consecrated to the ancestral spirits and ceremonially consumed by the members of the household,[1] no person who is not a member of this group may eat of these crops lest his stomach should swell and he should die. Should a visitor come while the family is eating this first meal of eleusine (the so-called *ovolo vwomusambwa*), the owner of the homestead must tell him: 'You cannot eat with us because we are eating the *ovolo vwomusambwa*.' The visitor then goes away immediately. Also, should a person pilfer some ears of eleusine from the field before the owners have eaten the 'first-fruits' and observed the accompanying rites, he would suffer the same fate. Afterwards, a little pilfering in another person's garden is not thought to be followed by any supernatural punishment. If a person falls ill at harvest-time after having partaken of a meal of eleusine porridge, he would attribute his illness to the same cause and would suspect his host of having tried to kill him by offering him of the first-fruits before they had been consecrated to the ancestral spirits.

Among the Vugusu no such first-fruit rites and prohibitions are observed. Only male twins or men who have begotten twins must refrain from eating of the new millet crop until it has become thoroughly dry, as otherwise they would get ill. When they eat the first meal they must kill a sheep or a goat and invite their kinsmen and neighbours to come with a basketful of porridge on which they put a piece of the slaughtered animal for them to take home.

(c) *Miscellaneous Avoidances and Prohibitions*

Finally there are a number of ritual prohibitions which are difficult to classify within any wider category of observances. However, as they may prove of importance in connexion with questions arising in the course of further research I shall briefly refer to them.

1. Among the Logoli a youth who carries on a courtship with a girl may not tear up the bead necklace of his sweetheart or pour or sprinkle water over her. If he does so and the girl later marries another man she will

[1] See the chapter on consumption, vol. ii.

remain lean and, in particular, will have abnormal deliveries when bearing children. They will be born with their feet first or they will be weaklings (*evironze*), and the mother will not succeed in bringing them up unless the youth who has violated the prohibition can be persuaded to perform a ceremony that will neutralize the effects of his offence (see below, p. 271).

2. When a cow has calved, strangers may not enter the hut in which the cow and the calf are kept until the following day. For it is thought that if a visitor were to enter the hut and see the cow 'his body would turn pale'. As a sign of warning the owner suspends a sandal (*ekilato*) from the frame of the door. Apparently this prohibition is an extension of the avoidance observed towards young mothers, as in other situations also cows are identified with women. Also the first milk that a cow yields after having calved must not be drunk but poured away, 'because it is too rich and does not taste well'. I am not certain, though, whether this prohibition has a ritual significance or not.

3. Besides observing food taboos some clans among the Vugusu refrain from doing or using certain things. Thus the members of one clan must not wear finger-rings of coiled iron wire. In explanation of this rule it is said that some generations ago an elder of that clan suffered from a sore and swollen finger caused by wearing such a ring. His whole hand became inflamed, and he ultimately died without having been able to remove the ring from his finger. Before his death he is supposed to have said that it was a bad thing for the people of his clan to wear iron finger-rings and that all who did so in future would die as he was now going to die. Some of the so-called 'totems' mentioned in Dundas's account of the Wanga clans are prohibitions of a similar nature.

4. On certain occasions people must practise ritual continence, as their cohabitation is thought to cause physical suffering to certain other persons or to increase the pain from which they suffer. Thus during the first night after their son has been circumcised a husband and wife must not cohabit lest their son should feel increased pain in his wound. Similarly, a dispenser of medicines who has been summoned to treat a patient's ulcer or another open wound must practise continence the night before he goes to see his patient as otherwise the latter would suffer additional pain in the night following the herbalist's visit. Among the Vugusu, husband and wife must also abstain from cohabitation for the first night after they have planted eleusine; otherwise the young shoots will not grow but wither away in the sun. When a near kinsman has died, and in particular after the death of one of their children, the parents must refrain from having intercourse until after the burial, but they must cohabit during the night following the burial. Continence was also practised during the night before a man started out for a war-raid. But this rule is said to have been observed merely for preserving the warrior's strength and not because any ritual significance was attached to it.

(5) GOOD AND BAD OMENS

It is a common belief among the Bantu Kavirondo that the outcome of an undertaking or any important event that will happen in the near or not too distant future may be forecast by omens or portents. Some of these omens are auspicious and encourage the person or persons engaged in an activity to be confident and carry on with it. Others are inauspicious and thus serve as a warning to abandon what one is doing or planning to do or at least to take precautionary measures to ward off the evil forces that are threatening. As distinct from oracles (see below, p. 225 sq.), which are consulted to find out the causes of events that have already happened or are in the process of happening, omens exclusively foretell events or their outcome. They are never made to happen by man as a result of ritual manipulations but always occur on their own account.[1] The following is a list of good and bad omens which I have noted down both among the Vugusu and the Logoli.

1. If a person starts out for a journey or goes to see somebody about an important matter and, while walking along the road, he hears a certain bird singing on his left, it is a bad sign, and he must return home and postpone his journey or visit for a day. If, on the other hand, the bird sings on the right side of the road, this is an auspicious sign for the success of his trip (Logoli, Vugusu).[2]

2. Among the Vugusu, when somebody has left his house in the morning to go somewhere he must ask the first person whom he meets if his firstborn child was a boy or a girl. If it is of the same sex as the first-born child of the person who has asked the question it is a good omen; if, however, the first-born children of the two persons are of different sex, it is a bad omen, and one should return home and do nothing of importance that day. If one's business is very urgent and cannot be postponed, one must at least pass the person questioned at a considerable distance to minimize the inauspiciousness resulting from having met the wrong person.[3]

Actually, the traveller does not put his question in a straightforward manner, but he asks: '*Olila lugendo sina?*', 'What journey do you eat?' The other one, if his first-born child happens to be of male sex, replies: '*Ndila lugendo lusedja*', 'I eat the right journey.' If the traveller's first-born child is likewise of male sex he shakes hands with him and salutes him emphatically with repeated outbursts such as *mulembe, mulembe, vulahi*,

---

[1] Cf. E. E. Evans-Pritchard's definition of Zande omens, *Witchcraft, Oracles, and Magic among the Azande*, pp. 374–5: 'They are natural happenings and not initiated by man and give him prognostications not deliberately sought by him.'

[2] K. Dundas (1913), p. 47, reports the same omen from the Wanga tribe, but according to him it is a good omen if the bird sings on the left side and a bad one if on the right. As, however, among most Bantu Kavirondo tribes the right side is regarded as the lucky side and the left side as the unlucky one, it seems very unlikely that it would be different among the Wanga. Dundas adds that if the bird is singing straight ahead it is an extremely bad omen.

[3] K. Dundas (1913), p. 47, reports the same omen from among the Wanga.

vulahi. Otherwise he just replies: '*Ndila lugendo luxasi*', 'I eat the left journey', and then turns away. If the first-born child of both of them is of female sex, they also greet one another and say: '*xulira lugendo lulala*', 'We eat the same journey'. According to another informant one may also say: 'My arm is up' if one's first-born child was a son and 'My arm is down' if it was a girl. Accordingly, if both arms are up or both arms are down it is equally good, but if one arm is up and one down it is bad. People also say that 'Women pull men down, because they are slow and backward and always keep their heads down in shame'. Similarly, among the Logoli, it is considered a good omen when starting out for a journey if a man whose first-born child was a son meets two boys walking together or in rapid succession, or two girls if his first-born child was a daughter. He says in that case 'I have met my arm'; but if he returns home because the omen was bad and the people ask him why he has come back he tells them: '*Sinyoye omukono gwange mba*', 'I did not find my arm.'

3. Stumbling is a bad omen among the Logoli, but it is worse to stumble with one's left foot than with the right one. In the latter case one returns home only if it happens twice in succession. If one stumbles with both feet in succession it means that two different troubles are in store. Among the Wanga, according to Dundas, 'it is lucky when going on a journey to stumble with the left foot but unlucky to stumble with the right. When returning home from a journey the opposite holds good' (1913, p. 47).

4. If one meets with a certain rat called *elivengi*, it is a bad omen in a general way (Logoli).

5. Meeting a small antelope (*ekisusu*) is a very good sign. Also if one meets a silver squirrel with a long, bushy tail (Logoli).

6. Meeting the *esimindwa*-bird[1] (red hawk) is a bad sign (Logoli).

7. If the *enyiru*-bird[2] twice crosses a person's path just in front of him and 'whistles', he must return home at once as this is a very bad omen (Logoli).

8. If an owl (*elikuli*) cries near a homestead, one of the persons living there will die soon. To prevent this from happening the owl is driven away with a firebrand (Logoli).

9. If one hears a big fox, called *ekivwi*, this is an omen forecasting the death of an important person in the tribe or clan (Logoli).

10. Among the Vugusu, if one comes across a certain kind of big ants called *náfusi*, this is a sign that one will be given plenty of beer and food by the person whom one is about to visit. Even if not visiting anybody, one thinks that something pleasant is in store for one if one meets *náfusi* ants.

11. Sneezing is generally considered a bad omen, and if a person

---

[1] This bird was described to me as having a long, curved bill and a predominantly red plumage with some black and white feathers. According to Hobley to see the red hawk is a bad omen among the Wanga also.

[2] This bird was described to me as having a short, straight bill and small, short tail-feathers with a striped design.

sneezes repeatedly before taking up an important activity, he puts it off for some time if he can possibly do so. With regard to the Wanga Hobley (1903, p. 341) makes the same statement, but adds: 'If a person plans to visit a friend who is said to be sick unto death, and if a sneezing fit comes on before he starts, then he knows that his friend will certainly recover from his illness.'

12. If two people clear their gardens and their hoes or axes by accident hit one another, this is a bad omen indicating that they will quarrel over their land. They must, therefore, stop their work and go home for a day. Obviously the hoes of the two neighbours can collide only if both work very close to their common boundary. This they would do only if they are each afraid that the other might encroach upon his land. By paying heed to the omen they actually ease a strain which would very likely end in a fight.

13. If in succession one sees two fig-trees (*emikuyu*), the leaves of which are hanging down, the harvest of one's crops will be plentiful.

14. If an antelope crosses the road (from either side) in front of the marriage-cattle while they are being driven from the place of the bridegroom's father to that of the bride's father, it is a bad omen indicating that the cattle will die.

The amount of attention which people actually pay to these various omens differs considerably. Some of them, particularly numbers 1 and 2, appear to be taken seriously by everybody, while others are considered more lightly. Old men and women who have plenty of leisure pay more attention to omens than young people, who would shun the inconveniences of putting off an undertaking because they had met with a bad omen. When walking in the company of young or middle-aged people I occasionally met with one or other of the good or bad omens quoted above. In every case I was told about them in a half-laughing, half-serious way, but no one ever suggested that we should return home or take some other measures to prevent the omen from coming true. The people in my company, however, insisted that the old people would take a more serious view of such incidents. This is borne out by the following incident: One day when I was visiting the old woman Xasoa she told me that I would not have met her at home if it had not been for two bad omens which she had come across that morning. At first she had wanted to visit her daughter, but soon after leaving her hut she met a woman whose first-born child turned out to be a girl while her first-born child was a son. Later on she started out in another direction to visit someone else, but again the first person she met was a girl (instead of a boy). She then decided to stay at home. When she greeted me she said quite seriously: 'You have tied me to stay home to-day.' According to Nandoli also younger people would take omens seriously if they had experienced bad luck after disregarding an omen or if within a short time they came across the same omens repeatedly. On the whole, the response to omens seems to be a matter of personal temperament. Some people with whom I discussed these things spoke about them in a perfectly serious manner while others—even pagans—said (or pretended) that they did not really believe in them.

Apart from omens in the proper sense of the word, i.e. auspicious or inauspicious incidents that happen by chance, people believe in lucky or unlucky happenings that they can partly or fully control. Thus among the Vugusu the number seven is considered unlucky, and whenever they can avoid this number they do so, in the same way as many west Europeans avoid the number thirteen. If a person has seven children he never admits the fact but either says that he has six or eight children. Similarly, a person would avoid possessing seven cows, seven goats, or seven objects of any sort. If a party of men goes hunting or raiding cattle they would see to it that they are not seven but either six or eight, as otherwise their trip would be ill fated. When they have to refer to the number seven they avoid the proper numeral which is *varano na vavili* (in the human class) and say instead *vavandu musafu muvi*—the bad luck (number of) people.[1]

In a similar way, both among the Logoli and the Vugusu, the right side of anything is considered the lucky side and the left the unlucky one. They also say that the right side of one's body is the strong one and the left side the weak one. An inferior person, therefore, should not stand on the right of a superior person as he would take his strength away. When natives see a European couple, and the woman walks on the right of the man, they shake their heads in surprise as they say that the woman will thereby sap the man's strength. Owing to the same notion, the rules of good manners demand that one must pass a person on his left side (so that my left shoulder is near the left shoulder of the person I pass) and never on the right. When doing things with one hand the right one should be used as the left hand is the unlucky one.[2] It also brings bad luck to a person if one passes behind his back instead of in front of him, as this is likewise thought to sap his strength.

To ensure good luck in an enterprise one must get up quickly in the morning. If one rises slowly everything else will go slowly that day. When leaving one's house to visit a person one ties a knot in a blade of grass that grows by the side of the path. This 'ties' the people to stay home or keeps them from eating their food or drinking their beer before one has arrived.

Significance of Dreams and Dream Prophecy

To ordinary dreams (*amaloto*) the Bantu Kavirondo do not attach much importance. As has been stated in a previous chapter (see above, p. 160), the commonly accepted view is that it is a person's 'heart' that makes him dream. It leaves his body while he is asleep and visits the various places

---

[1] In the various Bantu Kavirondo dialects the numeral 7 is formed either by adding 5 and 2 (—*tano (rano) na—vili*) or 4 and 3 (—*ne na—taru*).

[2] When shaking hands both hands are used, however, and also when accepting a gift—even a small one—it is good manners to stretch out both hands, shaping them into a cup, lest the donor would think that his gift is not appreciated. There is also a proverb which runs: 'If you are given with one hand take with both.'

MEASURES OF PROTECTION AND PREVENTION

which he sees in his dream. Vice versa, the 'hearts' of other people, and in particular the spirits of deceased persons, may come and talk to a person while he is dreaming. If such dream-visitations from ancestral spirits recur frequently, and if they are of an unpleasant nature, the person who suffers from them consults a diviner to find out what kind of sacrifice or other rite he should perform to pacify the troublesome spirit. Other dreams, in which no ancestral spirits are involved, are deemed to be significant only if they have been very vivid and unpleasant and if one has the same dream repeatedly. People then begin to talk about their dream, but there are no specialists who can be consulted to interpret dreams, nor have I discovered any symbolic interpretations of dreams the meaning of which is obscure. However, if somebody dreams that another person has died or is seriously ill he will try to discover next morning whether the dream is true, but he will not divulge his dream, lest he might be suspected of having caused the other person's death or disease. If the person concerned is a near kinsman or someone for whom one cares a great deal one would try to perform a rite over him which would prevent the dream from coming true. Thus Christopher Mtiva of Maragoli told me that one morning, when he was a boy of about seventeen, he came to his mother's hut to eat his morning meal. He saw his mother standing by the door, and as he was entering she hit him with the *elundu*-switch, that he had held behind his back while he was circumcised and which his father had since then kept in his hut. Then she threw a banana against his chest and told him to roast it in the fire and eat it. When he inquired what it was all about she told him that she had dreamt he had died and that what she had just done with him would prevent the dream from coming true.

Another means of preventing a bad dream from coming true is to beat the person concerned with a switch of the *elisazi*-tree. This was described to me in the following text:

'If a person has been dreaming that his child has died he leaves his hut very early in the morning and searches for an *elisazi*-tree; then he cuts off a switch and goes to meet his son; he beats him with the *elisazi* before he tells him: "I was dreaming that you had died"; later on, when he has finished beating him with the *elisazi*, he can tell him. And this rule applies to all people: even if a woman dreams or if a child dreams about its mother. It must leave the place where it has slept and come with an *elisazi* and beat its mother. Then the mother knows: this child was dreaming that I have died.'

People also believe that dreams can disclose hidden knowledge to them, e.g. who has committed adultery with one's wife, who has stolen something from him, &c. One would then go to the person whom the dream has pointed out as the offender and ask him to admit his guilt and offer compensation. If the other person does not admit the offence on the strength of such evidence one would call the *omuségetili* (see below, p. 275) or another specialist to administer an ordeal. If the outcome of the ordeal confirms the dream, the evidence would be considered quite convincing, and the clan-head would enforce the payment of the fine by the offender should he refuse to render it on his own account.

Apart from believing in the ominous nature of their own dreams, both the Logoli and the Vugusu consult specialists[1] who can foretell important events both of a public and a private nature by the inspiration which they derive from their dreams. This art of dream-prophecy is of rare occurrence, and the persons who possess it jealously guard their knowledge and hand it on to their own sons only. They do so by pronouncing a blessing over that son whom they have chosen for their successor, saying to him: '*Nguheye edzingulu dziange*', 'I give you my strength.' By uttering these words in the appropriate situation and in the proper context the father is actually thought to transmit his power of prophecy to his son. Together with his inherited disposition the paternal blessing will now enable him to succeed his father in the office of a dream-prophet. No medicines, secret rites, or spells are used in connexion with dream-prophecy (*ovuŋoli*) to increase the power of prophesying. Among the Logoli there is said to have been only one family of dream-prophets; it belonged to the Saniaga clan. Nagweya, the last member of this family who practised the art of prophecy, died in 1918, and his son disclaims having inherited his father's knowledge. Nagweya's fame is said to have extended beyond the borders of the Logoli tribe as he was consulted also by Luo, Tiriki, Nyole, and people from other neighbouring tribes. As a striking example of his prescience the following story is still circulating among the Logoli:

'One day when Nagweya and some other elders were sitting round the beer-pot he said he had dreamt that there was a certain light-skinned man in their clan who would be killed by the Nandi on the following day. Next day a party of warriors actually had an encounter with the Nandi, and the only person who was killed was a light-coloured man of Nagweya's clan called Kibviandja.'

Another striking prediction with which Nagweya is credited concerned the death of a boy who was attacked by a leopard. After having had a dream to that effect he instructed the elders of the tribe to exercise care and tell the people to stay home after dark. Nevertheless a short time afterwards a youth was badly mauled by a leopard and soon died from his wounds.

Among the Vugusu there seem to have been more dream-prophets than in Maragoli, but most of them are said to belong to two clans, the Gwangwa and Itu. Of one of these prophets it is told that he predicted the coming of the white man and the construction of the railway which in his prophecy he described as a shiny snake of iron that would stretch through the whole country from east to west.[2] Another dream-prophet of former times is said to have foretold the eastward migration of the Vugusu

---

[1] Called *omuŋoli* among the Logoli and *omuŋosi* among the Vugusu.

[2] Actually the railway from Nakuru to Kampala in Uganda passes through Kitosh from east to west.

MEASURES OF PROTECTION AND PREVENTION

(from the neighbourhood of Tororo to the southern slopes of Mt. Elgon), which must have taken place some seventy to a hundred years ago.

Among neither of the two tribes was I able to discover a legend accounting for the origin of dream-prophecy or any other theory explaining how those particular families who nowadays practise as *avaŋosi* have come to enjoy the reputation of being able to foretell future events from their own dreams. The invariable answer to such questions is that they have done so since long ago and that it is the spirits of their ancestors who inspire their dreams. This answer at least explains why an outsider who did not have the support of a long row of reputed dream-prophets in his ancestry would not be likely to be credited with the power of prophecy unless he succeeded in establishing such a reputation by a series of striking predictions which then came true.

Among the Logoli the dream-prophets use no particular technique, such as rites or medicines, but they either tell their dream-prophecies unsolicited when sitting together with the elders, or they are consulted by public or private clients. They listen to their inquiries, and then tell them to come back again the following day, so that during the night they may have a dream answering their questions. Among the Vugusu the *avaŋosi* do not only prophesy from actual dreams but they also enter into a state of meditation, smelling at a buffalo tail from which they claim to derive additional inspiration. Such a consultation then lasts through the greater part of a day as the prophet needs several hours before the inspiration enters his mind.

The dream-prophet is consulted both on matters of public and of private concern. The clan-heads among the Logoli are said formerly to have consulted him regularly towards the end of December or early in January (before the eleusine is planted, which marks the beginning of the new agricultural season) to find out what important events were in store for the whole clan during the coming year. If the *omuŋoli* prophesied an epidemic, a drought, or devastation of the gardens from hail-storms or locusts, the clan-head at the appropriate time consulted a diviner (see below, p. 222) to find out what counter-measures should be taken to prevent the prophecy from coming true. The dream-prophet never gave such advice himself but merely foretold the future. Similarly, the leading warriors consulted him on the probable outcome of a contemplated raid or other war-expedition. If he forecast that many would die this would induce them to postpone the raid and to wait until the auspices were more favourable. Among the Vugusu the consultation of the dream-prophet seems to have been a regular observance before embarking on any raid. After scouts (*vayoti*) had reconnoitred the position in the enemy's kraals and villages they reported their findings to the *omuŋosi*, telling him in detail what they had seen in the enemy villages. He would then give them specific advice as to how to approach the enemy. He would also disclose to them from which huts the counter-attacks would be made, what tactics the enemy would employ in doing so, and how they should respond to them. He would even tell them that in a certain kraal there would be a cow of a certain colour. If the warriors then succeeded in obtaining that cow they would give it to him as a payment for his information. The dream-prophet himself never joined in the actual fighting even if he was still young enough to be physically able to do so.

When people consult the dream-prophet on private matters they do so before embarking on an important but hazardous undertaking, such as a long journey, or the circumcision of their son. They would never consult him in cases of sickness or on minor matters (such as the outcome of a pending law-case, a courtship, &c.), nor does he ever prophesy an individual disease but only death in warfare or from accidents, such as the assault by a leopard, a snake-bite, and so forth. Unlike most other specialists, the dream-prophet is always consulted in the open, and there is no secrecy about the things which he tells his client. (Only if he predicts the death of another person, his information is usually withheld from the person concerned to spare him from being frightened.) Owing to the public nature of his office the dream-prophet can be visited in broad daylight, and the gifts which his clients take to him are openly handed to him. It appears that his special knowledge is never put to any anti-social ends. As a payment for his services he receives basketfuls of sorghum or eleusine, and in more important cases a sheep, a goat, or even a cow.

Forecasting the Future from the Inspection of Entrails

Although, as far as I could discover, animals are never killed merely for the purpose of divining from their entrails, this form of divination is an important feature of any ritual killing. Thus an inspection of entrails takes place, not only when an animal is killed for an ancestral sacrifice on behalf of a sick person, but on many other occasions as well, e.g. after the birth of a child, in connexion with the naming rite, at circumcision, before marriage, at the setting up of the new household for a young couple (*sitexo*-rite), and at the various sacrifices performed for the welfare of the whole clan or tribe (see below, p. 290). As on these various occasions different kinds of animals are killed, the divination of entrails is not restricted to cattle alone (although the technique of inspection seems to be most elaborate in the case of cattle), but it comprises also goats, sheep, and fowls and—in connexion with hunting—various kinds of antelopes. As formerly domestic animals were only slaughtered if an occasion for a ritual killing arose, the entrails were inspected every time an animal was killed. Only in the case of animals that had died from disease or had been killed because they were sick was no significance attached to the condition of their intestines.

All my informants insisted that faith in the divination from entrails is still very strong, in spite of the fact that at the various ritual killings which I witnessed the matter seemed to be taken fairly lightly, i.e. the remarks made by the elders during the inspection remained of a vague and

MEASURES OF PROTECTION AND PREVENTION

general nature and not much attention seemed to be paid to them. I was assured, however, that this has always been the case and that the elders would not pronounce all their findings right away in everybody's presence, but that they would make a few and rather insignificant remarks only and keep their real knowledge until later, when they would be privately consulted by the owner of the slaughtered animal or the person who had arranged the killing on his behalf. At one such ritual killing which I witnessed and which took place to 'confirm' the ancestral name of a girl about to be married, only the following words were spoken by the elders as they were pointing their sticks at the different parts of the intestines:

Hano, hano, hano, omundu omutai sio, neyuno mulalagula, neyevuno vulwale muntju, naye tjino tjilomo waxodjawe namwe kalava xúmusedje.

'Here, here, here, the first person (i.e. here child) is nothing (i.e. will die), and this here (means) you will always go to the diviner (i.e. there will be much trouble and sickness about). And this here (means) sickness in the house. And these are the words of her maternal uncle or perhaps with her husband (i.e. either she or her husband will quarrel with her maternal uncle).'

This prognostication of the bride's future was said to have been rather on the bad side, but nevertheless the marriage was not postponed or called off on account of it, a step which would only be taken if the entrails forecast the bride's death in case of her marriage or a similar major misfortune. She would, however, be warned to take particular care with her first child and to avoid anything that might provoke quarrels with her maternal uncle.

Among the Vugusu faith in the divination from entrails is based on the theory that the ancestral spirits have the power to produce the various symptoms in the intestines of domestic animals so that they become signs by which the people can foretell the future. 'The spirits change the entrails so that they help the people to know the future.' As far as the signs are bad it is thought that the spirits who produce them are different spirits from those that will cause the illness which the entrails predict. One and the same spirit would not send illness and at the same time also the omens which would enable the people to take timely measures of precaution and prevention.

Among the Logoli some relation is apparently thought to exist between the condition of the intestines and the *ombila* or *omulogi* who will cause the disease, for the bad symptoms can be 'returned' to them and then make them sick instead of the intended victim, if it is possible to administer to them a concoction which contains the inauspicious intestines.

The immediate purpose of the inspection of entrails is not only to discover the future but also to find ways of evading a misfortune and of preventing disease. According to the outcome of the inspection three different responses are possible.

1. If the signs are good one looks into the future with confidence and carries on what one has contemplated, e.g. a name-giving rite, a marriage,

or a war-expedition. If a ritual killing has been performed for a sick person, one trusts that he will recover without further steps being taken. Should things go wrong after all, e.g. should the patient die instead of recovering, the inspection of the entrails would not be blamed for having been misleading, but the dead person would be blamed for having caused his own death by himself performing evil magic which has then been returned to him. The divination from entrails is thus not conceived of as an infallible indicator of *any* future happening regardless of its cause, but it reveals a limited range of future happenings caused by certain agents (spirits, sorcerers, &c.). The idea seems to be that at the time when the entrails are inspected these agents have already set to work and that by some occult connexion between the agents and the entrails the state of the latter betrays their plans which otherwise have not yet become apparent.

2. If the signs are bad, one goes to the diviner to consult him as to the most appropriate steps to be taken for averting the disease or misfortune that has been forecast by the entrails. The procedure in this case is strictly parallel to that adopted after having met with an inauspicious omen or after having been forewarned of evil happenings by the dream-prophet.[1]

3. If the signs are altogether bad, people are said to submit to their fate or to that of the person concerned unless they can still evade the situation for which such bad prognostications exist. Warriors, for example, would postpone a contemplated raid or a bride would refuse to be married should the entrails predict her early death. There would, however, be no consultation of the diviner as he would be powerless to give any advice in the face of altogether bad signs. Unfortunately I could not obtain data on actual situations in which such a course of resignation was adopted.

The elders who inspect the entrails, the so-called *avaloli vemunda*, are not specialists in the usual sense of the word, but the majority of old men know the meaning of the different signs and marks which the entrails show, although some elders have the reputation of being better versed in their interpretation than others. The fact that they do not divulge all their findings while the people stand round the slaughtered animal indicates, however, that they observe some secrecy about this knowledge. They get no special payment, but are always given the intestines to eat and a fair portion of the meat of the slaughtered animal.

Among the Vugusu the following parts of the intestines of a cow are distinguished by special terms and, if they show any particular features, may become significant omens:

1. *Gámala*, small intestines.
2. *Sisiandja*, colon.
3. *Tjimburendje*, mesenteric lymph-glands of small intestine (also bronchial lymph-glands).

[1] It is for this reason that I have not classed the inspection of entrails with other kinds of divination (which will be dealt with in the following chapter) but with omens which always precede divination.

MEASURES OF PROTECTION AND PREVENTION

4. *Tjingeo*, (branch of) anterior mesenteric artery.
5. *Endulwe*, gall-bladder.
6. *Eyalamasi*, pancreas.
7. *Embotji*, caecum (also called *liesi*).
8. *Luvululusie* (also *lwavai*—of the herd because it is given to the herd-boys), terminal portion of colon.
9. *Lusilindja*, oesophagus.
10. *Ekokopi*, trachea.
11. *Lisombo*, big stomach.
12. *Navutundu*, small stomach, attached to big stomach.
13. *Tjimbiko*, kidneys.
14. *Luima*, spleen.
15. *Sini*, liver.
16. *Gumwoyo*, heart.
17. *Gumusuva*, rectum.
18. *Sitelwa*, part of liver.
19. *Livombo, gama*, big parts of entrails.

Wefwafwa, an elder of South Kitosh, who himself frequently officiates as an *omuloli wemunda*,[1] gave me the following examples of the divinatory meaning of intestinal conditions and peculiarities: (1) To see whether sickness is imminent they look first of all at the edge of the small intestines (*gámala*). If they are full this is a sign that sickness is threatening or—if the person concerned is already suffering from it—that it is still rampant. If they are empty it means that sickness is remote or that it will quickly subside. It is also a sign of threatening disease if the *gámala* are bulging out like swellings and if they are of a dark grey colour (i.e. full of excreta). If they are of a pink colour it is a generally good sign. (2) If one can see small pointed swellings (*tjisala*) on the small intestines this is a sign that all the other cattle of the person who owns the slaughtered animal will soon develop a disease called *lukata* (mange). (3) If the *sisiandja* (colon) is of even thickness like a well-stuffed sausage and of a dark colour, this is a sign that the owner of the slaughtered animal will enjoy good health and long life; if it is alternately thick and thin the owner will die in the near future and his possessions in cattle will be scattered among his relatives. (4) If they see the mesenteric artery (*tjingeo*) shine through this indicates that the wife of the owner will loose much blood when giving birth to her next child. (5) If the gall-bladder (*endulwe*) is very tense the person who has suffocated the cow will get rich. The opposite is likely to happen if the *endulwe* is limp. For this reason people who are rich in cattle never suffocate a cow themselves but engage for this task a person who owns few cows only and therefore runs only a slight risk should the cow have an empty gall-bladder. (6) If the *embotji* (caecum) is very narrow at the base and full at the end and pointed instead of rounded off, a person in the neighbourhood will die soon. (7) If the colon (*sisiandja*) looks very red the wife of the owner or any other person who cleans the cattle kraal and throws

[1] Lit., 'seer of belly', i.e. inspector of entrails.

out the manure will be fatally kicked or gored by a cow or a bull. (8) When a bull is killed on the occasion of a wedding and the terminal end of its colon is very full, this is regarded as a sign that the wife will soon be pregnant. (9) If the *embotji* (caecum) is very empty and limp this is a sign that the wife will be barren. (10) To find out whether the couple will live together happily or if they will quarrel much and separate again, the heart of the slaughtered bull is touched. If strong and firm it is a good sign, if soft and limber it is a bad sign for their matrimonial relationship. (11) If the edges of the small intestines (*gámala*) look very white and empty the young husband will not beget children for a number of years. (12) If warriors kill a cow before going on a war-expedition (the so-called cow of *lukari*) and they see that its small intestines are full and dark, they will have success in raiding cattle.

It will be seen from these few examples that the meaning attached to the shape, colour, and other condition of the intestines varies according to the nature of the occasion on which the killing has taken place, but the general principle on which the interpretation is based is the common principle of analogy or homoeopathy.

Among the Logoli I obtained the following list of more or less standard interpretations of peculiarities of the intestines and other internal organs. If the small intestines (*amakoyogoyo*) are found to be covered with small whitish blisters (called *dzimbula*) that look like drops and are filled with a watery liquid, this is a very bad sign foretelling the death of the person on whose behalf the sacrifice is performed. The meat of the animal is then eaten unceremoniously without an offering being made to the spirits and another animal must be killed after three days. Next to the small intestines the inside of the stomach is examined for worms (*dzinzoka*). These may be of white, red, or black colour. If they find white worms the patient will recover, although it will take a long time if the worms are very numerous. The presence of a few *red* worms means that the patient will ultimately recover but that someone else in the neighbourhood will die in the near future. A great number of red worms forecasts a serious epidemic, and if the same sign is found at the inspection of the stomach of several sacrificial animals it would be a serious warning to break down the village and move somewhere else to evade the threatening danger. The presence of black worms in the animal's stomach forecasts the death of the patient, and the greater their number the more certain is his death. A very great number of black worms, finally, would indicate that more people in the village are likely to die. If worms of all three colours are found in the stomach this means that the future of the patient is still uncertain and that the diviner should be consulted for further advice.

The colour of the liver (*elikúdumani*) is also significant. If very dark it indicates that danger is threatening from a near relative or, if a person is ill, that his illness has been caused by the evil magic of a close kinsman; if it is red, the illness has been caused by a stranger. An examination of the shape of the spleen (*embigu*) determines whether the illness (or the threatening danger) is caused by a man or by a woman. The spleen is also examined for its colour. As in the case of the worms, a whitish colour means recovery, red means persistent danger and is a warning to move away, while black means death. If the point of the animal's heart, finally, looks inflamed or as if it 'decays' (*kugunda*) it is a sign that the medicines used to cure the patient do not help him and that the reasons which the diviner has detected for his illness were wrong and his advice therefore useless.

D. THE TAKING OF COUNTER-MEASURES AND THE APPEAL TO HIGHER AUTHORITIES

THE measures of protection and prevention which we have discussed in the preceding sections are—as is implied in their name—taken *before* any untoward event occurs. In the present section of our investigation of the magico-religious we shall describe those measures which aim at counteracting mystical forces by combating, neutralizing, or destroying these forces *after* they have begun to be active. In the struggle against these forces, the measures to be discussed in this section present, so to speak, the second line of defence which has to be resorted to after the first line—protection and prevention—has failed.

Functionally closely related to the defensive measures of a magical nature against occult forces is the cult of the ancestors and of the Supreme Being. This cult aims at gaining influence over the powers emanating from these superior beings, to neutralize them as far as they are evil and, on the other hand, to enlist their services as far as they are deemed to be helpful.

(1) DIVINATION

In order effectively to fight in a concrete case any hidden force of a magico-religious order it is necessary first to discover what particular agent is responsible for the illness, accident, or other misfortune that has occurred. We have seen that in practice the same illness or disease may be due to quite a number of different causes or agents, so that, as a rule, the disease as such does not permit any conclusion to be drawn regarding the nature of the force or agent responsible for it. However, just as a physician cannot treat his patient with any chance of being successful in his efforts until he has made his diagnosis, so the taking of counter-measures against the activities of hidden forces can meet with success only after it has been possible to detect the particular force or agent causing this particular case of illness or misfortune. Now the art of divination, which is so widespread in Africa and occurs in such a great number of varieties, among the Bantu Kavirondo is almost exclusively employed in detecting the causes responsible for any given case of illness or misfortune and, on the strength of such a diagnosis, to indicate the appropriate countermeasures. Divination (Lurogoli: *ovukumu*; Luvugusu: *vufumu*) thus aims at discovering mystical causal connexions rather than at predicting future events which is predominantly the domain of dream-prophecy as well as of the inspection of entrails. While it is the first and foremost aim of divination among the Bantu Kavirondo to detect causes, its second, subordinate aim is the discovery of the appropriate measures which will serve to combat and neutralize the causes that have been detected. This second aim of divination is of subordinate importance because it is generally assumed that each cause has its definite counter-measure. Accordingly, once the cause of a misfortune or a disease is known, the counter-measures which it is appropriate to take are more or less automatically determined. It is then merely a question of establishing minor details of the course to be adopted, or discovering by means of divination whether in a particular case slight deviations from the norm will be called for.

This definition of the scope of divination enables us to deduce by a logical procedure the various situations in which one must go to the diviner as well as those in which it would be futile to consult him. In cases where the symptoms of the disease clearly and unambiguously point to the agent responsible for it and where, at the same time, the appropriate counter-measures are definitely laid down by tradition, leaving no choice between alternatives, a consultation of the diviner is obviously superfluous. Typical examples of such cases are the various states of ritual contamination as well as violations of the rules of avoidance (cf. above, p. 198 sq.). Another case in point would be a disease to which a person succumbs immediately after he has had a quarrel with a suspected *omulogi* (witch). If the whole circumstances of such a situation admit of no other cause than the hostility of that particular person, the victim immediately resorts to the appropriate counter-measures (see e.g. p. 266), without first consulting a diviner. If he decides to consult him even in such a case, then it is only after the customary counter-measures have failed to produce the expected result or after new complications have arisen. Similarly a mother whose child is suffering from diarrhoea will refrain from going to a diviner if she feels certain that her child's condition was preceded by the visit of an *omulasi wevikoko* (cf. above, p. 126). Instead of losing any further time she will resort to the only counter-measure possible in that case, viz. sucking the *evikoko*-particles by means of the cupping-horn (cf. below, p. 263). In the case of a harmless and quickly passing illness (e.g. a cold, a light attack of malaria (*oluhuza*), a headache, &c.) one would likewise refrain from consulting a diviner, as one would not attach any great importance to such complaints and, accordingly, would not attribute them to any ulterior magical causes. Only if they recur at frequent intervals or tend to become chronic would one pay closer attention to them and perhaps even consult the diviner about them. If, on the other hand, an illness overcomes a person all of a sudden, takes on a violent form, and ends up with death before the kinsmen of the patient have an opportunity to consult a diviner, one would, as a rule, refrain from visiting the diviner *ex post*, for, once the patient has died, the *omukumu*'s advice would no longer serve any purpose. As the saying goes: 'Who wants to go to the diviner should do so in time.' In a proverbial sense this means that in the case of threatening danger one should take quick resolutions and lose no time by hesitating. It is true that even after a person is dead his kinsmen are bent on detecting the agent responsible for his death, so that they may level indictments against definite persons, but such charges are usually based on suspicions harboured by the kinsmen themselves or on gossip circulating among the neighbours and not on any information obtained from a diviner. Only if a number of deaths occur in the same family or among a group of neighbours at strikingly short intervals, a diviner would be consulted even *after* a person's death, for in such a case it is believed that the evil agencies responsible for the deaths that have occurred might continue their harmful practices indefinitely unless counter-measures were taken to render them innocuous.

The decision whether, in any given case, a diviner should be consulted or not depends, of course, largely on the individual taste and disposition of the person concerned. Women, for example, are generally said to consult the diviner more frequently than men, as they tend to suspect ulterior agencies to be at work even in the case of insignificant events. Nobody is blamed for consulting a diviner if he has a weighty reason for doing so. But a person who goes to see him for every trifle will provoke the disapproval of his relatives and neighbours, and if he persists in his habit he will finally himself be suspected of practising evil magic. For, it is argued, if he had a clean conscience he would not need to live in permanent fear of evil powers threatening either himself or his relatives.

The following situations furnish generally acknowledged and approved reasons for consulting the diviner:

1. Sudden and violent illness, e.g. dysentery or other stomach and intestinal trouble, inflammations, skin-eruptions, eye-diseases, &c.

2. Persistent diseases even if only moderately severe, particularly if the person afflicted always used to be strong and healthy before.

3. Chronic ailments or a gradual physical deterioration (e.g. consumption) and regularly recurring pains which do not leave off despite a treatment with medical herbs.

4. Repeated bad dreams in the course of which the patient suffers from appearances of the spirits of the dead, as well as hallucinations and auditions (cf. above, p. 164). Also if a person has talked in his sleep or been restless, one of his close relatives will consult a diviner about the causes of his kinsman's restlessness, even if the latter can no longer recollect what he has dreamt.

5. If at night somebody hears noises outside his hut sounding like those made by an *omulogi*, and if on the following morning he wakes up with a headache and feels tired and worn out.

6. If somebody believes he has met with an *ombila* and some time afterwards notices the symptoms of approaching illness.

7. Sterility in a woman or, if she has already given birth before, an undue delay of her next pregnancy.

8. Complications arising during pregnancy or at delivery.

9. Impotence of the husband.

10. Sudden possession or insanity. It is believed in such a case that the person afflicted has either become the victim of a curse or has had a 'call' from an ancestral spirit to submit to training by an expert in some magical practice or other art of a mystical order (cf. below, p. 243).

11. Death caused by lightning.

12. Accidents, in certain circumstances even fatal ones.

13. Deaths of any kind, if the relatives of the deceased feel a very strong desire for revenging themselves by applying counter-magic.

14. Disease or sterility of one's cattle, or any other kind of misfortune suffered by one's herd of cattle or by an individual animal. For instance, if a cow repeatedly throws bull-calves.

15. Repeated harvest failures on one's own lands (while the fields of the neighbours yield ample crops), especially if the field concerned had previously lain fallow for several years.[1] If, on the other hand, one obtains a poor crop on an *isolated* strip of land, one would explain this fact by the poor quality of the soil (or a similar reason of an empirical order) and would select a new piece of land without bothering to consult a diviner. The same attitude would be taken if one noticed a marked deterioration of one's crops after having cultivated the same piece of land for several seasons in succession. Damage caused by drought and hail is exclusively attributed to the rain- and hail-magician, so that in these two cases a consultation of a diviner would, likewise, be unnecessary.

16. Repeated adultery of one's wife or other ill fortune in one's human relations, particularly in the case of unreturned love after the various kinds of love-magic (cf. above, p. 99 sq.) have failed to produce the desired effect.

17. Repeatedly occurring bad omens.

18. Disasters or dangers threatening the entire clan, e.g. epidemics, cattle diseases, pests and blights, or if the dream-prophet has predicted unfortunate events.

The art of divination is practised exclusively by specialists.[2] To qualify as such a specialist one must (1) possess an inherited disposition (cf. below, p. 242) and (2) have been specially taught and initiated by another diviner. A knowledge of the technique of divining would in itself not enable a person to practise the art of divination. The majority of diviners are men, even though occasionally a woman may inherit the disposition neces-

---

[1] Among Vugusu individual fields are frequently laid out in parallel rows climbing up the gentle slopes of the valleys, so that in the majority of cases adjoining plots of land (*tjindalo*) are of the same quality. A very uneven yield can therefore, in the eyes of the natives, have only mystical causes.

[2] Luvugusu: *vafumu*; Lurogoli: *avakumu* or *avalaguli* (derived from the verb *okulagula*, to consult the oracles).

sary for becoming a diviner, and, after having undergone the necessary training, may then practise in the same way as men do. Like her male colleagues, she would be consulted by clients of either sex and, if clever, would enjoy the same reputation as a man. The number of diviners nowadays varies considerably in the different locations. Among the Logoli, who for a long time have been exposed to strong mission influence, there appear to exist between fifteen and twenty diviners. Some of them, however, have given up practising as they have accepted the Christian faith. This means that there is only about one diviner for every two or three thousand inhabitants. Among the Vugusu of South Kitosh, on the other hand, there are still between forty and fifty diviners, or one for every five to eight hundred inhabitants.

In contrast to the dream-prophet, the diviner is only rarely consulted by the clan-elders in matters of public concern, but his clients come to see him either on their own personal matters or on behalf of their close relatives. Men as well as women may consult the diviner. In the case of a man's illness, however, it is the duty of his brother to do so, and only if he is prevented from going or if the patient has no real or classificatory brother living in the neighbourhood, may he send his wife. Since, however, it would be a violation of the rules of etiquette[1] if a woman during her consultation of the pebble oracle were to come into physical contact with the diviner—as the technique of consulting the oracle demands—she must be accompanied by another man who during the actual consultation takes her place. This rule is emphasized also in a text on divination:

'If a man and his wife live all by themselves and if he suddenly falls ill and nobody is near who can go to the diviner for him, then his wife must go to another homestead where she finds somebody who can go with her, for a woman cannot throw the pebbles with the diviner.'

A further rule demands that in the case of a child's illness it is not the child's father who goes to the diviner but its grandfather.[2] If he is prevented by illness, the child's grandmother may go in his place. Wealthy and influential people may also summon the diviner to come to their homes; as a rule, however, he does not go to see his clients, but they come to him.

A visit to the diviner being a weighty undertaking, a number of ceremonial rules must be observed in connexion with it. The most appropriate time for going to consult him is the early morning before dawn (the time of day which the Logoli call *makúvakuvi*), partly because one can then be certain of meeting the diviner at home, but chiefly because the early

---

[1] This, at least, was the reason given to me, but it may, of course, have a different and perhaps deeper significance. Cf. in this connexion the notion that magical power loses its potency when passed on from the male to the female sex (or vice versa); see pp. 130, 165.

[2] This corresponds to the rule observed in connexion with sacrificial offerings. A father cannot perform the sacrifice for his own children but must leave this function either to his father or to his elder brother (cf. p. 285).

morning is still 'clean' and one therefore runs less risk of meeting with bad omens. If an illness breaks out in the morning hours after sunrise it is better to wait until evening before going to the diviner, because in full daylight the risks of meeting the wrong kind of people on the way and of encountering other bad omens would be too great.

As an initial payment for the diviner the client takes with him a small basketful of eleusine, sorghum, or 'mash' which he adorns with the leaves of the *elilande*-creeper. Upon leaving his hut he spits twice in the direction of the rising sun (cf. above, p. 172) and, as soon as he has walked a few steps, bends down to his right and ties a knot in a blade of grass, thereby 'to tie the diviner to his hut' (i.e. to prevent him from leaving his homestead) and to ensure that his visit will prove successful. He must then follow the shortest route and not interrupt his journey. According to the nature of his mission, he must pay attention to various kinds of signs and omens while on his way. If he wishes to consult the diviner about an illness, he must not meet with any persons except a child, for a child signifies health, whereas an adult person might be a portent of disease. If it is his wife's barrenness which is responsible for his visit to the diviner, he must take particular care to avoid a certain kind of small rat with white stripes (*elivende*) crossing his path, as meeting such a rat would be a bad omen for the success of his mission. On the other hand, he would in this case have nothing to fear from meeting other people, though he must not return their salute. If, finally, his visit to the diviner is due to a misfortune of an economic nature, he must circle his hut twice before leaving and take great care that nobody witnesses his departure, as otherwise he would have to postpone his visit for a whole day. Once on his way, however, he has nothing more to fear.

Upon his arrival at the diviner's homestead the client's behaviour likewise varies in accordance with the nature of his visit. In most cases the diviner will see him coming from a distance, for early in the morning he usually sits in front of his hut warming himself by the fire which he has kindled in the yard. If the client has come to consult him about an illness of a kinsman, he places the basketful of millet in front of the diviner and without any further preliminaries briefly informs him of the matter he has on his mind, saying, e.g. '*nzizi hano kigira mwana wange numulwaye ligali, simanyimba kivune, nduki hano*' (I have come here because my child is very ill; I do not know the reason; (that is why) I have come here). In another text the client's arrival at the diviner's place is described in the following words:

'When this person (i.e. the client) arrives at the homestead of the diviner, he stands there without saying a word. The diviner then immediately knows: in this person's house there is sickness. He then says to the client: "Ah, why is it that the sickness troubles the people every day? Who has again fallen ill in your house?" And that one replies, "I have come so that you may consult your hides for me, for at home a small child is ill." If the client has come about the sterility of his wife, he will say nothing at all but approach the diviner with his back bent like an old man, as he feels too much ashamed to salute him. The diviner can thus tell already by the behaviour of his client for what reason he has come.'

After the diviner has received his gift he begins by questioning the client for some time so as to gain an idea in what direction the cause of the illness or of the misfortune has to be looked for. He asks, for instance, what kind of animals the client is keeping at his homestead, what sort of pots and implements he has in his hut and in what way he has acquired them, for each of these objects may have been employed by a malevolent sorcerer to serve as a vehicle for his evil magic. Furthermore, he questions his client about all the people with whom he is on bad terms or with whom he has recently quarrelled, and he asks him whether he has met with any people who have the reputation of being *avavila* (sorcerers) or *avalogi* (witches) of one kind or another. Finally he inquires if any of the client's relatives have died within the recent past or even a number of years ago and asks him if he has perhaps neglected to perform the duties arising from his ancestral cult.

While from the point of view of a European observer this questioning of the client by the diviner would largely deprive the latter of his prestige and his reputation of having an insight into hidden causes, the natives do not appear to look at it that way. At any rate, they willingly answer all the questions put to them by the diviner and, nevertheless, seem to be genuinely surprised at the way in which the diviner will diagnose, as being responsible for their troubles, that cause which they themselves have already considered the most likely one. Their confidence in the diviner (or in his oracles) is so great that ordinarily it does not even occur to them that it might perhaps not be the oracle and the inspired knowledge of the diviner which confirm their own suspicions concerning the cause of their misfortune, but merely the common-sense reasoning of the diviner himself. It would obviously require the existence of an intellectual doubt of the honest intentions of the diviner to induce a client to subject the method employed by the former to an intellectual control, e.g. by withholding relevant information from him or by supplying misleading answers to his questions. Such an intellectual doubt, however, seems to be very rare (cf. however, below, p. 241), or, at least, used to be so in the past. To-day a sceptical attitude is rapidly spreading among the younger generation, as many diviners, who have come under mission influence, have abandoned their old practices and publicly disavowed the methods formerly employed by them. In so far as the information dispensed by the diviners has always been subject to doubt on the part of the client, this concerned primarily the reliability and infallibility of the oracles consulted, and not the basic honesty of the whole procedure.

The Bantu Kavirondo know quite a number of different techniques of divination. Among the Logoli the most customary one consists in throwing stones and pebbles. As oracular implements the diviner employs a number of small smooth pebbles (*amagina amatérere*) as well as a rectangular piece of cow-hide (*kisero*) which must be taken from an animal killed in sacrifice. This piece of cow-hide he spreads on the floor when throwing the pebbles, so that they may not fall on the ground. Besides, he frequently has a large cow-hide (*esiru*) which he leans against his legs. These paraphernalia he keeps in a basket, called *endahi* or *endede*, which he also uses as a container for his grain when sowing the first seed and which differs in shape from all other kinds of baskets. The pebbles he keeps in a special bag (*emuya*). When he is not divining, the *endahi*-basket with its contents must lean against the base of the centre post of his hut. This ensures that the oracular implements will be under the continuous inspiring influence of the ancestral spirits who, as we have seen, are believed to have one of their favourite abodes at the centre post of a hut (cf. below, p. 282). Every morning before dawn he takes the basket with its various utensils outside the door of his hut where he kindles a fire. Sitting in front of the fire, he then takes every individual pebble in his hand and for some time rubs it up and down his chest, firmly pressing it against his ribs while doing so. Then he puts the pebble to his ear 'to listen what is going on in the country'. It is said that as a result of this procedure he knows already beforehand in what homestead sickness has broken out, who has been the victim of misfortune, and who will come to consult him in the course of the day.

When the diviner has finished questioning his client he can begin to throw the pebbles. The way in which he fetches the *endahi*-basket from the hut and carries it to the yard depends, likewise, upon the nature of his client's mission. If the latter has come to consult him about a case of illness, he fetches the basket unceremoniously from the hut, taking it to the front yard by the main door. Then he either *squats* down and tells his client to do the same opposite him, or they both *sit* down facing one another, so that their feet are touching or their legs crossing one another. The diviner then spreads the *kisero* between himself and his client and, at first, takes four pebbles from his bag and places them on the hide, pressing them with his hands firmly against the ground. Then he picks them up again one by one, and while shaking them between the palms of his hands begins to recite in a loud voice (*nomwoyo gwe dzingulu dzinene*) something like the following:

> *Endolaga, endolaga yeee hee*
> *endolaga, engoko*
> *endolaga, engoko.*
>
> 'I may see, I may see, *yeee hee,*
> I may see (whether) a fowl.'

The client repeats the last word 'fowl', whereupon the diviner continues: '*Endolaga endolaga emisambwa, yee emisambwa yee*' (I may see (whether) the ancestral spirits, yes, the ancestral spirits). The client always repeats the last word which suggests the agency that might perhaps be responsible

THE TAKING OF COUNTER-MEASURES

for the illness. In this manner the diviner mentions quite a number of potential causes, continuously shaking the pebbles between the palms of his hands. If a pebble drops from his hand on the hide while he is uttering one of these words, the particular object, person, ancestral spirit, or whatever other agent the word signifies has thereby been detected as the cause of the illness. The pebbles oracle has thus supplied its first answer.

An alternative technique of handling the pebbles oracle consists in letting all the pebbles drop on the hide whenever a new potential cause is named. In that case the answer is supplied if one pebble comes to lie apart from the others. To put it in the words used by my informant:

'When they proceed with the stones in this manner (i.e. when the diviner lets the pebbles drop on the hide) they (the pebbles) do not give an answer until, finally, one pebble falls down away from those others. They have just chosen to utter the words "white fowl", there a pebble rolls away; then they know: "Yes indeed, this it is (i.e. the white fowl) that is about to kill the sick person."'

This first answer supplied by the oracle, which in the above case has stated a white fowl to be the cause of the disease, must now be confirmed by a repeated consultation of the pebbles. If one of the four pebbles has fallen down or rolled away three times in succession at the mention of the same potential cause, the answer given is considered to be reliable, and the diviner can now proceed, by a renewed consultation of the pebbles oracle, to find out what sort of a white fowl it is. Thus he continues:

Endolaga, endolaga
engoko endavu
mundu wawalia ku engoko yeye
engoko yolususuni lutambi
embuli mwamu.

'I may see, I may see
(whether) a white fowl,
(whether) a person whose fowl you have shared with him,
(whether) a fowl with a long crest,
(whether) a black goat.'

As during the first consultation, the client now repeats every keyword mentioned by the diviner. If the consultation—as in this case—finally yields the information that the agent responsible for the illness is a white cock with a long crest which the patient has eaten while he was visiting somebody, the diviner can now proceed to consult the oracle as to the appropriate counter-measures to be taken. This, however, he does by quiet meditation or by murmuring obscure words which remain unintelligible to his client. In many cases the counter-measure automatically results from the kind of the agency detected, as in this particular case where the diviner would give his client the following advice: 'Go home and kill a cock with a long crest which is drooping to the right side. When you have roasted it, let nobody eat of it with whom you are on bad terms. If you let him eat of it, good health will not be restored to your home' (cf. however, below, p. 272).

In another Logoli text the consultation of the oracle in a case of illness is described as follows:

'The diviner asks his client who has come together with the wife (of the sick man): "What kind of trouble do you have?" And the client replies: "This woman has come here because her husband is very sick; she came so that you may divine for her (*umulagule*); she came in order to learn what it is that made her husband ill." And the diviner says: "Yes, we shall try, we may see whether the ancestral spirits wish that he may recover." Then he goes to fetch his basket in which he keeps the pebbles and the hide of divining. Now he begins (to speak): "I may see, I may see whether it is the ancestral spirits or perhaps the 'grain-picker'.[1] Perhaps it was his father who after his death wished that the patient should brew beer for him; if now he brews the 'beer of death' (cf. below, p. 498), then he (the spirit of his deceased father) will rejoice." After he has spoken thus, he lets the pebbles drop on the hide; then one of them falls down away from the others and he says: "Yes indeed, the pebble has said so." '

In this case, then, the spirit of the sick man's deceased father has been detected as the agent responsible for his illness. He has sent the illness to his son, as the latter had failed to brew for him the so-called 'beer of death' (*amalua golukuzu*) as the death customs prescribe. The diviner, accordingly, advises him to make up for his failure and thus to reconcile his father's spirit. When mentioning the potential causes of the disease the diviner, however, does not utter any actual names (either of the ancestors or of living persons), but only kinship terms or other circumlocutions which usually are ambiguous and leave the client a certain choice of interpreting their meaning according to his own discretion.

If the client has come to the diviner to consult him about the sterility of his wife, he first places the *endahi*-basket containing the paraphernalia upon his bedstead (*ekideli*) and not at the base of the centre post. Later on, when he goes to bring the basket to the front yard, he crawls with it through the so-called *vwasi*-partition (i.e. the part of the hut that is reserved for women) and then leaves the hut by the back door (*tjandango*) which ordinarily is only used by women. As soon as he has left the hut he raises the basket up into the air, spits three times in the direction of the rising sun, and says: '*Oh, oh, oh, nivava nivaveye avakuza mbolololi!*' (Oh, oh, oh, if it is the dead people, may they let her free!) He thus implores the spirits of the deceased to lift the curse with which they have afflicted the woman and which prevents her from conceiving (cf. above, p. 165). After the diviner

---

[1] During the oracular consultation the alleged cause of the trouble is frequently alluded to by a circumlocution so as not to arouse its anger. *Embozi*, 'picker', stands here for chicken.

THE TAKING OF COUNTER-MEASURES

has uttered this spell he goes with his basket to the front yard and, squatting down opposite his client, begins to consult the oracle:

> *Endolaga, endolaga, endolaga,*
> *vambika, vambika, vambika,*
> *mgesegese, mgesegese, mgesegese,*
> *mkinyaliru, mkinyaliru, mkinyaliru,*
> *muhiru, muhiru, muhiru,*
> *mulusimbu mulusimbu,* &c.

> 'I may see, I may see,
> (whether) they are hiding her
> in the apex of the roof,
> in the urinating hole,[1]
> in the living-partition,[2]
> in the eaves, &c.'

This manner of questioning the oracle is based on the notion that the ancestral spirits have cut off a small piece of the barren woman's loin-cloth (*ekevoya*) and have then hidden it somewhere in the hut after having uttered an appropriate curse over it. To discover the exact place where this piece of the woman's loin-cloth has been concealed, the diviner, while shaking his pebbles, mentions all the likely places in the hut where evil magic is usually supposed to be placed. The answer thus obtained must then be corroborated by a repeated consultation of the oracle. The diviner thereupon advises his client first to call an *omuliuli* (cf. below, p. 258) to come and remove the hidden object for him and destroy it and secondly to perform a rite of lustration over his wife (cf. below, p. 246).

As a rule—i.e. provided the symptoms of the disease do not from the very beginning indicate a definite course of procedure which would make a further consultation of the oracle superfluous—the diviner when consulting the oracles begins by mentioning insignificant causes and only gradually proceeds to name more weighty ones. In the case of an illness, for instance, he would, as a rule, first attribute the trouble to the anger of a neglected ancestral spirit, a situation which it is comparatively easy to remedy. If the illness persists even after the sacrifice, which he has advised offering to that spirit, has been performed (see below, p. 280), he would, in the course of a subsequent consultation, attribute the trouble to the evil magic wielded by a malevolent sorcerer or to other noxious agencies wielded by living persons. Similarly the counter-measures suggested will increase in importance only gradually and after repeated consultations.

Among the Vugusu the general course of procedure adopted by the diviner is basically the same as that employed among the Logoli, although the technique of divination and, accordingly, the oracular paraphernalia are different. The consultation always takes place inside the diviner's hut,

---

[1] At the bottom of the outer wall of the *ekego*, the partition of the living-hut in which goats, sheep, and calves are kept, there is a hole for the urine of the animals to drain off.   [2] The front partition of the hut.

the diviner sitting next to the centre post—provided there is one—and facing the door, while his client squats down near the door, either to the right or to the left of it. After having questioned the client about the reasons of his visit as well as the circumstances connected with the illness or whatever other trouble he may have come for, the diviner goes to fetch his requisites which he always keeps at the base of the centre post. Before he begins to consult the oracles he sings in a monotonous voice a long-winded song in which he proclaims that the art of divination has been honestly acquired by him. While doing so he enumerates his various tutors who have instructed him in this art as well as his ancestors (cf. below, p. 234), so as to impress his client with his authority. Then he takes in each hand a large gourd containing a few pebbles, and rattles them in a varying rhythm, at the same time imploring the ancestral spirits in a song to come and assist him or the oracles to discover the truth. In addition to his own ancestors he also summons those of his client—as far as they are thought to assist the latter as his guardian spirits—requesting their support in something like the following words:

Évamagombe mutima lugali,
omundu wenyue avue gexupe endja
nali omundu namulixo enyoxeyo
nali Wele yeeŋene namulixo aone.

'Ah, ancestral spirits, come quickly,
may your person recover, may he come out (from his misfortune),
if it is a human being who is "on" him,[1]
may he give him peace;
if it is God himself who makes him ill, may he recover.'

The noise made by the gourd-rattles serves to drive off any evil-wishing spirits that might be hovering about and thus to prevent them from interfering, for it is believed that the *visieno*-spirits (cf. above, p. 177) are very sensitive to the loud noise made by the rattles and thus will flee, leaving the scene to the helpful spirits. So as to banish them even from the most remote corners of the hut the diviner walks to and fro, swinging the rattles and taking care to penetrate into every nook and corner. The further procedure entirely depends on the technique of consulting the oracles in which the particular diviner has specialized or—in case he practises several techniques—which is given preference by his client. The oracle most frequently used among the Vugusu is a flat, oval-shaped wooden tray (*siie* or *sihe*) which is about 10 inches wide and 15 inches long. This tray contains four or six pebbles (*gámavale*), the tip of the horn of an antelope, several small pieces of charcoal, and maybe also some other paraphernalia, according to the individual taste of the diviner. Mumbling the names of the various ancestors of the client, the diviner begins to swing the tray with his right hand, at first slowly and gradually gathering speed. If in

[1] Meaning: who is bewitching him.

PLATE 9

A. *A widow wailing for her husband in front of a sacrificial hut: North Kitosh*

B. *Offering meat on a spear-point to ancestral spirits: South Kitosh*

PLATE 10

Skinning a sacrificial calf: South Kitosh

the course of this procedure the pebbles drop on the floor, this means that the ancestral spirits are ruled out as potential agents responsible for the illness or whatever the trouble may be. As long as the pebbles move about on the tray, the answer is still undecided, and the diviner must recite further names or continue to repeat the same names. As soon, however, as the pebbles seem to stick to the tray—an effect easily produced by the centrifugal force of the pebbles—the answer is in the positive. This means that the ancestral spirit whose name was mentioned by the diviner just at that moment when the pebbles ceased to move about in the tray has been detected as the cause of the illness. Accordingly the diviner every time he mentions the name of an ancestral spirit (or of another potential cause) repeats the following formula:

*Sisindu nesilixo olume
nesitataxo ogwe.*

'If it is this that weighs on him,[1] stick to it;
if it is not, fall down.'

The first answer which has been thus supplied by the oracle must again be corroborated by repeating the same procedure. This must be continued until the same result has been obtained three times in succession. When confirming the original answer in this manner the diviner, however, does not repeat all the names of the potential agents or causes but merely that name which has been detected by the first consultation. Accordingly all that is necessary to get the first answer confirmed is that the pebbles shall stick to the tray. As, with some practice, it is quite easy to make the pebbles stick to the tray even if it is swung back and forth at great speed and most violently, it will be the rule and not the exception that repeated consultations of the oracle confirm the answer obtained in the first place. As among the Logoli, the various questions which the diviner puts before the oracle lead from the general to the specific. Once the diviner has ascertained the name of the ancestral spirit responsible for the trouble, his next question concerns the motive for his hostile attitude; then he inquires what kind of sacrifice must be offered, then what kind of a sacrificial animal should be selected (whether a fowl, a sheep, a goat, or even a cow), and, finally, he consults the oracle as to the sex, colour, or any other qualities which the sacrificial animal must possess to be acceptable to the spirit. The diviner employs a corresponding procedure if the oracle has not detected an ancestral spirit as the responsible agent but such causes as the evil magic employed by an *omulosi*, the violation of a taboo, or the malevolence of one of the black gods (*wele gumali*). The consultation is over when the oracle, by the various answers which it has supplied, has indicated the whole course of procedure which must be taken by the client to combat the illness or the misfortune that has come over him. The whole range of counter-measures which, according to the cause that has been

[1] i.e. if this is the cause of the illness.

detected, may be taken—sacrifices, purification rites, counter- and destructive magic, rites of reconciliation, &c.—we shall describe in detail in the following chapters.

During the consultation of the oracles the client remains quite passive. He does not repeat every word uttered by the diviner, as is customary among the Logoli, but merely nods his head every now and then or shows by repeated gestures of consent or by calling out '*yee, yee*' that he agrees with the information supplied by the oracle. These occasional remarks as well as his facial expression are, however, quite sufficient to establish a close contact between him and the diviner and to show the latter whether his client has confidence in him and is satisfied with the information given or whether he responds with a sceptical attitude.

In addition to the swinging of the *siie*-tray several other methods of divination are practised by the Vugusu. They consist of consulting various other oracles, but the procedure of doing so in each case follows the same pattern. Thus the second oracle used by them is called *lúengele*. It consists of a board about 4 inches wide and 30 inches long, shaped like a willow-leaf and slightly bent upwards at its lower end, with a carefully carved groove in the centre extending over its entire length. Into this groove fits a small stick or peg which is about 2 inches long. To consult this oracle the diviner squats down. Holding the *lúengele*-board with his left hand by its upper end, he presses the lower end against the floor and with the thumb and the index-finger of his right hand moves the peg up and down in the groove. The peg is cut from the bark of a special tree, and a particular medicine is applied to it. While the diviner mentions the names of the various potential agents the peg suddenly sticks to the groove and does not come off, even if he knocks the board against the floor. This then has the same significance as if the pebbles get stuck on the *siie*-tray. The *lúengele*-board, accordingly, corresponds in principle to the *siie*-tray.

A third technique of divination consists in balancing the two gourds (the same which served for summoning the good spirits and for driving off the evil ones), one on top of the other. These gourds are particularly large and evenly shaped specimens which when used as oracular paraphernalia are called *tjísasi*. While the diviner enumerates the various potential causes of his client's trouble, he constantly endeavours to balance one calabash on top of the other. If it rolls down again, the spirits or persons mentioned by him are thereby ruled out as possible causes; if, however, it stays in position, the particular agent mentioned by him at that particular moment is held responsible for his patient's trouble.

The fourth and last technique employed by the Vugusu diviners differs from those previously mentioned in that it does not offer the client any visible sign of the decision reached by the oracle. The oracular instrument used by the diviner is a buffalo tail (*gumuxinga*) at which he smells, dipping it every now and then into a vessel containing milk, or holding it above the fire. After he has repeated this procedure for a considerable length of time, steeped in meditation, he slowly and hesitatingly imparts to his client the knowledge which the buffalo tail by its particular smell has revealed to him.

Each of these four oracular techniques can give information on any kind of question put to the oracle by the diviner. It is also possible to control the answer supplied by one oracle, for instance the *siie*-tray, by questioning another one, for instance the *lüengele*-board. Some diviners make use of all four techniques, others specialize in one technique only. Thus Wanami of South Kitosh, who in that whole area is reputed to be the most reliable and also the most wealthy diviner, exclusively employed the buffalo tail as an oracle. The various methods are, however, not considered to be equally reliable. The greatest confidence appears to be placed in the *siie*-tray oracle, 'because everyone can clearly observe how the pebbles stick to the bottom of the tray'. Then follows the buffalo-tail oracle which, apparently, owes its reputation to the fact that nowadays only very few diviners possess a tail of this animal which is no longer to be found in the densely populated Kavirondo District. The third place seems to be occupied by the technique of balancing the two calabashes, while the least popular oracle is the *lüengele*-board, of which my informants said that the diviner, by applying a stronger or weaker pressure of his fingers, can easily influence the behaviour of the peg which he moves back and forth in the groove.

To give a more concrete idea of the whole procedure I shall, in the following, describe in some detail consultations of two different diviners which I personally witnessed. In both cases the client was an elderly man from South Kitosh, called Wefwafwa, who had several wives. The reason for his desire to consult a diviner was the apparent barrenness of his youngest wife. After having given birth to one child, she had not conceived again in the course of the last three years. On his first visit which he paid to Mbita, a diviner of the Mwaya clan, Wefwafwa was accompanied by his youngest wife. As he had already told me on the way, he had no great confidence in Mbita's art, but having made several vain attempts to consult Wanami whom he had never met at his homestead, he now wished to try his luck with Mbita.

After Mbita had welcomed us to his hut and told us to sit down, he went to fetch his oracular paraphernalia from the centre post. Taking a calabash in each hand, he rattled them for at least fifteen minutes, first standing up, then sitting down again, at times performing excited gestures and at times relapsing into a monotonous rhythm. Every now and then he suddenly stopped rattling and assumed a tense facial expression and an absent-minded gaze, as if perceiving things hidden to the rest of us. Then again, while rattling his gourds, he made strange hissing and whistling noises or mumbled unintelligible sounds. At intervals, he chanted the following song, which he frequently repeated:

Vuvuefwe vuxale
sexwagula vwamundu ta'
vuvwefwe
vwama xunyandja
efwe vasinde vexunyandja.

'It is ours since a long time ago.
We have bought it from nobody,
(but) it is ours;
it came with us from the Lake (Victoria Nyanza),
from us, the uncircumcised ones of the Lake.'

By chanting this song he wished to convey to us that the art of divination had already been practised for a long time by his ancestors and had not been acquired by them by purchase; furthermore, that his ancestors had been diviners in those very remote times when they were still living on the shores of Lake Victoria and did not yet know the custom of circumcision. The Mwaya clan of which Mbita is a member is said to be of Nilotic origin. Its members claim to have migrated in a north-easterly direction until they met with the Vugusu, by whom they were finally assimilated. The last line of Mbita's song 'we the uncircumcised ones' emphasizes the fact that the Nilotes, in contrast to the Bantu, do not circumcise.

Furthermore, Mbita mentioned the name and the clan of his mother, emphasizing that she had come from the Kakalelwa tribe. As the Kakalelwa are well reputed as specialists in the arts of divination and magic, this emphasis on his mother's descent was intended further to underline his competence as a diviner.

After these preliminaries Mbita for some time engaged in an apparently commonplace conversation with Wefwafwa, asking him how things were at home and thus incidentally learning from him where his troubles lay. Then he picked up the *lúengele*-board and began to operate it, at the same time murmuring unintelligible words to himself. Now and again the peg stuck to the groove, but every time he forcefully knocked the board against the floor it fell off. When I asked Mbita what he was trying to find out by consulting the *lúengele*-board, he replied that he was going to determine if it was an *omulosi* who was responsible for the barrenness of Wefwafwa's wife. However, as the peg persistently refused properly to stick to the board he discarded this possibility, put the *lúengele*-board back in its former place at the centre post, and instead took up the two *tjisasi*-gourds. Before making a first attempt at balancing one on top of the other, he took the horn of an antelope from the basket in which he kept his paraphernalia and leaned it against the centre post as an invitation to the ancestral spirits to rally round and take up their temporary abode in this horn (cf. below, p. 283). Then, placing one calabash on top of the other, he said: 'If it is you, Malava, if it is you, if the *esasi*-calabash has been yours since long ago, you (addressing the calabash) may balance! Don't fall down! However, if you (addressing Malava) have merely bought it, you may fall down! Then do not stick on! The strangers are here in the house, don't refuse, don't waver!' Having thus admonished the calabash to answer the questions addressed to it by behaving in the proper way and after his protestation that it was already Malava (one of Mbita's ancestors) who called the calabashes his own oracle, he endeavoured for the next fifteen minutes to balance one calabash on top of the other, again murmuring unintelligible words while doing so. Several times his efforts seemed to be successful, but apparently the result obtained did not satisfy him, and so he finally resorted to the consultation of the *siie*-tray. He took it from its resting-place at the centre post and, after having added a few pieces of burning charcoal to the pebbles, began swinging the tray up and down, so that the ensuing draught caused the charcoal to be fully aglow in the semi-darkness of the hut. At first a few pebbles fell down on the floor; after some time—the rhythm of the swinging tray quickening and becoming more regular—they almost ceased moving until, finally, the pebbles stuck to the tray without showing the slightest movement. Throughout this procedure Mbita, in a soft but insistent voice, at times hesitating and interrupted by long intervals, put the following questions before the tray:

'What is it that has touched[1] this woman? Is it, perhaps, the black god (*wele mali*) or the ancestors (*vámagombe*) who died a long time ago? Is it they who have touched her, or perhaps her father's sisters (*vasenge*)? If it were her grandmother, she would bewitch the child (literally: the calf), so that she could eat of it.[2] If, however, it were her father's sister, she would bewitch the child when it sits on its mother's lap, so that she might find something to eat. Who would be such a fool as to fell a tree and then abandon it without warming himself at the fire?[3] Or is it perhaps her *xotja* (mother's brother) who has caused her to become barren, because he is annoyed that he hasn't been given anything to eat? (meaning that he had not received his share in the bridewealth paid for Wefwafwa's wife). If it were so, he would bewitch the small child when it sits on its mother's lap, for then he would get the things of the others (meaning the things that are due to him). Or is it perhaps the ancestral spirits of her husband, his paternal aunts (*vasenge*), his grandmother, or anyone else belonging to his kin who has touched the woman? In that case she may admit what she has done to him (i.e. her husband), so that we may know (where we stand). Since long ago the people say: "You should look for the open door and not go to the door that is closed to you" (meaning that a wife should not pay visits to the huts of the other men who might seduce her to commit adultery).'

Addressing Wefwafwa's wife Mbita continued: 'When you go to the

---

[1] The verb *xuiamba*, 'to touch', stands here for 'to bewitch', and in this particular case, for 'to render sterile'.

[2] Meaning: that she would benefit by the sacrifices offered for this child.

[3] This simile suggests that it would be foolish of the wife's deceased grandmother or aunt to prevent her from conceiving, for if an ancestral spirit prevents his descendants from having issue and thus continuing the clan, there will be nobody to offer sacrifices to it.

stream to fetch water you pray to God; when you go to collect firewood you pray to God.' And then, turning to Wefwafwa himself:

'When you go hunting you pray to God, and when you go to war you pray to God that you may find a cow, for otherwise (so you say) "The salt will kill me,[1] the poverty will kill me." And when you come home, you may find your child there, so that you may ask it, "Where has mother gone?" And it will reply, "Mother has gone to the garden to hoe." Then you may ask (your child) for water, and it will give you to drink and you thank it and say to it, "Thank you, little father, or thank you, little mother." '[2]

After Mbita had directed all these questions to the oracle in a clearly audible voice, he ceased swinging the tray for a short while, snuffed at the small antelope horn in the tray, asked Wefwafwa's wife to show him the palms of her hands, and, after having carefully examined them, renewed the glowing pieces of charcoal in the tray. Then he stood up and resumed swinging the tray, speaking now in an abrupt, staccato voice, seemingly in the highest state of exultation. After another ten minutes, when the pebbles and the bits of charcoal had, for a while, stuck immovably to the bottom of the tray, the consultation of the oracle was over. Mbita resumed his sitting position and, speaking in a voice of apparent exhaustion, communicated the following information to his client Wefwafwa:

'Wefwafwa, this (your) wife has surprised the "black gods" at the stream while they were bathing. Whereupon they said, "Ah, you have found us bathing! Now we shall pursue you, we shall go with you and stay in your house until you will have made a payment to us; then we shall cool off again!" Now they are staying in your house, Wefwafwa; you are sleeping with them on the same bedstead, and when you cohabit with your wife, they penetrate first (*in vaginam*), they spoil your sperm (*vusedja*) and your wife cannot be with child. If you go to pay them (*xuonga*), they may, perhaps, soon give peace to your wife. Go home and call a clever diviner; then you must look for a black goat and kill it. And the diviner may then catch the black gods; some of them he may banish into a pot and others he may throw into a stream, near the rapids, so that the water may quickly carry them away, and those (of the black gods) which you have trapped in a pot together with the rubbish from your hut, you may bury in the swamp before dawn. Furthermore, you must kill a fowl; you must take out its stomach and tie it to your right leg, and its head you must bury at the very spot where you have roasted the fowl. Then your wife will give birth to a boy. And you must cut a strip off the goatskin and sew four cowrie-shells on to it, two on the upper and two on the lower side, and this your wife must wear (as a necklace). One day, when you will have found (the child), you will salute me with joy and say, "Vagogi,[3] you have spoken the truth." '

[1] This means that he would have to be satisfied with salt instead of getting meat to eat.
[2] These last few sentences obviously are meant to implore the oracles and thereby the ancestral spirits and Wele to fulfil Wefwafwa's desire for a child.
[3] i.e. age-mate; cf. p. 376.

Wefwafwa, who still seemed to have his doubts, replied by quoting two proverbs: 'Yes, but he who does not get enough to eat cannot say "thank you" (*ori*)'—'What one does not have, cannot cause any joy!'[1] Whereupon Mbita finally retorted, 'True enough, Vagogi, but you will see, it is like I have told you; sure enough you will come and salute me with joy.'

A week later Wefwafwa went to consult another diviner, viz. Wanami whom, at last, he chanced to meet at his homestead. From earlier visits which Wefwafwa had paid to him Wanami was already well informed on Wefwafwa's affairs at home; besides, he knew all about our previous visit to Mbita. He therefore did not need to question his client in order to learn the reason for his visit or to obtain further details for sizing up the situation. So, after a short welcome and the customary exchange of the local gossip, he immediately began to consult the oracles. First, he produced his buffalo-tail, the possession of which added considerably to the prestige which he enjoyed. Then followed almost three hours of unbroken divinatory efforts before he was in a position to communicate the results of his labours to Wefwafwa, who looked on quietly remaining completely passive. During all that time Wanami appeared to be wholly absorbed in his efforts to detect the cause of Wefwafwa's trouble, again and again examining every conceivable possibility. To begin with, he smelled repeatedly at the buffalo tail which he shook violently every time he inhaled its fragrance and which he then dangled before his face like a fan. Then he told his wife to bring a small jug with milk into which he dipped the tail before smelling at it again. Every drop of milk sprinkled on the floor when shaking out the tail he touched with his index-finger with pedantic care, then putting it to his nose and smelling at it, as if the smell of each of these spilled drops of milk had a special significance. Every time he smelled he muttered unintelligible sounds, shook his head, or pensively gazed in front of him. When he had engaged in this procedure for about forty-five minutes he sent his wife into another hut to fetch the *siie*-tray. After having carefully cleaned it he rubbed each of the six pebbles for a long time between the palms of his hands, finally adding some bits of glowing charcoal to the tray. Then he began to rotate the tray, at first close to the floor and with such abrupt movements that every now and again a pebble dropped to the floor. Every time this happened he shook his head and tapped with the index-finger of his left hand against the tray, conveying the impression that he attributed a meaning to the sound made by the tray. Next he began to swing the tray up and down in the same manner as Mbita had done, at first sitting down and then standing up, until he appeared to be completely exhausted. His continuous muttering was interrupted only by occasional grunts and hisses. From time to time he stopped swinging the tray, emptied the pebbles on the floor, and again carefully cleaned the inside of the tray, particularly those spots which had been charred by the burning coal. Then, all of a sudden, he went outside and

[1] These two similes express the idea that one should not rejoice prematurely.

for a few minutes peered into the sun, shaping his hands like a telescope, before he came back to resume swinging the tray. After a while, he went outside again, this time to pluck a blade of the *luxafwa*-grass growing near his sacrificial hut (cf. below, p. 282). This blade of grass he chewed into tiny shreds which he then spat on the buffalo tail. Having once more smelled at the tail for a good length of time, he finally put it down and, turning to Wefwafwa, related to him the outcome of his long-drawn-out consultation:

'Wefwafwa! A black goat, black, black, black. This you must kill on the back yard of your hut; you must erect there a *wetili* (a certain kind of sacrificial hut; cf. below, p. 283). And those who have "caught" (i.e. bewitched) your wife, they are her co-wives. It is your big wife who has caught her. When she (i.e. the young wife) had a miscarriage your big wife, together with the second one, (secretly) removed some of the earth on which her blood had dropped. Of that (earth) they put some into the granary and some into the socle of the pot (*sitetwe*);[1] the remainder she (the big wife) has hidden near the ant-hill down by the stream and covered with her faeces; she has already completely covered it. And she has "caught" your young wife and put her underneath the hearth-stones (cf. below, p. 260). She has trapped her in the internodium of a reed grass and covered her with cattle manure. About this cow they are now going to Bungoma to buy there the salt for cooking it.'[2] At this point Wefwafwa interrupted Wanami's speech and said, 'Indeed, father, what you are saying about my cow is true. My cow is ailing. Is that the reason then? Well, father, if the country were still what it used to be, I really should drive this (wife) away, or should I, perhaps, keep her? But, let it go like that; it may be as the custom of the Europeans demands it.[3] It must, indeed, be those evil-minded women who are destroying her fertility and who, when they see that she has conceived, bewitch her, so that she cannot give birth.' Wanami then continued: 'Quite right, and now you may go and do as I have told you. Kill a black goat and also call an *omuliuli* (see below, p. 258), so that he may come and remove the *gamalogo* (the evil substances). And then you must cut a strip of goatskin and sew two cowrie-shells on the top side and two on the bottom side. Always, always these two women are sitting together, talking about nothing else but how they have "caught" (your youngest wife). And when you have removed the evil substance as I have told you and when you have killed the goat, then let the matter rest at that. When you hear your wives quarrelling with one another, let them quarrel; don't interfere with them but let them quarrel among themselves. I wonder why your big wife is always crying? You are not saying any bad things to her. Always she is crying, without any reason at all!'

[1] *Sitetwe* is the circular socle of clay which serves as a support for the pots. The hollow space inside these socles is regarded as a favoured hiding-place for magical substances, as the big and heavy pots are only seldom removed from them.

[2] That is to say, as a consequence of having thus abused the cattle manure, one of Wefwafwa's cows has fallen sick and will die soon, so that his wives are already on their way to Bung'oma (the market) to buy the salt which they will need for cooking its meat.

[3] According to the law which is now in force Wefwafwa can no longer drive away his great wife on the grounds of such a charge.

Being in complete agreement with everything that Wanami had told him, Wefwafwa replied: 'Indeed, father, all your words are true, you have spoken as if you had been there yourself.'

On our way home Wefwafwa, who was highly satisfied with the result of his consultation, told me that Wanami had already divined for him on three previous occasions and that the advice given by him had every time led to the desired result. Once he had married a woman who had run away from her former husband. She did not, however, bear any children for him. So, when he finally went to consult Wanami he told him that his wife's former husband had 'tied her down' by means of harmful magic he had administered to her. Following Wanami's advice, he dispatched an *omuliuli* to search for and remove the evil substance from the former husband's hut. Only a short time afterwards his wife was with child.

About one week after our visit to Wanami an *omuliuli* (see below, p. 258) came to Wefwafwa's homestead to remove the evil magic from the various places indicated by Wanami. On that day Wefwafwa, under some pretext, sent his two elder wives away, so that the *omuliuli* could search undisturbed under the socle of the pots and underneath the hearthstones of their huts. As I left Kavirondo soon afterwards, I could not find out whether on this occasion again Wefwafwa's confidence in Wanami's art was justified by producing the hoped-for result.

It will be seen from these two accounts of actual consultations of the diviner that—at least among the Vugusu—the questioning of the oracle as well as the answer which it gives cannot be controlled by the client. All he himself can see is that the diviner manipulates the *siie*-tray, the calabashes, or the *lüengele*-board and that they respond to the questions in a varying manner. But, as the diviner addresses all his salient questions to the oracle by muttering unintelligible words in a very low voice (cf. above, p. 227, and p. 235), he learns of the information supplied by the oracle only subsequently and indirectly from what the diviner tells him when the actual consultation of the oracles is over. The client, accordingly, although he is present during the entire proceedings, must have faith in the diviner's honesty and credibility, and the whole procedure is far less mechanical than a merely theoretical account of the technique of divination would indicate. Moreover, every diviner appears to embellish the basic elements of divination with all sorts of features he personally fancies (e.g. examining his client's hands, peering into the sun, tapping the tray, emphasizing the legitimacy of his knowledge, &c.), thereby enhancing the mysterious atmosphere which characterizes the whole seance and adding to the impression gained by his client that he actually *does* communicate with hidden forces and agencies. The degree to which he succeeds in conveying this impression and the skill he shows in guessing the innermost thoughts and wishes of his client appear to determine the confidence which the client places in the advice given by him. Obviously Wanami was more clever than Mbita in detecting just those causes for the barrenness of Wefwafwa's youngest wife which Wefwafwa himself was anxious to hear and ready to believe. To learn that the 'black gods' were responsible for her condition and to be told that he might (temporarily) destroy or banish them did not offer him an outlet for his strained emotions. To frustrate, on the other hand, the wicked scheme harboured by his jealous wives was bound to meet with his unrestricted approval, particularly as his 'great wife' by all her baseless grousing and complaining had already for a long time got on his nerves. The question whether the measures proposed by Wanami will actually produce the hoped-for effect, viz. the pregnancy of his youngest wife, thus becomes an issue of only secondary significance. The clever diviner, accordingly, when putting his preliminary and seemingly casual questions to his client, will try to learn as much as possible about his client's affairs at home and about any strains prevailing in his relations towards his nearest relatives, and will then make use of such knowledge when dispensing his oracular advice. Thus Wanami had found out from Wefwafwa not only that he was not on good terms with his great wife, but also that in the strife prevailing between his three wives, the two elder ones always conspired against their younger co-wife. He had even found out that one of Wefwafwa's cows was sick and that his wives had already gone to the market to buy the salt which they would need for cooking the meat of that cow.

Unfortunately I could not discover whether the diviners rely for the information they require solely upon what their clients themselves tell them in reply to their questions and what they can pick up from the daily gossip that is circulating or whether they employ a definite plan for gathering additional information prior to the consultation. The fact that on some pretext or other they frequently send their clients home again when they call for the first time, telling them to come on the following day, would suggest that such a policy is employed by them. My informants, however, including some former diviners who had become Christians, denied this, although they readily admitted that they used to obtain their information not by the answers given by the oracles but by the manner in which they questioned their clients.

It would appear then that the confidence which people place in a diviner does not depend so much upon the ultimate results obtained by following his advice but, to a large extent, upon the immediate emotional effect which the diviner is able to produce, i.e. upon his ability to relieve his clients of their emotional strain by convincing them that he has diagnosed the situation correctly. Accordingly the various diviners enjoy a widely differing reputation, even if they use the same oracles and can boast of belonging to equally old-established families of diviners.

As these facts indicate, the consultation of the oracles is not looked upon as an infallible, let alone mechanical, device for discovering what is concealed from ordinary persons but rather as an instrument which assists the diviner in getting his inspirations, as a medium through which God and

THE TAKING OF COUNTER-MEASURES

the ancestral spirits reveal their superior knowledge, provided that they are willing to do so. Neither do the diviners themselves claim to be infallible. They believe that what the oracles and their own inspiration tell them indicates the probable cause of their client's trouble or misfortune, but they do not pretend that what they reveal must necessarily and always be the one and the only cause. They rely a good deal on their *sugani*, their luck, as one of my informants put it. Accordingly, when they have given their advice, they usually say to their clients, 'Go home and try to do as I have advised you', but they would by no means hesitate to make a new diagnosis and to suggest different measures if the first ones should prove ineffective. Their own attitude towards the efficacy of their detective magic is most clearly revealed by the fact that at their client's departure they raise their hands in an imploring gesture and address the following prayer to God:

Wele, oxoyele wandjeta nemuxove nevamagombe gumusange gwase
Omundu oyo atjie ave omulamu
Vuno nivwo vulilo vwase.

'Wele, may you help me in my "sacrifice" (i.e. in my divination) together with Muxove and the ancestral spirits,
May this man (the client) go home and everything turn out right.
It is this which is my food (i.e. it is my profession to divine).'

Just as not all diviners enjoy an equal reputation, so the confidence placed in the art of divination differs considerably among different people. There was a consensus of opinion among my informants that women not only consult the diviner more frequently than men do but that they are also more firmly convinced of the merits of divination than most men who occasionally are—and always have been—sceptical about the whole procedure. Thus Nandoli told me that when he was still a small boy (i.e. before mission influence began to make itself felt in Kitosh) he listened to a conversation which at that time made a deep impression on him. He was herding cattle together with an elderly man by name of Nadjongali when a man came by who told them that all his children were ill. To detect the cause of their illness he had consulted every diviner in his neighbourhood, but every one of them had given him different advice. He himself, so he went on, had never thought very much of the knowledge dispensed by the *vafumu*, but his wife had been constantly pestering him, saying that the illness of their children was aggravated by his tardiness in going to a diviner. Nadjongali replied that he, too, did not believe in the wisdom of the *vafumu*. Even his father had never consulted them with any sense of conviction. He himself had once been there to find out who had caused his wife to be ill. On that occasion the *omufumu* had told him that his best friend was an *omulosi* (cf. above, p. 112) and that it was he who wanted to kill his wife. But when he turned to go home, the *omufumu* whispered behind his back, 'Now I have separated two real friends.' When he heard him say that he had turned round again and asked the *omufumu* to repeat his words which he had refused to do. Thereupon he had taken the present intended for the *omufumu* and gone home. His wife had died soon afterwards, but he had never gone to consult a diviner again.

The gift made or rather the fee paid to a diviner for his services varies not only according to his reputation but also according to whether the client is a neighbour or kinsman of the diviner or a stranger. In the first case he either pays him nothing at all or merely makes him a small gift. To quote from a text:

'If there is a diviner living in your neighbourhood and you wish to consult him about somebody's illness, you do not need to make him a present. For (the diviner will think), if a man of my neighbourhood finds my cows grazing on his fields, he must help me to drive them away. That is why he cannot pay when he comes to see me. If such a person comes to consult me I must help him without (being paid for it); but if somebody comes from a long distance, he must bring grain with him.'

Formerly the fee for a diviner consisted of a small basketful of eleusine which the client brought along the first time he went to consult him (cf. above, p. 224). No further payment was then made (not even after the patient's recovery); vice versa the client could not retrieve his gift should the advice given by the diviner prove ineffective.[1] In such a case, however, the client could consult him a second time without paying again. Nowadays, where the payment is mostly rendered in money, the customary amount given in the case of minor troubles and of diviners of average reputation varies between 30 and 50 cents. Diviners, however, who enjoy a particular reputation and are consulted by clients from far and wide are paid considerably more, in some cases as much as 5/- shillings. As will be seen from these rates, even the highest payment made to a diviner is considerably lower than that charged by an *ombila* or an *omulogi* (cf. above, pp. 140 and 122).

The inherited faculty or disposition required to qualify as a diviner is always passed on from a father to his son or from a mother's brother to a sister's son or, indirectly, from a mother to her daughter. It cannot be transmitted to an unrelated person, even if he should be an intimate friend of the diviner or offer him a large fee. But this disposition can remain latent for one or even several generations. This means that the art of divination can, in a certain family, fall into oblivion for several generations and then suddenly be revived, provided, of course, that the fact that one of the ancestors possessed the knowledge of divination has not been for-

---

[1] Nandoli, however, told me that in the year 1927 he happened to be paying a visit at a certain homestead when a diviner was called there in order to divine for a sick child. When the consultation had ended and the diviner was just about to depart, the child died. Having already collected his fee of 4/- shs. the diviner wanted to beat a hasty retreat. Nandoli, however, took the money away from him and returned it to the child's father who, after some hesitation, took it back gladly.

gotten. To-day there are a number of clans among the Vugusu which have no diviners of their own, but even among them the art of divination may at any time be revived since the required disposition—as we have said—can be passed on in the maternal line as well.

The first diviner among the Vugusu is said to have been a certain Maina. According to the tribal tradition he acquired the knowledge of divination from one of the neighbouring tribes, the Masava (Gishu) who nowadays live on the western slopes of Mount Elgon. Originally, when the Masava and the Vugusu were still one and the same tribe (cf. above, p. 23), the Vugusu—so they claim—already possessed the art of divination, but later on, when they seceded from the Masava and became a tribe of their own, they lost it until Maina learned it anew. Before addressing the oracles the Vugusu diviners frequently invoke Maina as a sort of guardian spirit.

Which one of the sons or nephews of a diviner (or of the daughters of a female diviner) has inherited the disposition qualifying him to learn the art of divination is revealed—as is the case with most such offices—by a state of possession. Its symptoms are of a manifold nature. Frequently the 'victim' suffers from dreams which are caused by the ancestral spirits and from which he awakes trembling and covered with sweat. Or his arms and legs are seized by sudden and violent spasms which are said to occur particularly while his father or uncle are practising their activities as diviners. Another widespread symptom indicating that the latent disposition is about to break forth is a spell of hiccups said to have been sent by the spirits. Even a protracted illness or a chronic ailment may, in some cases, be interpreted as having the same meaning. Nicola, for instance, a former diviner who later adopted the Christian faith, told me that his disposition to become a diviner had manifested itself by a violent illness which overcame him at the age of fifteen after he had eaten some sugar-cane. It persisted for several months and caused him to grow very lean. As only he himself was afflicted by this illness and none of his playmates who had eaten of the same sugar-cane it was sure to have a particular significance.

To ascertain the exact significance of all these symptoms—each of which, taken by itself, may be due to a variety of causes—the patient's father or another near relative consults a diviner.[1] If he confirms that the patient's condition is due to the 'desire of the latent power of divining to become active',[2] it is decided that he must receive instruction. He cannot, however, be taught by his own father but only by another relative, e.g. his real or classificatory mother's brother (if he happens to be a diviner) or, better still, by a diviner to whom he is not related at all. It is considered particularly auspicious if a male candidate is taught by a female diviner and a female candidate by a male diviner. About two or three months are

[1] This, however, must not be the father or the maternal uncle of the person concerned, but a stranger.
[2] One also says in this case: *vufumu vwamuamba*, 'the divination has caught him'.

required to teach a pupil the art of divination. During this time the pupil goes to his tutor every other day or the latter comes to instruct him in his father's hut (as in Nicola's case, who was taught by an old woman). The pupil does not have to observe any ceremonial rules, nor is the fact that he receives such instruction kept secret, although no one may be present in the hut while he takes his lesson. Prior to the first lesson the pupil's father pays the teacher a living bull and, besides, kills an ox (*exafu eye xuxuingisia vufumu*, 'the ox for letting the divination enter') as well as a goat which is either called *embusi eye naxatama*, 'the goat of the oracles', or *embusi eye sisia*, 'the goat of the *sisia*-necklace', for on this occasion the candidate is given a necklace made from *livombwe* leaves, called *sisia*, which he wears as a sign of his new status. Furthermore, the pupil's father celebrates the occasion by brewing beer and inviting his neighbours for a feast.

After the meal the teacher and his pupil repair to the hut, all the other persons remaining outside, and after they have barred the door the teacher dances for a while, rattling the *tjisasi*-calabashes, uttering grunting and hissing sounds, and occasionally beating his pupil on the head. Having in this way summoned the ancestral spirits, he speaks to them,[1] '*Vamagombe* (spirits), where have you gone? I have been calling you for a long time!' Whereupon the spirits reply in a high-pitched and weak voice, 'We, the *wamugoya*, have come, we had a long way to go, we are coming from Waxatelesia.' Then again the diviner: 'Here is your house in which you may stay.'[2] The spirits: 'Well, then, we are satisfied, we are already here.' Now the teacher hands his pupil the *tjisasi*-gourds, and he in turn begins to rattle them and to speak to the spirits: 'I am glad that you have come to stay here with me; here you are to let me know the rites (*ano muxandakeenge kimisango*) when the people come, so that I may divine for them (literally: *xulagulwa*, to be divined for).' And the spirits (i.e. the teacher with a disguised voice) reply, 'We, too, are glad to stay with you.'

Having thus welcomed the spirits, the teacher reaches for the oracular implements which up to now have been left lying by the door and hands them to his pupil, who thereby is immediately relieved of his state of possession from which he has been suffering up to that moment. Before handing him the paraphernalia the teacher spits some of the beer, which the pupil's father has brewed, on the various implements (the *siie*-tray, the pebbles, the *liengele*-board, &c.). In addition to the oracular implements he also hands him a new *endahi*-basket to serve as a container for the implements and the horn of an antelope which must have been killed by a person unknown both to the teacher and to the pupil. This horn, which

---

[1] According to Nicola's report.

[2] According to the version of this interview which Mbita gave me, the teacher addresses Maina in the following words: 'Maina, if it is you (who has come), may my pupil (lit., my person) recover (from his obsession); I dedicate this house to you, so that you may stay here.' This means that this house will from now on be devoted to the art of divination and thus will be a welcome abode for Maina.

THE TAKING OF COUNTER-MEASURES

during the consultation of the oracles must be placed against the centre post of the hut, in a vertical position and with its pointed end downwards, is to serve as the temporary abode of the spirits who—as we have seen—are summoned by the diviner before he begins to engage in his activities. Every Vugusu diviner has two particular spirits to assist him, a male one called Siorawule and a female one called Namagoya, which are also referred to as 'man' and 'woman'. Siorawule acts as a mediator between the diviner and the male ancestral spirits, and Namagoya between him and the female spirits.

After the pupil has deposited the horn and the basket with the oracular implements at the base of the centre post, the teacher opens the door and the visitors may enter and inspect the candidate. After this first lesson, which is called *xuxuingisia* (to let the spirits enter), the teacher instructs his pupil in the technique of manipulating the various oracles and, in particular, tells him what different causes he may detect and what counter-measures he must suggest to his clients in the various situations that may arise. Furthermore, he instructs him in the art of questioning a client and finding out if he has already consulted other diviners and what these have told him. This is to prevent him from giving the same advice, which has already proved to be ineffective, all over again.

Having thus been instructed by his teacher, the novice in the art of divination can begin to practise his new profession without any further initiation.

(2) RITES OF PURIFICATION AND RECONCILIATION

The consultation of the diviner has cleared the way for the taking of counter-measures in the proper sense of the word. As the mystical forces intervening in the life and well-being of men are of various kinds, so various means are employed to counteract these forces. In the following chapters we shall discuss and analyse these counter-measures in detail, observing in what way they differ from one another, on what occasions each of them is employed, and on what principles their alleged efficacy rests. We shall see that, as a rule, each category of active mystical forces is combated or neutralized by a specific type of counter-measure. But there are other counter-measures that are employed in a large variety of situations, while some elements of ritual procedure are of nearly universal significance. In describing the different counter-measures we shall proceed in the same order adopted in the first part of this section. We shall accordingly begin by discussing lustration from the state of *ritual impurity* as well as the lifting of *curses* and the ceremonial reconciliation that terminates an *avoidance* or a *blood feud*. Then we shall proceed to describe the various means of combating and neutralizing the noxious effects of *sorcery* and *witchcraft*. Finally we shall give an account of the cult of the *ancestors* and the *Supreme Being* as constituting a set of practices which likewise primarily serve the purpose of counteracting harmful forces of a mystical nature in the sense of our definition, even though the means employed towards this end—sacrifice and prayer—differ very much from those employed to combat ritual impurity or harmful magic.

The various states of ritual impurity or contamination (cf. above, p. 106), the affliction with a curse (cf. above, p. 101), and the state of ritual avoidance resulting from a quarrel or a feud (cf. above, p. 190) are, from the native point of view, all very closely related to one another. The persons who have become the victims of one of these conditions have all come under the influence of a mysterious power which, both for the persons afflicted and for everyone who comes into contact with them, either entails immediate dangers or at least hampers them in a particular direction and curtails the normal functions of their lives. Thus one says, 'the *luswa* (ritual contamination) keeps him in bondage' or 'the curse ties him'. Similarly the state of avoidance that, following a quarrel or a feud, is maintained between two individuals or two groups of persons is regarded as a curtailment of their ritual status and thus of their vitality. In all these situations the primary aim is to restore the disturbed ritual status and thus once more to become an *omwirongo* (Lurogoli) or an *omuravola* (Luvugusu), i.e. a person with a completely unblemished ritual status. This aim is attained by ritual observances which, though differing in detail, show the same basic features.

The time at which such ritual counter-measures must be taken depends on the particular state which they are to counteract or neutralize. If somebody has violated a taboo (*omugilu*) or has 'fallen into a state of *luswa*', a purification rite is performed as soon as possible after the victim realizes what has happened to him. In the case of the ritual contamination, on the other hand, which afflicts a widow, a warrior who for the first time has killed an enemy, or a circumcision novice, a definite period of time must elapse before a rite of lustration is performed, as otherwise it would remain ineffective. If somebody has become the victim of a curse, he usually resorts to counter-measures only when he begins to suffer from its effects and after a consultation of a diviner has confirmed his suspicion that the symptoms from which he is suffering are, indeed, a consequence of the curse that somebody has levelled against him. A feud or a mutual avoidance, finally, is ritually ended only when both parties feel the desire to resume friendly relations with one another.

Lustration from the State of Luswa

If the latent disposition of a person to fall *luswa* becomes active in one of the different ways which we have described in the first part of this section (cf. above, p. 107), the person concerned must immediately undergo a ritual procedure which aims at banishing or at least suppressing the *luswa* and thus averting its evil consequences. If, for instance, a small child cuts its upper incisors before the lower ones (cf. below, p. 322), an old man who must be of the child's clan kills a sheep, and the child's paternal grandfather pours some of the sheep's stomach content into the child's

THE TAKING OF COUNTER-MEASURES

mouth. Thereupon all the people who sleep in the same hut as the child must eat the sheep on the premises.

A grown-up person afflicted by a state of *luswa* is treated in a corresponding manner. Somebody, for instance, may have had the following experience:

'In the middle of the night when for some reason or other he stepped outside his hut, he saw the "sun" in the sky as it quickly returned from the west to the east. Then he knows that he has fallen *luswa*, and, on the following morning he must go to his father and tell him, "Last night I stepped outside my hut and in the sky I saw a bright thing which dragged many stars and claystones[1] behind it." Then his father replies, "We must immediately look for something with which we can put you right again (*okulomba*)." '

They must not let a single day go by but must right away procure a fowl, a goat, or a sheep, to perform with it a rite of lustration. If they choose a fowl for that purpose, the father must at first 'flutter' or sweep his son's body with it (*okweya nengoko*); then he must kill it and tie one wing to his son's neck; finally he must spit or blow (*okuvida*) the fowl's stomach content (*ovosé*) on his son and his children. After which he roasts the fowl and all the members of the family who have assembled for the occasion eat it on the premises, taking care that nothing is left over. If this rite of lustration is performed with a goat or a sheep, the father must kill the animal by strangling it and then cut a strip off the skin which he ties to his son round his right wrist. Thereupon he spits some of the animal's stomach content on his son's chest and on those of his grandchildren and hangs its entrails round the former's neck. While doing so he says, '*luno luswa luwela ano*' (now the *luswa* comes to an end right here). After four days the son may take off the entrails and the strip of skin as he is now fully immune against any harmful effects which might result from the *luswa*.

If an animal has fallen *luswa* or *kiragi* (see p. 108, examples 12 to 14), no purification ceremonies are performed over it, but one either kills it or tries immediately to sell it to a stranger. If, for instance, one discovers a hen perched on the roof of one's hut or if one hears a cock crowing in the evening, one calls a small child to catch the animal and strangle it; then one cuts off its head and buries it at a lonely spot in the bush. The remainder of the animal is cooked (it may not be roasted like a sacrificial animal) and consumed by the inhabitants of the hut, care again being taken that no meat is left over. The same procedure is taken if one has not personally observed the abnormal behaviour by which the animal has become *luswa*, but has learned about it only indirectly when consulting a diviner about a case of illness in the family. As soon as the animal has been killed and eaten it is said that the illness caused by its abnormal condition will leave the house.

[1] The clay stones are small balls of clay which are squeezed between the cooking-stones and the bottom of the cooking-pot to adjust its height above the fire. In this context the word refers to the tail of a comet.

An exception to the general rule that animals that have fallen *luswa* must be killed exists in the attitude taken towards bees. If a swarm of bees is unusually wild, stinging both men and livestock, this is regarded as a sign that the bees have become *luswa*. The father of the owner of the beehive then takes some of the stomach content of a sheep killed on a previous occasion[1] and scatters it over the hive or the barrel (*okunyita omulinga*). This rite frees the bees from their *luswa* and causes them to cease stinging, so that one can take the honey from the hive.

Lustration from Contamination by Death and Human Blood

In a similar manner as in cases of *luswa*, a rite of lustration must be undergone by all persons who have fallen into a state of ritual impurity from contact with human blood or with death (cf. above, p. 109 sq.). Before a widow can again freely mingle with other people and remarry, a goat must be killed for her. Among the Vugusu it is called *embusi eye xusinga ligoxe*, the goat of washing off the ashes, i.e. the ashes with which the widow had smeared her body as a sign of her grief. This ceremony is performed about one year after the husband's death. Apart from the usual beer-drink and the eating of the goat, its main ritual feature is that the widow's father smears the goat's stomach content (*vuse*) all over her body and then tells her to step into the *vuse* that is left over, so as to make sure that the *vuxútjakáli* will be completely removed. He also cuts a small strip off the skin of the goat and ties it round her right index-finger. The children of the dead man and everybody who nursed him shortly before he died are likewise smeared with the goat's stomach content, though not as thoroughly as the widow. A corresponding purification rite is performed with a widower; but as his contamination is considered to be of a much slighter nature than that of a widow, he can undergo this rite as early as the fourth day after his wife's funeral. He may then resume sexual relations with his other wives.

Among the Logoli a widow undergoes a lustration rite only a few months after her husband's death, the ceremony consisting essentially of the same features as among the Vugusu (killing a sheep and spitting its stomach content on her face and body). On this occasion the so-called *amalua gedzinduhu* (the beer of the holes) is brewed, after which the widows need no longer be sexually avoided but may enter into marital relations with the successors of their deceased husband.

Even a merely temporary contact with a dead person or with his remains makes it necessary to perform a rite of lustration, though only of a more or less perfunctory nature. Should somebody happen to come upon a corpse lying by the roadside, he may not pass by but must pluck a particular kind

---

[1] Part of the stomach content of a sheep killed for a sacrifice or a rite of lustration is always saved up and stored away to be used again on subsequent ritual occasions of minor importance. The stomach content is wrapped up in a piece of banana-bark and then tucked away in the roof of the hut.

THE TAKING OF COUNTER-MEASURES

of grass (*vululu*) and throw it on the dead person, protesting at the same time that he has only met him by chance and is in no way whatever responsible for or connected with his death. Should he fail to do so he would not have any peace of mind, but the dead person would pursue him wherever he went. Similarly a hut in which a human being has been killed must be sprinkled with the stomach content of a sheep before its inhabitants may enter it again. Should this rite be omitted, the blood of the killed person would haunt the house (*ekisahi kyomukuzu kinyala kulonda enyumba*).

A purification rite must, finally, also be performed over the so-called *guyavi*, the man whose business it is to excavate and burn the bones of a deceased person whose spirit is persistently troubling his living relatives and refuses to be pacified even by repeated sacrificial offerings; the idea of burning his bones being to render the spirit of that person innocuous (cf. below, p. 288). As soon as the *guyavi* has finished his unsavoury job he must bathe in a swift stream and immediately after having returned home must have the stomach content of a fowl spit on his body. The sheep which he has been given as a payment for burning the bones he must kill immediately; he may not even wait until he has reached his homestead but must kill it on his way. The relatives of the dead person whose bones the *guyavi* has burnt must all assemble and every one of them must chew a handful of eleusine lest they fall ill and be suffocated by the other ancestral spirits. If there is a small child among them which cannot yet chew the grains, its mother must do so for it and spit the chewed grains into its mouth.

Ovukāli, the particular kind of contamination or ritual impurity which affects warriors who for the first time have killed an enemy, must likewise be removed by a special ritual procedure performed at the end of their ritual seclusion (cf. above, p. 110). In a Logoli text this ceremony is described as follows:

'When the warriors (*avakāli*) have for three months lived in (ritual) seclusion, they know "now the time has come where we may leave the hut of seclusion". They light a fire and roast a little bunch of bananas which must be of the kind called *endahúlulwa*, for if they cut these bananas they know that it is their custom to do so. When they leave their hut of seclusion they must repair to the house of an old man who then may perform the lustration for his children (i.e. for the warriors). They must all line up and the old man then begins to stir eleusine flour in water and to spit upon the warriors, one after the other, this stuff which is called *ovwanga*, and this elder who functions as the *omuvidi* (the spitter or blower) must be somebody who is not guilty of any offence; he must indeed be an *omuhotjya* (i.e. a man with an unblemished character). Furthermore, he must kill a fowl, and when all the warriors have been blown with the *ovwanga* they must roast the fowl and eat it. When all this has been done they are permitted to return home, for when they were still staying in the hut of the *avakāli* they were under a taboo (*omugilu*). Now, after the *ovwanga* has been spit on them, they may again go to the girls; now they are no longer under any restriction.'

Among the Vugusu, warriors who for the first time have killed an enemy may return home after only five days. To lustrate them the father of one of the homecoming warriors must kill a goat (the so-called *embusi eye xuxuiosia*) which must be without any blemishes. Then the clan-head (*omugasa*) must smear all the warriors with the goat's stomach content, speaking the following words while doing so: '*Luno mwavene vigele viangwa negamaxona gosi kanguwe, musole lilova*', 'Now you are (again) on swift feet and all (your) hands are quick, may you save the country.' The meat of the goat is then roasted and consumed jointly by the young warriors and the old men as well as the women who are past the age of child-bearing. The clan-head cuts the skin of the goat into narrow strips which he ties round the wrists of the warriors' right hands. After this ceremony has been performed they may return home, as the contamination of their bodies caused by the blood of the slain enemy has now been removed (cf. above, p. 193). The weapons themselves are cleaned by the warriors immediately after the fight is over by dipping them into a swiftly flowing stream in such a way that the spears point up-stream.

Initiates must undergo a twofold rite of purification. Before they are circumcised the candidates must endeavour to acquire an unblemished ritual status by making confessions, by taking a ritual bath in a stream, and by shaving their heads (cf. below, p. 343). Upon leaving the hut of seclusion the novices must submit to the second rite of purification. All objects used by them during their sojourn in the hut of seclusion are ritually destroyed, the novices take a bath, shave their hair, and put on new clothes. Then they are ceremonially given commandments by their fathers, who on this occasion spit beer on them (cf. below, p. 365).

Lustration after the Violation of Taboos (emigilu)

When rules of avoidance or ritual prohibitions (*emigilu*) have been violated, a rite of lustration must be performed to avert the harmful consequences which would otherwise result from such a violation. In the case of a slight infringement an atonement can be effected by offering a present or making a payment to the persons involved. If, for instance, somebody unwittingly intrudes while people are thrashing grain or while they are firing pots and if he fails to stop at the proper distance, he must volunteer to pay them a fowl or a basketful of grain. It would be regarded as an offence of a similar nature if a wife should allow her husband to see her without her loin-cloth while taking a bath, or if a man should let his mother-in-law see him in the nude. In the first case, the wife must pay her husband a fowl (which she gets from her father), and in the second case the man must make his mother-in-law a present of tobacco and grain. If the guilty party neglects to atone for his offence by such a present, evil consequences (of a similar kind to those entailed by a curse) will ensue for *both* parties concerned. The guilty party is therefore merely serving his own interests if

THE TAKING OF COUNTER-MEASURES 251

he willingly renders the payment which custom demands; if, however, he refuses to do so, the other person involved may bring the matter before the clan-elders (*kuvulavu*—before the public place). The fact, however, that the present or the payment is to avert consequences of a mystical order clearly shows that it is not in the nature of an ordinary compensation but constitutes the most simple form of lustration.

In most cases where a ritual prohibition (a taboo) has been infringed, the atonement consists of the same ritual observances, viz. spitting the stomach content of a sheep upon the offender's body, putting a strip of skin round the wrist of his right hand, and ceremonially consuming the sacrificial sheep. If not only a person but also a material object has been contaminated or otherwise affected by the violation of a taboo, this object must likewise be smeared or sprinkled with the *ovosé*. If, for instance, a father has slept or sat down on his son's bedding and if, as a consequence of this infringement of an important ritual prohibition, his son henceforth proves himself unable to beget healthy children (cf. above, p. 198), both his son and the bedding must be purified with *ovosé*.

If somebody has killed an animal in violation of a taboo, the rite of lustration must be performed at the very spot where the animal has died. Among the Logoli, for instance, it is taboo to kill the *evaga* snake (python), and it is believed that any violation of this ritual prohibition will cause the offender to become impotent. If a man suffers from this complaint and if the diviner has detected the killing of a python as the cause of his impotence —it would make no difference how many years had passed in the meantime—three old men together with the man who has killed the snake must go to the place where the act has been committed. There they must kill a white cock, and while spitting the cock's stomach content first on the impotent man and then on the ground they must say, '*mwana wetu agase ombiri*', 'may our child recover in (its) body'! Thereupon they roast and eat the cock and drink the beer which they have specially brewed for that occasion and brought with them.

A special rite of lustration is performed over a man and a woman who, after their marriage, discover that a remote relationship exists between them—for instance, that their mothers belong to different sub-groups of the same clan. By such an infringement of the exogamous rules of marriage (cf. below, p. 383) they have both become *luswa*, a condition which in this particular case would entail harmful consequences for their children if no counter-measures were taken. To remove or neutralize the power of the *luswa* an old man must kill a sheep or a goat in the usual manner and then smear the couple with the animal's stomach content while speaking the following words: 'Now your two clans are separated. The sheep (or goat respectively) has been killed so that your children may live.' Then the woman must procure an old pot of the kind called *eningilo*, such as is used for cooking vegetables. It must be a pot which from frequent use has got cracks and holes, and under no circumstances a new pot. At night, soon after darkness has set in, the wife's brother must climb the roof of the hut in which the couple live and place the pot over the *sísuli*-staff which, as a symbol of the male owner of the homestead, protrudes vertically from the apex of the roof. By the performance of this rite the power of the *luswa* is broken and the blood-relationship existing between the husband and his wife annulled. The danger that their offspring might be weak or abnormal is removed, and friends and relatives can visit the couple at their homestead without any longer having to fear any harmful effects from the *luswa*.

If a girl has become pregnant after incestuous sexual intercourse (e.g. with a man of her own or of her mother's clan), the child is killed immediately after it is born, while the child's mother is lustrated not only by having *ovosé* spit on her but also by being sprinkled with the blood of a sheep specially killed for that occasion. Moreover, the girl's father must procure honey from wild ground-bees (*dzingote*) of which the girl herself and all the inhabitants of the hut in which she lives must eat. Then she can again freely mingle with other people who up to now have strictly avoided her.

Lustration after having committed a Crime

Although, as a rule, purification rites are performed only when taboos (*emigilu*) and not when prohibitions of a profane nature[1] (*amalago*) have been infringed, there are a few exceptions to this general rule. If, for instance, somebody has set fire to another person's hut and if he has failed to confess his misdeed and to pay compensation to the owner of the hut, it is said that his offence will constantly haunt (*okulonda*, follow) him and put him into a frame of mind which resembles that of ritual contamination. In a Logoli text this state of mind and the rite performed to remove its effects are described in the following words:

'Day by day the house pursues the criminal. Wherever he goes and wherever he stays, even in his sleep, he must see the house in his head. Now when he sees it like that, he must look for a sheep and take it to the remains of that house. There he must kill the sheep and smear the place (i.e. the charred poles and rafters) with its stomach content. Then he can live in peace again without becoming a madman.'

Similarly a woman who has killed her husband out of jealousy or spite must submit to a purification rite to recover her normal ritual status. To quote from another Logoli text:

'If a girl has been married to a man against her will and if she has then killed him by poison (*embodoka*) without having reconciled herself with him before his death (thereby neutralizing the effect of the poison, cf. below, p. 256), she must be killed without pardon. But if she flees at night and returns to her parents without telling anybody (of her crime) she cannot bear

[1] Profane prohibitions are distinguished from ritual ones in that they are sanctioned by law. Infringements of *amalago* comprise theft, physical assault, adultery, inflicting of material damage, &c.

THE TAKING OF COUNTER-MEASURES

a child until a "sacrifice" has been performed for her (*kusalisa*). Then she may bear a child.'

In both cases the offender's bad conscience puts him into a state of mind which impairs his ritual status in the same way as the other states of ritual contamination which we have discussed, and it therefore calls for a corresponding rite of lustration. In the second case, the woman would also have to fear the revenge of her husband's spirit, and it may be that the sacrifice referred to in the text is, at the same time, intended to pacify his spirit.

Lustration after having come into Contact with Harmful Magic

Contact with lethal magical substances (*amalogo, ovovila, gimisala,* &c.) likewise necessitates ritual purification. While ordinary persons must undergo such a rite whenever they have come into contact with such substances, taking care, at the same time, to purify the spot where they have found them, professional sorcerers and witches need to do so only if they have handled particularly dangerous magic; an *omulosi*, for instance, when he has just bought *gímisala* (cf. above, p. 116), and an *ombila* when he has removed the *vila*-plants, sown by another *ombila*, from his client's garden, particularly if he has done so while they were in blossom and thus in their most dangerous condition. It appears, therefore, that the professional sorcerers must purify themselves particularly when they have come into contact with harmful magic issuing from other sorcerers, whereas they are to a large extent immune against the magical substances which have been collected and prepared by themselves.

The rite of lustration employed in all these cases consists in spitting or smearing the contaminated persons and objects with *ovosé*, and in the subsequent consumption of the raw or cooked meat of the slaughtered sheep. After the destruction of the particularly dangerous *gímisala* (cf. above, p. 116) the spot where they have been found is, in addition, sprinkled with the blood of the sheep. Professional sorcerers can administer the rite of lustration to themselves (*kwégongoya* or *kwésalisa*). Ordinary persons must be lustrated (*okunyita, kugóngoya*) either by the *ombila* whose services they have enlisted for the removal and destruction of the *vila*-plants growing in their garden or, if they have come into contact with *amalogo*, by any old man of unimpaired ritual status, as in the case of all other rites of lustration.

Lifting of Curses

The lifting or neutralizing of curses is based on very much the same ideas as the lustration from a state of ritual contamination. Like a person who has fallen *luswa*, the victim of a curse suffers from a strong impairment of his ritual status, and, like the rite of lustration, the ceremonial lifting of the curse aims at restoring this status to normal. As in the case of a person who has fallen *luswa*, the misfortune that overcomes the victim of a curse is always of a specific nature, depending upon the particular things which the originator of the curse has mentioned in his spell. We have seen that illness, poverty, impotence, barrenness, insanity as well as weak or abnormal offspring are the most usual misfortunes which the author of a curse may bring down upon his victim (cf. above, p. 104 sq.). If a person afflicted with one of these various kinds of misfortune has found out by consulting a diviner that his trouble is due to a curse levelled against him, he does not need to submit to his fate, but he can make an attempt to get the curse lifted. As a rule the victim of the curse will know who has cursed him and why he has done so, because—as we have seen—curses directed against definite persons are usually uttered in their presence. But even if he has become the victim of a curse uttered in his absence against an unknown offender (cf. above, p. 102), the consciousness of his guilt will tell him so. However, should he harbour any doubts as to the author of the curse, he can find out by consulting a diviner. The next step which must be taken is to induce the person who has uttered the curse to come and take part in the rite by which the curse will be lifted. The cursed person does not go himself to the curser (*omulami*), but he sends a mediator with a present (usually a fowl or a basketful of grain) who asks the *omulami* to come to the victim's homestead and there 'give back his mouth' (*kwilanyia omunwa gwigwe*), i.e. lift his curse. If the *omulami* has uttered the curse to punish an unknown thief (see above, p. 104) he will, as a rule, be willing to comply with this request, provided that the thief offers to make amends for his offence either by returning the stolen property or by paying an adequate compensation. If, on the other hand, the *omulami* has uttered the curse against a definite person towards whom he harbours a serious grudge or a strong resentment, it will often require a good deal of persuasion and repeated offers of gifts before he finally agrees to come and lift the curse. This latter attitude is aptly expressed in a text on removing a curse of barrenness pronounced by a woman over her brother's daughter, because she had felt offended at not having received an adequate share of the meat distributed on the occasion of her niece's wedding:

'They ask her to come and they take to her millet, porridge, and fish, so that she might lift the curse (*okuhóliza*). But she does not come with a willing heart; they keep on urging her until finally she agrees to come. But (even) after she has come she does not want to perform the ceremony. So they cook food for her, and when she has eaten she is glad in her heart and no longer feels any resentment.'

As my various informants assured me, it never happens that an *omulami* who is implored to lift his curse persistently refuses to comply with this request. Were he to do so, he himself would at last be suspected of being an *omulogi*. Besides, it is said that if somebody died without having lifted a curse he has uttered, he would stay in his grave without finding any rest and the other spirits would avoid his company and despise him.

The ceremonial procedure by which a curse is removed differs according to the nature and the seriousness of the curse. In every case, however, the essential feature of the rite is that the *omulami* reconciles himself with the victim of his curse and that he performs an act by which the original act that caused the curse to become effective is undone or reversed. In the case of the woman, for instance, who had afflicted her niece with barrenness, the efficacy of the curse was due to the fact that she did not eat the meat which she was sent on the day of her niece's wedding but—after having uttered a spell over it—concealed it in the roof of her hut.[1] The meat thereby acquired the potency of harmful magic, giving out, so to speak, the power of the curse and thus preventing her niece from conceiving. To lift the curse she has to remove the dried-up meat from its hiding-place, soak it in water before her niece's eyes and then consume it together with the millet-porridge which they have cooked for her. While eating she must address her niece in something like the following words: 'My anger has ended, if it was my curse which has "tied you", may you now bear a child.'

In a corresponding manner a curse is lifted which a man had imposed upon a herd-boy, because while herding he had killed one of his cows without subsequently confessing his misdeed (cf. above, p. 104 sq.). If now the herd-boy falls ill and the *omulami* is called to come and lift the curse, he must fetch the skull of the dead cow from the secret place where he has hidden it, as the curse derives its potency from the mystical power emanating from the skull. The curser (*omulami*) must burn the skull in the herd-boy's hut and then pour the stomach content of a sheep, specially killed for the occasion, first on the herd-boy's head and then on the charred skull. While doing so he must speak the following words: '*Ugase ukomele niguva niguveye omunwa gwange gukungahizanga madiku gosi lelo ukomele*', meaning: 'May you recover, may you get strong again; if it is my curse (lit. mouth) which has caused you all that time to be sickly, may you now recover your strength.'

If somebody has cursed a thief wishing him to die, he must come to the sick-bed of the cursed person to lift the curse he has uttered. The patient's father in that case concocts a medicine from the stomach content of a sheep, the leaves of the *elineke*-plant, and the honey of wild ground-bees (*edzingote*). The liquid he first hands to the *omulami* to drink of and then pours some of it into his son's mouth. While the *omulami* partakes of this medicine he says: '*Yive ove mulamu kandi okumere kuli avandi*', 'May you get healthy and strong again like the others.'

As a final example we may give an account of the lifting of a curse which somebody has imposed on a cow which he had to part with against his will. If the cow then fails to calve and a diviner has attributed this fact to a curse having been levelled against the cow by its former owner, the latter must be asked to come and beat on the cow's back. While doing so he must say: 'Ah, ah, I am speaking with my mouth, the cow may recover, may you now get milk from it! If its back was hard,[2] may it now soften, may the cow

---

[1] Whoever accepts and consumes the share offered to him when meat or other food is distributed can no longer harbour any ill will against the donor without thereby coming himself to grief.

[2] Sterile cows are said to have a 'hard back' (*omugongo mudinyu*).

calve and when I come here again, may I then find it in good condition.' The former owner of the cow is then offered some beer which must be specially brewed for the occasion, and he is also given a present to take home with him.

Now it may happen that the curser is already dead when the curse begins to take effect or that somebody utters a so-called dying curse, so that it is not possible for the *omulami* himself to lift the curse. In such a case, too, there exists a remedy. A dying curse can be rendered ineffective by killing a sheep before burying the curser and placing in his hands a tray which contains some of the sheep's meat and blood. Then the cursed person must step up to the corpse and eat of that meat and blood, while at the same time a few bits or drops of it are put into the dead man's mouth. If, on the other hand, a diviner attributes a certain illness or misfortune to a curse uttered by a person who has died some time ago, the curse can be neutralized either by burning the bones of the dead man (as among the Logoli, cf. below, p. 288) or by catching and trapping his spirit (as among the Vugusu, cf. below, p. 289).

Reconciliation to terminate a State of Mutual Avoidance

If two persons or two social groups (e.g. clans) live in a state of mutual avoidance because they have had a quarrel, and they both feel a desire to terminate their avoidance, they can do so only by performing a special rite. As a consequence of their quarrel their mutual relations have, so to speak, become ritually contaminated, and if they were to resume their former relations unceremoniously, i.e. without previously restoring their normal ritual status, evil consequences would ensue for both parties concerned. The rite of reconciliation (Lurogoli: *okuhólizana*; Luvugusu: *xúosia*) thus closely corresponds to the lifting of a curse, the only difference being that in the former case the whole procedure is mutual. The simplest and most frequent form of such a rite of reconciliation is that which is performed between a husband and a wife who have showered abuse upon one another (cf. above, p. 190). If they wish to resume their former relations the husband must kill a goat and, in his wife's presence, must sprinkle its stomach content all over their hut. Thereupon they must jointly eat of the goat and send the remainder of the meat to their parents as well as to their neighbours. Now the wife may cook again for her husband and they may both resume their marital relations. While staying among the Vugusu I witnessed the case of a man who had sued his father-in-law to pay him such a goat of reconciliation (*embusi eye xúosia*). As he stated before the tribal court, his wife's bad temper had provoked serious quarrels between them already on three occasions since they had been married, so that every time he had been compelled to kill a goat to restore their matrimonial peace. He therefore thought it reasonable enough that this time the goat should be furnished by his wife's father.

Two clans which have maintained a state of ritual avoidance, or even have carried on a blood feud with one another, terminate that state in a similar manner. To quote from a Logoli text:

'When they see that four people have died (as a consequence of their mutual feud or of a reciprocal curse) they say to one another: "It is good that we look for a sheep and perform a rite of reconcilement (*elihólizana*)." When they have procured a sheep, they reach a mutual agreement and say, "You may all come, so that we may terminate our avoidance, for our people have been dying indeed." Then they must all come to the father of the man who had quarrelled with that other person. When they have all assembled the father must kill the sheep by strangling it with an *ekikunyi*-rope. Then they take the stomach content and mix it with the leaves of the *elineke*-plant and the honey of the *ngote*-bees and scatter this stuff all over the yard of the father's homestead.[1] When they have done so, they may all disperse and go home again without avoiding one another any longer. They are now glad and in good spirits. From now on when they meet on the road they salute one another with "*milembe, milembe*".'

(3) COMBATING AND NEUTRALIZING HARMFUL MAGIC

If as a result of having consulted a diviner one has learned that the illness or whatever other misfortune a person is suffering from is due to an act of witchcraft or sorcery practised by an *omulogi* or an *ombila*, one can choose between a number of possible counter-measures. Altogether five different kinds of such counter-measures may be distinguished:

1. One can try to locate the harmful substance (*amalogo* or *ovovila*) which sends forth the destructive power and then render it innocuous by destroying it.

2. By performing a certain rite one can reverse the direction in which the magical power will strike, so that it will harm its originator instead of the intended victim.

3. One can employ counter-magic (in the narrow sense of the word) by actively combating or neutralizing the *potency* of the magic directed against one without getting hold of the magical substance itself.

4. One can try to induce the perpetrator of the harmful magic (if an *ombila*) to undo or take back his magic by performing a rite to that effect.

5. One can try to punish or even to destroy the author of the harmful magic (*a*) by compelling the suspected person (or persons) to submit to an ordeal, (*b*) by lynching him if one catches him in the act of performing seriously incriminating magic, or (*c*) by accusing him before the clan-elders or, nowadays, the tribal court.

Which one of these different courses of procedure will be employed in a given case depends partly on the circumstances in which the act of harmful magic has been committed, and partly on the advice given by the diviner who, as we have seen, does not merely detect the cause of the

---

[1] According to another version the two parties drink jointly from a tray containing a concoction prepared from the leaves of the *elineke*-plant.

S

trouble but also consults the oracles as to the most appropriate counter-measures that should be taken. Of the five different methods of combating evil magic three are directed against the magical substance and only two against the human agent (the witch or the sorcerer) who is wielding these substances. We have seen that any suspicion of sorcery or witchcraft raised against a definite person, or even merely hinted at, would meet with an emphatic and indignant denial on the part of the suspected person and merely serve to increase his evil intentions towards his victim. Most people, therefore, would avoid having any direct dealings with the suspected witch or sorcerer, let alone levelling an outright accusation against him, but would prefer measures directed exclusively against the magical substance. On the other hand, any measure directed against the perpetrator of the harmful magic himself are bound to have a more lasting effect, because they go —so to speak—right to the root of the trouble and, if they actually lead to the extermination of the witch or sorcerer, will put a final stop to his evil practices. Accordingly the diviner will advise those of his clients who do not fear an open conflict with the suspected sorcerer or witch to request him to submit to an ordeal which, if he is guilty, will destroy him. His other clients he will advise to refrain from challenging the suspected perpetrator himself and to combat instead the magical substance in one way or another. Of the various methods employed, that of detecting and destroying the evil magic takes the first place. A reversal of its effect will be possible only if the affliction with the evil substance is discovered at an early stage (cf. below, p. 266). Counter-magic (in the narrow sense of the word), finally, is only seldom resorted to and appears to be limited essentially to such cases in which there exists no clear notion as to the perpetrator of the magic (cf. below, p. 268).

In the following sections we shall describe these different methods of combating harmful magic.

(a) Detection and Destruction of Harmful Magic

The method employed in detecting and destroying hidden magic depends on the kind of the substance which the diviner has declared to be responsible for the misfortune by which one has been overcome.

Okulíula

In a case of evil magic wielded by an *omulogi* (*omukingi* or *omurori* respectively, cf. above, pp. 114 and 125) one summons an expert, the so-called *omulíuli*, to detect and remove the magical substance as ordinary people would not succeed in doing so. Frequently the *omulíuli* works in collaboration with the diviner who instructs him as to the different places where he should look for the magical substance and what objects he is to produce as a result of his search. Accordingly the diviner refers his client to a definite *omulíuli*. Outwardly the *omulíuli*, however, acts independently and not as an apprentice or helpmate of the diviner.

THE TAKING OF COUNTER-MEASURES

If one wishes to engage the services of an *omulíuli*, one first pays a preliminary visit to his homestead, to present him with a fowl or a basketful of grain and to inform him about the particular matter on which one has come to see him. Just as when consulting a diviner, one calls on the *omulíuli* always early in the morning, so as to make sure of meeting him at home; but there is no need to observe any particular rules or omens. After the *omulíuli* has listened to the client's story, he sends him home and announces his visit for the following (but never for the same) day. He usually comes in the company of two or three neighbours who will protect him should anyone start to quarrel with him while he embarks upon his task of removing the evil magic, and who later on help him to drive home the goats or whatever objects he receives as a payment for his services. The search for the hidden magical substances takes place either at or near the client's homestead, in the bush, near a stream, or else in the house of the alleged *omulogi*. As we have stated in the first part of this section (cf. above, p. 111 sq.), the *omulogi* can hide the substance at any of these places, and it can send out its poison both from near by and from a distance. At which one of the different localities, considered as potential hiding-places of the magical substance, the *omulíuli* begins his search likewise depends upon the information dispensed by the diviner. If this has been kept in vague terms, he first searches the house and the yard of his client, then the surrounding bush, and finally the homestead of the suspected *omulogi*. In the latter case he must proceed with great circumspection and, if possible, wait for an opportunity to slip unnoticed into the *omulogi*'s hut. For the latter would, of course, not willingly submit to having his hut searched. With the help of his neighbours and clansmen, he would give the *omulíuli* a good beating and then drive him away. Formerly, serious clashes are said to have frequently arisen on such occasions between the *omulíuli* and the alleged *omulogi* if the *omulíuli* was taken unawares in the execution of his job. Nowadays the *mlango*-headmen, in accordance with the regulations laid down in the so-called 'Anti-Witchcraft Ordinance', would take police measures against these house-searching practices of the *avalíuli*, so that this side of their activities has been practically stopped and they are content to search for the evil substances in the bush or at their client's homestead.

Before the *omulíuli* begins to search for the hidden objects he takes off his clothes, as these would impede him in his freedom of moving about, for it is deemed necessary for the success of his endeavours that he runs about in wild ecstasy, penetrates into the most remote corners of the hut, climbs the loft as well as the roof of the hut, and even crawls into the narrow grain-bins. Moreover, by conducting his search completely in the nude he convinces his client and the other onlookers that he has not brought the objects which he finally produces with him but has actually found them on the premises. Before embarking upon the actual search (*okulíula*) he dances for some time in the yard, holding in his right hand a spear and in his left hand a club (made from wood or from the horn of a rhinoceros) as well as a certain medicine at which he smells every now and again and which, as he claims, shows him the direction in which he has to look for the evil substance. He performs wild antics, running excitedly and with abrupt movements to and fro in the yard, trembling all over his body. As soon as the medicine has 'pointed out to him' the place where his search might be successful, he thrusts his spear into the ground, into the roof of the hut, into the wall, or wherever else it may be and repeatedly pounds the spot with his club. Then he digs up or scratches that spot with the spear-point or stirs up the grass of the roof until he has found the *gamalogo* or the *ovukingi* concealed there. Usually he searches at several different places and then throws the objects, which are only a few inches in size, upon a heap in the centre of the yard where the onlookers behold them with exclamations of wonder and surprise, calling out words like '*e, e, ayivi viosi evindu via vakolelana hano,*' 'oh, oh, all these things which they have hidden here to commit sorcery with!' The places particularly scrutinized by the *omuliuli* are the gate (*ekilivwa*) in the enclosure of the homestead, the posts on either side of the entrance to the hut, the hearthstones, the bedspread, and the apex of the roof where the *sisuli*-staff (cf. above, p. 252) protrudes from it. Sometimes the *omuliuli* throws whole chunks of earth or a whole bundle of grass from the roof on to the yard, asking the onlookers to examine them for any magical substances that they might find in them. If the *omuliuli* discovers the *gamalogo* (or *ovukingi*) in a pot with grain or other stores, he has the right to take the pot home with him and to keep it, as its owner would not dare to touch its contents for fear of being contaminated by the substances contained in it. My informants said that the *valiuli* in this way often appropriated the best things which they could find at their client's homestead, e.g. his stores of ghee, sesame seed, tobacco, honey, &c. Sometimes the *valiuli* also insist on searching one of the members of the client's family to produce the evil substance from his hair, his clothes, &c. The person concerned has then no other choice but to submit to the wishes of the *omuliuli* and let himself be searched from head to foot, as his refusal would be tantamount to admitting his guilt. Especially women are occasionally suspected of keeping the *gamalogo* with which they intend to kill their husband concealed under their clothes.

When the *omuliuli* has extracted the evil substances from their hiding-place and thrown them all on a heap his duty is done and, after having received his payment, he can go home. The destruction of the substances is left to the client himself who takes them to the nearest stream where he burns them and then casts the ashes into the water to be carried away by it. He must take care that the smoke rising from the burning substances is not blown towards the hut where the patient lies, as to inhale it would aggravate his condition. Other persons against whom the evil magic was not directed do not need to fear either the *gamalogo* or the *ovukingi* themselves, or the smoke rising from them.

THE TAKING OF COUNTER-MEASURES

As a payment the *omuliuli*, in addition to the present which the client takes to him when he goes to summon him, receives among the Logoli another fowl, while among the Vugusu he is given a number of fowls, a piece of iron, several goats or even a young bull-calf, the value of the present depending upon the gravity of the case. The much higher pay which the *omuliuli* gets among the Vugusu indicates that the latter attach a greater importance to his services than the former. This tallies with the fact that the Vugusu know only *ovulosi* and not *ovuvila* and that, accordingly, combating *ovulosi* among them occupies the same place as combating *ovuvila* among the Logoli (cf. below, p. 264). After a patient's recovery no further payment is rendered to the *omuliuli*. If, however, the patient dies despite the alleged removal and destruction of the *gamalogo*, the presents given to the *omuliuli*, or part of them, are demanded back from him.

The confidence placed in the *omuliuli* and his activities is—as in the case of the diviners—not equally great among the various natives. Already the fact that he is closely watched while performing his task indicates that one thinks him capable of trying to deceive his client. Some of my informants too (e.g. Nandoli and Wefwafwa) expressed certain doubts as to the honesty of the whole procedure, pointing out that the *valiuli* never responded to their client's summons until on the following day, so that they might use the night to hide the *gamalogo* at the various places whence they would subsequently extract them. Visudje, a former *omuliuli* among the Vugusu who had been converted to the Christian faith, confirmed these suspicions, adding on his own account that he had often kept the *gamalogo* concealed between his fingers or toes. When I visited him at his own homestead he staged for me a demonstration of the activities of an *omuliuli* and on that occasion performed this sleight of hand so skilfully that despite careful observation the illusion was created that he actually produced the objects from the places where he pretended to have found them. As he further remarked, the *valiuli* laugh about the credulity of their clients when they sit among themselves. Nevertheless, he assured me that the majority of the patients actually recovered after the alleged removal of the *gamalogo*, a fact which he attributed to the assistance and blessing granted to the *valiuli* by their ancestral spirits.

The office of the *omuliuli* is hereditary like that of the diviner, being handed on either from father to son or from a maternal uncle to his nephew. Women cannot become *valiuli*. Among the Vugusu there is a whole clan which bears the name *valiuli*, and it is said that all *valiuli* of the tribe either belong to this clan or are 'nephews' (*avifwa*) of it. If a boy, who by virtue of his descent, possesses the required qualifications feels the desire to become an *omuliuli*, he behaves like a person possessed by a spirit: he trembles all over his body, dances about wildly, ejaculates all sorts of strange sounds, refuses his normal food and instead insists on being given the most unusual things to eat. When he has displayed these unmistakable symptoms for about a week his father or his maternal uncle respectively decide to instruct him in the art of *ovulíuli*. The tuition, which must be given in the seclusion of the teacher's hut, lasts for several weeks. When the novice has acquired the necessary knowledge and skill, his teacher hands him a club and a special pot in which to keep the medicine which, as we have mentioned, shows or inspires him in which direction to search for the evil substances. Before being used by the novice these objects must be blessed by the ancestral spirits. For that purpose they are placed for four days against the centre post of the father's or the maternal uncle's hut. To mark the end of the candidate's apprenticeship his father kills a goat which he consumes jointly with his son. If the instruction was given by the candidate's maternal uncle, he sends him one-half of the animal.

If (among the Logoli) the diviner has attributed the illness of a small child to the evil magic employed by a female *omulogi* (*omulasi wevikoko*), he usually advises his client to have the evil substance (*evikoko*, cf. above, p. 126) removed from the *omulogi*'s hut. In this case, however, no professional *omulíuli* is summoned, but the child's mother goes herself to the hut of the female *omulogi* and tries to remove (*okulíula*) the *evikoko* from there, as is described in the following text:

'... When the diviner has finished divining, he says to the father of the child: "Who has bewitched (literally, taken) your child, is a female person; she has concealed the child underneath the hearthstones of her hut" (cf. above, p. 128). In this way the mother of the sick child gets to know it is the wife of so-and-so who is killing her child. She leaves her hut and goes there (i.e. to the hut of the female *omulogi*) to do as the diviner has said. She must (however) wait until that *omulogi* leaves her hut to dig in her garden or to go somewhere else. For, if she is at home she cannot go there to remove (*kulíula*) the evil substances, for she is afraid to enter the hut. The owner of the hut could beat her and say: "Why are you coming here to remove *evikoko*? I am not an *omulogi*!" (So, when nobody is at home) she enters the hut and when she has stepped inside she looks in all directions. Thereupon she quickly goes into the cooking-partition where the hearthstones are, for the diviner has said: "Go there and tie the evil substances (*evikoko*) together with the medicine of the *ekitátula*-tree." Her husband has prepared this medicine for her and given it to her, and so she now goes with it to remove the *evikoko*. When she has arrived with those medicines at the hearthstones, she thrusts her bill-hook into the ground and dabs the medicine from the *ekitátula*-tree on the floor where she has dug it up with her bill-hook. She takes nothing away from there but merely bedaubs the spot with her medicine, which is also called "the medicine for tying knots"[1] (*evisala viokukúndikila*) or "the medicine for smelling out" (*lifunya*). When she has finished doing so[2] she quickly leaves the hut and hurries back home with the "knots".

[1] The medicine consists of flexible branches or sprigs into which knots have been tied. The idea is that by sweeping the spot concerned with these sprigs the woman will tie the evil substances concealed there into the knots.

[2] According to another version she also takes some of the soot from the roof of the hut.

THE TAKING OF COUNTER-MEASURES 263

Having returned home she performs a rite of lustration with herself (*kwégongoya*) and then waits until the evening. Then an old man comes and places (a pot) of water beside the centre post of the hut. And that woman hands him the knots (*vikúndikilu*), and he pounds them together with the evil substances (*evindu viokulíula*, the things that have been removed), which are tied up in the knots. Then he carries them (i.e. the powder) down into a valley and throws them into the water (of a stream). When he has done so he goes home again.

'Now the mother (literally, the owner) of the child waits to see how the child gets on. And she sees that the child laughs again like the other children. Then she is full of joy and speaks: "Oh, oh, indeed, that woman had bewitched (taken) my child." Then they all rejoice. From now on they closely watch the *omulogi wevikoko* without, however, accusing her on the public place (i.e. before the clan elders), for they say: "If we accuse her she may perhaps kill the child later on; we therefore cannot say anything." '

Removing vílasila *or* evikoko *by Means of the Cupping-horn*

If a child or an adult person suffers from a violent stomach-ache and the diviner attributes the cause of the complaint to the presence of *vílasila*- or *evikoko*-particles in the patient's body (cf. above, p. 127), an alternative method consists in removing these particles from the patient's body. For this purpose one calls a woman (*omulúmiki*) who is an expert in the use of the cupping-horn (*ekilúmiku*). As long as the patient suffers but moderate pain she tries (among the Logoli) to combat the effect of the *evikoko*-particles by a vigorous massage of the stomach, applying a certain ointment prepared from ghee (*amaguta*) and tobacco, or from the pounded leaves of a bitter-tasting herb called *ehálahaliza*. If this treatment does not alleviate the pain, the woman returns on the following day and now resorts to the cupping-horn. She begins by tapping the aching parts of the body with her fingers, calling out repeatedly: 'Oh, oh, she is an evil woman, she has cast *evikoko* into you, oh, oh, &c.' Then she takes a small knife (*olugembe*), makes two or three incisions (of 0·5 or 1 inch in length) into the abdomen and sucks the blood from the wounds. As a cupping instrument she uses the tip of the horn of a cow which must have been killed in sacrifice. The woman places the lower end of the horn on the wound and then sucks the blood through a small hole near the tip of the cupping-horn. Over the hole she places the paper-like web of a certain kind of spider (Logoli: *enyumba yoluvuvi*; Vugusu: *luvuvi*) to avoid getting any blood into her mouth. The idea is to suck the *vílasila* or *evikoko* respectively from the patient's stomach and thus to restore him to health. If the patient suffers also from a violent headache, the *omulúmiki* makes several incisions at both temples and also sucks blood from them. In a Logoli text the healing effect of cupping is described in the following words:

'They suck the blood and then they say: "Now the illness is over." And, in fact, you feel all right again. Before the *omulúmiki* made the incisions in your belly you were suffering from violent pain; now you find rest again, you can eat food which previously you have refused. . . . You cannot be ill for many days, for it was the illness which comes from the *evikoko*.'

Among the Vugusu the *omulúmiki* collects the blood into a leaf and then hides it at a secluded spot out in the bush, so that nobody can use it for any harmful purpose. Among the Logoli the blood is collected in a small potsherd and is first shown to the parents and relatives of the patient. They look at it startled and full of dismay, especially if they see that it contains tiny hairs which they interpret as *evikoko*. Then the potsherd with the blood is kept in the loft of the hut. Should the patient later suffer from another attack of the 'illness of *evikoko*', the blood is administered to him as a medicine.

The removal of the *vilasila* or the *evikoko* by means of massage and cupping is always performed by women, usually by the patient's mother or wife. As it does not require any secret knowledge or particular dexterity, there are many women who know how to administer this treatment and it is therefore not customary to render them any special payment for their service.

If the illness of a small child is diagnosed by the diviner as having been caused by a female *omulogi* and the child's mother suspects a definite *omuxupi owe vilasila* or *omulasi wevikoko*, it will frequently happen, so my informants claimed, that she gives vent to her rage and indignation by going to her house and trying to beat her up, by setting fire to her hut, or by otherwise inflicting damage on her. It appears, therefore, that the revenge of the *omulasi wevikoko* is not feared like that of other *avalogi*. On the other hand, I obtained a text on the subject which states that the enraged mother would ask to be accompanied if possible by the wives of an influential elder, an *eligutu*, and that they would first challenge the *omulasi wevikoko*, 'for if the child's mother were to go by herself, the *omulasi wevikoko* would intensify her magic and cause the other children of the woman to fall ill as well'.

Burning of vifúndilila-*particles*

The *vifúndilila*-particles which an *omufúndilili* has caused to enter his victim's body (cf. above, p. 117) do not have to be removed by any particular measures, as the patient will vomit them up on his own account. To render them ineffective a kinsman of the patient carries them into the bush and burns them, whereupon the patient will soon recover.

Destruction of ovovila

If the diviner has attributed a person's illness to the poisonous emanation of *vila*-plants growing in the vicinity of the patient's hut and planted there by an *ombila* who wishes him evil, the plants must be pulled out and destroyed, so that the patient may recover from his illness. The relatives of the patient, however, cannot do so themselves, but must enlist the services of another *ombila*. They must do so because only an *ombila* can with certainty identify the *vila*-plants as such and because only he can dare to touch them without thereby himself running any risks to his life. The removal and destruction of *ovovila* is described in the following text:

'At first (i.e. after the client has sent for him) the *ombila* performs an ancestral sacrifice[1] (*omusango*) at his own homestead. Then before going to his client to pull the *vila*-plants he makes all his children lick a certain medicine (*olunyasi*) and he himself also licks at it, for he thinks to himself: "If I go there without (having first licked the medicine) the *vila*-plants which I want to pull out might kill me." Then he starts out, carrying with him the utensils which he requires for his task; these are baskets of the *ndede* kind and a side-bag (*emuya*); furthermore, he is accompanied by a number of people—about six—who carry his utensils for him. When they are on their way like that to pull out the *vila*-plants and they meet somebody, he will be very much afraid of them and think: "Perhaps they will kill me (with their magic), for they are *avavila*." But they must salute him, for they know themselves: "If we meet with somebody and we do not wish him *milembe* (i.e. peace, the customary salute among the Logoli), this will not be good." Finally, they arrive at the homestead of the client who has summoned them. First they all sit down on the yard, the *ombila* together with his people and also the owner of the homestead. Then the *ombila* says: "Give me some water," and they go to fetch water in a calabash and give it to him. He puts the calabash down and peers into it. Then he sees what the situation is like and says: "It is a case of *ovovila* which is bringing a bad disease (*vuluasi*)." When he has seen this (by contemplating the water) he leaves the yard and examines the place near the back door (of the hut) to see where the *ovovila* are and how they grow (i.e. what stage of their growth they have reached). After having inspected everything he says to his client: "These here are *ovovila* and things look bad indeed for you, for they are ripe." Then he continues: "If you want me to pull these *ovovila* you must pay me; only then can I begin to pull them out." Then the owner of the homestead brings a heifer and shows it to the *ombila*. Besides, he produces a sheep with which to perform a rite of lustration (*lisálisa*). Only now the *ombila* begins to pull out the *ovovila*. When he has finished doing so, he throws all the *ovovila* on a heap and waits, together with his men who have come with him, until the food (which the client cooks for his guests) has been prepared. Then they eat and when they have finished the *ombila* says to his men: "Now you may go home." And he himself waits until the afternoon; then he takes the *vila*-plants down into the valley where a stream flows and throws them into the water. This he must do all by himself without a single person accompanying him, for at the place where he carries the *ovovila* they might kill other persons. And when he comes home, he again licks the medicine, for if he were not to do so, he would die.

'When they go to pull out *ovovila* they must wait for the (proper) time to come; they cannot pull them out when it rains, but they wait until the weather

[1] By offering a sacrifice he wishes to secure the favour of the ancestral spirits for his undertaking.

is dry. For they are afraid and say: "If we pull the *ovovila* while it rains, they might perhaps kill all the people; so we'll have to wait." '

(b) *Reversing the Direction in which the Evil Magic will Strike*

A second method of combating harmful magic is to reverse the direction in which it will strike, so that it harms its original perpetrator instead of its intended victim. This method, however, is restricted to the combating of *ovulogi*, particularly to that of the *gamalogi* or *amalogo*. Moreover, it can only be resorted to if the presence of the harmful magic is discovered before it has begun to take effect. Among the Logoli a typical case in point is when, after having been in the company of another person, one dreams of having become an *omulogi*, that is to say, in cases where one suspects a definite person of having infected one with his *ovulogi* (cf. above, p. 130). One believes in such a case that a certain object (e.g. tobacco, grain, an armlet, &c.) which one has been given as a present by the suspected person has been 'poisoned' by *amalogo*, thereby transferring the power of the *vulogi* to the victim. To reverse this process one must follow a certain procedure described in the following text:

'... When the *omulogi* has given his neighbour something, e.g. tobacco, to put into his pipe, the latter will dream like this: "Your friend whom you have visited to-day has given you *amalogo*." Thereupon he instantly says to his wife: "Wake up and go with me to our neighbour. I feel that there is something wrong with my body." He leaves his hut right away without any clothes around his loins. Then he calls his father[1] to go with him, but he (his father) does not need to be in the nude. When they arrive at the house of that *omulogi* he calls him. The son to whom he has given the *amalogo* must himself call him; he must not ask his father[2] to call the name of that *omulogi*. When they go to the homestead of that *omulogi*, they carry things with them which are called *evivi* (i.e. the bad ones), and these are *evigege* (white ants), leaves of the *tembe*-tree (Erithrina tomentosa) and of the *gaka*-bush (a kind of aloe) as well as *lande*-creepers. All these things they must collect by night to bring trouble to the *omulogi*'s house. When he (i.e. the son who has been afflicted with the *amalogo*) has called the *omulogi*, and he has replied from inside, "Who is there?" the son must shove all these *evivi* together with the *amalogo* under the door and call out: "Here I return your things to you!" And the *omulogi* cannot reply anything, he can just wonder.

'In the same night the son and his father start out for the lake (i.e. Lake Victoria). They do not want to arrive there while it is yet dark but only early in the morning, at dawn. When they have arrived at the lake, they must throw everything belonging to the son into the water. Even if he had shoes, he must take them off and leave them there in the water of the lake. Then he returns home together with his father, early in the morning when the country is still clean.

---

[1] Lit.: somebody whom he calls father, i.e. not his real but a classificatory father.

[2] This is particularly mentioned as in the case of most of the ceremonial acts the rites are performed by the classificatory father. It is therefore exceptional that the classificatory father on this occasion maintains a completely passive attitude.

'When he comes home, his father must procure a sheep for a rite of lustration, for it is a rule: When you have returned the bad things to an *omulogi* and you have been at the lake, they must perform for you a rite of purification (*elisálisa*), and that is what we call *okunyita*. When they have done so he can re-enter his house. He can no longer be an *omulogi* but can be called an *omwílongo* again, i.e. a good person (*omundu mulahi*). Now all the people know about it, and they say: "True enough, that man (who has given him the tobacco) is really an *omulogi*! Now we know him, we have always thought so." From now on they fear to look at him and to use his things.'

Among the Vugusu the direction of the evil magic which has been sent forth by an *omulosi* is reversed in the following manner. First, the alleged victim offers a sheep or a goat as a sacrifice to the ancestral spirits in order to enlist their help and sympathy. Next he takes the stomach of the sacrificial animal, fills it with small pieces of meat which he cuts from all parts of the animal's body, and then hides the stomach in the path leading to the homestead of the suspected *omulosi*. As a result of this procedure not merely is the intended victim of the *omulosi*'s evil magic saved from it but, like a boomerang, it will now turn back against its perpetrator. According to some of my informants the same purpose will be achieved if one hides a chicken-egg in the *omulosi*'s path.

It is important to note that the return of the harmful magic to its perpetrator (with the implication that it will strike at him instead of at the intended victim) is not effected by returning merely the original substances, but these must be coupled (tied up) with other substances specially prepared for this purpose by the intended victim. The point about these substances is that they stand in a clear contrast to the evil magic sent forth by the *omulogi* (or *omulosi*). Thus the various objects tied up with the tobacco (containing the alleged *gamalogo*) and pushed underneath the door of the *omulogi*'s hut are all plants which not only have no harmful qualities but, on the contrary, are reputed for their ritual purity. So is the stomach of the sacrificial animal that has been filled with pieces of its meat. The destructive effect which these objects have upon the *omulogi* when they have been tied up with the evil substances (*gamalogo*) and then returned to him or placed into his path, appears to be based upon the general principle that the forces of goodness (of ritual purity) act like an antidote against the forces of badness. It is the same basic principle which underlies the idea of lustration, but its effect goes one step further: the counter-magic does not merely destroy and thereby neutralize the *gamalogo*, but it also brings trouble to their perpetrator.

In this connexion some ritual observances in which the moon is involved may be mentioned as they correspond to the return of evil magic to an *omulogi*. If somebody suffers from a deficiency of speech, such as lisping or stuttering, he is led outside at full moon and, facing it, is made to speak against it as loudly as he can. It is said that this will make him lose his impediment and enable him to speak fluently and clearly.

Another rite performed by a mother over her new-born child appears to be based on an association between pregnancy and the moon. At the first full moon after the birth of the child she goes to the bush, carrying the child in her arm and, holding a sprig of the *kitátula*-tree in her hand, spits in the direction of the rising moon. Then she hurls the sprig of the *kitátula*-tree with all her strength towards the moon calling out: 'May the body of my child always be healthy!' As soon as she has called out these words she must run home with her child as quickly as possible without even once turning back to look at the moon.

(c) Combating Evil Magic by Antidotes (Counter-magic)

The counter-measures against harmful magic which we have so far discussed are based on the principle of directly destroying the harmful agent or returning it to its author; we shall now turn to those measures which combat the hidden forces by employing active antidotes, i.e. counter-magic in the proper sense of the word. The reversal of harmful magic by means of substances with positive qualities which we have discussed in the preceding pages presents already an intermediate stage between the destruction of evil magic and the use of counter-magic. The efficacy of the latter, however, rests on magical virtues of its own, without having to be brought into contact with the evil substances sent forth by the *omulogi*.

Harmful magic is combated by independently acting antidotes chiefly in those cases where one feels uncertain as to the author of the evil magic or where its power is of a general, diffuse nature and not materialized in definite substances. A typical case in point is the method employed in 'driving away' an earthquake. To quote from a text:

'When the earth shakes the people do not really know why it does so. But many people say: It is death which comes to kill men. When the time comes where they hear the earth quaking, the hearts of all people are filled with fear. And when the earthquake is over, somebody must go out (into the bush) at dusk; he must have a small hide (drum) on which he beats with great noise, shouting: "Death go down towards the west!" He raises a great noise and calls in a high-pitched voice, "*vu-u-u-vi-i-i-i*." Then the neighbours also go outside with their drums, beating them and calling in the same manner, until the noise penetrates everywhere and they all shout: "*vu-u-u-vi-i-i-i*, death, go down towards the west, go down to the Lake!" By doing so they drive death away, so that it may kill our enemies (instead of us). They begin shouting and beating in the east and (continue to do so) towards the west.'

On the same principle rests another ceremony known as *okuvímbula*. If a family is harassed by frequent illness, if the cattle grow lean and the crops are poor, the owner of the homestead goes to consult a diviner who will, as a rule, advise him to call an *ombímbuli*. He will say to him: 'If you call the *ombímbuli* and he performs *vímbula*-magic at your homestead, the sickness will leave your house, and you will find health and food again; both will be as plentiful as among other people.' First it is necessary to brew large quantities of eleusine beer to offer to the *ombímbuli* and the people who come in his company. When the beer is ready for consumption, one begs the *ombímbuli* to come. After he and his people have for some time feasted on the beer, which must be offered to the party in lavish quantities, the *ombímbuli* asks the members of the homestead to gather round him. He dips a bundle of leaves from the *omusembe*-tree into the beer-pot and, while sprinkling with it all the inhabitants of the homestead, he speaks to them: '*Mugase mumbuki mugende kuli avandi vagendanga.*' 'May you get well again, may you wake up, may you go about like the others are going about.' Thereupon he resumes drinking beer until the afternoon. In the meantime he eats a chicken and eleusine porridge of which, likewise, ample helpings must be placed before him. When he has eaten and drunk enough to feel 'replete and drunk' (*wiguti kandi uhambiki*), he repairs to the cooking-partition (*evwasi*) of the hut and, holding a twig of the *omusengeli*-tree in his hands, dances about in a noisy fashion, stamping with his foot against the wall (*olugitu*) which divides the cooking-partition from the front room (*ehiru*) of the hut. Then he continues his dance in the *ehiru*, and with his *sengeli*-twig beats or taps upon every object that he can get sight of. When he and his companions have finished drinking all the beer that has been prepared for them, the *ombímbuli* asks to be be given a chick which the owner of the homestead has already kept in readiness for that purpose. With the chick in his arm he then slowly proceeds to the nearest stream, followed by the inhabitants of the homestead who carry their old clothes and other utensils of daily use with them. Having arrived at the stream, he dips the *sengeli*-twigs into the water and sprinkles with it all inhabitants of the homestead. They throw all the things they have brought along on a heap and then cast them into the water to be carried off by the current. Then the *ombímbuli* takes the chick which he has carried with him, and flutters it over each of the persons present in turn (*okweya nengoko*, cf. below, p. 282), thereby removing from their bodies any traces of the *ovodékele* (poverty) with which they might still be afflicted. Then the *ombímbuli* tells the whole party to return home, warning them to go as quickly as they can and not to look back. When they have returned home, they kill a sheep and perform for themselves another rite of lustration (*okwésalisa*).

As a payment for his services the *ombímbuli* receives a fowl and a basketful of grain. If the effect of his counter-magic begins to show within a short time by the homestead being restored to health and prosperity, the owner of the homestead sends him a goat as a sign of his satisfaction.

Counter-magic in the narrow sense of the word is performed also by the *ombila*. If somebody has fallen ill after having met with an *ombila* (cf. above, p. 134), his kinsmen call another *ombila* who administers special medicines to the patient or massages his body with various ointments which are to act as antidotes against the potency of the *ovovila* which the first *ombila* had pointed at him. As distinct from the *ovovila* these antidotes are called *amahonya* (from *okukonya*, to help) or *olunyasi lwovovila* (medicine of *ovovila*). It is said that they always contain a certain quantity of the same *vila*-plants which were contained in the *liveye*-fruit which the first *ombila* had pointed at the victim, thereby causing his illness. These antidotes are clearly distinguished also from ordinary medicines (*edzinyasi*) which are administered by herbalists and which can be handled by any ordinary person.

Among the Vugusu the *omulíuli* too occasionally performs countermagic. He does so particularly in cases where the information dispensed by the diviner has shown that the *omulosi* keeps the *gámalogo*, employed to bring illness to his victim, in his own house and he has no opportunity to enter the *omulosi*'s house and remove them. He then prepares antidotes (which likewise are called *gámalogo*) and takes them by night to the *omulosi*'s hut, where he either pushes them under the door or hides them in the straw of the roof. The idea is that these antidotes destroy the potency of the *gámalogo* employed by the *omulosi* and thus cause the patient to recover.

Reparation by the Perpetrator of the Harmful Magic

Another method of undoing the effects of harmful magic is to induce its author to cancel or annul the act of evil magic performed by him. How one must go about to attain this end depends on whom one has to deal with. If it has become evident from the consultation of the diviner that the act or magic which is causing the trouble was performed by an ordinary person (cf. above, p. 96 sq.), the best procedure is to approach that person directly. As in the case of the lifting of curses, it is, of course, essential that the alleged perpetrator of the evil magic should not deny his authorship and that he is willing to revoke his spell or otherwise undo the effects of his magic.

If a man, for instance, ceases to be successful in his courtships and the diviner has attributed this fact to an act of magic directed against him by a rival (cf. above, p. 101), he can go to the latter and frankly discuss the case with him. If they come to terms with one another the rival will promise to undo the effect of his magic. For this purpose the father of the 'bewitched' person must procure a live mole (*embuku*) while the rival's father must gather branches of the *ekigusa-* and the *kisávasavi*-trees, i.e. of the same two trees from the pounded leaves of which the original potion had been prepared (cf. above, p. 101). With these twigs he builds a fire over which the father of the 'bewitched' roasts the live mole. In addition, the rival's mother must cook eleusine porridge. When everything has been prepared, all people present partake of this meal (the so-called *ovukima vwokuholiza*), first the victim of the magic himself, then his father, then the rival (the author of the magic), and finally his father. The two mothers eat only of the eleusine porridge and both hang a toe of the roasted mole round their necks. When they have finished eating they may all go home, for the effect of the harmful magic is now considered to have been removed.

THE TAKING OF COUNTER-MEASURES

If a boy has torn up a girl's necklace (to make her yield to him) or if he has sprayed water on her while she was fetching water from a stream (cf. above, p. 205) and if later, when she is married, she repeatedly suffers from miscarriages or difficult deliveries, this is considered to be a consequence of the act committed by the boy (cf. above, p. 206). To cancel these effects the youth must go to the house of the woman whose necklace he had torn up. Together with her child the woman must then stand in front of the door, while the youth must climb the roof of the hut and urinate down upon her. If it is not possible to summon him personally, his part in this rite may be taken by any uncircumcised boy, who is then given a fowl as a payment for his service.

An *omusohi*, too, can undo the effects of her 'evil eye' (cf. above, p. 127). If, for example, food does not get done despite long cooking as a result of an *omusohi* having cast the evil eye at it, she must herself bring firewood and kindle the fire with it. Should she cast her evil eye upon a gourd growing in the kitchen garden so that her glance would cause it to crack, the *omusohi* can prevent this from happening by covering the gourd with the leaves of the *elivililinzu*-plant. Should she cause a child to fall ill and should she later regret having done so, she can neutralize the effect of her evil eye by chewing a certain grass and spitting it on the child while saying to it: '*Nendise oxwira ove omulamu osakuluxe*', 'If it is I who am killing you, may you recover your health!'

In a similar way an *ombila* can undo the effects of his harmful magic. Having first demanded a goat for payment, he takes a small knife and makes with it a number of incisions in the patient's body. Rubbing his curative medicine (*olunyasi lwovovila*) into the wounds, he says: '*Ndali ninyenyanza okukwita, kandi nguhonyanga*', 'It was I who wanted to kill you, (but) now I am curing you again.' He thus frankly admits his former intention. Should the patient die despite this application of counter-magic, this particular *ombila* would no longer be held responsible for his death, as he had undone and thus rendered ineffective the evil magic originally performed by him.

If the diviner has detected an *omulosi* as the perpetrator of harmful magic, it would be quite futile to approach him with a straightforward request to undo his witchcraft, for—in contrast to an *ombila*—an *omulosi* would never admit having committed an act of bad magic. Moreover—so people say—he would never voluntarily lift the effect of his magic. To evade this difficulty and to coerce an *omulosi* even against his will to revoke his witchcraft and to destroy the *gámalogo* which he has concealed, the patient's relatives kill a goat or a bull-calf and invite all kinsfolk and neighbours, including the suspected *omulosi*, to divide the meat of the animal among them. If the *omulosi* accepts the meat and eats of it, he must also destroy the *gámalogo*, as otherwise he would fall ill and die (as a result of having eaten of the meat). If, on the other hand, he refuses the meat or passes it on to someone else, he thereby incriminates himself.

The reason for distributing the meat is obviously not to pacify or please the *omulosi* by making him a present, but rather so that none of the people who share in the common meal can any longer harbour ill feelings towards one another, as the joint meal is symbolic of their fellowship and their sense of solidarity. It acts like an oath which destroys him who breaks it.

Ordeals and Punishment of Sorcerers and Witches

Still another method of combating harmful magic, finally, consists in rendering the originator of the magic himself innocuous, i.e. to destroy him. For this purpose it is first of all necessary to convict the suspected *ombila* or *omulogi* of his crime. It will, however, only in the rarest cases prove possible to catch an *omulogi* in the act of performing his witchcraft, for instance by surprising him while he is dancing in front of his victim's hut or while he is engaged in the very act of hiding the *amalogo* in his victim's path. The suspicions harboured against an *omulogi* or an *ombila* can, however, be confirmed by compelling the suspect to submit to an ordeal (*elilama*).

There are two different kinds of ordeals. One of them merely finds out whether the suspect actually *has* committed an act of evil magic or not. The second kind automatically entails the punishment of the guilty person. In order to make a suspected *omulogi* submit to an ordeal it is not necessary to single him out for that purpose, a procedure which would be tantamount to an outright accusation. In most cases it would not even be necessary to let the suspected witch or sorcerer know that he is made to submit to an ordeal. Among the Logoli, for instance, the simplest kind of ordeal by which one can detect an *omulogi* and render him innocuous is to invite the suspected person under some pretext and then offer him a calabashful of beer to drink from. The administering and the effect of this 'ordeal' were described to me in the following words:

'If somebody on two or three different occasions discovers that eggs have been placed under the door of his hut, he goes to the "skins" of the diviner (to inquire who has placed them there in order to bring illness to his house). The diviner says to him: "It is your neighbour, the one who has built two huts for himself, you know who he is. Go and brew beer for this (man) who has bewitched you and call him to come to your house. When he has come he will drink of that beer, and you drink together with him. Then he goes home again, and ere long he will fall ill. Then (you know): indeed, he was the one who has brought those eggs. And he cannot know why he is ill, but he will always be ill or he will even die."'

The efficacy of this ordeal rests on the same notion which we have already repeatedly encountered, viz. that somebody who is harbouring ill will towards another person cannot accept food or drink or any other hospitality from that person without thereby coming to grief himself (cf. above, p. 271). As my informants expressly assured me, the beer offered

THE TAKING OF COUNTER-MEASURES 273

to the suspected *omulogi* would not contain any poison or other magical substances, but would be ordinary beer.

Among the Vugusu the following ordeal is performed for the detection and the destruction of an *omulosi*. The father, brother, or son of the sick person slaughters a goat and then summons all the neighbours, including the suspected *omulosi*. One of the clan-elders will throw in the full weight of his authority to make sure that all the neighbours come. When they are all assembled in the house of the sick person the latter is thoroughly washed and the dirty water is then placed before the guests who sit in a circle round the wash-basin. The patient's father then divides the meat of the goat. He dips every piece of it into the dirty water and then pierces it with a sharpened stick cut from the *lulurúsia*-tree, the exceedingly bitter taste of which immediately permeates the meat. Then he hands to each of the persons present a piece of the goat's meat prepared in that fashion, and while each of them eats of that meat he must say: 'If it was I who brought on the disease, may I fall ill and die.' If he has actually caused the patient's illness, he will die within a few months as a consequence of having submitted to this ordeal.

In a slightly different manner this ceremony is nowadays also performed as a rite of reconciliation or atonement. Instead of dipping the goat's meat into the patient's wash-water the *omulosi* washes himself in the water and says: 'If I have made him ill, may he recover.' The patient's father then roasts a banana, one half of which he gives to the patient to eat and the other half to the *omulosi*. The *omulosi* must then immediately destroy the magical substances which he had prepared with the intention of causing the patient's death, lest he himself should fall ill or die.

If in the course of a quarrel somebody is accused of being an *omulosi*, an *omuxupi owe vilasila*, or any other kind of a witch, he must endeavour to restore his good name by voluntarily submitting to an ordeal together with the person who has levelled the charge at him. For this purpose the old men procure an onion-like fruit (*ekolati*), the upper half of which they hollow out. On the public place of the village and in the presence of many witnesses the suspected witch must then spit into the *ekolati*-fruit and say: 'If I have gone to kill your child may the bitterness (*silula*) of the *ekolati*-fruit kill me (lit. eat me). If, however, you are accusing me of something which neither my father, nor my father's sister, nor my mother has done, then it (the bitterness) may turn against yourself.' Thereupon the person who has made the charge spits into the fruit and says: 'If it was not you who killed my child, if I have accused you wrongly, may the bitterness turn against me; but if you have touched it (i.e. killed the child by magic) may the bitterness turn against you and may you go with it (i.e. die as the child has died).'

After each of them has twice spit into the fruit an old man places it on a potsherd and carries it out to the bush. There it will strike roots and begin to grow. When the sprouting plant has reached a height of about

T

5 inches, one of the two persons who have taken the oath will fall ill. In most cases, it is claimed, the guilty person will even die and his own death will soon be followed by that of one or several of his children.

If the suspected witch refused to swear the oath or to submit to the ordeal, this was tantamount to a confession of his guilt and he had then to pay the denouncer 'blood-money', i.e. he had to give him several head of cattle as compensation for the damage inflicted upon him as a result of the alleged act of witchcraft. If, on the other hand, the denouncer refused to take the oath, because he felt that his suspicion was not well enough founded to justify the risk which the swearing of an oath implied for him, he had to pay the suspected witch compensation for libel, consisting usually of a bull or two goats.

Among the Logoli an *ombila* who was suspected of having abused his powers in a shameful way was summoned by the clan-head to appear before the assembly of clan-elders, where he was invited to make a clean breast of the offence attributed to him. If he denied his guilt, one of the old men stepped forward and levelled an accusation against him, whereupon he had to submit to the following ordeal. The old men took him into their midst and then began to dance around him, at the same time stamping the ground with long poles (*emidigilu*) in a slow, steady rhythm. While they were dancing like that the clan-head spoke words to the following effect: 'If you have been killing the people with your *ovovila*, may this dance kill you, but if you have not done so, may you go on living!' After the old men of the clan had danced round the suspected *ombila* for about one hour he could go home. If guilty of the offence of which he was suspected, he died under the influence of that dance on the same day.

The dance staged in connexion with this ordeal corresponds exactly to that performed by the circumcision novices at the end of the initiation rites during the feast of their discharge from the hut of seclusion (cf. below, p. 367). It appears, therefore, that on that occasion, too, its objective is to exorcize the forces of evil magic in a general way and thereby to fortify the ritual status of the initiates.

A similar ordeal was, among the Logoli, administered to a man strongly suspected of having caused a number of deaths by witchcraft (*ovulosi*). Upon orders given by the clan-head he was led to an *omutembe*-tree which, as has already been stated, is looked upon as a specific antidote against *ovulogi*. Eight old men specially reputed for their record as warriors then formed a circle round that tree. One of them handed the suspected *omulogi* a sort of dagger (*ekivavu*) which he had to thrust into the trunk of the tree using all the strength he could muster. Then while the old men beat with their spears against their shields, the clan-head (or the oldest one of the warriors) solemnly addressed him in the following words: 'If you have killed So-and-so you may die, but if you have not killed him, you may live.' This over, the suspected *omulogi* was told to extract the dagger from the tree and to return home. If he was guilty, his feet would begin to swell within a few days after having submitted to this ordeal, and he would gradually waste away until he died.

In all the cases we have quoted so far the ordeal did not merely decide the question, guilty or not guilty, but it simultaneously effected the punishment of the sorcerer or the witch if he had committed the offence of which he was suspected. There was, however, another kind of ordeal which merely established the question of guilt without automatically entailing the punishment of the offender. If, for instance, among the Vugusu somebody had accused somebody else of being an *omulosi*, the accused person would request the accuser to go with him to the meeting-ground (*luyia*) of the clan-elders so that they might jointly submit to an ordeal. For this purpose they summoned the so-called *owémbambio*, a man who possessed and knew how to handle a special knife (*embambio*) required for performing the ordeal. While the *owémbambio* heated the knife in the fire, the accused as well as the accuser took off their clothes and, stepping across them, each of them spoke: 'If I go about at night-time bewitching the people, these clothes may eat (i.e. kill) me.' Then they stood facing one another, holding in their right hand a stick and in their left hand a fowl which in the case of the accuser had to be white and in that of the accused 'red'. In the presence of the clan-elders as well as of numerous onlookers, the accuser began to plead his case, thrusting his stick into the ground immediately in front of the accused after every sentence he uttered. Winding up his indictment, he exclaimed that the red-hot knife might burn him if he had accused his opponent in vain. Now the accused had his say, solemnly protesting his innocence and likewise swearing an oath by the red-hot knife. When each of them had pleaded his case, the *owémbambio* rubbed a certain ointment on the outer side of each man's right thigh. Then he brushed the red-hot knife with its broad side over the anointed spot. He whose skin got most badly singed was considered guilty, i.e. either of an act of evil magic or of a wrong accusation. The amount of the penalty imposed on the guilty party was fixed by the clan-elders. For someone convicted of an act of witchcraft it is said to have amounted to five head of cattle, two goats, a sheep, a hoe, and a spear. This approximately corresponds to the compensation paid as so-called blood-money for murder. If the ordeal proved the accusation to be unfounded, the accuser was fined one or two head of cattle.

Ordeals and consultations of oracles respectively were also administered to people suspected of having committed adultery (with a married woman) or theft. In the former case the suspect was made, in the presence of the clan-elders, to pass between the legs of the woman concerned. It was believed that the sight of the woman's sex organs would, if he were guilty, automatically lead to his death. To find out a thief one summons (even to-day) the so-called *omuségetili* who in the presence of all the neighbours (including if possible the suspected thief) performs the following consultation of an oracle. Into a small pot which is filled with water he places a long, smooth staff the upper end of which he holds in his left hand. Then he takes some leaves of the *kitátula*-plant in his right hand and rubs them up and down the stick, mentioning while doing so the names of all the persons who might have committed the theft, e.g. 'If it was Adongo who stole the fowl, may this my medicine catch him.' As long as the *vitátula*-leaves slide up and down the staff without sticking to it, he must continue to mention further names; as soon, however, as the leaves get stuck, the person whose name he happened to be uttering at that moment has thereby been identified as the thief. If despite the 'evidence' furnished by this oracle the detected person refuses to admit his guilt, the *omuségetili* can utter a curse over him, saying: 'If it was you who has stolen the things belonging to So-and-so, hiding them now and refusing (to confess your misdeed), and if you fail to return the stolen goods, may you lose them; may the children you beget be thieves down to your great-grandchildren (*kuduka ku visukulului vivyio*).'

Ordeals to which a suspected witch or sorcerer must submit personally and on the grounds of an accusation levelled directly against him are to-day no longer resorted to. Even in former times they do not seem to have been frequent, as they provoked the revenge of the accused and, moreover, involved the risk for the accuser that he, too, had to submit to the ordeal or swear an oath.

Direct physical punishment of witches or sorcerers seems to have occurred only in cases where their acts of spiteful magic had aroused a spontaneous feeling of hatred and rage but not when the case had first been taken before the clan-elders and given a proper hearing. If after a person's death a strong suspicion of having caused his death by evil magic arises against a definite person, and if that person then dares to show up at the funeral rites, he may risk being beaten or clubbed to death by the enraged and revengeful clansmen of the deceased. In most cases, however (at least nowadays), such a suspected sorcerer or witch merely becomes a target for threats and abuse which would still leave him a chance to escape should he feel the resentment against him rise to an undue pitch. Moreover, the old men of the clan and especially the *omuseni* (the comforter, cf. below, p. 486) will use their full powers of persuasion to keep the resentment felt by the deceased's kinsmen within moderate limits and thus prevent actual clashes or the outbreak of a clan-feud.

If, however, an *omulosi* happened to be caught while performing his nightly dances and other antics in front of his intended victim's hut, he was killed on the spot, there and then, by thrusting a pointed pole into his anus. Nandoli's father told me that many years ago he had killed in this manner, with the help of three other men, a notorious *omulosi* by the name of Siswali, after laying in wait for him for weeks on end. Pierced on a long pole they had carried him back to his village where, on the following day—so Nandoli's father claimed—he was unceremonially buried by his clansmen who felt so much ashamed of him that they even refrained from demanding any 'blood-money' for his death. When he was buried his body was covered with a hide to conceal the wounds caused by the pole. The widow, so Nandoli's father added, in this case did not sing any of the customary dirges but a special song alluding to the fact that her husband had been killed because he had been found out to be an *omulosi*:

>   *Mulila vusa,*
>   *muxasimbula Siswali,*
>   *Siswali gatjia xuvina muvala.*

>   'You may cry only,
>   But do not uncover Siswali,
>   He went to dance in the Vala-clan.'

This story was confirmed by several other old men of the Vugusu tribe.

(4) THE CULT OF THE ANCESTORS AND OF THE SUPREME BEING

(a) *Family Sacrifices*

Having discussed the various methods by which the mystical forces wielded by human beings are either controlled, combated, or made to serve one's own ends, we shall now consider the attitude adopted towards the ancestral spirits and the Supreme Being.

In the first part of this section we have discussed the notions prevailing with regard to the spirits of the dead and their manifold ways of interfering with the fate of the living. We have noted that the spirits of persons who have recently died are feared because one attributes to them hostile intentions towards the living, but that one expects protection and help from the 'tame' or 'cooled-off' spirits, i.e. those spirits that have reconciled themselves to their life in the spirit-world. This ambivalent attitude towards the spirits of the deceased is clearly reflected in the cult of the ancestral spirits. In so far as the spirits of the dead are deemed to be antagonistic to the living, one merely seeks to appease them by means of sacrifices and other ritual observances. Inasmuch, however, as one believes them to be benevolent towards the living, one tries to establish close relations with them by regular sacrificial offerings and by imploring their active help and protection. Those ancestral spirits, on the other hand, who are regarded as fundamentally evil, who during their lifetime were notorious witches bent only upon the indiscriminate destruction of their fellow human beings and who now, after their physical death, continue their evil practices (the so-called *visieno*-spirits) do not form the object of any ritual observances, but one merely seeks to destroy them or at least render them innocuous by directing counter-magic or vengeance-magic against them (cf. below, p. 289).

The ritual observances towards the dead begin immediately after a person's death has occurred, with wailing, the watch of the dead, and the burial rites. Wailing and lamenting—apart from the moral relief which they bring to the bereaved kinsmen and close friends of the deceased—serve the twofold purpose of professing one's own innocence in connexion with the death that has occurred and of convincing the close relatives of the deceased that one has a clear conscience. For it is believed that the person responsible for the death (by having committed an act of sorcery or witchcraft) cannot step up to the corpse without betraying his guilty conscience by his behaviour or his facial expression. Among the Logoli it is also said that the deceased would suddenly open his eyes if the person who had caused his death were to come up to him. Moreover, one tries to give convincing proof of one's innocence by submitting voluntarily to a number of situations which act like ordeals by entailing automatic sanctions, should one be in any way involved in the person's death. Other ceremonial acts performed in the course of the funeral rites are to demonstrate to the spirit of the deceased that his living kinsmen honour and respect him and to make him forget his loneliness in the spirit-world. Thus the whole life of the deceased is represented in often very impressive pantomimic performances: by sham-fights his activity as a warrior, by rounding up the cattle of the whole clan his economic wealth, &c. The climax of these rites is formed by a large dance staged on the day following the funeral and attended by hundreds or even thousands of persons. It is believed that the spirit of the deceased, perched on a nearby tree or on the roof of his hut, watches these various rites and festivities performed in his honour and that they help to appease him.

A seeming contrast to these ceremonies is formed by others intended to sever the bonds with the deceased and to prevent him from returning to the world of the living. Thus among the Vugusu one tears down the hut of the deceased, while among the Logoli and the Nyole one buries—as a *pars pro toto*—a rafter of the roof in swampy soil. The widow who is considered to have been ritually contaminated by her husband's death is for a longish period of time isolated from contact with other people, and everyone who has been in close contact with the deceased immediately before his death must submit to a rite of lustration (cf. above, p. 248).

The same two seemingly contradictory ideas are found also in the sacrificial rites and ceremonies performed for the spirits of the dead.

Apart from seasonal sacrificial feasts taking place in special groves and staged by the entire clan or even the tribal community (as among the Logoli), the ancestral sacrifices are a matter which concerns chiefly the individual family.

As regards the motives from which ancestral sacrifices are performed, three different types of family sacrifices may be distinguished. The first are daily food libations offered to the spirit of a near kinsman during the first few months after his death. Without any special ceremonial the widow puts a small amount of the daily gruel or porridge into a small basket (*engungi*) and some vegetables into a potsherd (*oludju*), and when beer has been brewed she also pours some of it into a small pot. These food libations she places on the loft (*elilungu*) or beside the centre post of the hut as food for the spirit of the deceased (*ovukima vwekigingi*). One says that the *ekigingi* (the spirit of the deceased) will come to inhale the steam rising from the food offered to him and that this will sustain him. Moreover, these daily food libations are to demonstrate to the *ekigingi* that one has not yet forgotten him but that one still shares one's daily food with him as one used to do when he was still alive. The food itself is thrown away on the following day, unless it has meanwhile been eaten by rats. After several months—among poor people after a few weeks—these food libations become less regular until, finally, they are omitted altogether as it is believed that the ancestral spirit is no longer staying about the house but has by then settled down in the land of the spirits.

A second type of sacrifice is performed on all important occasions and turning-points in the life of the individual and the family. Whereas the daily food libations are addressed to a definite spirit, viz. that of the recently dead, sacrifices of this second type are addressed to all ancestral spirits to whom one attributes the power of affecting, either negatively or positively, the well-being of the family or the individual person on whose behalf the offering is made. These sacrifices aim chiefly at promoting the health and welfare of the person (or group of persons) in whose name they are performed by appeasing the antagonistic spirits in a general way and, at the same time, invoking the blessing and sympathy of the benevolent spirits (those that have already 'cooled off'). In the life of the individual, the most important occasions on which one offers sacrifices of this kind are: birth, naming, circumcision, marriage (in the case of a woman), the establishment of one's own homestead after the birth of several children (the so-called *sitexo*-ceremony among the Vugusu), death and, finally, in the case of a widow, the end of her period of mourning. On each of these occasions the sacrifice is connected with a number of other ceremonial observances. Thus the sacrifice performed after the birth of a child (the so-called *liswákila*-ceremony) is linked with its reception into the community of its paternal and maternal relatives. By offering the first ancestral sacrifice on its behalf the child which until then was still an *omusinde*[1] (an 'unconsecrated person') acquires its first ritual status. Similarly the ancestral sacrifice made after the circumcision of a young man is connected with the imparting of rules of conduct and with the admission of the initiate to a social status in the clan community. The sacrifice performed on the occasion of the *sítexo*-rite (from *oxutexa*, to cook) is to consecrate the newly established homestead and hearth and, at the same time, to bestow full marital status upon husband and wife. The sacrifice, finally, which is offered a few months after a person's death is to effect the reception of his spirit into the community of the dead and thus to terminate his existence as an *omusinde* in the spirit-world. This sacrifice, therefore,

[1] Cf. Wagner, 'Reifeweihen der Kavirondo Bantu und ihre heutige Bedeutung', *Archiv für Anthropologie*, Neue Folge, vol. xxv, p. 92.

is not addressed to the dead person himself, but to the spirits that have died a long time ago. It is, as it were, the last obligation which the living have to fulfil towards the deceased as to somebody who still belongs to the world of the living.

In the life of the family the most important ancestral sacrifices are performed in connexion with the sowing and reaping of the eleusine crop, with the consumption of the first-fruits, and with the erection of a new living-hut.

A third type of sacrifice, finally, takes place when illness or other misfortune has overcome the family, and the diviner has detected the anger of a definite ancestral spirit as the cause of the trouble. The occasions which give rise to such sacrifices of appeasement may be of many different kinds. They comprise all chronic diseases and ailments (sudden and violent outbreaks of illness, on the other hand, are, as a rule, not attributed to the spirits of the dead but to certain types of sorcerers or witches, cf. above, p. 112 sq.), bad dreams (particularly those in which the ghost of a deceased kinsman appears), barrenness of a woman, impotence or childlessness of a man, cattle diseases, and finally, crop failures affecting only the family gardens while the neighbours reaped a good harvest. As all these untoward events may also have other causes besides the animosity of an ancestral spirit, it is necessary to consult the diviner before performing the sacrificial rite.

On occasions of minor importance the offering consists of a pot of beer, a dish of eleusine porridge, or sometimes mere tokens. Thus the simplest kind of offering made for a child suffering from a minor complaint is to tie leaves of the *amalande*-creepers round the child's loins. This is said to please the spirit who has caused the child's complaint and to induce him to restore the child to health. If a beer offering is made it must always be the more valuable eleusine beer (*amalua govolo*) and not sorghum beer (*amalua gamavele*); on some occasions one does not offer the finished product but the germinated and fermented eleusine grain (*amamela govolo*) which forms an intermediate stage in the manufacture of beer.[1] Eleusine porridge (*ovukima vwovolo*) is seldom offered by itself but usually only in conjunction with an animal sacrifice. Among the sacrificial animals cows occupy the first place, but they are killed only on important occasions, e.g. after the circumcision of the eldest son, when performing the *sitexo*-rite, and in cases of grave illness or other serious misfortune. In all ordinary cases a sheep or a goat is sacrificed and in those of lesser importance a fowl. If the sacrifice is addressed to the spirit of a child, it is customary to offer merely a chicken-egg which is placed on a small tuft of grass and then deposited on a carefully cleaned path in the vicinity of the hut.

Among the Logoli the sacrificial animal must be without any blemishes; it must not be lame or have any scars, and its skin, its teeth, and its hoofs must be faultless; in short, it must be a perfect specimen of its kind.

[1] Cf. vol. ii, chapter on beer-brewing.

THE TAKING OF COUNTER-MEASURES

Among the Vugusu, no particular store is set by these qualities, unless the diviner has specially stated that the sacrificial animal, to be acceptable to the spirit, must be free from blemishes. The animal must be of the same sex as the spirit to whom it is offered. If the sacrifice is not addressed to any particular spirit, but is merely to invoke the general benevolence and assistance of the ancestors, a male animal is offered. The kind of animal chosen also depends on the importance of the spirit to whom the sacrifice is addressed and, furthermore, on the comparative wealth of the person who makes the offering. If he is very poor, the diviner will advise him to borrow a sheep or a goat from a neighbour and, instead of slaughtering the animal, merely to stroke its back and then to return it to its owner. The decision as to what kind of sacrificial animal will be appropriate in any given case always rests with the diviner.

The various sacrificial rites are designated in both dialects by a number of different terms, which, however, are not always mutually exclusive. Among the Logoli I have encountered the following terms:

1. *Okusanga*, to sacrifice (generic term), also *okukola* or *okumala emisango*, to make or to 'finish' sacrifices. The verb *okusanga* also means 'to gather', 'to assemble'. This term, accordingly, stresses the fact that a sacrifice offers an occasion for the kindred to rally round. Also used among the Vugusu (*oxusanga*).
2. *Okusálisa*, to sacrifice (a second generic term), sometimes also used with reference to rites of purification. Probably derived from *okusala*, to pray, to implore.
3. *Okusígisilila*, to sacrifice (literally: to throw for somebody). Refers to the throwing out or scattering of pieces of meat of the slaughtered animal as well as to the sprinkling of the sacrificial shrine with blood.
4. *Okuswákila*, to sacrifice for a new-born child. The ceremony itself is called *eliswákila*.
5. *Okunyíta*, to perform a sacrifice of appeasement. The sacrificial animal is always a ram. The term also designates rites of reconciliation that terminate a feud or an avoidance.
6. *Okukunya*, to perform a sacrifice for a seriously ill and weak person. The term seems to refer particularly to the sacrifice of a goat.
7. *Okugóngoya*, to sacrifice a fowl. Refers both to the killing of a fowl for an ancestral spirit and to a rite of lustration performed with a fowl. If administering such a rite to himself, the reflexive form *okwégongoya* is used.
8. *Okuhóliza*, to affect an appeasement or a reconciliation by performing a sacrifice or by another ceremonial act. The term seems to refer to the effect produced by the sacrifice. In other contexts the verb also means 'to fatten'.
9. *Okukola omuluka*, to perform a sacrifice after a harvest failure.

A number of other terms refer to particular ritual observances performed in the course of a sacrifice:

10. *Okuvida novwanga*, to spit or blow *ovwanga* (eleusine flour stirred in water) on a person.

11. *Okuvida novosé* or *okuvaka novosé*, to spit or rub the stomach content of the sacrificial animal on a person.
12. *Okweya nengoko* or *nekiminyu*, to stroke with a live fowl or chick.
13. *Okufwana ovwali*, to kindle a sacrificial fire.

Among the Logoli the sacrificial site or shrine consists of a set of three (sometimes also of four or more) stones (*amagina gemisango*), arranged in a triangular shape like the hearthstones and erected in the yard in front of the living-hut. Each of these stones is about 3 or 4 inches high, and the sides of the triangle formed by them vary between 10 and 15 inches in length. A sprig of the *olwovo*-tree, thought to be a favourite abode of the ancestral spirits, is placed in the centre of this stone setting.[1] Sometimes a circular arbour is erected above it, so that the sacrificial shrine looks like a miniature native hut without walls. When an offering is made, small pieces of the slaughtered animal are placed on top of the sacrificial stones or its blood is sprinkled over them. In the case of a beer-offering, one either places a small potful between the stones or pours the beer on the stones. It is believed that the spirits which one has invoked will alight on these stones and inhale the smell of the meat or the beer.

A second kind of shrine is the—already repeatedly mentioned—centre post (*etiru*) of the living-hut at the base of which one deposits all objects which one desires to be blessed by the ancestral spirits (cf. above, pp. 98 and 226). On certain occasions a sacrificial fire (*ovwali*) is kindled in front of this centre post with the branches of the *oluvinu*-plant, the rising smoke of which is said to please the ancestral spirits.

Among the Vugusu there are a number of different shrines consecrated to different kinds of spirits. Instead of a stone setting they have a sacrificial hut (*namwina*) which is erected either right in front of the entrance to the living-hut or on a nearby ant-hill.[2] The height of these huts varies between 2 and 7 feet. As a rule they have a centre post (*éndjeko*) and walls like a real living-hut. Instead of three stones, as among the Logoli, they have only one stone which is always placed to the left side of the entrance and which is called the 'stone of Wafula' (*livala lia* Wafula). Wafula is the spirit for whom, many generations ago, the first sacrificial hut of this kind is said to have been erected. To the right of the entrance one places a leafy branch of the *lunyuvuti*-tree to afford shade to the ancestral spirits sitting in front of the sacrificial hut.

While the sacrifices offered in the *namwina* hut are primarily addressed to the spirits of one's father and grandfather as well as to more remote

[1] I have seen such triangular stone settings also among the Tiriki, Nyole, Marama, and Tsotso. They appear to be typical for all tribes to the south of the Nzoia River.

[2] In former times the old men are said to have spent a great part of their time sitting on top of ant-hills on the look-out for the enemy. It is believed, therefore, that ant-hills are the favoured abodes of the ancestral spirits.

ancestors in the paternal line, the offerings made to the female spirits are deposited at the centre post of the living-hut. They consist of sesame seeds as food for the spirits or of live fowls tied to the centre post, as it is believed that the spirits of the female ancestors have a preference for residing in the bodies of fowls.[1] Possibly this is one of the reasons why women may not eat fowls or eggs, although I could not get any confirmation on this point. Furthermore, one can invoke the blessing of the ancestral spirits for all kinds of objects (e.g. the seed to be sown in the fields, the harvest implements, the tools used by the diviner, &c.) by leaning them for one night against the centre post and letting them 'sleep' there. Weapons and traps for animals, on the other hand, are placed beside the centre post of the *namwima*-hut, as for these tools only the blessing of the male spirits is required.

Behind the living-hut, under the eaves, another type of sacrificial hut, called *wetili*, is occasionally erected. It consists of a tunnel-shaped, vault-like structure which is about a foot and a half long, 10 inches wide, and 12 inches high. It is constructed from the pliable switches (*tjindaa*) of the *gumulaa*-tree. The sacrifices offered in this hut (a small gourdful of milk or the spleen and a portion of the sacrificial animal's neck called *éndjasi*) are addressed in the first place to Malava, a younger son of the tribal ancestor Muvugusu. When Malava was still alive—so the story goes—it was his duty to herd his father's cattle. This has earned him the reputation of wielding particular power over cattle, and a sacrifice is made to Malava whenever disease breaks out among the livestock. Besides, sacrifices are offered in the *wetili*-hut for the less important spirits of old women. Offerings to the ancestral spirits of the great wife of the homestead are made on the point of a spear which one plants on an ant-hill outside the enclosure. The portion of the sacrificial animal dedicated to them is the fine, transparent skin (*gumuvia*) which one scrapes off the hide. As an offering to Wele, the Supreme Being, finally, a chunk of meat is pierced on the *sisuli*-staff of the *namwima*-hut or even of the living-hut (cf. above, p. 252).

An indirect shrine for the ancestral spirits is provided by the *namwima*-hut for frogs which has already been described (cf. above, p. 199).

Among the majority of tribes the burial sites of ordinary persons do not serve as ancestral shrines. The Vugusu, however, on certain occasions, perform rites at the grave of a family head (see below, p. 502). Permanent ritual attention seems to be paid only to the burial sites of clan-heads where these enjoyed a formal status (see below, p. 478).

The stone settings (*amagina gemisango*) of the Logoli and the *namwima*-huts of the Vugusu may only be erected at the homesteads of men who enjoy the full social status of a family head. Bachelors and men who have married but a short time ago and who still take their meals at their mother's place must go to the homestead of their father, their father's brother, or

---

[1] One says: 'The spirits are walking in the fowls' (*vamagombe vagendanga mutjingoxo*).

their elder brother if they wish to have an ancestral sacrifice offered on their own or their wives' behalf. The putting up of the first sacrificial shrine at his own homestead is thus an important event in a man's life, not only from the religious but also from the social point of view. However, even if the above-mentioned prerequisites have been fulfilled, one defers building such a shrine until an occasion for offering a sacrifice arises. Then the husband looks for suitable stones, and his wife brews beer from eleusine. When everything has been prepared he calls his father's brother or another old man of his clan to choose the appropriate site for the shrine, to put up the stones (*kwómbaka amagina*), and to plant the *olwovo*-staff in the ground. He also invites some other clan-elders as well as all close kinsmen and neighbours to come to his homestead for the 'sacrifice of consecrating the stones' (*omusango gwamagina*). For this purpose the owner of the homestead must procure a white cock. His father's brother who officiates as a sacrificial priest (*omusálisi*) takes the live cock and flutters it over the heads of the husband, the wife, and the children who line up before the door of the hut, and then on his own feet. Next, another old man belonging to the clan of the owner of the homestead ceremoniously spits *ovwanga* (eleusine flour stirred in water) upon the chests of the various members of the family, beginning with the father. While doing so he says to him: *mugase amitu*, 'may you thrive, clan-brother!' Meanwhile the *omusálisi*, carrying the cock in his hand, enters the hut and flutters it over the walls, the roof, and, particularly, the door-posts. Then he suffocates the cock and pulls out some of its feathers which he ties round the children's necks (but not the wife's). Next he cuts a few small pieces of meat from the cock and scatters them over the sacrificial stones, simultaneously sprinkling them with blood. A small chunk of meat he pierces on the *olwovo*-staff. While consecrating the sacrificial shrine in this way he summons the ancestral spirits with the words: *liradji yimu*, 'eat here!' Finally, he roasts the cock over a fire kindled out in the open and divides the meat amongst all male persons present who eat it on the premises together with eleusine porridge. It is essential that no one is left out, even if he gets only a tiny bit. Should one of the close relatives be absent, a small piece of meat is saved for him and sent to his hut so as to let him, too, partake of the sacrificial meal.

The sacrificial shrine having been completed, the beer brewed for the occasion is taken out in the yard and put down beside the shrine. Then the eldest child of the owner of the homestead steps on one of the sacrificial stones and sips a few draughts of the beer, while the *omusálisi* ceremonially addresses the child as 'grandfather'. The next one to drink is the child's father, then its mother, and, finally, the other persons present.

On the occasion of this ceremony of consecrating the ancestral shrine a cock and a hen are sometimes selected from which to breed the chickens to be sacrificed on future occasions.

An ancestral sacrifice must always take place at the homestead of the man on whose behalf (or on behalf of whose children or wife) it is performed.[1] It would be futile to make an offering at the shrine of a close kinsman, a neighbour, or a friend. The sacrificial rite, however (i.e. scattering the pieces of meat, sprinkling the blood and invoking the ancestral spirits), can never be performed by the owner of the homestead himself nor can a physical father do so for his own children. The sacrificial priest (*omusálisi*) must rather always be a (real or classificatory) elder brother or father's brother, or else any other old man of one's own clan. The only argument which my informants could advance in explanation of this rule of ritual conduct was that the ancestral spirits would refuse to accept the sacrifice if it were offered by the head of the family himself or by his physical father. The underlying idea, however, seems to be that the efficacy of the sacrifice is bound up with the display of the solidarity and cohesion of the clan or at least of a major group of kinsmen within the clan, and that the manifestation of this solidarity will please the ancestral spirits. This view is corroborated by the term for sacrifice, *omusango*, which means a union, a gathering, a concerted action, as well as by the sacrificial meal, in which 'all' kinsmen must participate if it is to serve its purpose. The social status of the priest officiating at a sacrifice must be higher the more important the occasion for which the sacrifice is made. At a comparatively insignificant sacrifice the brother of the head of the family can officiate as *omusálisi*; in rather more important cases one calls an old and influential man from one's own close kin, while the offering of really important sacrifices (e.g. the *liswákila* ceremony for the first-born child, or in case of serious illness of the head of the family, &c.) is the prerogative of the so-called *omusálisi munene*. He is the chief sacrificial priest of the clan who, on the grounds of his wealth, his character, and his membership of the oldest lineage of the clan, is regarded as the proper representative of the clan-community before the ancestral spirits. To quote from a text:

'. . . And every clan (*ehili*) must have an *omusálisi munene*. If there is serious illness in a house he must perform the sacrifices, for they know we have our man here (in the clan) whom we call *omusálisi munene* and that is good so. If we wish to perform a sacrifice we must call him quickly. Then he comes right away. And also those people who belong to a small clan have their *omusálisi* whom they call when they want to offer a sacrifice.'

When going to the *omusálisi*'s place to call him one must observe the same rule as when consulting a diviner. One must start off at dawn, tie a knot in the grass upon leaving one's homestead, and on the way one must not meet with any bad omens.

Although the *omusálisi munene* must belong to the oldest lineage of the clan, his office is not hereditary but personal, and he is chosen exclusively for his personal merits, for his reputation as a man of unblemished character and conduct, and for the confidence which his clansmen therefore place in

[1] Except in the case of men who have not yet attained full married status, cf. above, p. 283.

him, and not on the grounds of any former privileges. Nor does he receive any pay for the services which he renders to his clansmen as a sacrificial priest.

If the sacrifice is addressed to a definite ancestral spirit (for instance, in the case of an illness) who does not belong to the clan of the head of the family but to his mother's or his wife's clan, the sacrifice must be performed by (or at least in the presence of) an old man of the spirit's clan. Sacrifices made on behalf of a man's wife are often performed at the homestead of the wife's father, especially during the first years of their marriage.

The details of ritual procedure vary, according to the kind of the sacrifice and the nature of the occasion. The ceremonial observances described on the preceding pages (see p. 284) are, however, typical for the majority of sacrifices performed in cases of illness as well as in connexion with the various critical events and stages in the life of the individual. In many cases special features are added to the ordinary ceremonial procedure, such as the inspection of the entrails of the slaughtered animal (see above, p. 214 sq.), the smearing or spitting of the animal's stomach content on all persons involved in the sacrifice, as well as the tying of strips of its skin (*dzingovo*) round their arms, &c.

If the sacrificial animal is a sheep, a goat, or a cow, the *omusálisi*, before suffocating the animal, must squat beside it in front of the sacrificial shrine and with his right hand gently stroke its back while calling the ancestral spirits and informing them on the nature of the trouble or other cause for which the sacrifice is offered. At a sacrificial rite performed among the Vugusu on the occasion of the imminent marriage of a young girl I heard the *omusálisi* summoning the spirits with the following words:

Hee baba omutai kavola ari:
omwana omuxana niye vuvwonga luxafwa silanda efuvuxo.
Livusi, Vugelembe, Mudonyi na Vagitwika vavandi
omundu wenywe niyoyu!
mwidje mumusangasie
mugende vwangu!
naye niye xwivilile
atime kedje
alie halala nevavasie!
vamagombe mulangane mwavene
vavasava ne vakitwika
mugende vwangu
mulie enyama yenywe
muŋone munda.

He, father, the first man[1] has spoken thus:
'Matrimony binds a daughter (to her husband's clan) like the *luxafwa*-creeper,
Livusi, Vugelembe, Mudonyi and you other ones of the Gitwika clan,
Your person is here!

[1] Referring to the legendary first man who gave commandments to the Vugusu and taught them their tribal wisdom.

You may come and join her,
You may come quickly!
And whomsoever we may have forgotten (to mention),
He may hurry here, he may come,
He may eat together with all the others!
Spirits! You may call one another,
You of the Vasava and you of the Gitwika clan,
You may come quickly,
You may eat your meat,
You may feel well in your bodies!'

While the *omusálisi* summons the ancestral spirits in this manner and strokes the sacrificial animal's back, the latter must stand still and urinate. If it behaves in the prescribed manner this is regarded as auspicious for the success of the sacrifice.

As the preceding account of the sacrificial ceremony shows, its main objective is the establishment of a community with the ancestral spirits. Compared to this, the ideas of feeding the ancestral spirits (so as to appease their stomachs) and of making an offering (in the sense of parting with a valuable and cherished object) form only secondary motives. Such community is sought not only with the 'tame' and benevolent spirits of people who have died a long time ago, but also with the antagonistic spirits; for one hopes that by being invited to share in the common sacrificial meal with the living they will forget their grievances against the latter from whose community they feel they have been expelled (cf. above, p. 166). With the same intention one continues to acknowledge to the spirits the rights which they used to have in connexion with the sowing of the eleusine crop (cf. above, p. 99). Thus after the harvest when throwing to them some of the porridge of the first meal prepared from the new crops, one calls out: *Vivio wo nivievio, oxaloma ori: wandjivílile wambele viekumwigo!* 'This is for you, this is for you. Do not say "you have forgotten to give me of the year (i.e. the first-fruits)".'

Now the idea of establishing by means of the sacrifice a community with the antagonistic spirits appears to contradict the tendency we have mentioned above (cf. p. 166), viz. to effect a separation from the dead, to consider dream apparitions, hallucinations, and other forms of visitations by spirits as portents of illness and misfortune. To explain this seeming contradiction we must refer to the above-mentioned idea that the spirits of the dead are desirous of making their living kinsmen join them in the spirit-world, because they feel lonely and desolate. To counteract this desire of the spirits one does, on the one hand, everything one can think of to sever as effectively as possible the former bonds which existed between the deceased and his kinsmen and neighbours, thus drawing a clear dividing-line between the dead and the living. But as, on the other hand, the spirits of the dead are believed to be shadow-like beings and therefore omnipresent, one does not attempt to drive them away, an undertaking that would be futile, but maintains towards them a ritual fellowship viz. that of a sacrifice, hoping that they will be satisfied with this kind of community. Both attitudes in the last resort aim at separating the dead from the living, but the means employed differ. In one case one endeavours to ignore the connexion between the dead and the living, while in the other case one substitutes the sham community provided by the sacrificial meal for a real community in the spirit-world.

The same idea of establishing a community between the dead and the living and appealing to the ancestors for protection is also found in the name-giving rites which will be discussed in detail in the section dealing with the rites of passage (see p. 313 sq.). The bestowal of an ancestral name upon a child does not serve merely to placate the spirit concerned, but it is thought that he will henceforth adopt the rôle of a guardian spirit towards his namesake, protecting him from dangers which threaten from various evil agencies, appearing to him in dreams and giving him useful advice, dissuading other spirits from sending harm to his ward, &c.

(b) *Warding off and destroying persistently troublesome Spirits*

As we have already mentioned, those ancestral spirits which are fundamentally evil and permanently antagonistic to the living are not sacrificed to. Instead of wasting one's time on futile attempts at appeasing them one rather tries to render them innocuous by warding them off or even by destroying them. If they are the spirits of convicted *avalogi*[1] they are not buried in the customary manner in front of their living-hut, but in the swampy ground near a stream, upside down and without ceremony, for it is hoped that they will thereby be prevented from returning to the world of the living.

In the majority of cases, however, the fundamental wickedness of a spirit becomes apparent only from the fact that, despite frequent offerings made to him, he persists in harassing his living kinsmen in the form of nightmares, or that the oracles of the diviner time and again attribute cases of illness and misfortune to one and the same spirit. If on the ground of such experiences further sacrificial offerings are held to be futile, one calls (among the Logoli) the so-called *oguyavi* (derogatory term for the gravedigger). Against the payment of a calf he undertakes to excavate the bones of the troublesome spirit and burn them. The care which the *oguyavi* must employ when setting out to perform this job and the circumspection which he has to observe towards his client are described in the following Logoli text:

'... And when they go to the diviner for the third time[2] he will say: "Listen, who is responsible for your trouble is that person who has died; he

---

[1] For instance, witches who have died after having submitted to an ordeal or persons struck by lightning.

[2] i.e. after he has on three consecutive occasions attributed cases of serious illness to one and the same spirit.

lies wrongly in his grave. You must go and burn black ants."[1] Then that kinsman (lit. owner) of the patient consults another diviner and tells him, too, about the illness in his house. And the sick man's relatives visit the patient every day, even the distant relatives. Their hearts ache and they call out: "Oh, our child! What is it that is wrong with that house! It is really a bad matter!" ... And when they see that he has many visions and is constantly talking about the spirits, what we call *elievózavoza* (to be delirious), then they say: "It is necessary that somebody goes to the diviner, so that we may consult the oracles." Then they visit another diviner ... and he says: "You must sacrifice black ants." Then they consult one another and finally they agree (to take the diviner's advice). They call the *oguyavi* and when he comes to the patient's house he must stop at some distance; he cannot come right up to the house like ordinary people. The patient's kinsmen then kill a fowl for him; this he eats before he sets out to dig up that deceased person (a woman). Then he goes to the burial site together with the husband of that deceased woman who is causing the illness. When they arrive at the grave the husband stays behind at some distance and lets only the *oguyavi* himself go right up to the grave. The *oguyavi* carries with him a digging-stick, cut from the *elisazi*-tree. First he cuts down the bush which has grown on the grave. Then he begins to dig until he finds the bones. Now he signals by gestures to the man to come, so that they may put the bones into a basket of the *ekihinda* kind which he has brought along. When he has collected all the bones, he goes to fetch some very dry grass from the roof of a hut. With that grass he kindles a fire inside the grave. While those two persons (the *oguyavi* and the husband of the deceased woman) are staying there, they must not speak but must preserve complete silence. If one of them wants to call the other one, he may do so only by signalling with his arms. When they depart from there, the man carries the fire and the *oguyavi* the basket containing the bones of the dead woman. While proceeding to the place where they want to burn the bones they must not meet anyone. If they see somebody they must warn him by waving a stick at him, without, however, betraying: "We have a dead person or a spirit with us." Having arrived at the spot (where they wish to burn the dead woman), they must first light a fire. Then they must use it to set fire to the bones. The *oguyavi* must take great care not to sit in the smoke that rises from the fire. And the old man who has come with him must stay behind at a great distance; he cannot go near the fire. When the bones are burnt up the *oguyavi* says: "Now I can scatter the ashes." When he has done so he goes to the stream to bathe.'

Among the Vugusu persistently troublesome spirits (the so-called *visieno*) are rendered innocuous by trapping them and locking them up in a pot. For this purpose one calls a diviner into one's house. He drills a small hole into the wall of the hut and then holds a small clay vessel against the hole. Pretending that he intends to offer a sacrifice, he implores the troublesome spirit to come. After repeated enticing calls the evil spirit (in reality the diviner) replies that he has come. Thereupon the diviner instantly closes the clay vessel with a lump of fresh clay, and the spirit who wanted to enter the hut through the hole has been trapped in the vessel. Then the

[1] A circumlocution for the burning of the bones.

diviner places the clay vessel in an old, cracked pot, and on the next morning—after the house has been cleaned and all the rubbish has been emptied into that pot—he goes together with his client to a stream and buries the pot with its contents in the swampy soil of the valley bottom. While on their way they must not meet with anyone nor may they talk together.

To keep the *visieno*-spirits away from the vicinity of a homestead a small hut resembling the *wetili*-shrines is erected on either side of the path leading from the nearest stream (where the spirits are staying at night-time) to the homestead. The section of the path where these small huts are put up is carefully cleaned, and several *lusulu*-twigs as well as the feathers of a fowl which has been killed and roasted there are stuck into the ground beside the two huts. If then the *visieno*-spirits come along that path they will be terrified at seeing the two sacrificial huts and will turn back again.

Another method of keeping the *visieno*-spirits away from a house is to bury a live mole whose teeth one has knocked out, together with the neck of an old pot and the broken handle of a hoe in front of the door.

(c) *Tribal Sacrifices*

In addition to the family sacrifices that we have discussed, an important sacrificial ceremony on a tribal scale is performed among the Logoli. It is of particular interest because—apart from the common tribute rendered to the rain-maker among the Nyole (cf. above, p. 157)—it furnishes the only occasion on which all clans of the tribal community unite for concerted action, submitting to the authority of a single man, viz. the highest sacrificial priest of the tribe. The ceremony described in the following pages is limited to the Logoli, and—as far as I could ascertain—none of the other Bantu tribes of Kavirondo perform sacrificial rites on a similar scale.[1]

The tribal sacrifice among the Logoli is held regularly twice a year, in March or April when the eleusine crop enters the principal stage of its growth, and in September or October when the sorghum crop is growing. The chief objective of the sacrifice is to secure an ample harvest or at least to avert the danger of a crop failure. As in the case of other sacrificial rites, the two ideas of warding off or appeasing antagonistic forces and of invoking the help of benevolent and sympathetic forces are so closely linked that it is difficult to decide which one of the two ideas furnishes the principal motive for offering the sacrifice. Although it takes place in good as well as in bad years, the various native texts which I have taken down on this tribal sacrifice all emphasize the warding off of a harvest failure (and hence the appeasement of antagonistic forces) as the principal objective of the sacrifice:

'. . . Then the old men gather and say: "These days our country is not good, the seed is not good . . . the people have cultivated their fields, but in

[1] This I can state with certainty for the Vugusu, Tsotso, Idaxo, Isuxa, Nyala, Nyole, and Tiriki.

THE TAKING OF COUNTER-MEASURES

some places the seed is not growing, the eleusine will not ripen ... it is (therefore) good that we go on the hill and offer the sacrifice."'

In addition to the regular, semi-annual sacrifices performed to ensure the proper growth of the crops, a sacrifice on a tribal scale is said to have been performed also in the case of repeated failures in warfare, the ceremonial procedure in both cases being the same.

The tribal sacrifice appears to be primarily addressed to the Supreme Being, Isahi or Emungu, but also to the ancestral spirits (*emisambwa*) in general as well as to a certain Aŋoma who is said to have lived a long time ago, before the tribe of the Logoli was founded, and who appears to be identical with the *wele muŋoma* of the Vugusu. Aŋoma is also said to have been the first person who offered sacrifices to the Supreme Being (cf. the song on p. 293), and after him the site where the sacrifice is performed is called *haŋoma* or *muŋoma*. The significance attached to Aŋoma and to the other ancestral spirits in connexion with the tribal sacrifice seems to be that of an intermediary between living men and the Supreme Being. The sacrificial ceremony itself is called *ovwali* (cf. above, p. 282), a name referring to the fire which is an important feature of the ritual procedure. The sacrifice is offered on the slope of a hill in a rocky cave situated in a grove (*ekelongo*) which may be entered only by the sacrificial priests themselves.

The sacrificial priests (*avasálisi*) are two men of the Nondi clan which traces its origin to the oldest line of descent from the tribal ancestor (cf. p. 59). One of these two priests occupies a much higher rank than the other one, and he is referred to either as the *omumali wemisango* (the finisher of the sacrifice) or as the *omufwani wovwali* (the one who kindles the sacrificial fire). It is his task to perform all the essential duties connected with the sacrifice and to utter the prayers, while the second priest functions as his acolyte. The office of this chief sacrificial priest is hereditary, and the present *omufwani wovwali*, an old man by name Keyoga, is the fifteenth in the number of sacrificial priests whom the old men can list. According to Keyoga's enumeration which—with only a few omissions—was confirmed to me by two other elders of the Nondi clan, he was preceded by the following fourteen sacrificial priests:

1. Kiviri
2. Lukudzedzi
3. Nondi
4. Vudzudzu
5. Ndemesi
6. Mulwani
7. Ngovelo
8. Yisa
9. Nagonda
10. Ligu
11. Ndiya
12. Nabemo
13. Kihugwa
14. Matjayo

Before he dies the chief priest appoints his own successor. If none of his own sons possesses the qualifications required for this office (see p. 79) to a sufficient extent, he can appoint one of his brother's sons or even a more distant classificatory son, but never a sister's son, as the office of the *omufwani wovwali* must always remain in the clan of the Nondi.

When the sacrificial priest, in joint consultation with the heads (*amagutu*) of the other clans, has fixed the day on which the sacrificial ceremony is to be held, he sends out a number of messengers who, on the eve of the ceremony, make a round through the tribal territory, blowing on antelope horns and shouting in a high-pitched voice in a manner closely resembling the yodelling songs of the inhabitants of the Alps[1] to announce that the semi-annual sacrifice will be held on the following day. The horns which they sound serve at the same time as a warning to all people to stop working in their gardens until the day following the sacrifice. The messengers see to it that nobody infringes this rule. To quote from a text:

'When they have sounded the horns and they still find anybody on the field they catch him and take his hoe away from him. They give it to one of the sacrificial priests when they go to the *muɲoma* sacrifice. Unless the owner of the hoe brings a chicken to retrieve his property, "the great one of the *ovwali*" (i.e. the chief priest) retains it without questioning (i.e. without paying any attention to the opinion of the owner of the hoe).'

On the following morning at day-break the singing groups of the various clans pour to the sacrificial grove from all directions, the men armed with long sticks or spears, their faces painted in bright colours, the women adorned with *lande*-creepers or, nowadays, bougainvillea. They all assemble on a large pasture near the grove which offers room to several thousand persons, for they may not proceed to the immediate vicinity of the sacrificial cave. Meanwhile the *omufwani wovwali* and his acolyte prepare the various ritual acts. Before setting out for the sacrificial grove they empty a pot of beer specially brewed for the occasion. It must have been placed for one night at the base of the centre post of the chief priest's hut, to be blessed by the ancestral spirits (cf. above, p. 282). The two priests drink this beer out of a special double-necked pot which is used only on that occasion.[2] While they are drinking no other person may be present in the hut. Other old men of the Nondi clan, however, may simultaneously partake of the same beer and even drink out of the same pot, if they possess very long beer-tubes through which they can suck the beer while themselves sitting outside the hut.

Before the sun rises the two priests repair to the sacrificial grove to kindle the *ovwali*-fire and to slaughter the sacrificial animal. The animal selected for that purpose (a white hen or a white goat) is supplied by an old man who, like the sacrificial priest himself, must be without blemishes (*dzimbala*); and so must be a second old man from whose hut the firebrand for kindling the *ovwali*-fire is procured. Besides, the chief priest selects two young girls (who must be virgins) to collect the firewood, grind the eleusine flour, and carry it to the place in front of the sacrificial hut.

First the chief priest goes to the pasture below the sacrificial grove on which a great many people have assembled in the meantime. There he

---

[1] They call: *holoyiu layie, holoyiu holoyie haye.*
[2] This pot must have been made by an old woman who no longer maintains sexual relations with her husband.

kindles the *ovwali*-fire, burning in it grains of sorghum and of a number of other plants and grasses[1] the smoke of which is to please and appease Isahi and Aŋoma. If the smoke ascends straight to the sky, this is interpreted as a sign that the sacrifice is welcome to them:

'When they kindle the fire they must watch the smoke: if it rises straight upwards, they can rejoice, but if they see that the smoke is bent or crooked, the people can say, "Our country is not good".'

As soon as the sacrificial priest has kindled the fire he sings a song addressed to Isahi or to Aŋoma in which all people join:

> *Aŋoma kitjyo uhu uhu*
> *asamba vwangoma ehe ehe*
> *otaleka Maina nahia aha aha.*
>
> 'Aŋoma himself, uhu, uhu,
> He kindled the fire at this place, ehe, ehe.
> Don't forsake Maina that he might perish, aha, aha.'

Maina, the younger brother or son of Aŋoma stands, in the context of this song, for the tribe of the Logoli. The song implores Isahi not to let the Logoli perish but to give them credit for the unbroken tradition of sacrifices which had begun already with Aŋoma. In other versions of the same song Aŋoma himself is addressed.

While the chief priest and his acolyte, after having kindled the *ovwali*-fire, repair by themselves to the sacrificial cave, the multitude continues to sing the same song (*okukélemana*). While they sing, each of the thousands of people present throws a few ears of grain which he has picked from his field into the fire. In addition to the above-mentioned song they sing a number of war- and victory-songs, at the same time brandishing their spears and pointing them towards the country of the Jaluo (the chief enemies of the Logoli) which they can see in the distance spreading out at the foot of the range of hills on which the sacrifice takes place. They continue singing these songs throughout the time during which the sacrificial priest performs the second part of the ceremonial procedure, viz. the killing and the offering of the sacrificial animal in the cave.

In the interior of the cave is a hut from the centre post of which a drum, the chief object of ritual importance, is suspended. This drum (*eŋoma*), which is about 2 feet high, is said to have been kept in the rock cave for many generations and to have been carved from the trunk of a tree which the Logoli felled in their former abode to the south of the Kavirondo Gulf and then carried across the gulf in a boat. It would appear that there is a connexion between Aŋoma, the mystical ancestral spirit, and this drum (*eŋoma*), a point, however, on which, despite frequent attempts, I could not obtain any enlightenment. In addition to the drum the cave—so I was told—also contains several beer-pots and antelope-horns.

[1] The names of these plants are: *omuguluka, omusundzu, ekilusu, oluvinu, ekisugi, eminu, elisazi*. Some of them are employed also as means of warding off evil magic.

Before the chief priest can begin to make the offering he and his acolyte must first clean the interior of the cave which they have not visited since the preceding sacrifice. They remove spider-webs from the pots and the drum, restore the horns that have dropped on the ground to their proper place in a horizontal rock crevice, anoint the drum with ghee (*amaguta*), and sweep the floor of the cave. Then the chief priest stirs some eleusine flour in water and blows the mixture (*ovwanga*; cf. above, p. 281) 'upon the chest' of the drum, uttering the following prayer while doing so:

> *Mwinye kumwamala kudzia milova*
> *mumenye milova nemilembe*
> *nakwinye kwatigala kumenye mwoyo nemilembe*
> *mugásidze omwana watigala*
> *akole miyindzi.*
> *mutavola kwamivilila mba.*

'We have placed you into the earth for good,
May you rest in peace in the earth,
And may we, we who have stayed behind, live in peace,
May you bless the child[1] that has been left behind,
May it perform (its work).
Do not say that we have forgotten you.'

As this prayer shows, the sacrificial priest implores the ancestral spirits to reconcile themselves to their fate and not to return to the world of the living, but at the same time to bless the living. It is said that the ancestors manifest their approval of the sacrifice offered to them by causing the drum to be filled with a roaring noise (*lifuma*).

Winding up the *ovwali* ceremony, the second priest roasts the sacrificial animal in the yard in front of the sacrificial hut, where the two priests consume it jointly with the clan-heads and the other influential old men.

While formerly all clans of the Logoli tribe assembled at the same rock cave at the place called *ekelengo*, in the course of the last few decades a second sacrificial shrine of a similar nature has been established on a hill called *itavwongo muguva*. Here the clans living in the eastern part of the tribal territory perform a corresponding sacrifice at the same times. In their cave, however, they do not possess a drum, but merely pots and horns. The setting up of this second sacrificial shrine was attributed by my informants to the rivalry between the two clans of the Nondi and the Lógovo which resulted from the claim of the Lógovo to participate in the office of tribal priesthood.

---

[1] Referring in this context to all living persons.

PART IV
THE RITES OF PASSAGE
A. BIRTH
(1) INTRODUCTORY

THE event of childbirth has a twofold social significance. Through it a new individual enters the community and has to be socially accepted and accorded a place in it, and through it a man and a woman acquire the status of parenthood. These two aspects of childbirth form an integral unit and cannot be dealt with separately. As childbirth establishes a system of new social relationships, the analysis of the observances connected with this event must view this change in relationships and all that it involves, as well as focus its attention upon the infant who enters the community. While from this point of view the social situation at the birth of the first child differs from that at the birth of subsequent children, the difference is one of degree rather than one of kind, as each new childbirth re-establishes and thereby strengthens the status of parents and grandparents, uncles and aunts, brothers and sisters, and so forth. The chief task of the present chapter is to show how these relationships first become established and what functions their ceremonial enactment fulfils.

(2) CONCEPTION AND PREGNANCY

The conventional attitude towards having children, the differential valuation of male and female offspring, and the economic place taken by children in the family organization are general factors which form the wider background of the cultural situation of childbirth as distinct from its biological aspect. As these factors are discussed in other sections of this book (cf. p. 47) we do not need to restate them in detail, but it may suffice to indicate their general implications. They indicate that childbirth is a highly welcome event, that it enhances the husband's and the wife's status in their respective groups of kinsmen, that the ceremonial procedure connected with it differs according to the sex of the child, and that, in its wider ramifications, the new situation will affect not only the immediate family but the kindred of both parents and, particularly, the father's lineage and clan. The following analysis of observances connected with childbirth will show to what extent and in what manner these indications are confirmed.

Owing to the fertility of Kavirondo women, conception, in the vast majority of cases, takes place without any resort to artificial measures such as the taking of medical herbs or the performance of magical rites. As records show, most women conceive during the first year of married life, but there is no feeling of alarm if pregnancy does not occur within that time. It is usually not until fifteen to eighteen months have passed since the consummation of marital relations that anxiety is felt that 'something might be wrong with the husband or wife'. The varying periods of time which elapse before a married woman is pregnant for the first time were attributed by my informants to differences in the capacity of women for sexual enjoyment. It appears from accounts given to me by a number of married men that the psychological state of shame and fear which has been induced in the bride by all the circumstances of the marriage procedure (cf. below, p. 427) often causes a long initial period of frigidity during which the young wife is supposed to be less likely to conceive. I am not able to say, however, whether this view is generally held or not. It is thought that frequent cohabitation increases the probability of the wife's conception, and this belief appears to be one of the reasons why indulgence in excessive intercourse by newly married couples is socially approved of and why the husband's real brothers may have sexual access to his wife before she has conceived for the first time. The first days after the end of the wife's period are regarded as the most favourable time for conception as then 'she would feel an increased desire for sexual intercourse and quickly experience orgasm (*xuxuinyala*) which would cause the seminal fluid (*vutíu*) to enter the womb (*nasáiye*)'. As an aid to conception women are said to remain lying on their backs after cohabitation while if they do not want to conceive they stand up and shake their bodies in a quick jerking rhythm.

If a woman does not conceive in due course, the husband consults a diviner, as her failure may have a number of different causes each of which calls for a different method of cure or counteraction. These causes are all of a mystical order, and counteraction is, accordingly, limited to a magical procedure. I have never heard of any attempts to remove the causes of barrenness by administering medicines alone or by performing any manipulations with the reproductive organs. The cause most frequently 'detected' by the diviner is alleged sorcery by a co-wife or another woman who harbours misgivings or feelings of jealousy towards her; other supposed causes are the breach of a taboo (avoidance) by the wife or the anger of the ancestral spirits. If repeated efforts to detect and counteract these various causes remain futile, the husband, if he is still childless, may suspect that he himself is responsible for his wife's failure to conceive. He will then tacitly agree to his wife's taking a lover. This may be either his brother or a person of the wife's own choice who, however, must belong to the husband's clan and with whom she must have no further relations after she has conceived. As far as I could discover, the husband does not submit to any treatment of a magical order to remove the cause of his disability, nor does there seem to be any native theory that accounts for it.

Women soon know that they have conceived, not only from the cessation of their monthly period, but also from a number of other signs which girls are instructed by their mothers to observe when they get married. Thus

PLATE 11

Idaxo novices dancing in their grass masks

PLATE 12

Dance of the novices: Idaxo

a darkening of the breast-nipples, a slight protrusion of the navel, recurrent morning-sickness, and chills in the evening are considered early signs of pregnancy. When the wife knows that she is pregnant she tells her husband about her condition, as she knows that the news will please him and cause him to be friendly towards her. It would, however, be considered bad manners to mention the fact of the wife's pregnancy in the presence of children or strangers, but there is no particular secrecy about it, nor is the wife considered to be ritually unclean or dangerous during the time of pregnancy. It is common knowledge that it takes nine months to bear a child and that the time of parturition can, therefore, be approximately predicted by the expectant mother. The most common method of doing so is by keeping count of the agricultural seasons. If a woman has first noticed her state at the time of the first 'digging for millet', she knows that the child will be born when the millet gets ripe; if at the time of the millet harvest, the child will be born during or soon after the weeding season, and so forth. Some women are also said to count the 'moons' by placing nine sticks in the roof of their hut and removing one at every new moon.

As this account of the ideas regarding conception shows, the Kavirondo realize that the child is the joint product of both husband and wife. Although, as we have seen, conception can, in native opinion, be prevented by the interference of spirits and other mystical agents, these agents can never positively become the cause of pregnancy, nor is it thought that the child's mental or physical characteristics are in any way subject to the influence of mystical agents. It is thus realized that conception can only be caused by the sexual union of man and woman. Deficiencies or major abnormalities in a child are commonly attributed to incestuous intercourse. If it is beyond doubt that the marital relationship between husband and wife does not infringe the laws of exogamy, the birth of an abnormal child is quite logically attributed to incestuous adultery on the part of the wife. The child in that case is put to death and the wife—apart from being severely blamed for her alleged misconduct—has to undergo a purification ceremony, and a sacrifice is made for her before her husband resumes sexual relations with her. A miscarriage which occurs suddenly and without causing much pain to the woman is regarded as the consequence of an act of adultery committed by the wife during her pregnancy. It is said in that case that the child was killed in the womb by 'the thighs of her lover'. Suspicions of adultery are also raised if parturition occurs too soon (after seven or eight months) or if the child is stillborn. On the other hand, if a miscarriage occurs during serious illness of the wife, it is considered a consequence of her illness which is thought to have been sent by an *ombira* or an *omulogi*, and the wife is not held responsible for what has happened to her. In practice, I have never heard that a wife after a miscarriage was openly accused by her husband of having committed adultery.

Inquiries which I have made into the native ideas concerning the processes of conception and growth of the embryo in the womb have yielded vague results only. Those uncertain ideas which I have found to exist on these matters do not appear to be relevant from the point of view of social structure, that is to say, they do not affect the native ideas on kinship, paternity, or maternity and therefore do not interest the average native. Moreover, most statements elicited by me on this subject did not appear to be expressions of previous or even conventional lines of thought laid down by the tribal tradition, but rather seemed to have been made up *ad hoc*. As far as they go, they concur in claiming that the father's share in the child is the more essential one. From him comes the child's soul and its physical features (*evifánanyu*), while the mother's share mainly consists in bearing the body of the child. At the same time it is admitted that a child's features may take after both parents; it is then considered normal that a son should resemble his father and a daughter her mother. I have heard the retainers of the Vugusu chief joke to him because his daughter had to a remarkable degree inherited her father's face. The chief replied —rather embarrassed—that this could not be helped as it was 'a matter of God'. The determination of the sex of the child is likewise considered 'a matter of God' and not dependent upon the conditions and circumstances relating to conception and pregnancy. Nevertheless, as we have seen in a previous chapter, the wife is blamed if she bears daughters only. As Christopher Mtiva writes in his life-story: 'In our country a husband cannot feel friendly towards his wife if she bears daughters only. My mother was, therefore, very happy when I was born, because she knew that now my father would begin to like her again.'

Summing up these remarks, it may be said that the ideas of the Bantu Kavirondo on the respective shares of husband and wife in the process of procreation are essentially indifferent. They do not reflect the social structure to any marked degree, nor do they constitute a force that serves as a sanction for the rights and privileges resulting from the social stress on unilateral descent.

The pregnant woman (Lurogoli: *okuva nenda*, 'to be with womb'; Luvugusu: *xuésia*), not being in any way considered unclean or ritually dangerous, is not the object of avoidances, nor does she have to observe any avoidances herself. She continues her usual life, works in the field, grinds, cooks food, and stirs the porridge if she is physically able to perform these duties. During their first pregnancy many women are said to feel weak and lazy and incapable of doing much work. The only definite rules which pregnant women have to observe pertain to food. Some of these are intended to prevent the foetus from growing too big and thus rendering parturition difficult. Among the Vugusu a pregnant woman— particularly during the last three months before delivery—must drink no milk and eat no ripe bananas; among the Logoli she mainly lives on thin porridge and sorghum gruel and avoids the thick maize and millet (eleusine) porridge. If she has given birth once and has had an easy delivery, she may relax these rules during her next pregnancy. Apart from these rules, which appear to be of an empirical nature, there are others which are of a magical order. Everywhere a pregnant woman must avoid eating meat from the ribs and back as well as the heart of a cow. A violation of these food prohibitions is said to block the passage for the child and to prevent the placenta (*engovi*) and afterbirth from coming out. 'They would stick in the belly and kill the mother.' Most pregnant women also have their own individual food preferences and avoidances, because 'the child in the womb wants (or refuses) these things'. Thus some women refrain from smoking during pregnancy, others refuse every kind of meat, and others again feel a desire to eat clay off the walls of the hut or to chew certain roots that they pick for themselves. If a pregnant woman suffers much from constipation, she consults a woman herbalist (*omwahi wolunyasi*), who gives her a concoction of certain herbs. During the last stages of pregnancy a woman must not lift heavy things and must refrain from bathing, as this is thought to cause premature parturition.

The husband may continue to have sexual connexion with his wife until the seventh or even the beginning of the eighth month. From then on sexual intercourse is said to be harmful to the child, as it would make it 'weak and liable to die at the first attack of illness'. If the body of the newborn child happens to be covered all over with *vutiu* (literally: seminal fluid, but actually referring to the amniotic liquid), this is taken as a sign that the husband has disregarded the rule of continence and has continued to have sexual connexion with his wife until shortly before the child was born. He is then scolded and abused *in absentia* by the women who have come to assist his wife. However, no action is taken against him, nor is any rite performed for the child to neutralize any bad effects that the husband's alleged misconduct might have upon it.

If a woman gets very lean during pregnancy and generally feels weak and sickly, this is taken as an indication that she will bear a son; if, on the other hand, she stays plump and fit, she thinks that she will give birth to a daughter. This rule is claimed to work out in most cases, but no explanation for it could be given to me, nor do any definite ideas seem to be held as to the time when the sex of the embryo (*akilisiagali*—still a lizard) is determined.

If pregnancy takes its normal course, no ceremonies of any kind are performed for the benefit of the expectant mother. She does not even wear any charms to ensure an easy delivery or to protect herself against sorcery or the evil eye. It is remarkable that in spite of the numerous dangers and uncertainties inherent in pregnancy and childbirth, no need is felt for protective magic, although, as we have seen, miscarriages under certain conditions are attributed to sorcery.

If the pregnant woman frequently suffers from pains, her father-in-law performs an *okugásidza* (well-wishing)[1] ceremony for her. For this purpose he requires a hen, which is supplied by the wife's husband or father.

[1] Lit.: to cause to become well.

He tells his daughter-in-law to stand in the yard of the homestead in the presence of any relatives who care to be there and, fluttering the live hen over the pregnant woman's whole body, he says to her:

> 'You may recover,
> You may be well,
> You may bear the child well.'

Then, addressing the child in the womb, he says:

> 'If you are a girl-child you may be born well,
> If you are a boy-child you may be born well.'

After these ceremonial utterances of well-wishing over the pregnant woman and the child, the father-in-law sets the hen free again. Ordinarily, no further ceremonies or sacrifices are performed until the time of delivery arrives. Should pregnancy last beyond the month during which the birth of the child is expected the husband goes to ask an elder of his clan for his advice and the two together go to consult a diviner. Such a delay is always attributed to the interference of a troublesome ancestral spirit (*sisieno*), but the diviner has to detect which spirit is responsible and what sacrifice he demands. The sacrificial animal is then killed by the *omusalisi* (the sacrificer), who sprinkles its blood over the sacrificial stones, calls the names of the various ancestral spirits, and then divides the meat among the relatives who have come to witness the sacrifice. Unless the sacrificial animal is a fowl, the pregnant woman may partake of the meal.

(3) DELIVERY

No preparations of any kind take place when the time of delivery approaches, as it would be considered inauspicious to do so. This attitude falls into line with the general belief that it brings bad luck to anticipate the positive outcome of a risky and anxiously hoped for event by engaging in any preparations for it. This belief still prevails among many Christians, and missionaries complain that even Christian expectant mothers often cannot be persuaded to sew clothes for their child or to give any thought to other things which they will need as soon as the child is born.[1]

In Kitosh no definite place is prescribed where delivery must take place; it may either be inside the house or outside, wherever the labouring woman who feels restless and bent on moving about happens to be. Among the Logoli, Nyole, Tsotso, and Tiriki it is a definite rule that the child must not be born inside the hut, but either under the eaves behind the hut, in the back yard, or in the banana-grove behind the house. If, however, the woman is taken by surprise with a quick delivery while working in the field or walking on the road, this is not considered a mishap of magical significance. Nor is it held to be improper or unlucky if the child is born at the homestead of a stranger. I once took a labouring Logoli woman by

---

[1] Similarly the natives have a prejudice against repairing their granaries before having reaped the new harvest.

motor-car to a hospital, but owing to a breakdown of my car on the muddy road the child was born half-way at the homestead of a pagan Nyole. This did not cause any embarrassment on either side, and I was assured that 'according to old custom' also such a situation would not have necessitated any ritual action. It seems, therefore, that it matters little where the child is born as long as it is not born inside the hut.

When the woman begins to feel the pains of labour (*okulumwa*, to be bitten) she sends her husband to call her mother and sister and two or three old women from the neighbourhood who have experience in assisting women in childbirth. There are no real experts in midwifery, however, and these old women merely perform a neighbourly duty without receiving any pay for their services. The wife's mother-in-law and other relatives of the husband may also be present and help, but women in labour are said to prefer the assistance of their own mothers. The husband must be away while his wife labours, but he may see the child immediately after it is born and before other persons are allowed to come near it. His absence during the time of delivery is demanded partly because he observes a rule of avoidance towards his mother-in-law and partly because assistance in childbirth is considered a woman's job. My informants denied that it had any ritual significance, nor is it attributed to a feeling of shame on the husband's or the wife's part. This is confirmed by the fact that the husband may be called by the women to hold his wife if delivery should prove exceptionally difficult.

It is considered normal for a woman to be in labour twelve to fourteen hours before the child is born. No medicines are given for the purpose of shortening the intervals between labour pains. Only when there are indications that the presentation of the child will be abnormal, an old woman who has the knowledge of the appropriate medicine is called, and she administers a concoction of the dried and pounded leaves of a herb to the woman. This is supposed 'to turn the child in the womb, so that it gets into the right position'. The chief activity of the old women who act as midwives consists in preventing the labouring woman from resting; they urge and admonish her relentlessly to press and push as much as she can and scold her for her laziness whenever she wishes to relax. If the labouring woman gets exhausted and gives up all efforts of her own for lack of strength, she is held up in a kneeling position and one of the women holds her mouth and nose so that she cannot breathe, the idea being that the pressure of air in her lungs will then push the child out. When parturition occurs, the woman kneels on the ground, clasping one of the veranda poles or seeking support from the women who stand round her. The child is placed on a layer of banana-leaves and, as soon as the placenta (*engovi*) comes away, either the wife herself or her mother cuts the umbilical cord (*olulera*) with a blade of sharp grass (Lurogoli: *oluhu*; Luvugusu: *luxevétjwe*). Both are then buried by the wife's mother, either inside the hut near the wall or behind the hut at a secret spot, so that they may not be tampered with by an *omulogi*. The remainder of the umbilical cord is tied off with fibre and left to heal. No care is taken to prevent the navel from becoming ruptured; as a consequence one frequently sees children with a large protruding navel that sometimes reaches the size of an orange and is regarded by native parents as a welcome adornment of their children. Strangely, such protruding navels seem to disappear later in life, as one sees very few adults whose navel is of abnormal size.

If the placenta does not come away quickly, a woman expert is called who gives the mother a certain root to chew. As an alternative it is pounded and a concoction made from it is given to her to drink, while at the same time another specimen of the same root is beaten against her head and a third one rubbed along her back and then passed between her legs.

If the child does not come after twenty-four hours or more of labour, recourse is had to the fowl-fluttering and *okuvida*-rites. The woman's husband calls his father, who comes with a hen and a rooster. In the same manner as during her pregnancy he touches or strokes the whole body of his daughter-in-law, first with the rooster and then with the hen, uttering the following words as he does so:

> 'The baby how is it? Why is it not to be born?
> We married you, so that you may bear people!
> The child may come forth well from the womb!'

Then he sets the hen and the rooster free and, taking some millet flour and mixing it with water into *ovwanga*, spits the mixture over the woman's chest and utters the same spell again. If the child is not born after the performance of these two rites, nothing else is done and the woman is abandoned to her fate. The performance of an operation to create a passage for the child is unknown. If the mother dies in childbirth, no efforts are made to save and rear the child; it is left to die from hunger and exposure even if it was quite capable of surviving. My informants insisted that this attitude is not due to a belief that such a child would be unlucky or otherwise afflicted with some mystical disabilities, but that it is merely due to the difficulty of rearing it. As in a polygynous household there should be little difficulty in finding another woman who could suckle such a child, it appears, however, more likely that the true motive behind this sort of passive infanticide is the ambiguous status which such a child would have in the community.

(4) THE RITUAL SITUATION AT CHILDBIRTH

The birth of a child gives rise to a complex social and ritual situation which is characterized by a variety of notions: (1) The new-born child is deemed to be in a state of ritual dangerousness which becomes effective in two ways. The one is that the child is exposed to dangers that threaten it from contact with other persons who may have committed acts that, in a mystical way, are opposed to the child's welfare. The other is that the child itself becomes a source of ritual danger to other persons who come into contact with it. (2) The mother is in a similar ritual condition to the child, but the dangerousness of her condition is one-sided: other people have to avoid her, but she has nothing to fear from them. (3) The normal sex-relation between husband and wife, having been interrupted through the wife's pregnancy and the birth of the child, can only be resumed after the observance of particular rites. (4) The child has to be socially accepted by its father's and mother's relatives so that the kinship bonds between the child and its various relatives may be ceremonially established. A preliminary condition of this social acclamation is the testing of the child's legitimacy. (5) After the birth of the first child (and to a lesser degree after the birth of any subsequent child) the social relations between the husband and the wife and their respective in-law relatives undergo far-reaching changes which are given a ritual expression by the ceremonies following childbirth. (6) A bond between the child and the ancestral spirits must be established and the child accepted into the magico-religious community of its lineage and clan.

These notions, which together constitute what might be called the ritual situation at childbirth, form the basis of a complex ceremonial procedure which accompanies and ritually elaborates the biological processes of the mother's confinement and the early care and rearing of the infant. As empirical and ritual behaviour are closely interwoven, and as each stage in the ritual procedure derives its significance from a variety of notions and, moreover, contains other features which still evade any attempts at interpretation, I shall in the following give a descriptive account of the procedure in its approximate chronological order rather than attempt a systematic analysis of the ritual expression of each of the notions which I have mentioned.

The ceremonial procedure that follows childbirth comprises three major phases: (*a*) the period of seclusion for mother and child which coincides with the mother's physical confinement; (*b*) the termination of the period of seclusion and the presentation of the child to its relatives; (*c*) the performance of the first sacrifice for the infant.

(5) CONFINEMENT AND RITUAL SECLUSION

As soon as delivery is over and the afterbirth has been disposed of, the mother with her infant is led inside the house. Owing to their state of ritual contamination the two may not enter the hut through the front door but must use the side door (*ekyandangu*) which one of the co-wives of the young mother, or a person corresponding in status, opens for her. 'If they were to enter through the front door the infant would die' is the explanation offered for this rule. The same prohibition, however, applies to different people in a variety of situations[1] and on each of these occasions

[1] Similarly the newly appointed clan-head (cf. above, p. 82) enters the hut by the back door.

it has a different sanction. Inside the house, a bedspread has in the meantime been prepared for the mother and her infant at the usual sleeping-quarters, the *evulili*-partition (cf. vol. ii). It consists of several layers of banana-leaves of a special variety which the husband went to cut as soon as he heard that the child was born and which were carried home and spread out in the hut by the husband's sister. The women who have acted as midwives then go home and leave the mother and the infant in the care of one or two close relatives who sleep with her and generally look after her and the child. They also cook for the husband and do all the housework for the next few weeks, until the young mother again feels strong enough to resume her usual activities. The persons who perform this nursing duty (*avwalikilili*) are usually the unmarried sisters of the husband and occasionally the wife's sisters or even her mother, provided that she is an old woman who is past the age of child-bearing.

The mother's confinement in the hut lasts for two days if the infant is a girl and for three days if it is a boy. During that time no strangers may enter the hut to see the mother or the child. To warn any would-be visitors against entering the hut and to announce at the same time the news of the birth to passers-by, the husband suspends a small triangular piece of cow-skin (*ekesélo*) from the middle of the doorway if the infant is a boy, and a piece of calabash (*engogoto*) if a girl. During the period of confinement the wife may leave the hut only through the side door to go down to the nearest stream to bathe. Great care must be taken that no one sees her while she bathes or even while she is on her way to and from the stream, as anyone 'who was to see her would turn pale'. To ensure the wife's privacy, her husband clears a path through the bush leading to a section of the stream where its banks are hidden by dense bush or tall grass. He also closes the path against trespassers by marking it in such a way that people will know its significance and refrain from using it. During the daytime the husband may enter the hut and see both his wife and his child, but he must stay in the front partition, the *vuhilu*, where he also takes his meals. The nights he spends either with his other wives or, if he has only one wife, in the bachelor hut (*esimba*) of one of his clansmen. He is free to carry on courtships during that time (*okudzia mbavakana*, to go into the girls), but these sexual relations with other persons render it ritually necessary for him to stay away from his wife and his child.

Soon after the mother has entered the hut with her infant she is given a calabashful of water to wash herself and her child. Ordinary water is used for this purpose, but sometimes pounded roots are added by the mother which are supposed to protect the child from getting fever. After the child has been washed, it is wrapped in a soft and pliable piece of calf- or goat-skin and put on the bedspread of banana-leaves by the side of its mother.

By this procedure, however, neither the mother nor the child becomes ritually clean. The *ovwivu*-smell with which both are said to be afflicted for the next few weeks can only be removed by the performance of a rite and not by physical cleanliness.

In the case of a first-born child the mother waits for a whole day before she suckles the infant; any subsequent children may be suckled an hour or two after they are born. In explanation of this custom I was told that a mother who has given birth for the first time does not have milk right away and that, if she has milk, it is thin and watery and unfit for the child to drink. Apart from this physiological explanation, the custom also has its sociological meaning as it serves to differentiate between the first-born child and subsequent children. A mother always begins to suckle her infant at her right breast and then puts it to the left, irrespective of whether it is a girl or a boy. In the case of twins the first-born is always given the right breast and the second-born always the left. If a mother does not have sufficient milk of her own she drinks a concoction made of the dried and pounded leaves of a tree called *omusala gwamavele* (tree of milk). Besides, it is the husband's duty to see that she is given plenty of milk to drink, both fresh and sour. If, in spite of these aids, a mother cannot suckle her child, she is normally assisted by one of her co-wives or a neighbour who has more milk than she needs for her own infant. Occasionally infants are reared on cow's milk only. In that case they are given additional food, eleusine gruel and cooked and mashed bananas, as early as a week after they have been born. In areas where milk is scarce I was told that babies are fed with cooked bananas and gruel right away; the millet is then, however, ground several times.

In Kitosh an infant is given cow's milk to drink before its mother suckles it for the first time. A few drops are poured into its mouth through a funnel-shaped leaf or by means of a small calabash which is held against its chin. It is said that the reason for this initial feeding with cow's milk is 'to open the baby's mouth'. The baby is henceforth partly suckled by its mother and partly fed with cow's milk. Adult persons mention the fact that they were brought up on cow's milk when they brag and boast at beer-feasts to show that at their mother's home there was no scarcity of milk. It seems, therefore, that feeding small infants with cow's milk serves as a means of social (economic) differentiation and, at the same time, as a symbolic action by which the future wealth of the child is to be assured.

Infants are never fed at regular intervals but whenever they are hungry and cry.

During the ritual seclusion in the hut the young mother must strictly observe certain food rules. For the first two days she is given only thin gruel and cooked bananas and no heavy food like *ovukima*, a thick paste made from millet or maize. While eating she must take care not to touch the food with her hands, nor must she take her meals from dishes or trays which are to be used again by other persons:

'When they give her food she cannot eat from a plate (*oludjú*), nor from a wooden bowl, nor from a skin, but they bring her the leaves of a tree which we call *omusundzu*. She cannot "*okumega*" the food (i.e. take off pieces with the first two fingers and the thumb of her right hand, the usual way of eating thick porridge or paste), because she must not touch it with her hands, but her sister-in-law must feed her.'

Until she has regained her full strength a young mother is supposed to be given large quantities of strong and rich food, such as beef, strong beef broths made from the bones of the back and the legs, and plenty of milk. To provide such food for his wife is one of the husband's main duties during that time. If he fails in this respect and neglects his wife's need for extra rations, he may be sure to have this held against him on the occasion of future matrimonial quarrels, not only by his wife but also by his relatives-in-law. To supply his wife regularly with meat the husband goes round among his clansmen and neighbours and tells them that his wife 'got rid of her burden and now refuses to eat vegetables'. This hint that he is begging for meat is understood by everyone and he may count on being given a piece of meat wherever an animal is being slaughtered or where there is meat in the house. Besides, close relatives both on the husband's and on the wife's side as well as neighbours are expected to send meat and milk to the young mother on their own account.

Before the period of ritual seclusion in the hut comes to an end and the infant is presented to its kindred, the legitimacy of the child is tested. When the husband and his sister go to cut the banana-leaves for the wife's bedspread they obtain at the same time a bunch of bananas of the *endahúlulua* variety 'which must be pulled only and not cut with a knife'. The husband's sister who carries this bunch of bananas home must take it into the hut through the side door, while the husband himself enters through the front door. Then his sister hands him the bunch of bananas and he suspends it either from the attic shelf or from one of the hooks (Lunyole: *sirenyelo*) which protrude from the wall of the sleeping-partition and are used by the wife for hanging up her skin and other personal utensils. The infant is then placed underneath this bunch of bananas so that the gum-like sap which oozes out of the stem where it has been pulled off drops down on its body. The test of legitimacy then works automatically: 'If the wife has conceived the child in an adulterous union, it will die, but if it was begotten by her legitimate husband it will live.' As an additional test the bananas are cooked and given to the mother to eat. If the child is the offspring of an adulterous union it will die as a consequence of the mother having eaten the bananas, otherwise it will be spared. There is no rigid time-limit within which the child has to be either alive or dead as the result of the test. If the infant happens to die within a few days of the performance of the 'test' its death will be attributed solely to this cause; as time passes, other causes would be recognized as well, until finally the test, or rather its implications, have been quite forgotten as a possible cause of the infant's death.

After the child's legitimacy has been tested the women who act as nurses cut some banana-leaves, likewise of the *endahúlulua* variety, into streamers and make them into a sort of skirt (*mulivu*) which they tie round the mother's waist. This *mulivu* she must wear until the end of her confinement, when she exchanges it for the customary garment, the tail and the belt of fibre tassels. Although no ready explanation of the significance of this custom was advanced by my informants, it seems obvious that it symbolizes the ritual condition of the mother and particularly marks the fact that during her confinement she must practise continence. This interpretation is supported by the fact that a woman must wear the same kind of skirt after her husband's death when she is in an analogous ritual condition and likewise must practise continence. Moreover, 'sexual status' is commonly marked by the garments that women wear round their loins. The size and length of the tassels differ for unmarried women, for married women who have borne children, and for old women who have passed the menopause. Furthermore, the fact that the skirt is made of the same plant which is used for the test of legitimacy suggests that it has a sexual significance.

(6) THE TERMINATION OF CONFINEMENT AND THE PRESENTATION OF THE INFANT TO ITS KINDRED

When the two or three days of the mother's confinement have passed, both the mother and the infant are presented to her kindred, an occasion which gives rise to an elaborate feast and to a ceremonial procedure. If the infant is the first-born child the feast furnishes the first occasion on which the husband's mother-in-law 'formally' visits the house of her son-in-law and 'establishes contact' with her daughter's mother-in-law. It is significant for the native conception of marriage that the social relation between the husband's and the wife's parents is not fully established at the time of their children's marriage, but only after the birth of the common grandchild. The wife's mother, accordingly, is the chief person among the visitors who come to see the child. While all of them bring small baskets with grain as presents for the wife, her mother comes with an elaborately prepared assortment of gifts. The importance of her gifts on this occasion is best conveyed by a quotation from a Nyole text describing the care with which the mother prepares for this first visit to her daughter's house:

'On the third day word is sent to the wife's kin, "Your daughter has finished to bear the child" (i.e. the time of her confinement is over). Then the mother of the "girl" (i.e. of the woman who has borne the child) buys eight *evivambala*-fish and meat in an *enduvi*-basket; she takes both raw meat and dried meat; she begins to fill a *sitinyilo*-basket with eleusine and an *enduvi*-basket with sorghum. Then she puts peas into a pot by themselves, simsim-seeds by themselves, beans by themselves, and also salt by itself. Next, the meat is put into the *sitinyilo*-basket and they pour the eleusine over the meat (so as to cover it). (Likewise) the fish are put into the *enduvi*-basket and the sorghum poured over them.'

All these small baskets and pots are then placed in a large basket and on top of it all is put the meat of a castrated goat. One of the mother's co-wives ties *amalande*-leaves round the basket and a young girl 'who is still to go to a husband' starts off in the morning for the daughter's place, carrying the basket with the gifts on her head, accompanied by another girl who carries a load of firewood.

In the meantime the child's mother, assisted by the women who look after her, sweeps her hut clean and rolls up the bedspread of banana-leaves which she hides away in a place where nobody will find it. Then she takes a bath in a stream and both she and the infant are shaved before the visitors arrive. While the young wife thus prepares herself and her hut for her visitors, her mother-in-law cooks food for them in her own hut near by.

When all the visitors have arrived the wife's mother and her party ceremonially enter the hut. The young girl, carrying the basket with the gifts, enters first, then follows the wife's mother, after her 'the tier of *amalande*', and finally, the girl who carries the firewood. They first stand in the front room (*vuhilu*) and then 'the tier of *amalande*-leaves' (*ombohi welilande*), after having tied the *amalande* to the centre pole, leads the party into the *evulili*-partition of the hut where they put down their gifts in front of the wife and the infant. Having presented their gifts, the visitors repair to the yard again.

When everything has been prepared for the further procedure the young mother takes her child and comes out with it through the front door. As she steps out she cuts off the string from which the piece of skin or calabash has been suspended (cf. above, p. 304). The period of seclusion in the hut is thereby brought to an end. Now the mother puts her child on a banana-leaf placed across the furrow formed by the water dripping down from the roof in front of the door. Standing in the doorway in front of her child, she shapes her hands into a cup and her unmarried brother-in-law pours some drops of water into it from a calabash. Then she opens her hands and clasps them, so that the water drops down on the baby lying in the furrow below. Then the mother steps across the child and picks it up again.

The next phase of the procedure consists of the ceremony of ghee-rubbing. The ghee (*amaguta*) which is used for this purpose must come from a 'cow of the yard' (*eŋombe yomugizi*), i.e. a cow which has either been caught in war or bought in exchange for grain, and not from a cow of the bride-wealth. While the ghee is being fetched from the hut of the husband's mother, the husband and his wife, together with the child, sit down in the doorway of their hut facing the crowd of visitors which has assembled in the yard. The procedure during the following ceremony shows some variations according to the different accounts given to me. Among the Tiriki and Logoli the husband's mother hands the tray with ghee to her husband (i.e. the infant's paternal grandfather), who then rubs in turn the infant, its mother, and its father, applying the ghee with a certain stick called *lúvaya*. Among the Nyole the ceremony is performed by the young girl who has carried the food basket from the home of the wife's mother. She first applies some ghee to the infant's mother by dashing it across her forehead with the palm of the right hand; then she does the same with the infant. Now she hands the tray to the infant's father, who himself rubs his face with ghee and then passes it on to his mother, who likewise rubs herself but applies the ghee to her feet only. With the remaining ghee the young girl finally anoints herself. Then trays with cooked bananas are brought for the people who have been anointed with ghee. When they have finished eating, the infant is again taken into the front room of the hut and the 'tier of *amalande*' takes the *amalande*-leaves off the centre post and ties them round the infant's body. As a payment for this service she is given a hoe.

Now food is brought for the visitors, many trayfuls of meat and porridge being placed in front of the various groups that sit together in the yard and inside the hut. Eleusine porridge is dished up in front of the honoured guests, such as the wife's mother and the other senior members of her kin, while the young and unimportant visitors have to be satisfied with the less tasty sorghum porridge. However, before the visitors begin eating, the husband's mother, the 'hostess' of the feast, showers abuse upon her guests, addressing the most staggering insults to the mother of her son's wife. In the presence of all the guests she defames her daughter-in-law as a lazy, good-for-nothing girl who, when she visits her people, never comes home with proper presents for her husband and her husband's relatives. She also accuses her daughter-in-law's family of stinginess and contrasts the poor assortment of gifts brought to-day by the mother of her daughter-in-law with the ample amount of tasty food which she herself has cooked for her guests and which, as all can see, is just being dished up. Winding up these rude remarks she says: 'Now let us give you food and when you have eaten you may all go home.' But now it is the turn of the wife's mother to take offence and to refuse (*okutumba*) the food by pushing away the dishes which have been placed in front of her. To *okutumba* food that has been specially prepared and offered to the visitor is ordinarily a grave insult to one's host and thus a proper retort to the preceding speech of 'welcome'. The husband's mother tries to persuade her guests to eat, but they insist on first being given a present. The usual payment on this occasion is a goat for the wife's mother and a fowl for her sister who has joined her mother in refusing to eat the food offered to them. When these payments have been made no further obstacles are in the way and the two groups of relatives can sit down to their first common meal.

When they have finished eating all the food cooked by the husband's mother, the food basket which the wife's mother has brought along is displayed. As the eleusine and the sorghum are poured out of their respective baskets the various kinds of meat and fish, as well as the pots with simsim, peas, beans, and salt, are revealed. The husband's relatives then show their approval of this pleasing variety of gifts, thereby admitting that they have been too rash in accusing the wife's mother of stinginess.

Before the wife's mother and the other visitors return home they kindle a fire in the wife's hut, using the firewood which they have brought along from their place. This fire must be kept going for the following six days during which the mother of the infant may not yet do any work in the house. Among the Nyole, visitors who want to smoke their pipes on the way home must light them at this fire as, on this particular occasion, they must refrain from lighting their pipes by 'borrowing fire' at houses which they pass on the way.

A few weeks after this ceremony, when the wife feels strong again and the infant's skin has become 'really black', she pays a visit to her mother, taking to her the bundle of banana-leaves which served as her own and her infant's bedspread during her confinement. This visit is called 'to take the *ovwivu*' (Logoli) or 'to send the leaf' (Tsotso) to the wife's mother. Her mother buries these leaves at a secret place. Among the Vugusu this visit paid by the wife to her mother and the sending away of the *ovwivu* indicates to her husband that his wife is now willing to resume sexual relations with him. It is followed by a small beer-feast to which neighbours and relatives on both sides are invited but at which no rites are performed. On the night following the beer-drink the husband for the first time touches the infant. As his wife hands it to him she says: '*Mayi* (or *baba*) *tjiánio rarao ali*', 'Mother[1] (or father), go to where your father is!' The husband holds the child for a moment caressing it and then hands it back to his wife. From now on he can touch the child whenever he wants to do so and even look after it and feed it when the mother is away and no other nurse is available. On the night after he has touched the child the father resumes sexual connexion with his wife.

The only restriction of a sexual nature which the parents must observe during the period of lactation is to refrain from sexual intercourse whenever the infant is sick, as otherwise 'the child would refuse to suck and eventually die'. With this exception, sexual intercourse between the parents not only does no harm but is even deemed to be beneficial for the health and development of the child. The period of continence should, therefore, not be extended for more than two months after the birth of the child, and it is definitely regarded as 'bad for the child if the parents have not resumed sexual relations by the time the child begins to smile'. In that case the husband must kill a sheep. He thereby neutralizes the evil consequences which the prolonged separation from his wife might otherwise have for the child.

Among the Logoli sex-relations between husband and wife may not be resumed until after the *liswákila*-sacrifice—which we shall presently describe—has been performed for the child. If, however, for some reason the performance of this sacrifice should be unduly delayed (for instance, if

---

[1] It is customary to address small children as 'mother' or 'father'.

the husband cannot find a suitable goat), the husband can evade the prohibition by having an iron wristlet made at a smithy and putting it on the child's right arm. This iron wristlet then protects the infant against the ritual dangers which its parents' sex-relations would otherwise have for it.

(7) THE LISWÁKILA RITE

When a child is about two or three months old it is deemed to be time to perform the *liswákila*-ceremony, the first ancestral sacrifice offered on behalf of the child. The occasion for this sacrifice is not determined by any unusual or alarming condition of the child, but it is performed with the general intent of inducing the spirits to adopt a benevolent attitude towards the child or at least to refrain from interfering with its health. In addition to its professed purpose the ceremony is hedged round with numerous other observances which, as we shall see, serve to initiate the child into the wider groupings of its paternal and maternal kin and to lend ritual expression to the husband's and the wife's new status of parenthood.

The proposal to perform the sacrifice comes from the husband. One day when he is sitting with his father and mother he mentions his desire 'to kill a goat for the child as it is still an *omusinde*' (i.e. a person for whom no sacrifice has yet been performed). If his father approves of his son's suggestion he looks for a male goat which he selects, if possible, from his own herd. It must be a fine specimen that has no blemishes or shortcomings (*edzimbala*), and it may therefore take him a considerable amount of time to find the proper animal. In further preparation for the sacrifice the child's father digs out an *oluvinu*-plant growing on his land, taking care that in removing it he does not cut off any of its roots or branches, as he must carry it home in perfect condition. The plant itself, like the goat, must be free from any flaws, such as diseased leaves or withered branches. When he has brought it to his yard he cuts it into many small pieces which he spreads out in the sun to dry. Then he starts off to summon the various people who have to officiate at the sacrifice. First he goes to the *omusálisi* (the sacrificer), an old man of his clan whose duty it is to dedicate the goat to the spirits and to make the offering to them. Next he calls on the *ombidi*,[1] the 'blower of *ovwanga*', another old man of his clan, then on a person 'whom he calls brother' (*omundu wolanga awenyue*), and whose duty it is to cut the skin-wristlets and to put them on the arms and round the necks of the persons taking part in the ceremony (Lunyole: *ombixi wexixova*; Lurogoli: *ombiki wedzingova*). When all these have agreed to come and perform their various duties he fixes a day for the sacrifice and invites all his kinsmen (*aviko*) to attend. On the afternoon before the sacrifice is to take place the 'blower' comes and ties the sacrificial goat to the centre post of the husband's hut where it remains until next morning.

[1] A noun derived from *okuvida*, to blow.

On the following morning the 'kinsmen of both sides', i.e. of both husband and wife, must assemble in their full number; 'as long as even one of the *aviko* has not yet come they cannot begin with the sacrifice'.[1] Then the husband unties the goat from the centre post and leads it through the front door out into the yard for the *omusálisi* to examine it. If he has satisfied himself that it is in perfect condition (having carefully inspected its teeth, ears, eyes, hoofs, &c.) he strokes its back while muttering words such as the following:

> *Ai, ai, mwana agase, gasa,*
> *ombili gukuhulilane vulani muno.*
> 'Ai! Ai! The child may be well, well,
> the body may become strong indeed!'

If the goat has behaved properly during this procedure, i.e. if it has stood quietly and urinated, he hands it to the child's father or to his younger brother to be killed. They slowly suffocate it (*okumiga*) by tying a string round its mouth and plugging its nostrils with the leaves of the *oluvinu-*plant. Then they skin and gut the animal and when the stomach and the entrails are exposed the *omusálisi* and the 'blower' together with the other old men inspect them for good and bad signs. They examine the walls of the stomach for blisters and the entrails for their colour as general signs of the auspiciousness of the sacrifice. Particular attention is then paid to the position of the spleen. 'If they see that the spleen lies down (i.e. flat along the wall of the stomach) they say that the "spearshaft" (*oluvango*, often used as simile for the clan) is crooked, and when they see that it stands up they say that the child will be healthy. But if they see that the spleen lies down they say that the child will die.'

When the entrails have been thus inspected the father of the infant or his younger brother performs the ceremony of piercing the stomach (*okufúdula ekifu*). First he inflates the stomach by blowing air into the oesophagus and tying it off with a piece of banana-bark. The old men then observe whether the stomach stands up properly, and if they have accepted the position of the inflated stomach as auspicious, the child's father (or his younger brother) taps its walls and utters words of well-wishing, such as:

> *Hango hagase!*
> *omwana aviruke!*
> 'The homestead may be well!
> The child may grow up!'

After he has done so an old man of the father's clan takes the infant and then the other children who are present and makes them all touch the inflated stomach. Then the child's father pierces the stomach with his index-finger, thus letting the air escape. The whole ceremony is addressed

---

[1] The full participation of the kindred of the person in whose name the sacrifice is offered is an essential prerequisite for its success.

to the ancestral spirits who are said to be hovering about the place and to be pleased when they hear the noise made by the escaping air.

The 'blower' now takes the stomach content (*ovosé*) which leaks out of the hole and rubs it first over the infant's chest and then over the chest, shoulders, and back of the mother, while the father takes only a little *ovosé* and rubs himself with it. Then the 'blower' ties the oesophagus round the mother's neck while 'the putter of the wristlet' cuts some long strips from the edge of the goatskin. These strips he makes into small armlets which he puts on the right arm of the infant and on those of the other children of that homestead.

Now it is the turn of the 'blower' to perform the 'blowing' or spitting of *ovwanga*. Both the water and the eleusine flour used for this ceremony must have been ritually consecrated by having been placed against the centre post of the hut during the preceding night. Both ingredients are taken from there by the child's father, who also makes the *ovwanga* by mixing the flour and the water to make a thick paste. When the *ovwanga* has thus been prepared the child's father and mother sit down in the doorway of the hut and the 'blower' stands in front of them, holding the calabash filled with *ovwanga*. He takes a small sip and, facing the rising sun, blows the *ovwanga* towards it and calls: 'The sun when it rises in the east brings milk and health with it, and when it sets in the west may it take the badness along with it to the west!' Then he takes further sips and in turn blows or spits the *ovwanga* over all the members of the family, beginning with the father, the infant, and the mother.

When this last phase of the offering has been performed the meat of the goat is roasted and dished up on wooden platters (*evivu*), together with eleusine porridge. After the *omusálisi* has fed the mother and touched the infant's lips with the roasted meat and porridge, all the people who have come to attend the ceremony join in the sacrificial meal. Before they disperse to their homes the *omusálisi* takes the head and the skin of the goat as well as the calabash with the remaining *ovwanga* and places them against the centre post of the hut where they 'sleep' for one night. Early next morning he returns, and with the dried branches of the *oluvinu*-plant kindles a fire at the base of the centre post to burn the things which he had placed against it. He utters no words while performing this rite, but silently watches the smoke which must rise straight into the roof of the hut if the sacrifice is to be accepted by the spirits.

(8) NAMING

In the chapter on the ancestor cult we have already pointed out the religious significance of one category of personal names, viz. the ancestral name (Luvugusu: *lisina lia guga*; Lurogoli: *elieta lia guga*). I shall now discuss more fully the whole range of names, their choice, function, and the manner of using them, as well as the procedure at the various naming rites.

In the course of his life every person is given three different types of name: (1) the name of his childhood, (2) the name of his adolescence (*elieta lie lusóleli*), and (3) the ancestral name. Frequently he is given not only one but several of each of these different kinds of name, so that an adult person may altogether have as many as eight or ten different names.

The first name, that of childhood, is chosen unceremonially by the infant's mother while she is still confined to her hut. As she caresses the child a number of pet names may come to her mind and will be casually used by her. These are heard by other children, her husband, or neighbours, and eventually one of these names is given preference and thus comes into general use. These names refer to particular characteristics of the season, to some conspicuous event that happened during the mother's pregnancy or delivery, or to peculiarities of the child itself. Although their choice is to some extent dictated by convention, the same names do not recur very frequently. The range of even the more customary names comprises several hundred, so that a wide margin is left to the imagination of the infant's mother. These informal names always have a meaning, but as a rule the noun or verb from which they are derived undergoes a slight change which is subject to convention.

Among the Vugusu boys' names frequently take the prefix *wa-* and girls' names the prefix *na-*. Thus a child who was born during a heavy rain might be named *Wafula* if a boy and *Nafula* if a girl; a boy born during harvest time might be called *Wegesa*, a girl *Negesa*.[1] One of my informants was given by his mother the two informal names *Wanyama* and *Xaoya*, the first one referring to the fact that there was plenty of meat (*enyama*) in the house when he was born, and the second to the rinderpest epidemic which was rampant at the time. Incidentally, this custom of naming a child after a conspicuous event that happened at the time of its birth in some cases makes it possible to trace the age of a person and to compare the relative ages of two persons. In other cases it enables the bearer to know at what time of the year he was born. However, as only a small fraction of the names given refer to events which would be remembered for years or decades to come, it seems very improbable that the idea of recording a person's age by his name enters as a determining factor in the choice of names. Persons are equally often named after pleasant, unpleasant, or indifferent events or objects, and no mystical relation is thought to exist between the (childhood) name of a person and the event or object which it signifies.

The second name, that of adolescence, is also given informally. A male youth receives this second name from his age-mates when he has passed through the circumcision ceremonies and become 'a new one' (*omuhia*). A young woman is given her second name by the girls with whom she sleeps in the same hut when she reaches the age of puberty, 'when her breasts begin to form'. Much the same as our nicknames, these names refer to

---

[1] The prefixes *wa-* and *na-* and the initial vowel *e* of the nominal stem are contracted to *we-* and *ne-* respectively.

physical or mental characteristics and peculiarities of the person upon whom they are bestowed. They are usually very coarse and realistic, but this fact never seems to cause embarrassment to their owners. Like nicknames, too, they are seldom given on a particular occasion but, as a rule, come into use gradually. Once they have become firmly established they replace the childhood names, and adult persons would regard it as disrespectful if they were still addressed by their former names, except by very close relatives and old people who have known them since their infancy. Among Christian natives the place of the traditional names of adolescence has been taken by the biblical names bestowed on them either at baptism or when they become registered members of the Church community. These biblical names have been accepted whole-heartedly and are commonly used, not only by the Christians themselves but also by their pagan friends and relatives. They offer a rare example of a change where the new element fits exactly into the traditional pattern.

The most important name, although the one least frequently used, is the ancestral name. In contrast to the other two names it is ceremonially bestowed upon the child and its choice has to be carefully considered. Among the Logoli the naming ceremony takes place within the first four weeks after the infant's birth, either as a separate ceremony or in connexion with the *liswákila*-rite. Among the Vugusu the time for ceremonially bestowing the ancestral name upon a person depends upon his physical condition. If a child grows up normally and its health never gives any cause for anxiety to its parents, the *lisina lia gugawe* (the name of his grandfather) is bestowed on a boy only when he has passed through the circumcision rites, and on a girl when she is betrothed and the wedding-feast is about to take place. This indicates that the possession of the ancestral name is a necessary condition for acquiring the status of an adult person, but that it is not absolutely necessary for the welfare and growth of the child. However, if an infant cries a great deal or refuses to suck, or if in later years the child suddenly gets ill, it is ceremonially given an ancestral name, as it is thought that its condition has been caused by a deceased ancestor who wants the child to be named after him. I was told that about seventy-five out of a hundred people are thus named during their infancy or childhood. If a child dies before it has been given an ancestral name it is remembered by its informal name of childhood only. No ancestral name is given to a child posthumously, nor is a child hurriedly named if it becomes obvious that it is going to die.

To reach a decision in a particular situation as to whether the child should be named and to discover the ancestor whose name should be chosen, the child's father or its maternal uncle consults a diviner. This preliminary procedure may be dispensed with only if the circumstances leave no margin of doubt as to what the appropriate name should be. This would be the case, for instance, if the child's paternal or maternal grandfather has died during the mother's pregnancy, as then his name would obviously be the one to be chosen. Also if the child's father died during the mother's pregnancy his name would always be chosen, regardless of any other persons who may have died during that time. If, however, the mother died in childbirth the infant, if a girl, is not named after her but is called *Mufuvi* (female orphan) and, if a boy, *Wafuvwa* (male orphan).

Even if a diviner is consulted in order to find out the appropriate name, the range of names from which he may take his choice is limited by a number of considerations. First of all, a male person can only be named after a male ancestor and a female person only after a female ancestor. This is in accordance with the belief that men can suffer harm from and enjoy the protection of male spirits only and women of female spirits only. Another general rule is that a child can never be named after the spirit of a person who has died without being married or who though married died without leaving issue. Furthermore, the number of spirits who are deemed to have a potential influence over the child and whose names must, therefore, be considered is restricted to the clans of the eight great-grandparents of the child. Of these again the spirits of its paternal and maternal grandparents are given preference, and of the remaining spirits again those with whom relationship can be genealogically established. Among the Logoli spirits are thought to 'cool off' after their bodies have been dead for about five years and the choice is, accordingly, restricted to spirits of those who died during the last few years before the child was born. In Kitosh, on the other hand, spirits of persons who have died ten or even twenty years ago may still be 'detected' by the diviner as wishing to have their name bestowed upon the child.

The qualities of character possessed by the spirits while they were still living beings are not taken into consideration when the ancestral name is chosen. I was assured that even the names of thieves who have been killed by lynching might be given to children to save them from being haunted by their spirits. Nor does the fact that a spirit during his lifetime had the reputation of being a sorcerer or a witch bar his name from being suggested by the diviner. The only ancestral spirits who are excluded from the choice are those who during their lives suffered from leprosy or who died from being struck by lightning. Such people are buried in the damp soil near a stream where 'their spirits cool off quickly, so that they cannot come back and trouble the living people'.

These various limitations of the choice of the ancestral name show that the margin of choice which the diviner has in making his suggestion is narrowed down to a comparatively small range of names. By skilfully interviewing his client he will soon be able to discover which of these spirits the latter thinks likely to be troubling the child or for what name he shows a preference for some reason or other. Even then the diviner does not actually mention the name of a particular spirit but gives ambiguous hints, the meaning of which can be stretched by his client so as to fit his own ideas as to what would be the most appropriate name for his child.

It thus appears—though this is hardly realized by the native himself—that the chief purpose of consulting the diviner is to have one's own choice confirmed and approved of by the diviner's authority rather than to leave the choice of the name entirely to the diviner and passively to accept his verdict.

If the child does not recover from its illness or its particular complaint after the naming ceremony has been performed, it is said that 'the spirit refused to have the child named after him'. In this case the father goes to another diviner who suggests the name of another spirit. This procedure may be repeated several times, and if the child finally gets well it retains as its permanent ancestral name the one which it was given just before it began to show signs of recovering. If a child dies shortly after it has been given its ancestral name, no other children will be named after that spirit as it is feared that they might suffer the same fate. If, on the other hand, a child thrives well after having received the name of a certain spirit, other children are preferably given the same name. Thus it happens that the names of some spirits become popular while those of others are dropped altogether. The number of children who may be named after the same spirit is not limited.

As spirits are thought to be jealous of one another the dilemma may sometimes rise that the naming of a child after one spirit causes another spirit to become angry, because he thinks that his name should have been chosen instead. This situation is most likely to arise when naming a child whose grandfathers are both dead. Theoretically the paternal grandfather should be given preference, but if the maternal grandfather has died more recently or if he was an influential person it is thought that his spirit may feel offended by being made 'to wait'. In that case the dilemma is solved by naming the child after both ancestors simultaneously. The one is then called the 'head' and the other the 'servant'. When the child is being named, the 'head' is implored to 'come and carry the sleeping-skin of the child' and the 'servant' to 'come and carry its milking-gourd'. The task of protecting the child is then divided between the two spirits: the one sits on the child's sleeping-skin and guards it against disease, while the other takes care of the child's milking-gourd and promotes its growth. Usually the honour of being the 'head' is reserved for the paternal grandfather but not always, the decision being left to the diviner who, I was told, takes the respective social positions of the two *vasagwa* into consideration.

What then is the particular nature of the bond which the bestowal of an ancestral name upon a child establishes between the spirit and the child? The fact that acute illness or a prolonged state of poor health furnishes the occasion for naming a child, and that in choosing the name no discrimination is made between the spirits of good persons and those of bad persons, seems to suggest that the bestowal of an ancestral name merely serves to placate a spirit who proves to be particularly troublesome. Naming would thus merely be a means of neutralizing an evil force. From the evidence I have this actually seems to be the prevailing idea among the Logoli. Among the Vugusu, on the other hand, this merely negative aspect is more than balanced by the notion that the spirit after whom the child has been named becomes its guardian spirit, the idea being that it will not only refrain from harming the child but that it will also protect it. The spirit wants to be remembered by his living relations and so 'he scratches the child' (i.e. he makes the child ill) to inform its father or maternal uncle of his desire to have the child named after him. The initiative to do so is left to the spirit; the child is, therefore, not named as long as it grows up healthily. If it were to be named anyway, the spirit whose name it was given might refuse to fulfil his duty of guarding the child and kill it out of spite.

Once a spirit has accepted the role of guardianship and has restored the child to health the latter has no more to fear from him. 'A spirit after whom a child has been named never harms his namesake.' Should the child get seriously ill again, it does so owing to the evil work of a sorcerer or another spirit and in spite of the protection granted by its name-spirit, but not because the latter has withdrawn his protection or even reversed his attitude by sending harm to the child. The kind of protection which the name-spirit will offer is the same as that granted by other spirits whose goodwill one has secured by the performance of sacrifices. He tries to dissuade other spirits from sending harm to his ward and even summons them for assistance if harm threatens the child from other mystical agents, such as sorcerers or witches. A person does not enter into any communication with the spirit after whom he has been named, nor is it necessary to make regular offerings to him. When sacrifices are offered to the ancestral spirits, the name-spirit is called along with the others to partake of the meal, but there are no special sacrifices addressed exlusively to him.

From what has been said about the relationship prevailing between a spirit and the child named after him it appears that there is no idea of a reincarnation of the spirit in the body of the child. The only features in the whole complex of beliefs and practices connected with naming which might suggest the existence of such an idea are: (1) that parents—especially on ritual occasions—often address their child as 'father' and 'mother' or 'grandfather' and 'grandmother', and (2) that a child is hardly ever named after persons who have died since it was born. On the other hand, the name relationship is characterized by a number of notions which appear incompatible with the idea of reincarnation: (1) The ancestral spirit continues to exist independently after the child has been named after him; he does not enter the child's body but moves back and forth between the various abodes of spirits and the child's sleeping-skin or milking-gourd and, later on, when the child has become a grown-up person, the roof of his hut. (2) The child is often named after two spirits, the 'head' and the 'servant', and the name of one spirit may be given to several persons who are alive at the same time. (3) It is not thought that any physical or mental similarity exists between the child and its name-spirit or that such a similarity gradually develops in the course of the child's life. (4) In connexion with the naming rites there is no feature which might be interpreted as a symbolic enactment of the ancestor's rebirth in the child, nor is there any linguistic evidence to that effect. In Luvugusu the expression *xutiuxa lisina* and in Lurogoli *kugúlika elieta*, 'to bestow a name', are used with reference to the ancestral name as well as to the informal names of childhood and adolescence. Of the spirit it is said that 'he wants to walk in the footsteps of the child' when he makes the child ill and that 'it pleases the spirit to hear its name used'.

The evidence which speaks against the existence of the notion of reincarnation of ancestral spirits thus clearly outweighs that which speaks for it. But even if the bestowal of the ancestral name upon a child is not based on the idea of reincarnation, it appears from the above data that it aims at something more than merely keeping the memory of the deceased person alive. By being assigned the active role of a guardian over the child named after it the name-spirit is given a purpose and a function among the living. The intimate relation that is established between the spirit and the child lets the former have an active share in the 'life of the living' and thereby bridges the dangerous gulf between the living and the dead. Psychologically, the bestowal of the ancestral name appears therefore as an attempt of the living to arrive—so to speak—at a *modus vivendi* with the weird phenomenon of death and the dreaded spirit-world. The custom of addressing a small child as *dada* or *mama* or even as *guga* or *guku* (grandfather or grandmother), respectively, would in this sense have to be interpreted as a 'gesture' towards the ancestral spirit which is thought to please it, just as it enjoys hearing the child being called by its name.

The rite of naming a child is simple. In Maragoli it is performed by the real or classificatory brother of the child's paternal grandfather. For a male child the naming ceremony takes place early in the morning. Standing in the yard in front of the door the mother holds the child, and in the presence of the child's father and any neighbours who care to come, the (classificatory) grandfather puts an iron wristlet (*engulikwa*) round the infant's right arm and says words like these:

> *Edzimoni dzikulave,*
> *nuloli omusigu omwanguhe,*
> *nanganga yive elieta lia dada wowo.*
>
> 'The eyes may be bright (to you),
> if you see the enemy you may be quick,
> I am calling you (by) the name of your father.'

Then he utters the name. When the child has outgrown the wristlet the father puts it into a small pot which he keeps inside the house.

A girl is named in the evening after the sun has set and not outside in the yard but inside the hut in the *vuhilu*-partition. The ceremony is likewise performed by the brother of the child's paternal grandfather, but no *engulikwa* is tied round the girl's wrist.

Among the Vugusu both boys and girls are named during the daytime and in the same manner. The mother stands or sits in the doorway holding the child and covering herself with her sleeping-skin. The ceremony is performed by the father's young brother or by the mother's brother, according to whether the child is going to be named after a paternal or a maternal ancestor. He stands in front of the child and, taking a sip of beer from a new gourd and spitting it against the sleeping-skin, utters the name of the spirit and in words such as the following implores him to come and to cease troubling the child:

> *E, baba Songwa widje xangu!*
> *Wava nive osolile ori,*
> *nafwa ndie ngá, omugumba,*
> *luno ogane Songwa,*
> *wamwene widje.*

> 'Oh, father Songwa come quickly!
> If you have grumbled thus:
> "I died as an *omugumba*" (a man without issue),
> now you may be pleased, Songwa,
> yourself, you may come!'

The spirit after whom no one has yet been named is here compared with a man who is childless, i.e. with a man who feels lonesome and neglected.

If a child is simultaneously named after two ancestors the ceremony is performed jointly by the 'young father' (i.e. the father's younger brother) and the maternal uncle. The two spirits are then called to come at the same time:

> *Wandjusi ne Xaemba munenwa ne munenwa*
> *lisielo lilala mwixale*
> *mugende xangu*
> *omwana axaxola kamatexele*
> *ne mulinywe mweŋene mwakame,*
> *omundu wase aole.*

> 'Wandjusi and Xaemba, friend and friend,
> you may sit together on one skin,
> you may walk (and come) quickly;
> the child may not suffer from weakness,
> if it is you only (who cause the weakness),
> you may stop to do so,
> my person (i.e. the child) may recover.'

After the names of the spirits have thus been mentioned and the spirits themselves have been implored to come, the young father (or the maternal uncle respectively) slips a wristlet of skin or iron (depending upon the diviner's orders) over the child's right arm if a boy and over the left one in the case of a girl. The wristlet is made anew for each child and is later preserved in a small pot as among the Logoli. When the naming ceremony is over the mother remains seated for a while, still holding the child and leaning with her back against the post and facing the rear of the hut. While she is sitting there a wicker door is placed against the centre post, so that she and the child are hidden from the view of other people. The ceremony ends with a beer-drink and the ceremonial killing of the 'goat of naming' (*embusi eye xutiuxa*).

If a boy has not been given his ancestral name during infancy or childhood he is named by his maternal uncle on the day when he leaves the circumcision hut (*ligombe*). The rite is performed in conjunction with the giving of commandments by the maternal uncle, the boy standing in front of the circumcision hut, holding a shield, sword, spear, and club. While uttering the ancestral name the maternal uncle spits beer from a new gourd against his nephew's shield, a procedure which corresponds to the spitting of beer against the mother's sleeping-skin. The ancestral name in this case is chosen by the father or maternal uncle without any previous consultation of the diviner.

A girl who has not previously been named receives her ancestral name either shortly before or on the day of her wedding (*siselelo*) while standing on her mother's sleeping-skin and being anointed with ghee (cf. below, p. 413). Otherwise the procedure is the same as in the case of a boy; the maternal uncle performs the naming rite and at the same time instructs the bride in her future duties as a married woman.

Among some Vugusu clans it is customary to 'confirm' the ancestral name that has been given to an infant or a child later on when it reaches the status of an adult person, i.e. at the wedding of a girl and the circumcision of a boy. Frequently also a child which grows up without illness is informally called by its parents by a certain ancestral name which then must be ceremonially confirmed.

Although there is no secrecy about the ancestral names, their use, both when addressing and when referring to a person, is restricted to certain near relatives. If a stranger or any unrelated person addresses somebody by his ancestral name he causes him embarrassment. Especially a girl when thus addressed by a boy would feel ashamed and pretend not to have heard the name. Moreover, children never call their parents by their names, neither by their ancestral nor by their informal names, but always 'father' and 'mother'. It would be considered disrespectful if they were to mention their parents' names, and they would be given a beating if they did so in the presence of their parents. Other senior relatives, like the *guga*, *guxu*, *xotja* (*omifwa*), and *senge*, are likewise addressed by their kinship terms and not by their personal names. A son-in-law and a mother-in-law must strictly avoid uttering each other's names until the initial period of avoidance between them has come to an end. Were a son-in-law to call his mother-in-law by her name or even to mention her name in the presence of his wife he would have to pay a goat to his mother-in-law. Parents- and children-in-law do not even address one another by their kinship terms (*masala, musani, navizala*) but as *omwana* (child) and *mama, dada, guga,* or *guxu* respectively. Husband and wife call one another by their informal names of adolescence until the *sitexo*-rite has been performed. On that occasion they ceremonially utter their respective ancestral names, which henceforth they may use whenever they talk together intimately or when no one else is present.

(9) CUTTING TEETH AND WEANING

An infant is supposed to cut its first teeth when about six or seven months old, but no ritual attention is paid to a delayed or to a premature cutting of the teeth. If, as sometimes happens, a child is born with one or two teeth, they are knocked out, 'as the infant would otherwise bite the nipples of the mother's breasts'. It is considered proper that the two lower incisors should 'sprout' first and that they should come out simultaneously. Among the Nyole the mother celebrates this event by brewing beer for her own relatives and her neighbours, but no ceremony takes place: 'They come to drink, they are walking only (i.e. they bring no gifts). Now there is no matter (no ceremony); they drink only.'

Among the Logoli and the Vugusu no social event of any kind marks the cutting of the first teeth as long as it occurs in the normal way. If, however, the upper teeth cut first the infant is considered to be *luswa* (see p. 107). The child's father must then sacrifice a sheep to avert the danger of a sudden death which threatens him and the other occupants of the house as a result of the child's condition. The sheep killed for that purpose is called *lixese liexuosia gameno gomwana*, 'the sheep of appeasing the teeth of the child'. An old man of the neighbourhood kills the sheep, and the infant's paternal grandfather squeezes the juice of its stomach content into the child's mouth. Then all the occupants of the house jointly consume the sheep.

The same rite is performed if the child cuts its teeth while the wife is staying with it at her mother's place, i.e. away from her husband. In that case the infant is not considered to have become *luswa*, but it is feared that it will die if its parents resume their interrupted marital relations without killing a sheep and squeezing the stomach content into the child's mouth.

A mother continues to suckle her child till her breasts dry up or till she is pregnant again. This is said to occur with great regularity about fifteen or eighteen months after the birth of the last child. Genealogical charts and other documentary data which I have collected confirm this statement, showing an average interval between two births of approximately two years. Only if the child dies soon after it was born the mother usually conceives again after a few months. Slight variations in the interval between pregnancies are, however, acknowledged by the natives as lying within the range of the normal. Linguistically these variations are denoted by the terms *omwanguhizi*, the quick one, i.e. the prolific woman, and *omulindagili* or *omuhaizi*, the one who comes late, the tardy one. Women of the latter type, it is said, do not have their first menstruation after delivery (*ovwada*) till a year or more after they have given birth, a delay which is not attributed to physical weakness but to a disease of the blood. Sorcery or other supernatural agents are not held responsible for the absence of pregnancy unless the interval between two pregnancies lasts longer than two years. We have seen in the case of one of Wefwafwa's wives that her failure to conceive again after the birth of her first child was attributed by one diviner to the evil magic which her co-wife had performed over the afterbirth and by another to the 'black gods'.

By the time children are weaned (Luvugusu: *xulatia*; Lurogoli: *okulugukila*) they have learnt to eat all the dishes cooked for adult persons, including the heavy eleusine porridge and meat which they are first given when they are about a year old. Nevertheless, a child is not weaned gradually but all at once. The mother decides to refuse her child the breast when she knows that she is pregnant again and when for the first time she feels distinct pain in her breasts while suckling the child. To continue to suckle a child during the following pregnancy is considered to be bad for the embryo in the womb. Male children are supposed to be more difficult to wean than female children, but according to my informants most children stop sucking on their own account when the time of weaning arrives. If a child cries a lot when it is prevented from sucking, the mother puts pepper (*xalalie*) or tobacco juice (*ekunieti*) on the nipples of her breasts or she beats her child and pushes it away when it tries to suck. Should the child prove very troublesome it is sent to its grandmother who then 'suckles' the child till it gets tired of sucking at her dry breasts. A child may, however, stay with its grandmother only if she is an old woman who has ceased to have sexual relations with her husband.

The weaning of a child is not marked by any social event, such as a beer-feast or a formal exchange of visits.

(10) ATTITUDE TOWARDS TWINS AND CEREMONIES CONNECTED WITH THEIR BIRTH

Diametrically opposed attitudes towards twins are taken by the Logoli, on the one hand, and by the Vugusu, on the other. The Logoli consider the birth of twins an unfortunate or at least an unwelcome event, for they think that twins will bring bad luck (in a general way) and that it will be difficult to rear them both. Unless they are equally strong and healthy the mother chooses the twin whom she likes best and devotes all her care and attention to him alone, to the exclusion of the other one whom she neglects to feed and generally to take care of till he dies. It is then said that 'one of the twins refused to live'. As far as I could discover, the Logoli perform no special ceremonies for twins in case the parents decide to rear them both. As I have several times met adult people in Maragoli who by their names were marked as twins it appears that even in former days both twins were permitted to survive.

The Vugusu, on the other hand, celebrate the birth of twins as a particularly fortunate event. It is considered by them to bring luck to the father's clan, and it enhances the respect which the mother enjoys amongst her relatives-in-law. However, like every happening that is out of the ordinary, the birth of twins involves certain potential dangers, both to the twins themselves and to the people who come into contact with them. These dangers have to be warded off by the performance of certain rites and ceremonies.

Whether they are of the same or of different sex, the first-born twin is always called *muxwana* and the second-born *mulongo*. The pair are known as *vaxwana*. These names correspond to the childhood names of other people, and they are used both as terms of address and of reference. Later on each twin is given his ancestral name like any other child, and there is no rule that the ancestral names of twins must have any connexion with one another. If one twin dies, the other one retains his ancestral name but changes the name which marked him as a twin; he is now called *mukavana*, 'the one who is separated'. As regards their respective status in the family and in the wider group of kinsmen, twins stand in the same relation to one another as an older and a younger brother, with the sole exception that both are circumcised at the same time, whereas ordinary brothers may not undergo this rite in the same year. The *muxvana* has the right to claim his marriage cattle before the *mulongo*, and in the distribution of the father's legacy he has the same privileges which are ordinarily enjoyed by an elder brother.

It is not thought that any mystical bond exists between twins linking their two lives together or otherwise co-ordinating their respective fates. Thus the death of one twin does not in any way endanger the life of the other, nor is it thought that the physical or mental similarity between twins is greater than that between ordinary brothers. I have not discovered any generally accepted explanation for the birth of twins; twinship does not form a theme in any of the legends which I have collected, nor does it seem to be in any way attributed to the influence of ancestral spirits or any other mystical agents. Accordingly, there exists no magic either for bringing about the conception of twins where twins are desired, or for preventing it where they are disliked. One old man in Kitosh suggested to me that the eating of twin-fruits might cause a man to beget, or a woman to conceive, twins. Another elder said that twins were caused by the manner of copulating: 'If the husband interrupts the ejaculation of the seminal fluid (*vutiu*) it would reach the *nasaiye* (womb or ovaries, but also used with reference to all internal female sex organs) in two separate impulses and thus two embryos would grow at the same time.' Such explanations, however, were hazarded by individual natives as the product of their own reflections on the subject, and they do not represent widely accepted views.

Ceremonies connected with the Birth of Twins

Among the Vugusu the ritual situation created by the birth of twins shows two new features as compared with the birth of a single child. (1) The emanation of an intense and prolonged ritual danger from the twins, and (2) the notion that the birth of twins means a blessing with fertility which must be celebrated and, above all, communicated to other people, so that through the performance of the appropriate rites they may participate in it. These two notions, in conjunction with the other features of childbirth, give rise to a complex set of ritual observances.

When twins have been born, both parents, together with the twins and the nurse, must remain inside their hut and firmly 'lock' the door by tying it to the door-posts so that nobody can enter the hut and see the twins. While staying in Kitosh I witnessed the birth of twins which took place in the hut of the wife's mother where the wife just happened to be staying for a visit. Although it was a distance of several miles, both the wife and the twins were moved to the husband's hut the same night, as the husband could not remain with his wife and the twins in the hut of his mother-in-law.[1] During the period of seclusion the hut may not even be opened to throw out dirt and rubbish, which the nurse carefully piles up in a heap inside the hut. The parents then wait till one of their near kinsmen sends a bull or young ox as a present for the twins. The obligation to furnish this animal does not rest with any particular kinsman but anyone in the husband's or wife's clan may do so if he can afford it. If the kinsmen of the twins are wealthy, they may send a number of animals and other presents as well, such as basketfuls of grain, ground-nuts, beans, mash of beer, &c. The bulls and oxen are kept for the twins as the nucleus of their future personal possessions, while the various other presents are consumed by the visitors who come during the course of the following days to celebrate the happy event.

When the presents have been piled up in the yard and the animals tethered to the granaries the brother of the twins' father comes 'to open the twins' (*xuxwigula vaxwana*). Before breaking into the hut he kills a sheep out in the yard and skins it. Then he opens the door by force and, upon entering, catches the father of the twins by his hands and hangs the sheepskin, which is still warm, over his body. Following him a clansman of the twins' mother enters the hut and hangs a net-like garment of *amalande*-leaves (*kamavombwe* in Kitosh) over her naked body. The father's brother then leads the parents out into the yard, telling them that they have brought the 'presents of opening the twins' and that they should now come out into the yard to see them. The father of the twins does not resist but thanks his brother for having come to open the door for him. If the husband's clans-

[1] Owing to the rules of avoidance between son-in-law and mother-in-law.

men have sent a bull and those of the wife have failed to do so, the wife leans on the husband's back while they are both being led out of the hut. If, on the other hand, the husband's clan is poor and cannot afford to send a bull, the wife goes in front and the husband follows her leaning on her back. To send the proper presents for the twins is thus a matter of competitive effort on the part of the husband's and the wife's kinsmen, both of whom are expected to show their joy over the birth of the twins in an equal measure.

When they are out in the yard the parents join the other visitors, who in the meantime have assembled and begun to dance 'the dance of the twins'. This dance is the most important feature of the whole feast. It is continued throughout the day and sometimes repeated again on the following day. It is one of the few ritually prescribed occasions for the performance of pronouncedly obscene dances and the indulgence in sexual liberties, indecent gestures, and the passing of obscene jokes between the sexes which ordinarily would be considered most serious breaches of the rules of social conduct. The dances are performed to the rhythm of a small drum which is beaten by small boys and girls. The dance-leaders are mostly old women who, even if ordinarily the most respectable old ladies who can boast of a good record of faithfulness to their husbands, on this occasion urge the younger men and women to overcome their shame and join in the singing and dancing, 'as this is the feast of rejoicing over twins'. At the dance which I saw in Kitosh there were far more curious onlookers than people who actively took part in the dancing, and the main job of the old women was to make these passive spectators join in the dance by beating them with switches and pulling them by their arms. As there were numerous mission boys and girls among the onlookers, the dance at first did not come into proper swing till all these passive elements had been driven away with the comment that they were 'spoiling the custom' by idly standing about. It thus appears that the songs and dances have a magical significance as fertility rites which can achieve their purpose only if all barriers of shame are overcome and if all people participate in the procedure.

Most of the songs sung on this occasion are said to have their own tunes, but the texts are improvised by the song-leaders, who are mostly women. Standing in the middle of the dancers they sing the leading words, often in a high-pitched and shrill voice, at the same time moving their limbs and bodies to the rhythm of the dance. The refrain is taken up by the whole group of dancers, all falling in at once at a sign given by the dance-leader. Each song is repeated about a dozen times, and after a short interval, during which the dancers rest, another song-leader steps forward and rallies another group of people round him (or her) for a new song and dance. As the feast gets into full swing several groups dance at once till eventually the whole yard is crowded with dancers. Occasionally a man and a woman dance together, acting the movements of copulation, or two women, the one

BIRTH

acting as husband and the other as wife. While single couples perform these dances the onlookers interrupt them by shouting obscene jokes at them which are accompanied by bursts of laughter.

The texts of the songs consist either of plain obscenities or of hints with ambiguous meanings which everyone understands. The following are examples of both kinds, the refrains in each case consisting only of the customary 'yeee ohee eee' which is common to all songs:

Wanamukwela
sokwela siefutuvile.

'Who is dancing,
he may dance like the *efutuvile*-fish.'

Xuxine vúmuranga eee ee
nanu owaluxola Fuamba owa Wasula.

'Let us dance the dance of shaking the shoulders
as Fuamba did, the son of Wasula.'

Vayala vusa
nemunyumba xunyanyagana.

'They play only (out here),
but in the house we chew one another.'

Galuxasia mayi wange,
Mugonambi alole xumberani.

'Turn round my mother,
Mugonambi he may see blisters.'

Ngéye ngína mwana,
ngeye salixúnyama Muyavi,
omwene vana ngeye salixunyama.

'The tail of the mother (is) the child,
the tail is following behind Muyavi,
the owner of the children; the tail is following behind.'

Okinga kinganga ogulenge
Ovoné ómutia wowalé?

'You carry carrying the big old leg,
but where is your lover to be seen?'

Otunda tundanga esilenge
Ovoné omugónesia wowalé?

'You shake shaking the leg,
but where do you see the one who sleeps with you?'

Omuniégwa vaxasi lugina
nandáxa úlila oxómaga.

'The vagina of the women is like a grinding-stone,
which does not hear (i.e. keeps silent) if you beat on it.'

Namuŋoŋoli ŋooo, omwana wa Nguvo,
negasoda omwana owa Luvoya,
wamuxundila xuítodje, ovwene nivusíla.

'Namuŋoŋoli, the son of Nguvo,
he copulated with the daughter of Luvoya;
he had intercourse with her at the veranda pole, then his own (sperm) was spilled.'

Throughout the ceremonies the twins must stay inside the hut, and no one may see them or even come near them, as they are afflicted with *vuxwana*, a mystical force behind twinship (cf. p. 110). This *vuxwana*, which is fraught with danger to everyone, including the twins themselves, the parents, and the nurse who looks after the mother, manifests itself in a falling-out of the eye-lashes, in blear-eyes, and other eye diseases. Objects which have been in close contact with the twins, especially their faeces, and also the ashes and rubbish in the hut, likewise become infected with *vuxwana* and thereby are as dangerous to strangers as the twins themselves. It is, for this reason, one of the nurse's special duties to collect these things every morning in a broken potsherd and to carry them outside and hide them somewhere in the bush while nobody is near. As payment for this service she is given a new hoe by the father of the twins. Should people happen to pass a heap of ashes or rubbish thrown out from a hut in which twins are staying, the *vuxwana* would 'burn their eyes'. As preventive magic against this danger every person who has to handle these things or who, by going near the twins, exposes himself to the danger that emanates from the *vuxwana* has a star-like pattern of *ovwanga* (millet flour mixed with water) impressed upon various parts of his face and body. At the dance of 'opening the twins' which I saw all the women and most of the men present underwent this protective rite which was performed by a maternal aunt of the twins. With a small calabash filled with *ovwanga* and a little stick shaped like a chicken-leg she sat at the door of the hut and stamped marks on the forehead, temples, cheeks, breasts, and the back of the neck of every person who wanted to get a glimpse inside the hut. Some women even entered the hut and looked at the twins after thus having safeguarded themselves, but I was told that this is a recent relaxation in the attitude towards the *vuxwana* and that in pre-European days nobody would have taken unnecessary chances with twins even after having been marked with *ovwanga*.

On the same day on which the twins are 'opened' an old man of the husband's clan kills a sheep by suffocating it as a propitiation to the spirits of people who have died recently, lest they come at night and kill one of the twins. No blood or meat is put on the spirit hut, and only the stomach content of the sheep is hung up in the granary as an offering. The old man then cuts some wristlets from the skin of the sheep and puts one on the right wrists of the father and the mother of the twins. Before the others eat the roasted meat the mother of the twins is given a small piece of raw meat which she must pick from a tray with her mouth without touching it with her hands.

On the day following the dance the father of the twins prepares a calabashful of fertility medicine, called *kamanyasi*. It consists of the dried and pounded pulp of the stem of a banana bunch, mixed with water and a secret medicine supplied by his wife. With this concoction he goes from house to house and, without discrimination, sprinkles all the people he meets at the various homesteads and on the road until his supply of medicine has given out. He utters no spell or blessing while doing so, but the accepted idea is that by his action he confers the fertility and the good luck of his own matrimony upon the other people and their homesteads. Although inquiries into the motives which a father of twins might have in undertaking such a neighbourly action elicited merely the general reply that it was 'the custom to do so', it seems highly probable that through this generous bestowal of his own favoured condition upon all and sundry he hopes to minimize the envy that other people, and particularly sorcerers, might feel towards him. This assumption would be in accordance with the fears of being grudged the possession of numerous children which parents display in other situations and also with the fact that, although the father does not restrict his dispensations to his own kinsmen, he neither asks for nor receives a payment for his benefaction.

Even after the ceremony of 'opening the twins' has been performed they are not permitted to come outside, and their seclusion in the hut lasts for several years; sometimes, I was told, till they are four years old, but in any case till they can walk properly. When in October 1937 I inquired about twins born in April 1936 I heard that they were still confined to the hut, but unfortunately I did not have an opportunity of visiting the place again to confirm this statement. Should a stranger enter the hut unawares he must pay a small trinket, such as an iron armlet or necklace, and, nowadays, money as a fine for having seen the twins. To prevent the twins from leaving the hut on their own account when they reach the crawling stage, the parents build a high threshold of banana-trunks in the doorway. Actually, if no strangers are near, the twins may be taken out in the yard, but the mother must take care to hide them as soon as a visitor approaches the homestead. As the twins grow older the *vuxwana* gradually loses its strength, and when it is thought to have disappeared altogether they may move about freely like other children. The transition being gradual it is not marked by any ceremonial event. When the twins are about six years old their father brews beer and kills a bull-calf or a goat 'for eating' (i.e. without performing a sacrifice with it), and a feast is arranged at which the twins are shaved for the first time in their lives. The relatives on both sides, as well as neighbours, are invited to come, and they again bring presents for the twins, although not as many as at the time of their first visit when the ceremony of 'opening the twins' was performed.

(11) CEREMONIES PERFORMED FOR WEAK AND SICKLY INFANTS

We have seen that the *liswákila*-sacrifice invokes the general benevolence of the ancestral spirits towards the new-born child and that the name-giving rite invites the guardianship of a particular spirit for a child. In addition to these general observances a number of other rites are performed for weak and sickly infants. They show that not only the ancestral spirits but also various other mystical agents are thought capable of hampering the normal development of a child. In all these cases the responsible agent must first be detected by consulting a diviner. Once the agent is known the ritual procedure to be taken is laid down by convention. Although to a certain extent the force or agent responsible for the child's condition can be discovered from the symptoms from which the child suffers, these symptoms are not considered unambiguous enough to make it possible to dispense with the services of a diviner.

If a mother has lost several children in succession and the diviner has in each case attributed their death to the malevolent attitude of an ancestral spirit, the mother tries to protect her next child against a similar fate by keeping the spirits in ignorance of the existence of the child. Instead of rearing it in her own hut and performing the *liswákila*-rite the mother, as soon as she has recovered from her confinement, takes the infant out to a lonely spot in the bush and puts it down in the grass near a place where two paths cross one another. Before doing so she makes an arrangement with a woman of her neighbourhood to walk down the path which crosses the one along which she intends to take her child, so that her neighbour will find the infant at the crossing a few minutes after she has put it there. As soon as the woman finds the child she breaks out into shouts of joy, dances round it and calls out: 'Now I have found my child, now I have found my child.' She then takes the infant home with her and rears it together with her other children till it is about four or five years old. The arrangement between the real mother and the foster-mother is made secretly, so that the impression is given that the infant has been picked up by chance by a strange woman who just happened to pass by there. Actually, however, the foster-mother is carefully chosen. She must be a woman who has been exceptionally fortunate in rearing her own children and she must belong neither to the clan of the infant's mother nor to that of its father, so that the malevolent spirit may not succeed in discovering the child's whereabouts. The real mother may regularly come to the hut of the foster-mother to suckle her child, but while she does so she pretends that it is not her own child which she is suckling but that of the foster-mother. Even at the home of the foster-mother the child is reared with particular care and the same precautions are taken over it as over twins. It is kept inside the hut as much as possible and nobody may see it unless he makes a payment in the form of necklaces, chains, or wristlets which are then worn by the child as charms. As in the case of twins such a child is not shaved until 'it has passed the tender age', i.e. until it is five or six years old. This fact is also indicated by its name: *omuvwélela*, 'the one that may not be shaved'. When the foster-mother has thus successfully reared the child to the age of about five years she goes with it to the house of its real parents where the father in the meantime has brewed the *gamalua gexuveka omuvwélela*, 'the beer of shaving the *omuvwélela*'. The kinsmen on both sides as well as neighbours are invited for this feast but no sacrifice is performed. Before they drink the beer the foster-mother shaves the child in the front yard, carefully collecting its hair which she then hides away in the bush. As a payment for her services the child's father kills a goat for her which she shares with some other women of her neighbourhood.

If an infant gets very thin and does not learn to sit up and crawl about in due time, the suspicion arises that its condition has been brought about by the spirit of a cobra (*mugóyavaka*) that has taken offence, either because the child's father had killed it during the mother's pregnancy or because the mother herself has crossed its trail or passed near the place where it has died. If the diviner confirms this suspicion a rite must be performed to pacify the spirit (*sisieno*) of the cobra. In the first case, i.e. if the father of the infant has killed the cobra, he takes the spear with which he killed it and goes with it to the top of an ant-hill near the spot where he speared the cobra. Putting the spear on the ground he says:

> *Mugóyavaka noliwe ósolile*
> *kamaxuva kowónono kavwéle hano.*
>
> 'Cobra, if it is you who grumbles,
> may your matter (i.e. grievances) be finished here.'

If, however, the infant's mother has crossed the trail of a cobra a more elaborate rite must be performed. Preparatory to it some old women go to a nearby ant-hill and with their billhooks clear a straight path leading from the top of the ant-hill to a path which has frequently been used by the child's mother. It does not matter which particular ant-hill is chosen, as all of them are considered to be abodes of the spirits of cobras whose favourite haunts they are also during their lifetime. While the old women clear the path an old man plaits a life-size image of a cobra, i.e. he plaits a ribbon of banana-bark about 5 inches wide and 4 to 5 yards long which tapers off into a narrow 'tail'. When everything is ready and beer has been brewed the old man ties the tail of the cobra image to the leg of the infant's father, to his right one if the infant is a boy and to his left if it is a girl. Starting off from the place where the cleared path joins the other one, the father slowly walks along the path towards the top of the ant-hill, dragging the 'cobra' behind him by its tail. A crowd of neighbours follows him joining in his frequently repeated song: *mugóyavaka wayandja*, 'cobra you are pleased now'. When he has reached the top of the hill the old man cuts the string with which the tail of the image was tied to the father's leg. The old woman who has cleared the path puts a tiny pot with beer on top of the ant-hill as an offering for the spirit of the cobra. Returning from the ant-hill the child's father and his neighbours again follow the cleared path, still singing the *mugóyavaka*-song and 'stepping down' to the rhythm of the song. In return for their services the old man who has plaited the image and the women who have cleared the path are given beer which is served them at the centre post of the father's hut. The image of the cobra is then left at the ant-hill till it rots away without any further attention being paid to it.

Should the condition of the infant fail to improve after the performance of this rite, a small, dome-shaped grass-hut, a few inches high, is erected on the ant-hill by the same women who cleared the path, and the beer-offering is repeated while the infant is 'fluttered' with a white hen.

Two other rites which are performed for a child that is thin and especially for one that cries a great deal are called *okufúmbela omwana*, to 'coax'[1] or cherish a child, and *okufúdula ogutu*, to pierce the ear. The condition of the child for which these rites are performed was described to me in the following text:

'A person has an infant which may be either a boy or a girl. Then the infant begins to cry day and night. It cannot stay quiet; it begins to cry at the time its nurse takes care of it, and when its mother comes back from her work (in the field) she still finds the child crying hard. The mother takes it and gives it the breast; it drinks and when it has finished drinking it begins crying again. Then the mother wonders and says: Now it is necessary that the sacrifices (*emisango*) of "coaxing" and of piercing the ear may be made for it.'

First the parents of the child brew beer from eleusine and sorghum which, for the purpose of the rite, must be freshly made, i.e. they cannot take *dzimbale* or *amamela* which they have kept in store. When the beer is ready the wife's parents are invited, together with an old man and an old woman 'whom the child calls grandfather and grandmother' (classificatory grandparents of either side). The child is then taken out to the trail that passes near the homestead, and the lobe of its ear—the right one if a boy, the left one if a girl—is pierced with a thorn. The classificatory grandfather first takes the thorn and points it at the child's ear; then he hands it to the grandmother who actually pierces it. The performance of this rite is then celebrated by a beer-drink. During the following weeks the hole in the lobe of the ear is widened by inserting grasses of increasing thickness, first *ekikálanzila*-grass, then *olunyolu*-grass. When the hole is sufficiently wide and has healed up properly, the old woman who has pierced the lobe inserts a small iron pluck (*eneno*) which the child's father has procured from a smithy. The magical efficacy of the *eneno*, its power of promoting the infant's welfare, lies in its attachment to the ear; it is not previously consecrated, nor is the act of putting it on marked by the utterance of a spell.

A few days after the *eneno* has been inserted into the lobe of the child's ear a number of classificatory grandmothers of the child are invited to

---

[1] The same verb denotes the careful coaxing of a tender plant and the laborious kindling of a fire which is only faintly glowing.

BIRTH

come to the mother's house to sing the *mbumbele*-song. They must be 'really old women' (*avadzílilu*), i.e. women who are past the age for having sexual relations with their husbands, but the degree of their relationship to the infant does not matter. Each of the women is given a small gourd into which the child's mother has put some simsim seeds, peas, groundnuts, and *dzimbale*, so that they can be used as rattles. One old woman who takes the part of the song-leader is given a larger gourd. Sitting in a circle inside the hut where the infant is sleeping and with no male person present, they sing the following song, shaking the gourd-rattles to its rhythm:

Leader: *Mbu—mbeleee, mbu—mbeleee,*
        ndole nigwaka
        likanga niyo enyama.
Others: *Mbu—mbeleee, mbu—mbeleee,*
        ndole nigwaka.
Leader: *Likere nigwo muyaga.*
Others: *Mbu—mbeleee, mbu—mbeleee,*
        ndole nigwaka.
Leader: *Isudzi niyo enyama.*
Others: *Mbu—mbeleee, mbu—mbeleee,*
        ndole nigwaka.
Leader: *Litunde dzie dzingudza,*
        inze Muyonga sindia kizálala,
        akana nikyo kindu,
        esikulu nikyo kindu,
        avavila vivwo vulasi,
        mugosi nikyo kindu,
        lisanga nilio kindu,
        misambwa nigyo lwanda,
        ovukonyi nivwo kindu,
        elineke nilyo milembe, &c.
        kufumbele kulole nigwaka.
Others: *Mbu—mbeleee, mbu—mbeleee,*
        ndole nigwaka.
Leader: *Avakele kuhodzelize.*
Others: *Mbu—mbeleee, mbu—mbeleee,*
        ndole nigwaka.

Translation
Leader: 'I may coax, I may coax,
        I may see if it blazes high!
        The guinea fowl is the meat.'
Others: 'I may coax, I may coax,
        I may see if it blazes high.'
Leader: 'The frog is covered with sores.'
Others: 'I may coax, I may coax,
        I may see if it blazes high.'
Leader: 'The *sudzi*-fish is the meat.'
Others: 'I may coax, I may coax,
        I may see if it blazes high.'

The leader sings as many verses as he knows, each being followed by the same refrain:

> 'The *litunde* are the vegetables,
> I am an Omuyonga; I do not eat *kizálala*[1] (fish),
> A little child is a good thing,
> The school is a (good) thing,
> The sorcerers are the stings,
> A gentle person is a (good) thing,
> The joining (of people for a feast or sacrifice) is a good thing,
> The sacrifice is the rock,
> Help is the thing,
> *Elineke*[2] is the peace, &c.'

The song is wound up with the following two lines:

Leader: 'We may coax, we may coax, we may see if it blazes.'
Others: 'I may coax, I may coax,
I may see if it blazes.'
Leader: '(We) old women we may tend with loving care.'
Others: 'I may coax, I may coax,
I may see if it blazes.'

After they have finished singing this song the women drink the beer which has been left over from the 'feast of piercing the ear'. Before the child's maternal grandmother goes home she is given a gourd filled with beer to take to her husband who drinks it together with his neighbours as he was not permitted to accompany his wife to the *mbumbele*-ceremony. As a result of singing the *mbumbele*-song the child is supposed to stop crying and to put on weight. The song thus appears to be a rare combination of promotive (or curative) and protective magic. It is not addressed to the ancestral spirits or to any other definite category of supernatural agents. Analogously to the 'piercing of the ear' the efficacy of the rite lies in the song itself and in the particular manner in which it is chanted. The fact that the song enumerates both good things and bad things suggests that by sympathy the good things are invoked and the bad things exorcized. It may be significant from this point of view that in the song which I have recorded the list of good things greatly outnumbers that of bad things.

B. CIRCUMCISION AND INITIATION RITES

(1) INTRODUCTORY

IN the life-cycle of the male individual circumcision, together with the elaborate initiation rites that surround the actual operation, is undoubtedly the most outstanding and important single event, even more so than the conclusion of marriage, as it involves a greater change in social

---

[1] The members of the Yonga clan may not eat the *kizálala*-fish.

[2] A concoction of the *elineke*-plant, a variety of saxifrage, is drunk on the occasion of rites of reconciliation.

status. Although in many of its ceremonial features it constitutes but one of several *rites de passage* which mark the entrance of the individual into every new phase of life, it differs from them essentially in that it is performed collectively and not individually like all the other rites of transition. Its significance, therefore, extends beyond the orbit of the individual's lifecycle even more than that of birth or marriage, although—as we have pointed out—these events, too, furnish the occasion for observances that affect much wider groups and serve far wider functions than those bearing directly and immediately upon the individual concerned.

Despite the obvious importance of circumcision as revealed by its lengthy and elaborate ceremonial, and despite the comparative ease with which its actual procedure can be studied and observed, it is by no means self-evident what are the salient features of the circumcision rites and what is their 'meaning'. Indeed, to formulate the question in this way, to search for one basic idea behind circumcision and to expect that its discovery will furnish the clue for an interpretation of the whole multitude of rites and observances would, from the outset, stultify the inquiry.

The distribution of circumcision and initiation rites throughout Africa, and the frequent resemblance between details of ceremonial procedure in areas thousands of miles apart, indicate that the circumcision ritual has an old tradition behind it and in its present form is the result of a long process of development. Like any other major institution of native life, it has, in the course of this process, acted as a focal point to which new features have tended to converge, as changes in the conditions of life called for new adjustments in the political and social organization and, accordingly, for new mechanisms of preserving and transmitting knowledge, of grading authority and making it valid, and of creating effective relationships between groups of people for co-operation in the various tasks of social life. The initiation rites have—to use another simile—formed a receptacle which, in the course of time, has received many different streams of ideas and practices that have issued from various quarters of the cultural realm. To ask for *the* meaning of circumcision and the accompanying rites in any given society would thus mean to misjudge the nature of the problem, as circumcision cannot possibly have *one* meaning but must have several, each of them determined by the point of view from which we look at the rites.

First of all, there is the problem of the 'meaning' of the actual operation of circumcision, the question 'Why do people consider it desirable or even necessary to remove the prepuce of the male member?' Here again we must distinguish between the original motive which many generations ago led the people to adopt the custom, and the purpose which the operation is intended to fulfil to-day. Next, there is the problem of the 'symbolical meaning' of the numerous rites and ceremonies and of the whole system of thought into which the various ideas may be synthesized. Finally, there is what might be called the functional meaning of circumcision, i.e. its contribution towards the working and maintenance of tribal culture. This functional meaning, again, it will hardly be possible to render by a single formula but only by a careful analysis of all the aspects—economic, political, religious, educational, and so on—that enter into the various phases of the procedure. In a study such as the present one, the ultimate aim of which is to lay bare the structure of Kavirondo society and to assess the significance of the various elements that build up this structure, this last type of meaning is the one which it is of foremost importance to determine. The problem of symbolism enters in so far as the symbolical and metaphorical meaning behind the various rites is consciously experienced by those people who actively and passively participate in them. The first-mentioned problem, on the other hand, that of the purpose of the actual operation, is only of minor significance. The operation and the whole initiation ceremonial having become an integral unit, the traditional native mind does not detach the operation from its ritual and ceremonial context to ponder over it *per se*. His statements about it are therefore only incidental. Nevertheless, we shall see that the state of being circumcised has, under modern conditions, acquired a meaning by itself and the problem thus has its own significance in respect of the 'modern' native.[1]

To obtain the basis required for a discussion of these various meanings[1] I shall in the following give a straightforward analytical account of the circumcision rites among a number of Bantu Kavirondo tribes which is based partly on personal observation and partly on texts and oral accounts that I have taken down.

Male circumcision is practised among all Bantu Kavirondo tribes, including the Gusii of South Kavirondo, but it is less general among the tribes living along the border of the Nilotic and Teso-speaking groups who do not circumcise. Among the Wanga, as a rule, only the eldest son in every family is circumcised. It is said that formerly only the ruling Hitsetse clan which had split off from the Tiriki practised circumcision and that the subsequent adoption of the custom by other clans was due to the influence of the neighbouring Vugusu. If that is so, it is probable that one might still find two types of circumcision rites among the Wanga, viz. the Vugusu and the Tiriki types. I was not able, however, to investigate this point by fieldwork among the Wanga. Among the Nyole, there exists a commonly accepted historical tradition according to which circumcision was suspended for six age-classes and taken up again in 1917, but it is not practised among all clans, and even among the clans which do practise it I have found a number of uncircumcised people of middle age who, although with some reluctance, admitted that they had adopted the Luo custom and evaded circumcision. With the exception of the Vatadjoni none of the Bantu tribes of Kavirondo practise female circumcision or any other form of female initiation such as is common among the Nandi and all the other Nilo-Hamitic tribes living to the east and north-east of the Bantu Kavirondo.

[1] See vol. ii.

CIRCUMCISION AND INITIATION RITES

In the opinion of numerous elders whom I have questioned, circumcision is an old custom in Kavirondo; there are no legendary accounts of its supposed origin or its diffusion. Only among the Logoli I was told by one informant that many generations ago a man named Musa introduced circumcision and the ceremonies connected with it, but his statement was denied by other elders. The Vugusu say that their tribal ancestor, Muvugusu, was not circumcised, as 'throughout his life he was harassed to such an extent fighting against the Teso and Nyole that he had no time to undergo the rite'. His brothers whom he had left behind in Embai (said to be in the Karamodja country) had already been circumcised when Muvugusu detached himself from his tribe and migrated southwards. When after a few generations the Vugusu had come to rest near the Tororo Rock, a certain person, named Kolongolo, remembered that circumcision had been an old custom among his people and revived it again.

Although, of course, the absence of origin-stories does not necessarily prove that the circumcision ceremonies are of a very great age, it would seem to me that the following accounts of the ceremonies and the age-grades and, in particular, the fact that the ceremonial has become differentiated into a number of tribal variants, leave no doubt that circumcision was generally practised when the first Europeans came to Kavirondo. Sir Harry Johnston's categorical statement, made in 1902,[1] that 'the Bantu of Kavirondo do not practise circumcision', which he maintains in spite of Hobley's reports to the contrary, must therefore obviously be based on a misunderstanding.

(2) CONDITIONS OF CIRCUMCISION AND PREPARATORY OBSERVANCES

The decision to hold the circumcision rites is taken by the elders of the clan when they see that sufficient time has passed since the last circumcision for a new generation of young men to have reached the age when they are fit to become warriors. The average interval between two circumcisions is three or four years, but the occurrence of such events as an epidemic or a poor harvest or, on the other hand, an exceptionally good harvest, are said to have occasionally lengthened or shortened the interval by a year or two. The decision of the elders is also influenced by the pressure of the young men who pester their fathers to be initiated when they are grown up and feel strong enough to face the pain of the operation. Although, with the exception of the Tiriki, there are no tribal meetings at which the decision to hold the circumcision rites is reached by an agreement between representative elders of all clans, the same interval between two circumcisions is observed by all clans of the tribal unit. It seems that uniformity in this respect is achieved by the tradition that has been set by the age-grade organization. Besides, it is said that if the elders of a strong clan agreed to hold a circumcision before the customary interval of time had passed, the other clans would follow its example, as otherwise they would suffer a

[1] See Sir Harry Johnston, 1902, pp. 256 and 728.

shortage of warriors in comparison with the clan whose young men have been initiated that year. Circumcision is not held at annual intervals, partly because the number of candidates would not be large enough to make the ceremonies a tribal event, and partly because the elaborate feasts connected with initiation were too great a drain on cattle and grain to permit them to be held at very frequent intervals. The last two circumcisions in North Kavirondo took place in 1934 and in 1937. In the latter year circumcision ceremonies were held among the Avisuxa, Avidaxo, Tiriki, and Vugusu, but not among the Wanga, Logoli, and Nyole.

Among the Tiriki, in order to decide whether a circumcision should be held in a given year, the head (*eligutu*) of the largest clan asks the principal elders of all clans to assemble at a certain place, called Mukabukolosi. This is a clearance in a dense part of the forest, the access to which is kept secret from women and uncircumcised boys. The elders bring a male goat with them which must be supplied by a member of the oldest age-grade in the tribe. It is killed in the presence of all the elders, and the oldest man present inspects the stomach and the entrails to see if the omens are favourable for the intended circumcision rite or not. If the outer surface of the stomach and entrails is smooth and free from blisters and pimples, this is taken as a sign that the lads will soon recover from the operation and that none of them will die from his wound. If the opposite is the case, they will suffer pain for a long time and their wounds will be likely to become inflamed. If the inspection of the entrails yields such an unfavourable result the elders adjourn their decision and after a few days hold a second meeting, killing another goat. Should the entrails of this second goat show the same inauspicious signs, circumcision is postponed until the following year. In any case, the elders eat the goat on the spot without leaving anything over or taking any pieces of meat home with them. The skin of the goat is cut into long narrow strips (*vixanda*), a section of which every elder wraps round the third finger of his right hand where he leaves it for about a week and then throws it away unceremoniously. Only the stomach and the entrails are taken home and eaten by the elder who has inspected them. He must not share this food with his wife or children, although his wife may cook it for him. When the elders return home from their meeting at Mukabukolosi they sing a certain song or rather hum a tune—for it is said to have no words—which serves as an indication to all young lads in the tribe that the circumcision operator will soon arrive and that they have to prepare themselves for the occasion.

Among the other tribes no such preliminary consultation of omens by representative elders of the whole tribe is known.

The conditions which a boy has to fulfil before he can qualify as a candidate for circumcision are not very rigid. The circumcision age varies considerably, leaving him a wide margin of choice. Among most Bantu Kavirondo tribes the average age is said to have been eighteen to twenty years, i.e. the age when a boy has reached full physical and mental maturity and is fit to become a warrior. In Kitosh, where warfare was a more serious affair than in most other parts of Kavirondo (owing to the frequent and ruthless raids by the Masai and Teso), the average age of the candidates is said to have been twenty-two years or even more. An age of twelve or thirteen years is usually given as the lower limit below which both the father and the operator would refuse to circumcise a boy. The upper limit seems to be around thirty years. A slight difference in age among the candidates is, of course, inevitable as the circumcision ceremonies do not take place every year. For the most part, however, the range in age is due to the varying response shown by the different boys towards circumcision. Courageous boys will urge their fathers to permit them to be circumcised when they are still quite young. Small boys of eight or ten years of age begin to brag about their courage to face the operator's knife, and to volunteer for the operation at an early age is the best way for a boy to gain respect among his fellow herd-boys and to impress the girls. Actually, most of the influential elders with whom I discussed circumcision claimed to have been circumcised well below the customary age. Lads, on the other hand, who are afraid of being circumcised let one occasion after another go by until ridicule by their age-mates or by the girls eventually induces them to muster up their courage and submit to the operation when the next circumcision takes place. All uncircumcised boys are called *avasinde*, but to be called by this term has a derogatory connotation only after a young man has passed the age when he should have been circumcised. When the time of circumcision approaches and he does not join the other candidates in their preparatory observances, the girls sing songs like the following when they meet him on the road:

> *Waria ingwé adzie evunyólo!* (repeated)
> 'Who fears the medicine[1] may he go to the Luo!'

If a boy persistently refuses to be circumcised, his father or his circumcised brothers eventually catch him and have him circumcised by force, especially if he is the eldest son. Nowadays, boys who fear circumcision frequently run away from the reserve and seek employment with Europeans on farms or in towns. But even there they are not entirely certain of having escaped their fate, as even after many years their clansmen may follow them and force them to be circumcised, if they do not yield to persuasion. Nevertheless, one finds in most clans one or two elderly men who have successfully evaded circumcision. They are referred to as *avasinde* throughout their lives, and they never attain to full status in the tribe. At a beer-drink they cannot occupy the prominent place near the door, they will never be recognized as leading elders of the clan (*avagasa*), and formerly, when intertribal wars were not yet prohibited, they were not permitted to fight in the front ranks. Otherwise, they are not made to suffer public ridicule

[1] That is to say, the medicine which is put on the fresh wound of the circumcised penis; cf. below, p. 357.

once they have reached middle age, and their age-mates might even politely salute them as *vagogi*, a term which strictly refers only to their circumcised age-mates.

However, unless a boy is past the proper age for circumcision he is—at least among some of the tribes—not urged by his father and his clansmen to join the other candidates, but the initiative to do so is left entirely to him. Among the Vugusu, a father actually forbids his son to be circumcised; he quarrels with him and even beats him when he gets ready to join the other lads by putting on the ornaments that are worn by the candidates (*vésaile*). It is said that a father acts in this way to test the strength of his son's character and will-power. If his son is easily intimidated by his protests, he has reason to fear that he will flinch when the moment of the operation arrives. For a boy to show fear on this occasion would be a serious disgrace to the father who would then have to listen to abusive remarks by his 'joking-friend'. Stories are even told of fathers who have attempted to commit suicide because their sons behaved as cowards during the operation.

Whereas a boy must always be circumcised before he is permitted to carry and use the weapons of a real warrior and before he can take an active part in fighting, circumcision is not necessarily a prerequisite of marriage. Although the majority of men marry only after they have been circumcised, there is no direct connexion between the two events, and a girl would not refuse to marry an uncircumcised man, provided he was still young. A man, however, who is past the proper age when he should have been circumcised obviously has shirked the operation and would, therefore, find it difficult to get a wife. He would, as a rule, have to be satisfied with a widow or with a girl who for some reason or other did not find a more desirable suitor.

The procedure during the circumcision ceremonies comprises three major phases which we shall now discuss in their chronological order. The first phase consists of preparatory observances by the candidates and leads up to the actual operation. The second phase comprises the life of the circumcised boys in the *etumbi* or hut of seclusion where they stay while their wounds are healing up and for a further period of time during which they are instructed both in practical and theoretical knowledge. The third phase, finally, begins with the 'feast of coming out of the hut of seclusion', is then followed by a series of further rites and festive occasions, and terminates with a round of visits by the initiate to all his relatives, analogous to the round of visits that a boy undertakes after the rite of teeth-knocking.[1] The entire procedure takes between three and six months or even longer, depending mainly upon the length of the stay in the *etumbi* which differs among the various tribes. The actual operation usually takes place in July or August, after the harvesting of the eleusine crop, of which great quantities are needed to feed the initiates and to brew the beer for the various feasts during and after the stay of the novices in the hut of seclusion.

[1] Cf. vol. ii.

CIRCUMCISION AND INITIATION RITES

Among all tribes the actual circumcision is preceded by a number of preparatory observances on the part of the candidates. They serve to get them into the proper spirit that is necessary if they are to face the operator courageously, and to ensure that they are not afflicted with any ritual impurities which would increase the dangers of the operation both to themselves and, through magical contamination, to their fellow candidates and even to their senior clansmen. The duration and the details of these preparatory observances, however, differ from tribe to tribe.

Among the Vugusu the lads who wish to be circumcised that year begin, about two months before the operator is due to come, to tie several chains of iron beads (*vútundi*) round their loins so that the ends hang down in front covering their genitals. They usually buy these chains from a smith, paying for them with the fowls which have been given to them during the years of their adolescence by various relatives and especially by their maternal uncle. After they have walked about in that attire for a month, defying their fathers who try to prevent them from putting on the *vútundi*, they beg some elderly clansmen to give them smooth iron wristlets (*vírere*) which they slip over both wrists. Then they borrow some cow-bells for which they have to pay another fowl. To these bells they attach a stiff handle made of string, so that they can hold them like hand-bells. Also, they fasten to their belts some curved teeth of wild pigs and sharp pieces of iron which protrude sideways from their waists. In this attire they go and dance about all day in groups of eight or ten, trying to scratch one another with the pig-teeth and the iron pins and making a rhythmic noise by beating the iron wristlets against the cow-bells. They visit in turn the homesteads of their respective fathers and classificatory fathers, each of whom has to kill a goat or fowl for them and offer them plenty of porridge after they have danced. As a result of their daily feasts the candidates (*vésaile*) get quite fat and are thus properly prepared to stand the operation and the loss of blood which it entails. The *vésaile* themselves do not sing any songs during this period of preparation, but a member of their clan who has been circumcised some age-grades ago (called *omuósi* or *omuhóli*) sings songs to them to which they have to reply by grunts and groans. In these songs, which usually consist of a few words only, he warns them not to fear the circumcision operator, hints at the shame which cowardice would bring on them, and encourages the candidates to be happy and carefree:

> *Omusinde oteremaka*
> *atjiá evunyolo haahá, haaahó,*
> *émbalu elumá vuví*
> *elimatávula haaa hoooó.*

> 'The uncircumcised boy who always fears
> he may go to the Luo (country), haaha, haaho,
> the knife (when) it hurts badly,
> (the pain) is near to come to an end.'

*Xusányenge ovuónya
xaoya eeeeé.*

'We must play joyfully,
(never mind) the rinderpest.'

*Háridji masewáya hahá háhiya,
háridji omusínde, haháhahi; ya háridji.*

'The coward is light like husks, haha, hahiya,
the coward (remains) an uncircumcised boy,
haha, hahiya, the coward!'

*Olumbe luomugongo luxoya sívitari,
xunyánye, váyia háh, xunyanye.*

'The sickness of the back it needs the doctor,
let us eat, please, let us eat.'

*Haha, hoho, haha, hoho,
xunyama mbolo Murunga wálila ari:
éndjala evuwanga haha, hahé,
xunyama mbolo Murunga walila
gímiva giase haho, hehé,
xunyama mbolo.*

'Haha, hoho, haha, hoho,
about the rotten meat Murunga cried like this:
The hunger (is great) in the Wanga country!
About the rotten meat Murunga cried:
My sugar-cane haho, hehe,
about the rotten meat.'

Shortly before the operator comes each candidate asks his father to supply him with eleusine or sorghum, so that he may brew 'beer' for the first time in his life. Each boy by himself thrashes the millet, then he gives it to his sister to grind, and finally prepares the beer up to a stage where it is called *gamalua gexutjúxila*.[1] He gives some of this porridge-like stuff to his mother who makes beer of it for the visitors who have been invited to come on the day before the circumcision takes place. The remainder of the *gamalua gexutjúxila* the boy keeps for himself and makes it into a thin gruel by pouring cold water over it. Then he invites his fellow candidates and the older men to come and drink this 'beer', which is poured into a beer-pot and sucked through hollow reeds like real beer. This feast serves as a sign that the father has now permitted the boy to be circumcised. Afterwards the *vésaile* go to their various paternal and maternal relatives, beginning with the father's sister, and tell them to come and drink the beer which their mothers have prepared to celebrate the forthcoming circumcision. When paying these visits to their relatives they have to appear very fierce and defiant, pretending not to have the slightest fear of the operation which will now take place in another day or two. They again take their wristlets and

[1] Cf. vol. ii.

hand-bells along with them and dance about wildly. The relatives whom they visit rub ghee on their bodies and sprinkle them with simsim seeds.

The evening before the operation takes place the *vésaile* may eat as much porridge as they like, but they may not drink of the beer which is offered to the visitors. They dance till late in the night, bragging and boasting, and get up early in the morning, again dancing and making a lot of noise to show their impatience. After they have eaten a plentiful breakfast, consisting again of meat and thick porridge, those *vésaile* who are going to be circumcised together at one homestead go down to the nearest stream, followed by many people but not by their own fathers. After they have bathed in the stream an adult person, specially chosen by the elders for the courage that he displayed when he himself was circumcised, covers the body of each candidate from head to foot with thick brown mud, leaving a free space only round the eyes. On the head, which has been shaved the preceding afternoon by the boy's *senge* (father's sister), he places a lump of clay, about 5 inches high, into which he sticks long feathers that wave in the wind and make the appearance of the candidate resemble that of a warrior. If the maternal uncle has killed a bullock for his nephew (*omwiwana*), as he always does for that nephew whose mother's marriage-cattle has enabled him to marry,[1] the candidate takes a piece of the bullock's breast-meat and hangs it like a collar round his neck, with flaps of meat hanging down on his chest and the upper part of his back.

The lads are now ready to appear before the operator. Shrieking and yelling loudly to show their impatience to be circumcised, they run back from the stream to the homestead where the operation will take place. On their way home they must follow a different route from the one they had taken when they went down to the stream, as is the practice of warriors who thereby mislead their enemies. About half-way home they are met by their fathers, who again try to dissuade them from facing the operator's knife and who test their courage by telling them to go back to the stream wash off the mud, and return home. Thus they give their sons a last chance to change their minds and save the whole lineage from the disgrace which would descend upon it if they flinched or ran away from the operator's knife in the presence of all the onlookers.

Among the Tiriki, the boys who have reached the age to be initiated get their first intimation that the time of circumcision is approaching when the elders of the tribe return from their secret meeting at Mukabukolosi. At dusk that day all the would-be candidates go to the meeting-place (*oluhia*) of their sub-clan where, soon after darkness has set in, they begin to sing circumcision songs. Any clansman who has been circumcised with the last age-grade can take the part of a teacher and song-leader (*omwémeli*). They sing and walk about all night, beating with sticks against small shields or a hard piece of cow-skin which they beg from their fathers for this purpose. They continue these nightly gatherings for several weeks and extend them

[1] Cf. vol. ii, chapter on cattle law.

through a great part of the night whenever the moon is shining and the ground is dry. During the period of preparation the candidates of one *oluhia* sleep together in the hut of an old woman, including even those candidates who are already married, as they have to stay away from their wives and practise continence during that time. In the daytime the boys may stay about their fathers' homesteads and carry on their usual activities, herding cattle or helping their mothers in the field. They must, however, refrain from visiting girls, observe a number of food taboos, and exercise particular care not to do those things which are prohibited to all uncircumcised boys, such as the killing of the *ivaga* snake (cobra), of dogs, and of certain small birds (*efidjondjo* and *elidudu*) that build their nests under the roof of the hut. Small mishaps to which ordinarily not much attention would be paid are looked upon as bad omens if they happen to a circumcision candidate, e.g. if he cuts his finger with an axe while splitting wood. Such mishaps as well as the violation of any of the prohibitions and food taboos must be reported by the candidates on a particular day arranged for that purpose shortly before the operator is due to come. This 'confession' takes place in the presence of the assembled elders of the clan who come to the house of the old woman where the candidates sleep. To frighten the lads into telling the truth and confessing everything they have done, their fathers and other circumcised people make them believe that the elders have placed a lion in the hut which will detect and punish them for any lies they may tell or for any omissions in their confession. To simulate the presence of the lion, the elders carry a huge water-pot[1] into the hut and tilt it slightly backwards. A man squats behind the pot and, covering both the rim of the pot and his head with a sheepskin, blows into it, imitating the roaring of a lion. The candidates are then led into the hut one by one, and after each of them has made his confession he is told to touch the sheepskin on the pot, being warned beforehand that should his confession be incomplete the lion will jump out of the pot and maul him while otherwise it will do him no harm. If the candidate is not at all afraid to touch the skin the elders know that he has reported all his misdeeds and he is permitted to face the operator next day without suffering any punishment. Should he plead guilty to having killed a dog his father must pay a goat which the elders eat after the confession is over.

On the eve of the operation the candidates are given a meat feast by their fathers, the meat being provided by the wealthy fathers who can afford to kill a cow for the occasion. This is the last solid food the boys get for some time, as on the following days they are given only soft gruel to drink.

To dispel their fears and to keep them from running away when they see the operator, the boys are told that they are not actually going to be circumcised with a knife, but that the operator will fix a metal ring round their member. At night, while they sleep, this ring will cut through their prepuce and make it fall off without causing them any pain. Without any

[1] The Bantu Kavirondo make pots with diameters up to 1 yard.

further ceremony, they are, on the following day, led to a secluded place in the forest from which all women and uncircumcised boys are strictly kept away. They do not bathe or cover their bodies with clay but go quite naked, except for a cover of leafy branches which they cut from the *emihalia*-bush.

Among the Idaxo, the boys begin to gather only a few days before the circumcision takes place and, like the Tiriki, sing circumcision songs and spend the nights together in the hut of some old man or woman. The elders choose for each hut a guardian or tutor (*omutili*) who looks after the candidates, leads their songs, and performs numerous services for them throughout the course of the ceremonies. The candidates must observe rules of conduct resembling those of the Tiriki lads, but, instead of making a confession of their misdeeds, they undergo a purification ceremony on the morning of the day on which they are circumcised. To quote from a text:

'When the time reaches eight o'clock in the morning, they look for an old woman who may grind six measures full of millet (eleusine). Then the flour is mixed with water and an old man puts it into a pot; then he draws it with a calabash and blows it on the boys' chests. If there is one among them who has made a girl pregnant he "is blown" all over his body with that flour which is called *ingosia* or *fivudu*. And at that time each boy must kill a fowl (which he gets) from his home and which he may eat together with all the other boys. When they have finished eating and being blown, they may leave the house and sing: "*Wohée, wohée*, they said we are no men, *wohée, wohée*, they said we are no men." Now the tutors who have been chosen must listen for the operator; if they hear him beat a thing called *mudidi* (a small drum) they can take the boys into the bush. There they root up the sticks which are called *dzinundu*[1] and the tutors can give them to the candidates to take into their right hands. They dance with them and sing: "*Wohée, wohée*, they said we were no men, &c." until the tutors lead them to the open place where the circumcision takes place.'

Among the neighbouring Tsotso, the preparatory observances are very much less elaborate. The candidates sing no songs, sleep in the boys' huts as always until the day of circumcision arrives, and they neither observe special rules nor do they undergo a purification rite. They merely take a bath in a stream and have their heads shaved before they assemble at the place where they are to be circumcised.

Among the Logoli, finally, the candidates sleep in the open for the last three nights, small groups from neighbouring homesteads staying together in a valley in the neighbourhood of a stream. They remain there also during daytime, sitting round a fire which they keep going continuously, singing circumcision songs and boasting of their courage. In the daytime an old man (*omukulundu wemisango*, the elder of the sacrifices) stays with them and gives them instructions as to how they must behave when they stand before the circumcision operator and what they have to do later on

[1] i.e. the Raffia palm.

when they will be living in the hut of seclusion. While they stay in the valley each boy chooses a special friend (*omírongo*) whom he rubs with white clay all over his face and body and who, in turn, performs the same service for him. These two boys then remain close friends for their whole lives and support one another like brothers when they are in need. They also contribute to one another's marriage-cattle. As a rule, they belong to the same clan, but if they belong to different clans they henceforth behave in some ways like clan-brothers towards one another, i.e. they cannot marry each other's sisters, although the children would be permitted to intermarry.

On the last morning the candidates bathe in the stream, wash off their paint, and throw away the belts made of the leaves of sweet potatoes which they had tied round their loins while they stayed in the valley. They appear completely naked before the operator carrying only the *dzinundu-*sticks.

(3) THE DAY OF THE OPERATION

After the candidates have been ritually prepared by the observance of taboos, by confessions and purification rites, and after their morale has been tested and stiffened by the psychological effect of the common boasting and singing of songs, they are now considered ready to face the operation and the considerable pain which it involves.

The expert who performs the operation (*omukevi*) is a man of ordinary social status. He belongs to the same category as other experts who perform various services for individuals for payment. But, although his office is not linked up with the alleged possession of special magic or other supernatural virtues, the number of circumcision operators is quite small. Succession to the office of *omukevi* is restricted to sons and, exceptionally, to maternal nephews. The art of circumcising is never taught to outsiders for payment. Only a few clans in each tribe thus have *avakevi* of their own. Among the Tiriki, who number 17,000 people, there are only four operators, three belonging to the Loxova clan and one to the Mbo clan. The Idaxo have two operators with their sons as helpers who belong to the Masava clan which is said to have held the office exclusively from the distant past. Not only do they circumcise all the candidates of their tribe but they also tour the country of the Logoli and Nyole who have no operators of their own. The Tsotso, likewise, have no operators in their own tribe but engage the services of the experts of the Kakalelwa and Kabras (Nyala) tribes who, they say, possess more skill than the operators of the Idaxo.

Among the Vugusu, the number of operators is slightly larger, but they also are limited to a few clans only. With the exception of the Tiriki who claim that the circumcision operators are rich people, they are not supposed to amass lasting wealth through the performance of the operation, as they give away most of the fowls and goats which they collect as payment for the operation and as fines for any misdemeanours of the candidates.

The fact that not all tribes have circumcision operators of their own may possibly be due to a differential age of the ceremony among the different tribes. This explanation is supported by the fact that at the present time the Vugusu, Tiriki, and Idaxo cling far more tenaciously to the performance of the circumcision rites than the Logoli and Nyole, among whom circumcision has become rather erratic during the last twenty years. The Logoli themselves explain the absence of operators in their own tribe by pointing out that it requires particular skill and long experience to perform the operation without causing fatal injuries to the patients and that for a long time there has been no clan or family in their tribe which has had this experience. Besides, it appears that fear prevents a would-be operator from experimenting with the circumcision knife, as stories are told about operators who were beaten to death because some of their patients had died from loss of blood. Among the Vugusu, one clan which formerly 'owned' the office of *ovukevi* has given it up altogether owing to a succession of ill-fated operations. Actually it should not be very difficult for persons other than the hereditary experts to acquire the manual skill necessary for the performance of the operation, for onlookers are not kept at a distance[1] but may watch the operator at close quarters while he circumcises the boys. But, as with any other native craft which is in the hands of experts, a person could not successfully and auspiciously practise it unless he had rightfully acquired the knowledge pertaining to it and had obtained the consent of his master and teacher to make use of it. In this sense every native craft has its magical aspect, even if it does not involve the possession and the handling of a specific magical substance or the uttering of secret spells. A further possible reason for engaging the services of operators from neighbouring and even hostile tribes is that the hatred which the candidates feel towards them should preferably be directed towards strangers and not towards members of their own clan or tribe.

The operator does not, as far as I could discover, perform any preparatory magic before he sets out to circumcise the candidates. He is accompanied by his sons or some neighbours who serve as his helpers, carrying his knives and collecting the fowls and the meat which he receives for his services. To notify the elders and the candidates of his impending arrival, he sends a drum-beater (*omukubi*) ahead who with one stick continuously beats a small, high-pitched drum, the monotonous rhythm of which can be heard over a considerable distance. It is easily recognized as the signal of the operator's approach and feared accordingly by the candidates. The operator and his entourage do not waste much time at each locality but quickly proceed from place to place. On the one occasion when I saw the operation performed I had to follow the sound of the drum for over an hour until I caught up with the operator who within that hour had operated upon boys at three different places. The operator is in such a hurry, partly because he has to circumcise hundreds of boys within as short a space of time as possible, so that all the subsequent ceremonies can be

[1] Except among the Tiriki, cf. below, p. 348.

timed to coincide, and partly because the different operators compete with one another, each anxious to circumcise as great a number of boys as he can.

The operator's attire is very much the same among all the tribes. He dresses himself up so as to look as fierce and awe-inspiring as possible. His face, the upper part of his body, and his arms and legs are painted with streaks of white, red, and black paint; round his face he ties a head-dress of colobus monkey-skin (*enduviri*), round the waist a leopard-skin, and iron rattles round his legs. Only the attire of the Tiriki operators is different: they merely cover their bodies with leaves of the *emihalia*-bush like the candidates, but otherwise go quite naked.

While the candidates line up to be circumcised the operator dances about wildly, jumping up and down in an abrupt rhythm and dashing towards the boys brandishing his knife, thereby showing his impatience 'to be let loose' on the boys. The candidates, however, must not be intimidated by his antics. Among the Vugusu they are even expected to rush forward individually and try to beat the operator with their *dzinundu*-sticks to show that they defy his challenge.

Among the majority of tribes the operation is performed in a large open pasture, a sort of village green or common, where all big feasts and dances as well as the judicial sittings of the clan-elders take place. Among the Vugusu, however, the candidates are operated upon in small groups in the front yard of their father's homestead, the boys of one lineage assembling at the homestead of their 'eldest father'. Among the Tiriki the operation is performed at a clearing in the forest,[1] the access to which can be easily guarded and so the presence of women and children prevented. With the exception of the Tiriki, the ceremony is performed quite publicly, the candidates being surrounded by a large group of onlookers of either sex and all ages who shout encouraging remarks at them and closely watch for any signs of flinching or faltering.

A number of devices are employed which help the candidates to show courage and remain steady while they undergo the operation. Among the Vugusu a man who knows where to find a rare root (*tjitiaɲi*) which is supposed to lend courage to anyone who comes in contact with it is engaged by the father of the candidate. For the payment of the stomach of the cow of *lúvaga* this man digs a little hole in the yard and puts the root inside, one branch of it protruding from the ground like a stick. The candidate then stands on the spot where the root has been buried and grips its protruding part between the big and the second toe of his right foot. This is supposed to enable him to stand straight on the spot without flinching.

With the exception of the Tiriki, among whom the candidates, having been led to believe that nothing serious will happen to them, are caught by force and held down to be circumcised, the boys stand up while they are operated upon, without being supported by anybody. With both hands

[1] The particular site is called *Mukavunyondje*.

CIRCUMCISION AND INITIATION RITES

raised up to their shoulders they hold the raffia switches (*dzinundu*) behind their necks. This is supposed to help them to stand erect and to maintain a straight and steady look in their eyes.

The Tiriki candidates, having assembled at various places, walk in single file to the forest, singing songs and carrying shields which they have been given by their fathers. When they are still about a hundred yards away from the operator they kneel down and, upon a sign given by him, crawl towards him and then stand up again. The operator walks along the whole row of boys, pretending to cut off the foreskin of each but actually touching it only. Then he gives a quick sign to all the fathers to catch their respective sons from behind and, each of them being caught unawares, he performs the real operation.

The Idaxo candidates line up for the operation in several concentric circles which they form round a special long-lived tree (*musembe* or *musutsu*). Quite a small tree is chosen for the purpose, but its growth marks the advance in status of the age-grade that has been circumcised under it, and it later serves as a meeting-place for its members. The candidates stand close together, their arms interlocked and thus supporting one another in maintaining a courageous attitude.

Among the Vugusu, the first boy to be circumcised is always the oldest one in the lineage; among the other tribes he is the one who displays the greatest amount of courage by challenging the operator to come to him first. He then enjoys a favoured and honoured position throughout the subsequent ceremonies. Among the tribes where no confession is made to the elders beforehand, the operator asks each candidate whether he has violated any taboos or disregarded any of the other prohibitions. To induce the boy not to withhold anything, he whets his circumcision knife in front of him and tells him that the operation will be painless if he confesses all his misdeeds, but that it will hurt him very much and possibly even cause him to die if he omits anything from his statement. Besides averting a magical pollution of the knife and the dangers this might entail for the other candidates, the operator has a material interest in insisting upon the candidate making a full confession, as he levies a special fine from the candidate's father for every misdeed committed by his son.

With the exception of the Vugusu, among whom the operator's assistant (*omuvingilisi*) sprinkles some white powder (dried and pounded clay) on the candidate's penis to prevent the prepuce from sliding forward again, no medicine is applied to the penis before the operation takes place. Should the penis be too small from fear or exposure to the cold to permit performing the operation properly, the operator beats it with a stick to cause a slight erection.

The manner in which the operation of circumcision is performed shows minor variations among the different tribes. Among the Idaxo, Isuxa, Logoli, and Nyole the operator first pulls forward the prepuce as far as it goes and then feels with the nail of his left thumb where the glans of the penis ends. Then he releases the foreskin momentarily and, pulling it out again, cuts it off with a quick downward stroke of the circumcision knife (*eŋembe*) which he holds in his right hand. To prevent the severed foreskin from twitching, he quickly steps on it with his foot. Next he cuts a slit, about ¾ inch long, along the dorsal side of the remaining part of the prepuce. Through the hole thus made he pushes the tip of the glans and then, beginning at the end of the dorsal incision, quickly cuts round the base of the foreskin, first to the right then to the left and, finally, severing the remaining part with a quick forward stroke underneath the penis.

A second method which is followed among the Vugusu and Tiriki is to fold back the remainder of the foreskin (the first part having been cut off in the same way as has been described), then to make an incision (not a slit) on the dorsal side up to the corona and, finally, to cut round at the base (*lúsinga*) of the foreskin while the assistant holds the glans and turns it slowly as the operator cuts. He either cuts a complete circle or first to the right, then to the left, and then severs the foreskin at the bottom. Among the Tiriki the operator lets a flap of foreskin stand underneath the glans. As this device is followed only among the Tiriki it serves as a distinguishing tribal mark.

The instrument used by the operator is either a single- or a double-bladed knife. Though of ordinary shape it is never employed for any other purpose. Among the Logoli, the operator carries with him only one knife, and it was stressed by my informants as an important rule that he must not wash the blood off the knife nor off his hands or his body until after he has finished circumcising all the boys of the tribe. This rule stands in direct contrast to the practice prevailing among the neighbouring Nyole where the operator has a whole basketful of knives, and must use a different one for each clan, a rule that is carefully observed by the clan-elders who inspect the knife before the first boy of their clan is circumcised. Among the Idaxo, the operator cleans the knife after every operation by dipping it into a calabash of water which one of his assistants carries for him. In Kitosh, where double-bladed knives are used, one knife always serves four candidates, the older two being circumcised with one blade and the younger two with the other. Later in life, the two boys who were circumcised with the same blade of the knife refer to this fact when they wish to stress their mutual friendship by saying: 'We are both of one blade.' The older one also assures the younger one, rather inaptly, 'When I was circumcised the knife was too sharp, so I have made it easier for you.'

Thus among all tribes the number of candidates circumcised with the same knife and the manner of cleaning it are ritually significant factors. We shall examine later on[1] how far the variations mentioned can be correlated with other differences in the respective tribal cultures and how far they must be considered merely different, fortuitous expressions of

---

[1] See vol. ii, where a special chapter will be devoted to the discussion of tribal variants and the problem of their interpretation.

CIRCUMCISION AND INITIATION RITES

the same basic idea, viz. that it is necessary to handle the blood-stained knife with ritual care.

Boys who suffer from a disease, though not necessarily a contagious one according to European notions, are generally circumcised with a special knife which is kept separate from the others. In that case the boy's father has to pay an extra fee to the operator.

On the one occasion where I saw the operation performed the whole procedure took only slightly over ten seconds and impressed me as being carried out with great skill and dexterity. The edge of the blade of the knife used was perfectly smooth and seemed at least as sharp as the blade of a penknife of good quality. Although there are various indications that the sensitiveness to physical pain is less acutely developed among natives who have not been under the prolonged influence of civilization than among Europeans, it is considered by the natives a severe test of manhood to endure the operation of circumcision without flinching or showing pain by facial gestures. Generally, more than half of the boys are said to display more or less pronounced signs of fear, but I never heard of boys having fainted during the operation. If one of them tries to catch the operator's hand or to run off at the last moment he is held by his clansmen and afterwards has to listen to songs of derision, sung by the girls and women who dance in front of the initiates while they sit in the shade of a tree waiting for the wound to stop bleeding. Moreover, to stamp such a boy as a coward, the operator bedaubs his face with streaks of blood which he must not wash off for several days.

No medicine is applied to the wound to stop the bleeding which commonly continues for thirty or forty minutes after the operation has been performed. To prevent the penis from touching the thighs and thus irritating the wound, the tutor hands each boy a string made of banana-fibre with a noose into which he puts his penis, thus holding it up in a horizontal position. If the wound bleeds excessively this is considered a sign that the candidate has committed a theft at some time in the past, and his father must then render an additional payment to the operator who stops the bleeding by uttering a spell over it, saying or singing: 'My son, I have disabled you; my son I have disabled you.' The operator is also supposed to be able to tell the boy's father from looking at his son's blood whether he will become a courageous warrior and 'a begetter of many children' or not. If the blood is 'hot' it is a good sign; if it is 'cool' it is a bad sign and the father will urge his son to start an early courtship to test his manhood.

While a boy is being circumcised, his father stands close by and encourages him to keep steady, at the same time admonishing the operator to be careful with his knife. The operation is thus almost as critical a moment for the father as for the son. If the son's behaviour is cowardly, the father's shame is so great that he runs away from the crowd and hides in the bush. Later he will refuse to send food to his son, and their mutual relations might even be seriously disrupted for years. Women and children watch the performance of the operation from a distance, while the boy's mother runs into her hut and clasps the centre pole with her arms and legs as this 'will help her son to keep steady'.

Among the Vugusu, immediately after a boy has been circumcised, a girl who is in love with him or who has already been courted by him rushes towards the boy and from behind throws her arms round his hips, thereby claiming him her future husband. The boy's father then has to act up to the girl's advances and give or at least promise her a 'heifer of friendship' which, if actually given to her, publicly seals the betrothal. However, if the boy does not like the girl he can later refuse to marry her, although this would bring disgrace and ridicule upon her. The other girls would then make up songs like the following about her:

> *Naliaga wenakweyendelo*
> *keyendela hali vusa, vakulova*
> *gwaŋoŋáŋoŋa.*
>
> 'Naliaga chose for herself;
> she chose in vain (because) they refused her,
> now she feels ashamed.'

As a rule, however, only those girls would claim a boy who had some secret understanding with him that he would marry them. This custom was abandoned at the circumcision rites in 1927, 'as the girls were getting too shy to claim the boys of their choice in public'.

For about an hour after the boys have been circumcised they sit down quietly in the shade of some bushes or leafy branches that their guardians have stuck in the ground behind them to make them feel more comfortable. If a boy still has enough energy left he may run after the operator, beat him with a stick, and try to tear off his head-dress. If he succeeds in doing so, the operator must give him three chickens as a reward for his pluck.

While the boys are resting, their sisters and mothers dance in front of them, praising their courage in various songs and shrieking with delight. At the Nyole circumcision I saw some mothers dancing in front of their sons for half an hour without stopping, shaking gourd-rattles right under their noses, and making a frantic noise to which their sons responded only with increasing apathy. Occasionally the women began to quarrel, each taunting the other that her son had trembled, but their voices were soon drowned again by the singing and rattling of the other women.

As soon as the last boy has been circumcised the operator moves off to another place, accompanied by his assistants, who carry the fowls and drive off the goats and sheep which he has collected. Usually the operator is paid one fowl for performing the operation and another one later on for giving the boys permission to wash themselves and for administering a disinfectant medicine to them. To this 'basic fee' is added a large variety of fines which differ from tribe to tribe. The usual charge is one fowl for each item in the candidate's confession and a sheep or goat for weightier

PLATE 13

A. *Taking gifts from bride's to bridegroom's place: North Kitosh*

B. *Dancing at a wedding in the* lidegeriza *fashion: South Maragoli*

PLATE 14

A. *A maternal uncle giving rules of matrimonial conduct to the bride: North Kitosh*

B. *Beer-drinking in the shade of a banana grove: South Maragoli*

CIRCUMCISION AND INITIATION RITES

offences, e.g. if the candidate has caused a girl to be pregnant or if he suffers from a venereal disease. The candidate's father must also pay another fowl after the operation if his son had to be held down by force or if the operator had to devote special attention to him to stop his wound from bleeding. At the end of each day's work the operator is entertained with beer and eleusine porridge but, as he has become ritually unclean through the performance of the operation, he and his helpers must eat in a separate hut from their hosts. They must not touch the food with their fingers but eat with small sticks. Among the Vugusu the operator also gets the head of the bullock which the father of each boy kills for his own age-mates.

(4) THE LIFE OF THE INITIATES IN THE HUT OF SECLUSION

After all the initiates have been circumcised and after they have duly rested in the shade of the trees, they proceed—in single file but in no particular order—to the hut of seclusion (Lurogoli: *etumbi*; Luvugusu: *ligombe*) where they will spend the next few months. Among the Tiriki, where, as we have said, the operation takes place in the presence of men only, the initiates must not be seen by women and children on their way to the initiation hut. Among the other tribes, there is no secrecy about this and all the onlookers may accompany the initiates continuing to sing their songs of praise. From now on until the performance of the ceremonies which mark the end of the period of initiation the lads are called *avakulu* and their behaviour and activities during the following months are governed by numerous rules and observances. They are from now on separated from their relatives and live under the care and control of a number of tutors or guardians (*avadili*). These *avadili* perform numerous services for them, especially during the period of convalescence and, at the same time, maintain discipline among them and instruct them both in general knowledge and in the particular ritual observances which are demanded from the initiates. The only other persons with whom the initiates regularly come into contact are young girls, the *avadili vakana* or 'female guardians'. Their main tasks are to bring food to the initiates and to provide them with water and firewood; but they also perform a number of duties in connexion with the further rites and ceremonies.

The tutors or male guardians are, as a rule, youngish men who have been circumcised one or two age-grades before the present initiates. They are appointed by the elders of the different clans, their choice being determined by their qualification for leadership and the courage they showed when they were themselves circumcised. In addition they must have a good all-round knowledge of those tribal crafts which every man should know as well as skill in hunting and in the handling of weapons. Once chosen, the tutors are left to themselves by the elders, who do not interfere with their activities or their treatment of the initiates. The number of initiates who are under the care of one such tutor varies among the different tribes, as does the number of boys who stay together in one hut. In Kitosh, on an average, five or six boys stay in one hut under the care of one tutor. Among the Lugoli and Tiriki the huts are occupied by twenty or even more initiates, all under one tutor or guardian, while among the Idaxo and Isuxa each guardian looks after only two boys and there are four or five guardians in charge of each hut. It appears that this large number of tutors among the Idaxo is due to the fact that they have to perform far more services for their pupils than is the case among the other tribes. The nature of the relations that prevail between the tutors and their pupils will become clear from the subsequent account of the life which the initiates lead at the *etumbi*-hut and the rules and regulations which they have to observe.

The female guardians must always be young girls 'who have not yet entered into wifehood'. No particular stress, however, is laid on their virginity as is the case with young girls who assist in the performance of sacrificial rites. There is usually one girl for each initiate. Although, as we shall see later on, the contacts between the initiate and his female guardian are such that they would easily offer scope for love-making between the two, it was emphatically denied by all my informants that this aspect entered into their relationship at all. It was maintained that a courtship between them would be regarded as just as serious a lapse from the prescribed norm as the offence of incest. The female guardian calls the initiate *omwana wange*, 'my child', and he calls her *mama wange*, 'my mother'. It is left to the initiate to choose his female guardian. It makes no difference whether the girl he chooses is related to him or not. In many cases the initiate will choose his real or a near classificatory sister, but if he prefers to choose a girl from another clan he may do so; only he cannot later marry her 'as he has called her *mama*'.

The lads who stay together in one hut do not necessarily belong to the same clan. However, as in all Kavirondo tribes the clans form territorial units, it naturally comes about that the majority of inmates of one hut do belong to the same clan. Lads whose fathers live as so-called *avamenya*[1] in their wife's clan or that of their mother do not join up with their own clan-mates but stay with the boys of the clan in which they live. In Kitosh the boys who have been circumcised in the same yard usually stay together in the same hut and the inmates of one hut, therefore, tend to belong to one lineage, but there is no strict segregation according to lineages. A boy who happens to be staying with his maternal uncle or at the homestead of his father's sister can be circumcised at the place 'where he is visiting' and then stay in one hut together with his cousins or his friends. Formerly, the boys who belonged to one *lúgova* (walled village) were all circumcised together, and if they were too many to find room in one hut they were distributed at random over two or three huts. Among the Tiriki where all boys of the tribe—usually several hundred—are circumcised at the same

[1] Cf. above, p. 56.

place they split up into arbitrary local groups of thirty or forty lads who stay together in one hut irrespective of their clan or kinship affiliations.

The rules concerning the initiation huts and the sites where they have to be built vary slightly among the different tribes. Among the Tiriki the huts must be put up at lonely spots in the forest, as far away from other homesteads as possible, so that women and children can be prevented from coming near them. They must be newly built for each generation of initiates a few weeks before the operation takes place. The tutors direct the work and help the initiates to cut the poles, while the female guardians mud the walls and beat the floor so that it may become hard. In Kitosh, likewise, the initiation huts must be newly built, a task that must be performed by the novices themselves. They are, however, put up near other homesteads, formerly even within the walled villages, and not at a secluded spot. Among all the other tribes, the elders look for a respected old man, preferably a widower, who agrees to vacate his own hut and put it at the disposal of the initiates, who then build a new hut for him to live in. In explanation of this custom I was told that by staying in the hut of an old man his knowledge and wisdom would be communicated to the initiates. No special arrangements are made in the interior of the hut, nor does its outer appearance differ from ordinary living-huts. Before the initiates enter it the tutors collect banana-leaves and bark which they spread out for the boys to sleep on, while the female guardians fetch wood and build a big fire in the centre of the hut. When the initiates first enter the hut they must do so backwards and using the side-door by which they must always enter and leave until 'the feast of coming out' when they are for the first time permitted to use the front door. A day or two after the boys have entered the hut the operator returns for a visit and 'locks' the front door of the initiation hut by stopping up all the holes and slits with banana-bark and placing a number of banana-trunks against the wicker door, which he firmly ties to the door-posts. When he has thus ceremonially shut the initiates in, he sings the following song:

> *Vana vandje, vana vandje,*
> *maswétjela yese,*
> *maswétjela.*
>
> 'My children, my children,
> it (the operation) made you stay inside,
> it made you stay inside.'

Then he leaves the initiates without seeing them again.

While staying in the initiation hut the boys are under the constant control of their tutors who are with them all day and who, among some tribes, also sleep in the same hut as the boys but on a raised bedstead (*ekidali*), while the initiates sleep on the floor. The female guardians spend the nights as always in the hut of the unmarried girls, except among the Nyole, where they sleep in the loft of the initiation hut.

Soon after they have entered the *etumbi*-hut the initiates are given their first meal, which has been prepared and brought to them by the female guardians. As long as the boys have not yet been ceremonially cleansed by the operator they must not touch the food with their hands. Thus the tutors either supply them with sticks which serve them as eating-implements (Vugusu, Tiriki), or they give them thin gruel only which they can drink from calabashes (Idaxo, Logoli). Among the Logoli the guardian feeds them with cooked bananas for the first day to make them urinate as seldom as possible as this is said to be painful while the wound is still fresh. During the period of convalescence the initiates' staple food is eleusine, which is considered to have a better flavour and to taste 'sweeter' than the more frequently grown sorghum. The initiates must avoid eating starchy and spicy food (especially potatoes) for some time, as such food is said to cause pus to form in their wounds. After they have fully recovered they can eat every kind of food and are plentifully supplied with a large variety of foodstuffs by their mothers in addition to what they bring home from their own hunting- and raiding-excursions.

While they are staying in the *etumbi* the initiates must observe special eating rules which teach them restraint and a willingness to share things with others. At every meal they must obtain the tutor's permission before they may begin to eat, and if he happens to be away when their food is brought, they must wait till he returns, even if this should take several hours. Besides, although each boy is sent his own meals by his mother or female guardian they all pool their food and eat it together, so that they all get an equal share. Among the Logoli and Isuxa, the novices for a whole month are given nothing but gruel, which they pour into a sort of trough (one half of a honey-barrel which an old man has given the initiates as a present). Holding their arms behind their backs, they all kneel down in front of the trough and drink the gruel 'like cows', i.e. without using a calabash. Explaining this custom to me, one elder said: 'During their stay in the *etumbi* the initiates must act like cows in many ways, because cows are very helpful giving us milk and meat and skins. The initiates behave like cows, so that they may become useful like cows.'

When the initiates have stayed in the *etumbi* for several days, the operator comes and ceremonially washes every boy by pouring a calabashful of water over his hands. If the operator had to circumcise a large number of boys, a few weeks may pass from the day of circumcision until he returns to perform this 'washing ceremony'. In that case the initiates may wash themselves in the meantime and even bathe in a stream, but they do not thereby become ritually clean. They must, therefore, continue to use sticks or otherwise avoid touching the food with their hands until the operator has performed the ritual cleansing, a service for which he charges another fowl. Often he collects all the fees and fines only on this occasion. In Kitosh the fathers of the initiates brew a special 'beer of washing' to which they invite the operator but of which the initiates themselves do not get a share.

CIRCUMCISION AND INITIATION RITES

On the third day after the operation—either before or after the ceremonial washing—the tutors collect the leaves of a certain medicinal plant, called *ingói*. These are then dried and burnt and the tutors or the initiates themselves either put the ashes on the wound with a chicken-feather or strew them on a piece of banana-leaf which is then wrapped round the penis. Apparently this medicine, which is used by all the Bantu Kavirondo tribes, acts as a disinfectant, for it is said to prevent pus from forming in the wound and to quicken the process of healing. Its application to the wound is said to cause severe pain; some people even claim that it hurts more than the operation itself. To be able to stand the initial pain, which subsides after a few minutes, the patients distract their minds by scratching their knees and legs till they bleed. Among the Idaxo, the operator administers a further medicine (*amasambu*) to the initiates when he has finished performing the 'ceremony of washing'. This medicine is said to neutralize the dangerous effects which the violation of one of the taboos that have been imposed upon the candidates might otherwise have: 'It prevents even those boys from dying after the operation who have committed bad deeds.' It thus apparently strengthens the redeeming effect of the confession which among the Idaxo does not take place before the operation but simultaneously with the 'washing ceremony'. In accordance with its magical purport, the medicine, in order to be effective, must be administered and taken in a specific manner. Each initiate in turn licks it from the operator's hand; next he spits it into his right, then into his left hand, and finally he swallows it.

As long as the initiates are still suffering from their wounds they stay in the *etumbi*-hut most of the time and only walk about a little in the yard outside the hut, supporting themselves on sticks which their tutors cut for them. Ordinarily the wound caused by the operation heals up within a fortnight. Serious infections are, apparently, very rare. Following the operations performed on several hundred boys of the Idaxo and Isuxa tribes in the autumn of 1937 not a single case of death or serious illness seems to have occurred. Although such cases would be hushed up, they would certainly have come to the notice of my Christian informants.

Should an initiate die from the effects of the operation his death is not bewailed but passed over in silence. His relatives are not properly informed of his death but are only given a hint of what has happened by being told by the tutor that they do not need to bring food for him regularly or that it will be sufficient if they cook smaller quantities of it. Moreover, the initiates on their daily walks sing the following song which indicates to everyone that a death has occurred among them:

> *Mbue, vana vandje,*
> *nyende nambeya.*
>
> 'Mbue, my children,
> the worm is the eater.'

The song refers to the fact that the worms are eating the decaying body of the deceased boy. A mother who suspects then tries to make certain what has happened by secretly watching the initiates when they sit in the morning sun to warm themselves; if she fails to recognize her son among them she knows that it is he who has died. But even then the mother and the other relatives of the deceased must sing circumcision songs only, for 'if they were to wail over their child's death, their wailing would cause all the other initiates to die as well'. If a boy gets seriously ill while staying in the initiation hut he may be removed to the place of a very old woman but not to his mother's place, unless she is past the child-bearing age. 'Should this rule be disregarded, the mother could never bear another child.'

As soon as the initiates have recovered from the operation they are free to move about. First, however, they weave long grass-masks and dresses which they must wear whenever they leave the hut. This rule is based on the belief that if their faces were seen by other people the *avakula* would be attacked by a disease. Besides, the masks are said to make good ornaments for dancing with. They are made in two different styles. The more elaborate ones which one finds among the Tiriki, Logoli, and Nyole are woven from the rind of switches cut from the *imásia* and *umbure*-trees which have a greyish and brownish colour respectively. To add a third colour, the *umbure* switches are dyed black by putting them for one night into black muddy soil. The top part of the mask consists of a bell-shaped 'helmet' covering the whole head and neck and having only two openings for the eyes, with a tube-like rim protruding about an inch. When weaving the mask the different coloured strands of bark are intertwined in such a way that broad horizontal ribbons of grey, brown, and black alternate. The only other decoration of the top part of the mask is a small piece of monkey-skin which is sewn on between the holes for the eyes. The vertical strands of the top part continue into long plaited fringes covering the body down to the waist or even further. The tutors teach the initiates how to weave the masks and how to plait the strings, a task which is said to take the initiates nearly two weeks.

The other type of mask which is found among the Isuxa and Idaxo is a semi-stiff grass cloak stretching in one piece from above the head to just below the knees. It has a pointed top to which a number of 'handles' (*mihambo*) are attached which are said to be merely decorative. The cloak is made of *fivembe*-grass in the fashion of a mat and is of a texture loose enough to permit the initiates to peep through although it has no special holes for the eyes.

Among the Vugusu, the initiates do not wear such masks or grass dresses. Instead they rub their whole bodies with white clay (*lulongo*) and smear the milky juice of Euphorbia leaves into their hair till it forms a thick sticky mass.

Besides masks and cloaks the initiates wear short skirts of *amavinu*-leaves round their loins (Idaxo, Isuxa, Logoli), or they are given skins of young heifers or bull-calves (*esumati*) which reach down below their knees (Vugusu, Tiriki). Round their legs the Tiriki initiates wrap string, and to the top of their masks they tie tall tufts of grass. About a month before they leave the circumcision hut they replace these tufts by elaborate wooden head-dresses (*igwálo*) which they carve in the shape of buffalo horns and which they richly adorn with grass streamers.

When going out for their walks the initiates must observe a number of rules. They cannot enter the houses of their relatives and accept food there, nor must they talk with their parents who are forbidden to enter the *etumbi*. When they meet other initiates or circumcised men they do not salute them with the customary *milembe* (peace) but by beating against their shin-bones with the sticks they carry. Among the Tiriki they are said to do this with such vehemence that the older men run away when they catch sight of the initiates. This attitude might suggest that a feeling of hatred and revengefulness prevails among the initiates, because they have been deceived by the old men who had assured them that no pain would be inflicted upon them. This interpretation, however, was not endorsed by my informants who insisted that this form of 'salute' was not spontaneous but in accordance with the instructions the initiates had received from their tutors. Among the Vugusu, on the other hand, it is the privilege of the old men to hit the initiates against their shin-bones whenever they meet them or when they come to visit them in their hut. Their visits are therefore not welcome to the initiates who may retaliate only by a weak stroke, as respect for the elders prevents them from hitting hard. Nowhere may the initiates salute one another or other people with words as, if they were to do so, 'they would not marry but become madmen'.

When the initiates meet grown-up men who are not yet circumcised or those of their age-mates who ran away from the operation at the last moment, they give them a good beating or threaten them with songs, such as the following:

> *Nembona sigonela eé eé,*
> *nembona sigonela wanangali*
> *gumuxono gwárenga,*
> *nembona Muxalisi owavurema*
> *gumuoyo gwárenga,*
> *sigonela eé, eé.*
>
> 'If I see a coward, Oh, Oh!
> If I see a coward who is to be despised,
> my arm is shaking (to beat him);
> if I see Muxalisi (the operator), the one who cut,
> my heart is shaking (with anger),
> the coward, Oh!'

But a *sigonela*, a coward, can make friends with the initiates if he regularly supplies them with milk, eggs, and honey or other pleasant things. They will then refrain from beating him and will protect him from being molested by other initiates. A boy who has been circumcised together with the others but who behaved like a coward and had to be held down by force may stay in one hut together with the other initiates, but he has to endure many humiliations from the other boys. Among the Vugusu they continue to call him *omusinde* like an uncircumcised boy and they do not take him with them when they go to the stream to rub themselves with clay, claiming that his presence would increase the pain caused by their wounds. Among the Logoli the boys who have flinched during the operation are not permitted to take part in the sham fights in which the warriors engage with the initiates and they are taunted if they try to join the others in their various activities.

After the initiates have recovered from their wounds a good deal of their time is devoted to the acquisition of theoretical and practical knowledge imparted to them by their tutors. The teaching of the theoretical knowledge consists chiefly in the recital of certain general rules of behaviour and etiquette which a grown-up person must obey and which a father would feel ashamed to talk about with his son. The tutor tells them, for instance, that a circumcised boy must not enter the cooking- or sleeping-partition of his mother's hut; he warns them against the various forms of incest and instructs them in the rules of exogamy. He also tells them how they have to behave in the presence of men of higher age-grades. Some of my informants also insisted that he warns them against all the more common anti-social offences, such as adultery, assault, theft, &c., but no instruction is given in the laws and rules that govern the ownership of property, inheritance, and succession, as 'every boy learns these rules from his father as he grows up'. Other informants claim that the tutor also discusses matters of sex life with the initiates, e.g. how to proceed when visiting the hut of the unmarried girls, &c. Among the Tiriki, where most of the circumcision procedure is kept secret, one of the main points of the tutors' instruction is to warn the initiates against betraying any phase of the ritual to the women and the uncircumcised.

As none of my informants was able to give me any set forms of such instruction and as the accounts of what is taught vary considerably, the scope and character of the instruction do not seem to follow any rigid pattern but to depend to a large extent upon the tutor himself. Leading a common life with the initiates, he would naturally talk with them as men talk among men, even without having the explicit duty of imparting particular knowledge to them. Only one of my Logoli informants (Christopher Mtiva) claimed that the tutor gives regular lessons every morning before sunrise as well as every evening and that he appoints five initiates who have to repeat every morning what he has told them the night before. As this form of systematic instruction was not confirmed by any of the older men who were circumcised in pre-mission days it would appear that the particular tutor to whom my informant referred had adopted European teaching methods.

CIRCUMCISION AND INITIATION RITES

The practical knowledge which is imparted to the initiates appears to be of far greater importance than the theoretical. Besides being taught by the tutors to weave their circumcision masks, they are instructed in various other crafts which are common knowledge among all men, such as basketry, skin-dressing and sewing, and the building of huts and granaries. The main stress, however, seems to be laid on hunting and shooting. Among the Vugusu the initiates make their own weapons—bows and sharpened sticks (as arrows)—with which they practise shooting every afternoon, using banana-trunks, which they stick into the ground at increasing distances, as targets. Each boy shoots in turn and acclaims his success with long-drawn-out shouts as he would do in actual fighting. The girls may look on and encourage the initiates by praising the good shots and laughing at those who fail. The importance attached to these shooting practices is shown by the fact that they are preceded by a special feast, the 'beer of target-shooting' (*gamalua gétoa*), which the initiates brew for their fathers and relatives without, however, themselves participating in the beer-drink. Among the Logoli the tutor, likewise, instructs the initiates in the use of the different weapons and during the daily excursions into the bush practises with them the various methods of approaching the enemy, how to use the shields for making signs, and how to abduct cattle. Shortly before the 'feast of coming out of the initiation hut' is due to take place, the initiates challenge the leading warriors of their clan to a sham fight, summoning them by blowing horns as warriors do when they get ready for an actual raiding expedition. Formerly the bravest and most skilful boys were then selected by the warriors and they were permitted to accompany them when they started out for their next raid.

During their daily hunting excursions the initiates may also steal fowls from the homesteads of their fathers and of other people. These fowls they roast themselves, sharing them with their tutors, who are given the roosters while the initiates keep the hens. Such stealing expeditions have to be carried out with cunning; although they form part of the prescribed activities of the initiates, they must take care not to be caught in the act of stealing and must run away as soon as the owner of the fowls discovers them. To prevent the fowls from cackling, the Vugusu initiates tie long strings round their waists, with an iron hook (*gumulovo*) at the end to which they attach a grasshopper as bait. Among the Idaxo the initiates knock the fowls down with long poles (*tsimbú*) specially procured for them by the tutors who hide the poles again after they have been used, apparently to mark the stealing expedition as a special ceremonial occasion. In Maragoli the initiates may also steal crops from the fields.

The hunting excursions of the initiates mainly serve to teach them skill and co-operation in hunting and to provide them with plenty of meat. Such meat they may roast at their own yard, whereas the porridge and the beef which they receive from their mothers' homes are cooked there and brought to them by the female guardians. As a rule, the hunting excursions are undertaken in small groups and they are not connected with any ceremonial observances. The only hunting activity conducted in a semi-ceremonial manner is the 'beating of rats' which is undertaken jointly by all the initiates soon after they have recovered from their wounds. For this purpose the initiates cover themselves with the leaves of the *elilande*-creeper and stay out for three days killing rats which they roast and then store in the roof of the *etumbi* to eat them on various subsequent occasions as a relish with their porridge.

When the initiates have spent about half of their time or slightly more in the initiation hut a ceremonial event of a sacrificial nature takes place among most of the tribes. Its detailed procedure and significance, however, vary considerably from tribe to tribe. It is most elaborate among the Tiriki, where it consists of a ritual enactment of the death and rebirth of the initiates. The procedure at this rite was described to me in the following account:

'About a month before the initiates leave the initiation hut they assemble on the same clearing in the forest where they have been circumcised. They arrive there towards evening, each group being led by its tutor. The elders then carry big loads of banana-trunks to the forest, telling the women and children that they are going to kill the initiates with these trunks but that later they will pour water over the boys which will restore them to life. While the initiates are being led to the place of circumcision they really believe that they are going to be beaten to death and, accordingly, they are very much frightened. However, after they have all assembled, the elders tell them that nothing will happen to them but that they are merely going to deceive the women and children and that they must act their part. The elders then hit the banana-trunks against one another and against rocks, and the initiates cry and moan as if they were dying. The women are carefully kept out of sight, but they may follow the proceedings by staying within hearing distance. While the initiates are alleged to be killed they line up and, one by one, pass the heap of banana-trunks. As each boy passes it, the elders burst forth into a loud wail and shout the name of the boy who has just "died", e.g. *mixula wa Muxangula, goyiiii!*, "the son of Muxangulo oh!" The women who hear the shouts from a distance then join in the wailing. When all the boys have thus been "killed" they sit down with the elders and, for the first time in their lives, are permitted to feast together with the elders on the beef and beer which the latter have carried down to the forest for the occasion. During the feast the boys must keep perfectly silent to dispel any suspicions which the women might have that they are not really dead. Only the elders continue to wail or to imitate the noises made by hyenas.

'Before daybreak the elders and the tutors fetch the water which the women have been ordered to bring to a certain place near by and which is supposed to be poured over the "dead-ones" to bring them back to life again. A few hours after sunrise the initiates return to their respective huts, singing circumcision songs but walking "like persons who are just recovering from death", i.e. they frequently tumble and have to be lifted up again and supported by the elders and tutors who accompany them. The mothers who

CIRCUMCISION AND INITIATION RITES

may look on from a distance then feel certain that their sons have actually died and come back to life again. On that occasion the initiates still wear their circumcision masks.

'When they have returned to their huts the tutors instruct them never to tell the women and the uncircumcised boys what actually happened during the night, warning them that any offender against this rule would be certain to die.'

Among the other tribes no such ceremonial death and rebirth of the initiates is enacted, but at approximately the same time a purification ceremony takes place which apparently serves a similar purpose. Among the Idaxo the clan-elders hold a meeting when the initiates have stayed in the *etumbi*-hut for about a month, choosing an elder who is able and willing to supply a sheep for performing a sacrifice (*xwátisa*) on behalf of the initiates, 'so that they may remain well'. The sheep is skinned and then suspended at the front door of the initiation hut. The initiates line up in single file and then pass by the sheep, each boy biting off a piece of the raw meat without using his hands which he must keep behind his back.

The Logoli perform an analogous rite at about the same time. At the homestead of each clan-head (*omukulundu woluhia*) a cow is killed; its skin is then cut into narrow strips from which they make wristlets (*edzingova*) as well as necklaces for all the initiates. The hump of the cow is given to the initiates by their tutor while the other meat is eaten by the clan-elders themselves.

During the remaining weeks of their sojourn in the *etumbi*-hut the initiates practise the circumcision dance and learn the songs which they will sing at the 'feast of coming out'.

(5) THE FEAST OF COMING OUT

The life of the initiates in the *etumbi*-hut is terminated by a series of elaborate ceremonies and a period of feasting. Although the general pattern of these ceremonies is the same all over Bantu Kavirondo, the detailed procedure differs considerably from tribe to tribe. To demonstrate these differences I shall, therefore, give separate accounts of the procedure followed among the Vugusu, the Idaxo, and the Logoli.

When the Vugusu initiates have stayed in the circumcision hut for several months the elders of each lineage meet and agree to brew the *gamalua gexuxualuxa*, 'the beer of getting out', with which the elders celebrate the conclusion of the period of initiation. The proper time for the coming feast and ceremonies is determined by the round of agricultural activities: they usually wait until the second digging for the eleusine crop has been finished,[1] as then the women have time to attend to the preparation of the beer and to the grinding and cooking of the vast quantities of porridge that are required for the feast. On the day before the initiates leave the *etumbi* they build a small, dome-shaped hut (*lisali*) in a nearby banana-

[1] i.e. November–December.

grove, such as the herd-boys put up in the bush to give shelter from rain and storm. After their evening meal each initiate makes a long torch for himself. Then they collect the bloodstained banana-leaves which have served as their bedspreads and, outside the hut, pile them up in a big heap to which they set fire. When the fire is ablaze they light their torches at it, turning their backs to the flames while doing so. As soon as the torches have caught fire the parents who are looking on shout at them to hurry off. Then, without looking back at the fire, each boy rushes off with the burning torch towards the *lisali*-shelter, near which all torches are thrown upon a heap, thus starting a fire which the initiates keep going all night. As each lad rushes off with the burning torch he calls out the name of the operator who circumcised him, finishing off with long-drawn-out shouts and yells. They spend all night in the *lisali*, warming themselves at the fire and making love to the girls who, on this occasion, have permission to join the initiates. They are warned, however, not to go beyond the customary limits of premarital sexual enjoyment. During this night the initiates also have licence to hack off as many banana-bunches as they like; they may even indulge in wilful and conspicuous waste by hitting one another with the bananas which they have roasted over the fire. After they have enjoyed themselves all night in this manner they must take care to leave the banana-grove and the *lisali* before sunrise and continue the same activities in the bush, 'lest they should die soon'.

Early in the afternoon the initiates walk down to the nearest stream and wash off the white clay with which they were painted while they lived in the initiation hut. Then they exchange their old skins for new ones which their fathers have prepared for them and which are either given to them by the female guardians (*namaxala*) who meet them down at the stream or brought there by the girls the preceding night when they came to join the initiates in the banana-grove. These new skins are usually nicely tanned and decorated cowskins. The old skins are given to the girls. They take them to the initiates' paternal aunts or grandmothers who carefully clean them with ghee and then wear them themselves.

Washed, shaven, and clad in their new skins, the initiates are now called *vátembete*, the 'new and soft ones'. They are now ready to return to their fathers' homesteads where all their relatives and neighbours have gathered to drink the 'beer of getting out'. When they arrive there they are served with large quantities of cooked bananas which are poured out for them on a wicker door. They eat till they are replete and then again hit one another with the hot banana mush.

When the initiates have finished their meal their fathers or other elders hand them shields, spears, clubs, and other weapons. Holding these weapons like a warrior and standing straight and steady, one boy after the other moves to the centre of the yard of his 'old father'[1] where, in the order of seniority, every initiate is given extensive rules of conduct by his father.

[1] i.e. his father's eldest brother.

When addressing his son the father stands in front of him and, before every sentence he utters, takes a draught of beer from a new gourd, swallowing some and spitting the remainder at his son's face and chest. He gives him the following rules:

'My son, you have left behind "the mother's cloth" (i.e. the prepuce), but now you are given the father's cloth.

'If you come to a house and it is closed do not open it to enter. The closed door is not for you, only the open door is yours. If you find an old woman who has one eye,[1] go and build (a hut) for her. She will cook food for you in peace. If you see an old man call him father and treat him as a father. If he tells you to go on an errand for him accede to his request. If you find him cutting or carrying the grass help him. If you "sit in the beer" (i.e. if you are attending a beer-drink) and you are a strong boy and you see another boy troubling an old man, help the old man and fight the strong boy who is troubling him. If an old man calls you "my strength" reply to him, "Here I am, your strength." If you meet an old woman carrying water or wood or other heavy things, help her as you help your mother and call her "mother". If she begs you to cut grass for her or to help her digging do not say, "Who are you, old woman, do not trouble me!" but go and help her in peace. A good boy will always eat the secret[2] things. Friendship is always better than (to have) many things in the house or the possession of many cattle.

'Now you are a man. If you see the people quarrelling tell them: "Do not quarrel," and if you find the people hurting each other stop them.

'Now you are a man. No longer ride on a cow or an ox! Do not dance about standing on one leg, because this is childish and a disgrace for a man. If you see the children doing bad things, take them to their father but do not beat them yourself! Do not join the women when they sit together and talk about their own things. If you go there you will hear foolish things and become a fool yourself. Go where the old men are sitting and join them!'

When the father has finished his exhortations he hands the gourd to his son who takes some sips of the sour-tasting beer and then returns the gourd to his father. He does not say anything in reply to his father's speech.

Among the Logoli the preparations for the 'feast of coming out' likewise begin with a meeting of the fathers of those lads who live in one *etumbi*-hut. They discuss at this meeting who shall furnish the grain and brew the beer for the feast. About the same time a cow is set aside which the initiates themselves choose from the wealthiest elder by singling it out from his herd and hanging *amalande*-leaves round its neck. The owner usually protests against this 'requisition', but the other elders persuade him to yield to the initiates' choice, warning him that the spirits of his clan ancestors might get angry and kill him if he were to cling to his refusal.

Some time later when the initiates have stayed in the *etumbi*-hut for about three months and shortly before they are due to come out they are taught by the tutors to weave small rings, called *dzisume*, which they keep

---

[1] Meaning a woman who is still unmarried.
[2] Meaning morsels of choice food which are not offered to any ordinary visitor.

for two days. In the evening of the third day when the sun is about to set the initiates take the *dzisume*-rings down to the valley, using a path which the tutors have specially prepared for them. When they have reached the stream that flows down the valley they dig a deep pit in the clayey soil along its banks. Then, one by one, they throw the *dzisume*-rings into the pit, beginning with the *navihaya*, the lad who was circumcised first. Before they return to the *etumbi*-hut the tutor warns them not to look back at the pit into which they have thrown the rings but to run straight to the *etumbi*. Then they must go to sleep immediately and for the next two days are confined to the *etumbi*-hut 'like prisoners without having permission to walk about'.

The day before the initiates leave the *etumbi*-hut they go down to the valley and bathe. Then they cut long poles (*dzindanga*) and, having spent the whole night in the valley singing songs and practising the initiation dance, they return to the *etumbi* in the morning. Under the supervision of the tutor each initiate thrusts his pole into the roof of the *etumbi*, throwing it like a spear with the intention of piercing the roof and making the pole stand upright on the floor of the hut. While doing so each initiate shouts: 'My spear-shaft is of the so-and-so clan' (mentioning the name of his father's clan). Each pole has been marked and the tutor afterwards announces to the initiates which one of them has thrust his pole with the greatest force and marksmanship. Then the initiates carry all the things and paraphernalia which they have used during their stay in the *etumbi* inside the hut, piling them all in a heap: the trough or manger from which they used to drink the gruel, the calabashes and gourds, the bedspreads of banana-leaves, and their skirts of *amavinu*-leaves. The father of each lad brings some *egisugi*-medicine as well as *ovosé* (stomach content of a sheep) which he has retained from the last ritual killing and hands it to the tutor, who places it near the centre pole of the *etumbi*-hut. The initiates then finally leave the hut, this time through the front door, and assemble in the yard outside.

Now the tutor, or more properly a classificatory maternal uncle of the initiates' clan, sets fire to the hut, lighting the roof just above the front door. The initiates must not look at the burning hut but turn their backs to it. As soon as the hut is fully ablaze the tutor shouts to the initiates: 'The hut is now nearly falling down.' This is the signal for them to rush off and, shouting loudly, they run to a prearranged place in the bush. Here their sisters await them, having brought the new skins which the initiates put on after they have been shaved and anointed with ghee by an elder who receives a payment from the father of each boy for performing this service. Now the *avasikulu*,[1] as the initiates are called after they have left the burning *etumbi* and put on the new skins, run in a group to the dancing-ground, singing the second set of circumcision songs which they

[1] Derived from the verb *okusikula*, to drag from the mud, to cleanse, to free from dirt.

CIRCUMCISION AND INITIATION RITES 367

have practised during the preceding days and the frequently repeated refrain of which runs, 'Ye, ye, ye, the white chicken is nearly hatched out; our children did like that.' On the dancing-ground, where the initiates of several circumcision huts assemble, they dance for several hours, moving slowly in a circle, each lad holding in both hands a strong pole (*omudigelu*) with which he pounds the ground in a slow rhythm. After they have danced for a while, the cow which they have selected is led into the centre of the circle formed by the dancers. While they dance round the cow it gradually gets weaker and weaker and finally collapses, spreading out its legs to all four sides. Should it fall sideways this is considered a bad omen for the initiates' future life as warriors and begetters of children, but no other cow is killed in that case. If it falls down and dies in the prescribed manner, everything will go well with the initiates; they will live long and multiply and their clan will be strong. I was told that to bring about the proper collapse and death of the cow it is fed with a certain medicine called *esámbakulu*[1] and that small red-hot iron beads are put into its ears. However, both these methods which jointly produce the described effect are used secretly by the elders, and the initiates are made to believe that the cow gradually dies under the spell of their song and the monotonous rhythm of their dance. As they dance round the cow they sing the following song: 'Ye, ye, ye, you may come and hear (us) rejoicing (about) the cooling (i.e. dying) of the cow; it suffers, the *evembe*-grass causes suffering of the swelling.'

When the cow has died the initiates skin it. After the *omusálisi* (sacrificer) has sprinkled some meat and blood on the ground as a libation to the ancestral spirits the meat is eaten by the elders and the initiates, but in separate groups. No meat is given to the women.[2] The skin is cut into strips from which wristlets and necklaces are made for the *avasikulu*. They wear them for a time and then give them to their mothers, who place them into small pots which they hide under the roofs of the huts.

After they have all eaten, the old man who has sacrificed the meat to the spirits speaks to the initiates, telling them that they are now grown up and that they must teach their children the same things which they were taught while they stayed in the *etumbi*. In reply, one of the initiates, whom the others have selected beforehand, says that they have listened to his words and that they will follow the rules and customs which they have been taught.

A third type of procedure, most phases of which I can describe from personal observation, is followed among the Idaxo. When the day on which the initiates are to leave the hut has been appointed by the 'elders of the ridge' (*volugongo*) their fathers and mothers begin to brew large quantities

---

[1] The leaves of a plant growing near the water which cause a violent itch when they touch the skin.

[2] Women and children may not participate in the meal, nor do they later receive a share in the meat of the sacrificial animal.

of beer, while the male and female guardians as well as the initiates themselves get busy procuring and preparing the various paraphernalia which they will need in the course of the following ceremonies. The tutors cut poles of the *mudóvolo*-tree with which the initiates dance when they rehearse the *vuxulu* or initiation dance. They decorate them by peeling off the bark in such a way that a spiral pattern results. Then the tutors go and recover the *tsimbú*-sticks or poles which had been used by the initiates to kill the fowls and which they have afterwards taken away from them and hidden in the bush (cf. above, p. 361). They clean them and peel off the bark and then hand them to the initiates, who will use them again when they perform the initiation dance. To the ends of these sticks they tie iron rings (*masili*) which each tutor fetches from the home of the initiate's father. These rings are later returned again to the father, who keeps them for his next son's initiation dance.

The female guardians have the duty of collecting a certain fibrous plant (*lisidzi*) from which they make long white tassels to tie to the *tsimbú*-sticks together with the *masili*-rings. They also carve large stirring-paddles, both for themselves and for the tutors, with which they dance at the initiation dance.

The initiates themselves go to collect a certain reed-grass from which they weave a sort of apron which they wear in the manner of a sheepskin on the day of the dance. When all these things have been prepared and the initiates have rehearsed the *vuxulu*-dance for a few days, they begin one night singing the *vuxulu*-song. While passing their parents' homesteads they sing:

> 'Yeee yehé, we come out, O mother!
> The one who gave birth (to us) she rejoices, O mother!
> We may rejoice upwards, O mother!
> Where Kisumu is I shall look.
> Where Mumia's is I shall look.
> We may rejoice, O mother!'

This song serves as a sign for their mothers to prepare a festive meal, consisting of porridge, meat, fowls, and vegetables which the female guardians carry to the initiation hut soon after sunrise. The tutors in the meantime gather together all the objects which the initiates have used during the past few months: the grass dresses (*amavembe*), the *amavinu*-skirts and belts, the *midóvolo*-sticks with which they have practised dancing, the feathers of the fowls which the initiates have killed and with which they have adorned their grass dresses, the banana-leaves on which they have slept and, finally, all their eating- and drinking-utensils. All these things the tutors put outside under the eaves of the *etumbi* where they remain for a few days.

Early in the morning the initiates shave one another and wash themselves with water which the female guardians have brought to the *etumbi*. Then they eat the food which their mothers have prepared and which is served

CIRCUMCISION AND INITIATION RITES

and dished out to them by their tutors who share this meal with the initiates. When they have eaten they put on their reed aprons in preparation for the big dance. At the *vuxulu*-dance which I saw all the initiates wore red shorts underneath the reed aprons which the female guardians had made for them. I was told, however, that formerly on this occasion they merely wore the aprons, which left their genitals uncovered, so that all onlookers could inspect their members and convince themselves that the operation had been properly performed. Upon my arrival at the initiation hut that day I found the yard filled with onlookers of both sexes and all ages. They are now for the first time permitted to come near the initiation hut and see the initiates at close quarters and without their grass dresses. Groups of relatives and neighbours attend to each lad as he gets ready for the dance. The general rejoicing of the people over their reunion with the initiates expresses itself in frequent outbursts of shrieks and laughter, in a constant blowing of horns by the warriors and the old men, and in improvised dancing and collective shouting performed by various small groups of spectators which form and re-form every few minutes. While the initiates are still getting ready, the tutors dance for a while, at times in a compact group, at times running back and forth between the initiation hut and the gate of the enclosure, swinging their paddles and shrieking loudly every time they reach the gate. Then the initiates, each accompanied by his tutor and his female guardian, one by one dance, or rather run, along the passage stretching from the hut to the gate of the yard and lined on both sides by onlookers who by now number many hundreds. As each lad proceeds along the passage he is loudly cheered and acclaimed by the onlookers, especially if he has behaved courageously during the operation or if he comes from a well-known family and has many friends and relatives. Next all the initiates, together with the tutors and the female guardians, form a group near the *etumbi*. After having danced in a circle for a few minutes they proceed in close formation, running and singing, to the dancing-ground on the large 'common', where the initiates of the various clans assemble in quick succession. Those who come from several huts of one clan join up, but the various clans dance in separate groups, each unit forming a wide circle about a hundred feet or more in diameter. In the centre of each circle the female guardians, stripped to the waist and with their heads and shoulders painted with white clay, clap their hands to the rhythm of the dance, constantly repeating the refrain of the *vuxulu*-song. Facing the initiates and dancing with them are the tutors, whose task it is to lead the songs and encourage the initiates to dance properly and vigorously without getting slack in their movements. The initiates dance side by side, in an anti-clockwise direction, gripping their *tsimbú*-poles with both hands and pounding the ground with them at each step they make. A further but less regular outer circle of dancers is formed by the ordinary people. They dance in a clockwise direction and may leave off and rest whenever they please. Thus, with short breaks every ten or fifteen minutes, the dance goes on from noon-time till about 4.30 p.m. Then, again in close formation, the initiates return to the *etumbi*-hut.

For the next two nights the initiates must sleep outside, as they may not enter the *etumbi* again, having, in the morning, ceremonially left it through the front door. The following three or four days are given over to indiscriminate dancing and feasting in which all the other people, circumcised and uncircumcised alike, join. On the third or fourth day the initiates are given rules of conduct by the elders, and on the same evening the tutors kindle a fire in the yard of the *etumbi*, burning all the objects which they had put under the eaves of the hut a few days before. All the objects that have been used by the initiates are thrown into that fire, with the exception of the *tsimbú*-sticks. These the initiates take down into the valley in the middle of the night, accompanied by their tutors. After they have taken off the *masili*-rings, which they return to the initiates' fathers, the tutors throw the *tsimbú*-sticks into a deep pit which they and the initiates have dug near the stream. When all the poles have been deposited there the initiates must leave the spot in a hurry and run straight off without looking back, as the Logoli do after they have buried the *dzisume*-rings. They run till they come to a banana-grove which the tutors have previously pointed out to them. Using certain poles, called *ludaro*,[1] which they were given the same night by their tutors, they begin to hack at the banana-bunches and leaves until the whole grove has been devastated. Then they return to the yard of the *etumbi*, spending the remainder of the night in the company of their female guardians. They talk together and warm themselves by the fire that is still burning in the yard of the *etumbi*, but they must not make love to the girls.

In the morning they are again given an ample meal. This is the day of clothing the initiates, and again, as on 'the day of coming out', a large crowd of relatives and onlookers assembles at the *etumbi* to celebrate the event. First, each boy puts on the new skin which his female guardian has brought for him. Then, standing at the front door of the initiation hut, each boy receives a shield and a spear from an elder of his clan but not necessarily from his father. Beginning with the lad who was circumcised first, the initiates, one by one, proceed from the *etumbi* to the gate, holding their weapons like warriors who are approaching the enemy. The first time each boy merely aims at the gate-post and then runs back to the *etumbi*. The second time he actually spears it. If he succeeds in doing so the onlookers break forth into loud cheers and, lifting him up on their shoulders, carry him back along the passage in triumph. If he misses they laugh at him or, if he is the son of a well-known elder, pass over his failure in silence. When all the initiates have gone through this procedure, which takes several hours, they line up again to be anointed with ghee and to have simsim seeds thrown over them. This is done by a married woman whose moral conduct must be above reproach. Likewise, only those initiates

[1] Plural: *tsindaro*.

may line up to be anointed with ghee who have kept the rule of continence while they lived in the circumcision hut as 'otherwise they would get lean and weak'. While they are being anointed the crowd rejoices again and shouts 'our children have come out, they have come out without dying', the warriors blow their horns, and the people shriek and dance spontaneously to give vent to their feelings. Thus the ceremonies come to an end, and the people disperse to the various homes of the initiates' fathers, where relatives and neighbours are invited to drink beer and to feast on meat and porridge.

The initiates are now called *avahia*, 'the new ones'. Before they are permitted to return to their fathers' homes, however, a sheep must be killed for them at the place of the elder whose hut served as the *etumbi* and the sheep's stomach content sprinkled over them. If the initiation hut is still in good condition the previous owner then moves back to it; otherwise it is broken down and only the poles are used again.

After this last ceremony has been performed for them the *avahia* are free to go wherever they like. During the next few weeks they carry the *ludaro*-poles with them on all their walks as a visible sign of their new status. Then each sticks his pole into the roof of his father's hut, where it is kept for many years without being put to any other use.

Among the Tiriki the feasts and ceremonies which terminate the stay of the initiates in the *etumbi*-hut[1] are far less elaborate and lack many of the features which are common to the Vugusu, Logoli, and Idaxo. When the elders of the whole tribe have decided that the initiates should be dismissed from the *erumbi* and the father of each lad has prepared beer and porridge for a feast at his homestead, he goes to the *erumbi* early in the morning and gives his son the new goatskin (*isiru*) which he is to wear from now on. This is the skin of an ordinary goat which has not been killed in sacrifice. His old things, the cow-skin, the mask, and the head-dress, the father takes away with him. The mask and head-dress he suspends from the roof of his hut to show that he has a circumcised son, the cow-skin he wears himself, and the streamers or fringes of the mask he wraps round the handle of a hoe. Before the initiates put on the new goatskins they roll them up and tie them round their waists. In this attire they run to the *oluhia*, where a large crowd, including women and children, has gathered to inspect the initiates' bodies and to see whether they have been properly circumcised. This display of their bodies (*fialoxu*) is particularly intended to give the unmarried girls of the tribe an opportunity to make a choice of their future husbands, although they do not publicly acclaim their lovers as the Vugusu girls do immediately after the initiates have been circumcised (cf. above, p. 352). When the inspection is over the initiates return to the *erumbi*, where they put on the skins properly. Then they all disperse to their fathers' homesteads, where they join in the beer- and beef-feast without any further observances. Next morning the tutor visits all the initiates in

[1] Or *erumbi*, as the hut of seclusion is called in Ludiriki.

turn and shaves their heads. There is no ceremonial burning of the hut or of the various paraphernalia used by the initiates, nor are there any of the other features which ceremonially mark the initiates' dismissal from the initiation hut.

The procedure among the Isuxa is, with the exception of a few details, identical with that followed among the Idaxo. The Isuxa initiates do not have their heads shaved before they come out for the initiation dance; at the dance they adorn themselves with beaded ribbons which the female guardians have made for them and cover their genitals with small pieces of goat-leather instead of wearing reed aprons like the Idaxo, and their *tsimbú*-sticks are rough poles without any adornments, such as the iron rings (*masili*) and the tassels (*amasidzi*) which characterize the Idaxo dancing-poles. On the morning before they are given their new skins they wear small pieces of banana leaves in front, but otherwise go completely naked.

Among all tribes the initiates, after having returned to their bachelor huts (*dzisimba*) and having stayed there for a few days, start out for a round of visits to all their relatives. They either go alone or in groups of two or three. It is essential that each boy visits his maternal uncle first; the order of his further visits is not strictly prescribed, but as a rule the novice visits his paternal grandfather next, then his father's brothers in order of their age, then his paternal aunts, next his other maternal relatives, and, finally, his various affinal relatives and his parents' neighbours. All the kinsmen whom he visits must honour his new status by making him a present. From his maternal uncle he receives the largest gift, usually a bullock. He is also given plenty of meat and porridge to eat, and when visiting his close relatives (i.e. his maternal uncle, grandfathers, and father's brothers) he stays overnight and is treated by his hosts with the formality and etiquette which it is customary to show to an adult visitor. The gifts which he receives—mostly goats, sheep, and fowls, and occasionally also hoes and basketfuls of millet—are 'his own', but he must save them as they are intended to serve as a basis for the accumulation of his bride-wealth. Although his father usually keeps these gifts in trust for him he has no rights of disposal over them.

Among the Logoli the round of visits is preceded by the ceremonial conclusion of a further friendship between two initiates (cf. above, p. 346). The choice of this friend, who is likewise called *omírongo*, rests largely with the initiate's father. He will usually suggest a son of his own *omírongo*, though not necessarily so. When the choice has been made and the willingness of the *omírongo* and his father to accept the offer of friendship has been ascertained the former is invited, together with the first *omírongo* who was chosen at the clay-rubbing ceremony that took place on the day of circumcision. The three boys then partake of a common meal which consists of a conically shaped pile of eleusine porridge to which some buttermilk has been added. This dish is ceremonially put before the three *virongo* in a deep *eŋuŋi* basket, the space between the sides of the basket and the

CIRCUMCISION AND INITIATION RITES

pile of porridge being filled out with *amalande*-leaves. The peculiar way of serving this dish is said to ensure long life to each of the three *virongo* and to bind them together in friendship. The son of the house where the ceremony takes place eats first, taking off the top of the pile, while the other two eat the porridge from the sides.

Among the other tribes no such ceremonial friendships seem to be concluded in connexion with the initiation rites.

(6) CIRCUMCISION AGE-GRADES

The initiates who have been circumcised during the same year are all grouped together into one age-class,[1] of which they remain members throughout life. As succeeding circumcision generations are initiated, each such age-class moves up in rank, till it finally becomes the oldest age-grade alive. As the interval between two circumcision years varies from tribe to tribe the number of such grades which one can compile among the different tribes ranges between eight and fifteen. Among the Logoli the meaning of the names of most of the grades can be ascertained, and it is evident that they were chosen after some outstanding event which characterized the conduct of the initiates or which happened during the time of the circumcision ceremonies. As the last age-grade to be properly named and distinguished was that of 1911, I have found it impossible to obtain a more definite account of the manner in which the names of the age-classes were chosen and adopted. It seems, however, that there was no particular authority responsible for the choice of the names, but that they came about in the same way in which current events are constantly reflected in beer and dance songs, i.e. various names were suggested in the songs sung at the initiation dance and made up *ad hoc* by the song-leaders. Of these names one became popular and then generally came to designate the age-grade.

Among the young and middle-aged men the names of the age-classes are no longer generally known. They can seldom mention more than four or five and are always uncertain about their order, although they can usually tell to what age-classes their fathers, grandfathers, and other near male relatives belong. The lists which I obtained from the old men of the tribe agree with one another,[2] although with regard to the older age-grades, which are no longer represented by living persons, there is some uncertainty as to their proper order. These are the names:

1. Save
2. Angaya
3. Kigwamiti (or Kivwambiti)
4. Edzimangule
5. Gamunenezi
6. Ngulu-Ngulu

} order disputed among the elders

[1] Lurogoli: *elikula* (plur. *amakula*); Luvugusu: *lúvaga* (plur. *tjimbaga*).

[2] I have compiled lists from five elders belonging to different clans and age-grades: Paulo Agoi, Olungafu, Djairo, Keyoga, and Mutiva.

7. Nyongi
8. Aluse
9. Likuvati (age-grade of Dumbaya and Yisa)
10. Kihongila (were old men when Government was established, *c.* 1895)
11. Esavili (age-grade of Vusisa, son of Dumbaya)
12. Evagale
13. Engengele
14. Olulolo (age-grade of present chief)
15. Kitjiti (also Kigedi).

If the statement is correct that the men of the Kihongila age-grade were old men when British rule was first established, it would confirm the claim of the elders that formerly the intervals between two circumcision years were much longer than they are to-day. Provided the initiates were of an average age of twenty-five years the Kihongila age-grade must have been circumcised some time round 1850–5. This would indicate an average interval of eleven years for the subsequent age-grades up to 1911.

The meaning of most of the age-grade names among the Logoli is quite clear. As the following examples show, it is mostly seemingly insignificant peculiarities in the conduct of the initiates which have furnished the names. The initiates of 1911 are known as *kitjiti*, which is a Swahili adaptation of the Anglo-Indian word 'chit'. This word is commonly used in Kenya to denote a piece of paper with a short written message and in this particular case commemorates the issue of tax receipts which were first introduced in 1911. After 1911 the age-grade system broke down as the majority of lads began to be circumcised in mission hospitals where they went individually and whenever they liked. All people circumcised after 1911, including those who underwent the traditional ceremonial, are therefore indiscriminately referred to as *embalabala* (a wide road), 'as they were circumcised on the road', i.e. without any ceremonial and without the traditional seclusion in the *etumbi*. *Olulolo*, the name of the age-grade preceding *kitjiti*, means 'flea' and is said to have been chosen as the name of an age-grade because the *etumbi* was infested with unusually many fleas which caused the initiates much suffering; *engéngele*, from *kukéngela*, 'to peep out', commemorates the fact that the initiates used to make small holes in the walls of the *etumbi* through which they looked outside; *evagele*, from *okwivagala*, 'to bask in the sun', signifies the habit of the convalescing initiates to sprawl in the sun; *esavili*, from *okusávila*, 'to ask for', refers to the initiates' constant desire for food, &c.

Among the Tiriki I have compiled a list of twelve age-grades. In contrast to the Logoli the twelve age-grades formed a cycle which repeated itself indefinitely. As will be seen from the following list, five of the age-grades have the same names as those of the Logoli:

1. Djibudjulu
2. Sawe
3. Ngolo-Ngolo

4. Andalo
5. Isavile
6. Gwayimedi
7. Evagale
8. Gamulalagi
9. Musalagani
10. Σidjoso
11. Nyongi
12. Mayina.

The age-grade system among the Tiriki is still intact, and the *Mayina* grade was circumcised in 1929. The last circumcision took place in 1937, but I was not able to discover whether the name *Djibudjulu* was actually chosen to designate this age-grade, as I was told in 1935 that it would.

In Kitosh, where, as we have seen, circumcision takes place every two years, the age-grade system is more complex, showing a close similarity to the Nandi and Masai systems. Altogether there are eight major age-groups (*vívingilo*), each of which comprises a period of approximately twelve years. As among the Tiriki they form a cycle, so that the eighth age-class is followed again by the first. As the whole cycle would normally comprise 8×12 or 96 years it would work out in such a way that the name of the oldest age-class would recur soon after its last representatives had died. It was stressed by my informants that the name of the oldest age-grade could not be used again as long as any of its members were still alive. These eight major age-grades (*vívingilo*) are:

1. Kikwameti
2. Kánanatji
3. Ginyigewu
4. Nyange
5. Mayina
6. Tjuma
7. Sawa
8. Golongolo.

There is some disagreement as to the proper order of the first four grades. The last member of the *Mayina* grade died in 1936; the *Vatjuma* are the oldest living now, and the chief, a man of approximately sixty years, belongs to the *Omusawa* class. The *Omugolóngolo* class was circumcised between 1900 and 1911. It should have been followed by the *Omukikwameti* and *Omukánanatji* classes, but as circumcision after 1911 became sporadic these age-grades are no longer clearly distinguished. Each of these major age-groups or *vívingilo* is again subdivided into six circumcision groups or *tjímbaga* (sing. *lúvaga*), of which again every two form a pair, the members of which observe certain obligations towards one another. The six *tjímbaga* of the *Omugolóngolo* class are:

1. Nandemu (*a*)
2. Naviswa (*b*)

3. Visudje (*a*)
4. Manyonge (*b*)
5. Vidjeti (*a*)
6. Xaoya (*b*).[1]

This organization of the age-grade system into main grades and subgrades corresponds closely to the age-grade organization of the Nilo-Hamitic tribes with which it is obviously historically connected.

An attempt to discover the significance of the age-grade organization, by following up the occasions on which the age-grades come into action as well as the rules of behaviour, rights, and privileges that prevail within each age-grade and between the members of different age-grades, leads only to meagre and inconclusive results. In Kitosh the members of one age-grade salute one another as *vagogi*,[2] 'age-mate', a term of address which is said to express friendliness and goodwill, 'to make the person thus addressed feel happy and welcome'. Properly its use is restricted to persons who belong to one of the two *tjímbaga* which form a pair, but less formally it is used as a term of address to every stranger, even of another tribe, who by his outer appearance seems to be of the same age as the person who salutes him. Among the Idaxo the term *vamuai* is used with the same meaning and in the same way as *vagogi* among the Vugusu. Among the Logoli and Tiriki the age-mate relationship can be linguistically expressed only by a circumlocution. The name of one's age-class is said to have been mentioned formerly by persons who visited a strange village. They would utter it along with their clan-name to identify themselves and would then find a friendly welcome among their *vagogi*. It is said, however, that clan feelings were stronger than age-class solidarity, and that a young person who suddenly found himself at the mercy of members of a hostile clan would not find protection from or asylum among his age-mates merely on the strength of that fact.

Nowadays a man would mention the name of his age-class when sitting with others round the beer-pot and boasting about his wealth in cattle. But even on such occasions the age-class is mentioned only along with one's personal and clan-name; there are no special songs of praise for one's age-grade or any boasting of military or other achievements on an age-grade basis.

Among the Vugusu economic obligations between age-mates are restricted to the killing and distribution of a cow (the so-called *éxafu eye lúvaga*) on the occasion of the son's circumcision. The meat is distributed among

[1] These names have the following meaning: (1) *endemu*, a big snake which was frequently seen at that time. (2) *Nasivwa*, name of a Masai from whom the Vugusu captured many cattle; (3) *visudje*, wolves (hyena) which were numerous that year; (4) *gamanyonge*, iron trinkets which the Vugusu bought from the Vahayo in exchange for grain (1907); (5) *vidjeti*, receipt tickets for poll-tax; (6) *xaoya*, rinderpest which was rampant in 1911.

[2] The term '*vagogi*' is never used in the singular. Thus a person saluting an age-mate would say to him, '*milembe vagogi*'.

members of the two *tjimbaga* which form a pair, but both *tjimbaga* sit in separate groups and the members of the host's *lúvaga* are entitled to receive their share first. As regards marriage, a man cannot take the daughter of his age-mate (i.e. of the same pair of *tjimbaga* or of the same *elikula*) for his 'young wife'. This prohibition is also reflected in linguistic usage, as a man addresses his *vagogi*'s daughter as 'my daughter'. This marriage prohibition, however, applies only to the daughters of one's own age-mates and not to those of either younger or older men; its purpose, therefore, obviously cannot be to set a limit to the difference in age between husband and wife.[1] Moreover, as a marriage between a son and a daughter of two age-mates is not only permissible but even considered particularly appropriate, the marriage prohibition cannot be taken as an indication of the existence of economic, legal, or military bonds between age-mates which would let the age-grade relationship appear as something similar to the clan-relationship and therefore require the observance of exogamy as an analogous safeguard of that relationship. The only significance of this prohibition seems to be the maintenance of a perfectly equal status among the age-mates which would be upset by the establishment of a father- and son-in-law relationship between them.[2]

The only other formal rule which I could discover in the relationship between age-mates is that the circumcision operator must not operate on sons of his *vagogi*, a rule which is sanctioned by the belief that its violation would cause the initiate's wound to become inflamed. I was not able to obtain further data which would reveal the significance of this rule and thereby throw further light upon the nature of the age-grade relationship.

Besides these more tangible features, the age-grade organization becomes manifest in the observance of various rules of etiquette, especially at beer-drinks, where the members of the older age-grades are given the best seats inside the house or in the shade of the banana-grove. These rules, however, are not very definite and in practice do not amount to more than a display of formal respect to seniors by their juniors. Small groups of persons who have been circumcised in the same year and on the same *oluhia* are said to have tended formerly to go together on hunting and war expeditions, and they still unite and support one another in many activities that require concerted action or the pooling of resources, such as house-building or informal beer-drinks. Such groupings, however, are not formally organized and have no leadership. Furthermore, the age-grades do not seem to have fulfilled any formal functions in the conduct of warfare, nor did I discover that the gradual advance of each age-grade in the

---

[1] Such a limitation, it might be argued, would be socially valuable as the marriage of young girls to old men leads to a number of anomalous situations in the kinship structure.

[2] Unfortunately I was not able to discover a case where this rule had been broken or to study the reaction to such a breach.

whole cycle, brought about by the dying off of senior grades and the formation of new ones at each circumcision, carried with it any increase in explicit rights and privileges, such as one might expect in connexion with clan jurisdiction or with the performance of magico-religious ceremonies. The only ceremonial significance of the age-grades is that the office of the *omuseni* (the comforter and spokesman at a funeral) can only be held by a member of the oldest age-class of which representatives are still alive.

It appears from this discussion of the age-grade organization that it was not so much in itself a system of social or political organization in which each age-group formed a unit with definite functions, but that it chiefly served as a means of reckoning age. We have seen at various junctures throughout this book that among the Bantu Kavirondo seniority counts as a grading principle in economic, political, and magico-religious activities. The notion—to a certain extent universal—that advance in age means a rise in status is strengthened by the characteristics of Kavirondo clanship and its corollary, the ancestor cult. It is obvious that in the absence of a calendar some system of time-reckoning is imperative to provide an objective criterion for determining seniority. Even though, in view of the wide latitude in the age of the circumcision candidates, age-grade seniority is not necessarily equivalent to seniority by years, it is the former which matters culturally. The rule (*omusiru*) that two real brothers must be circumcised not in the same year but one after the other according to their ages shows, however, that the age-grade system does not overrule the relationship patterns that prevail in the family but falls into line with it. Rather than cutting across the clan and kinship organization, the age-grade system thus serves as a framework to support the proper working of one of the chief implications of that organization, viz. the principle of seniority.

It is only natural that in a society in which seniority is socially, legally, and ritually significant, people with equal age-status should tend to engage in common activities and practise mutual hospitality. But the looseness and informality of the bonds between age-mates and the fact that a mutual obligation between them exists only on one occasion, viz. at their sons' circumcision, seems to leave little doubt that the chief function of the age-grades is not a horizontal grouping of the tribal society but a means of defining seniority in individual relationships.

The only feature which remains unintelligible in the whole system is the complex grouping of two *tjimbaga* into a pair and of six *tjimbaga* into a *sisingilo* which we have found among the Vugusu. Ostensibly this is a formal feature without a functional meaning. Unless further research reveals a significance in this system which I was unable to discover, we have here a case of a formal feature borrowed from a group of neighbouring but structurally quite different tribes which has not been functionally integrated into the structure of the recipient society.

C. MARRIAGE

(1) ATTITUDE TOWARDS MARRIAGE

IN the course of previous chapters we have seen that all rights and duties of the individual—economic, religious, and political—either exclusively or predominantly work through the channels of kinship. The individual who wishes to obtain a maximum degree of protection by the community in which he lives and to attain influence and prestige in it must aim at securing for himself a prominent place in the elaborate network of kinship relations. This he can do only through marriage and procreation, for matrimony and parenthood are necessary steps in the process of acquiring social status. Seniority which, as we have seen, acts as the grading principle in nearly all human relationships among the Kavirondo, derives its validity from the fact that authority is closely linked with kinship status and that this again is based on kinship ties. The older a person gets, the wider becomes the group of people related to him by blood and by marriage, and the wider, accordingly, extends his sphere of influence. The *social* significance of seniority, therefore, does not consist in the mere accumulation of years, but in the increasing number of effective kinship relations which is involved in the process of ageing.

While this fact, in a vague and general way, stresses the social valuation of matrimony and suggests that early marriages are favoured, there are a number of considerations which modify this general tendency and which, according to the particular combination of circumstances, may induce the individual native to hasten or to postpone his own marriage or to take an approving or disapproving attitude towards his child's or sibling's marriage.

From the point of view of the prospective husband, every consideration speaks in favour of an early marriage. Economically the unmarried youth is dependent on his parents: he tills his father's land and eats his mother's food and is thus under his parents' authority, having no independent personal status with regard to property. Marriage for him means the gradual gaining of such a status; it involves—in its early stages at least— no extra burden but, on the contrary, the acquisition of help, both for his mother and for himself. As he does not set up a new household right away, the economic side of marriage is for him no hazardous undertaking by which he has to give up a well-established routine of work and economic co-operation with a definite group of people in exchange for a new and untried arrangement. By taking a wife the husband merely adds to what existed before, and while this addition might turn out to be of little or no advantage, it can hardly be a change for the worse. From the sexual point of view, matrimony, likewise, involves no decisive change in the life of a man. The youth who decides to marry does not thereby give up his privilege of carrying on courtships and of paying visits to the unmarried girls' hut. It is true that this privilege is frequently curtailed by his wife's jealousy, especially during the early years of matrimonial life. During a year's stay among the Logoli I heard of three suicides committed by youngish women who had been jealous of their husbands' courtships. However, as a married woman gets older and as her domestic duties increase with the size of her family, she generally welcomes her husband's courtships, provided that they lead to his taking another wife. The young wife will then help the older wife in the cultivation of crops and in the care of the livestock, and she will share the 'great wife's' burden in preparing food and brewing beer for visitors. But even if in actual practice marriage to some extent limits the sexual freedom of a man, he is compensated for these limitations by the advantages of a legitimate sex-life, whereas all premarital sex-adventures had to be carried on *sub rosa* and under conditions that generally involve inconveniences and often, especially in former times, even dangers. Moreover, the social segregation of the sexes continues after marriage much in the same way as before, so that the youth who marries does not have to forgo his former pastimes and pleasures. He may continue to go to dances and spend the evenings with his friends, and if through marriage he becomes more 'domestic', he does so by his own choice and not under the moral pressure of conventional attitudes. In traditional circumstances, therefore, a male youth is anxious to marry as soon as he can fulfil the various conditions on which marriage depends.

From a girl's point of view, the incentives for an early marriage are not quite as strong. Marriage means for a girl that she has to leave her parental home and join a group of persons who will make numerous demands upon her and who often will show a very critical attitude towards her accomplishments and her conduct as a wife. For the first year or two of her married life she will have to submit to her mother-in-law's authority or, if she is a junior wife, to that of her husband's 'great wife'. She must perform all the least pleasant duties of a wife, such as fetching wood and water, grinding grain, and cleaning the cattle kraal. If she was fortunate enough to have been married off to the husband of her choice and if she can adjust herself to her new surroundings, her status in her husband's family will soon become similar to that of a daughter. However, if she was forced into a marriage she despised and shows herself obstinate, her life often becomes miserable. Attempts by young wives to run away from their husbands and relatives-in-law and to return to their parents are by no means rare, but usually the parents will not encourage their daughter's reluctance to remain with her husband, especially if they have prompted her to marry. The only way out of such a dilemma then is for the wife to elope with another man, but there is little chance that her parents and brothers will acquiesce in such a course, unless the new husband is in a position to pay the marriage-cattle in full.

For a girl marriage also means the complete change-over from promiscuous courtships to a closely guarded marital faithfulness. Unwillingness to abandon her sexual freedom is often said to be the chief cause of a girl's reluctance to marry. The wish to preserve their freedom rather than the fear of social ostracism also appears to be the main reason why unmarried girls apply what contraceptive knowledge they have and why occasionally they even practise abortion. When I asked some elderly pagans whether pregnancy or the birth of an illegitimate child would decrease a girl's chances to find a husband, they seemed genuinely surprised at my question. Instead of answering it to the point, they merely insisted that such a girl would marry soon, as she would no longer care to reject suitors but be quite willing to become a married woman for, having a child to look after, she would no longer be able to lead the life of an unmarried girl. As long as a girl's premarital sex-conduct is not excessively promiscuous, so that she acquires the reputation of being an *omuheyi*, a 'wanton woman', by whose pledges of marital faithfulness little store can be set, she has no reason to fear that she will remain a spinster if she extends her girlhood as long as she can.

All this does not mean, of course, that the prevalent female attitude towards marriage is to consider it a necessary evil. It merely means that girls cherish their state of being single to a greater extent than men and that, as we shall see, the initiative in breaking off a marriage is more frequently taken by the wife than by the husband.

Love often forms a powerful motive for marriage and sweeps aside all other considerations, as is shown by the large number of young girls who voluntarily elope from their parental homes with men whose proposals have been rejected by the girls' fathers or brothers. These girls often are brought back by force half a dozen times, but they continue to run off to the husbands of their choice in spite of the drastic punishments and prolonged material hardships which they may have to undergo.

The attitude taken by parents towards their children's marriage is chiefly determined by considerations connected with the payment or reception of the bride-wealth. A son's desire to marry is often frustrated by his father's reluctance to pay the marriage-cattle for him. As a proper marriage cannot be concluded until the full bride-wealth has been handed over, it is a necessary condition of marriage to procure a sufficient number of cows. Even if the father's herd is large enough to enable him to furnish his son with the required number of animals, he often objects to or delays the marriage, because he feels reluctant to part with his cattle. In Kitosh, where the wealth in cattle is greater than in Maragoli but where cattle also play a more important part in the family economy, this tendency seems to be more pronounced than in Maragoli. When a father hears of his son's visits to the girls' hut he scolds him for carrying on a courtship and warns him to dispel any thoughts which he may harbour with regard to marriage, pretending that he has no cattle which he could give him. In pre-European days fathers are said to have disliked the early marriage of their sons, as they feared that once they were married they would cease to go out on cattle-raids. It seems, however, that such paternal objections to a son's marriage were only maintained until the latter had reached full manhood (i.e. the full status of a warrior) and that then even an unwilling father yielded to the pressure of his clansmen who would persuade him not to withhold his cattle from his son.

For the same reason for which a father frequently exercises a restraining influence upon his son's desire to take a wife he is eager to marry off his daughter as early as possible, provided that the prospective husband suits his taste and is in a position to pay the marriage-cattle. 'To see the feet of the cattle' which are offered for his daughter is a sight which few fathers can resist for long. If the first-born child is a daughter, the bride-wealth received for her is frequently used by the father to marry a second wife. He will then be particularly anxious to see his daughter married at an early age, so that he may have a few years' time to replenish his herd before his eldest son puts forward his claims for marriage-cattle. In families, moreover, where the 'cattle of the yard' are few in number and where, accordingly, the cattle needed by the sons for their marriages has to be furnished by the daughters' marriages, not only the father but also the brothers will bring pressure to bear upon a girl to get married whenever they themselves wish to marry.

To a mother the marriage of her daughter means, as we have seen, the loss of a companion and a helper in her daily work in the field and in the house. For, although a daughter frequently returns home for longish visits after she has been married, she spends at least half of her time at her husband's place and increasingly more as she sets up a household of her own. Nevertheless, I have never heard that mothers dissuade their daughters from marrying on these grounds or that they show any signs of grief at their final departure. On the contrary, mothers think and talk about their daughters' marriage for many years before the latter reach the marriageable age. It seems, therefore, that a mother's vanity in seeing her daughter courted and betrothed is stronger than the feeling of the loss which she thereby incurs.

Thus the typical attitude of parents towards their children's marriages runs counter to the typical wishes of the children themselves. Whereas a son is anxious to marry at an early age, his father tends to restrain him. Conversely, a daughter would, as a rule, like to prolong the freedom of girlhood, but her father and her brothers have an interest in seeing her married off and thus often urge her to matrimony. While in actual life this antagonism of attitudes is frequently offset or modified by other considerations, it nevertheless appears to be one of the chief causes of strife between members of a family to which marriage gives rise.

(2) CHOICE OF THE MARRIAGE PARTNER

Apart from the general attitude towards marriage, the actual decision to marry is subject to a complex set of notions relating to the choice of the marriage partner. Most of these notions have the effect of ruling out marriage between certain persons and groups of persons. They negatively

PLATE 15

A. *A widow decked out in her husband's clothes: North Kitosh*

B. *Driving cattle to a funeral feast: South Maragoli*

PLATE 16

B. *Decorating a grave: North Kitosh*

A. *Accordion player accompanying ovukana dance: South Maragoli*

MARRIAGE

limit the categories of people who are eligible as mates rather than lay down positive rules by which the marriage between certain individuals would be particularly desirable or preferential. Listing these notions roughly in the order of their prominence and character, we can distinguish the following marriage prohibitions and restrictions:

1. The laws of exogamy.
2. Mutual marriage prohibitions between clans which have entered into a ceremonial friendship (*ovuvute*) with one another.
3. Temporary marriage prohibitions between clans which live in a state of mutual avoidance, usually pending a feud.
4. Marriage restrictions between certain relatives of circumcision friends (*virongo*).
5. Disapproval of the simultaneous sororate and related forms of marriage.

By far the most important set of regulations which restrict the choice of the marriage partner among the Kavirondo are the laws of exogamy. Formulated in the most concise manner, these laws prohibit marriage between a man and a woman if any one of his four grandparents belongs to the same clan as any one of her four grandparents. A native whom one questions about the laws of exogamy would not, of course, define them by such a general formula. He would say that when a lad wants to find out if a certain girl is eligible for marriage with him he must, to begin with, inquire to what clan she belongs and 'where her mother came from'.[1] Further, he would continue, he must ask of which clans the girl's parents are *avifwa* (i.e. sister's children). If he discovers that the girl's mother is an *omifwa* of the same clan of which his own mother is an *omifwa* he cannot marry the girl, as his and her mother would call one another 'sister'. Nor can he marry the girl if her father is an *omifwa* of the same clan as his father, as then the two fathers would call one another 'brother'. Finally, the prohibition would apply if the girl's mother is an *omifwa* of the same clan as his father (or her father of the same clan as his mother), as in these cases her mother and his father (or her father and his mother respectively) would call one another *mbozwa* (i.e. sibling or parallel cousin of opposite sex). In short, a lad whose four grandparents' clans are A, B, C, and D must ensure that the clans of the girl's four grandparents are E, F, G, and H:

$$A\triangle \!=\! \bigcirc C \quad B\triangle \!=\! \bigcirc D \quad E\triangle \!=\! \bigcirc G \quad F\triangle \!=\! \bigcirc H$$
$$A\triangle \!=\! \bigcirc B \qquad\qquad E\triangle \!=\! \bigcirc F$$
$$A\triangle = \bigcirc E$$

According to these rules any two persons who can trace a connexion with

---

[1] i.e. to what clan the girl's mother belongs.

one another through the clans of their four grandparents are considered to be too closely related to marry one another. Linguistically this relationship is denoted by the term *vuleve* which, significantly, is used with reference both to persons of the same and of different sex. If I refer to a person of my own sex as 'my *omuleve*' I thereby imply that I cannot marry his 'sister' or, if I am a girl, that I cannot marry her 'brother'.

The border-line beyond which relationship is not considered a bar to marriage lies between the generation of the grandparents and that of the great-grandparents. As a term of address all great-grandparents are called *visoni*, but when speaking of the rules of marriage the term refers only to the clans of the four great-grandmothers. Although a relationship with these four clans is still recognized, it is permissible to marry into them. If one says of a person 'he is my *ekisoni*', one thereby states that he is just outside the group of clans into which one is debarred from marrying. Beyond the clans which are *visoni* no further grades are distinguished. My Vugusu informants, however, insisted that formerly marriage even into the clans of one's *visoni* was permitted only after everybody belonging to their generation had died, as the old man of that generation would have objected to the marriage and refused to come to sacrifices performed for the children that were born from such a union.

While the full rules of exogamy are actually taken into consideration when a marriage is contemplated and the question of a girl's or boy's eligibility is discussed before the betrothal and the wedding are arranged, the stringency with which they are observed and with which breaches of them are dealt with tends to decrease with the increasing remoteness of the relationship. Thus the notion of incest is primarily limited to the occurrence of sexual relations between members of the *same* clan, and even within the same clan the attitude towards the offenders is not the same in the case of 'real' (i.e. physical) siblings or a 'real' parent and child as in that of classificatory clan relatives. As regards marriage, we find that similar distinctions are made. Between persons of the same clan, marriage is ruled out under any circumstances, no matter how large the clan and how distant the actual relationship (i.e. the relationship which can be genealogically traced) between the two persons concerned. In numerous genealogical inquiries I have never encountered a single such marriage, and there was a general consensus of opinion among my informants that a couple persistently living in such an 'incestuous' union would be not merely socially ostracized but driven away from the clan-land, as their mere presence would endanger or 'destroy the clan' (*kwónonya oluhia*). Nowadays there are said to be a few such couples on European farms or in European towns like Nairobi, but they are 'lost', i.e. they maintain no connexion with their relatives at home.

Marriage with a girl of one's mother's clan would, likewise, not be tolerated, although it is definitely regarded with less horror than marriage within one's own clan. An illegitimate child resulting from such a union would be allowed to live, but some mental or physical deficiency, such as crippled limbs, squint-eyes, or even imbecility would be feared. A pair living in such a union would be cursed by the husband's father and avoided both by the husband's and the wife's kin, but neither clan as a whole would take action. Actually, no concrete case of such a marriage has come to my notice, so that I cannot say to what extent the practical attitude would conform to these theoretical statements. A marriage, on the other hand, between a man and a woman whose mothers both belong to the same clan would be tolerated if the two mothers came from different sub-clans and if the relationship became known only after the marriage had been concluded. This might happen in the case of an elopement marriage or if one of the marriage partners were an orphan who had been reared in the house of one of his father's co-wives and had thus lost contact with his real maternal uncle. It would, however, still be feared that the offspring of such a union would not grow up healthy but that the children would be weak and die from the *luswa* with which the parents had become afflicted as a result of having disregarded their *vuleve*. This *luswa* is thought to enter the hut in which the pair live through the *ekisuli*, the stick that protrudes from the apex of the roof and forms a symbol of the husband's procreative power. To prevent the *luswa* from entering and harming the children, the following rite is performed which apparently is common to all Bantu Kavirondo tribes. The sacrificer (*omusalisi*) is called to kill a goat or a sheep and to smear both husband and wife with its stomach content. While he does so he says to the couple: 'Now your clans are separated. The sheep has been killed, so that your children may live.' Then an old pot for cooking vegetables (*eningilo*) must be procured. It must be a cracked one with holes in the bottom from having been frequently used by the wife and not a pot that has been broken by force. Soon after nightfall the wife's brother climbs on the roof of the hut and sticks the pot upside down on the *ekisuli* where it is left for all people to see. The cracks of the pot 'break' the *vuleve* that exists between the husband and the wife and thereby keep the *luswa* away from the hut. I was assured that the married couple feel no shame or reluctance at having this pot placed on the roof of their hut and that their kinsmen and neighbours would harbour no ritual fear or social disapproval with regard to them. They would freely enter their hut and accept food and beer from them as from any other people. It appears, therefore, that the placing of a pot over the *ekisuli* of the hut merely serves as a magical antidote and not as a means of publicly marking or stigmatizing the homestead and its inhabitants as something to be avoided.

If the relationship, finally, can be traced through one of the grandmothers' clans only, marriage is tolerated without any ceremonial safeguards, provided again that the relationship is too distant to be genealogically traceable. Such marriages provoke 'grumbling' among the elders of the clan by which the relationship between the couple is established. They can, therefore, not be concluded by the celebration of a wedding feast, but they are subsequently condoned, especially if they are not followed by any unlucky events. Should, however, the children resulting from such a union be weak or sickly, then the *eningilo* pot would in this case also be placed upon the roof of the hut as an antidote against the *luswa*.

The widespread belief that a violation of the laws of exogamy results in mentally or physically defective offspring seems, at the first glance, to suggest the existence of a native theory on the adverse biological consequences of in-breeding. A closer examination of native attitudes and beliefs, however, does not confirm the existence of such a theory, much less its use as a basis for the widely ramified net of exogamous marriage prohibitions which we have just discussed.

Observation of native methods of cattle-keeping as well as inquiries into their knowledge of the processes of nature reveal only a meagre amount of biological insight. It is, therefore, very improbable that the mental or physical anomalies which offences against the laws of exogamy are supposed to produce in the offspring of such 'incestuous' unions have actually been observed as the results of excessive in-breeding. On the other hand, we find that in native belief any deviation from an important norm of social behaviour, and in particular any violation of an *omugilu* (taboo), is supposed to be followed by some kind of mental or physical abnormality. We have seen that a violation of the *emigilu* which relate to widows or young mothers causes the offender's body to 'turn pale' or 'his hair to fall out', or that a breach of the *omugilu* relating to twins produces an eye disease. It appears to be analogous to these beliefs that the rules of exogamy are supposed to be sanctioned by a weak or abnormal offspring. The fact that in Kitosh alleged abnormalities in children resulting from the marriage of two *valeve* are attributed to the influence of *luswa* shows that the rules of exogamy fall into line with the wider concept of *emigilu* and that they do not form a category by themselves. Moreover, we have seen that the term *vuleve*, which denotes the particular quality of relatedness that serves as a bar to marriage, not only applies to the relationship between persons of opposite sex but also to that between persons of the same sex. This fact further seems to indicate that the power and the significance of the *vuleve* relationship is not restricted to the sexual or procreative sphere, but has a social significance also.

Finally, while it might perhaps be possible to argue that some of the rules of exogamy derive their significance from an unformulated native belief in the biological consequences of incestuous marriage, one could hardly explain the whole set of exogamous marriage regulations on that basis, for they rule out marriage between thousands of people between most of whom no genealogical relationship can be traced at all.

It appears, therefore, that the rules of exogamy have a social rather than a biological significance. Native interpretations of the laws of exogamy confirm this point of view. Thus the nature of the *vuleve* relationship is

MARRIAGE

mainly expressed in terms of social and economic ties. Two *valeve* say: 'We cannot marry one another, because our kinsmen still visit each other', or 'because we still see the people over there', or 'because we eat of the same cow'. The latter remark means that when the 'cow of splitting'[1] is killed by one of the related clans, the relatives of the boy and those of the girl still share in the distribution of the same meat. Similarly, when summarizing the rules that govern the choice of the marriage partner, the natives say 'one must not marry one's friends but one's enemies'. Although, taken literally, this is a gross overstatement, it signifies the idea that marriages must not be concluded between persons who have any social or economic interests in common. Positively speaking, those persons (or groups of persons) should intermarry who have never maintained or at least have ceased to maintain effective kinship bonds with one another. In a society where social groups based on kinship (clan and lineage) actually are political units, all persons who are outside these groups are, in a sense, 'enemies' (*avasigu*).

An important consequence of this far-reaching set of exogamous marriage prohibitions is that by ruling out every form of cousin-marriage, extending to the most distant trace of relationship, the establishment of continued or preferential marriage relations between any two clans is prevented. If a man of clan A marries a woman of clan B this means that none of his ancestors in direct paternal or maternal line for two generations upwards have married into clan B and that none of his children or grandchildren will be able to do so again. The same holds true of the ancestors and offspring of the woman of clan B with regard to clan A. Thus, as the generations change, the clans that intermarry must likewise constantly change, and the members of any given clan are simultaneously linked by marriage with a great number of different clans. The laws of exogamy thus ensure that the network of relations which becomes established through intermarriage is as widely flung as possible. This fact has two important implications as regards social structure. On the one hand, it constitutes a strong force making for tribal integration and, on the other hand, by keeping the affinal relatives of the members of one clan in as diverse groups as possible, it clearly stresses the social preponderance of the paternal kin (and clan) over the maternal kin. It thus prevents the growth of too strong rival loyalties in the individual which, in the course of time, would weaken the principle of unilateral descent.

While the laws of exogamy rule out marriage within the clan and between a given individual of one clan and all members of another clan (owing to his relationship with that clan through his parents or grandparents), there are two other types of marriage prohibitions between two clans which affect all members of the clans concerned. They are thus

[1] Luvugusu: *éxafu eye luluasago*, a term referring to the ox or bull which a wealthy clan-elder slaughters for the benefit of his clansmen and kinsmen, cf. vol. ii.

permanent or temporary marriage prohibitions between two groups as groups.

These two types of prohibition are based on diametrically opposed conditions. In the one case they arise from the conclusion of a ceremonial friendship between two clans which are in no way related to one another. Having maintained good neighbourly relations towards each other for a long period of time, they have decided to seal their friendship and their mutual assistance in the performance of certain rites and in the conduct of warfare by refraining from intermarrying. Among the Logoli, two clans which have concluded such a friendship are the Yonga and the Muku. They live in adjoining territories and their mutual assistance in warfare was probably fostered by the need for co-operation against the frequent night raids which the neighbouring Tiriki and Nandi used to undertake against them. The Muku are a much smaller clan than the Yonga, and it seems that the initiative to conclude the mutual friendship was taken by the former when they felt the need for seeking the protection of their more powerful neighbours. Lubanga, an elder of the Yonga clan, gave the following account of how their friendship and mutual agreement to refrain from intermarriage originated:

'Long ago the Muku and the Yonga lived on swampy ground. Nowadays this place is called the hill (?) of the Yonga. They used to sit together to eat the meat and to drink the beer. Then one day they said: "We, the Yonga, and we, the Muku, we do not want to take from one another the girls (i.e. to intermarry); it is good that we may become *avavute*." Then the Yonga killed a goat and divided it into equal halves (by cutting it lengthwise); the Yonga took one half and the Muku the other. And they also divided the skin of that goat in two and said: "Now we cannot take from one another the girls any longer. If we take each others' girls we shall die; they may perish together, (because) now we are brothers."'

The names of the elders of the two clans who concluded the agreement are not remembered, nor can the time when the friendship was first established be defined by reference to circumcision age-grades. As in all legendary accounts, the beginning of the *vute* friendship is vaguely referred to the distant past by the adverb *kale*, long ago. As regards their marriage relations, the *vute* friendship has welded the two clans into one, with the difference however, that the exogamous bond between them extends to the *avifwa* of the two clans only and not to the maternal grandchildren. That is to say, while a Yonga is debarred from marrying a girl whose mother is a Muku (and vice versa), he can marry a girl whose maternal grandmother is a Muku. The two clans also enter into a close ritual relationship by performing services for one another in connexion with the circumcision rites. In all other respects, however, they have remained independent clans. They have retained their separate names and they have continued to occupy distinct territories and to administer their internal justice separately.

The other type of marriage prohibition between two clans is not based on a bond of mutual friendship but on its opposite, the existence of a blood feud between them. Such a feud may be continued for several generations and, as we have seen, nearly always arises from a case of murder or a quarrel over alleged witchcraft or sorcery. While the feud lasts, the two clans avoid one another in all social and ritual matters and, therefore, must naturally also refrain from intermarrying. When the event that originally started the feud and the sequence of mutual slayings that often —though not always—followed it, have completely passed out of the personal memory of all living members of the two clans, a gradual reconciliation takes place and the former marriage relations are resumed. Among the Vugusu, two clans that until recently refrained from intermarrying are the Mueya and the Sombi, because several generations ago the Sombi killed Namunya, a clansman of the Mueya.

A further type of marriage prohibition which is based on the same notion as the *vute* friendship is the rule that a man may not marry the real or classificatory sister or daughter of his *virongo* (circumcision friend), even if he chooses the latter from a clan to which he is in no way related. Here again, the fact that the two *virongo* become like 'brothers' who may freely call upon one another for economic help is considered to be incompatible with the relationship in which they would stand to one another as brothers-in-law. In contrast, however, to the *vute* relationship, the marriage prohibition established by the *rongo* friendship is purely personal: it does not extend to the brother of one's *virongo* who is free to marry one's sister, nor does it continue through succeeding generations. On the contrary, a marriage between the son and the daughter of two *virongo* is particularly welcomed, for, as the people say, 'two *virongo* will be friendly towards one another as *vasagwa* (parents of a married pair)'. This fact throws an interesting light upon the standardized emotional relations that prevail between people related through marriage. Although with regard to the legal claims and obligations which arise from the payment of marriage cattle two *vasagwa* stand in much the same relation to one another as two brothers-in-law, the differential attitude of two *virongo* with regard to these two relationships seems to show that the antagonisms which are expected to arise between brothers-in-law do not extend to the older generation of the *vasagwa*.

The prohibition of marriage between a man and his age-mate's daughter, which has already been referred to when discussing the age-class system, is based upon similar considerations. The establishment of a father- and son-in-law relationship between two age-mates would upset their equality of status and, moreover, would erect the bar of the father-in-law avoidance between them. Marriage with the daughter of an age-mate would thus interfere with the pattern of social relations that characterizes the age-grade organization.

Finally, there are two types of marriage restrictions which are not laid down as rigid rules but which are raised as weighty objections when a proposed marriage comes for discussion before the forum of relatives on both sides. The first of these restrictions consists in the disapproval of the marriage of two sisters to one husband as long as the sister who was married off first is still alive. An objection against such a marriage would be voiced both by the girl's and by the boy's kinsmen. The girl's kinsmen, particularly her brothers, would object 'because they like their *avifwa* (the children of their sisters) to belong to different clans or at least to different lineages of the same clan'. As one elder in Kitosh put it to me: 'If I have three daughters who are married to three clans and I have a quarrel with somebody, then the *vaxwe* (relatives-in-law) of three clans will come and help me. But if my daughters are all married to the same clan, then only one clan will come and help me.' The same argument would apply with regard to the ordinary exchange of kinship gifts and the fulfilment of the various mutual obligations that exist between a maternal uncle and his sisters' children.[1] If a man's sisters are married to one and the same husband, he will find it more difficult to obtain the 'cow of the maternal uncle' which he is entitled to claim from the marriage cattle given for *each* of his maternal nieces, for his brother-in-law will be likely to attempt to 'contract' his obligations towards the brother of his two wives. In other words, if one has affinal relatives in several clans, the potential help which one may expect from them will come from a wider group of persons and, accordingly, will be more substantial than it would be if they all belonged to the same clan, and, on the other hand, a disruption of one's relations with a brother-in-law will be of less consequence if only one sister is involved.

The man's kinsmen, too, would object to his marrying two sisters as, for reasons of the same nature, they like to see the marriage cattle with which they furnish their brother (or son) go to different clans. Besides, if a man marries two sisters, his sons by his 'great wife' could not marry his young wife after he has died, as such a marriage would involve a breach of the laws of exogamy. The father's young wife would, therefore, have to remarry into another family. Although, as we shall see, a young widow may always remarry into another family or even clan if she prefers to do so, the normal arrangement is for her to be taken over by her deceased husband's eldest son. It would, therefore, be against the interests of the husband's sons if, owing to the sororate, such a marriage should be ruled out.

The *successive* marriage of two sisters to one husband, on the other hand, is not only tolerated but quite common, especially if after the first wife's death her kinsmen are not in a position to return the marriage cattle (or the part of it that is still returnable) or if the children borne by the first wife are still very young, the mother's sister being considered the best substitute for the mother.

The other type of marriage restriction coming under the same category

[1] Cf. vol. ii.

MARRIAGE

as the one just discussed is the objection to the marriage of two sisters by two full brothers or by classificatory brothers of the same lineage. As a man's legal and economic relations towards the relatives of his own wife are very similar to those maintained towards his brother's wife, practically the same considerations would arise if two brothers marry two sisters as if the same person marries two sisters.

Comparing these different prohibitions and restrictions which narrow down the choice of the marriage partner, we notice that they are all based upon one general idea. This is to exclude from intermarriage all those persons or groups of persons who are either linked together by definite bonds of a social, economic, ritual, or political nature or who stand in a hostile relationship towards one another. In other words, a marriage may be concluded only between persons and groups of persons whose relations towards one another are perfectly neutral. We may assume, therefore, that the conclusion of a marriage establishes a particular set of claims and obligations as well as of emotional attitudes between the persons directly and indirectly affected by it which is incompatible both with any other form of social relationship and with the relationship established by a previous marriage. In the following analysis of the marriage ceremonies and of the attitudes displayed between relatives-in-law we shall examine the nature of this particular set of rights, duties, and attitudes which characterizes affinal kinship.

Before discussing the various stages of the marriage procedure we have to examine some further considerations affecting the choice of the marriage partner which are of a more personal and, hence, elastic nature.

While I was staying among the Logoli, taking down genealogical records of a number of individuals and their kin-groups, I noticed the unusual fact that in one particular clan, the Gimuhia, there were a number of middle-aged women who had remained unmarried. Inquiring into this matter among the Gimuhia themselves, I received merely evasive answers. It did not seem that these women suffered from any noticeable shortcomings which could serve to explain why they had failed to find husbands. Continuing my inquiries among persons of neighbouring clans, the information gradually oozed out that the Gimuhia had the reputation of being *avalogi* and that this fact made it difficult for them to marry off their daughters. This view was subsequently confirmed by identical statements made by a number of informants quite independently of one another. Moreover, the Gimuhia were pointed out to me as notorious *avalogi* in various other contexts which had nothing to do with marriage. This fact makes it very unlikely that 'being suspected of practising witchcraft' is merely a general explanation which is given for want of a better one whenever a person remains unmarried who has no obvious physical shortcomings or deficiencies.

To a certain extent the marriage discrimination affects all members of the clan afflicted with *ovulogi*, but it becomes a serious bar to marriage only for the sons and daughters of those persons who for some reason or other are reputed to have put their latent disposition of *ovulogi* into actual practice. To find a husband or a wife, the children of these persons then have to go far afield, if necessary to a different tribe where their alleged disposition is not known. As slanderous remarks about other people's witchcraft are always a dangerous undertaking for the person who makes them, there would be little chance that the alleged possession of witchcraft would become known to a suitor or a bride from far away.

The most striking example of the working of this discrimination which came to my notice was the case of a wealthy Gimuhia elder who had four grown-up daughters. One of these he married off to a 'detribalized' Logoli living at Nakuru, a European town over a hundred miles away from the girl's home. The second daughter found a husband who had spent all his life in Nairobi and who, therefore, contemptuously ignored what he called 'local gossip'. The third was married to a Christian teacher of another tribe (Vugusu) living about eighty miles away. The fourth daughter had an illegitimate child by a Christian youth who was quite willing to marry her and who had even handed over the marriage-cattle but whose father and other kinsmen subsequently refused to sanction the marriage as their suspicions about the father's *ovulogi* increased. After a prolonged lawsuit for the return of the marriage cattle, which came before the Native Appeal Court and even the Court of the Provincial Commissioner, the girl's father won his case. Even then the father of the lover forfeited his cattle rather than let his son marry the daughter of an *omulogi*.

Certain diseases are likewise a bar against marriage, especially if they are contagious or thought to be so. Thus persons afflicted with epilepsy, leprosy, serious ulcers, and similar diseases generally remain unmarried and often have to live by themselves in the bush at a safe distance from other homesteads.

Other factors which, apart from sexual attraction, determine the choice of the marriage partner to a greater or less extent are the comparative wealth of the two families concerned, the distance at which they live from one another, the respective ages of the man and the woman and, finally, their personal qualities and achievements. Although Kavirondo society is not formally graded on a basis of rank or wealth, the institution of the bride-wealth has produced a tendency for families of equal or approximately equal means to intermarry. The number of cattle demanded for a girl depends *inter alia* upon the amount of cattle possessed by the girl's father. In the majority of cases, therefore, a wealthy man's son marries a wealthy man's daughter and a poor man's son a poor man's daughter. Among the Logoli, the amount of the bride-wealth varies between one and four cows (and a corresponding difference in goats, hoes, or money) and among the Vugusu between five and fifteen head of cattle. The fact, however, that this tendency for people of equal wealth to intermarry has—with the possible exception of the Wanga tribe—nowhere led to a formally

MARRIAGE

marked differentiation of the tribal society into 'commoners' and 'aristocrats' indicates that wealth in cattle was only rarely stable enough to become associated with one family or lineage for a number of succeeding generations.

While, owing to the territorial grouping of clans, the people who intermarry are only in exceptional cases close neighbours,[1] a mother does not like to see her daughter married off to a husband living at a great distance. For in that case it would be difficult for the daughter to visit her mother at frequent intervals, and for the mother to summon her daughter if she were in need of her services. The average distance between the husband's homestead and that of the wife's parents appears to be between two and three miles among the Logoli, whose tribal population of nearly 46,000 people lives crowded together in an area of ninety-five square miles, and between five and ten miles among the Vugusu, whose slightly smaller population is spread over a territory nearly seven times as large. Thus marriages tend to be concluded between people living within a limited section of the tribal area, in so far as the numerous exogamous marriage restrictions permit of such residential preferences. The spatial distances over which people marry also tend to be limited by the fact that boys and girls meet and become acquainted with one another at dances, feasts, and similar occasions which take place between neighbouring clans, so that the majority of youths find their marriage partners without looking very far afield. If a man takes a girl from a territorially very distant clan, he usually does so only after he has made several unsuccessful attempts to court a girl closer to his home or because he has committed some offence or suffers from some other disability which causes him to be rejected as a suitor by the people who know him.

Intertribal marriages are said to have been very rare in pre-European days, at least between tribes which were traditional enemies or which occasionally waged war against each other, like the Nyole, Logoli, and Tiriki. Most intertribal marriages which I encountered when taking down genealogies had been concluded either with female war-captives who had been taken as children and raised in the family of the man who had captured them or between people living near the tribal boundaries. Apart from the distance factor which is often involved in intertribal marriages, the main objections raised against them relate to differences in custom. Thus the marriage arranged between a Vugusu youth and a girl from Maragoli who became acquainted with one another at a mission boarding-school was postponed for over a year because the bridegroom's relatives disapproved of it. When inquiring into the motives for their disapproval, I learnt that the bridegroom's mother was doubtful about her prospective daughter-in-law's knowledge of the tribal ways of cooking and of cultivating the fields, while his father and his brothers feared that the girl's kinsmen would fail to fulfil the various obligations which, among the Vugusu, arise from

[1] e.g. if one marries the daughter of a clan-stranger (*omumenya.*)

the acceptance of the bride-wealth but which are not known among the Logoli.[1] Another objection formerly raised against intertribal marriages was the difficulty of obtaining justice for both parties if a legal dispute arose between them.

On the other hand, an incentive for the conclusion of intertribal marriages is given where, owing to a differential status of wealth among neighbouring tribes, the average amount of bride-wealth differs considerably between them. In these cases the marriage relationship between the two tribes remains essentially one-sided, and the women of the poorer tribe who are married off to the wealthier tribe must be satisfied with an inferior social status as compared with the native women of that tribe. Thus many Luo men among whom the average amount of the bride-wealth is ten head of cattle or more take wives from the neighbouring Logoli. These they can marry for a bride-wealth of three or four cows and, moreover, the Logoli women have the reputation of being better agriculturists than the Luo women. A Logoli father, on his part, is quite willing to marry his daughter to a Luo as even the three or four cows which he will get from him still mean a higher bride-wealth than the majority of his own tribesmen would be able to give. If, on the other hand, a Logoli elder marries a Luo girl he does so in order to increase his prestige in his own clan and tribe, for such a marriage presents a visible sign of his wealth. Among the elders of the large and influential Yonga clan in Maragoli there was only one who some years ago indulged in the luxury of paying ten cows for a Luo girl. She was only fourteen years of age, but soon became his favourite among his eight wives. He built a particularly roomy hut for her and made her do no work except feeding and taking care of some gazelles, guinea-fowls, and quails which he kept as pets. One of his sons talked to me about this marriage with a mixture of pride and disapproval, the latter mainly concerning the visits of her Luo kinsmen who frequently came in groups of twenty or more and whom his father entertained on a lavish scale, killing a goat for them on nearly every occasion and making his other wives brew large quantities of beer.

The *age* of the bridegroom and, to a lesser extent, that of the bride also enter into the considerations which determine the choice or rather the approval of the marriage partner by the parents of either of them. Apart from a grudge that is often felt by the young men against the wealthy elders of their clan when they see them snatching away the young girls as 'junior wives', there is no general feeling that marriages ought to be concluded between persons of approximately equal age. I have attended pagan weddings where a girl of seventeen or less was married to an old, decrepit man, without noticing any signs of disapproval among the adult men and women present. Conversely, a man may marry a widow who is much his senior, although such cases are far less frequent. Among the Vugusu, some young men complained to me that most fathers preferred to marry their

[1] Cf. chapter on cattle law, vol. ii.

daughters to middle-aged men, not only because the older men can pay more marriage cattle but also 'because they know how to look after women' and because they prefer a son-in-law who is socially and economically well established to a youngster of whom they do not yet know how he will turn out. This preference given by the fathers of many girls to middle-aged suitors appears to be one of the chief causes for elopement marriages, as the girls themselves naturally prefer to be married to a youngish man. Among the Vugusu, a lad whose sweetheart had been betrothed against her will to an elderly man collects some friends and secretly goes with them to where the girl is working in the field. In the presence of the bride and her girl friends they sing songs of ridicule and shout derogatory remarks (*xusekeya*) about the bridegroom. The idea is to incite the girl to such a pitch of contempt for the man to whom she is betrothed that she will run home and drive the marriage cattle back to the bridegroom's place as a sign of her refusal to marry him. Once married, however, many women seem to reconcile themselves to the fate of being the wife of a man who is twenty-five or thirty years their senior. Provided that they are treated well they often even prefer the life of a junior wife to that of a 'great wife', as it means less work and less control of their activities by their husband.

Finally, personal qualities of character count as weighty factors in the competitive efforts of finding a husband or of being accepted as a suitor. I have repeatedly heard of cases where a man, although he had cattle enough to pay the bride-wealth, had for a long time tried in vain to find a wife because he had a reputation for cruelty or stinginess. Most of the standardized considerations, however, refer to the qualities which make a desirable wife. Young men are taught by their mothers and their maternal uncles not to choose a wife for her looks but to court a girl who is industrious, modest, and physically strong, so that she can stand up under the strain of the heavy work that is expected of a wife. The various emissaries who are sent to the girl's place to negotiate the betrothal and, later on, to hand over the marriage cattle, take these opportunities to inquire into the girl's character and achievements. Moreover, the work which both the bridegroom and the bride perform for their respective parents-in-law during the period of betrothal serves *inter alia* to test their willingness and ability to work. Among the Vugusu, a father whose daughter has industriously cultivated a large garden of her own and filled a granary or two with the fruits of her own labour usually asks for an extra cow to be added to the bride-wealth when he negotiates the amount with the suitor's father. I was told that formerly the bridegroom used to go with his friends to the girl's garden where, standing at one end of the strip of cultivation, he would shoot off an arrow with all his strength to measure the length of her garden. If the arrow fell down at the end of the garden or even beyond it, the girl would be considered lazy and this fact would be used as an argument when settling the amount of the bride-wealth.

Virginity, as we have seen, is likewise regarded as a special virtue in a bride, particularly in Kitosh, but, being the exception rather than the rule, its lack is not regarded as a serious shortcoming. A girl, however, whose premarital sexual adventures went far beyond the customary two or three love affairs considerably weakens her chances of getting properly married, especially if she has once eloped with a man without having been properly married to him. When listening to court cases I was impressed by the number of cases where women had changed their husbands half a dozen times within a few years, the bride-wealth given for them decreasing at every new marriage till, finally, they were satisfied to stay with any man who was willing to take them.

(3) COURTSHIP AND BETROTHAL

We see, then, that the choice of the marriage partner is governed by a complex set of culturally determined notions, ranging from rigidly formulated rules to considerations of a flexible and imponderable nature. As one might expect under such conditions, the desire of two people to marry one another, arising from their mutual sexual attraction, frequently comes into conflict with these culturally imposed restrictions. As a result of such conflicts, the majority of marriages do not conform to the theoretical norm. They are, accordingly, concluded in a manner and under circumstances which imply a greater or lesser deviation from the marriage procedure followed in cases where all rules of marriage are complied with and all prerequisites have been properly fulfilled and where all relatives on both sides who have a say in the matter have given their full approval. These deviations from the 'norm' are too important—both in view of the frequency of their occurrence and as indications of strain in the working of a cultural institution of foremost significance—to be briefly disposed of as mere variations of a pattern. I shall, therefore, discuss seriatim the major ways in which marriages are concluded, examining in each case the particular circumstances responsible for each variant.

Among the Vugusu three major ways of concluding marriages are distinguished:
1. *liaxa*, the marriage with the full wedding procedure, i.e. the type which represents the theoretical norm according to which a marriage should be concluded.
2. *liveyia*, marriage by elopement, and
3. *lixuesa*, marriage by abduction or capture.

The second way of concluding a marriage is the only one which sometimes leads to prolonged bad relations between the kinsmen of both partners, but once the marriage-cattle have been handed over, no serious stigma is attached to such a marriage.

Apart from these major types the differences between the marriage of a first wife and that of a plural wife, between the marriage of a girl and the remarriage of a divorced wife or a widow, &c., give rise to further variations in the wedding procedure.

I shall begin with an analysis of the *liaxa* type of marriage, the 'full' form, and follow it up through its various stages, as it leads from courtship via betrothal and the various wedding festivities to the actual consummation of marriage. The conclusion of a marriage is thus not a single event but rather a long-drawn-out process, in the course of which a network of relationships becomes established and in which such phases as the 'betrothal' and the 'wedding' have a significance that is analogous to but not altogether identical with the meaning of these words in European societies.

As will be discussed in the chapter on premarital sex-life (see vol. ii), the 'institution' of the unmarried girls' hut provides the chief opportunity for the two sexes to get to know one another, as all the ordinary activities of everyday life and even most recreational pastimes, such as games and partly even dances, are characterized by a far-reaching segregation of the sexes. Nevertheless, it appears from all the evidence I have that the nightly visits to the girls' hut do not predominantly or ostensibly serve the purpose of facilitating courtships which are expected to lead to betrothal and marriage. They rather offer means of sexual gratification and of gaining experience which lead up to marriage only in so far as, sooner or later, they inspire, in both boy and girl, a desire to end the life of adventurous and more or less promiscuous love-making and seriously look for a marriage partner. In contrast to the informal behaviour of a youth who carries on a playful love-affair, a man who seriously courts a girl does not, as a rule, enter into intimate relations with her but displays towards her a formal and restrained behaviour. Frequently, he will not even propose to her directly but approaches her indirectly through a third person. This does not necessarily mean that he is ignorant of the girl's qualities of character or even of her conduct in sexual matters, for he may have observed her while he was making love to other girls and he may have heard other lads talk about her who had a more personal knowledge of her. Such a formal and impersonal relation between a boy and a girl who contemplate marrying one another is not merely maintained for a show, because it is demanded by the rules of convention, but appears to be a genuine (although culturally determined) expression of their mutual psychological attitude. The boy refrains from making love to the girl to show thereby that he seriously intends to marry her, and the girl is careful not to make any advances to the boy and even displays an exaggerated modesty towards him, as she fears that otherwise the boy may refrain from proposing to her. A girl who fails in this respect, and permits the prospective bridegroom to make love to her, is said to have to suffer for it after she is married, as her husband will despise her as soon as his passion for her has worn off. The peculiar feature of this attitude is that the idea is not so much to convey to the suitor the impression that the girl whom he is courting is more virtuous than other girls, for the girl makes no secret of her former love-affairs; it is rather the particular nature of the situation, the fact that the pair intend to get married, which makes it desirable that they should observe initial reserve and self-restraint in their behaviour towards one another. It is, of course, difficult to say what percentage of betrothals actually conform to this pattern of behaviour. But even if it should not be typical by its numerical prevalence, it is, nevertheless, significant. For it shows that, where such an important undertaking as marriage is concerned, the sexual aspect is from the very start subordinated to the social aspects, i.e. to the need of a proper adjustment of husband and wife with regard to their future social, legal, and economic status. It would obviously be prejudicial to this process of adjustment if informality and intimacy were to prevail between the marriage partners before the matrimonial relationship has been finally established. The importance attached to such self-restraint is evident from the fact that even if the betrothal results from an intimate friendship between the boy and the girl, their behaviour towards one another becomes entirely formal as soon as their betrothal is publicly made known.

The initial procedure, then, is for the boy to find out if the girl to whom he wants to propose is eligible for marriage and, if so, if she herself is willing to marry him. As questions about the clans of her mother and of her two grandmothers—being tantamount to a proposal—would be bashfully evaded by the girl if put to her by the boy himself, he must engage the services of a third person whom he sends to her as a mediator. This service may be performed by a friend, or, more often, by the old woman in charge of the girl's hut who, if she favours the boy's proposal, is in the best position to influence the girl and to break down any resistance which she might feel. Old women 'whom one calls grandmothers' are the most suitable persons for acting as mediators in the arrangement of betrothals, as neither the boy nor the girl feels any of the reluctance to discuss matters of sex with them which they would have towards persons of their parents' generation, or even their own. As a gratuity for her help, the suitor presents the old woman with a blanket or, among the Vugusu, with a gift of meat, tobacco, or white ants; he may also send a ring or an armlet to the girl herself. At the same time he talks with his father about his desire to marry, or preferably with his mother, with whom he feels more free to discuss such matters and who is also more likely to approve of his intentions and to persuade her husband to consent to his son's marriage.

From accounts given to me by several Logoli of their own betrothals, it appears that a father himself often chooses the girls whom he wants his sons to marry provided that he has a strong enough personality to impose his will upon them. He does so especially at the first marriage of his eldest son and if he has made a previous arrangement with a friend that their son and daughter should one day marry one another. Sometimes also his wife may tell him about a certain girl, and if he considers her suitable for his son he may urge him to marry her. Christopher Mtiva, the son of a wealthy elder of the Yonga clan in Maragoli, thus writes about his own betrothal:

'They [his parents] were paying the bride-wealth for me without asking me; I had not even seen the girl. Our customs are that your parents are the ones who can arrange the matters of the bride-wealth. They are good customs but very difficult (to follow). To know a girl before you marry her is very good. To marry her if you do not know her is very difficult. I tried to refuse a present, Rispa Agwona, without any reason. My parents and our sister had a good reason to choose this girl to become my wife. She is a very likeable girl who is kind to everybody.'

The average age at which girls are betrothed is about eighteen to twenty years, but girls of fifteen or sixteen are occasionally married off, if the father or the brothers are anxious to get the marriage cattle, as they want to marry in turn. Child-betrothals of girls who have not yet reached puberty do not seem to occur, but sometimes girls of fourteen years of age are promised to a man who hands over a cow as the first instalment of the bride-wealth and takes the girl to the hut of one of his wives to prevent her from being snatched away by someone else. The natural increase of this cow is returned to him when he hands over the remainder of the bride-wealth before marrying the girl.

After the suitor has ascertained the girl's willingness to marry him, and after his father has promised to furnish him with the marriage-cattle, another emissary (*omutevi*, asker) is sent to put the proposal before the parents of the girl. The *omutevi* is always a woman, usually the suitor's mother. She starts off to the home of the girl's parents early in the morning to be certain of finding them still at home and without any other visitors. After the customary salutations she sits down near the door in the front partition of the hut and puts forward her proposal by saying: 'I have come about the handle of a hoe.' From the time and the other circumstances of her visit the parents of the girl know that she has not actually come to borrow the handle of a hoe but that she is making a marriage proposal. Even if her question does not come as a surprise to them, and if they are quite willing to give their consent, both pride and modesty require that they should not immediately agree to the proposal but pretend 'to have no handle for a hoe'. The suitor's mother, however, insists that she knows they have a handle and a very good handle at that. If the parents of the girl are willing to marry off their daughter, they finally give in and say: 'Indeed, we may see, perhaps the handle of the hoe may be there.' No further details are discussed on this occasion, but the visitor is offered food and a fowl to take home with her.

If the parents refuse to give their consent, they will continue to pretend that they have no handle of a hoe and finally will talk about something else. In this case also they offer food to the *omutevi* and present her with a small gift. If their refusal does not appear to be final, the *omutevi* repeats her visit after a few weeks and perhaps even tries for a third time. Only if she consistently receives negative answers does she eventually give up.

If the reply is favourable, the suitor's father begins to brew the 'beer of *enganana*'.[1] The festive drinking of this beer marks the first occasion on which the girl's father comes to the house of the boy's father for the purpose of negotiating the amount of the bride-wealth. While the prospective groom may be present and take a few sips of beer to please his father and his future father-in-law, he does not actually take part in the beer-drink nor in the ensuing negotiations. These are carried on exclusively between the boy's father and the girl's father and a few invited neighbours belonging to the age-classes of the two fathers and acting as witnesses. The girl's maternal uncle may also be called if he lives near, but his participation is not essential as his share in the bride-wealth is in any case fixed. When the beer is ready for consumption, the boy's father sends some messengers to the home of the girl's father, to invite him to come and drink the beer of *enganana*. These messengers also take two pots of beer along, the so-called *gamalua gexusuta*, 'the beer of carrying home'. This is a gift by the boy's father to the girl's mother and her neighbours to compensate them for not being invited to the beer-drink and the subsequent discussion, for this is a man's affair only at which no woman may be present, with the exception of the boy's mother whose duty it is to attend to the guests and to pour hot water into the beer whenever the supply runs low in the pot. Later, when the girl's father returns home from the beer of *enganana*, he will still find his wife and her neighbours drinking and he joins them to finish the 'beer of carrying home'. As Nandoli suggested, this gift of beer to the girl's mother is not merely a gesture of goodwill, but is intended to serve the useful purpose of making the girl's mother well disposed towards her prospective relatives-in-law and less likely to quarrel with her husband when he comes home for not having pressed his claims hard enough. Thus it will be seen that, although the girl's mother has no official say in the question of her daughter's marriage, her attitude towards it is by no means considered negligible.

The two fathers and their respective neighbours assemble in the hut of the boy's mother. After they have been served some cooked fowls and eleusine porridge they sit down, forming a circle round a huge beer-pot which contains the beer of *enganana*. Having tasted the beer, the host hands the beer-pipe to the girl's father to drink, but the latter refuses to take it, implying thereby that he wants to be presented with a new pipe. His host begins to look round everywhere pretending to search for a pipe, though actually he has taken care to make a new one and put it aside for this occasion. It must be a particularly neatly made specimen, so that it may please and honour his *navana* (i.e. his son's father-in-law). As Wefwafwa and Nandoli both volunteered in explanation of this request for a new pipe, 'the girl's father shows thereby that from now on he and his *navana* will be friends and that the two may ask things from one another as is customary between friends'. Since the main feature of their future relationship consists in inviting one another for beer-drinks, this gift of

[1] The following account refers to the Vugusu.

a beer-pipe appears as an appropriate expression of the nature of their friendship.

When the drinking has been going on for a while, the girl's father asks his *navana* for a few sticks (*visala*), so that he may count the things which he intends to demand for his daughter. The boy's father then hands him a bundle of sticks which he has likewise prepared for this occasion. If the bundle contains a few sticks only, the girl's father may refuse to take it and insist on further sticks being added. He then begins to make his demands by putting down a stick for each cow that he wants. Every time he takes a stick from the bundle, he raises it up in the air and shows it, so that not only the suitor's father but all the other people present can clearly follow what claims he is making. In this way he puts down between ten and twenty sticks and then says: 'This is the cattle for our clan.' Raising another stick and putting it down by the side of the first heap he continues: 'And this is a stick for my daughter's *xotja* (maternal uncle).' Next he puts down another stick by itself which represents a hoe to be given to his wife, the girl's mother. Adding still further sticks he asks for a goat for his sister (the girl's *senge*) and for one or two goats for the two grandmothers. Finally, he puts down a stick representing a spear that he wants for himself. If the suitor's family is rich, the girl's father may even claim separate goats for both the paternal and the maternal grandmothers, for his own sister, and for his wife's sister. He knows that the boy's father will in any case attempt to make deductions from the demands put forward by him and, therefore, always asks for more than he expects eventually to be given.

It is now the turn of the boy's father to drive a bargain by trying to whittle down his *navana*'s demands as substantially as possible. He begins by arguing about the cow for the maternal uncle. As the girl's father does not benefit from this cow in any case, he will be likely to agree that its payment may be postponed and that the suitor's father may settle the matter directly with his daughter's *xotja*. Next they talk about the cattle for the father's clan. The suitor's father takes off a stick for every head of cattle which he refuses to give and, pointing at the remainder, he says words like the following: 'I shall give you these sticks, but as regards those (pointing at the others) my arms are short.' After a longish argument during which the girl's father stresses the virtues of his daughter and the boy's father his poverty in cattle, the former may finally agree to let off two or three cows and to accept a young bull where he had demanded a heifer, or a few goats where he had asked for a calf. Winding up the discussion and getting ready to go home he says: 'Now we have counted the sticks, but we have not yet seen the cows and goats with our eyes; to-morrow I shall send my people to see all the things which we have talked about.' Although the neighbours of both fathers have witnessed the agreement reached by them over the beer of *enganana*, it does not yet have any binding force but is merely a preliminary arrangement which still leaves room for minor changes and adjustments.

According to legendary accounts given by the old men, the average amount of the bride-wealth has varied considerably throughout the past, the fluctuations depending upon the often very rapid changes in the tribal wealth in cattle. Thus stories are told that at one time in the distant past the Vugusu were so rich in cattle that when negotiating the bride-wealth they did not haggle over each animal as they do to-day, but settled the amount by a very quick and simple procedure. The girl's brother came to see the bridegroom and went with the latter as he drove his herd of cattle down to a stream in single file. Looking up and down the row of cattle, he took his club and, standing by the side of one cow, hurled it as far as he could. All the animals which were between him and the place where the club had fallen were then claimed by him and handed over by the bridegroom without any further argument. Another story, referring to a different phase of the past, relates that the Vugusu were so poor that they could not marry for cattle at all but merely handed a few rats to the father- or brother-in-law when they wanted to marry. Provided that these stories are not merely legends without any background of historical fact, they would indicate that such far-reaching differences, both in the kind and amount of the bride-wealth and in the manner in which it was 'paid', must have been paralleled by far-reaching changes in its function and significance.

On the morning after 'the beer of *enganana*' the girl's father sends a party of about four or six persons to the suitor's place 'to see the things' (*xulola vivindu*), i.e. to inspect the cows and goats which the suitor's father has promised to hand over as bride-wealth. The party is usually made up of the girl's brothers and one or two neighbours, but it does not include the father or the girl herself. The bridegroom and his brothers welcome the visitors and, after having offered them food (porridge) and a fowl, they take them to see the animals which in the meantime have been led to the yard. The delegates of the girl's father choose those cows and goats which they like and refuse others which they think are too small or too lean or otherwise unsatisfactory. Then they return home without as yet taking any of the cattle along with them and report to the girl's father what they have seen and which animals they have accepted and which they have refused. After a week or two, the boy's father invites the party for a second inspection, sending a message to the girl's father that in the meantime he has looked for other cows which, he thinks, will please him better than those he had offered the first time. If the second inspection leads to a mutual agreement or if only one cow is still under dispute, the girl's father will authorize his sons to accept the animals. Accompanied by some neighbours they go to fetch the bride-wealth cattle, goats, and sheep (*xuxuaula*), the boy's brothers going with them for a mile or two but not all the way to the girl's father's place. The party having returned, the girl's father inspects the cattle and they all sit down 'to talk them over'. Should the father not be pleased with the choice made by his sons, he still has the right to refuse one or the other of the animals and tell his sons to drive them back and exchange them for others.

Among the Logoli the betrothal is not marked by a beer-feast as in Kitosh. After the preliminary and secret agreement has been reached between the boy and the girl and after the parents' attitude has been sounded by the visit of a female mediator, a meeting is arranged between the brothers of both the groom and the bride at which they negotiate the amount of the bride-wealth. This meeting (*okololana*, to see one another) is usually held under a tree somewhere between the boy's and the girl's home and the negotiations take only a short time, as the generally much smaller amount of bride-wealth given in Maragoli leaves less room for bargaining. When an agreement has been reached, the boy's father assembles the necessary cattle and goats and sets the day on which he is ready to hand them over to the girl's father. There is no preliminary inspection of the bride-wealth by the girl's brothers. They either take the cattle the first time they come, or else the boy's father summons a large group of male and female kinsmen (as many as twenty in the case of a well-known family) to drive the bride-wealth off and hand it over to the girl's father. Before parting from the cattle, he beats each cow on its back with his right hand. This he does in the presence of the assembled relatives and neighbours to show that he is handing over these cows to his son, so that he may take them for his marriage-cattle. If one or several of the cows of the bride-wealth are jointly owned by (or earmarked for) two sons, the father stresses this fact while he beats such a cow on its back, saying: 'If this cow calves, the calf must return to your brother.' He thereby publicly states the claim which his younger son still has to the increase of the cattle which are being handed over.[1] The recognition of this claim by the girl's kinsmen has already been obtained on the occasion of the *okololana* meeting.

When the party arrives at the yard of the girl's father, he inspects the cattle and, if he approves of them, asks his guests to enter the house where porridge and meat and sometimes beer are kept ready for them. He also gives them a large cooked hen and a basketful of eleusine porridge to take home with them as a present for his *navana*.

The various considerations and the procedure leading up to a betrothal among the Logoli were described to me by a Logoli elder in the following text:

'... When a boy has seen in the girls' hut "this girl is good", he must go and tell his mother, so that she may know, "I found a wife". He cannot tell his father like (he can tell) his mother. She may begin to know when his father does not yet know "my son is wanting a wife". Later on, the mother tells the boy's father: "This our son wants a wife." Then the father asks, "Did he find a girl or not?" The mother of the boy replies, "Wait, let me ask his friends." Then she asks them and they say, "Yes, we know that girl"; then they also say, "She is the daughter of So-and-so." Now the mother of

[1] Cf. chapter on cattle law, vol. ii.

the boy wants to know the name of that girl, and when she has found out the name she can walk (i.e. here "proceed") secretly and inquire further, because she does not yet know the ways (*emima*, customs) of the girl and those of the home where she comes from. To those people who live near the girl she says: "I want to see the daughter of So-and-so." Then the old women tell her: "We know the girl; she is good." They also tell her of which clans they are (i.e. the relatives of the girl); perhaps the girl may be of the clan of the boy.

'Then (after having inquired into everything) the mother of the boy returns home, and when she has returned home she speaks to her neighbour who is an old woman and says to her: "I wish that you may go to the house of So-and-so to take there the words of our son, for he wants a cook." When that old woman reaches the day of going to the place of the girl, she must first send words there like a letter: "I may come to have a talk", but she cannot talk about the purpose of her visit beforehand. When she arrives there she says: "I have come here, because the son of my neighbour has sent me here to ask for a cook." And those people ask her: "Whose boy is he?" And they also want to know well who they are (*vulahi ayivandiki*), i.e. the clan of the boy's father and so forth. Then that old woman who has been sent there can tell everything to the people of the girl: how they are living and if they are rich people. But she cannot finish the matter; she can only say all these things. Then the mother of the girl can say to the old woman: "Go, you may tell the owners of the boy, it is good for them to send two old women again; then we may finish the matter." When those old women arrive at the girl's place they must observe (lit. be with) a small rule (*omwima*) with which they must be careful indeed: They may enter the house, but they must not pass through the *muhilu* (front room) into the *evwasi* (cooking-partition); they may sit down in the front room only. Then the girl's mother begins to talk: "What have you come here for? We do not have a thing which we can offer you to eat!" The old women reply: "We have come here with a matter", and the girl's mother asks: "What matter?" She is asking although she knows why they have come, but it is their custom to do so. Even if they know beforehand, it is good that those who came begin with their story, lest it be different (from the message of the first woman). When they hear that the words are altogether the same, the girl's mother begins to "pretend poverty" (*okwégamina*) and she says: "We, we are poor; we do not have a thing. But anyway, we shall make gruel." Actually, she will not cook gruel only, but she cannot say openly "to cook food" (*okudeka kyokulia*). It is our custom to say those things.

'Now the two old women must begin the talk that they have come to ask for a cook. The mother of the girl says: "How do you know we have a daughter who can do the work well? a' a'!" But they insist and say: "We know, because a girl who came from here has told us so; so we came to know what we did not know before." The girl's people agree and say: "It is good that you may give us an account (*elivaliza*) of the cattle which you have." Then they reply: "We have two cows and a bull and twelve hoes." And the owners of the girl agree, because the girl has already agreed with the boy.

'Now they arrange the day of sending the people who belong to the girl to go to the place of the boy; they are called *avahuli*, which means "those who fetch the cattle". Those who go there are three men and when they are going they cannot go straight to the boy's place, but they begin to go to the place of the first *omutevi* (the emissary). The reason is that the *omutevi* knows where to go (i.e. how to lead them to the boy's place). Now the three men, together with that woman (the *omutevi*) makes four; then they begin to go (to the boy's place). When they arrive there they stand in the yard and the woman only passes and enters the house, because only she has permission to go inside the house. And the men "have permission" to remain in the yard, because while they stand there they want to see how the boy's father unties the cows from (the *ekego*) inside the house. Then they may choose those cows which they want. They stand for about ten minutes while they are not yet offered stools; finally the boy himself brings stools for the visitors and they sit down. Then the boy's father "begins" to call two of his neighbours. And those are witnesses to see how they give those *avahuli* the cattle. The boy's father says, "I have here two calves which I shall bring. You may see them and look at them." While he is yet to bring them, the two neighbours must begin to talk with those *avahuli*. They want to know the ways (*emima*) of the girl, and whether she is a lazy girl (or not). And also those old men (the two neighbours of the boy's father) are talking about matters like these. They begin showing the *avahuli* how one cow (of the bride-wealth) is owned jointly and whether it is the betrothed who shares it with another person or the father. Then they say: "It is good, you may take it, and if it calves you may return the heifer-calf because the cow is owned jointly."

'Those men (the *avahuli*) then have a fowl cooked for them and that woman (the *omutevi*) a fish. When they have finished eating they ask for permission to leave. The boy's father brings the cows and gives them to the *avahuli*. Later, when they are going, those two old men must choose some people who belong to the boy's homestead to drive those cows (to the place of the girl's father). They must be two boys and four girls, and the things which will be cooked for them (at the girl's place) are fowls for the boys and meat for the girls. It is a big rule (*elilago*) for the mother of the girl that she may stir (i.e. cook) the food for the boy who will marry her child. The girls who helped to drive the cows must carry food and a fowl from the girl's to the boy's place. He cannot eat that food (at the girl's place), because this is the custom. He must wait until the girls return home bringing the food. Then now the boy can begin eating the food which came from the place of the girl.'

The transfer of the bride-wealth from the boy's place to the girl's place marks the beginning of their betrothal. The length of time during which a pair is betrothed varies considerably, as it depends upon a number of circumstances. Among the Vugusu it is said that formerly a year generally passed from the time of handing over the marriage-cattle until the beginning of the series of feasts that lead to the consummation of marriage. Among the Logoli, the interval between betrothal and marriage never seems to have lasted for more than a few months. To-day it is generally shorter among both tribes, often lasting only a month or even less.

An important factor upon which the length of the betrothal depends is the ability of the girl's father to procure the things required for the wedding-feast. He needs large quantities of meat, grain, beans, and other vegetables for the lavish hospitality with food and beer and the numerous presents to the boy's parents which, as we shall see, are among the most important features of the wedding-feast. For this reason most weddings take place soon after the eleusine harvest, in October or November, when food is most plentiful.

Besides offering an opportunity for accumulating things for the wedding-feast, the period of betrothal serves the important purpose of testing the industry and the qualities of character of the future son- or daughter-in-law respectively. The prospective son-in-law during this time comes regularly with two or three friends to help his future parents-in-law with any kind of work that may turn up, particularly in clearing the bush, cutting grass, and repairing huts and granaries. As, however, the main share of such work is done by his friends while he himself 'only touches everything', the purpose of these visits is not to impress his future father-in-law with his own industriousness but to show him that he has friends who are willing to help and support him. Owing to the prescribed avoidance of his future parents-in-law, especially of his mother-in-law, the son-in-law cannot sit down and accept food or any other hospitality in his mother-in-law's house. While at the end of every day's work the future wife cooks meat and porridge for his friends, her fiancé must either go straight home from the work in the field or else go and eat with some of his father-in-law's neighbours. Among the Logoli, the future wife likewise goes, together with her friends, to help her future mother-in-law digging, planting, and weeding. As a sign that they have no claims of ownership to the produce of their labour, the girls do not bring their own hoes along but come empty-handed, being supplied with hoes or other implements by the boy's mother. Like the boy at her place, the girl cannot accept any food at her fiancé's place. While her friends are offered porridge and vegetables or other relishes at the end of the day's work, she goes home by herself and later eats the food which her mother-in-law has 'stirred' for her and which one of her friends carries home for her. Among the Vugusu, on the other hand, a betrothed girl does not do any work for her future parents-in-law. She continues to help her mother as she used to do before she was betrothed, but she is given no hard work to do, so that she may look 'nice and plump' when the time for the wedding arrives. If she is still young and inexperienced in household work her mother teaches her to cook properly, to grind the grain to fine flour, to economize with water and firewood and so forth, so that she may not fail when later on her skill and knowledge are scrutinized by her mother-in-law. During the time of her betrothal she is not yet called *omwéa* (bride) but still *omuxana*, girl, or *waxévwa*, 'the one who has been given marriage cattle for'.

The work done for the future parents-in-law during the period of betrothal is not considered as a 'payment' or 'service' by which the man 'earns' his wife (in the sense that he thereby acquires any such rights with respect to his future wife as he does by having handed over the bride-wealth) as appears to be the case in some other parts of Africa. Among the Logoli it is obvious that no such idea is implied since an approximately equal amount of work is performed by the boy and the girl and their respective friends. But even in Kitosh where a girl does not work for her future parents-in-law, the boy's services rendered to his father-in-law have nothing to do with his claims to his wife. If a man elopes with a girl or 'captures' her soon after the bride-wealth has been handed over, his father-in-law demands no compensation for his failure to work for him, nor is this point ever discussed when a marriage is dissolved. This would certainly be the case if the services rendered by the betrothed to his (or her) parents-in-law should entitle him (or her) to any definite claim. It rather seems that these services are intended to establish a social relationship and to promote a mutual feeling of trustworthiness between the two groups of people who will soon become related through the marriage of two of their members. This point will be discussed more fully and in a wider context after the various other phases of the wedding procedure have been analysed.

The behaviour of the betrothed couple towards one another is of a particular nature. All visits which a boy pays to a girl's hut *before* the marriage-cattle have been handed over must be undertaken secretly and under cover of darkness. *After* the cattle have been paid, the boy and his friends may freely visit his fiancée's hut whenever they feel inclined to do so. The purpose of these visits, however, is not to give the betrothed pair an opportunity of making love to one another but, on the contrary, to guard the girl's chastity. Even if, prior to their betrothal, the girl had been on intimate terms with her future husband, she must now display a very bashful and reserved behaviour towards him which reaches its climax during the wedding-feast. During his nightly visits to his fiancée's hut the future husband must never lie (*okugonya*) with her but with one of her girl friends, while his friends must in turn lie with the future wife. This arrangement is to prevent the betrothed couple from entering into any intimacies with one another and, at the same time, to ensure that no outsiders will try to make love to the girl. Apparently the future husband can trust his friends not to go beyond the customary *okugonya*-relationship when sleeping with his fiancée. Should one of them, however, indulge in sexual relations with her or make her pregnant, he (the future husband) will refuse to marry the girl and will ask for the marriage cattle to be returned.

Whenever the future husband and his friends do not sleep in the girl's hut, the old woman in charge of it is held responsible for guarding her chastity. In return for this service she receives occasional gifts of tobacco, meat, or white ants from the future husband and his friends.

During their betrothal both parties are still free to break off the engagement either by returning the bride-wealth or by demanding it back. No cattle or goats are deducted by the girl's father if the betrothal is thus dissolved, nor does either of the two parties need to have any particular reason for calling off a betrothal. While nowadays it occasionally happens that even before a marriage has been consummated the girl's father refuses to agree to a demand for the return of the marriage cattle, all my informants insisted that formerly such a refusal was practically unheard of. If a father had refused to return the bride-wealth voluntarily, the boy's clansmen would have fetched it back by force and no father in his senses would then have resisted them.

While it is said to happen that girls harass boys for having broken off a betrothal, they find little sympathy in such a case but rather become the laughing-stock of the young people of the neighbourhood, both boys and girls. When I stayed in Kitosh I heard of a girl who had continued to implore a boy to marry her for a long time after he had cancelled their betrothal and, eventually, had committed suicide by hanging herself at his mother's house. If it is the girl who wishes to terminate the betrothal she returns the ring or armlet which her lover had given her. This frees her from her promise to remain faithful to the boy. Should he later make abusive remarks about her, she could justify herself by pointing out that she had returned the armlet.

During her betrothal a girl still has the chance of escaping from a marriage into which she is to be forced. Although in such a case her opinion is not asked, she has several means of drawing public attention to her refusal and of enlisting the sympathy of the elders of her lineage or clan. Her ritual status as a promised bride ordinarily prevents her from drinking the milk from the cows of her bride-wealth or accepting food at her future husband's place. Thus one of the strongest means of expressing her refusal to marry the person to whom she is betrothed is for her to drink from the milk of the bride-wealth cows or to eat from the gifts of meat or white ants which her prospective husband from time to time sends to his father-in-law to please him. As another sign of her refusal she will attempt to drive the cattle back to her fiancé's place, or again she will run off to her paternal aunt or to a more distant relative and hide there for a few months. While some fathers yield to such demonstrations and break off the betrothal, especially if the girl is very persistent, others bring pressure to bear upon her. If an ordinary beating by her father or her brothers has proved to be of no avail, her resistance—so my informants stated—would be broken by more drastic methods. One of these is to dig a deep, narrow hole in the yard in front of the hut. Some red-hot charcoal is then thrown into this hole and the girl's left arm is forced into it and kept there by filling in the remaining space with earth and beating it hard. Another method is to put both her arms into two narrow holes in the ground and to press down the soil so tightly that she cannot free herself again. If the girl's mother sided with her too openly she would be subjected to the same treatment or at least be beaten severely.

Should a girl commit suicide in order to escape a forced marriage or because, owing to her father's refusal, she cannot marry the boy she loves, her maternal uncle can claim a cow from his brother-in-law as a compensation for his niece's death.

(4) THE WEDDING-FEAST AND THE CONSUMMATION OF MARRIAGE

The transition from betrothal to marriage is marked by a series of festive occasions which already by their outward features—the number of participants, the amount of economic display, and the wealth of ceremonial observances—clearly present themselves as the climax of the marriage procedure. The main sequence of festivities and events appears to be the same throughout the Bantu Kavirondo area. An initial feast, celebrated separately but simultaneously by both the bridegroom's and the bride's kinsmen, is followed by a series of visits by the bride and her people to the bridegroom's place and by counter-visits by the bridegroom's people to the bride's place. In the course of these visits a number of ceremonial actions are performed which 'enact' the main social and biological features of the process leading up to matrimony: the mutual adjustment of the two clans to one another, the departure of the bride from her home, her social acceptance by her relatives-in-law, the new duties awaiting her in her husband's family, the formation of bonds between the bride and her sisters-in-law, the fertility of the bride, and finally her daily work in the house and in the gardens.

Although alike in all its major features, the details of the marriage procedure differ slightly, not only from tribe to tribe and from clan to clan, but even from occasion to occasion. Every phase of the procedure is, so to speak, characterized by a dominant notion which then finds manifold expression in a variety of actions and attitudes. Certain features of modern native life are being liberally incorporated into the traditional marriage procedure, a fact which shows that the details of the procedure are not rigidly laid down but are to a large extent flexible. Moreover, at the various wedding-feasts which I attended, the inclusion of one feature or the omission of another was often a matter of expediency, depending in each case upon such factors as the presence or absence of certain persons required for performing a certain rite, the availability of the necessary paraphernalia, or the social and economic status of the two families concerned. A description of the marriage procedure, even for a limited area, would therefore have to omit most details to be of general validity. However, it is the details which furnish the best clues for an understanding of the significance of the entire procedure. It seems preferable, therefore, to forgo the attempt to give a representative account and to include the details as far as they have come to my notice. While it is possible that a systematic study of the marriage procedure over a larger area would reveal a deeper significance in local variations by leading to the discovery of correlations between such variations and local differences in other aspects of culture, it is by no means certain that such a result would ensue. It may just as well be that what appear to be local variations are only accidental concatenations of features which by imitation tend to be repeated on a number of successive occasions. As my material does not warrant any attempt to formulate hypotheses in that direction I feel justified in including in the following account all the features I have observed on the various occasions on which I have attended weddings or that have been related to me in the form of narratives.

The initiative in setting the beginning of the wedding festivities rests with the bride's father. He has to make the preparations for the first big feast which is to celebrate his daughter's forthcoming marriage and to which chiefly the people of his own and his wife's clan are invited. When he has collected sufficient quantities of grain and beans and obtained one or two bulls for slaughter, he sends out his daughter, the bride, to collect firewood for cooking the food and roasting the meat. This serves as a sign to all neighbours and kinsmen that the time of the wedding is drawing near. Should the girl's father unduly delay making preparations for the wedding, the future husband would show his impatience by sending an old woman of his clan to the girl's father to ask him that 'he should give his daughter permission to cook the food of the wedding'. As we shall see later, this is a hint that the bridegroom's people might abduct the bride unless he speeds up his preparations for the feast.

When the bride goes to collect the firewood she must pay attention to unlucky signs (such as the singing of a bird on the wrong side of the road), as any mishap that she might meet with on that occasion would be regarded as inauspicious for her marriage and therefore would necessitate the postponement of the wedding. For her protection two of her clansmen accompany her, for 'it is not good if anybody quarrels with her or if she is beaten by strangers'. Before the party actually begins to collect the firewood they go to the bride's maternal uncle to tell him of the forthcoming feast and to choose a lad from there to complete the bride's escort during her wood-gathering expedition.

When sufficient wood has been collected and the beer is ready for consumption the visitors 'from the girl's side' come and, for a day or two, celebrate the happy event of their 'daughter's' *ekiselelo* with feasting and dancing. Neither the bridegroom nor any of his kinsmen are present at this feast. The full attendance of the relatives of the bride, however, is, as on other occasions, a necessary condition of the auspiciousness of the feast: 'If they are all not there, the girl who is going to be married will not get a child quickly; then they will grumble about a person who did not come there.' '*All* relatives' means in this case the members of the bride's lineage and of her mother's lineage, as well as those neighbours with whom the bride's parents maintain effective relations.

The celebration of the bride's forthcoming marriage, the *ekiselelo*,[1] does not revolve round a set of ritual observances but, for the most part, is merely a social gathering. Its chief attraction for the visitors is the killing of a bullock in the course of the first or the second day. The procedure at

[1] Vugusu: *siselelo (oxusélela)*.

such a feast is rather uncoordinated. There are many categories of guests, each group keeping more or less by itself and having a good time in its own way. The age-mates of the bride's father sit round the beer-pot inside the great wife's hut; the senile old men assemble round a second pot in the shade of a granary; groups of warriors with their leaders occupy a third place, perhaps in a neighbouring hut or under some shady tree near by, while some stray individuals, usually uninvited and unwelcome guests, wander about from group to group, either making themselves a nuisance by begging for beer or providing entertainment for all by joking and jesting. Among the women, a similar differentiation into rough age-groups prevails. The very old women rest somewhere in the shade and gossip or join the old men sitting round the beer-pot; the middle-aged married women sit round the hearth and talk with the bride's mother, and the younger girls are busy round the grindstone or go in parties to the nearest stream to fetch water. Children, finally, from infants up to young lads, also form a number of groups, some playing, some eating, some helping, while others stroll about by themselves, gazing or crying. Amidst all these different categories of guests, each pursuing its own pastimes, the bride and the bridesmaids are by no means the centre of public interest, but meekly fulfil their duties fetching water, keeping the pots filled with beer, and dishing out porridge or gruel to the various groups of guests.

At most present-day feasts the differentiation of the visitors into several groups is further marked by the segregation of pagans and Christians or 'old-timers' and 'moderners'. At a half-Christian, half-pagan wedding which I attended near Broderick Falls in Kitosh, the generally picturesque scene afforded by the traditional setting was further enlivened by the presence of three or four decidedly modern groups of visitors. Under the eaves of the hut there were half a dozen unmarried Christian girls sporting gaudy dresses and shawls and sitting all by themselves on a bedstead ostentatiously displaying an air of superiority. At intervals of an hour or so various detachments of schoolboys, led by their 'captains', marched in formation to the yard and in the midst of beer-drinking groups of elders gave short drill-performances or sang songs in English. A little farther off, in the hut of one of the co-wives, young men and girls in European clothes, obviously 'on leave' from labour contracts in towns or on farms, danced in European fashion to the accompaniment of an accordion, a drum, and a triangle or had a musician sing songs of praise for one another.

The type of entertainment offered on such an occasion may best be illustrated by quoting at random a few passages from my note-books, referring to some detail or episode observed, to remarks overheard, or to the gist of a talk round the beer-pot:

'As I arrive at the wedding, a few miles from Lugulu,[1] the "bull of eating" is just being killed in the grass next to the hard-surfaced yard. About half a dozen men are standing round the "skinner", constantly criticizing his manner

[1] A mission station in North Kitosh.

of handling the knife but not actually interfering with him. While he cuts up the meat, dozens of children come near, snatching tiny pieces of meat which he throws into the air for them. Men and women crowd in from all sides, looking hardly less eager to get their share but waiting for their turn. Every time a piece is thrown to someone he jokingly complains that it is too small. Some eat the meat raw, still standing round the carcass; others pierce it on little sticks and walk off with it to one of the dozen small fires which have quickly been kindled all over the yard and in the bush near by when the distribution of meat began. An elderly warrior, carrying a shield and a Masai spear, solemnly watches the cutting up of the meat; suddenly he jumps up and down and, shaking his head, calls out "*a*' *a*', cattle are a disease which kills us in the war, which kills us in the war indeed!",[1] his remark provoking shouts of approval and laughter from all the people who hear it.

'As I follow the bride's *mulamua* (i.e. her brother's wife) who has just filled a big, flat basket with entrails and is carrying it into the house where the elders sit round the beer, I hear some guests joke about the smell of the entrails. The woman's husband who is sitting there among the guests gets up and, taking the tray away from his wife and putting it outside, calls aloud in Swahili: "Oh you women have always short brains." This remark again provokes great hilarity. His wife just shakes her head and with the customary click: *a*', *a*', expressing wonder and displeasure, sits down near the fire-place where the bride's mother is stirring some porridge. Her husband gets busy again driving off all the people who were merely sitting round the fire, and complaining—again in Swahili—that the women are crowding the men out and that only those may remain inside who are really busy working. Then the drinking goes on again.'

At another wedding a dance and beer-feast in progress in the hut of the chief's junior wife attracted my attention. It was the wedding of Mutjambala, one of the chief's daughters, to Guxolome, who was marrying her as his second wife.

'The large hut, dimly lit by a fire and a few rays of daylight coming in through the low door and a few cracks in the wall, is filled with people sitting round a huge beer-pot in the centre of the hut. A musician (*omupi owe litungu*) plays the lyre (*litungu*) and in a long-winded song names all the chief's ancestors. This pleases the chief so that he finally stands up and dances a solo dance which all applaud with shouts and shrieks. In another song the musician praises the good qualities of the wives of long ago. Then he bewails the fact that they have all died and that the wives now living in the country are no good but a lazy and unfaithful lot. In response to this wholesale indictment one of the chief's wives gets up to dance in front of him and to insist in a shrill voice that "the present wives are still doing as the wives of long ago used to do". Another woman stands up and, taking the chief by his wrist, raises his right arm and praises him as "the trunk of the tree" and "the stone of the road". As soon as she sits down, a third woman, one of the chief's senior wives, steps forward. Dancing for him she sings: "When I married you I thought that I married just an ordinary man; I did not know that I was

[1] Meaning that the desire for meat drives the men to raid cattle from the enemy, a pursuit in which they might get killed.

marrying a chief." This pleases the chief (who formerly was only a *mulango* headman) and in good humour he replies to his wife: "I conquered your people (the Wanga) and I nearly killed your father in battle. But I spared him and so I came to marry you."

'Now it is the turn of one of the chief's sisters to get up and dance. Pleased by her dance, the chief beckons to her and her sisters and invites them to sit down by his side: "Come here and drink this beer; you are of my clan, but the others are my enemies. Now they are drinking and praising me, but in the end wives always kill their husbands." As his wives hear him say this they all stand up together, tie their loin-cloths tightly and dance in the centre of the hut. The musician again strikes up the tune to which one of the wives previously sang "You are the trunk of the tree" and all the wives sing and dance together until the chief finally joins in with them. The song being finished, the chief resumes his seat and, by now being rather drunk, admonishes his wives: "Now you are dancing and praising me, but when the time comes that I shall die, the people will try to inherit you. When I give you things, share them well and do not be selfish. Then you will live happily and when you have another husband you will cry for me and remember me." Seeing that the chief is 'fading out', the musician takes his lyre and leaves the hut, joining now one of the other groups that have assembled outside or in other huts.'

These few passages may suffice to convey an impression of the nature of Kavirondo sociability on the occasion of such a big feast. We shall now go on to describe the part which the bride takes during the further course of events.

At the beginning of the feast the bride's chief task was to help provide the guests with food and drink. In the afternoon of the second or third day, when the feast at her father's homestead draws near its end, the bride pays her first visit to the bridegroom's place, escorted by a few young men and a great number of bridesmaids. Preparing for this important event she first chooses her bridesmaids. They may be as many unmarried girls as she can muster, usually some twenty or thirty. They must all be girls who are skilful in grinding grain, for this will be one of the main tasks they will have to perform at the bridegroom's place. Two or three of them are her close friends who stay with her throughout the further wedding procedure, and she must take care to choose one of them from her maternal uncle's clan. On the morning of her visit to the bridegroom's clan the bride takes a bath in a stream and then has her hair shaved, together with all the other bridesmaids. When she is ready to go, her mother's sleeping-hide is placed in the yard in front of the entrance to the mother's hut. The bride and two of her best friends among the bridesmaids step on this hide, and the bride's sister-in-law (*mulamua*) anoints them with ghee and simsim seeds and adorns them with a necklace of pleasant-smelling roots (*edzindago*). The avowed purpose of this rite is 'to make the bride conceive quickly'. The stepping on the sleeping-hide is to transmit the mother's fertility to her daughter; for analogous reasons the anointing with ghee, &c., must be done by a *mulamua* who has given birth to several children. If the wife of the bride's physical brother does not fulfil this condition, the rite must be performed by a *mulamua* of 'another house', i.e. by the wife of one of her classificatory brothers.

Among the Logoli the bride formerly went naked, adorned only with some *amalande*-leaves which her father hung round her neck and shoulders after she had been anointed with ghee. In Kitosh she wears the same fibre-tassels round her loins which she used to wear before she became a bride; they are, however, cleaned and anointed with ghee for the occasion. In addition, her mother sometimes gives her a new garment made by sewing together two goatskins which have been softened and from which the hair has been scraped off by a specialist.

The bride is now called *omweha* (Luvugusu: *omwea*), a name which she retains for the following three or four months. As she takes leave of her mother there is no display of grief on either side, nor is her departure marked by any ceremonial feature. The time of departure is always fixed so that the bridal party will arive at the bridegroom's place just at sunset or even shortly after darkness has fallen. The bridesmaids assemble in the yard and after one of them has been appointed to be a song-leader, they take the bride between them and run off singing towards the groom's place. Now and throughout the following days the bride puts on a shy and meek behaviour, casting down her eyes and showing herself entirely unresponsive to everything that goes on round her. This is not a sign of her grief or fear at leaving her accustomed surroundings but of the shame which she is supposed to feel in her role as a bride. '*Olukosi nduvera*', 'the bashfulness kills them', say the Nyole of the bride and the bridesmaids who to some extent adopt the same behaviour.

As the party proceeds to the bridegroom's place, the bridesmaids, headed by the song-leader, sing songs of praise for the bride, extolling her good qualities and her sexual advantages as well as her father's wealth. To mark the rhythm of their songs they beat an iron armlet which they hold in their right hand against the blade of a hoe which they carry in their left, raising both arms above their heads. If the distance between the bride's and the groom's place is short, they make a detour to give more 'publicity' to the event and to take the opportunity of ridiculing couples who have married without following the proper procedure. In Kitosh a bridal party which I accompanied thus went out of its way to pass the house of a young man who had worked on a European farm and had recently settled down with a girl with whom he had eloped. As the bridesmaids approached the house they sang a song denouncing girls who had married by elopement and ridiculing their husbands as lazy and good-for-nothing persons. Presently the husband came out, armed with a *kiboko* (a whip made of hippo-skin), at the sight of which the whole bridal party quickly dispersed. Resuming their procession towards the bridegroom's place, they sang songs which anticipated the hospitality they would meet with and in which they raised doubts as to whether the bridegroom and his people would prove worthy of the honour of getting such an excellent wife as they were now taking to him.

At the bridegroom's place preparations have been made in the meantime to receive the bridal party and to offer the bridesmaids generous hospitality. When the bride's father killed the 'bull of eating' for his daughter's *siselelo*, he sent a front leg and the hide to the bridegroom's father. Besides, he presented his *vasagwa* with the 'bull of *naŋeso*', either alive or slaughtered, together with about eight large basketfuls of eleusine flour. So it is now up to the groom's father to retaliate. Thus a bullock is killed, beer is brewed, and several basketfuls of eleusine porridge are cooked in expectation of the bridal party.

The atmosphere in which the two parties, the groom's people and the bride's people, meet on this occasion is one of the most curious but also most significant features of the whole wedding. In place of the cordiality and mutual politeness which ordinarily prevail between hosts and guests, both parties in this case adopt an exceedingly contemptuous and haughty attitude towards one another. Each group provokes the other by showering every kind of abuse upon it. The bridal party displays the greater initiative in these efforts, amply outdoing the bridegroom's people. The abusive remarks made by the latter are mainly retorts to the insults hurled against them. This essential one-sidedness of the aggressive attitude was borne out both by my own observations on several occasions and by statements made in the narrative of a Logoli elder. Speaking about the first visit of the bride and her people to the bridegroom's place he said:

'When they (the bridal party) arrive at the bridegroom's place they can abuse (*okunyegela*) his people by singing songs, and this can show the people of the groom: "*a' a*', perhaps they call us poor people." Then over there the people of the bridegroom can "worry in the stomach" as they sleep and think like this, "What can we do for them, because now they will be calling us 'the poor ones'." Then they must make an effort and increase the things (the food and gifts to be offered to the visitors), so that they become many because of the abuse by the despisers.'

In such a spirit of apprehension a party from the bridegroom's place starts out to meet the bride and her escort when they have come within a mile or less of the homestead of the bridegroom's father. It consists of a few boys and a dozen or more real or classificatory 'sisters' of the bridegroom. As the two parties meet, the bridegroom's sisters try to take the bride between them and conduct her to their yard, but the bride passively resists and the bridesmaids put up an active fight, beating and scratching the bridegroom's sisters but finally surrendering to them. At the three Vugusu weddings where I have seen this fight performed it was never more than a feeble pretence, a sham fight lasting only for a few minutes and provoking at least as much laughter as angry comments on both sides. I was assured, however, that formerly the bridal party would have persistently resisted the attempts to 'lead the bride home' and would even have returned to the bride's place, should the bridegroom's sisters have turned up in much smaller numbers than the bridesmaids. Such a failure to lead the bride home would have compromised the bridegroom's whole lineage and clan and made it the laughing-stock of all neighbouring clans, as it had clearly demonstrated that its people were few and weak and incapable of holding their own against the bride's family and lineage. Thus the encounter between the two parties, although not a serious fight, has nevertheless a deeper significance. It ensures that the bride is received at her new home with the same honour and respect—as shown by the number of sisters-in-law who turn up to greet and 'capture' her—which she enjoyed in her own clan and lineage. The sham fight from the very beginning strengthens her position in her husband's kin-group, for it furnishes her with proof that she is not merely tolerated but that she is a person who has been fought for. If subsequently her husband quarrels with her or if she feels ill-treated, she can say to him: 'Did I elope with you or did all my people come and "step on your father's yard"? So why do you treat me like this?' Or if her sisters-in-law behave arrogantly towards her, she can remind them that it was they who wanted her to come and that she did not come on her own account because she had no other place to go to. We shall see how this same problem of adjusting the rights and duties in the husband-wife relationship determines the attitude adopted by the two parties towards one another throughout the wedding festivities. The marital position of the wife being weaker than that of the husband—owing to the residential arrangement as well as to her inferior social and legal status—the conduct of the bride's people throughout the wedding is provocative and overbearing, as if to balance thereby the inequalities of the subsequent matrimonial relationship.

As soon as the bridesmaids have reached the yard of the bridegroom's father they resume singing their songs of mockery and abuse. Some of their insults are merely grotesque, while others exaggerate actual shortcomings of the bridegroom's family or of the way in which the feast is managed. At the wedding of a young farm-labourer which—his own father being dead—took place at the homestead of his 'young father',[1] the house and the yard looked indeed rather badly kept. Commenting in their song upon the things they saw, the bridesmaids derided the deserted cattle kraal, the high grass growing round the homestead, the empty granaries, and the scarcity of food of which the first trays were just being carried outside by the *vamulamua*. Retaliating, the bridegroom's paternal aunt joked about the beer which the bride's father had sent over earlier in the afternoon, remarking that he must have boiled a corpse in it as it was so thick. The bridesmaids, without much ready wit, replied that the beer had been good when it had left their place and that it must have been the bridegroom's sisters who had boiled a corpse in it. Suddenly one of the

[1] i.e. one of his father's younger brothers.

bridesmaids discovered the bridegroom, standing at a distance and unobtrusively watching the proceedings. As he would be made to suffer the brunt of the bridesmaids' slanderous remarks if he were present at the arrival of the bridal party, he usually either hides in the bush or goes to the house of a friend. In this case, however, his curiosity had got the better of him and had induced him to put in an appearance. As soon as the girls had spotted the bridegroom, some of them rushed forward to catch him while others quickly improvised songs of ridicule about him: 'Look at his big eyes and his swollen head! A fool like him wants to marry our daughter! And he has only paid one cow [actually he had paid the bride-wealth in full], but then his clan is weak and powerless! There are no men in his clan. Just look! Nobody is coming to stop us [i.e. rebuke us for these songs]!'

In the meantime the bridegroom's sisters had dished out porridge and meat to the bridesmaids, and so their abusive remarks turned again to the scarcity and the poor quality of the food and the slowness with which it was forthcoming.

Among the Logoli the songs of the bridesmaids and the replies by the bridegroom's sisters sometimes take the form of virtual singing competitions, both groups, under the guidance of their respective song-leaders, improvising songs and dances for hours on end. The main body of the bridesmaids forms the chorus; in front of them and facing them is the song-leader who, with two or three other girls, accentuates the song by dancing in the *lidegeriza* (shoulder-shaking) fashion, slowly moving forwards and backwards. The tunes of these songs are conventional, but the words are often made up *ad hoc*. The following are some songs which I heard at the wedding of Olisa, a girl of the Gonda clan, to Adalo, a Tembuli of South Maragoli:

> *Anderéeye, Anderéeye,*
> *lelo naŋone mukampi wowonyoli,*
> *Anderéeye, Anderéeye, Anderéeye, Anderéeye,*
> *lelo naŋone mukampi yadego* (repeat).

> 'Andereye, Andereye,
> to-night I may sleep in the camp of Wonyoli,
> Andereye, Andereye, &c.,
> to-night I may sleep in the camp of Adego.'

This song refers to the fact that some bridesmaids will spend the night in the hut of Wonyoli, others in the hut of Adego who are both unmarried daughters of the bridegroom's great wife. The implication is that it will be a night of licence for the bridesmaids.

> *Adego kindu kya kutonyele oyaya, oyaya,*
> *sumanyi oyaye, oyaye,*
> *menyi wanyaligi oyaya,*
> *djavugula oyáya, djavugula oyaya,*
> *oeréye oyaya, oereye oyaya,*
> *djavugula oyaya.*

> 'Adego, the thing of to let drop, *oyaya*,
> you do not know, *oyaye*,
> I live at Wanyaligi, *oyaya*,
> of which she takes, *oyaya*, &c.'

The bridesmaids tell Adego that she does not know the 'real' oil for anointing one's body (*kindu tja kutonyela* stands for *amaguta*, oil). The bridesmaids live at Nyaligi, an Indian trading centre where they can buy vaseline, whereas Adego, the bridegroom's daughter, is still using the old-fashioned ghee for anointing her body.

> *Adego ndakugaya, Adego ndakugaya,*
> *Wonyoli ndakugaya, Wonyoli ndakugaya,*
> *Adalo ndakugaya, Adalo ndakugaya,*
> *Oside ndakugaya, Oside ndakugaya,*
> *Seseme ndakugaya, Seseme ndakugaya,*
> *Oyaye mamboleo, oyaye mamboleo.*

> 'Adego, I prevent you, Adego, I prevent you,
> Wonyoli, I prevent you, Wonyoli, I prevent you,
> Adalo, I prevent you, Adalo, I prevent you,
> Oside, I prevent you, Oside, I prevent you,
> Seseme, I prevent you, Seseme, I prevent you,
> The new thing, oyaye, the new thing, oyaye (I want).

The speaker refuses all these people as lovers (or sweethearts respectively) and only wants to see the 'new thing' (*mamboleo* (Swahili)) now, i.e. the bridegroom or the bride, respectively. Some of the names mentioned in the song are those of boys, others those of girls. This song is also sung by girls in the girls' hut when they are tired of the visits of the same lover and desire to exchange him for a new one.

> *Oereya oyaya, oereya oyaya,*
> *teve Adego oyá, teve Adego oyá,*
> *oereye oyá, oereye oyá,*
> *muteve Seseme oyá, muteve Seseme oyá,*
> *engóyi yatuma oyá, engoyi yatuma oyá,*
> *oeréye oyá, oereye oyá.*

> 'Oereye oyaya, oereye oyaya,
> you may ask Adego,
> you may ask Seseme,
> the leopard growls,
> oereye oyaya, oereye oyaya.'

In this song the bridesmaids accuse the bridegroom of keeping a leopard in his house for a pet. The singer quotes Adego and Seseme, who are daughters of the bridegroom, as witnesses for her indictment. As keeping a leopard in one's hut is regarded a habit characteristic of an *omulogi*, this song is a grave insult.

> *Ndeda oyere, ndeda oyaya,*
> *ndeda oyere, ndeda oyaya,*
> *avana va Mnubi,*
> *oyala soludenga,*

MARRIAGE

> *ndeda oyere, ndeda oyaya,*
> *otundu twa Seseme,*
> *oyala soludenga.*

> 'Ndeda oyere, ndeda oyaya,
> the children of Mnubi,
> you accuse of slimness (?)

> Ndeda oyere, ndeda oyaya,
> the small person of Seseme,
> you accuse of slimness (?).'

The literal translation of the last line is not clear, but the whole song is said to infer that the people of the bride's clan (the children of Mnubi) are tall while those of the groom's clan (the children of Seseme) are short.

> *Ooyera, ooyera,*
> *lilova lyalega lindi,*
> *amakono amaterere* (repeated).

> 'Ooyera, ooyera,
> Another country is the winner,
> the arms are smooth (or slippery).'

This last song has nothing to do with the wedding but refers to the fact that the Government has taken possession of the country and that its native inhabitants no longer carry weapons (causing their arms to be smooth, i.e. empty).

When the bridesmaids are tired of singing they sit down and eat the food which the bridegroom's sisters have cooked for them. The bride, too, is offered food but she refuses to eat. If she were to accept any food at the bridegroom's place it would mean that she is not willing to join him as a wife. Together with her two or three best friends, the bride is then led to a bachelor's hut belonging to one of the bridegroom's friends. As they did during the time of her betrothal, these friends sleep with her, guarding her chastity, while the bridegroom himself sleeps in the hut of some other friend. The bridesmaids spend the night in groups of two or three in the various huts of the unmarried girls of the neighbourhood. For the youths of the bridegroom's clan this visit of so many unmarried girls furnishes a welcome opportunity for love-making and the girls, too, look forward to this night as to a time of licence. Although they have been warned by their mothers to practise self-restraint, I was assured that a girl who became pregnant after having acted as a bridesmaid would be dealt with more leniently by her parents than if the same thing had happened under ordinary circumstances.

On the following day the bridesmaids are given work to do by the bridegroom's father or mother, such as digging or weeding, grinding grain, or fetching water. The bride herself does not join in these activities but stays inside the hut in which she has spent the night. She remains there until in the course of the following day the bridesmaids come 'to open the bride'.

This means that they dance round the hut showering abuse on the bridegroom's people as on the previous day, and demanding that the bride be released. If the bride's family does not live too far from that of the bridegroom, this ceremony is repeated a number of times. During the days of the bride's first visit reinforcements of bridesmaids come over to the bridegroom's place without warning and 'open the bride' when there are only a few people to guard her.

In the afternoon of the second or third day, the bride and the bridesmaids return home, the length of their stay at the bridegroom's place depending upon the amount of work they have been given to do and upon the general elaborateness of the wedding. During all this time the bride is supposed to starve, as she must not accept any food at the bridegroom's place. Actually, however, food is secretly brought to her from her mother's place and she eats at odd moments when nobody is watching her. The bridesmaids, on the other hand, may eat as much as they like. Besides, it is their privilege on this occasion to beg for small presents, such as iron wristlets and other trinkets which the bridegroom's sisters must keep in store for them to avoid being talked about as being poor or stingy. At one wedding I saw a married sister of the bride who was accompanying the bridal party carrying one of her father's spears. Later she asked the bridegroom to put a shilling on the spear, 'because his father-in-law's spear had done him the honour of paying him a visit'. In such and similar ways the bridesmaids and other people of the bride's clan may pester the bridegroom's people for little gifts which must not be refused them.

The signal for returning home from the bridegroom's place is given by the bride, who suddenly dashes away heading straight for her mother's home without looking back once. The bridesmaids follow immediately after her and, a little farther off, the bridegroom's brothers and sisters who, at a given sign, make an attempt to catch the bride and delay her, although they do not actually try to lead her back to the bridegroom's place. At a wedding which I attended near Kimilili the bride chose a moment for running off when most of the bridegroom's people were inside the hut looking for a hide on which they wanted her to stand to be rubbed with ghee before she returned home. Nevertheless, the surprise displayed by the groom's people at seeing the bride suddenly dash away appeared to be largely faked. Even Nandoli, who was a stranger there, told me several minutes beforehand that the bride would now soon run off, and presently she did so.

While the bride runs back to her mother's home she must observe a number of rules and signs, lest her matrimonial life be haunted by adverse luck. Thus she must, if possible, avoid running home while it rains, as being caught in the rain on this occasion would cause her to become jealous of her co-wives. Actually, at the above-mentioned Kimilili wedding a sudden shower completely drenched the bride. But while jokes were made about this mishap when she reached her mother's place, it was obviously not considered a matter of great consequence. A more important rule is

MARRIAGE 421

that the bride must avoid stumbling while she runs home, lest 'she will die soon'. Accordingly the bridesmaids constantly shout warnings to her to watch her step, a feat which is not easily accomplished in the high grass in which numerous stones and ditches are hidden away. Should the bride stumble or fall down, a sheep must be ritually killed for her to ward off the effects of the evil omen. If she has to cross a stream on her way home, she must be careful not to touch the water with her feet 'as this would cause her to become barren'. Should there be a stream too wide for her to jump across, either her sister or one of her 'young' father's wives must wait there for her and carry her across on her back.

When the bride is about half-way home she is met by one of her younger sisters, who hands her a bunch of grass which she has pulled from under the roof of her mother's hut. As soon as the bride has taken the grass she must leave the bridesmaids behind and, increasing her speed, run home as quickly as she can. This is the sign for the bridegroom's people to run after her and catch her. At the Kimilili wedding to which I have referred, the bride succeeded in running a few hundred yards only and then was caught by two boys of the bridegroom's clan who grabbed her by her arms. She tried to wrest herself away, quietly without crying or talking. Now the bridesmaids interfered, bearing down on the two boys with switches and shouting at them to release the bride. In the meantime, however, more boys, both of the bridegroom's and of the bride's clan, had appeared on the scene, and a general fight ensued between the two parties which lasted for about ten minutes. Finally the bride freed herself and ran on home while her people successfully prevented the bridegroom's friends from following her. This, I was assured, is the usual outcome of the encounter. Should, however, the bridegroom's friends win the fight, they would merely delay the bride's return to her mother, frequently sitting down with her and thus keeping her hungry; for the bride is now supposed to be starving for a meal, having theoretically gone without food for two or three days.

On arriving at her mother's homestead the bride is met by a party of paternal aunts who come towards her dancing and singing. The father's sister rubs soot, which she has taken from underneath the cooking-pots, all over the bride's face. Then she hangs pieces of raw meat over her ears or, like ear-ornaments, suspends them with string from the lobes of her ears and, finally, gives her a stirring-paddle that has been dipped into gruel to lick. All this has a magic significance, for it is supposed to ensure the bride's prosperity in her future life as a housewife and a cook.

Now, together with her best friend among the bridesmaids, the bride runs towards the entrance of her mother's hut stopping, however, just in front of it, facing the doorway. This is the occasion for the bride to demand gifts from her own kin and to pester her parents for any particular objects to which she has taken a fancy or which she wants to give to her friend for a present. Thus she stubbornly stands in the doorway and refuses to enter her mother's hut until all her wishes have been satisfied. Moreover, this is also an occasion to make voluntary gifts to the bride. When Mutjambala, the chief's daughter, thus stood in front of her mother's hut, her kinsmen and neighbours came and piled hats, dresses, blankets, and sheets all over her. When she had been laden with things her father's sisters told her and her friend to enter the hut and eat the food which the mother had cooked for them. Both, however, refused to do so, Mutjambala saying that she had made an agreement with her friend that she would give her a cow on the day of her wedding and that her friend had promised to do the same for her at her own wedding. So she would not enter the house until her father had given her friend the cow which she had promised her. Her father, the chief, remained inside the hut but after a while sent out one of his askaris with two shillings. When his daughter refused to accept the money, he sent him out again after a while, this time with five shillings. But Mutjambala stubbornly insisted on being given a cow before she would move from where she was standing. Now the chief became angry or at least pretended to be so and, coming out of the hut himself, scolded his daughter for her impertinence, telling her that he had spent everything he had on the wedding-feast and that he was now a poor man and had no cows left. The bride, however, remained unperturbed by her father's outburst and still insisted upon her demand. Her father, by now shouting excitedly, threatened to leave the wedding-party and to go to his other village at Kimilili where he would not be continuously pestered and troubled. Seeing, however, that his daughter showed no signs of changing her mind, he finally gave in and, in the presence of all the people, promised that he would 'look for a cow'. Actually, I was assured, he knew of his daughter's agreement beforehand and merely put up a sham refusal to test her strength of will and the firmness of her friendship.

When all her demands have been fulfilled or at least promised to be fulfilled in the presence of witnesses, the bride finally enters her mother's hut, together with her friend and the other bridesmaids, to eat the food which the bride's mother has cooked for them. This meal has a special significance, as the bride is now for the first time permitted to drink of the milk which comes from her future husband's marriage cattle. A special gourd with such milk is set aside for her and handed to her by her mother before she eats of the other food.

In the meantime, the boys from the bridegroom's place who had followed the bridal party arrive at the bride's homestead. They are received with derogatory remarks by the young men of the bride's clan and in rude words are told to stay away. They reply in the same manner and must not permit themselves to be intimidated by the unfriendly reception which they are given. If they feel strong enough they may even provoke another 'fight' with their hosts, in the course of which the two parties hit one another in the face with the thick sticky stuff that settles on the bottom of the beer-pots. At Mutjambala's wedding the bridegroom's people came nearer after a brief exchange of abuse and, forming a circle and dancing round the hut in which the bride and the bridesmaids were eating, sang the following song:

> *Nonda olugele, nonda olugele,*
> *aŋombe yátjia,*
> *eŋombeeee, eŋombe,*
> *wióya.*
>
> 'I follow in the step, I follow in the step,
> the cow it went,
> the cow, the cow,
> gently.'

By singing this song they—so to speak—justify their visit to the bride's place, for it means that they are following in the footsteps of the marriage-cattle and that they have, therefore, nothing to fear from their *vaxwasi* (brothers-in-law). As the song-leader later explained to me: 'The cattle which have been handed over by the bridegroom's clan have made friends for them.' After they had sung this song the bridesmaids came out with many dishes filled with porridge, meat, and vegetables. Having put them down first in front of the bridegroom's friends and then in front of the visitors of the bride's clan, the two groups joined in the common meal. This meal appears to be the main feature of the visit paid by the bridegroom's people to the bride's place, for the whole visit is referred to as *xulia vusuma vanga omuxana*, 'to eat the porridge at the home of the girl'.

On the same day on which the bride has returned from her first visit to the bridegroom's place or—less often—on the following day, the sleeping-hide of the bride's mother is brought outside and put down in the yard in front of her hut. The bride, together with her friend, steps on the skin and, facing the doorway of her mother's hut, is given rules of matrimonial conduct by her maternal uncle or her 'young' father, or by both in turn. If these rules are given to her immediately after her return from the bridegroom's place, she throws the bunch of grass which her sister had pulled out for her on the hide and stands on it while the rules of conduct are being imparted to her. According to the information volunteered by an old man, this observance ensures that the bride will soon have a house and a hearth of her own and that everything will be well in that house. When the ceremony is over, her paternal grandmother picks up the bunch of grass and takes it back into the hut of the bride's mother, where she hides it somewhere in the roof.

While the bride's uncle gives her instructions for her marital life he holds in his right hand a new gourd which is filled with beer that has a very bitter and unpleasant taste as it attracts the flavour of the new gourd. The uncle first takes a sip himself. Then he hands the gourd to the bride and, after having made her taste the beer, makes a solemn speech, clearly reciting rule after rule in a voice like that in which the clan-elders sum up the evidence of a legal case at a sitting of the tribal court. The following rules were given at the wedding of a young girl of sixteen to an elderly man who had three wives already and who was now taking his fourth wife to live with him on the European farm where he was working. The younger brother of the bride's father spoke first. Taking a sip before each sentence and spitting a few drops into the bride's face, he said:

'I have given you the beer and you have tasted it. Now, the important thing to make the people (i.e. husband and wife) live happily at their home is *xuxualana* (polite verb referring to sexual intercourse). When you are going to the river carrying the water-pot and you hear your husband calling behind you because he wants to sleep with you, put the water-pot down and return to the house to sleep with him. Afterwards you can go on with your work. When you are working in the garden and your husband calls you, go to the house and do as he wants. When he has finished, you may return to the garden. When you are going to fetch wood and he calls you, go and follow him. When you are roasting millet on the fire and your husband wants you, do not say that you must dry the millet first, but let it burn and go and sleep with your husband. Now, this old man (i.e. the bridegroom) has grown-up sons. If they come to your house, cook food for them. Then let them go. If they want to stay and speak to you, say to them: "No, you better go." If you sit and talk to them, your husband will think you have slept with them. If you are gathering the firewood in the bush and another man comes and asks you to sleep with him in the bush, refuse him. We do not wish to hear that you have committed adultery; we do not wish to hear that you are selfish; we do not wish to hear that you are a thief.'

Having given these rules, the 'young father' passed the gourd on to the bride's maternal uncle to continue the instructions. He repeated the same points, stressing the importance of the wife's yielding to her husband's wishes and then added:

'When your husband copulates with you you must move your hips and play (*xusegenya*). When your husband copulates with you and he is near to finish, hold him tightly and embrace him but don't lie there only. If you embrace him he will be happy.'

At these words some Christian girls who were standing near by ran away shrieking, some pagan boys calling after them: 'Why do you run away? This is the way of the people.' This incident rather abruptly ended the maternal uncle's instructions to his niece.

At another wedding, that of Wambulua, the bride was standing on a skin together with six bridesmaids. Her maternal uncle gave her the following instructions:

'Now you are marrying a husband and you will be his strength (i.e. you will work for him). He is an old man; if he calls you, go quickly. Do not wait for him to call you twice or three times. If you wait too long when he calls you, he will say, "This wife was not given any rules by her maternal uncle." If you have gone to fetch the wood and he calls you to come back, return quickly and work for him. You are marrying an old man who has two wives. When you fetch the water you must take it to them first; then you may go and carry your own water. If your co-wives send you to gather wood for them, go and gather it. Do not think that they are troubling you. If the old women give you something with one hand stretch out both hands to receive it.'

The maternal uncle then handed the gourd to the bride's paternal aunt, an old woman, who took a sip and added:

'If you do not understand what your *xotja* has said to you, you will be a bad wife and one day you will sleep on the trees and in the bush (i.e. you will have no home).'

Apparently this reminder was deemed to be appropriate in this case, for I heard that the bride had refused to marry her prospective husband as he was an old man and as she resented the idea of having to work for his other wives.

After these rules of matrimonial conduct had been given to the bride a curious ceremony was performed which—as far as I could discover—is peculiar to the Vugusu tribe or even to *some* of their clans only. While the bride was still standing on the hide, facing her mother's hut, one of her classificatory sisters stepped in front of her, looking in the same direction as the bride. Picking up a basket with eleusine porridge and a piece of raw meat which the bride's mother had put in front of her, she lifted it up first to her own head and then, without turning round, passed it on to the bride standing behind her. The bride, in turn, placed the basket on her head and after a few moments handed it on to her *mulamua*, the bridegroom's sister, who was standing back to back with her, facing the gate. She, too, put the basket upon her head. Then, reversing the process, the bride's sister-in-law handed it back to the bride and the bride again to her 'sister' who was still standing in front of her. The latter now took the basket and, describing a semicircle round the bride, handed it again to the bridegroom's sister. The bride then walked straight into her mother's hut; the bridegroom's sister, carrying the basket, made one circuit round the house and then, likewise, entered it, while the bride's 'sister' followed behind her as the last person to go inside. The bridegroom's sister then had to eat the food that was in the basket, taking care that she did not spill any of it on the ground or if she did so that any such bits were carefully hidden away, so that nobody could get hold of them. The food which she left over she gave to the bride's mother, who finished it.

The symbolism of this rite is so lucid that it hardly requires any commentary. Nevertheless, it may be added that its obvious meaning was confirmed to me by a native elder who stated that 'it was to show that henceforth the bride's relatives and the groom's relatives will help one another with food and freely give things to one another without quarrelling about them'.

Before the bridegroom's people return home they further celebrate their visit to the bride's place by dancing and beer-drinking. If the distance between the two homesteads is too far, the bridegroom's people stay overnight visiting the bridesmaids in their various huts and continuing their courtships with those girls with whom they had already made friends during the previous nights when the bridesmaids stayed at their place.

The bride now stays at her mother's place for a few days—up to a week—to give the bridegroom's people a chance to brew more beer and make other preparations for the bride's second visit, the *sifóroro*. After the bridegroom's people have sent a message that everything is ready, the bride leaves her mother's place again, this time escorted by a few bridesmaids only. Her departure is again timed so that she will arrive at the bridegroom's place at sundown, as on her first visit. As a present for her mother-in-law the bridesmaids carry some basketfuls of eleusine flour and the meat of a bullock or a goat. The bride wears the same attire as before. She carries her mother's sleeping-hide on which she had been standing while she was given the rules of matrimonial conduct. She will use this hide to sleep on after she is married, but not during her wedding-night.

On arriving at the bridegroom's place the bridal party stops at the gate of the enclosure singing wedding-songs. They refuse to enter until the bride has been given a hoe and the bridesmaids various small presents, such as wristlets or finger-rings. While the bridal party is standing in the yard, still singing and begging for further presents, a new sleeping-hide is put down, either in the front room of the bridegroom's mother's hut or outside in the yard, and the bride is told by her mother-in-law to step on it to be anointed and adorned for the wedding-night. The bride agrees to do so only after a further hoe has been paid to her. She is then stripped (except for her skirt of fibre-tassels) by her future co-wife or her husband's sister, and her face and body are anointed with ghee. Her head is adorned with ribbons of banana-fibre, blackened in mud and softened with ghee (*gimisindixa*), while iron coils or rings are put round her arms and ankles. After the bride has thus been adorned the bridegroom steps on the same skin to undergo a similar treatment by his *woluvango* (literally: his spear-shaft, i.e. his real or classificatory brother whom he regards as his close friend). He anoints the bridegroom's head with a mixture of ghee and red ochre. Should any ghee be left over it is used up by the bride's co-wife (if there is one) and by the bridesmaids who dab it on each other's faces.

When the evening is well advanced and food has been served to the bridesmaids (the bride herself still refuses to accept food at the bridegroom's place) the sisters-in-law lead the bride to their brother's *esimba* or bachelor hut for the marriage to be consummated. If the bridegroom has no hut of his own the pair may spend the wedding-night in any old and empty hut (*ekidioli*) placed at their disposal by a friend or neighbour. If a man is marrying his second or third wife he will sleep with his bride in his 'great wife's' hut. Under no circumstances would the bridegroom build a new hut until after the pair have been married for a few weeks or even months. To put up a house beforehand would be considered inauspicious for the success of the marriage.

Besides, as the betrothal is not binding but may be broken off by either side, the bridegroom would expose himself to ridicule if he were to make elaborate preparations and the marriage should then fail to come off. 'You cannot sharpen the spit before you see the meat' is a saying with which a Muvugusu aptly characterized the situation when explaining this custom to me.

While the bride is being led to the hut to join the bridegroom she shows the same indifferent and bashful behaviour which she had displayed throughout the wedding procedure. She keeps her eyes cast down and her features show no trace of response to what is going on round her. Male informants with whom I discussed the bride's behaviour insisted that it is not merely conformity to convention which determines her attitude but that she actually feels greatly embarrassed, even if she has had sexual experience before. I have not heard, however, that at this juncture the bride would make any attempt to run off or that the bridesmaids would try to prevent the bride from joining the bridegroom. She follows him passively and only before she agrees to lie down she asks him to give her 'the goat of her *senge*' or 'the goat of girlhood', i.e. the goat which the bridegroom has to pay for depriving the bride of her virginity. The bridegroom, however, before making this payment is supposed to raise doubts as to her virginity and to reply to her: 'Before I look for the goat let me see first whether this pot is not open.'

The amount of privacy or publicity in which the defloration of the bride takes place varies considerably among the different Kavirondo tribes. It appears that the higher the bride's virginity is valued the more importance is attached to its public demonstration. Thus among the Vugusu a fire is kindled in the hut in which the bridal couple sleep. When the fire is blazing high the bridegroom has to deflower the bride in the presence of the bridesmaids and the youths of his own clan, so that everyone present can see whether the bride has preserved her virginity or not. Nowadays this custom is being abandoned as even pagan bridegrooms refuse to join the bride before the eyes of other people, knowing in most cases from previous relations with the bride that she is no longer a virgin and fearing to expose themselves to ridicule by submitting to a public 'test'. The discontinuance of this public proof of the bride's virginity also causes the girls to discard all precautions in their premarital sex-relations. Thus an old woman, lamenting modern times, said to me: 'The country is changing now, the girls do not guard their virginity any more, as they no longer fear to be put to shame when their wedding-night comes.'

Among the Logoli the bridesmaids and youths of the neighbourhood remain outside the hut, but they stay near by as they are eager to know whether the bridegroom will be successful in his attempt to embrace the bride. Among the Nyole the bride has to pay a price for the privilege of privacy, for her *woluvango*, her best friend among the bridesmaids, will only leave her alone and consent to sleep in one of the girl's huts after she has been given (or promised) a female goat.

It is customary for the bride to put up a strong resistance before she yields to the bridegroom. Like her bashfulness during the wedding festivities, this resistance appears to be a mixture of a conventional attitude and a genuine resentment and fear. That her conduct is at least partly determined by convention seems to be indicated by the fact that the bride is supposed to show the same resistance in every case, whether she is joining the husband of her choice or an old man to whom she is being married by force. Moreover, it is said that her motives for resisting are partly to test the bridegroom's manliness and partly to give proof of her own chastity. Both these motives would appear to be of a sociological rather than of a psychological order.

The bride's behaviour during the wedding-night was described to me by a Logoli husband in the following words:

'In the night the husband takes the bride into his *ekidioli* hut and offers her eleusine porridge and meat. His mother or sister brings the dishes and puts them in front of the bride. But the bride sits there only and "listens"; she looks over her left shoulder and neither faces the bridegroom nor the food that has been placed in front of her. This is because "she is with shame and fear" (*nedzisoni nende novuti*). The bride continues to refuse the food, so the husband finally eats by himself. Now the husband prepares the bedspread and says to the bride, "Come and sleep". But she remains sitting on the floor, her head turned away. She does not move. Then the husband catches her by the wrist and drags her to the bedspread where he has put down the sleeping-hide. She stands up and follows reluctantly but remains standing by the sleeping-skin and refuses to lie down. The husband talks to her with persuasion but she just stands there and "listens". Finally, he wrestles her down by force calling out, "I want to find you" (*nyenya kukunyola*), but the bride still refuses, telling him that he has not yet paid her (the goat of defloration). The husband replies that he has strength enough, and so he embraces her by force. When he lies with her she cries out aloud like a person who is dying. The boys who are waiting outside hear the bride crying and they say to one another "Now he has found her" (*kalunu yakadukaga ku*). After the bride has been embraced she is quiet and now she has no other matter against the husband.'

If the bride has proved to be a virgin, the bridegroom, in the morning, folds up the blood-stained sleeping-hide and, together with the 'goat of defloration', hands it to the bridesmaids who take it to the bride's paternal aunt (*senge*). She washes the hide in a stream and calls a few old women of her neighbourhood and, if they live near, the two grandmothers of the bride to share the goat with her. They kill it by beating it to death and eat it without any other people being present or sending any of the meat away. Both the sleeping-hide and the goatskin are kept by the bride's *senge*. Among the Logoli and Tsotso the sleeping-hide is first taken to the bride's mother by the bridesmaids who show her the blood-stained hide saying,

MARRIAGE

'Come and see who has taken her virginity (*ovugima*).' In Kitosh, on the other hand, the bride's parents see neither the goat nor the hide, 'because they do not want to know what their daughter has been doing'.

After the wedding-night the bride stays with her husband for two days and then returns once more to her mother's place. During these two days the bride may help the bridesmaids who work in the mother-in-law's garden, but she still refuses to accept food which her mother-in-law has cooked or to perform any of the duties which are subsequently expected from her as a daughter-in-law. But from now on she no longer resists her husband, unless she dislikes him and intends to run away from him. While during the first night the husband may cohabit with his bride only once, he may join her again the following night and then may have repeated intercourse with her.

After having spent a few days at her mother's place the bride goes to the husband's place for a third time, and this time she comes to stay. Again she takes fowls and flour along as presents from her own mother to her husband's mother. However, before she agrees to settle down and take her part in the life of the husband's family she demands a number of presents from her parents-in-law. Among the Vugusu, to make the bride eat her first meal, the husband's father must kill a bullock and send part of the meat over to the bride's mother. If he is rich he sends a whole bullock and, besides, kills a goat for themselves. The bride then takes the food which is put before her, but for the first year or so (until the first child is born) she eats either by herself or together with her husband's sister in a small hut near her mother-in-law's house. Among the Logoli the husband's mother induces the bride to eat by putting a hoe (*embago yokulágila*, hoe of making her eat) next to the dish of food which is placed before the bride. For performing various other duties resulting from her new life as a married woman and a daughter-in-law the bride likewise demands an initial payment of a hoe, an armlet, or a chicken, the number and value of such gifts depending upon the economic status of the parents-in-law. Thus when the bride enters the front room (*vuhilu*) of her mother-in-law's hut for the first time she refuses to sit down until her mother-in-law has presented her with a second hoe (*embago yokwikala*, hoe of sitting down). When she returns from the well carrying water for the first time she stands in front of the hut with the water-pot on her head and refuses to put it down until another hoe is forthcoming. Before smoking her first pipe the bride holds it in her hands and refuses to light it and suck at it until a hoe or a fowl has been given to her by her sister-in-law. Similarly, she may demand a hoe before washing her hands for the first time, before sweeping the yard or grinding grain. Only for cleaning out the cattle partition she may not demand a further payment as this has become her duty through her father's acceptance of the marriage cattle.

These various gifts of hoes, fowls, &c., are really part of the previously arranged bride-wealth. Like the marriage-cattle, they are not kept by the young wife but are handed over to her father. Among the Nyole the handing over of the *evilisio*, as these subsequent gifts to the bride are called, furnishes the occasion for a further elaborate feast which is described in the following narrative:

'Then the people of the bride come (to the husband's place) to count the *evilisio*-gifts. These may be twelve hoes and three goats or, if these are not there, it may be a heifer "which jumps the stream"[1] or which is near to calve or big enough to bear a calf. When the six people from the girl's place have seen the *evilisio*-gifts, they return to take the matter to the girl's father and when he agrees and the gifts are enough then the bride may go and eat the food (at the bridegroom's place). Then the girl's father may begin to soak the "yeast" and to thresh the millet; it may be ground and when the mash of which they will drink is enough, then they may begin to brew the beer. When it has well fermented they may go to the leader and tell him he may go and give orders to "those of the bridegroom" that they may bring the *evilisio*-gifts. Then the bridegroom's mother may choose the women who may take the gifts to the girl's place next morning. They may begin their journey at eight o'clock; at that time they start from the bridegroom's homestead. One of the women who have been chosen must be one who knows "the words of the marriage", and when they go she is the one who may speak with them. When they arrive they may enter the house and sit down; the stock (i.e. the goats and the heifer if any) may be tethered in the yard and the hoes may be taken into the house. Then the visitors may be served beer and when they have drunk the beer, porridge and meat and fish may be dished out for them, and also a castrated goat may be killed. Each person gets a tray with porridge and a dish with meat and one with fish; each person gets his (own), and the food which remains over may be carried home, the porridge, the meat, and the fish, and the dishes may be covered with banana-leaves. And a dishful of meat may be given to the leader. And the bride herself carries a basketful of food on her head which she takes to her mother- and father-in-law. She puts it down at the place of her husband. When she has arrived with the meat which she has taken to her father-in-law she may stay there for three weeks. Then she may take the baskets and the dishes back to her mother and "those of her husband" may put in a fowl which she may take to "hers"; then she may stay home again for six days. When these days are finished she may return (to her husband) with a basketful of grain and a fowl and with a pipe and tobacco. The bride may return to the home of the husband in the afternoon and she may put down there the things which she came with. And the husband's mother may keep them and show them to her (the bride's) father-in-law. He may look at them to see how they are and then they may keep them. Now the bride stays with her mother-in-law all days. They rejoice with her (*mbasangala nnaye*) and she helps with the work and cooks the food and grinds the grain and takes out the manure and sweeps the rubbish well.'

(5) THE ECONOMIC ASPECT OF THE CONCLUSION OF MARRIAGE

The preceding narrative clearly shows the importance which, in connexion with marriage, is attached to the exchange of gifts, especially food,

[1] i.e. which is big enough to jump across a stream.

MARRIAGE

between the wife's parents and those of the husband. Beginning with a series of formally arranged exchanges of gifts during and immediately after the wedding festivities, the mutual gift-making between the two groups of affinal relatives continues in a more or less formal manner for many years, although it gradually becomes less as the new family which results from the marriage establishes a homestead of its own and acquires full social and economic status.

The economic aspect thus plays an important part in the conclusion of a marriage. Although the bride-wealth proper appears as the most outstanding item in the list of economic transactions that take place in connexion with marriage, its economic value is almost equalled by the aggregate of numerous gifts exchanged between the two parties as well as the frequent display of reciprocal hospitality, both in the course of the wedding festivities and on a number of subsequent occasions which we shall describe in their respective contexts. The following compilation is a list of gifts and counter-gifts which appears to be typical as regards families of average means among the Vugusu:

(A) *Expenses incurred and gifts made by the bridegroom's kin*

1. At the betrothal: Four or six pots of beer brewed for the beer of *enganana*; two pots sent over to the bride's mother (*gamalua gexusuta*). Fowls and flour for the meal offered to the bride's father; new beer-pipe and tube for the bride's father (small value only).
2. When handing over the bride-wealth: A fowl and porridge for the first party which comes to inspect the marriage cattle. The same if a second inspection takes place.
3. At the *siselelo* (first visit by the bride to the bridegroom's place): Two bullocks; one killed for the relatives of the bridegroom, some of the meat (front leg) sent over to the bride's place. The other bullock (bullock of *naŋeso*) sent alive or slaughtered, either before or a few days after the *siselelo*. Two basketfuls of porridge for the guests and bridesmaids; about six large pots of beer, some for the bridesmaids and others sent over to the bride's place during or after the bride's first visit. Small presents for the bridesmaids.
4. At second visit of bride (*kámafura* or *sifóroro*): Porridge and meat for the bridesmaids as well as small presents. Goat of defloration.
5. At third visit of bride: Bullock 'to make the bride eat'. Hoes, fowls, &c., for making her perform other 'duties'.
6. At subsequent visits: Small gifts of food (porridge, meat, fish, fowls) whenever the wife pays a visit to her parents.

(B) *Expenses incurred and gifts made by the bride's kin*

1. When asking for 'handle of hoe': Food (fowl and porridge) offered to emissary from bridegroom.
2. Betrothal: Nothing.
3. Transfer of marriage cattle: Nothing, unless the bridegroom's people

accompany the cattle all the way, in which case they are offered hospitality at the bride's place.
4. *Siselelo*: A small granary full of sorghum for brewing beer. One 'bullock of eating', the hide and foreleg sent to the bridegroom's father. About eight basketfuls of eleusine flour sent to the bridegroom's place together with the cow of *naŋeso*. About four basketfuls of eleusine flour for porridge to be served to visitors and bridesmaids before they start off to the bridegroom's place.
5. Second visit of bride: About four baskets of eleusine flour and slaughtered bullock or goat as present for the bridegroom's father. No feast at the bride's place.
6. Third visit of bride: Fowls and flour taken by the bride as a present for her mother-in-law.
7. The bride's granary handed over to her father-in-law.
8. The bullock or heifer of *kumuoulo* paid to the husband.
9. The ox or bullock of *sitexo* killed by the wife's father. Also a goat which is eaten in the house of the wife's parents.[1]
10. Small gifts of food given to the wife by her mother whenever she returns to her husband's place after a visit to her mother's place.

A comparison of these two lists of gifts and expenses incurred for hospitality shows that they are to a large extent reciprocal, the slight preponderance on the bride's side being mainly due to the bullock of *kumuoulo* which is a return gift expressing the satisfaction of the wife's kin with the marriage cattle. The reciprocity on some of these occasions is almost immediate. The bull of *naŋeso* has hardly been sent from the bride's place to that of the bridegroom when a return gift of the same nature and even of the same name passes from the bridegroom's father to the bride's father. It differs from an actual returning of the gift only in so far as the bull which is handed over as the counter-gift must be a different animal. Similarly, the baskets of food carried to and fro between the two parties at every visit exchanged between them are, both in quality and in quantity, as nearly alike as possible, although here again it would be considered a gross violation of good manners if the same instead of different grain were returned as a counter-gift.

Being strictly reciprocal, these gifts must have a different meaning from the handing over of the bride-wealth, for this is clearly a one-sided transfer of material objects in exchange for the acquisition of rights and privileges concerning a human being. The care with which the actual quantities exchanged are listed in narratives on the subject, and the ostentation with which the gifts are transferred and displayed in the yard of the other party are significant. Here are two groups of people, hitherto entirely unconnected by any specific social ties, even expressly devoid of any joint interests save their common tribal background[2] who now, through the marriage of two of their members, enter into a particularly close relationship with one another. To make it a success this relationship must be balanced;

[1] See p. 43.   [2] Cf. above, p. 387.

each side must feel and be made to feel that the other side is its equal. Accordingly, as the two groups establish their mutual relations, each side tends to be suspicious and jealous of the other, lest it might try to assume a superior attitude and consider itself of higher standing. The dominant feeling in each group seems aptly expressed by the lines which we have already quoted: 'Then over there the people can worry when they sleep and think: what can we do for them, because now they will be calling us the poor ones?' Hence, as one group demonstrates its wealth by sending presents to the other, the other group answers the 'challenge' by returning a gift of the same nature, either immediately or on a subsequent occasion laid down by convention. Thus the primary significance of the exchange of gifts appears to be the demonstration by the two parties, both to each other and to outsiders, of their equality of economic status.

But there are other elements involved as well. The fact that both parties test each other's economic resources by challenging one another with presents implies that the conclusion of marriages according to the full tribal norms between persons of unequal wealth tends to be discouraged, as the economically weaker party in the long run could not maintain the reciprocity on the scale established by the stronger party. The fear of being put to shame by the generous gifts of the in-law relatives thus induces people to intermarry with their economic equals, and counteracts the temptation which a father might feel to marry his daughter off to the wealthiest suitor, as he can offer the largest amount of bride-wealth.

Moreover, the economic burden which the wedding festivities entail is generally distributed over the different 'fathers' of the bridegroom or the bride respectively, i.e. their real fathers and their various paternal uncles as well as their maternal uncles will each furnish a gift. Thus the real father will pay for the *liaxa* or *siselelo*, one of his brothers will bear the expenses connected with the *kámafura*-visit, still another will provide the ox of *sítexo*, while both paternal and maternal uncles will contribute towards the bull of *kumuoulo*. This sharing of expenses among the various kinsmen on both sides clearly serves to extend the group of people who take an active part in the arrangement of the marriage, and thus to strengthen the bonds established between two groups of people by the marriage of two of their members. The exchange of gifts and hospitality—as we shall point out more fully in one of the subsequent chapters—is one of the chief means of establishing and maintaining a relationship. The variety of reciprocal gifts and the number of people participating in the exchange are thus an indication of the strength and the scope of the relationship that is being established.

(6) OTHER TYPES OF MARRIAGE[1]

The full wedding procedure which we have described in the preceding chapters is followed in less than 30 per cent. only of all marriages that

---

[1] The following section refers primarily to the Vugusu.

are concluded. Even apart from the remarriage of widows and divorced women, or other unions where the particular status of one of the marriage partners would suggest some deviation from the ordinary procedure, there are two types of marriage which, for a variety of reasons, are chosen as alternatives to the full procedure. One of these is marriage by elopement (*líveyia*), and the other marriage by abduction (*líxuesa*). Both forms of marriage are resorted to so frequently that they can hardly be labelled deviations from the norm, even if the full procedure (*liaxa*) is theoretically considered the ideal which should be followed if all the conditions of marriage have been properly fulfilled.

(a) Marriage by elopement

A man may decide to elope with a girl for one or several of four different reasons. The most important of these is the poverty of the suitor and his kinsmen, making it impossible for them to assemble the full number of cows which they know the girl's father would be likely to demand if the suitor were to make a formal proposal and invite him to the 'beer of *enganana*'. The second reason is the rejection of the proposal by the girl's father when the suitor's emissary comes to ask for the 'handle of the hoe', either because he has someone else in mind whom he prefers for personal reasons or because he dislikes the suitor's clan. A further motive for a marriage by elopement would be the existence of a distant relationship between the boy and the girl. This would render the conclusion of a marriage in full style impossible but would not prevent the marriage from being tolerated *ex post*. Finally, a man may elope with a girl merely because he is impatient to have her and unwilling to wait until the long-drawn-out proceedings of an elaborate wedding have taken place. Thus nearly all men with plural wives have married one or even several of their junior wives by eloping with them, even if they had enough cattle and no cause whatever to fear that the girl's father would have raised any objections. Besides, such a marriage adds to the bridegroom's reputation of manliness, as his clansmen will say of him with pride that 'the girls run after him'. Only when taking his first wife a man prefers to 'marry in full style', as otherwise she would not have the standing and respect among his kinsmen which a 'great wife' should command.

The manner in which a marriage by elopement is concluded and subsequently sanctioned by the kinsmen on both sides differs according to the degree of tension which the elopement has produced between the two parties concerned. If the bridegroom decides to follow this course merely because he is too impatient to wait for the *siselelo* he does not, as a rule, elope with the bride until after the cattle have been handed over. Even so he would only have to wait a week from the time the first proposal had been made. He then arranges with the girl that following one of his nightly visits to the girl's hut she should come with him to his own *esimba*. If the girl agrees to this plan they choose a time when the old woman in charge of the hut is absent, so that the news of the elopement may not leak out until the following day. The pair then enter into marital relations with one another and leave it to the girl's father to take the next step. He comes on one of the following days, professing in the presence of his son-in-law's kinsmen that he had plenty of things to stage a proper wedding, and lamenting that now, after his daughter's marriage has been so rashly concluded, the people will think him stingy. Having thus publicly proclaimed that his daughter has eloped against his own wishes he will, as a rule, acknowledge the *fait accompli* without harbouring any further grudge against his son-in-law. No wedding-feast is celebrated in such a case, but the conclusion of the marriage between the two parties is recognized by ceremonially exchanging the bullock of *naŋeso*. Besides, the bride refuses to eat at her mother-in-law's place until the 'ox of making her eat' has been slaughtered by her father-in-law. Then she returns to her parents' place for a few days and when she finally comes to her husband to stay she is accompanied by half a dozen bridesmaids who carry the baskets with flour and meat which the bride's parents send over to those of the bridegroom. But there are no mutual provocations or sham fights, no dancing and singing, no anointing with ghee, nor any of the other ceremonies which characterize the full wedding procedure; nor does the bridegroom pay the goat of defloration. To this form of marriage no public stigma is attached, except that the young men of the bridegroom's clan regret that their chance of making love to the bridesmaids has been spoilt and that there is a general disappointment among the 'would-be guests' that a welcome occasion for feasting has been missed. Unless, however, a father permitted all his daughters to be married off in this fashion he would not be made to feel any public resentment by becoming the butt of slanderous beer-songs or of other forms of gossip.

A far greater tension between the two parties arises if the elopement takes place for one of the other reasons, i.e. if a man runs off with a girl without having paid any marriage cattle. Nowadays this is one of the most frequent offences, which accounts for a large percentage of all civil litigation. As the girl's whereabouts would have to be kept secret for a longish period of time to obtain the final consent to the marriage by the girl's father and brothers, such elopements are often staged with a considerable amount of skill and cunning. First of all the suitor must find out if the girl really means to elope with him, for it has happened that girls have first agreed to elope and then either maliciously or through an indiscretion have allowed their brothers to follow them and catch the boy. Thus he repeatedly asks the girl to make a solemn pledge that she is willing to go through the whole adventure with him and, if necessary, 'to die' if their plan should fail. Further, to make sure that the girl will not change her mind at the last moment or betray their plans to another girl who might spread the news, the suitor first arranges a secret meeting with her in a friend's house, which would not compromise him if it did not come off. If the girl turns up at this meeting they agree on a new place where they will meet shortly afterwards. From there, under cover of night, they run off to the house of a distant cousin, a *senge*'s or a *xotja*'s son who has declared himself willing to hide the girl in his house for a couple of months. To dispel any suspicions, both the boy and the girl take their evening meal in their usual company, laughing and singing and appearing as carefree as possible. If the elopement has been successfully staged the boy pays nightly visits to the girl at her hiding-place, but takes care to return before dawn so that no one in the neighbourhood may suspect him. During the following days, when the girl's disappearance has become known and caused a stir in the neighbourhood, he even joins in the search for her and tries to mislead the girl's brothers by putting them on to wrong tracks. In this way his secret marriage may last for several months or even a year, until the girl is pregnant or until her lover has other reason to think that the resistance of her parents is broken. As a rule, however, the girl's hiding-place sooner or later becomes known to her family. Her brothers will watch the nightly excursions of all the boys whom they suspect and secretly follow them until they are on the right track. Or again, the neighbours of the cousin in whose house the girl is hiding give the secret away when they sit round the beer-pot and exchange the local gossip. Having lost their restraint when they are drunk they will say that there is a 'black cow' living amongst them and that they wonder who is missing it. Such talk will then spread and finally lead to the discovery of the girl's whereabouts. Her brothers, assisted by their clansmen, will then try to fetch her back by force, but the boy opposes them, if he can muster sufficient support among his friends and clansmen. After a more or less serious encounter between the two parties the girl is either retrieved by her family and quickly married off to another man who can pay the marriage cattle, or her father gives in and negotiates with his daughter's lover about the payment of bride-wealth. If he and his family are poor he usually accepts payment in instalments, which he would never do if the marriage had been properly arranged beforehand.

The planning with which such elopement-marriages are concluded, and the prolonged hardships and tensions which the two lovers are willing to endure, especially the girl who through her action incurs the hostility of all her paternal relatives, clearly show that sexual attraction among the Kavirondo often takes the form of a deep-seated and persistent desire, and not merely of a sudden flaring-up of passion.

Frequently the place to which a pair have eloped is discovered after a few days and the girl brought back to her home. Girls who have once eloped in vain almost invariably repeat their attempts, and if they are married off to other men by force they make an arrangement with their lovers to continue their relations secretly and to run off together as soon as a chance offers itself. Owing to the prevalence of this attitude the clan-elders usually persuade the girl's father to let his daughter marry according to her choice and to be satisfied with a smaller number of marriage cattle rather than force her into a marriage and face the endless troubles and embarrassing situations which his daughter's improper marital conduct would entail. If the girl's father objects to the marriage for other reasons than the bridegroom's poverty the elders will argue with him that, after all, a girl is only a girl and that he would do better to let her go and give the cattle to her brothers so that they can marry in turn and beget sons for the clan.

A typical case illustrating the gradual breaking down of the father's resistance is that of a pagan Logoli boy, Anona, and his Christian girl, Rebecca. Anona had courted Rebecca for a long time and wanted to marry her, but he had neither the 24/- shs. (the present-day money part of the bride-wealth which has taken the place of the twelve hoes) nor the cattle for the bride-wealth. After having secured the girl's consent to come with him (by presenting her with a shirt which she accepted), he ran off with her to a friend's *esimba*. After a few days, Rebecca's father and two brothers found out their hiding-place and, disguising their voices, induced the boy to open the hut. Upon entering, the brothers grabbed the girl and gave her a good beating, while the father beat down on the boy with a stick, constantly repeating his demand: 'Where are the cattle for my daughter?' But as Anona had nothing to offer, Rebecca was taken back and carefully guarded for a few days. Less than a week later she ran off again; but she was soon caught and both she and her lover were given an even more severe beating than the first time. Other boys of the neighbourhood joined in, as they disliked her for never having given a chance to any other boys but Anona. However, when Anona made a third attempt to run off with Rebecca, her father finally agreed to talk to Anona's father, who came to his house to plead for his son and to ask him for time 'to think about the cattle'. In the end Anona handed over one cow and Rebecca was permitted to stay with him on the understanding that the remainder would gradually be paid off over a number of years.

(b) *Marriage by Abduction*

Marriage by abduction (*lixuesa*) is resorted to when both the bridegroom's and the bride's family cannot afford or are too stingy to provide the food and meat required for a proper wedding. At first the bride's father merely delays making preparations for the *siselelo*. When his prospective son-in-law comes to work at his place he hints at his poverty by complaining about the poor harvest or the losses which he has sustained from wild animals or disease killing off his livestock. Later on when his son-in-law talks to him about the *siselelo* he will say to him: 'If you are so impatient why don't you come and fetch your wife?' pretending, of course, that he is merely joking. The bridegroom then knows that his father-in-law has made no preparations for the wedding-feast and so he sends some of his friends secretly to follow the bride when she goes to fetch wood or water and to carry her to his house by force. She resists with all her might, screaming and pretending that she was entirely unaware of the plot to abduct her. If any of her clans-people are near they must come to her assistance, but once she has been carried to the bridegroom's house they will make no further effort to get her back by force. As soon as the news of her abduction has become known, young girls from the neighbourhood come as bridesmaids and sleep at the bridegroom's place, without, however, bringing gifts along or singing and dancing there. They work for the bridegroom's father for two days and sleep there while the bride displays the same behaviour as she would have done in the case of a full wedding, i.e. she does not yet enter into sexual relations with the bridegroom, nor does she accept food at his place. Before she returns home the bridegroom provides a goat or a young bull of *sitiso*, i.e. the 'goat of abduction', which he sends to the bride's father, keeping one front leg for himself. After the bride has stayed home for a week she returns to live with her husband, accompanied by a few bridesmaids, who carry some basketfuls of grain and meat as a present from the bride's parents to those of the bridegroom. The further procedure is the same as that of a full wedding.

The prevailing motive behind most weddings by abduction appears to be to economize on the expenses which the two parties would have to incur if they celebrated a full wedding, and to screen this motive by giving the impression to the public that the bride has been abducted by force.

(c) *Various other Forms of Marriage*

If a boy has made a girl pregnant while courting her he will, as a rule, deny being responsible for her condition until after the child is born. The reason for such a denial, however, is not that the lover fears punishment or refuses to marry a girl who has given birth, but rather that he would have to pay the full amount of marriage-cattle if the girl died in childbirth. He therefore waits to see if everything goes well. When the child has been born and both mother and child are alive and healthy he will be quite as willing to marry the girl as he had been before she became pregnant, or even more so, as the girl in the meantime has given proof of her fertility. That the birth of an illegitimate child by no means lowers the girl's chances of finding a husband is borne out by the fact that, as I was assured, the girl's father will accept his daughter's lover for a son-in-law only if he is in a position to pay the full bride-wealth. Moreover, at the beer of *enganana* it would not occur to the boy's father to offer fewer cattle on the grounds that the girl had given birth. Nevertheless, a full wedding would never take place in such a case, as both parties concerned would regard it as inappropriate to celebrate a marriage concluded under such circumstances by a public feast. It seems that the feeling in this case is less one of moral than of social disgrace. The girl's failure to resist her lover's advances obviously makes it impossible for the people of the bride's clan to maintain their attitude of haughtiness and boastfulness towards the bridegroom's clan, an attitude which, as we have seen, in a marriage with full procedure pervades the whole wedding ceremonial and characterizes the atmosphere between the two parties. The marriage of a girl with an illegitimate child is, therefore, concluded in the *lisindixa* style, i.e. after the cattle have been handed over the girl is merely sent off by her father to join her husband without any further feast or ceremony.

The marriage of a divorced wife (*nasigogo*) takes place in a similar manner to the marriage of a girl with an illegitimate child. The proper conduct for a woman who has been driven away by her husband or who has left him for his cruelty or similar reasons is first to return to her father's place or to go to one of her brothers and stay there until the marriage cattle have been handed back to her former husband. If then another man intends to marry her he may approach her directly, talking to her on the road or at the spring, as, unlike an unmarried girl, a divorced woman does not feel ashamed to talk about her marriage. Nevertheless, the suitor would use figurative language only when proposing to her and discussing the amount of the bride-wealth, addressing her in words such as: 'You are living here by yourself only, but we need women to build the fire for us.' If she feels inclined to accept the proposal she answers: 'Perhaps your hands are too short' or 'look at your fingers', i.e. count on your fingers how many head of cattle you have to pay as bride-wealth. If, on the other hand, she wants to reject the proposal, she insists that she must stay and help her parents, or that she is an old woman. In the first case, i.e. if she accepts, the suitor replies: 'The bird that flies from one tree to another knows where it will alight', or 'If a man tightens the strings of his lyre he knows what he is going to play', implying that he has thought about the bride-wealth before he came to propose to her. Finally, the *nasigogo* will say to him: 'Well, it is your matter, you may go and see my father (or brother).' Having thus secured the woman's consent, the suitor talks to her father, speaking about the number of cows in a matter-of-fact way without using figurative language. The cattle are then handed over in the usual manner, and about a week later the wife comes to his place accompanied by a few 'bridesmaids' (who may be either married or single) carrying baskets with flour and meat. At the bridegroom's place they are given food and a similar amount of gifts to take back to the wife's mother. No cows of *naŋeso* are exchanged between the two *vasagwa*, nor does the wife show the behaviour of a bride when she first visits her new husband's place. The marriage is consummated right away, and the wife immediately begins to work and cook without observing any initial avoidances. Thus the marriage of a divorced wife involves none of the irksome observances—avoidances and many gifts—which characterize the marriage of a young girl. This form of marriage is, accordingly, quite popular, unless the woman has acquired a reputation for wantonness. A favourite song which the musicians sing at beer-feasts to the accompaniment of their lyres, goes: *nasigogo axila omuxana*, 'the divorced wife is better than the young girl'.

If a widow marries a person of a different clan from that of her deceased husband the procedure is exactly the same as in the case of a divorced wife's marriage. If, however, she has agreed at the hair-shaving ceremony to be 'inherited' by her deceased husband's real or classificatory brother, he simply steps into the former husband's place. Apart from the 'change in the individual person' this is socially not considered a new marriage, as through it no old relationships are severed and no new ones established.

At first the new husband comes and helps the widow in her garden and does various other kinds of work that used to be her former husband's duties. The widow cooks for him and serves him with food when he has finished the day's work, but he goes home again and sleeps in the hut of one of his other wives. After this has gone on for a couple of days the widow delays preparing the meal till after dark. This serves as an invitation to her new husband to spend the night with her, a sign that she is now willing to enter into marital relations with him. Among the Vugusu, the new husband either now or in the course of the following weeks sends a cow to the widow's father (or brother if the father is dead) and he in return kills the 'cow of the fibre skirt' (*exafu eye djinyindja*), which signifies that the widow has now put away the widow's attire and wears again the fibre skirt which is the mark of a married woman. The meat of this cow is sent to the house of the former widow, who cooks it together with porridge, and dishes it out to all relatives and neighbours who care to come. Thus the feast of the cow of *djinyindja* socially marks the termination of widowhood and the beginning of matrimony between the former husband's brother and the *omukali omutiga*, the inherited wife.

(7) DISSOLUTION OF MARRIAGE

As one would expect from the elaborateness of the marriage procedure, matrimony among the Kavirondo on the whole tends to be a lasting union. The different features which characterize the matrimonial relationship, as well as the general factors which serve to integrate and stabilize marriage, have been discussed elsewhere in their respective contexts. The stability of the marital union varies, however, with the type of marriage. Genealogical charts and other records show that matrimony with the first or 'great' wife tends to be of the most permanent nature, while subsequent marriages with junior wives tend to be less stable as the number of wives increases. This fact is not due to a notion that marriage with a junior wife is of a different order from that with the first wife, as seems to be the case in some other regions of Africa, where the marriage of plural wives is regarded more or less as a socially recognized form of concubinage. It rather appears to be due to a marked increase in occasions for matrimonial friction as the number of wives increases. Owing to the nature of these frictions younger wives generally tend to be the losers while the 'great' wife is able to maintain her position. As the overwhelming majority of people live in monogamous matrimony, the number of dissolutions of marriages by divorce is by no means as great as it would appear to be from the matrimonial records of a few prominent polygynous elders.

In dissolving a marriage, either of the two marriage partners may take the initiative. Actually, the presence or absence of a plausible motivation for the divorce enters as an important factor in the procedure of dissolving a marriage, but it is not a necessary condition of effecting the return of the bride-wealth and thereby a 'legal' dissolution of the marriage.

On the part of the husband the most frequent overt reasons for divorcing his wife, i.e. for driving her away, are her repeated unfaithfulness and her persistent laziness and failure to fulfil her chief duties in the household. For a single offence of adultery a husband would, as a rule, send his wife back to her father's place for a few weeks, but in the end would permit her to return to him, provided that she brings a cow from her father's place as a compensation for her improper conduct. Similarly, her laziness has to be very persistent and provocative to be considered sufficient reason for a divorce. Thus a wife's repeated and intentional absence from the homestead when she should be there to prepare and cook the evening meal, or her refusal to offer hospitality to her husband's kinsmen or friends, are often quoted as the causes of a quarrel or a separation when matrimonial conflicts come before the tribal court.

On the wife's part the most frequent reasons for seeking separation from her husband are persistent ill-treatment, failure to be supplied with meat and milk, and—especially if the wife has been married to an elderly man and against her will—the desire to live with another man. In polygynous families jealousy and strife between co-wives, not only for the sexual attention of the husband but also for a proper share in the distribution of food and other material values, furnishes a strong additional cause for matrimonial strife. To minimize the occasions for such quarrels each wife has her own sphere of economic rights and duties, and frequently the different wives are kept in separate homesteads. On the whole, it may be said that the initiative in seeking a separation is taken more frequently by the wife than by the husband. This is quite natural, as the nature of the matrimonial relationship plays a much more decisive part in a woman's than in a man's life. The latter can always take an additional wife (or at least openly carry on courtships) if he finds fault with his first wife, while the former depends solely upon her husband.

Besides, there are a number of other causes for matrimonial tensions and conflicts which are seldom or never admitted as causes for the dissolution of a marriage when the matter is brought before the forum of elders but which, nevertheless, are at the root of many a divorce. Thus barrenness of the wife will cause a husband to ill-treat her and all the members of his lineage to make her life at the husband's place miserable, especially if she is the first wife and the husband does not have sufficient cattle to be able to marry a second wife. Among Christians who have made a pledge to live in monogamous matrimony, barrenness of the wife gives rise to even more serious conflicts. The Christian husband who puts up with a barren wife will have to remain childless, a state which is regarded as one of the greatest misfortunes which a man can suffer. In Christian families, likewise, a husband who gets tired of his wife and wishes to marry another woman must first seek a cause for driving his wife away. Sometimes he baselessly accuses his wife of having a lover, until she finally *does* run away with another man.

The suspicion that either the husband or the wife practises sorcery or is afflicted with witchcraft is another indirect cause for divorce. Such cases occur especially in polygynous families, as the diviners like to attribute the sickness of one wife or her children, or the childlessness of another, to the sorcery alleged to be practised by one of the co-wives. Finally, incurable or contagious diseases, as well as repeated and serious criminal offences, may cause a husband to drive his wife away or a wife to desert her husband.

Whenever a marriage is terminated the bride-wealth or that portion of it which is considered still to stand to the husband's credit must be returned by the wife's kin to the husband or his heirs. By this procedure the marriage becomes legally dissolved, i.e. the husband thereby relinquishes all further rights over his former wife. As regards this purely legal aspect of the dissolution of marriage, it makes no difference whether the dissolution has been caused by the death of one of the marriage partners or by divorce, whether the wife has been driven away by her husband or whether she has left him on her own account, whether the husband is the guilty party or the wife. Even if the husband had been sincerely devoted to his deceased wife it would not occur to him to waive his claim to the bride-wealth, and the argument would be appreciated by everyone that 'he will need the cattle to marry again'. Vice versa, it would not occur to the wife's kinsmen to say that the husband had forfeited his claims to a return of the marriage cattle if he had ill treated and driven away his wife without any misconduct on her part. Cattle among the Bantu Kavirondo are much too weighty a possession for a claim to them to be forfeited by such vague and intangible offences as ill treatment of or cruelty towards one's wife.

When assessing the amount to be returned, several factors are taken into consideration. Provided that the marriage has lasted beyond the initial stages, only that part of the bride-wealth is deemed to be returnable which has been paid in cattle and not the hoes (or nowadays the money) which are given to the bride in instalments to break down her resistance to the various household duties which she has to perform. The value of these hoes (or the money) is considered to have been equalled by the numerous gifts which the newly married wife brings with her every time she returns from a visit to her parents' home. The wealthy and hospitable Vugusu in any case consider it below their dignity to keep count of such petty gifts and counter-gifts. Among the Logoli, however, it is customary for both sides to compare the gifts which they have made to one another when the amount of the returnable part of the bride-wealth is assessed at the hair-shaving ceremony (*olovego*) that follows the funeral or at the informal meeting that seals a divorce. Thus at the *olovego* which took place after Isaka's death the husband of one of his sisters, whose wife had left him some months before, claimed a sum of 50/- shillings from Isaka's property, saying that he had not yet redeemed 40/- shillings which he had paid as the money part of the bride-wealth and another 10/- shillings which represented various presents sent to Isaka and his father. When the elders asked Isaka's widow about this claim she admitted that the money had not yet been returned but produced a piece of paper with a long list of counter-gifts by Isaka to his brother-in-law, comprising numerous chickens and basketfuls of grain, meat, fish, and various other items. All these items were confirmed by witnesses and their value was assessed according to current prices. When added up, the total value of the counter-gifts was found to be 60/- shillings. Consequently the former brother-in-law's claim was dismissed amidst laughter.

From the cattle part of the bride-wealth animals are deducted for the various major feasts, killings, or gifts of cattle which the wife's family or kin have made for the husband and his father while the marriage lasted. Thus among the Vugusu a bull is deducted for 'the beer of the wedding', if the wife's father has made a big *siselelo*; if the bull of *kumuoulo* had been given and the *sitexo*-rite performed by the wife's relatives further bulls or bullocks are deducted for each of these two occasions. If the husband's father has 'opened the wife's granary' a heifer is deducted as being equivalent in value, its size depending upon the amount of grain that the granary contained. If the wife should die after she has cultivated a garden for one or two seasons, the crops raised by her are divided equally between her husband and her father, because they say that the crops were raised both with the husband's bill-hook and the father-in-law's hoe. This means that the husband has cleared the garden and thus prepared it for cultivation with his bill-hook, while the wife's father has furnished the hoe for digging it. In subsequent years, when the wife cultivates her husband's gardens with her husband's hoes, her own kinsmen have no claim to any of the crops raised by her.

The cow of *naŋeso*, however, being a reciprocal gift, is only deducted from the bride-wealth if it had been handed over by the wife's father but not yet by the husband's father. Such a delay in reciprocating sometimes occurs, as a liberal margin of time is left to each party for making the counter-gift. Furthermore, if the marriage has been terminated by the death of the wife, the wife's kin take off 'a bull of the shaving ceremony' (*éxafu eye lúvego*, or *eye ligumba*), as they will have to make a ritual killing on that occasion.

Cows are, finally, deducted from the returnable part of the bride-wealth, if the deceased or divorced wife leaves children behind. The number set off is determined by the number of children, but is agreed upon in each case. It partly depends upon the total amount of marriage cattle that have been handed over and partly upon the circumstances in which the marriage was dissolved. If the wife has died, the deduction of cattle for the children borne by her tends to be more liberal than if she has left her husband or has been driven away for having committed an offence. Generally speaking, one cow is taken off for one or two children, two cows for three or four, while no marriage cattle are returned at all if the wife leaves five children or more. This means that the duties of the wife resulting from the payment of marriage cattle for her are considered to have been fulfilled if she has borne a sufficiently large number of children for her husband and his clan. The tendency is to deduct more cattle for sons than for daughters, not only because sons are more highly valued, but also because sons will cause additional expense to the mother's brother who will have to give them cattle at the time of their circumcision and marriage. Daughters, on the other hand, are an economic advantage to the mother's clan, as at every daughter's marriage the mother's brothers can obtain a cow from the bride-wealth that is given for her.

Thus it will be seen that when all these deductions have been made there will not be much left to be returned when a marriage that has lasted for a number of years is terminated.

The husband and his heirs can and usually do ask for the same animals to be returned to them which have originally been handed over to the wife's father.[1] If—as often happens—the animals have in the meantime been passed on to serve as bride-wealth at the conclusion of another marriage, the father- or brother-in-law of the first claimant must go to the person in whose present possession the cows are and offer him cattle in exchange for those which he has to return. The present holder cannot refuse to conform to this request as long as the animals offered him in exchange are of equal quality. Should he try to do so the claim can be enforced before the tribal court. This state of affairs clearly confirms the fact that cattle handed over as bride-wealth by A to C for his daughter B do not actually become C's property but are rather in the nature of a deposit made by A and held by C, at least for a number of years, until the marriage between A and B has become fully established and several children have been borne by B. The marriage cattle being a deposit over which C has not full rights of disposal, obviously the best use to which he can put them is in turn to pass them on as bride-wealth when he or his son wish to take a wife.[2]

Among the Vugusu the recipients are entitled to keep the natural increase, even if the marriage is dissolved and the marriage cattle themselves are returned. The same applies in principle to the Logoli, unless it

---

[1] Provided that the marriage was not concluded so long ago that the animals meanwhile have become old and worthless.

[2] The functions of the bride-wealth among the Bantu Kavirondo will be more fully discussed in vol. ii (chapter on cattle law).

has previously been arranged that the first calf or two must be returned to the wife's husband. This is usually done if the husband owned the cow in partnership with his brother or friend (cf. above, p. 405).

As we have stated above, the husband or his heirs under no circumstances relinquish their legal claim to a return of the bride-wealth if the marriage comes to a premature end. Nevertheless, it is in practice far more difficult for a husband to 'divorce' his wife, i.e. to recover the marriage cattle given for her, if she has done no wrong than it would be if she had left on her own account or been driven away for a matrimonial misconduct that is generally considered sufficient cause for a divorce. In the former case the wife's father, as a rule, at first refuses to return the marriage cattle and, instead, persists in sending his daughter back to her husband. He adopts this course partly because it means considerable trouble and—if he is poor—even difficulty to recover the animals which may have changed hands several times, and partly because he knows that, once his daughter has become a *nasigogo*, a divorced wife, he will not be able to marry her off again for the full bride-wealth, even if she has been divorced through no fault of her own. If the husband stubbornly continues to send his wife back to her clan (which, of course, he would only do to recover his bride-wealth for marrying another girl), the wife's kinsmen will keep her until she has found another husband who is willing to pay bride-wealth for her. When this has been received they will return the cattle given by the first husband and the former marriage would thereby be terminated.

What the position would be should the wife find no other husband I have not found it possible to discover with certainty. I have never heard of an actual case of this kind, which obviously would be of very rare occurrence, as a wife who had done no wrong would easily find another husband unless her husband's behaviour towards her drove her at last to commit some offence which would justify his demand for a return of his cattle. To discuss with native informants in a purely theoretical way an imaginary legal situation is seldom of value as it is difficult for them to see and formulate legal principles when abstracted from actual situations which they have experienced or heard about. Nevertheless, my theoretical inquiries into this situation yielded the one positive result that when it comes to a legal conflict between the husband and the wife's father over the return of the marriage cattle, the support given to each of them by his clansmen will be a decisive factor. If the husband's case is unreasonable, the elders of his clan would persuade him to let his wife return to him rather than try to recover his marriage cattle by force. Similarly, the elders of the wife's clan would encourage her father to remain obstinate in his refusal to return the cattle. As the elders of both clans are primarily concerned to maintain a mutual relationship of fairness and neighbourliness between their clans, they tend to apply pressure to individual members of their clan to keep them from making unreasonable demands. Thus we see that a man's theoretical right to dissolve his marriage whenever he pleases to do so may in practice meet with serious obstacles if he has no proper cause for seeking a divorce. Nevertheless, it makes a great difference whether a husband who ill treats his wife and drives her away without reason, thereby *forfeits* his legal claim to his marriage cattle and loses his wife as well, or whether he remains in any circumstances the lawful husband of his wife, as long as his marriage cattle have not yet been returned to him. While in the first case the bride-wealth serves as a guarantee for the wife's proper treatment by her husband and his kinsmen, it has almost the opposite effect in the second case, as it induces the wife's father to persist in sending her back to her husband irrespective of the ill treatment to which she may be exposed at his place.

If the desire to dissolve the marriage comes from the wife's side and her intentions are endorsed by her father or her brothers, the husband has no means of forcing her to stay with him or to return to him if he does not wish to relinquish her. She owns no property and he holds no possessions belonging to his wife's kin which would be in the nature of a pledge of her good behaviour. Once his wife has left him, there are only two things for a husband to do: either to reconcile himself to the situation and demand his cattle back, or to make an attempt to recapture his wife by force. Provided that she is supported by her kinsmen it is thus considerably easier for a wife to leave her husband without valid reason and to terminate her 'marriage contract' than it is for a husband to drive off his wife without reason and to recover the marriage cattle.

Under ordinary circumstances, of course, it seldom happens that a wife's unjustified and selfish desire to leave her husband meets with any approval on the part of her own kinsmen. The brothers of a wife who has run away with a paramour will, as a rule, make every effort to fetch her back and to hand her over again to her lawful husband, provided that the latter is willing to take her back. They will do so particularly if they hear that their sister's lover is not willing or able to pay the bride-wealth, for in that case the wife's brothers would be the losers if their sister's first marriage were dissolved. The deposit of the bride-wealth, therefore, does in fact strengthen the husband's hold over his wife, as the unpleasant prospect of having to hand it back to the husband in case of a divorce induces the wife's kinsmen to use their influence in maintaining the marriage and to compel the wife to return to her husband if she has run away with a lover.

Occasionally, however, it happens that the brothers of a wife (or, more rarely, her father) are anxious to see their sister's (or daughter's) marriage dissolved, as they wish to remarry her to another man whom they prefer as a brother-in-law, either for personal reasons or because he is able to give a higher bride-wealth. As a sign that they wish to terminate the marriage they would then send the marriage cattle back to the husband and retain their sister when she comes to their place for a visit.

Two very similar cases of this sort were pending at the native tribunal when I left Kavirondo for the last time. In the one case a wife had been abducted by her brothers who wanted to marry her off to a friend. Her husband to whom she had been married for six months, and with whom she had lived quite happily, refused to take his marriage cattle back and accused his brothers-in-law of having 'kidnapped' his wife. In the second case the wife's brother had tried to return the cattle, pretending that they were getting lean and had brought a case against his sister's husband, demanding that he should take his cattle back and surrender his wife.

According to the statements of elders such cases were unknown under traditional conditions. However, if a case of this kind had occurred and the dispute been brought before the elders of the two clans concerned they would have supported the husband's case, provided the wife wanted to stay with him.

D. DEATH AND MOURNING

(1) INTRODUCTORY

THE notions which we have seen to prevail among the Bantu Kavirondo with regard to the existence and activities of the spirits of the dead[1] imply that the event of bodily death is not thought to terminate the existence of the human individual and his spiritual life but rather to transform the *nature* of his existence. In the chapter on ancestral spirits we discussed which aspects of the human individual are believed to vanish or perish and which to live on when death occurs, what changes the phenomenon of death brings about and in what manner this process of transformation is thought to take place. We have seen that physical death is looked upon as a decisive break in the spiritual existence of the individual, a turning-point which involves a definite change for the worse and, consequently, evokes a feeling of initial restlessness and of resentment towards the surviving relatives whom the deceased tends to hold responsible for the fate that has overtaken him. At the same time, we have seen that physical death does not sever but merely transforms the bonds that existed between the deceased and his friends and relatives. These bonds in many ways assume an even greater importance after death, as the power and influence wielded by the deceased over the living are thought to be even greater than that wielded by the living over their fellow human beings. It is a natural consequence of these notions that a close community is maintained between the living and the dead.

The event of death thus signifies a beginning as well as an end. The person who dies leaves one phase of his existence to enter another one, not only as regards his own individual existence but also as regards the place which he will henceforth occupy in the community of the living. This last point is sociologically relevant, for obviously the idea of 'life after death' has a different social significance if it entails the notion that the deceased

[1] Cf. above, p. 159 sq.

continue to wield power over the living than it would have if they were merely thought to live on in a remote spirit-world which has no effective connexion with the world of the living. Inasmuch as death means the transition from one phase of existence to another, both of which involve the maintenance of close relations with the living, its social significance is analogous to that of the various other 'crises of life', viz. birth, initiation, marriage, &c. Death chiefly differs from these other 'crises' in that it is forced upon people against their will, and thus produces a (real or supposed) psychological reaction, both in the bereaved and in the deceased himself which, likewise, is fundamentally different from the psychological situation arising in connexion with the other crises of life. The subsequent analytic account of the rites and observances connected with the event of death will clearly prove that this analogy is by no means a theoretical construction imposed upon the facts to make them fit into a system, but that it cogently results from the ritual procedure.

Like all the other rites of transition, the observances and ceremonies performed after a person's death are expressions of the complex situation which the dissolution of relationships of a varied nature and the establishment of new relationships entail. For the purpose of analysing this situation, which is the task of the present chapter, we must distinguish between the various aspects of this situation. There is, first of all, the material or physical aspect of death, the need for a disposal of the body. Like the biological processes of birth and of the physical care for the new-born child, this aspect is not altogether biologically determined but has a material basis which then becomes culturally elaborated and thereby significant. Thus the time and manner of burial, the position and set-up of the grave, and many other features connected with the disposal of the body are such cultural elaborations in that they go far beyond the mere physical necessity for disposing of the corpse. Next, there is the social aspect of the situation. Through the death of a person his social and economic relations with other persons are severed and the place hitherto occupied by him in the social group becomes vacant. This fact gives rise, on the one hand, to the need for filling the gap in the social group, i.e. to succession, and, on the other hand, to a distribution of his property, i.e. to inheritance. Perhaps most important of all is the emotional response which the situation of death evokes. Here again the psychological reaction to bereavement as a sentiment rooted in human nature is culturally shaped by the notions which are held with regard to the causes of death and its consequences for the living. The emotion of grief over the departure of the deceased from the living is thus coupled, on the one hand, with a feeling of hatred and vengeance towards those whom the bereaved hold responsible for the death, and, on the other hand, with a feeling of apprehension that the deceased might blame an innocent person for his death or that he might try to return and take other people with him.

These various aspects which jointly constitute the situation at death differ

DEATH AND MOURNING

according to the former status of the deceased in the community. Thus the social aspect of death, the regulation of succession and inheritance, is obviously of much greater importance in the case of a wealthy and influential polygynous clan-elder than in that of a youngish man; it differs for a man and a woman, and it is wholly absent if the deceased person is a child. Similarly, the magico-religious notions which determine the attitude of the people towards the spirit of the deceased differ according to his former status in the community and, particularly, according to the extent to which he was credited with the possession of magical or other mystical powers.

With such differences in the range and nature of the various aspects of the situation at death, the ceremonial procedure varies accordingly. In the subsequent account we shall describe the observances after the death of a fully established polygynous elder, for they present the most elaborate form of the 'typical' ceremonial. From it simpler forms of ceremonial can easily be deduced by omitting those features which particularly refer to conditions of polygyny and by reducing others to a smaller scale. The procedure followed after the death of a clan-head, of a woman, and of persons with real or alleged abnormal qualities will be described separately, in so far as it deviates from the general pattern.

As in the preceding chapters, we shall present the following analysis of the death and mourning rites in their approximate chronological order and discuss tribal variants at their proper places in the chronological sequence of events.

(2) THE APPROACH OF DEATH

When a person is dangerously ill and his condition takes a turn for the worse, a last effort to save his life is frequently made by moving him from the hut of one wife to that of another one in the hope of leaving the sickness behind in the previous hut. This is done especially if it is thought that the sickness is due to the emanation of an evil substance which a sorcerer has hidden in or near the patient's hut. Among the Vugusu, the brothers or sons of the sick man sometimes move the patient to an open arbour (*lisali*) which they erect in the bush. The idea in doing so is to protect the sick man from visitors who might want to aggravate his condition by practising sorcery over him, pretending that they are visiting him to show their sympathy. The *lisali*-shelter is, therefore, erected at a hidden place from which undesirable visitors can be kept away. While the patient is being carried there, attention is paid to good and bad signs. If the *exisi* animal (a small buck) crosses the path in front of the party or if they hear a certain bird singing by the roadside, it is taken as a sign that the patient will die, and he is then carried back again to his homestead.

Everywhere, the proper place for a man to die is the front partition of his house (*ovuhilu*), and if he has several wives, he must die in the house of his great wife. As death approaches, the patient is accordingly carried home again from the *lisali* or moved back to his great wife's hut if previously he had

G g

been moved to that of another wife. However, if death overcomes a person away from his house, no rite is performed to counteract the unfortunate consequences which this might entail for the spirit of the deceased.[1]

When it appears that death is imminent, all relatives and close friends of the patient are summoned by messengers. They stop their work and come to see him before he dies. The persons particularly required to come are his children, his brothers and sisters, and the children and grandchildren of his father's sister and his mother's brother. Before they arrive the patient calls his brother to his bedside and tells him that he feels the end coming. His brother ruefully replies that there is nothing they can do for him; so the patient asks him to kill a cow he wants to distribute among his clansmen while he is still alive. His brother then selects a big fat ox from the dying man's herd and kills it as soon as all kinsmen have assembled in the yard. When the ox has been skinned and cut up, he taps its stomach with a stick and while doing so utters the following spell over it: 'Whoever is trying to kill the sick man may die when he eats of this stomach.' Having thus prepared everything, he enters the house together with the other brothers or sons and, supporting the patient under his arms, they slowly conduct him outside to the yard to perform the sacrifice and to divide the meat amongst the visitors. He pierces the stomach and, throwing bits of meat and of the stomach content to the spirits,[2] asks them to come and participate in the meal, saying: 'All the people who died may come to eat of this meat. You (mentioning the names of some spirits) may come and give us health.'[3] Having performed the sacrifice, he is carried back to the hut to die, leaving it to his brother to divide the meat of the stomach among the visitors. While doing so the brother makes sure that each of them receives a piece and eats it on the premises, lest he should be suspected of having tried to kill the patient by sorcery. Should anyone fall ill after having eaten of the meat this would be regarded as due to the spell uttered over the meat while it was eaten, and his guilt would be considered to have been firmly established. Likewise, if one of the sick man's neighbours or relatives fails to appear, his absence is attributed to his guilty conscience with regard to the sick man's disease and his fear of falling a victim to the spell uttered over the meat. In the first case the punishment for having applied sorcery to the sick man follows automatically, as the eating of the meat of the stomach acts as an ordeal. In the second case, special efforts will be made to induce the absent kinsman to come and renounce his evil actions and intentions and thereby save the patient.

After the meat of the stomach has been eaten, the sick man's brother divides the remaining meat of the ox among the relatives. Each of them may take home the share which he has been given.

---

[1] Cf. the rules concerning delivery, p. 301.
[2] i.e. either on the roof of the sacrificial hut or to various parts of the yard. Text: *avukule yinyama afuvile emisambwa djilie xuo*—he may take the meat, he may throw to the spirits, they may eat on.   [3] Cf. above, p. 312.

If the patient still has enough strength left, he then calls his sons to his bedside and tells them how to divide his possessions in cattle and other livestock. Otherwise he delegates this duty to his brother, who discusses the question of succession and inheritance at the hair-shaving ceremony that takes place three days after a person's death.

Thus it will be seen that the killing of an ox just before a person's death has a threefold significance: it is a last sacrifice performed by the dying man for the welfare and well-being both of himself and of his kinsmen; it is his last participation with them in a common meal, and it also serves as a means of detecting and punishing persons who may be responsible for his illness.[1]

This last sacrifice having been performed, no further ritual or other actions take place until death (*olukuzu*) occurs. The wives and sisters who attend to the dying man sit about in silence, crying softly and throbbing but they do not yet wail. If the patient suffers from fever, they keep bathing his head with cool water until the end. Otherwise they leave the patient without further treatment once they have given up hope, which is often several hours before death actually occurs. When the patient begins to fight the death-struggle (Nyole: *oxurá'tsana*) the women begin to wail aloud, but the men remain silent until he has actually died. That death has occurred is recognized by the fact that the patient has stopped breathing and by the sudden stare in his eyes (Tsotso: *edzimoni dzimalile oxukaluxana* —the eyes become different). His eyes are then closed and his mouth is shut, a duty which may be performed by anyone who happens to be near the dying man.[2]

(3) WAILING AND CEREMONIES PERFORMED IN HONOUR OF THE DECEASED

The moment of death is marked by a sudden and violent outburst of wailing (*okwikula*) joined in by all the people who are assembled in the house and in the yard. The wailing noises may be described as drawn-out cries of a melodious but melancholy tinge intermingled with high-pitched, discordant shrieks and screams. The sudden outbreak of wailing where there was complete silence only a second before is, especially at night, somehow eerie and terrifying. Although the shrieks and screams sound emotional enough, they appear to be largely determined by convention, and one would never for a moment mistake them for the screams of a person in sudden physical danger or suffering acute bodily pain. That, although conventional, the urge to start wailing at the moment of death is genuine is shown by the case of a woman whose dangerously wounded

[1] I cannot say whether or not the offering of the stomach to the spirits is thought to affect them in the same way as a living sorcerer if one of them has caused the man's illness.

[2] Among the Nyole it is said to happen that a dying person is suffocated by tightly closing his mouth and his nose. The reason for doing so is to make his spirit stay in his body and so preventing it from visiting the living. I was not able, however, to check this piece of information which I was given by a missionary shortly before my departure from Kavirondo.

child I once took to a hospital by car. While speeding along the road the child died, and the mother immediately began to wail in the customary fashion although no other native was in the car with us and we were passing through the territory of another tribe. When they have wailed for a few moments by the side of the deceased, the widows strip and, taking their bush-knives and one of their husband's weapons or beer-tubes, run about in the neighbourhood and to their parents' homes, all the time wailing loudly and, in short and abrupt sentences, shouting the name of the deceased and the words of the customary dirges. While doing so they hold their right arm over their head, which is the typical manner of wailing for a female mourner, while men raise their left hand to the back of their neck, a custom, however, which seems to be observed only by elderly men. Like the widows, the brothers of the deceased, too, run from homestead to homestead to spread the death message among their clansmen,[1] while his sisters run to their respective husbands' places. Among the Idaxo and the Logoli, the news is furthermore announced by beating a dancing-drum (*endumba*) as soon as death has occurred.[2] While the mourners run about wailing, the corpse is left to itself, only a few neighbours and the children who beat the drum remaining at the homestead. After an hour or more the relatives begin to return from their 'round of wailing' and they now kindle a fire in the house and another one in the yard. Clansmen, friends, and in-laws of the deceased begin to arrive from all directions and the yard is quickly filled with mourners, even if the death has occurred in the middle of the night. Old men run about and sound their horns, so that the death message can be heard for many miles.

During the first night the corpse remains in the front room of the hut where the widows keep the death watch. Among the Logoli they take the corpse between them and leave it there all night. Among the Nyole the wives all sleep on one side of their dead husband, lying in the order in which they were married to him, i.e. the great wife sleeps next to him, then the second, the third, &c. As they say that the deceased will stick to the sleeping-hide if he is allowed to rest on one side only, they turn him round every few hours, and the widows then change their positions accordingly. The brother of the deceased has the task of tending the fires which have been kindled inside the hut and out in the yard. The sons keep him company, and the sisters who had come to nurse their brother during his illness sleep in nearby huts—either in those of the younger wives or of neighbours—as it is their task to look after the widows during the following days. No work must be done in the house where the corpse rests; not even may the rubbish be swept outside until after the burial has taken place.

[1] *Xasule nasilikwa nalakaya nakoma mbaluhia*, he may come out with screaming and he cries and runs wailing 'into' the clansmen.
[2] Among the Logoli this custom seems to have been copied from the Idaxo. It has now been made compulsory by chiefs' orders to announce every death by drumming.

Early next morning an old widowed woman whose former husband belonged to the clan of the deceased enters the hut to hand the eldest widow (the great wife) the dead man's cow- or goatskin or to place his spear and shield in her hands. Then she hands another spear to the second wife, a bush-knife to the third, a beer-pipe or stool to the next, and so on till all the objects which the deceased used to wear or carry about with him have been distributed among the widows. Led by the great wife and accompanied by the old woman, the widows start off to run all across the country, wailing and singing dirges. After a while they stop at the bank of a stream where the old widow rubs them with mud (*litohi*), beginning with the great wife. Upon their return home they are joined by the sisters of the deceased and now they all assemble in the yard to dance and to sing. Some dance in a sitting position, moving only the upper part of their bodies (*vexayendje basi mbasalama*), others in the *lidegeriza* fashion, i.e. their shoulder-blades quivering and their bent lower arms raised up to the height of their breasts. Others again scream in a shrill and high-pitched voice (*kukuba evigalagala*) as warriors do when they see the enemy rushing towards them. At intervals both the widows and the sisters of the deceased, wailing passionately and running about wildly brandishing their bill-hooks, tear the grass off the roof of the hut and hack down the banana-grove behind the house. Among the Vugusu and the Nyole the widows put on a belt adorned with cowrie-shells with one or several cow-bells tied to it, so that the bells constantly jingle while they are dancing. Each woman keeps the bells for a few minutes and then hands them on to another woman standing near by.

In the meantime, while it is still early in the morning, the men prepare everything for the big cattle-drive, the *elisona*.[1] The manner in which this cattle-drive is staged varies considerably from tribe to tribe and from occasion to occasion, but everywhere the basic idea seems to be to pay homage to the spirit of the deceased by driving one's entire wealth in cattle to his homestead. As a rule, an *elisona* is held only after the death of a well-reputed clan-elder or a man who at least had the full status of a family head, although among the Logoli I have seen cattle-drives on a smaller scale also after the death of well-known and respected old women. In accordance with the general rule to stop working during the time between a person's death and his burial, all the people who mourn for the deceased also refrain from milking their cows on the morning of the cattle-drive, letting the calves suck all the milk they want. Preparatory to the *elisona*, everyone who wishes to join in it runs down to a stream and paints his face and body with white, red, or black clay, no definite pattern being prescribed but everybody choosing an individual design according to his own fancy. The women cut *amalande*-leaves with which they adorn their own bodies as well as the horns and the humps of the cattle.

If the deceased was himself the owner of a large herd, his brothers start driving off his cattle soon after daybreak, the widows and sisters of the

[1] Among the Marama and Tsotso the cattle-drive is called *efiremba*.

deceased running in front, wailing and singing, and various old men of the neighbourhood accompanying them, blowing their horns and shouting war-cries to announce far and wide that the cattle-drive is on its way. As they run along, the cattle from other homesteads join the procession and when the party finally comes back, having covered a distance of several miles, hundreds of cows and mourners have joined in. At the same time, further parties of people arrive with their cattle from all directions, having first assembled at the 'public places' of their respective sub-clans and villages. In groups of twenty or more, depending upon the size of the yard (*omugizi*) in front of the deceased's house, the cattle are then driven past the dead man, who has by now been moved to a place under the eaves of the hut. After they have thus 'honoured the spirit of the deceased', the cows are driven back by the herd-boys to graze in the pastures as usual. These are the characteristic features of the cattle-drive as I have observed it on numerous occasions among the Logoli, Marama, and Tsotso.

In a Nyole text which I recorded from the narrative of an old man, another feature of the *elisona* is related. According to that narrative, the clansmen of the deceased, on the eve of the cattle-drive, agree on a place where they will assemble their cattle. There they meet at daybreak next morning, each of them taking some porridge, milk, sweet potatoes, and gruel with him. Thus equipped, they drive the cattle to the *sitsimi*, i.e. the uninhabited zone of country between their own tribal territory and that of the neighbouring hostile tribe. There they 'throw the food to the spirits' (*vafuve emisango*) and graze the cattle to provoke their enemies, for ordinarily both tribes would refrain from grazing their cattle in the border-zone. If the enemies accept the challenge, they quickly untie the grazing cattle and tell the herd-boys to drive them back, while the men remain to fight the enemy, 'the reason being that the dead man was a warrior'.[1] My informant assured me, however, that they would not enter into a serious fight but mainly shout abuse at the enemy and boast of their own courage and fierceness.

By far the most impressive cattle-drive I ever witnessed took place after the death of Vigeti, a well-known polygynous elder of the Tadjoni tribe and a member of the tribal council of elders. In contrast to the Logoli custom, the cattle-drive among the Tadjoni is staged not *before* but the day *after* the burial. However, as the spirit of the deceased is believed to hover about his former homestead for the first few days after death, the exact sequence of events makes little difference. From early in the morning till about one o'clock in the afternoon, herds of cattle were almost incessantly driven across the homestead of the deceased. Coming in a constant stream from all directions and from distances up to five miles and even more, the different herds were first assembled on a large pasture adjoining the deceased's enclosure. Then one[2] herd after the other—i.e. either the cattle

---

[1] *Esifune yali omundu owelihé.*
[2] Comprising between 60 and 100 head of cattle.

DEATH AND MOURNING

belonging to one elder or the combined herd of a sub-clan or a lineage—was driven from the pasture to the yard inside the enclosure where they were rounded up by the herd-boys. As soon as the animals were huddled close together, all the men and women present began to dance round them in a heavy, thumping rhythm. They were dancing in two or even three concentric circles, the men holding their spears and rattling the iron rattles attached to their legs, and the women carrying sticks and rattling gourds which they were holding in their left hands. Moving slowly in an anti-clockwise direction, they sang a number of songs, beginning invariably with the following one which was repeated dozens of times:

>   1. *Mama iŋombe heee iŋombe*
>   *mama iŋombe heee iŋombe.*
>
>   'Mother cow, hee cow!'

By addressing the cows as 'mothers' they mean that their fathers married their mothers in exchange for marriage cattle and that this cattle made it possible for them to be born. Among other songs sung on that occasion I recorded the following ones:

>   2. *Nesivela siefu, nesivela heee*
>   *sia vahaviyia, nesivela, rep.*
>
>   'With our sorrow, with sorrow, heee,
>   of the Naviyia clan (the clan of the deceased).'

This song, which was likewise repeated dozens of times, voices the sorrow that death has brought to their clan. In contrast to the previous one which praises the cattle as a means of increasing the clan, this song implies that death keeps the clan small.

>   3. *Xavanga Iseve xulugulu, Iseve xulugulu,*
>   *xavanga Iseve,*
>   *xuali avaumbwa xulugulu,*
>   *xuali avarua xulugulu*
>   *xavanga Iseve xulugulu, Iseve xulugulu.*
>
>   'I search for Iseve on the hill, for Iseve on the hill,
>   I search for Iseve,
>   We were the enemies on the hill,
>   We were the Masai on the hill,
>   I search for Iseve on the hill, for Iseve on the hill.'

According to the commentary given to me, this song recalls a war-deed in which the warriors of the deceased's clan searched for an enemy called Iseve whom they wanted to kill. They went about their task as cleverly as the Masai, the acknowledged masters of warfare. Possibly this song recalls a war expedition in which Vigeti took part and earned special praise for himself.

4. *Xwenyala omunyolo gwasiko?*
Ha vayayiwa!
Xwenyala omunyolo.
Omwami yenyalile omunyolo gwasiko?
Ha vayayiwa!

'We urinate the chain of what?
Ha alas!
We urinate the chain.
The chief he urinated the chain of what?
Ha alas!

5. *Musaya omwami owe lugongo,*
xusaya omwami hee,
musaya omwene.

'You beg the chief of the ridge
we beg the chief, hee,
you beg him himself.'

In the last two songs the word *omwami*, chief, refers to the dead man. The meaning of the first song is obscure. The second one stresses the wealth of the dead man to whom all people came to beg things. It is one of the main duties of a wealthy and influential man to be generous and helpful to people who come to his homestead to beg things from him.

6. *Iŋombe yauya hahá*
iŋombe yauya hahá!

'The cow it moves, hahá!'

The song was sung whenever the dancing and singing round one herd of cattle had come to an end and the cows were driven off the yard to make room for the next herd. Before each herd was driven off, some of the dancers picked out a large ox and, grabbing it firmly by its horns and tail, adorned its back with rags of clothes and its hump with beads and a hat. Then they made a small boy ride on its back and danced round the ox till it tore itself loose and dashed away. In explanation of this ceremony my informants merely stated that it serves to express their joy over their cattle. The lifting of an uncircumcised youth (*omusoleli*) on the animal's back seems, however, to possess a deeper significance, the idea possibly being to secure continuity from the dying to the rising generation in their respective relationship towards cattle. Other ceremonial features connected with these dances round the various herds of cattle appear to be expressions of similar notions. Thus, while the people dance round the cattle, an old woman sprinkles milk over the backs of as many cows as she can reach, using for that purpose a branch of the raffia palm which she dips into a milking-gourd. The milk must be taken from one of the dead man's cows and the professed aim of the ceremony is to increase the milk yield of the cows. Also, during the intervals between the songs the young girls smear each other's faces with cow-dung which, as they say, increases their fertility. They call this mutual smearing with cow-dung 'to eat the guts', and it seems, therefore, to have the same significance as the anointing with the stomach content of cows, sheep, and goats which forms a standard feature of every ritual killing. It thus appears that, among the Tadjoni at least, the cattle-drive does not merely serve as a homage to and entertainment of the dead man's spirit but it also benefits the cattle themselves and furthermore lends strength, in a magical sense, to the mourners and to the deceased's clan as a whole.

Among the Vugusu, the cattle-drive (*liiyia*) does not take place before or immediately after the burial but after about a year, when it is held in connexion with the feast that terminates the widow's period of mourning (the cutting of the *gimigoye*).[1]

The second outstanding ceremonial event of the funeral rites is the sham fight (Lurogoli: *elifuliana*; Lutsotso: *oxutunguya*) which is performed by the age-mates of the deceased. Whereas the cattle-drive re-enacts the life of the deceased as a herdsman and owner of cattle, the *elifuliana*, by a pantomimic performance of fighting, recalls his life as a warrior. To quote from an account by a Logoli elder:

'They can perform a sham fight showing how that person fought in the war when he was (still) alive; then those of his age-class make a sham fight against (others of) his age-class. And they carry the weapons which they were fighting with, like that person (the deceased) was fighting with: horns, bugles, spears, sticks (clubs), shields, and bow and arrow.'

Accordingly, the *elifuliana* is only staged after the death of a man who has taken part in fighting, and the greater his reputation as a warrior and the number of enemies he has killed[2] the more impressive is the scale on which the sham fight is performed. As nowadays most of the youngish or middle-aged men cannot boast of any record as warriors, the *elifuliana* is, as a rule, only performed after the death of old men 'who have still seen the days of fighting'. The only time I have seen a sham fight performed in honour of a youngish man (of about 35 or 40 years) was at the funeral of a man from the Matioli clan of North Marama who for nine years had been a member of the Kenya Police Force and who had died while he was home on leave. The initiative in staging the sham fight is always taken by the age-mates of the deceased, i.e. by the people who belong to his circumcision age-class (*elikula*). They are also the people who primarily take part in the performance of the fight, although, as it gets into full swing, other people of both older and younger age-grades may join in. As the members of the older age-grades are no longer very numerous, the sham fights nowadays performed after the death of old men are rather skimpy affairs. They last but a few minutes and only a handful of people take part in them. The

---

[1] Cf. the sacrifice of a bullock at the father's grave which is also called *liiyia*.

[2] The number of enemies killed by a warrior seems to be one of the chief means of assessing his fame. Among the Vugusu it also makes a difference whether the enemies killed were Masai, Tero, or 'merely' Elgonyi.

proper time for performing the *elifuliana* is in the morning after the burial, i.e. on the day following the *elisona*, but I have frequently seen it take place immediately after the cattle-drive or during the interval between the departure of one herd of cattle and the arrival of the next.

The most elaborate *elifuliana* I have ever witnessed was performed at the funeral of the man of the Kenya Police Force in Marama. It was staged in the spacious yard of the dead man's homestead on the morning after his burial. As—to judge by other descriptions of warfare—it gives a fairly realistic impression of the manner in which fighting-encounters took place in former days, the procedure may be recorded in some detail:

'Upon our arrival we find hundreds of onlookers of both sexes and all ages lining the yard, many of them perched on trees or sitting on the framework of an abandoned and half-dilapidated hut. While the "warriors" are assembling on an adjoining pasture, putting on their head-dresses, painting themselves with clay in various colours and adorning themselves profusely with the vines of the *elilande*-creeper, the last phase of the cattle-drive and dance which had begun on the previous day is still going on. Then immediately the yard has been cleared of the cattle and the dancers, about eighty to a hundred men dash in through the narrow gate of the enclosure, some of them carrying a spear and a huge shield and others clubs or sticks or bows and arrows. After several minutes of general turmoil during which everyone performs individually, brandishing his spear, swinging his club, or blowing his horn, the warriors fall into two groups, each lining up at opposite sides of the yard. Those who carry shields stand in the front line, forming a solid wall. Uttering the high-pitched war-cries, both groups slowly proceed towards one another till the two front rows are only a few yards apart. Now a few men individually dash forward and thrust their spears against the shields of their opponents. This serves as the signal for a general attack, and for the next few minutes there is a confused scuffle, shield clashing against shield and club against club. Then both groups resume their former positions, lining up at opposite sides of the yard, and after a short pause the same performance is repeated all over again. Occasionally a "warrior" falls down and is carried outside by the onlookers while others, seemingly in a state of ecstasy, throw down their clubs or shields and for a few seconds utter shrill sounds and dance in the *lidegeriza* fashion, i.e. by shaking their shoulders. After the sham fight has gone on for about thirty minutes, the "warriors" all assemble in the shade of the banana-grove to the side of the yard. There they form a solid column, deeply echeloned, and, their spears and clubs raised high up, they slowly dance across the yard. At the centre of the yard they lay down their weapons as well as all their drums, horns, and ornaments, piling them up in a large heap. Then they form a circle and for another thirty minutes dance in an anti-clockwise direction round the heap of weapons, singing victory songs (*okukélemana*). As the dance comes to an end, they pick up their weapons and file out again through the same gate by which they had entered the enclosure.'

The cattle-drive and the sham fight are the two chief dramatic events of the mourning rites, as far as the bulk of the mourners is concerned. But

DEATH AND MOURNING

these two events are accompanied by a number of other features which throw light upon the attitude towards death and the response which it evokes. From the moment of death onward, a constant stream of visitors pours into the homestead of the deceased. They come and go at all times of the day and usually stay for several hours. The majority of the mourners come in their ordinary attire, but a few, especially old women who are themselves widows as well as (real or classificatory) sisters of the deceased, paint their faces white and adorn their bodies with the vines of the *lande-*creeper or with the leaves of the *sazi*-plant. Whether to don such a mourning-attire or not is left entirely to individual taste: at the numerous funerals which I attended among the Logoli it was mostly the same old women, turning up at every funeral regardless of their kinship affiliations to the deceased, who were decked out in the most fantastic mourning garb, while I often saw close female relatives of the deceased wear their ordinary clothes. The behaviour of the mourners is quite informal, the old men sitting together in the front yard, gossiping or sucking beer through long reed-pipes from a pot in their midst, provided that the relatives or neighbours of the deceased have supplied them with any. The young men and women stand or sit about in groups, some munching at long pieces of sugar-cane which on these occasions are always brought along in great quantities, as the mourners are not provided with any other food. Boys and girls welcome the occasion to flirt together, chatting loudly and laughing or even shouting from group to group. Children run all over the place, chasing one another entirely unconcerned, and no one ever admonishes them to be quiet or show restraint.

As each visitor arrives, he first goes to look at the corpse which, as a rule, is put on a bier under the eaves of a hut or in the shade of a granary. Standing beside or leaning over the corpse, the women wail or sing dirges, while the men gaze at the deceased in silence or, in a low voice, utter a few words of sorrow and grief. People do not fear to touch a corpse, at least if they have no guilty conscience towards the deceased. But it is said that if the person who has employed witchcraft or sorcery against the deceased and is, therefore, responsible for his death, were to come and look at him, the latter would quickly open his eyes and stare at him for a moment. A kinsman or neighbour, therefore, who failed to come and look at the deceased would be suspected of having a guilty conscience. The fact of his absence would be publicly mentioned at the hair-shaving ceremony when accusations of having killed the deceased by sorcery or witchcraft are levelled against various people (cf. below, p. 486). Likewise, a widow who has been unfaithful to her husband as well as her secret lover must avoid coming near the corpse, as this would cause both of them to die. At the funeral of a Roman Catholic native in Kitosh I heard some visitors commenting accordingly on the widow's apparent reluctance to approach her dead husband while she was wailing.

Although the body of the deceased is treated with much formality as regards the way in which it is laid out in state and the observance of certain prescribed rules of ritual behaviour, the general attitude to a dead person does not differ fundamentally from that shown to a living one. He is not treated with any religious awe or reverence as one might expect since he is the seat of the *ekigingi*, or the spirit of the dead, which henceforth becomes the object of the ancestral cult. He is talked to as if he were still a living person. At a funeral among the Logoli I even heard a widow scolding her dead husband for the pungent smell of his body. Interrupting her wailing noises for a moment, she stepped back from the deceased and shouted at him in an angry voice: 'Why are you smelling at us[1] like that? What have we done to you? Haven't we cared for you well? Do you think we have killed you?'

Another peculiar feature of every funeral is the hilarious behaviour displayed by some of the mourners who suddenly leave off wailing to perform some clownish or obscene gestures in front of the deceased or to burst forth into loud and sustained yells[2] ending up in roars of laughter. Their behaviour provokes unrestrained mirth among the visitors, but merely a faint smile on the faces of the widows and other near relatives. Everyone, except the near kinsmen of the deceased, is entitled to act the part of such a joker (*omwésekeli*) at a funeral, the professed idea of such a display of merriment being to cheer up the bereaved and to please the spirit of the deceased.

The generally unconcerned or even cheerful behaviour of the bulk of the mourners thus stands in marked contrast to the feelings of grief and sorrow shown by the widows and other close relatives of the deceased which bear all the symptoms of a genuine emotion. This contrast lends the whole scene a peculiar atmosphere which apparently impresses the native mind in quite a different way from that of the European. The general behaviour of the crowd strikes the European observer who endeavours to identify himself with the emotions felt by the bereaved as tactless and indifferent. The native mourners, on the other hand, as I was able to assure myself by frequent and careful observations, are in no way offended by the behaviour of the crowd of visitors, nor does it cause the latter any embarrassment to joke in the immediate presence of the deceased or to laugh right into the faces of the grief-stricken and weeping relatives.

The people who attend a funeral form as motley a crowd as their motives for coming are varied. The bulk of them usually consist of members of the deceased's clan, whether he be a man or a woman. Unless they are in European employment, people attend the funerals even of distant clansmen, especially if the latter have been well-known and respected old men. If a middle-aged man dies who has not been conspicuous for his wealth or his personality, only the people of his own lineage will come to his funeral, as well as those of his clansmen who live in his immediate neighbour-

[1] She used the transitive form *okufunyila*, to emit a smell.
[2] The sounds uttered by them which provoke the greatest laughter closely resemble the manner of Swiss and Tyrolese yodelling, e.g. *agodei i, ahi'*.

hood. If the death of a well-known elder should coincide with that of a person of no consequence in the same clan, the latter's funeral is completely eclipsed by that of his better-known fellow clansman, for merely a few dozen people will come and look at his body for a short time. The attendance of in-law relations and distant kinsmen at a funeral is not subject to any definite customary rule. If a male person dies, his wife's brothers and sisters will certainly come, even if they live some distance away, while the husbands of his sisters and the wives of his brothers only come if they live near by or if they have been on particularly good terms with the deceased. If a young woman dies, or one of middle age, the number of mourners who come from her own clan is often larger than that belonging to her husband's clan, but if she is an old woman with numerous offspring, she is given as big a funeral in her husband's clan as she would be in her own. Neighbours, as a rule, attend funerals regardless of their clan or kinship affiliations with the deceased, and, besides, there are always a few dozen people who spend their days loafing and who are to be found at every funeral far and wide even if they have to walk for miles following the sound of the funeral drum.

Age-grade solidarity, though not organized, also to some extent comes into action at a funeral. If an old man dies, there are far more old people present than at the death of a middle-aged or young man, while, if the deceased is a man of thirty-five or forty, most of the mourners, too, are of approximately his age.

The chief avowed motive for attending a funeral is to give vent to one's feeling of sorrow over the loss sustained and one's desire to see the deceased once more before he is buried. Closely linked with this motive, however, appears to be the fear of incurring the anger of the dead man's spirit by failing to be present at the funeral rites (especially in the case of near kinsmen), as well as the anxious wish to allay any suspicion on the part of the bereaved that one might be in any way responsible for the death that has occurred. In addition, the dances, the sights provided by the cattle-drive and the sham fight, and the general entertainment which any gathering of a large crowd offers, even though no food is distributed, serve as strong enough incentives for going to a funeral, especially for the crowd at large which is not connected with the deceased by any bonds of kinship or by personal sympathy.

Dirges

In the preceding account of the funeral rites we have already repeatedly referred to the dirges or laments which are sung or rather chanted by the mourners. There exist two types of these songs: the first are the dirges proper (*edzindzikulu*) which, as a rule, consist of short exclamations of sorrow over the bereavement, giving vent to the feeling of loneliness and helplessness which has overcome the mourner. Although in their general structure and in the manner in which they are chanted they all follow the same pattern, the actual wording is often made up by the singer *ad hoc*. Mostly, the dirge consists of a single line (or of two or three lines, each being a slight modification of the same idea) and a refrain. Preceding and following each line and between the frequent repetitions of the dirge, the mourner, in a low-pitched voice, chants the monotonous wailing tune: *yee yee ohe' yehe*, varying the pitch only by a semi-tone or a tone. The dirge itself is sung in a slightly higher pitch and in a faster rhythm, the melancholy monotony of the wailing-tune changing over into a more emotional although restrained outburst which has an undertone of a challenge or reproach. The dirges of this first type are sung by people of either sex, but more frequently by women than by men. They are usually sung by one person only, but sometimes a woman who runs along the road wailing is accompanied by other women who then join in the dirge, singing the refrain. While chanting them, the wailing attitude, which has been described above (p. 452), is adopted.

The second type of dirge (*elyimbu*, song) consists of songs with conventional texts either lamenting in a general way the sadness of death or the havoc wrought by the 'enemy disease', or commemorating the deeds of the great warriors or the courage of the whole tribe, thereby implicitly paying a tribute to the deceased. These dirges often consist of several lines, each expressing a different idea, both the wording and the melody being fixed. They are always sung by a group of people in accompaniment to a dance (*efiremba*), the song-leader (Lurogoli: *omuleteleli* or *omwimbi*; Tsotso: *omureresi*) singing the stanzas, while the chorus repeats the refrain and hums the preceding and the following tune. The song-leaders are young men who have gradually gained a reputation as clever singers and dancers by having shown their talents at funeral dances. They have no 'rights of ownership' in the various songs and appear to practise their art chiefly for the sake of their own enjoyment and the praise they get. They receive no pre-arranged payment for their services, but if they perform well, people throw things to them (pieces of clothing or money) to make them go on. The following are examples of both types of dirges which I have heard and recorded at various funerals:

1. *Edzindzikulu:*

> 1. *Vamenya voilele*
> *ludoye ekeyoyo Magui*
> *edzingulu dzianze vamali.*
>
> 'Strangers *voilele*,
> it (the sickness) chose a good person (of) Magui,
> they have finished my strength.'

This dirge was sung at the death of Manero, an elder of Magui (a place name in Maragoli), by one of his classificatory daughters. While chanting it she stood near the corpse and danced in the *lidegeriza* way, i.e. by vehemently shaking her shoulders. By the word 'strangers' she addressed the visitors from other clans who had come to the funeral. *Ludoye*, it chose, refers to *oluluaye*, 'disease', which had chosen a person of good character for its victim. *Ekeyoyo* is commonly used with reference to a good, pleasant, useful thing. The personal pronoun *va-* in *vamali*, 'they have finished', refers to the people who have caused Manero's death (cf. below, p. 486). The song thus bears witness to the prevailing idea of double causation, as it blames both the disease and human beings for Manero's death.

2. *Baba ma ondeki kunzila*
   ingadamba oyeye, oyeye,
   Orogo ondeka vava!

   'Father (then) you have left me on the road,
   it (the road) troubles me, oyeye, oyeye,
   Orogo, you left me oh, oh!'

One of Orogo's daughters sang this lament as she was running along the road wailing. 'To be left on the road or path' is a frequently used simile for 'to be left without support, without a home'. *Ingadamba* from *okudamba*, to trouble, to neglect, as people neglect orphans.

3. *Yeye yeye baba yakugoha,*
   sumbila avamiti.

   'Yeye yeye, father he is lost,
   please tell me who has killed him.'

The old woman who chanted this lament was no relative of the deceased, but it is customary in a dirge to call the dead person *baba* or *mama* respectively. The relative pronoun *ava-* which refers to the living class indicates that she suspects other people to have killed him by sorcery.

4. *Omukulundu wange, omivuli wavana,*
   kuvunaniki lelo!
   Omukulundu wavagonda
   kuvunaniki lelo?

   'My old man, begetter of children,
   what do we want now?
   Old man of the Gonda (clan),
   what do we want now?'

Leaning over the corpse and shaking her shoulders, the singer asked her dead husband in an angry voice, 'What is left for us to do?' The deceased was an elder of the Gonda clan who had left many children behind, and the widow is wondering how she is to rear them without her husband's help. It is customary for a wife to address and refer to her husband as 'my old man' instead of *omusaza wange*, my husband.

5. *Omulina wange ovoye oye oye*
   ma onyagi na inze nkolendi?
   Omulina wange ovoye oye oye,
   oleganyi ndayinga vudzwa
   omulina wange.

'My friend, ovoye oye oye,
then you took (him) away by force and I what can I do?
My friend, ovoye oye oye,
you left me behind (now) I shall wander about in sorrow only,
my friend.'

This dirge was sung at the funeral of an unmarried youth by one of his clan-sisters just before the corpse was lowered into the grave. 'You took him away by force' means here 'you killed him out of spite'. The words are addressed to the unknown sorcerer whom she accuses of killing the boy. *Oleganyi*, from *kuleganya*, which also has the connotations, 'to refuse someone's company, to leave behind by death, to defy'. Used in this connexion, it seems to express the idea that the deceased yielded to the sorcerer's scheme because he did not care sufficiently for his living friends. Otherwise he would have tried to recover.

6. *Nyinga ngoni kunzila*
 nyinga nalye' navo?
 Nyinganga, Avayose! ngoni kunzila
 nyinganga naŋendange navo?
 Nyinganga.

'I wander about, I lie (helplessly) on the road,
I wander about, with whom may I eat?
I am wandering about, Avayose! I lie on the road,
I am wandering about, with whom am I going to walk?
I am wandering about!'

The verb *okuyinga* is also used with the following meanings, 'to become a fool, to worry desperately, to disregard all rules of good behaviour owing to mental distress'. *Okugona kunzila*, 'to sleep on the path', is a frequently used simile for 'to be homeless, to be without economic support'.

The dead man to whom this dirge was addressed was a Christian, Isaka, who had left two unmarried daughters but no sons. The dirge was sung by one of them while her father's brother nailed the coffin. She stood at the head of the coffin clenching her bill-hook with both hands (one of the conventional wailing attitudes) and chanted the lament in a low, monotonous voice. When she had finished, her sister stepped forward and in the same manner chanted the following two songs:

7. *Yeyeyeye Avayose yeyeye,*
 nakorovolane navo?
 Avayose aviko vava,
 nanyingele nayi lelo,
 mboganga lelo
 vangose vange mulilova novudinyu
 ndinanga lelo.

'Yeyeye Avayose yeyeye,
with whom may I talk?
Avayose, (my) kinsmen oh!

DEATH AND MOURNING

where may I enter now.
I am wandering now,
my sisters in the country it is difficult.
I am an orphan now.'

8. *Mboganga lelo,*
   nanyingele hayi lelo?
   Isaka omugosi
   nanyingele hayi lelo?
   Ehili yange Isaka enyangala
   Isaka omudelua
   nanyingele hayi lelo?

   'I am wandering now,
   where may I enter now?
   Isaka (was) a gentle person,
   where may I enter now?
   my clan Isaka a single person,
   Isaka the only one,
   where may I enter now?'

The end of the last dirge stresses the fact that Isaka left no sons, so that his daughters are now abandoned to their fate having no near relative to take care of them. Actually, of course, Isaka's brother steps into his place, but it is customary in a dirge to overstate the economic distress that follows in the wake of death. The other relatives will not take offence if those immediately bereaved complain in the lament of being left entirely without help and sympathy.

9. *Yeyey ohé yeyeye,*
   nyenyanga vudzwa mma!
   yeyeye, &c.

   'I am wondering only, mother!'

This short lament was sung by a young woman a few minutes after her mother had died. As she sang it, tears ran down her cheeks and she ran along the road, obviously in genuine distress.

10. *Yaa ahá amiru alahunya*
    amiru alahunya
    yaa ahá vasomi namulole
    mwana weru ovwungi yaa aha.

    'Yaa aha (our) sister she will decay
    (our) sister will decay,
    yaa aha, readers, you may see
    our child is a (lifeless) heap,
    our child is a heap.'

The deceased in this case was an unmarried Christian girl of the Tiriki tribe. The lament was sung and danced by her pagan sisters, the eldest one leading the song and the others repeating the refrain (lines 2 and 5). While

H h

dancing they formed a semicircle round the corpse. The song was addressed to the Christian mourners who filled the yard singing hymns and listening to the sermon of a preacher. The word *avasomi*, 'readers', is often indiscriminately used by pagans with reference to anyone who 'follows the mission way' whether actually Christian or not. By telling the Christians that their sister is a lifeless heap, they want to drive home to them the futility of their faith which failed to save their sister, a young and strapping girl, from succumbing to the powers of evil magic.

11. *Mayi iwe*
vasamula sevalota.

'Mother, you
who went to the garden they are not coming home.'

I heard a Vugusu husband singing this dirge as he went about wailing shortly before sunset a few weeks after his wife's death. Apparently the second line expresses the idea that his wife is now not coming home from her daily work in the field as she used to do when she was still alive. It is not clear, however, why he refers to her in the plural.

2. *Edzinyimbu* (dirges of the second type)

Some dirges of the second type have already been quoted in connexion with the account of the Tadjoni cattle drive and dance. Here are some others which I heard at funerals among the Logoli and Marama:

1. *Haha Aliero, haha Aliero*
Aliero asananga wagarani
Aliero ahinganga hahá
ye Aliero hinganga,
asavanga wagarani haha oroyo!
omilu gwe ligungu haha oraye!
asaluma haha oroyo!
wiganya mufumbwa wange,
asananga wagarani
haha Aliero, haha Aliero.

'Haha Aliero, haha Aliero
Aliero is asking you to fight
Aliero is (always) boasting, haha
ye Aliero is boasting
he is asking you to fight, haha oroyo.
The tail feather of the *ligungu*-bird (Egyptian stork), haha oraye
it bites, haha oroyo,
mind my enemy who comes at night
he is asking you to fight,
haha Aliero, haha Aliero.'

Aliero is the name of a legendary enemy who is supposed to have been so strong that he could not be killed. The tail feather of the Egyptian stork is the symbol of the warrior going out to meet the enemy. It is fastened to the headgear, so that it sways in the wind. The word *mufumbwa*, 'the enemy who comes at night', refers to Aliero who apparently was a Nandi, for they are said to have come exclusively during the night to raid the villages of the Bantu Kavirondo. This song was sung at Manero's funeral by a group of warriors of his age-class while performing a sham fight shortly before he was buried. In this particular context the song is intended as a praise of Manero's courage, for he used to put on the tail feather of the *ligungu*-bird when meeting his enemies, as did the man in the song who answered the challenge of the boastful Aliero. The wording of the song, however, is conventional, and it was formerly also sung as a war and victory song.

> 2. *Salanga eŋombe evuhando*
> *ehindanga ſigo.*
>
> 'I am begging the cow at *vuhando*
> (but) it is waiting in the cattle partition.'

Like the previous one, this song praises the activities of the deceased as a warrior. 'The cow of Vuhando' stands here for the hostile warrior at Vuhando (a place-name in the country of the enemies) who failed to accept the dead man's challenge for a fight and stayed at home. His behaviour is compared with that of a cow which refuses to leave the cattle partition of the hut when the people come to fetch it to be slaughtered.

> 3. *Vuhingu vwange ita embezi kerumbesi*
> *ita embezi kerumbesi.*
>
> 'My bow and arrow kill the bush-pig, the bush-pig,
> kill the bush-pig!'

The word *embezi*, bush-pig, stands here for enemy. The singer implores his bow and arrow to kill the enemy; in its primary context the song probably served as a magic spell spoken or chanted over the weapons before starting out for a fight. *Kerumbesi* is merely a euphonic elaboration of *embesi*.

> 4. *Ayiyohe ayiyohe asava ovulwani,*
> *engo engo elalila*
> *ayiyohe asialuma.*
>
> 'Ayiyohe ayiyohe, he begs for a fight,
> the leopard will howl,
> ayiyohe he'll maul everyone.'

The challenging warrior is here compared with a fierce leopard.

> 5. *Singila ngeleka*
> *Muŋole yasingila ngeleka*
> *akasambila Maina,*
> *siya omilu*
> *dembela ngeleka.*

'Stand over yonder,
Muŋole stand yonder,
he burns (a lethal herb) for Maina,
Clean the tail feather,
Wave (it) over yonder.'

Muŋole is an old magician who destroys the enemy Maina by burning certain herbs the smoke of which will kill him. The last two lines refer to the custom of cleaning the tail feather of the Egyptian stork (cf. above) after a successful fight and dancing with it to a victory song, looking towards the country of the enemy and waving the feather in the rhythm of the dance.

6. *Omufumbwa wange ahongeranga oludwalo oroyo*
   omilu gweligungu ragongoraye oroyo
   embwa gadigadi embwa
   embwa gadigadi embwa
   ndola evugwe amayai galimala oho.

'The enemy (who comes at night) is always roaming about, oroyo,
(with) the tail feather of the *ligungu*-bird ragongoraye oroyo,
the dog is barking, the dog,
the dog is barking, the dog,
I see the blight (i.e. enemies) from the east they will finish (us) oho.'

This song contrasts strangely with the preceding ones. Instead of making reassuring statements on their own strength and success in warfare, it is a gloomy vision of destruction by the enemies from the east (Nandi and Masai) who are always roaming about at night and who betray their nearness by causing the dogs to bark.

The following four songs I have heard at a funeral in the Marama tribe. It is said that they are the four traditional mourning songs which have been handed down to the people by their forefathers. They are chanted by the members of the dead man's age-grade as accompaniment to the dance which they perform before the sham fight. They must only be sung, however, at the death of a person who has no elder brother living, as 'otherwise the singing of these songs would cause the elder brother to die as well'.

7. *Haha nisié inzofu*
   inzofu iſevungwa xumaxanda.

'Haha I am an elephant,
the elephant is being cut on the skin.'

According to my informants this song means that the deceased man was strong and fierce like an elephant, but even the elephant succumbs to death when his skin is ripped open by spears. It expresses the idea that even the strongest people are not immune from death.

8. *Nisie wetete*
   ahandzia nimbimwa.

'I am (like) a grass-hopper,
wherever I go I am hunted down.'

DEATH AND MOURNING

This song, likewise, although in a different way, stresses the helplessness of man in his struggle against death and disease.

9. *Yimbwi ilalila omusika nomumira*
yimbwi ilalila
ilalila omusika nomumira.

'The wildcat will cry tear(s) and snivel,
the wildcat will cry,
it will cry tear(s) and snivel.'

The meaning of this song is that the mourners will cry for sorrow and anguish like the wildcat. A mourner who is furious over the death of a friend and bent on revenge is called a wildcat.

10. *Haha omwenya haa,*
hayaya haha omwenya haa
ha omwenya.

The only word in this song which has any meaning is *omwenya*, joy. It is always sung at the end of the dirges and is said 'to make the hearts of the people glad and to help them to overcome their grief'. While singing it the people dance in a circle, holding hands and waving their arms up and down as an expression of joy.

(4) BURIAL

The procedure followed when burying a person shows a number of variations according to the sex, age, and social status as well as certain peculiarities of the deceased. Further, the present-day modes of burial even among pagans differ in some essential points from traditional custom, the innovations being partly due to the influence of Mohammedan burial customs and partly to regulations passed by the British authorities for reasons of hygiene. The tribal variations, on the other hand, appear to be negligible, at least as far as the traditional modes of burial are concerned.

Among all the Bantu tribes of Kavirondo the traditional manner of disposing of the dead is by interment in fairly deep graves.[1] Among the Vugusu the 'throwing of the naked corpse into the bush' was occasionally practised as an alternative to interment, if the deceased had expressed a particular desire not to be buried. In explanation of this peculiar deviation from the norm I was told that 'some people disliked the idea of the soil being thrown on their bodies and of other people trampling on their graves'.[2] In such a case, therefore, the corpse was merely carried into the

---

[1] Among the Vugusu the graves are said formerly to have had a depth of about 3 feet; the majority of graves which I have seen, however, had a depth ranging between 5 and 7 feet.

[2] It is possible that the throwing of corpses into the bush has some connexion with the cannibalism with corpses which has been reported from the Bagishu and which, as some Vugusu elders admitted to me, was practised among some Vugusu clans.

bush, laid on the ground, and covered with leaves, but no precautions were taken against its being devoured by hyenas and vultures.

According to traditional custom, the burial of an ordinary person takes place on the day following his death, so that there is one full night for keeping vigil by the dead and to permit even those of his relatives who live at a distance to receive the death message and to come and see their dead kinsman before he is buried. Elders of higher social status are buried on the second or third day after death, and in the case of the clan-head the burial may even be delayed until the fourth day. Such a delay is founded on the belief that it will please the spirit of the deceased to remain in the company of the living as long as possible, so that he may 'see' the mourners and watch the performance of the cattle-drive and the sham fight while he is not yet in the grave. Infants and small children, on the other hand, are usually buried a few hours after they have died, a custom which is in accordance with the prevailing notion that the spirits of children are 'powerless' and that it is therefore unnecessary to take much trouble over them.

The customary time of day for burying a person is either in the morning or late in the afternoon when the sun sets. The latter time is considered to be appropriate for persons of higher standing, and it is also the time which naturally results from the fact that the digging of the grave usually takes the greater part of the day. My informants always insisted that a person must not be buried in the heat of the day (although I saw this happen on various occasions). This rule appears to be based on the belief that the deceased will be more willing to part from the living, sleep in the grave, and generally submit to his fate when he is buried as darkness falls than he might be in the middle of the day.

The grave (Lurogoli: *kilindwa*) may be dug anywhere in the hard-trodden yard in front of the living-hut, but it is usually to the right of the entrance in the case of a man and to the left in the case of a woman. Women were always buried outside in the yard, but men were sometimes interred near the centre post inside the hut, if they had uttered a particular desire to that effect (cf. below). The grave of a polygynous elder was always inside or in front of the living-hut of his great wife, while a married woman was buried in front of her own hut. Women who had not been married for very long were, and occasionally still are, buried at their father's or brother's homestead, if their own relatives insist on fetching them back to their place.[1]

The duty of digging the grave rests with the brothers of the deceased; in the case of a woman, both her own brother and near clansmen of her husband join in the work. Persons directly bereaved (such as sons or husbands) are not expected to help dig the grave, 'as they would have no strength in their grief', nor have I ever seen a woman join in the work of

---

[1] Thus the only sister of my cook, Amiani, was buried at her father's homestead although she did not die there. Her husband's place was about three miles away. It was her father's wish that she should be buried at his homestead.

making a grave. Under ordinary circumstances people are not afraid to dig the grave or to handle the corpse; but in the case of a person who has committed suicide or been struck by lightning, the grave-diggers fear to be infected or contaminated by the evil power which had taken possession of the deceased. They can, therefore, claim a special payment for their services and must afterwards undergo a rite of purification (cf. above, p. 248).

Among the Nyole the digging of the grave is preceded by the pantomimic performance of a beer-drink, and the tools used for digging the grave are ritually prepared, as is described in the following text:

'One old man may ask the people that an old hoe be tied to a handle. The one who is called "his brother" (i.e. any classificatory brother of the deceased) may ask the wife herself, and she may tell him where the hoe is in the loft (*elilungu*). He may go and take it together with a handle and a piece of string. When he has finished (fetching these things) he may bring them out to the yard where the "blower" (*ombidi*) is and he may then tie the hoe to the handle. When he has finished doing so, he may also cut a digging-stick and put it together with the hoe. The great wife may then be asked (to supply) a pot of the kind called *olusumbi* which may be broken into pieces. And she may also tell them where an *esipala* (a wide-necked pot) is. And the *sumbi*-pots are two: one which may be broken into pieces and another one which may be placed on the ground together with the *esipala*; the beer-pipes may be put in; then they act as if they pour beer into (the pots), and the dancers dance and the singers sing the songs of the beer. Then they beat against the (*sumbi*) pots and rap against them with sticks. Then the sister (of the deceased) may take the *sumbi*-pot and break it into pieces. Then she may pull the grass off the roof; she may wail, and when she has finished wailing, an old man may sweep off the potsherds and they may begin to dig the grave.'

The shape of the grave is either rectangular or oval, and the walls are dug vertically to a depth of about 5 or 6 feet (nowadays 7 or 8 feet). One or two men dig simultaneously, standing in the grave, but as they take turns with others, there are usually four persons engaged in digging the grave, whose task it also is to lower the body into the grave.

Both in Kitosh and in Maragoli—provided that no coffin is used—the corpse is not placed at the bottom of the grave proper but in a special burial-chamber. In Kitosh this chamber consists of a trench (with vertical walls) which extends along the centre of the bottom of the grave and is just long, wide, and deep enough to receive the corpse. When the corpse has been placed inside on a bedding of grass the trench is covered with a layer of sticks flush with the bottom of the grave proper. The sticks are then covered by a layer of grass which must be freshly plucked for this purpose and not pulled from the roof of a hut, lest 'the widow or one of the children of the deceased will die'. On top of the grass a layer of mud should, in turn, be put, but this does not appear to be essential, for at two Vugusu funerals which I attended it was dispensed with, as the soil was very dry and there was not enough water to turn it into mud.

Among the Logoli a similar burial-chamber used to be constructed in former days, but, according to the description which I was given, the chamber was cut into the side of the grave instead of the bottom. These burial-chambers, which, under Mission influence, are rapidly being replaced by coffins, appear to be a fairly recent feature of the Bantu Kavirondo burial customs. Some of my informants claimed that they were introduced only a few generations ago by natives who had adopted the Moslem faith, but I did not inquire very thoroughly into that matter.

An ordinary person is buried entirely naked. Even his ornaments, talismans, and amulets are taken off, and none of his personal belongings or utensils of daily use are placed in the grave with him.[1] The body is always laid on its side, the head resting on one hand as in sleep. It faces the direction whence the clan of the deceased is believed to have come originally, and whither the spirit of the dead person is eventually supposed to go. Among the Vugusu the dead are thus usually made to face the north-west, as they think that their original tribal abode lay in a north-westerly direction from their present home (cf. above, p. 23); a Wanga man whose funeral I attended near Kimilili was buried with his head pointing to the south-east which was in keeping with the Wanga tradition that they originally lived in the country of the Tiriki (cf. above, p. 24). Theoretically the corpse should always rest on its right side. Among the Vugusu I was told in explanation of this rule that 'if the shadow of the deceased wants to leave the grave, he needs the strength of his right arm to get up and force a passage for himself through the soil of the grave'. In practice, however, no great importance appears to be attached to this point, for I have often seen corpses lying on their left shoulder. Among the Nyole the head of the deceased, to protect it from being covered with soil, is sandwiched between two large leaves through which holes have been pierced to provide a passage for the spirit when it desires to depart from the body through the ears. All these customs, though differing locally in detail, are based on the general idea of facilitating the movements of the dead man's spirit and so pleasing and appeasing it.

Before the corpse is buried, a short ceremonial speech is addressed to the deceased imploring him not to bear any grudge against the living, while the actual moment of lowering the corpse into the grave is marked by a renewed and violent outbreak of wailing. The sequence of events at a Nyole burial is described in the following narrative by a Nyole elder:

'When they have finished digging (the grave) they may appoint two buriers (*avari*) who may bury him. The one who seizes him by his head is his clansman (*omundu omuluhia wavue*), and the one who seizes him by his feet is his

---

[1] Only among the Tsotso the switch of the raffia palm which the deceased held behind his back while he was being circumcised is placed in the grave with him. Into a woman's grave they put the stalk of the *ilivanze*-plant, a weed growing among the eleusine crop.

maternal cousin (*omufiala nyene*).¹ Then they may carry (the body) out of the house with screams, and when they wail the children and sisters (of the dead man) must leave off (wailing). . . . And the men (only) may take the corpse from the house with screams and laments (*netsixwisi netsilakaya*). And the horns are sounded, the shriekers shriek, the youths stamp the ground, and also those of his age-class may "step down" and say: "We have been overcome; we said you would sleep in the enemies' (country),² we did not know that you would die from the disease of wailing.³ It is (the disease) which came with the people from long ago, and it will come with us (too)."⁴ And when they have finished (saying) those (words) the corpse may be laid out on top of the grave-soil; and an old man who passes them all (in age) and who has killed two people⁵ may stand up, and when they see him standing up they must all sit down. There may not be even one who may stand or speak; only the horns may wail and the shriekers may shriek. And who has killed eight people and who has killed six people or four people, they may follow behind his back.⁶ And even who captured five cows in the war or two only and some goats, he may be there. The reason is that they are of one age-class; they belonged to one herd of cattle (which they used) to herd and also they began to wage war in one year. Then the old man will lament and say: "Our brother, I was always saying you will be killed in the war, I did not know that you would die the death of wailing. It is that which came with the country."⁷ Then he bids him farewell: "You may go and cool off,⁸ and we who remain, may we stay in peace, we who remain outside."⁹ Then he (the corpse) may be put into the grave and they may bring the leaves and pierce two holes in them, one (leaf to be placed) on top of one ear and the second underneath the other ear. His adornments, the iron-rings, armlets and necklaces with which he used to go, may all be taken off, and the one who takes them off is the person who is going to wear them (i.e. his brother or his eldest son). Then he will look as he did when he came from his mother's womb. When they have finished (stripping the corpse) they may bury him¹⁰ and, standing on the soil of the grave, all the people start wailing; then they wail the wailing cries. The widows may stand under the eaves of the hut, but they cannot wail, because

---

¹ The term *omufiala* also refers to a father's sister's son, but here it means the (real or classificatory) son of the mother's brother.

² i.e. you would be killed in the war.

³ i.e. from sickness instead of from a wound inflicted by a weapon in the war.

⁴ This assurance to the deceased that disease has always caused people to die and will also kill those who still live implies that he should not bear any grudge against the living as being responsible for his death. Cf. below, 'Death came with the country', i.e. death is as old as the country in which we live.

⁵ i.e. he must be a renowned warrior.

⁶ i.e. they may sit behind the old man who addresses the dead person.

⁷ Cf. note 4.

⁸ *Onyire* from *oxunyira*, to get cool (like porridge or any hot food). It is generally said of spirits that they cool off after some time, i.e. they become appeased and reconcile themselves to their fate, cf. p. 167.

⁹ That means, in the world of the living.

¹⁰ The body is carefully lifted and received by several men standing inside the grave. They gently put him down in the proper position and then climb out of the grave.

(if they did so) they would turn pale.¹ And he (the dead person) cannot be buried if the cattle which belong to him are out on the pasture; the cattle, the goats, and the sheep may all be driven to the yard, and the granaries may be opened, and the eleusine may be taken out and given to the singers. The sorghum and the beans, too, may be given away: sesame, peas, black peas, and bananas, everything may be taken outside and given away, together with other things which had already been brought outside to where he (the corpse) was lying on the skin anointed with ghee.'

The last sentence refers to the custom of taking the dead man's sleeping-skin out to the yard on the morning after he has died. It is anointed with ghee and the corpse is laid out on it. Then heaps of sorghum, eleusine, and other stores from the dead man's personal granaries[2] are piled up by the side of his body and sesame seeds are thrown over him. After the burial the mourners, especially the old women, may freely help themselves to these foodstuffs and also to other objects and utensils which have been placed beside the corpse. This generous distribution of the deceased's personal grain-stores and other possessions is to reward the mourners for having come and shown their sympathy with the bereaved. Besides, it is said to bring misfortune to the widows and their children if they were to keep such property of the deceased for themselves. The members of the dead man's family apparently fear to appropriate for their own use the cherished personal belongings of the deceased, because he used to guard them so jealously during his lifetime.

The foregoing account of the traditional burial rites among the Nyole tallies almost completely with the accounts given to me among the Logoli, Tsotso, and Vugusu.[3] The comparison of the naked corpse in the grave with a child 'when it comes from its mother's womb' was rendered in exactly the same words by my Logoli and my Vugusu informants, and it seems, therefore, to imply more than a mere circumlocution for the state of complete nakedness. It is significant in this connexion that a new-born infant, a person who has recently died, and the initiate who has just been circumcised are all called *omusinde* and that they must all be completely naked.[4]

Before the grave is filled in the near relatives of the deceased drop a handful of soil on the body. When they have done so they say, 'Now I have put you into the grave.' If a widow refuses or hesitates to perform this rite

---

[1] That is to say, her skin would turn pale and spotted and would look like an over-ripe banana.

[2] Every man has one or two granaries of his own which his wife may not touch, the contents of which he uses mainly for brewing beer (cf. vol. ii).

[3] Only the wailing customs differ among the various tribes. Thus the prohibition for the widows to wail while the body of their deceased husband is lowered into the grave applies only to the Nyole.

[4] These analogies will be discussed more fully in a special chapter of the second volume where an attempt will be made to define the meaning of the various rites that mark the crises of life.

she thereby tacitly admits having been unfaithful to her husband, for in that case the throwing of the soil into her husband's grave would entail for her the same dangers as standing by the side of her husband's death-bed. At a funeral near Kimilili I saw how a child of about fifteen months was carried to the edge of its father's grave and made to throw a handful of soil into it, 'so that later when it is grown-up it may remember the time when its father died'.

The burial-mound is usually left bare and becomes a favourite spot to which the widow and relatives or friends of the deceased repair to wail or sing dirges. To keep hyenas from digging up the grave the buriers cover it with branches of the *ovurala*-plant and quantities of a certain grass (*lixa*) the smell of which is said to be loathsome to hyenas. In some cases, objects belonging to the deceased and valued by him are placed on the grave for a few days. On the grave of a wealthy Tadjoni cattle-owner I saw, for instance, a milking-jug and gourd, the branch of a raffia palm, a switch of the *gumudjandjasi*-tree, and the hoe which had been used for digging the grave. In Maragoli the four corners of the burial-mound are often marked by sticks, stuck vertically into the ground (about 3 feet high), but this is said to be a Moslem custom which has been introduced only recently.

Should the relatives of the deceased harbour any suspicions that the death has been caused by sorcery or witchcraft, they keep a close vigil near the grave for several nights, as it is thought that the person who committed the evil act will visit the grave under cover of darkness to perform there a certain rite which will protect him from the revenge of the dead man's spirit. Thus, if an *omulogi* has caused the death, he is supposed to come on the second night after the burial and jump over the grave, thereby 'tying' the spirit of the deceased, so that he cannot harm him (Maragoli). An *ombila*, on the other hand, is said to protect himself from the spirit's revenge by visiting the grave on the first night after the funeral and collecting a handful of soil from it. This he takes home with him where he grinds it into fine powder and mixes it with a certain medicine which serves as an antidote against the spirit's revenge. This mixture he must soak in water and then drink it out of a calabash like gruel. An alternative method[1] is to dig a narrow hole in the grave where the head of the corpse is and pour boiling water into it. This is supposed to frighten the spirit, so that he will refrain from avenging his own death. Stories are told both in Kitosh and in Maragoli according to which the vigil by the grave actually *has* led to the detection of witches and sorcerers.

The burial of a clan-head (cf. above, p. 76) differed in many respects from that of an ordinary person. These differences are particularly significant, as they present one of the few instances among the Bantu Kavirondo where social and political leadership finds a clear outward recognition by a differentiation in ceremonial behaviour. From the information which I have been able to gather it appears that, in contrast to the burial customs

[1] Among the Vugusu.

pertaining to ordinary persons, the manner of burying a clan-head showed considerable tribal differences, corresponding to the varying degrees of political integration and authority among the different tribes. Among the Wanga, who had attained to the highest degree of political integration, we encounter the most elaborate burial customs for the heads of their major clans.[1] The following two accounts of a clan-head's burial refer to the Logoli and the Tsotso, the latter being neighbours of the Wanga and very closely akin to them both as regards language and custom. Among the Vugusu, I could not discover any formal differences between the burial of ordinary elders and that of the *omwene lugova* (the owner of a walled village) or the *omugasa munene* (the big leader or clan-head). The burial of their leading men is said to have been marked merely by the attendance of a larger crowd and the full observance of all ritual details which in the case of a person of lower status are often omitted or curtailed owing to a lack of the necessary paraphernalia, such as ghee, animals for slaughter, &c. This fact, again, corresponds to the complete absence, among the Vugusu, of any formal symbols of political authority.

The burial of a leading person or clan-head among the Logoli is described in the following narrative of a Logoli elder:

'According to our customs of long ago the following things were done when a leading person (*omundu mudúkilu*) was very ill and near to die. His eldest son together with his "little fathers" (i.e. the younger brothers of the sick person) must go and build a small hut at the fire-place[2] near the house in which the father is lying ill. This little hut then "waits" until he has died. And at the time he has been defeated by the illness and died, it is not good that any person may wail, not even at a distance; they must all tell one another to remain silent. When his people have received the death message they may come, (but) they must not come to the house (of the deceased), they all must listen[3] only at the fire-place near the house of that dead man. Now when that father (i.e. the clan-head) has finished dying, he must first be put on a skin in the house in which he has died. Then his son and the "little father" must go into the small hut which they have built and dig the grave near the centre pole of that small hut. After the digging is finished, all people, even the dead man's wives and children, except his great wife, his brother, and his eldest son, must remain there.[4] Then they must take the corpse and put it into the grave they have dug inside the little hut which they have built at the fire-place near his homestead. The reason why they do so is that they do not want any person who is still young to see the corpse.

When the sun is near to set, they must call his eldest grandson and they must give him the dead man's cooking-pot (*nyambeva*) in which he used to

[1] These have been described by K. Dundas (1913, pp. 28-29), but as I have done no fieldwork among the Wanga I cannot expand his account.
[2] Round this fire-place, *oluhia*, the elders of the clan meet every morning to discuss the news of the previous day and to serve as arbitrators in disputes brought before them. The term *oluhia*, therefore, also designates the clan (cf. above, p. 55).
[3] i.e. they must sit there quietly.
[4] i.e. away from the hut where the body of the deceased is.

cook the fowls.[1] Then his grandson must go with that pot to the fire-place. Later he must leave there with the pot and wail until he reaches the dead man's house. When he has arrived there he must break (the neck off) the pot. While he is there he gives permission to everybody to wail. Before he breaks this pot nobody may wail. When the neck of the pot has been broken off, they must take the *oludju* (the pot minus its neck) of that pot and place it over the dead man's head. All these things are done before they fill up the grave with soil. When the grandson has finished doing so, they can throw the earth on him (i.e. the corpse). And later they must plant trees on his grave and these must be *emigumu* and *emivuti* trees only. When these things have been done, all people must blow calabash bugles and horns and play on the lyres and flutes. This will tell the people that a person has died who was a person of power.'

As this account shows, the burial of a clan-head among the Logoli differed in four major respects from that of an ordinary person: (1) He was not buried in his own private or family yard in front of his hut, but near his *oluhia*, the fire-place round which he and the other clan-elders used to sit in council. This *oluhia* among the Logoli is not yet a 'public place' in the sense that it has been permanently set off as a 'common' for clan functions irrespective of family rights, for it is the same kind of fire-place which every ordinary elder has near his homestead and where he cooks fowls for religious and social ceremonies or meets his age-mates to gossip with them. In the case of the recognized leader of the clan, however, his fire-place becomes, in fact, a centre of clan-life to which all elders have the right of access and which thereby acquires a communal and political significance. The burial of the clan-head on the *oluhia*, the erection of a special burial hut on that spot, and the planting of certain trees, so that the burial site may be permanently marked, all serve to emphasize and maintain beyond his physical death the superior social status of the clan-head and thus are instrumental in strengthening the political integration of the clan. (2) In contrast to the funeral of ordinary elders where—as we have seen—the sons of the deceased have no ceremonial functions to perform, in the case of a clan-head's burial both the eldest son and the eldest grandson have specific duties assigned to them. The son assists his father's brothers in building the shrine and digging the grave, and the grandson is the first who has the right to wail and to break the cooking-pot of the deceased. (3) The deceased is buried with a pot placed over his head. Among all the Bantu tribes of Kavirondo, where clan-heads are formally recognized, this trait constitutes the chief means of differentiating the burial of a leading person from that of commoners. It seems probable that a cooking-pot has been chosen as such a symbol of differentiation because the ability and willingness to offer food and drink to one's clansmen is one of the chief means of acquiring prestige and political leadership (cf. above, p. 79). (4) The superior status of a deceased clan-head finds a further expression in the

[1] Meaning the fowls he offered to his guests.

mass of the mourners being prevented from seeing the corpse from near by (the corpse is not laid out in the yard like that of an ordinary person but kept inside the burial hut and the mourners may not enter the hut but must stay at the *oluhia*) and in the prohibition of wailing until his eldest grandson has chanted the first lament and broken the pot, thereby giving the general signal for wailing.

Inquiries into the significance of these customs yielded—as usual— merely the general reply that it was the rule handed down from the ancestors to behave in this manner towards a deceased clan-head. Whatever their original meaning, however, the prohibition of wailing immediately after the clan-head's death and the keeping of mourners at a distance from the corpse are clearly instrumental in preventing a political crisis from arising in the clan-community; for it is particularly those moments when the kinsmen of a dead person begin to wail and when they look at the corpse which evoke those outbursts of uncontrolled passion which may easily lead to quarrels and mutual accusations and thus to a disruption of the clan community. The risk of such an outbreak is reduced when these passions are restrained until his son's and grandson's rights of (ultimate) succession to their father's office have been concretely demonstrated and established by the performance of definite ritual duties in connexion with the clan-head's burial.

The prohibition against the mourners seeing the corpse has, moreover, a significant parallel in the behaviour towards twins who are, likewise, secluded in the hut, as it is thought to be fraught with danger to others to see them until they have reached a certain age.

The burial of a clan-head among the Tsotso is characterized by essentially the same features, although the procedure differs in some respects from that described for the Logoli.

The grave is not dug inside the hut or in the yard of the clan-head's homestead, but at a secluded place in the bush where former clan-heads have already been buried. Burial sites of this kind, which after some persuading I was shown by some Tsotso elders, are located at the base of large old trees with widespread crowns, but no preference seems to be given to any particular kind of tree. These sites are approached only through dense bush and along hidden paths kept in bad repair, so that they can only with difficulty be detected by strangers or unauthorized persons. The burial site itself is marked by two beer-pots into which small libations of beer are poured for the spirits of the dead whenever a beer-offering is made. A beer-tube is placed in each of the two pots, so as to enable the spirits of the deceased clan-heads to suck the beer consecrated to them in the same manner as they used to do when they were still alive. On the other hand, I did not discover any sacrificial stones or huts at these burial sites; the offerings of meat, blood, and porridge are made on three flat trays (*efixowovwe*) made from banana-bark which are placed next to the pots.

When the clan-head feels that his end is approaching, he summons his sons to his sick-bed and appoints one of them as his successor, not necessarily the eldest one but the one whom he trusts most and whom he considers best suited to administer his estate. The son who has been appointed as the father's successor must then select an ox from his father's herd, killing it by means of a spear while a second son holds it by a rope. The animal's meat is then divided between the two sons who dig the grave.

In contrast to the ordinary dead, the clan-head is buried in a sitting position. His sleeping-skin is spread out for him to sit on. Then his youngest wife shaves his head, on which one of the clan-elders places a cap which is adorned with cowrie-shells and with the long, red tail feathers of the *Yixu*-bird. This head-dress (*efimuata*) reaches on either side over his cheeks and is tied together under his chin. After he has been lowered into the grave, a beer-pot (*indenyexo*) is placed by his side and a beer-tube inserted into his mouth. Finally, his eldest grandson climbs down into the grave and places a pot (*likyo*) over both his head and the head-dress. At the place where the eyes of the deceased are, holes have previously been drilled through the walls of the pot, so that he may be able to peep out. His head, however, does not protrude from the grave—as in the case of the deceased chiefs among the Wanga—but is about one yard under the surface of the ground. For the first three nights after the burial the grave remains open and during this time is guarded day and night by two members of the dead man's clan.

Just as the manner of burying a clan-head differs from that of interring commoners, so the burial of confirmed witches, criminals, persons afflicted with physical abnormalities, and people who have died under unusual circumstances or in an unwonted manner differs from that of ordinary persons. My Logoli informants, for instance, assured me that habitual criminals (murderers, incorrigible thieves, or *avalogi* caught in the act of performing their witchcraft) in former times were buried at a secluded spot in the bush in a vertical position, with their heads pointing downwards and their feet sticking out of the grave. The grave, in such a case, was hurriedly dug by hired grave-diggers who demanded a sheep or a goat from the deceased man's herd or from his nearest clan-relatives as payment for their services. After having performed their duty they had, moreover, to undergo a purification rite so as to escape the revenge of the dead man's spirit. The nearest relatives and clan-members of the deceased, accordingly, no longer considered the deceased as a member of their community and therefore denied him the death-rites and the care to which any ordinary dead person is entitled.

Hunchbacks (Lurogoli: *vekiguku*), too, are said formerly to have been buried without the usual rites being afforded to them; they were placed in the grave by strangers who could claim a goat for their service.

At the funeral of a barren woman all young men and women who were still unmarried or without children had to keep away from the corpse and from the grave for fear that they likewise might become sterile.

If a pregnant woman dies among the Vugusu, she must not be buried with the child in her womb, for it is feared that this might entail the death of further members of the clan. In such a case, the foetus—even if it is only three or four months old—must be removed from the womb by a specialist, the so-called *omuari*, and buried in a special grave. After the deceased woman has been placed in the grave which, in this case, must be dug by a female person (either by the mother or the mother-in-law of the dead woman), the *omuari* approaches the grave at dusk, imitating the wailing sounds made by a hyena. Then he climbs down into the still open grave and excises the foetus together with the whole womb. While he does so, the relatives of the deceased woman stand at some distance from the grave and by appropriate gestures and noises act as if they want to drive 'the hyena' (i.e. the *omuari*) away from the grave. They are, of course, only pretending and actually do not interfere with the *omuari*'s job. As payment for this operation the *omuari* is given a bull and a sheep. Before he may enter his hut again he must kill the sheep and smear his entire body with its stomach content (*vuse*), so as to cleanse himself from the ritual contamination with which he has become infected by performing the operation.

The burial of a twin differs only slightly from that of an ordinary person. Among the Vugusu a bull (an ox or an old cow) and a sheep are slaughtered for the deceased twin. The hide of the cow is then cut into two halves and the corpse sandwiched between them. The meat of the two animals is then distributed among the mourners. No ritual attention is paid to the surviving twin; like any other brother, he may even help to dig the grave.

(5) THE CEREMONIAL CONDUCT OF THE WIDOWS DURING THE FUNERAL RITES

In the preceding account of the funeral customs reference has repeatedly been made to the part played by the widow, or the widows, respectively, in connexion with the various funeral rites. We have seen that it is their duty to keep watch over the corpse while it is laid out in the hut, that they put on the garments of their deceased husband while singing their dirges, and that they perform a special dance, holding his weapons as well as the various objects which he had in daily use, and, finally, that the widows run to the bank of a stream where they are rubbed with clay by an old woman. In the following we shall describe some tribal variants of these customs as well as a number of further ceremonies performed with widows which I have either observed myself or of which I have been given an account by my various informants. As far as possible I shall describe these ceremonies in their chronological sequence.

Among the Nyole the widows and the children of the deceased have broad strips of banana-bark, which must be taken from a particular kind of banana called *sindalo*, tied round their foreheads and their loins by an old widowed woman. While the grave is being dug they must, for this purpose, all stand in front of the death-hut. Their next duty, while sitting under the eaves of the hut, is to grind some eleusine which is then ceremonially dabbed on their heads. Meanwhile, all the clothes (*tsinguvo*) of the deceased husband as well as his weapons are carried out of the hut and piled up in a heap. Each of the widows is then given a goatskin or another garment worn by her deceased husband. In addition, the senior widows receive a shield and a spear each, while the junior ones have to be satisfied with a grass-cutting knife (a bill-hook), a stool, or even such a trifle as their deceased husband's beer-tube. Armed with these objects, the widows, under the lead of the 'great wife', run towards the gate of the main enclosure. There they dance for some time, jumping into the air with both feet at the same time and uttering shrill sounds. After a while they simultaneously raise their spears and thrust them into the ground, then raise them for a second time, and point them towards the roofs of the various huts of the homestead. When they have finished brandishing their spears in this manner, they lean them against the walls of the huts, while the men, amidst a great amount of wailing and lamenting, carry the corpse out of the death-hut to place it in the grave, the digging of which has in the meantime been completed.

After the deceased has been buried and the grave filled in again, all the widows must sit down under the eaves of the hut, to the right of the entrance, and wait there until the first meal which they may partake of after their husband's death has been prepared. The sisters of the deceased, whose duty it is to look after the widows during the next few days, grind some eleusine and pick some vegetables of the *tsimboka*-kind which they cook in an old, broken pot and on a fire quickly kindled in the front yard. When the vegetables are half done, they begin to cook the eleusine porridge on the hearthstones inside the hut. The two dishes are then served to the widows on a potsherd and not on a flat tray as is the usual custom. Before the widows begin to eat properly, they take one bite which they spit out towards one side, and then a second bite which they spit towards the other side. Only the third bite they may chew and swallow.

After the widows have finished their meal, the grave-diggers go to the banana-grove behind the house where they cut the leaves of a certain variety of banana called *sindalo*. During the following nights these leaves serve the widows as a bedspread. After they have slept in their huts for two nights, they are led to the nearest stream where, however, they may not bathe but merely dip their little fingers in the water. On their way home they sing the so-called *litoma*-song.[1] On the following day they secretly go to the banana-grove and cut off two bunches of bananas. After four days they go again, this time in order to fetch a great quantity of bananas. One of the grave-diggers goes with the 'great wife', while the second one accompanies the junior wives. They visit all the banana-groves in the

[1] From *oxutoma*, to call. The words of the song are: *ndomele omutjeni ndoma*, 'I call the visitor, I call' (i.e. I call for my husband).

neighbourhood and everywhere cut off as many bananas as they can find without being interfered with by the owners of the bananas. After they have finished, horns are sounded to serve as a signal for the boys and girls of the neighbourhood to come and collect the bananas that the widows have cut off. Following the widows in a sort of procession, they carry the bananas to the dead man's homestead. It is considered important that they should all arrive there at the same time, forming a long queue of about a hundred persons, headed by the grave-diggers who are followed by the widows and these, in turn, by the carriers of the bananas. The bananas are then distributed among all persons present; what remains over is kept for the hair-shaving ceremony which will take place on the following day (cf. below, p. 485 sq.), as well as for those guests who did not have their share on the previous day because they were prevented from coming. On this occasion it is the privilege of the grave-diggers to distribute the cooked bananas among the guests; if anybody helps himself to these bananas he must pay the grave-diggers a chicken as a fine. If he fails to do so voluntarily, the grave-diggers send a few girls to his place to collect twice the fine by catching two of his chickens.

During the first few days after the burial the widows, as well as all other persons who used to sleep in the same hut as the deceased, may not move about freely. In particular, they are strictly forbidden to do any work in their gardens. Should any one of them infringe this rule, two chickens are taken away from him.

Towards evening of the day when the widows have gathered the bananas, the 'grave-digger of the head' (i.e. the man who held the head of the deceased while he was lowered into the grave) loosens a rafter from the roof of the death-hut so that it can easily be removed. He shows the widows the rafter which he has loosened and, during the second half of the night when all people are fast asleep, awakens the widows to tell them they must go and pull the rafter off the roof. As soon as they have done so, they follow him to the nearest stream carrying the rafter; there they dip it into the water and then hide it in the dense undergrowth (*muluevo*) near the bank. They also remove the ribbons of banana-bark which had been tied round their foreheads and loins and hide them in the bush together with the rafter. Now they wash their whole bodies and, as soon as they are dry again, hurry back to the death-hut under the lead of the grave-digger and singing the *yumba*-song. They must take care to return home before the first crowing of the cock, as otherwise the grave-digger may not kindle a warming fire for them.

The other inhabitants of the homestead who have stayed behind may not sleep while the widows are away, but must keep themselves awake by constant singing, as otherwise their skin would turn pale (*xuxanya embili*). Only after the widows have returned home may they snatch a few hours of sleep until daybreak.

The behaviour of the widows, as I observed it during the funeral rites staged for the repeatedly mentioned Vigeti of the Tadjoni tribe, corresponded to that just described with only minor deviations and omissions. After the cattle-drive had ended, the two widows, each of them standing in front of her own hut, were undressed by an old, widowed woman. This woman then tied strips of banana-bark right across the widows' heads, while round their loins she put a sort of skirt made from banana-leaves cut into the shape of triangular streamers. As among the Nyole, she now dabbed the widows' heads with eleusine flour which was freshly ground for the occasion. Another woman then fetched Vigeti's spear and his beer-tube container from his hut, dividing them among the two widows; on the head of the elder widow she placed the wreath (*engara*) on which the beer-pot of the deceased used to rest. Next they began to prepare the first meal for the widows which—as among the Nyole—must be cooked outside the hut in an old, broken pot. As soon as they had eaten, the widows, accompanied by all the women present, went to the nearest stream while the men stayed behind and performed a dance on a pasture nearby. Arrived at the stream, the majority of the women, led by the widows, plunged into the water. After having bathed the widows were rubbed with clay all over their bodies and then driven back to the homestead of the deceased, while the other women broke through the circle formed by the dancing men and then gave the sign for a new dance to start in which both men and women participated.

Among the Vugusu the widows (and frequently also the mother as well as the sisters of the deceased) put on the clothes of the deceased while the funeral is still in progress, and carry his personal utensils in their hands. At a funeral which took place in the neighbourhood of Kimilili I saw a widow sporting her dead husband's shirt, jacket, and trousers and walking about with a European saw in her hand (the deceased had worked as a carpenter) while singing the dirges; the mother of the deceased had put on her son's hat, while in her hand she carried an oil-lamp and to her skirt she had fixed all sorts of objects of European origin which had been among the contents of her son's hut. In all other respects the ceremonial behaviour of the widows among the Vugusu corresponds to that of the Nyole and Tadjoni which has been described above. In explanation of the ceremonial bath taken by the widows after the burial of their dead husband, I was told among the Vugusu that it serves to cleanse them of everything connected with their husband that is still sticking to their bodies. It is therefore essential that they plunge into the river where the water is deep, so that they can be completely submerged. Both when going to the river and when returning from there, the widows are constantly prompted by the women accompanying them to hurry. They shout to them to be as eager and light-footed as their husband who used to run about untiringly when it was a question of supplying them with meat and with the other things they needed. In the night following the burial the widows are awakened at the first crowing of the cock and sent down to the river a second time where they must bathe again to wash off the clay with which they are still covered from the previous day.[1]

During the first few days after their husband's death the widows may not partake of any food, except for the meagre ceremonial meal which is prepared for them in the front yard in a broken pot. Their fasting is to show that they are stricken with grief over the loss of their husband and feel no desire to eat. Even the ceremonial meal which is placed before them they must not consume greedily, gulping it down, but slowly and hesitatingly, indicating by corresponding gestures that they eat only with great reluctance. My informants assured me, however, that the women who during these days look after the widows secretly cook additional food for them which they deposit at some distance from the hut when nobody else is around. While one of the widows walks about, wailing and singing dirges, her sister or sister-in-law will unostentatiously point out to her that at a certain spot in the banana-grove or in the nearby bush an ample helping of millet-porridge is awaiting her.

As a parallel to the custom of collecting bananas which we have recorded for the Nyole, the widows among the Vugusu prepare a concoction from a number of specified herbs with which they go all round the neighbourhood, sprinkling the fields and the banana-groves. While they are doing so they may pull off as many bananas and pick as many fruits growing in the gardens as they care to without anybody preventing them.

At a funeral rite which I attended among the Marama the ceremonial procedure to which the widow was subjected consisted of the following features. Standing in front of her hut, the widow was first shaved by an old widowed woman, who then undressed her and smeared her from head to foot with white clay which she had mixed with water in a trough-like vessel made from a banana-trunk. Only around the widow's eyes, nose, and mouth a square spot was left free. Next the old woman tied strips of banana-bark round the foreheads and loins, first of the widow and then of her three children, and then placed an *engata* (a wreath-like support for a pot) upon the widow's head. Now she robed her with the clothes of her deceased husband and tied a cowbell to her belt, while the old woman herself put on the clothes of the widow and likewise tied strips of banana-bark round her head. Then she cut a couple of switches from a bush. Taking the widow by her shoulders and dealing her some gentle strokes with the switches, she pushed her into the hut, the widow at first offering a sham resistance but finally yielding to the pressure. In the same manner the old woman then pushed the children into the hut too. When all four of them were inside, the old woman entered the hut herself, repeating the same procedure all over again, or rather reversing it, pushing the widow and the children outside again. This rite having been performed, an old man handed the widow the spear and the stool of her deceased husband.

[1] The custom of removing a rafter from the roof of the hut is not observed by the Vugusu.

Holding the spear in her right hand and the stool in her left, the widow slowly walked to her husband's grave, where she performed a dance. On the following morning, at dawn, she went down to the river to bathe and wash off the clay. I may add that I failed to elicit any other comment on these ceremonial features save the general remark that they were 'the custom of the widows'.

As these variants in the ceremonial behaviour and conduct of the widows show, the principal features are the same among the various Kavirondo sub-tribes. The details, however, the completeness with which they are observed, and the sequence of the various customs and ceremonial features differ not only from tribe to tribe but from clan to clan and even from case to case.

(6) THE HAIR-SHAVING CEREMONY

Among all the Bantu Kavirondo tribes whose death customs I have studied, a so-called hair-shaving ceremony takes place three days after a person's death. The procedure at this ceremony is very similar among the various sub-tribes, a fact which indicates that it constitutes a traditional and basic feature of the death customs. The term 'hair-shaving ceremony' (Lurogoli: *olovego* from *okuvega*, to shave; Luvugusu: *livégana*, shaving one another) refers to the fact that everybody who has come into contact with the deceased during his last illness or who has been connected with the handling of his body must have the hair of his head shaved. This serves as a ritual purification, for it is believed that the disease from which the deceased suffered and which emanated from his body sticks to the hair of those persons who have been in close contact with him and thus causes the disease to spread. The Vugusu, therefore, sometimes refer to the hair-shaving ceremony as *mulufu nelulurire*, 'the sickness may come out', i.e. it may leave the hair. To prevent the shaved-off hair from being abused for purposes of evil magic, it must be hidden at a lonely place in the bush.

The actions performed on the occasion of the hair-shaving ceremony, however, are not limited to the shaving of the hair. This rite merely forms the preliminary to a debate which is usually drawn out over many hours and in the course of which all the questions arising from the death that has occurred are aired and settled. To begin with, the various claims which the deceased still had upon his relatives and neighbours with regard to cattle, fowls, grain, or other objects are voiced and, similarly, a list is drawn up of any debts that he might still have owed when he died. After all claims of this nature on both sides have been put forward and confirmed, the estate is distributed among the sons of the deceased and the other relatives entitled to a share in it. Or rather, a public announcement is made of the distribution of the dead man's property, for, as a rule, a father divides his property among his various sons shortly before his death (cf. above, p. 451), instructing them as to which of them must share in the possession of a certain cow, who will have the claim to the first calf, &c.

The subsequent public announcement (on the occasion of the hair-shaving ceremony) of the way in which the estate has been divided serves the important purpose of making sure that there will be as many witnesses as possible to the settlement which has been made. If, then, in the course of the execution of the settlement, which often extends over many years,[1] disputes arise between the heirs, each of them can refer back to the settlement as it was publicly announced on the occasion of the hair-shaving ceremony and produce witnesses who can testify to the justness of his claims. The public announcement of the division of the estate thus serves the same purpose as the making of the last will in writing does with us.

Furthermore, the hair-shaving ceremony offers a welcome opportunity to the close relatives and friends of the deceased to discuss the probable cause of his death and to level against definite persons more or less direct suspicions or even accusations of an act of sorcery or witchcraft committed against the deceased. To make such accusations, and to demand the punishment of the alleged sorcerer or witch as the one to be held responsible for the death that has occurred, is a kinship obligation which the near clan-relatives of the deceased owe to him or to his spirit. As we have seen, the Bantu Kavirondo are convinced that every death, even that of a very old person, is caused by a mystical agency, usually by an act of sorcery committed by a fellow human being harbouring ill will against the person concerned. In most cases these accusations give rise to a heated debate between the two parties, the relatives of the deceased and those of the accused or suspected sorcerer. Indictments of this nature, uttered on the occasion of the hair-shaving ceremony, are said to have led, in the past, to frequent outbreaks of open hostilities and even to family- or clan-feuds (cf. above, p. 70). If the suspected person belongs to the clan of the deceased, the indictment levelled against him may easily lead to a break up of the clan community. To prevent this from happening a clan-elder functions at every hair-shaving ceremony as a so-called *omuseni*, a comforter of the bereaved ones. It is his duty, by using convincing words and arguments, to calm down the excited minds, reminding them that from long ago it has been the common fate of all people to die and that the misfortune which has come over the clan by the death that has occurred would only be increased if the clansmen were now to accuse one another of sorcery or even to harbour thoughts of revenge and retaliation. The *omuseni* usually begins his harangue to the assembled mourners by reviewing the great deeds performed by the clan in the past and by exhorting his listeners, for the sake of the peace of the clan, to let bygones be bygones and to reconcile themselves to the inevitable. Such a speech made by the *omuseni* is not the spontaneously uttered conciliation of any clan-elder who may feel in the mood to talk reason, but is a definite office which can only be practised

---

[1] Especially if some of the sons were not yet of age when the father died or if the legacy was so small that some of the heirs were only assigned a claim for a calf not yet born.

by such elders who on account of their personality and their unblemished conduct throughout life have proved their ability to intervene in disputes and quarrels as arbitrators (cf. above, p. 78).

Now the fact that the *omuseni* points out that it is the fate of all human beings to die appears to contradict our statement that human beings only die if they become the victims of evil magic. To reconcile these two views with one another one would have to assume that, in native belief, all men sooner or later become the victims of lethal magic. Frequent conversations which I had with natives on this point have convinced me that they are quite ready to acknowledge the possibility of a death by natural causes as long as they deal with the phenomenon of death in a merely theoretical, detached manner. If, however, an actual death occurs which produces in them a powerful emotional reaction, they will account for it in terms of mystical notions. This tendency will be the stronger, the more intimate their contact with the deceased has been and the more suddenly and unexpectedly his death has come for them. Strictly speaking, they acknowledge two different causes of death: a general, theoretical cause, viz. the mortality[1] of all human beings which 'explains' the phenomenon of death in an abstract manner, and a special cause which explains why a particular, concrete case of death has occurred just at this juncture and under just such circumstances. The *omuseni*, whose own personal detachment and ripe old age enable him to persuade his clansmen to accept also the particular death which he is talking about as sufficiently accounted for by the fact that all men must die, would find his arguments the less convincing the more unexpectedly that death had come. If a family happens to be stricken by repeated bereavements, the survivors will not rest content until they have detected the alleged perpetrator of these deaths and have rendered him innocuous either by direct measures of retaliation or by countermagic, no matter how reasonably the *omuseni* talks to them and comforts them.

At the hair-shaving ceremony, as a rule, the question of who will inherit the widow or the widows is also discussed.[2] As we have already

---

[1] The origin of death is explained by the widespread story of the chameleon. Among the Vugusu I heard the following version of it: 'A long time ago the people did not die. One day, the chameleon came to the homestead of a certain man who was the son of Maina. He was sitting outside in the yard eating. The chameleon asked him to give it some of his food, but he refused to do so. When the chameleon did not stop begging him, he finally turned angry and drove it away. Thereupon the chameleon cursed the people and spoke: "I am leaving you now, but from now on you shall all die." Then the people began to breathe the air, to get ill and to die. When the chameleon had left the man it visited the snake which gave it something to eat. As a reward for its good deed the chameleon blessed the snake with eternal life. When the snake gets old, it merely casts off its skin instead of dying. Even to-day snakes die only when they are killed. Antelopes, too, live on for ever, unless they are killed.'

[2] As far as I could ascertain, it is only among the Marama that the question of the remarriage of the widow is not discussed on the occasion of the hair-shaving

stated in the chapter on marriage (p. 440), it is customary for the widow to be taken over by a real or a classificatory brother of her deceased husband. She is, however, at liberty to marry a man from another clan if she prefers to do so, but in such a case her new husband must give marriage cattle to the heirs of her deceased husband. On the occasion of the hair-shaving ceremony the widow has an opportunity to state her own wishes. To quote from a Logoli text:

'Before the people (who have gathered for the hair-shaving ceremony) part from one another, they first decide who is to become the successor to that woman (i.e. the man who "inherits" the widow). They (i.e. the successors—in case the deceased had several wives—that have been chosen) must then look after those widows, and if one of the widows refuses to recognize the man who has been appointed as the successor (of her deceased husband), then she may do so. The clansmen (of the deceased) cannot force her. If she chooses another husband, they must listen to her and say to her people: "Your daughter has refused the brother of her deceased husband; she has gone to another man and has left the dead husband's brother." If that one is not of the clan of the deceased he must begin to pay *ovukui* (bride-wealth), and the things which belonged to her former husband must be returned (i.e. the relatives of the widow return the marriage cattle that was originally given for her to the heirs of the deceased, while her new husband has to give them new marriage cattle).'

We shall now describe in some detail the procedure and the various ceremonial acts performed in connexion with the hair-shaving ceremony, the subsequent discussion of the property situation, the distribution of the inheritance, and the detection of the cause of death, quoting from a number of texts and referring to concrete cases.

The most complete account of the hair-shaving ceremony I recorded among the Nyole:

'... They begin to shave in the morning. The sister of the deceased who on the day of the burial has broken the *litjio*-pot, goes to fetch water from a swiftly flowing stream.[1] She carries the water home in an *olusumbi*-pot which she must carry on her head without a support (*yingara*), for the water used for the shaving of the hair must not be fetched on a support. This is taboo (*omusilo*). While returning from the stream she sings dirges, until she enters the gate of the deceased's homestead. Then she puts the water down on that side of the grave where the (deceased's) head rests. Meanwhile the hearthstones have been properly arranged for cooking bananas on them. Part of the water is then poured on the bananas, while the rest is used for the shaving of the hair. The first one to moisten his hair with the water is the "grave-digger of the head", who is always a clansman of the deceased. And the widows, clad only in their skins (i.e. without any ornaments and without a

ceremony but only two months afterwards. The father or a brother of the deceased husband then kills a goat, brews beer, and invites several clansmen and relatives of the wife. Then they decide who is to take over the widow.

[1] Water from a stagnant pool or a very sluggish stream would not offer a guarantee of being ritually uncontaminated.

loin-cloth), sit under the eaves of the hut.¹ Next, comes the second gravedigger, and after him it is the turn of the son of the deceased to moisten his hair. Then follow the brothers of the deceased, and finally all the clansmen of his lineage (*owesilivua siavue*) moisten their hair to be shaved. And then they ask one another, "Where did the sickness (*olufu*) which caused his death come from? We do not know where it came from." Then the horns will sound and they will all assemble. And an old man begins to perform a sham fight (*oxuhuliana*) on the grave and a singer sings. And the old man says (to the deceased): "I went with you to Lukolele; we stood there together on the fighting ground and there something big happened to you (i.e. you killed an enemy) and the same happened at Yiyi; but it is like that, (our) brother; death came together with the people. We always thought you would remain in battle, we did not know that you would die the death of wailing." He then cites all the war-deeds of the deceased and when he has finished doing so, he takes his spear with which he performed the sham fight and thrusts it into the ground. Then he leans the shield and the tail feathers of the deceased's headdress against the spear. Now the horns are sounded again, the singers sing, and all present remain standing for some time until they may sit down.

'He who begins to shave the people is a boy (*omundu omusiani*); then follows a married man, as a third a young girl, and as the fourth a married woman.² And all the kinsmen (*avexo*) must come to be shaved. And the widows and the nephews and nieces and the other clansmen may think, "If I fail to have my hair shaved, perhaps I will always eat together with the deceased."³ Then they dish out the bananas, so that each will get something. The last ones to eat are the widows, and when they have eaten too, they are adorned (lit.: tied) with *amanini* ribbons.⁴

'After the meal, the dead man's sisters (who during the past few days have taken care of the widows) may go home. And also one of the grave-diggers may go home; the other one remains there and looks after the widows; the two grave-diggers take turns in performing this duty.'

Several other reports on the hair-shaving ceremony which I was given by a number of old men among the Logoli, Tsotso, Marama, and Vugusu agree in all essentials with the above text. Furthermore, it is unanimously stressed in all these other reports that the *olovego* always used to take place three days after death had occurred and that it was therefore not necessary to fix a particular day as is nowadays done among the Logoli, especially if one of the kinsmen whose presence at the *olovego* is deemed necessary is in European employment outside the reserve and must first be recalled.

---

[1] In the various Logoli texts on the hair-shaving ceremony it is likewise stressed that the widows must be shaved at a certain distance from the other persons present, as their ritual contamination is particularly strong and continues also after their hair has been shaved.

[2] Among the Logoli the widows are always shaved by old, widowed women, as others would fear to come into close contact with them.

[3] Meaning: the spirit of the deceased would not give me any rest.

[4] *Amanini* are the tender fibres of a reed-grass (*litoko*) which are plaited into ribbons.

To illustrate the discussion of the unsettled demands and debts of the deceased, the following passage from a Logoli text may be quoted.

'... Then (when they have finished shaving one another) they ask if there is anybody who possesses a cow or a goat which is the property of the deceased. Whoever has such an animal must admit it and say: "Yes, I have a cow which he gave me to herd; it now has a calf." And if the deceased used to eat of the property of other persons (i.e. if he had debts), the widow must admit this and say: "Yes, indeed, the deceased went to our neighbour and borrowed a goat from him, so that he might perform a sacrifice for his child. This goat must still be returned to him." Then all the clansmen say: "Yes, it is good. As soon as there will be a goat, he (the creditor) will get it back, just as you now have promised him." '

The discussion of the cause of the death forms the subject of another Logoli text:

'There (i.e. at the hair-shaving ceremony) assemble also the old men whom one may not pass in front of.[1] Then they produce the knife (to shave each other's hair), and all the clansmen must ask at this hair-shaving ceremony in what way the deceased used to live until he fell ill. If he went to a beer-party and there had a quarrel with another man, they must trace the words spoken by that man and find out whether he had a good reason (to quarrel with him). If this man was somebody who lived in a state of avoidance with all other people (*wavagirana avandu vosi*), then they must believe that it was he who killed him. If he then fails to profess his guilt, the clan-elders must take him into their midst, right there and then, and must accuse him outright of having caused the death (*okumukugila*). If they speak like that and he is a sorcerer (*ombila*) who exterminates the clans (by his acts of sorcery), then he will die indeed. Then he cannot sleep in peace; he goes home and soon he will die. And then the people will say: "Really, it is he who has killed So-and-so." Everybody must then fear him.'

The way in which the various affairs of the deceased are discussed on the occasion of the hair-shaving ceremony can be gathered from protocols on the proceedings which I have taken down on several such occasions. These notes, at the same time, offer concrete examples of the manner in which traditional custom and new tendencies and observances are interlaced or clash with one another. Some passages from these protocols may therefore be quoted:

I. Hair-shaving ceremony (*mulufu*) after the death of Vigeti, an old man of the Tadjoni tribe (cf. above, p. 136), on 5 June 1936:[2]

In the course of the morning about sixty men, most of them from Vigeti's clan, have assembled underneath a shady tree near the dead man's homestead. Some 20 yards away a number of women, including the three

---

[1] The rules of etiquette demand that younger people must not pass in front of the men of the highest age-grades, but only behind their backs.

[2] Vigeti had died on 2 June, his funeral had taken place on the 3rd, and the cattle-drive (*liiyia*) on the 4th.

widows, are sitting on the grass. The hair-shaving had already taken place early in the morning, but only the widows and several sisters of the deceased have had their hair cut. About ten o'clock one of the clan-elders addresses the crowd, asking whether there is anyone who has claims to Vigeti's property. The first one to reply is a son of Vigeti's *xotja* (mother's brother), who says that he still has a claim to the *sivixo*-cow[1] from his deceased 'brother'.[2] One of the clan-elders, however, denies his claim, pointing out to him that his father (A), after the death of Vigeti's two brothers, had received, in the one case, a bull all for himself and, in the second case, a bull which he was to share with his brother (B). This time, therefore, the other *xotja* (B) is entitled to receive the *sivixo*-cow. It has—so he adds— already been sent to B on the previous day and that is why B has not shown up at the *mulufu*. The second elder to speak is a man by name of Kavudjanga. In a lengthy account he recalls how, in the year 1918, he had sold to Vigeti's brother Mavonga a granaryful of millet (eleusine) which he had owned jointly with Vigeti. This statement is confirmed by several witnesses. Mavonga had at that time given him a bull and, besides, had promised him a goat, equal in value to the millet. This goat Vigeti was first to give to Mavonga as payment for his share in the millet, and then Mavonga was to pass the goat on to him (i.e. to Kavudjanga). In the year 1924, however, Mavonga had died without having given him that goat. On the occasion of the hair-shaving ceremony that followed Mavonga's death, he had not raised his claim—so he said—because he thought that Vigeti, who at that time was working on a European farm, would not refuse to give him the goat. But so far he had been waiting in vain, and so he was now claiming it from Vigeti's estate. The clan-elders, however, reject his claim, too, arguing that he should have voiced it after Mavonga's death in the year 1924. Now, they say, there are no longer any witnesses who can confirm his claim. Vigeti's second wife, who at one time had been married to Mavonga, intervenes at this point, shouting from her distant place in the grass that she had never heard anything about this goat. An old man gets up and explains to Kavudjanga that times have changed and that nowadays he needs witnesses if he wants to claim a debt after so many years. He should just look at the Indians who ask to be paid on the spot when they sell you a pair of trousers. They would not wait for twenty years before it occurred to them to claim a debt. Kavudjanga replies that he will take his case before the tribal court, a procedure from which, however, a number of men try to dissuade him.

The next to voice a claim is an *omwitjuxulu* (grandson) of Vigeti's clan

---

[1] This term designates the cow to which a maternal uncle (or his legal successor) is entitled after his nephew's death. His claim to such a share in his nephew's legacy is derived from the various gifts which he has made to his nephew on the occasion of his circumcision, marriage, &c. (cf. vol. ii, chapter on cattle law).

[2] A term of politeness, for strictly speaking Vigeti is not his brother but his cross-cousin (*omwana wa senge*).

whose mother was a classificatory sister's child of Vigeti's lineage; he, too, asks for a *sitixo*-bull from Vigeti's estate. In justification of his claim he points out that one cow of the marriage cattle which had been handed over for his mother had been assigned to Vigeti's father who was to keep it for Vigeti who at that time was still a child. This cow, so he said, had then 'helped to give birth to Vigeti's eldest son', as Vigeti used it to make up the bride-wealth which he gave for his wife. Vigeti's clansmen at first reject this claim, too, arguing that it rests on too distant a degree of kinship. In the subsequent speech, however, the *omuseni* advises them to give their *omwitjuxulu* at least a sheep or four shillings, a proposition to which they finally agree.

Next, one of Vigeti's classificatory mother's brothers sets out to discuss the cause of Vigeti's death to which we have already referred in a previous chapter (cf. above, p. 136 sq.). After he has finished his speech of indictment, Magongolo, one of the three *avaseni* who have come, steps forward to administer a comforting message to the mourners who have gathered. While making his speech he walks back and forth along a path called *gumuse*.[1] While he is speaking nobody may cross this path; a violation of this rule would, it is said, automatically entail the offender's death. In a clear, resounding voice the *omuseni* announces:

'Illness has been spreading far and wide to kill the people, and we have just heard that it is Kavudjanga who is said to have killed Vigeti. But for a long time already the clan-heads (*vagasa*) and the other people as well have been dying; Lusueti and Sikulia, likewise, had to die. Sikulia's son, instead of singing dirges for his father, took a stick and beat another person with it, because he suspected him of having committed an act of sorcery against his father. As a consequence, they took a cow away from him, and so he had a twofold reason for wailing. To-day the people are fighting one another with words, saying, "Ah, you are deceiving us, but we shall get even with you!"[2] To-day the young men purchase many clothes which they wear on their bodies and in which they are hiding destructive magic substances (*vixu*). And they make arrangements with someone who is willing to throw these *vixu* into the water, so that they will kill somebody. But don't let this make you nervous! Since long ago the old people have been dying, one like the other, good people as well as bad people. But later on, still greater ones will come than those who have died. You may therefore proceed carefully. The first man (*omutai*) spoke thus: "He who walks slowly, arrives in the west" (i.e. at the goal of his journey). You may therefore walk about humbly. And those who will inherit the property (*gumuandu*) of the deceased are the

---

[1] Lit. 'basis, foundation'. The word signifies also the circular line on which the wall-posts of the hut are planted and nowadays also the foundation of a brick house. Because he walks to and fro on the path he is called *omuseni owe gumuse*, 'the walker of the path'. In a figurative sense this term signifies the idea of 'a layer of the foundation', i.e. after a death has occurred the *omuseni* lays the foundation for the future.

[2] '*Ah, ovea vusa xuxave nenawe.*' This is the customary form in which one threatens somebody whom one suspects of an act of sorcery or witchcraft.

"House" (i.e. the lineage) of Funguo and that of Lusamamba, but you others are his clansmen just as well (even if you do not inherit anything). Since a long time ago the sons of Tadjoni and the sons of Vugusu have been going together, but the Vugusu have swallowed the land; they swallowed the Mia (Teso) and they swallowed the Xayo, they swallowed the Wanga and the Nyala (Kakalelwa). But you, the sons of Tadjoni, why didn't you swallow the people of Kabras? Nor did you swallow the Savei.[1] You children of to-day are killing one another![2] You are always saying that the Vugusu are taking our chieftainship (*vuvuami*) from us, but you yourselves are living in discord with one another. You are living in your own country; what is it that the son of Mayegu[3] is taking away from you? I hear that they have put you in jail at Esieyue[4] (i.e. Kakamega). You neglect your beer. What's the matter with you? We, the sons of Tadjoni, have two headmen (*muliango*). That is quite enough. Formerly Sifuma used to be the clan-head (*omugasa*) under Chief Namadjandja,[5] and he was all by himself. But now, the son of Sifuma is a *muliango*, and so is the son of Mwasame. Why did you quarrel with the son of Mayegu? Let him rule! The others are learning English (*lusungu*); they are getting to know the affairs of the world, but you, the sons of strength (*wavana vegamani*), are just sitting round the beer-pot and do not know what the others are like.

'Now, to-day, Vigeti has left behind two sons. One of them, Kavudjanga, is to keep Vigeti's youngest wife; he may then look after the children of Vigeti's brother, and the second wife shall be taken care of by Guxuvilo. And Kavudjanga is the one who will look after the great wife, together with Vigeti's cattle.'

Magongolo having finished his harangue, several old men remark that he should have claimed one of the widows for himself instead of merely thinking of the other people. He replies that it is his task to divide Vigeti's estate but not to take anything for himself. To signify that they are in agreement with what has been said, they all get up and then disperse to their homes.

II. Hair-shaving ceremony after the death of Kidiya, a man of the Yonga clan (sub-clan: Yose) of the Logoli tribe, on 29 June 1935:

Kidiya had died on 17 June towards evening after having been ill for about two weeks (apparently he had been suffering from an inflammation of the lungs). On 18 June a large cattle-drive was staged which was attended by hundreds of people coming from all directions and in the course of

[1] A tribe living on the northern and north-eastern slopes of Mt. Elgon and related to the Nandi.
[2] Meaning, you are ruining one another by your mutual charges of sorcery, instead of being unified.
[3] Referring to Amutala, the present chief of the location of Kimilili of which the Tadjoni form a part.
[4] A number of Tadjoni men who refused to submit to the authority of the Vugusu chief Amutala, but demanded the appointment of a chief over the Tadjoni, were arrested for political agitation.
[5] Namadjandja was the first Vugusu chief recognized by the Government.

which far more than a hundred head of cattle[1] were driven past the corpse of the deceased. As the yard in front of the dead man's hut was too small to accommodate so many men and beasts, the corpse had been moved under the eaves of the nearby hut of his brother. In the afternoon a large dance was held on a pasture near the deceased's homestead, and on the next morning the sham fight (*elifuliana*) took place. Led by the widow, about eighty women, who had joined her during her tour through the entire clan territory of her dead husband, arrived at the homestead, forming a solid procession. Smeared with clay and adorned with *amalande*-creepers, brandishing clubs and sticks, they performed a dance in which they imitated the behaviour of warriors stalking and encountering the enemy. Towards noon Kidiya was placed in the grave, and in the afternoon another large dance was staged in which again hundreds of persons took part.

At to-day's hair-shaving ceremony about 130 persons have come together and have seated themselves partly in the open yard in front of the dead man's hut and partly in the adjoining maize-fields which have already been harvested. The actual hair-shaving has already taken place unceremonially several days ago, so that to-day's meeting merely serves to settle the claims and debts of the deceased as well as the question of succession. Although Kidiya had not been a Christian, the elders of his clan have asked two of the leading Church-elders of the Yonga clan, Thomas and Festo, to 'take the chair'. Thomas, accordingly, acts as the *we endeve*[2] (chairman) and Festo as *omuɲodi* (secretary). Sitting at a table outside the dead man's hut, Festo writes down the names of all persons who wish to voice claims to Kidiya's estate. On seeing the list of names grow, the widow, sitting at some distance in the grass, shouts across that she knows only of four people who still have any claims to Kidiya's property, but that there are a great many people who are still owing him something. She refrains, however, from mentioning any names. The first one from among the crowd to speak is an elderly man, by name of Anubi, who states that he had borrowed four shillings from Kidiya which he had not yet returned to him. Next, Lumadede, the headman (*muliango*) of the Yonga, proposes that everybody who during the last few days before Kidiya's illness had bought from him a calabashful of porridge and had not yet paid for it, should do so now.[3] When thereupon only a few people volunteer, one of the clan-elders admonishes those present to acknowledge their debts. Then an old man by the name of Donera registers a claim of 25 cents which, so he says, Kidiya still owed him for a bunch of cord he had lent him to tie his granary. He had frequently reminded Kidiya to repay his debt but had always been put off by him. At last, Kidiya had promised to give him a fowl instead of the money.

[1] The Logoli own an average of two or three cows per family.
[2] Lit. 'the one of the chair', a new word formed by analogy to the English word 'chairman'.
[3] Kidiya used to sell hot eleusine porridge at a nearby market.

Next, Otioko, Kidiya's elder brother, steps forward and says: 'Now my brother has died and shortly after him one of my cows too. This gives me food for thought, for one day Mwango and Adero were drinking beer with Kidiya. While they were sitting together, Adero produced the tail of a cow, swept with it once round the beer-pot and spoke: "I know, Kidiya, that you will not finish this year. And if you do not die, then the cow will die."' Lumadede interrupts him: 'Were you there yourself when Adero said this?' Otioko denies this and quotes Gusali as a witness. He had told him about it after Kidiya's death. Lumadede, however, rejects the indictment on the grounds that, in the first place, Gusali was not present and, secondly, that Otioko should take his case before the tribal court. The other clan-elders agree with him, adding that this indictment was 'a big matter' which they could not discuss to-day. Several old men want to ask for further details concerning the beer-party referred to by Otioko, but they are silenced by Thomas and Festo. When, nevertheless, still more people want to comment on this point, Lumadede cuts them short and says: 'I know that some of you are grumbling and say that I myself am an *ombila* (sorcerer) because I appear to be siding with the sorcerers by refusing to discuss them. However, I am not a sorcerer, but I know that if we listen to Otioko the whole thing will grow into a big affair and we will never come to an end. Besides, I do not believe that Kidiya was killed by an *ombila*. You are thinking that Adero has killed him, merely because he is an *ombila*. An *ombila*, however, who kills somebody would come from far away, he wouldn't be somebody whom we all know.' Several other old men enlarge upon the subject, all of them endorsing what Lumadede has said until, at last, Otioko appears to be satisfied.

The next one to speak is Mahagua, another of Kidiya's brothers. He states that he had visited Kidiya at his sick-bed and had left him his blanket, because he was cold and badly wanted a second blanket. Later on, when he came to the funeral he had seen Kidiya's body wrapped up in this blanket, so he had taken Kidiya's own blanket which he had found in the hut. This piece of information arouses the indignation of several of the old men, who drive it home to Mahagua that he should have given his blanket to his brother without bothering about getting it back. He was, after all, to inherit the widow and then could share Kidiya's former blanket with her. Mahagua, however, replies that he does not care to inherit the widow and that he is pleased to let somebody else have her. He is interrupted by Kikanda, the widow, who shouts across that she too does not care to live with Mahagua, as he is a bad person who is always quarrelling with her. Kidiya, on the other hand, had always treated her well. Several old men, however, remind her that she could not refuse Mahagua, as this very morning when he came to see her she had taken his blanket into her hut with her.[1] After a longish discussion as to whether or not Kikanda

[1] If somebody carries the blanket which his visitor has left in the front yard into his hut, he thereby lets it be understood that he welcomes his visit.

was still entitled to refuse to marry Mahagua, one of the elders finally suggests that Ekedego, Mahagua's younger brother, should inherit the widow. Kikanda, without passing a direct comment on this new proposal, repeats once more that under no circumstances will she go to Mahagua, adding that he already has two wives and that she refuses to become his third wife. Petro and several other Christians disapprove of the idea that Ekedego should marry the widow, arguing that he was already married and, being a Christian, could not take a second wife. Finally, the whole question of Kikanda's remarriage having been aired from every possible angle, Anubi sums up the position in the following words: 'We know that according to our custom a widow can choose between Mahagua and Ekedego; she has decided herself for Ekedego, and so Ekedego it will be. If we do not provide her with a husband and she stays by herself, her father-in-law (*navizara*) might come into her house, and that would not be good.'[1] This latter remark provokes roaring laughter, while it causes Kikanda great embarrassment. Festo, as a church-elder, at last declares himself in agreement with this solution, remarking that it was better for Ekedego to marry a second wife than for Kikanda to stay by herself. The question whether Ekedego will in that case be expelled from the Christian community is not discussed.[2] Reuben, another church-elder, winds up the *olovego* by a Christian prayer, and Donera, a pagan and one of the oldest men of the Yonga clan, 'blesses' the widow in accordance with the old custom by saying: 'May God (*Nyasai*) protect you; may you live in peace and no longer think of him who has died, for now you will live with the man whom we are giving to you, with Ekedego.'

Ekedego, who has thus been appointed Kidiya's successor, now asks everybody to stay on for a while to eat the 'millet porridge [*ovukima vwolovego*] and the fowls of the hair-shaving ceremony' which, meanwhile, have been prepared for them.

(7) THE RITUAL STATUS OF THE WIDOW AND THE WIDOWER

The state of ritual impurity with which a woman is infected after the death of her husband is not removed by any of the ceremonial acts performed over her in connexion with the funeral rites nor by the subsequent hair-shaving ceremony. The agent responsible for her impurity, the mystical force called *vuxútjakāli* or *ovukunzakāli* (cf. above, p. 109), continues to reside in her for the next few months. As during that time she constitutes a source of ritual danger for everyone who comes into contact with her, she must observe a number of rules of avoidance which are to keep her fellow human beings from being infected by her ritual impurity.

---

[1] Such a visit would be an infringement of the rule of avoidance prevailing beween father-in-law and daughter-in-law.

[2] As I subsequently learnt, the church-elders decided tacitly to sanction his second marriage, as he did not live inside a so-called Christian village.

DEATH AND MOURNING

The most important of these rules is that of sexual continence. Among the Vugusu the widow must practise continence for a whole year, even though she has been already assigned to her future husband on the occasion of the hair-shaving ceremony. Among the Logoli, however, the rule of continence extends only for two or three months. Furthermore, the impure widow must avoid visiting the homesteads and, particularly, entering the huts of other people, lest the things she might touch there become infected with *vuxútjakāli*. If other persons go near her, they must take care to avoid her shadow; children particularly must be warned not to step on it and otherwise to evade it. She must eat her food from a special tray. A further source of danger is formed by her excrement and by the water which she has used for washing or bathing herself. She must, therefore, avoid frequenting the same places in the bush which are used by ordinary people, nor may she bathe where other people bathe. A narrow path must be cleared for her leading to a secluded place in the bush and at the stream. This path is specially marked to warn other people against using it. A violation of any of these rules would in each case entail the same consequences: the *vuxútjakāli* would 'bleach' and 'soften' (*kwakanya* and *okwenga*) the skin of the infected person, so that he would finally 'look like an overripe banana'.

Apart from these rules of avoidance, the widow can move about freely and pursue her usual activities without particularly having to avoid the presence of other people. As a precautionary measure she must, however, drink a particular medicine which is concocted and administered to her by an old widowed woman on the day of her husband's burial. This medicine is said to reduce the potency of the *vuxútjakāli* to such an extent that other people can go near her and even enter her hut without thereby risking their health.

Outwardly a widow—as far as I could ascertain—is marked as such only among the Vugusu, where throughout the entire year of mourning she wears her goatskin, or whatever other clothes she may possess, inside out. Moreover, she weaves for herself so-called *gimigoye*, i.e. two-finger-wide ribbons of bast or glass-beads, which she ties round her forehead, her neck, her arms, and her ankles.

To give vent to her grief over her husband's death, the widow wails or sings dirges at his grave whenever she is overwhelmed by her loneliness, particularly in the evenings at dusk. Furthermore, until the end of the period of mourning a widow is expected to lead a quiet and retiring life, lest she should be suspected of having desired or even caused her husband's death.

Until her remarriage, a widow continues to live in her former hut. A few days after the hair-shaving ceremony, however, the deceased's sister's son comes to remove the rod (Luvugusu: *sísuli*; Lurogoli: *ekisuli*) which protrudes from the apex of the main hut and is a symbol of the male owner of the homestead. Before the sister's son climbs on to the roof he asks to be given a fowl from the estate of the deceased. Among the Vugusu he then takes the *sísuli* with him and either hides or burns it; among the Nyole he first places it on a hide which is spread out in the entrance of the hut and then on the grave where he leaves it, while he takes the hide home with him. Among the Vugusu the sister's son of the deceased also removes one of the three hearthstones, the so-called 'husband's stone'.

After several months have passed, a feast is staged which terminates the widow's state of ritual impurity. The names by which this feast is known and the details of the ceremonial observed on this occasion differ among the various tribes. Among the Vugusu it is called the 'beer of washing the ashes' (*gamalua goxusinga ligoxe*), among the Logoli the 'beer of death' (*amalua golukuzu*) or the 'beer of the holes' (*amalua gedzinduhu*) or else the 'beer of tears' (*amalua gamaliga*), and among the Nyole the 'beer of the grave' (*amalua kivilindwa*). In each case large quantities of beer are brewed, a task which is jointly performed by the widows and the sisters of the deceased. The eleusine required for this purpose must chiefly be provided by the man who inherits the widow (i.e. usually the brother of the deceased) and to a lesser extent by the father of the deceased and other near relatives. Furthermore, among the Vugusu and the Logoli the future husband of the widow must slaughter a goat and smear the widow from head to foot with its stomach content, so as to 'wash off' the *vuxútjakāli* from her. Among the Nyole, on the other hand, the lustration of the widow is effected by spitting *ovwanga* (eleusine flour mixed with water) on her as well as by slipping a strip of skin (*esixova*) over her arm. To quote from a text:

'If you wish to inherit the wives of the deceased you must kill a goat. Then you summon the widows together with your own wives to assemble in the yard and call the "blower" (*ombiti*), so that he may spit *ovwanga* on them. . . . Then when the goat has been skinned, they cut off a strip of skin and slip it on your own wife's arm, and then a second strip which is slipped over the outstretched arm of the woman left behind by your brother (i.e. the widow). This must be done with all the women, without anyone being omitted.'

These various ceremonies having been performed, the widow no longer needs to observe the above-mentioned rules of avoidance, for she is now no longer infected with *vuxútjakāli*. She may now also enter into marital relations with her new husband. Among the Vugusu, however, she continues to wear the *gimigoye*-ribbons until a whole year has passed since her husband's death. Then another beer-feast is staged, in the course of which the widow cuts and throws away the ribbons which signified her status of widowhood. To celebrate the termination of the period of mourning, the cattle of the clansmen are once again driven across the homestead of the deceased and another sham fight is performed. In the following night the hut of the deceased (*liguvili*) is torn down and the building-materials are burnt.[1] They must not be used for the building of a new hut—as is customary in cases where a hut is torn down because it is old and dilapidated—

---

[1] This is the case only among the Vugusu. Among the Logoli and the Nyole the widows continue to live in their former huts until these become dilapidated.

for it is feared that the further utilization of parts of a dead person's hut would cause the inhabitants of the new hut to die. The widow then either moves into a hut which her new husband has built for her or—if she is too old to marry again—into a widow's hut, known as *lisali*, which, as a rule, is put up for her by her youngest son.

In many respects a widow continues to occupy a special status, even after the period of mourning has ended. In a Nyole text this status which a widow retains for the remainder of her life is described in the following words:

'If you have taken a "woman who has been left behind" (*omuxasi womwandu*)[1] and you then see another such woman you cannot take (i.e. marry) her, as otherwise you would die soon. If you wish to marry yet another woman, she must be a young girl; she may then join your other wives. And for the widow you cannot build a hut in the middle of your homestead, but only at the side. The reason is that, if you die, the inherited wives cannot wail for you. Only your own wives can do so, and the inherited ones can follow only behind them. If you die, the inherited wives cannot behave like widows for a second time. It is they who will then tie the ribbons of banana-bast to your own wives, without being themselves tied by others.'

The ceremonial conduct and the ritual status of a widower on the whole correspond to those of a widow, though to a lesser extent. A widower is likewise called *omukunzakāli*, but his ritual impurity is supposed to last only for a very much shorter period of time. Among the Vugusu, for instance, a sheep is killed (*xuosia*) for the widower already on the fourth day or—at most—one week after his wife's burial. He himself and his children must then step into the sheep's stomach content to wash off the *vuxútjakāli*. After this rite of purification the widower may resume his marital relations with his other wives or marry a new wife. My informants quoted to me the names of various men who had remarried already within a month after their wife's death.

The difference in the ritual behaviour of widowers and of widows was explained to me by the fact that the *vuxútjakāli* which issues from the breath of a dying man is very much stronger than that issuing from a dying woman. In the case of a 'great wife' it is, again, believed to be more powerful than in that of a junior wife, a notion which is obviously derived from the fact that the relations between the husband and his great wife had been of a more varied nature and much more firmly knit than those with his junior wives and that the 'great wife' was older in years and enjoyed a higher social status than the other wives.

Apart from the rule of continence which he must observe during the first few days after his wife's death, a widower is not subjected to any

[1] This term (and the corresponding Logoli word *omukali omutiga*) is applied to a widow for the remainder of her life. The word *omukunzakāli*, on the other hand, refers only to the period of mourning during which the widow is considered to be ritually impure.

particular rules of avoidance; his presence, his shadow, &c., are, accordingly, not feared or avoided by other persons. Otherwise, however, a widower mourns in much the same way as a widow: he wears his 'clothes' inside out (that is the hairy side of his goatskin outside); when wailing he goes about carrying the handle of his wife's hoe or the stirring-paddle used by her; sometimes he also dons the clothes worn by his wife. Among the Vugusu, a widower terminates the period of mourning after about four months by brewing the so-called 'beer of the ribbons' (*gamalua gagimigoye*).[1] On the following day he tears down the hut of his deceased wife and from now on lives in the hut of one of his other wives or in a newly built one.

The death- and burial-rites performed for a woman are essentially the same as those we have described above. A feature which is completely absent from them is, of course, the sham fight, while a cattle-drive is only staged after the death of old and highly reputed women who have borne and raised a great many children and who had outstanding personalities. On the other hand, I have not discovered any ceremonial features which would be performed only after the death of a woman. The public meeting held in connexion with the hair-shaving ceremony is, in the case of a woman's death, usually limited to a discussion of the cause of her death. Only after the death of an elderly widow is there any property worth mentioning to be distributed, e.g. the cattle that used to be placed in her hut as well as her personal possessions, such as pots, cooking utensils, &c. The question, on the other hand, of returning part of the marriage cattle to the widower—an issue which arises particularly after the death of a childless woman—is not discussed on the occasion of the hair-shaving ceremony but is settled later on, when the widower thinks of marrying again, between himself and the relatives of his deceased wife.

If a widower does not have a second wife who can cook for him and look after his children and if he is too poor to marry again soon, he feeds with his mother or—in case she too is dead—with one of his brothers. He then sends his children to stay with various relatives, usually with the brothers of his deceased wife. If they remain there for many years, he must pay them a cow in return for what they have done for his children. As long as a father is alive, however, his rights and duties regarding his children can never be ceded to the foster-father, that is to say he can never forgo his claim to the marriage cattle given for his daughters, nor evade his responsibility for providing the cattle which his sons need to marry in their turn. If the wife of an old man dies, the widower frequently establishes a joint household with an old widowed woman without, of course, paying any marriage cattle in such a case and without observing even the most rudimentary form of the usual marriage ceremonial.

[1] A widower, however, does not wear *gimigoye*-ribbons during the period of mourning.

DEATH AND MOURNING

If an unmarried son or an unmarried daughter dies, the mother mourns for her deceased child in the same way as a widow mourns for her husband, i.e. she puts on its clothes for some time and—among the Vugusu—also adorns herself with the *gimigoye*-ribbons. After the death of an unmarried person, however, the bereaved are not considered to have become ritually impure and, accordingly, no hair-shaving ceremony or other purification-rite is held. When a circumcised son has died, the 'beer of the ribbons' is brewed after one year, but his former hut, the *esimba*, is not torn down. If after the death of a small child a mother continues to mourn for more than two or three months, her kinsmen and neighbours tell her to stop wailing and showing grief, lest the skin of her womb (*oluvelekelo*) should likewise 'cry' and thus prevent her from conceiving again.

(8) THE FIRST SACRIFICE FOR THE DECEASED AND THE CARE OF THE GRAVE

The first animal sacrifice offered to the spirit of the deceased is of particular significance, for it establishes, so to speak, his social status in the spirit-world. Like a new-born child before the first ancestral sacrifice has been made in its name, and like the circumcision novices, the spirit of a person who has recently died is called *omusinde*. In a Nyole text this state (*ovusinde*) is characterized as follows:

'. . . then they speak to one another and say: "So-and-so (i.e. the spirit of the deceased) is living like a small child, he is still like somebody who does not possess any cattle; he is still living in the spirit-world without a ritual killing having been made for him." His sons then ask one another whether there is a goat. When they agree that they have a goat, some of them object and say: "Do you think we may kill for him merely a goat and not a cow?" Then they consult one another and finally they agree that they have a cow to spare. Then the other people are talking to one another and say: "So-and-so is living like an *omusinde*, without a ritual killing having been made for him, he lives like an orphan." '

This first sacrifice for the spirit of the deceased is usually offered about three months after his death. Among the Nyole it is preceded by a beer-feast, the so-called 'beer of the blood' (*amalua kamatsahi*), in the course of which a second hair-shaving ceremony, to which particularly women and children must submit, takes place. Chiefly, however, the 'beer of the blood' is to furnish the sons of the deceased with an opportunity for discussing who is to provide the sacrificial animal and on what day it is to be killed.

The sacrificial animal must, in this case, be killed without any blood being spilled,[1] a task which must be performed by the two grave-diggers. Before skinning the animal they cut branches from the *oluvu*- and the *olutséyue*-bushes and pull out stalks of the *litoko*-reeds, the fibres of which

---

[1] In a text on the subject it is stated that the sacrificial animal is killed by means of punches with the fist.

they plait into a cord. Then they fence the grave, sticking the branches into the ground and tying the cord from branch to branch. This having been done, they skin the sacrificial animal, seeing to it that the 'grave-digger of the head' removes the skin from the front legs and the 'grave-digger of the feet' from the hind legs.

After about one month they begin to brew beer from eleusine, the so-called 'beer of the grave'. On the day on which this beer is to be consumed, the grave-diggers place branches of the same two kinds of bushes (*tsimbú* and *tsintséyue*) which were used for fencing the grave, on top of the fence, so that they form a kind of roof. Then they cover the branches and twigs with grass, part of which is taken from the roof of the hut above the entrance, and part of which must be freshly pulled out for this purpose.

Among the Vugusu it was formerly customary to surround the grave by a fence or a thorn-bush hedge, partly to keep hyenas away from the grave and partly to please the spirit of the deceased. Nowadays the widow or the widower respectively after several months brews the so-called 'beer of cleaning the grave' (*gamalua gexusinya silindwa*) to which any number of neighbours and relatives may be invited. They all help to clear the grave of weeds and then cover the burial-mound with an even and carefully applied layer of black clay which must be fetched from the bank of a stream.

A further ceremony is performed at a man's grave, if his eldest son had not attained the full status of a family-head when his father died. In that case the son postpones the *liiyia*-rite (the cattle-drive, sham fight, &c.), which usually takes place on the day of cutting the *gimigoye*-ribbons, until he is about forty-five years old. The Vugusu say that at that age a man has reached the climax of his manhood and he is then referred to as a *waxule* or a *wangale*, i.e. 'somebody who is fully grown'. Accompanied by as large a number of neighbours and kinsmen as possible (both of his own and of his wife's clan) he visits his father's grave. The grave is then cleaned for a second time and a bull is killed by suffocating it. A sacrificial priest, who must be a clansman of the deceased, then scatters the stomach content and pours the blood of the animal over the burial-mound as well as on the path leading to it. Furthermore, he deposits a pot of beer at the grave. The whole party remains for some time near the grave, drinking of the beer and eating of the meat of the sacrificial animal. The greater part of the meat, however, is taken to the homestead of the eldest son who lavishly supplies the guests with meat, beer, and eleusine porridge. Should the eldest son fail to perform this *liiyia*-rite for his deceased father, the spirit of the latter would revenge himself by sending sickness and trouble to him, to his wives, and children, as well as to his cattle.

Apart from this rite which, as far as I could ascertain, is limited to the Vugusu, and apart from the Tsotso custom of offering sacrifices at the burial-sites of their clan-heads (cf. above, p. 478), the graves of the dead are not the objects of ceremonial observances. Already one or two years after the burial the grave can hardly be identified as such, and soon after the inhabitants of a homestead have torn down their huts to rebuild them somewhere else, the graves of the abandoned homestead fall into oblivion. The only places consecrated to the spirits of the dead are then the spirit-huts, the sacrificial stones erected in the front yard, and the centre post of the living-hut (cf. above, p. 282).

INDEX

Abduction, see *lixuesa*.
Age, of circumcision candidates, 338; of marriage partners, 394, 399.
Age-grade organization, 376 seq., 461; and circumcision, 28, 77, 373; in Kitosh, 375, 378.
amalago, customs, 79, 252; see also *elilago*.
amalogo, evil medicines, 125, 127, 132, 257, 266, 272.
amaloto, dreams, 210.
amalua, see Beer.
amitu (plur. *avamitu*), half-sibling of same sex, 51 (n. 3); general term for clan-brother (or sister), 72, 87.
Amulets, 183, 184.
amwavo (plur. *avamwavo*), full sibling of same sex, 72; 'your brother', 87.
Ancestors (*vámagombe*), 99, 235, 244, 288, 315, 318.
Ancestral spirits (*emisambwa*), 167, 226, 277, 287, 288, 473; sacrifices to, 93, 278, 291, 294, 311.
Animals, sacrificial, 280; totemic-, 198, 201.
Asai (Isahi), Supreme Being, 168, 291.
avadili (sing. *omudili*), attendants, 192, 193; tutors or guardians of initiates, 353.
avafumu (sing. *omufumu*) (Luvug.), see Diviner.
avagasa (sing. *omugasa*) (Luvug.), clan-elders, 77, 250, 339.
avahálikwa, co-wives, 50 (n. 2), from *okuhálika* = to marry a second wife.
avahia (sing. *omuhia*), 'the new ones', 314; name for initiates after coming-out feast, 371.
avakáli (sing. *omukáli*), warriors who have killed their enemy first in battle, 110, 193, 249.
avakó (sing. *omukó*), general term for affinal relations, 43, 83.
avakulu, initiates, 193, 353, 356, 359, 361.
avakumu (sing. *omukumu*) (Lurog.), see Diviner.
avalogi (sing. *omulogi*) (Lurog.), witches, 76, 92, 111, 112, 113, 118, 120, 128, 129, 391, 475; combating magic of, 267, 272.
avaloli vemunda, inspectors of entrails, 216.
avalosi (sing. *omulosi*) (Luvug.), see *avalogi*.
avaluhia, 'those of the same tribe', 20, 154.

avamenya (from *okumenya*, to stay as a guest); clan-strangers, 56, 70, 81, 354; marriage with daughter of, 393; rights of residence of, 56, 84.
avasiala, cross-cousins, 56, 87.
avasigu, 'enemies', 387.
avasikulu, name for initiates after leaving *etumbi*, 366.
Avasuva, relatives of the Logoli, 25.
avavila (sing. *ombila*) (Lurog.), sorcerers, 92, 111, 132, 134, 141, 253, 475; protective magic against, 182, 225.
avifwa (sing. *omifwa*), reciprocal term of reference for mothers' brothers and sisters' sons, 56; 'nephews', 261; marriage prohibitions between children of, 383, 388.
aviko (sing. *omiko*), general term for genealogically traceable kin, 43, 83; ceremonial duties of, 85, 311.
avilongo, persons free of witchcraft, 129.

Bantu, distribution of, 3; — Kavirondo dialects, 26; influence of culture contact on, 30 ff.; migrations of, 25.
Beer, 280; *amalua gamaravula*, '— of the shadows', 98; *amalua gétoa*, '— of target shooting', 361; *amalua golukuzu*, '— of death', 228.
Blood, ritual impurity caused by contact with, 110; used in *ovulosi*, 124 (n.), 188.
Bride-wealth, *ovukui*; cause of strife between members of family, 381; *evilisio* gifts as part of, 429, 444, 447; responsibility for, 48; return of, 407, 442, 443; variation in amount of, 392, 402; *see also* Marriage cattle.
Buhayo, chieftaincy, 17, 21.
Buholo, chieftaincy, 17; population figures, 21.
Bukhayo, see Buhayo.
Bunyore, chieftaincy, 4, 15, 18; population figures, 21.
Burial, of *avalogi*, 288, 479; in bush, 469; -chambers, 475; in graves, 469; in sitting position, 479.
Butsotso, chieftaincy, 17, 21.

Cattle, 51, 382; *see also* Marriage cattle.
Cattle-drive (*elisona, liiyia, efiremba*), 278, 453, 457, 490, 502.
Charms, 93.
Chief, 'location chiefs', 36; *milango* chief, 36, 135, 259; paramount chief, 14, 21.

Circumcision, 28, 335, 336, 348, 349; age of circumcision candidates, 338; *see also* Age-grade organization, *vagogi.*
Circumcision operator (*omukevi*), 85, 344, 377; attire of, 348; avoidances of, 194, 353; payment of, 352; performs 'washing ceremony', 356.
Clan, *oluhia*, a patrilineal, exogamous, territorial unit, 53, 56, 76; blood feud between clans, 67, 389; ceremonial friendships between clans, 389; magical qualities, 76, 129; membership of, determined by birth, 57; names of, 53, 54, 58 seq.; origin of new clans, 58, 67, 68, 70; patrilineal clans named after women, 54; clan-strangers, see *avamenya*; solidarity, 72, 76; clan-elder, see *avagasa*; clan-head, 76, 79, 81, 82, 291, 363.
Colville, Sir H., 31.
Curses, *okutjena* and *okulama* (*xulama*), 102; lifting of, 254.

Dances at birth of twins, 326; in initiation rites, 367, 369.
Dead, 163, 277; *see also* Spirits.
Death (*olukuzu*), 95, 169, 200, 452, 487; life after death, 90, 163, 447; ritual death of initiates, 362.
Diseases, 180; as bar to marriage, 392.
Divination [*ovukumu* (Lurog.), *vufumu* (Luvug.)], 220, 225, 232; from entrails, 214.
Diviner, *omukumu* (plur. *avakumu*), consultation of, 91, 183, 220; how to become a, 222, 243; payment of, 224, 242; succession to office of, 85.
Divorce, 43, 441, 446.
Dream-prophet [*omuɲoli* (Lurog.), *omuɲosi* (Luvug.)], 212, 213, 214.
Dreams (*amaloto*), 160, 210, 211, 280.
Dundas, K. R., 66 *passim.*

efiremba, see Cattle-drive.
Egg, 202, 280; in magic, 98, 124.
ehili (plur. *edzihili*), tribe, 55, 285.
ehiru, front room of hut, 269, 304; see also *vuhilu.*
ekego (Lurog.), cattle enclosure, 188, 229.
ekegono, unmarried girls' hut, 41.
ekigingi (Lurog.), spirit of deceased, 162, 279, 460.
ekihungu, bird, 183.
ekilili (Lurog.), shadow, 160.
ekilivwa (*efilivwa*), 'gate', term for lineage, 55, 260.
ekilúmiku, cupping-horn, 263.
ekiruazo, council of clan-elders, 44 (n. 1), 81, 154.

ekisuli-rod (Lurog.), *sisuli* (Luvug.), 107, 385, 497.
Elgon chieftaincy, 4.
eliamwana, homesteads abandoned on account of evil magic, 123.
elidala (plur. *amadala*), homestead, 50.
elifuliana (Lurog.), sham-fight in funeral rites, 457, 494.
eligutu (plur. *amagatu*), clan-head, also supporting-post of hut, 80, 292, 338.
elikula (plur. *amakula*) (Lurog.), *lúvaga* (plur. *tjimbago*) (Luvug.), age-class, 373, 457.
elilago, custom, 41, 405; see also *amalago.*
elilimilu, fields, jointly cultivated by clansmen, 82.
elilogo, evil medicines used by *avalogi*, 126, 184, 188.
elilungu, loft, 279.
elisálisa, purification rite, 267.
elisona, see Cattle-drive.
El Kony tribe, 13, 16, 23, 31.
Elopement (*liveya*), marriage by, 396, 414, 434, 435.
emagombe (Luvug.), spirit-land, 163, 164.
embala, person without blemishes, 79.
embula, rain, 153, 155.
emigilu (Lurog.), ritual prohibitions, 79, 190, 198; taboos, 250, 252.
emisambwa, ancestral spirits, q.v.
Emongo (*emungu*), spirit-like being, 176, 291.
enganana, beer of, 400, 402, 431, 438.
engani, prohibition, 171.
enyumba (Lurog.), round living-hut, 40; term for lineage, 55.
esimba, bachelor hut, 41, 62, 304, 437, 501.
esoni (*tjisoni*), 'shame', 195.
etaso, extra bit, baksheesh, 199.
etumbi (Lurog.), *ligombe* (Luvug.), hut of seclusion, 321, 355; burning of, 366; ceremonial dismissal from, 363, 366; ritual confinement in, 193, 340, 353, 357.
eturi (Lurog.), centre-post of living-hut, 98, 226, 282.
Evans-Pritchard, E. E., 91 *passim.*
evikoko-particles, used in evil magic, 126, 220, 262, 263.
evilisio, gifts to the bride, 430; *see also* Bride-wealth.
evulili, partition in hut, 304.
evwasi (*evuasi, vwasi*), cooking-partition of hut, 42, 228, 269, 404.
Exogamy, rules of, 198, 383; in relation to clanship, 53, 54, 67, 70, 71; sanctions of infringement of, 251, 384, 386; social significance of, 386.

INDEX

Family, structure, 40 seq.; polygynous, 49.
Fasting, ritual, of initiation candidates, 205.
Father, authority over children, 46; provides marriage cattle for sons, 48, 381; functions of, at child's birth, 301, 401.
Father's brother, role of, in sacrificial rite for ancestor, 384; in rites for twins, 325.
Father's sister, see *Senge*.
Feast, wedding, 409 seq.
First-fruit rites, 205.
Firth, Raymond, 111 (n. 2).
Frog, 199.

gamadjumi, folds of skin, cause of *luswa*, 109.
gamalesi, poisonous roots, 114, 115, 120.
gamalogo, roots or pieces of bark used in evil magic, 114, 260, 266, 271; antidotes to, 238, 270.
Gedge, 30.
gimisala, poisonous objects used in evil magic, 116, 253.
gimisilu (Luvug.), taboos, ritual prohibitions, 74, 75, 79, 190; see Taboos.
Gimuhia, Logoli sub-clan, reputed to be *avalogi*, 76, 129, 391.
Gishu, Masai tribe, 12, 16, 54.
Givagi, sub-clan of the Logoli, 58; noted for being *avalogi*, 71.
God, High, belief in, 92, 167.
Grave, *kilindwa* (Lurog.), 470, 471; rites at, among Vugusu, 283.
guga, grandfather, 49, 73.
gumusilu (plur. *gimisilu*) or *gumusiru* (Luvug.), taboo, avoidance, 67, 200 (n.).
Gusii (Kisii), 3; specialists in witchcraft and sorcery among, 132.
guyavi, man who burns bones of dead person, 249.

Hair-shaving ceremony [*olovego*(Lurog.), *livégana*(Luvug.)], 137, 451, 485, 489; settling claims at, 443, 491, 494.
Hanga (Luhanga), dialect spoken by the Wanga, 26.
Hannington, Bishop James, 30.
hasi, 'down', abode of ancestral spirits, 163.
Hayo tribe, 22, 25.
Hobley, C. W., 6 (n.), *passim*.; on clan-taboos, 74, 200 (n.).
Holo tribe, 25.
Hut, see *esimba, etumbi*.

Idaxo, agricultural tribe, 27; chieftaincy, 21; circumcision among, 345; list of clans and lineages among, 63; patri-lineal clans named after women, 54; possess powerful *avavila*, 132.
Incest, 384.
Incisors, 27, 40.
indzu, lineage, 'house', 55.
Inheritance, claims to, 48, 52, 84, 487.
Initiation rites, 28, 334 seq.; *see* Circumcision.
Insignia, 82.
Intestines, list of native terms for, 216.
Isuxa tribe, 21 (n. 4), 22; possess powerful *avavila*, 132.

Jackson, 30.
Jaluo, Nilotic tribe, 3, 7, 8, 15, 16, 17, 28; migration of, 25.
Johnston, Sir Harry, 11 *passim*.
Joking relationships, 84.
Jopadhola, Nilotic tribe, 26.

Kabras, chieftaincy, 11, 16, 17, 21, 24.
Kakalelwa, chieftaincy, 17, 21.
Kakamega, gold-mining district, 7, 10, 17, 21.
Kavirondo, 3, 4; etymology of the term, 19.
kilindwa, see Grave.
Kimilili, 22, 23.
Kinship, avoidances in relation to, 84, 195; classificatory system, 72; manifestations of, 83; terms as, 73, 83, 86; behaviour as, 84; ceremonial duties as, 84; gift obligations as, 84; inheritance and succession as, 84; marriage laws as, 86.
kiragi, ritual impurity of animals, 107; lustration from, 247; see also *luswa*.
Kisa, chieftaincy, 21.
Kisienya, mythical ancestor of Tiriki, 24.
Kisii, *see* Gusii.
Kitosh, Masai name for Vugusu, 12, 17 chieftaincy, 17, 21.
Kitson, Sir Albert E., 38 (n. 3).
koza (*avakoza*), general term of address for mother's brother, 72.
kuvulavu, 'before the public place', 251.
kuyinga, to become a fool, 191.

Lago, non-Bantu tribe, 16, 22, 23.
liaxa, marriage with full wedding procedure, 396, 433.
ligombe (Luvug.), see *etumbi*.
liiyia, see Cattle-drive.
Lineage (*enyumba, ekilivwa, indzu*), 55; definition of, 54, 71, 83; lineage names among Idaxo, 63.
lisali, dome-shaped shelter, 363; sick man moved to, 449; widow's hut, 499.
liswákila rite, first ancestral sacrifice after birth of child, 279, 285, 311 seq., 315, 330.

508   INDEX

livégana (Luvug.), see Hair-shaving ceremony.
liveyia, marriage by elopement, 396, 434.
lixuesa, marriage by abduction, 396, 437.
Logoli, 20, 22, 25, 27; absence of clan taboos among, 74; attitude towards twins, 323; burial of clan-head, 476; circumcision, 345, 349; clan names, 58; dialect spoken by, 26; first fruit rites, 205; kinship terms among, 86.
Logovo, Logoli clan reputed to be avalogi, 76, 129.
lugova (plur. dzingova), walled village, 40, 56, 158, 354.
Luo tribe, 16, 24, 25.
Lustration, 246 seq.
luswa, ritual impurity of human beings, 107; avoidances of people suffering from, 191, 194; causes of, 109, 191, 322, 385; lustration from state of, 247, 251; manifestations of, 107.
lúvaga (plur. tjimbaga) (Luvug.), age-class, 373 (n. 1), 375 seq.

Macdonald, J. R. L., 25 (n.).
Magic, 75, 90, 93, 96, 97, 99, 179, 182; counter magic, 268; and religion distinguished, 90; rain-magic, 152.
Magician, see avalogi, avavila, omugimba; garden-magician, 99; see omukingi womulimi.
Malakisi, chieftaincy, 21.
Malinowski, 179 (n.), passim.
Marach, chieftaincy, 17, 21; origin of, 25.
Maragoli, chieftaincy of South Maragoli, 4; clan names in South Maragoli, 58; population figures of South and North Maragoli, 21.
Marama, chieftaincy, 17, 21, 22, 24; list of clan names amongst, 64; origin of new clans amongst, 68; ovulogi and ovufira among, 131, 143.
Marriage, attitude towards, 379; choice of partner, 382, 391, see exogamy, vuleve, vusoni; circumcision no condition of, 340; disease as bar to, 392; dissolution of, 442; of divorced wife, 439; exchange of gifts, 431; inter-tribal, 393; prohibition of, between clans, 388, 389; prohibitions for omirongo, 346, 389; vagogi, 377, 383, 389; of widow, 440.
Marriage cattle, father provides, for son, 45, 48, 381; given for sister used by brother, 45, 49, 51, 382; return of marriage cattle at divorce, 45, 442, 445, at death, 444, 500, to deceased husband's heirs at widow's re-marriage, 46, 488; raiding as means of acquiring, 48; settling of amount of, 401, 403, 436.
Masava, see Gishu.
Masks, used in initiation rites, 358.
Mavi, son of Mulogoli, 59; Logoli clan, 58.
mbozo, full sibling of opposite sex, 72, 87.
mbozua (mbozwa) (plur. avavozua), half-sibling of opposite sex, 51 (n. 3); general term of reference to half- or clan-sister of a man mbozua or (mbozwa brother) of a woman, 72, 87, 383.
Medicines, edzinyasi, 183, 270; used after circumcision, 357.
Mia (Kidi, Elgumi), 16, 22, 25.
milango, sub-headmen, chiefs, 36, 135, 259, 494.
milembe (Lurog.), 'peace', 257, 265, 359.
Milk, avoidance of, 203.
Mother's brother, omifwa (plur. avifwa) (Lurog.), xotja (Luvug.), 56, 72, 87, 321; claims at nephew's death, 491; claims at niece's death, 409; role of, in circumcision rites, 343, 372; role of, at niece's betrothal, 235, 390, 401, 410, 424, 433, 436.
Mourning, dirges in mourning rites, 461.
Mukulu, chieftaincy, 17, 21, 24.
Mulogoli, tribal ancestor of Logoli, 25.
mulongo, second-born twin, 324.
Mumia, paramount chief, 14, 24.
musambwa (Luvug.), spirit of deceased, 162.
Muvugusu, mythical tribal ancestor of Vugusu, 23.
muxwana, first-born twin, 324.
Myths, 169, 200, 487.

Name, importance of ancestral, 42, 315, 317; clan name, 53; naming rites, 288, 313, 319.
Nandi, Nilotic tribe, 16, 17, 22.
naŋeso, bullock of, 415, 431, 434, 439.
nasigogo, divorced wife, 439, 445.
navana, mutual term of address used by parents of married couple, 87, 400.
Ngoma, non-Bantu tribe, 16, 22, 23, 31.
Nilotes, distribution of, 3.
Nyala tribe, 11; dialect spoken by, 26; inhabitants of Kakalelwa and Kabras, 22; origin of, 24.
Nyasai, Supreme Being among Logoli, 168.
Nyole tribe, 20, 23; family of reputed rain-magicians among, 145.

okufunya, 'to emit poison', 142.
okololana, meeting where amount of bride-wealth is fixed, 403.

INDEX

okugasidza, to bless, 106.
okugila, food taboo, 204.
okhólina, to reconcile, forgive, 106, 139, 254.
okuhólinana (Lurog.), *xúosia* (Luvug.), to perform rite of reconciliation, 256.
okuhonya, to cure, 139.
okulama (Lurog), *xulama* (Luvug.), to curse, 102.
okulomolela or *okutjena*, to curse, 102.
okuyera (Lurog.), to observe personal food avoidances, 204.
olovego (Lurog.), *see* Hair-shaving ceremony.
olugaga (Luvug.), cattle enclosure, 40.
olugembe, knife, 105, 263.
oluhia (plur. *edzimbia*), exogamous clan-unit, 'fire-place on a meadow', 55, 476 (n. 2), 477; public meeting-place, 78, 82, 109, 194, 343, 377.
olukuzu, 'deadly danger', 197 (n. 2); death, 451; *see also* Death.
olunyasi, public magic and preventive medicines, 97, 135, 142, 147, 185, 265.
ombidi, blower, 248, 311, 471, 498.
ombila, see *avavila*.
ombili, body of the living, 160.
ombimbuli, expert in counter-magic, 268.
Omen, 207, 216.
omirongo (plur. *virongo*), circumcision friend, 346, 372, 383, 389.
omisukulu (plur. *avisukulu*), grandson, 73, 87.
omuari, burial expert, 480.
omufila (plur. *avafila*), term for sorcerer among Marama, 132, 143.
omufundilili, female *omulosi*, 113, 117, 264.
omugasa, see *avagasa*.
omugilu or *omugiru* (Lurog), avoidance, 67; 'totem', 200 (n.); taboo, 246, 249, 386; *see also* Taboo.
omugimba (plur. *avagimba*), rain-magician, 144, 147; prestige of, 158 (n.), 186; succession to office of, 84, 156.
omugizi, yard, 40, 41, 454.
omuhotjya, man with unblemished character, 79, 249.
omukaali, see *avakaali*.
omukali (Lurog.), wife, 42 (n. 2), 45, 87.
omukasa, ivory armlet of clan-head, 68.
omukevi, *see* Circumcision operator.
omukingi, type of *avalogi* among Logoli, 126, 128, 185, 258.
omukingi womulimi, garden-magician, 99, 185.
omukógoti, last-born son, 49, 139.
omukulo, joking relative, 109.
omukulundu, term of address for elder, 72, 86.
omukunzakāli, widow, 496; widower, 499.

omukuzu, dead body, 160.
omulatji, Nyole clan-elder, 81, 82.
omuliuli, expert in removing magic, 195, 229, 238, 239, 258, 261, 270.
omulogi, see *avalogi*.
omulosi, see *avalosi*.
omulúmiki, woman expert in the use of cupping-horn, 263.
omunoli (Lurog.), *omunosi* (Luvug.), dream-prophet, 212 (n. 1), 213.
omunyamusira, Gusii name for sorcerer, 132.
omurori, type of *avalosi*, 112, 114, 258.
omusalisi, sacrificial priest, 79, 284, 286, 291, 300, 311, 385.
omusango, sacrifice, 265, 285.
omuségetili, expert in discovering thieves, 211, 275.
omuseni, public comforter at death, 78, 95, 123, 276, 378, 486, 492.
omusilo (Lunyole), taboo, 488 (cf. Lurog. *omugilu*).
omusinde (plur. *avasinde*), uncircumcised boy, 88, 339, 360; person for whom no sacrifice has been performed, 279, 311, 474, 501.
omusindixilisi (Luvug.), type of *avalosi*, 112, 115.
omusiru (Lutsotso) taboo, 378.
omusohi, *omulogi* employing evil eye, 127, 184, 187; undoing effect of evil eye, 271.
omutevi, 'asker', female emissary in courtship, 399, 405.
Omuwanga, tribal ancestor of Wanga, 23.
omuxingi, type of *avalosi*, 113, 116, 186.
omuxondoli, female *omulosi*, 113, 117; protection against, 187.
omuxupi owe vilasila, 'beater of *vilasila*', female *omulosi*, 112, 116, 264, 273.
omwahi wolunyasi, herbalist, 183.
omwami, chief, 157, 173.
omwea (Luvug.), bride, 406, 414.
omwémilili, clan-leader in warfare, 82.
omwirongo (Lurog.), *omuravola* (Luvug.), person with unblemished ritual status, 120, 246.
omwitjuxulu (Luvug.), grandson, 73, 88, 491.
omwiwana (Luvug.), 'sister's daughter', 67; sister's child, 88; nephew, 343.
omwoyo, 'heart', 160.
ovinásitjula, type of *avalosi*, 112, 113.
ovodekele, poverty, 269.
ovosé, stomach content of sacrificial sheep, 188, 251, 253, 313.
ovovila, plant used in *ovuvila*, 138, 183, 257, 264; lustration after contact with, 253.
ovugima, virginity, 203, 429.

ovukāle, condition of *avakāli*, 110, 193; lustration from, 249.
ovukui, see Bride-wealth.
ovukumu, divination, 219.
ovulogi (Lurog.), *ovulosi* (Luvug.), witchcraft, 71, 79, 112; attitude towards, 121, 123, 129; combating of, 266, 274; instruction in, 120; origin of, among Vugusu, 119; transfer of, 129, 131.
ovulosi, see *ovulogi*.
ovululu, 'fierceness' of deceased spirit and of wild animals, 165.
ovuŋoli, dream-prophecy, 212.
ovuvila (Lurog.), sorcery, 79, 132, 133, 139, 261, 264; plants used as lethal medicines, 133; see also *ovovila*.
ovuti, fear, avoidances between in-laws due to, 195.
ovwali, sacrificial fire, 282, 292.

Patriliny, 53, 76, 83, 387.
Peters, Carl, 30.
Polygyny, 44, 49, 50 (n. 1).
Pregnancy, observances during, 298.
Prohibitions against killing animals, 198; ritual prohibitions between kinsmen, 197.
Property, *gumuandu*, husband's ownership of, 45, 52 (n. 1), 53; inheritance of, 492.

Raiding, to acquire marriage cattle, 48.
Rain-magician, see *omugimba*.
Ravenstein, E. G., 19.
Rebirth, ritual death and, of initiates, 362.
Rees, J., 168 (n. 2), 198 (n. 4).
Religion, distinction between magic and, 90.
Richards, Audrey, 122 (n. 2).
Rites, first-fruit, 205; funeral, 453; of passage, 84, 90, 335.
Ritual impurity, 95, 96, 106, 110; see also *luswa, kiragi, vuxútjakāli, vusixu*.
Roscoe, J., 26 (n.).

Sacrifice (*omusango*), to ancestral spirits, 93, 265, 279, 285; after birth of child, 279, see *liswakila*; by dying man, 450; tribal, 290.
Sacrificial fire, 282, 292; site, see Shrine; rites, terms for, 281.
Samia tribe, 16.
Senge, father's sister, 87, 118, 321; role in betrothal of niece, 401, 427, 436; in initiation rites, 343.
Seniority, as grading principle, 77, 379; significance of, 378 seq.
shambas, gardens, 9.
Shrine, *amagina gemisango, muravula*, *namwima*, 199, 282, 503; consecration of, 284; *wetili* shrines, 238, 283, 290.
Siblings, relationship between, 48.
siselelo (Luvug.), wedding, 321; bride's father responsible for, 410, 415, 431, 434, 437, 443.
sisinini (Luvug.), shadow, 160, 162.
Sisters' sons (*avifwa*), 87; marriage of children of, 383; residence of, 56; see also Mother's brother.
sisuli (Luvug.), *ekisuli* (Lurog.), staff on roof of hut, 252, 260.
sitexo, rite at the establishment of own homestead, 43, 197, 214, 279, 322; bullock of, killed by wife's father, 43, 432, 433, 443.
sivixo, cow due to mother's brother at nephew's death, 491.
Solidarity of age-class, 376; within the clan, 72.
Songs at birth of twins, 326, 327; in circumcision rites, 341, 343, 352, 355, 357, 359; in rites for weak infants, 333; *litoma*-songs, 481; *vuxulu*-songs, 368, (bridesmaids) 417, (funerals) 455, 461 seq., *yumba*-songs, 482.
Sorcery, see *ovuvila*.
Sororate, 383, 390.
Spire, F., 31.
Spirits (of the dead), 159 seq., 447; 'cooled off' (*okukinda*), 165, 277, 474.
Stam, N., 17 *passim*.
Stork, *makuyi*, large black and white, as totem, 202 (n.); tail feather of, as symbol, 466.
Succession, 84.
Sun (*liuwa*) god, 172; myths, 173.
Supreme Being, see Wele; belief in, 92, 167; sacrifices to, 291.
Swahili, 33.

Taboos, *emigilu* (Lurog.), *gimisilu* (Luvug.), observance of, on clan basis, 74, 202; origin of, 75; as protective measures, 179, 488; sanctions of, 74, 386; violation of, 250, 252.
Tadjoni, 22, 23, 454, 490.
Talismans used in love magic, 99.
Teso tribe, 13, 16, 23.
Thomas and Scott, 3.
Thomson, Joseph, 9 *passim*.
Tiriki, chieftaincy, 4, 18; circumcision among, 338, 343, 347, 350; clan names of, 62; origin of, 24; relationship to Wanga, 54; population figures, 21; tribe, 22.
tjisoni (Luvug.), 'shame', avoidances due to, 195.
Tola, sub-tribe of Teso, 23.
Totemic animals, 198, 202; avoidances, 67, 200 (n.).
Tsotso tribe, 22, 24, 64.

INDEX

Twins, *vaxwana*, avoidance of, 194; birth of, 325; burial of, 480; seclusion of, 325, 329; see also *vuxwana*.

Uasin-Gishu, *see* Gishu.

vagogi, circumcision age-mates, 236, 340, 376, 377, 457.
valosi, see *avalosi*.
vámagombe, ancestors, q.v.
vasagwa, husband of wife's sister; term of address between parents of married couple, 89, 415, 439.
vésaile, circumcision candidates, 340.
vilasila (Luvug.), poisonous objects used in evil magic, 116, 126, 263.
visieno, troublesome spirits, 177, 230, 277, 289, 300, 331.
volugongo, sub-headmen, 36, 135, 259, 367.
vufumu (Luvug.), divination, 219.
Vugusu, 12, 27, 33, 54, 87, 323, 341, 350, 375; clan names of, 64, 65; dialect spoken by, 26; distribution of, 22, 65; origin of, 23, 169.
(*o*)*vuhilu*, front-partition of hut, 304, 308, 320, 429, 449; see also *ehiru*.
vuleve (*valeve*), relations, 175, 387; a bar to marriage, 384, 385; social significance of, 386.
vulosi, see *ovulosi*.
vusixu (Luvug.), ritual impurity caused by blood, 110; lustration from, 248.
vusoni, relationships, 384.
(*ovu*)*vute*, ceremonial friendship between clans, 383, 388.
vuxútjakāli (Luvug.), *vukunzakāli* (Lurog.), ritual impurity caused by breath of dying person, 109, 496, 499; lustration from, 248.
vuxwana, 'twinship', 110, 194, 328.
vuxwe, fear, avoidances due to, 195.
vwasi, see *evwasi*.
(*o*)*vwivu*, smell emanating from new-born child, 110, 304, 310.

Wakefield, 19.
Wamia, *see* Mia.
Wanga, 14, 17, 20, 22, 24, 476; clan names of, 66; chieftaincies of, 21; paramount chief of, 14, 21, 24; relationship to Tiriki, 54.
Weapons, 27.
Wele, Supreme Being among Vugusu, 99, 168, 283; Wele *ómuwanga*, White God, 175, 177; Wele (*gumali*) *evimbi*, Black God, 175, 231, 235; Weles, 175.
Weller, 30.
Widow, 452, 480; avoidance of, 109, 191; behaviour of, at funeral rites, 482; status of, 499.
Wife, 41 seq., 45, 50, 51.
Witchcraft, see *ovulosi*.

Xotja, Mother's brother, q.v.
xúosia (Luvug.), to perform rite of reconciliation, 256.
xusutja, to feel desire to kill, 107.

Yigulu, 'above', Wele's abode, 172.

Ziba tribe, 23.

PRINTED IN
GREAT BRITAIN
AT THE
UNIVERSITY PRESS
OXFORD
BY
CHARLES BATEY
PRINTER
TO THE
UNIVERSITY